The Preobrazhensky Papers, Volume III

Historical Materialism Book Series

The Historical Materialism Book Series is a major publishing initiative of the radical left. The capitalist crisis of the twenty-first century has been met by a resurgence of interest in critical Marxist theory. At the same time, the publishing institutions committed to Marxism have contracted markedly since the high point of the 1970s. The Historical Materialism Book Series is dedicated to addressing this situation by making available important works of Marxist theory. The aim of the series is to publish important theoretical contributions as the basis for vigorous intellectual debate and exchange on the left.

The peer-reviewed series publishes original monographs, translated texts, and reprints of classics across the bounds of academic disciplinary agendas and across the divisions of the left. The series is particularly concerned to encourage the internationalization of Marxist debate and aims to translate significant studies from beyond the English-speaking world.

For a full list of titles in the Historical Materialism Book Series available in paperback from Haymarket Books, visit: www.haymarketbooks.org/ series_collections/1-historical-materialism.

The Preobrazhensky Papers

VOLUME III

Concrete Analysis of the Soviet Economy

Edited by
Richard B. Day
Mikhail M. Gorinov
Sergei V. Tsakunov

Translated by
Richard B. Day

Haymarket Books
Chicago, IL

First published in 2022 by Brill Academic Publishers, The Netherlands
© 2022 Koninklijke Brill NV, Leiden, The Netherlands

Published in paperback in 2023 by
Haymarket Books
P.O. Box 180165
Chicago, IL 60618
773-583-7884
www.haymarketbooks.org

ISBN: 978-1-64259-994-7

Distributed to the trade in the US through Consortium Book Sales and
Distribution (www.cbsd.com) and internationally through Ingram
Publisher Services International (www.ingramcontent.com).

This book was published with the generous support of Lannan
Foundation and Wallace Action Fund.

Special discounts are available for bulk purchases by organizations and
institutions. Please call 773-583-7884 or email info@haymarketbooks.org
for more information.

Cover art and design by David Mabb. Cover art is a detail from *Painting
26, Long Live the New! Morris & Co. Hand Printed Wallpapers and Kasimir
Malevich's Suprematism*. Acrylic on wallpaper mounted on canvas, (2016).

Printed in the United States.

10 9 8 7 6 5 4 3 2 1

Library of Congress Cataloging-in-Publication data is available.

Dedicated with Love and Gratitude to Judi

∴

Contents

Abbreviations

Comintern	Communist International
GARF	State Archive of the Russian Federation
Gosbank	State Bank
Gosizdat	State Publishing House
Gosplan	State Planning Commission
IKKI	Executive Committee of the Communist International
IMEL	Institute of Marx-Engels-Lenin
Komvnutorg	Commissariat of Internal Trade
Narkompochtel'	People's Commissariat of Posts and Telegraphs
Narkomprod	People's Commissariat of Food
Narkomtyazhmash	People's Commissariat of Heavy Industry
Narkomzem	People's Commissariat of Agriculture
NEP	New Economic Policy
NKF, Narkomfin	People's Commissariat of Finance
NKVD	People's Commissariat of Internal Affairs
OGPU	Joint State Political Directorate
Pomgol	Committee for Famine Assistance
Proletkult	'Proletarian Culture'
RAN	Russian Academy of Sciences
Revvoensovet	Revolutionary War Council
RKP	Russian Communist Party
RSDRP	Russian Social-Democratic Workers' Party
SNK	Council of People's Commissars
STO	Council of Labour and Defence
TsK	Central Committee
TsSU	Central Statistical Directorate
USSR	Union of Soviet Socialist Republics
VChK	All-Russian Extraordinary Commission for Struggle against Counter-revolution and Sabotage
VSNKh	Supreme Soviet of the National Economy
VTsIK	All-Russian Central Executive Committee

PART 1

[*The Problem of Economic Equilibrium*]

∵

[Preface]: The Problem of Economic Equilibrium in Concrete Capitalism and in the Soviet System[1]

In Volume II of *Capital*, Marx initially gives an analysis of simple reproduction in pure capitalism, i.e., in the sort of economic system in which capitalism has subordinated both industry and agriculture to itself, having squeezed out all pre-capitalist forms and become not only the predominant but also the sole form of production in society. Analysing the conditions of equilibrium in precisely this pure and abstract capitalism, in this part of his investigation Marx applied the customary methodological approach that he adhered to in all of his economic works. He began precisely with simple reproduction, because with simple reproduction the equilibrium between branches producing means of production and those producing means of consumption can be theoretically photographed with the greatest clarity, for equilibrium in the exchange of values here takes the form of mathematical equilibrium.

In the analysis of simple reproduction – which in real life can only exist as an exception – Marx clarified the most important part of the problem, namely, the equilibrium in exchange of means of production from Department I for means of consumption from Department II, which in terms of value means the balanced exchange of $s + v$ of I for c of II. Marx then proceeds to the much more complex problem of expanded reproduction in pure capitalism, when the entire system is in motion and the theoretically conceivable and actually observed possibilities for disproportion are incomparably greater than with simple reproduction. With the same volume of capital in society and all other conditions remaining the same (the organic composition of capital and the level of exploitation), here a completely different allocation of productive forces is required. Moreover, it must change with even the slightest fluctuation in any direction on the part of the rate of accumulation. A declining rate of accumulation, a steady rate or a rising rate each requires special proportions in the distribution of capital due to regroupings and alterations in the other conditions of reproduction.

But in his analysis of simple and expanded reproduction, as we know, Marx never left the terrain of pure capitalism. Meanwhile, in an investigation of real capitalism and the conditions of its equilibrium, the economist must apply

---

1 A chapter from Vol. II of *The New Economics* (published in the journal *Vestnik Kommunisticheskoi akademii*, No. 17–18, 1926).

Marx's scientific discoveries in conditions where capitalist reproduction is entangled with reproduction in simple commodity economy. On the one hand, this certainly complicates the entire problem, for in such an investigation one must add to Marx's Departments two additional ones for the pre-capitalist forms of economy and then consider the conditions of equilibrium between four sets of figures. But, on the other hand, the analysis of mixed capitalist and pre-capitalist reproduction also involves a certain simplification of the problem insofar as, for example, *with simple reproduction* in the petty-bourgeois sector of the economy the whole product is only divided between two parts, i.e., the income being consumed by small producers themselves on the one hand, and the part of constant capital[2] being replaced on the other. Conversely, the analysis becomes complicated again with expanded reproduction in simple commodity economy, since here it cannot be assumed that there is a constant value of labour power: the surplus product of small-scale production can go not just to the expansion of production but also to expansion of consumption by the independent producers themselves, and it can do so in varying degrees that are only indirectly regulated by the law of the value of labour power, just as under-consumption can also sink below the level of the average workers' wages.

Of course, in the analysis of reproduction in concrete capitalism, we cannot take a single step without relying on the analysis that Marx gave of reproduction in pure capitalism. On the other hand, without an analysis of equilibrium in concrete capitalism, i.e., without an analysis of equilibrium between capitalist and small-scale, independent commodity production, it will be very difficult for us to study equilibrium in the economic system of the USSR, where three forms of reproduction are interwoven in the conditions of commodity exchange: simple commodity economy, capitalism, and the state economy of the proletariat. A concrete attempt to study equilibrium in our economic system leads to the conviction that it is easiest to solve the problem after an investigation of the simpler forms of equilibrium in a mixed capitalist economy. This is required not merely for pedagogical reasons, or out of consideration for the convenience of the study, but by the essence of the question itself.

In the theoretical part of this discussion, we shall consider five basic problems: 1) the problem of simple reproduction with a mixed economy consisting of capitalism and simple commodity production; 2) expanded reproduction under pure capitalism in conditions of a rising organic composition of capital;

---

2 We use the word 'capital' with reference to the means of production of petty producers provisionally and only for the purpose of simplification, since according to Marx's terminology in *Capital* these do not in fact constitute capital.

3) expanded reproduction in *concrete* capitalism, i.e., in conditions where capitalist production is interwoven with petty-bourgeois production; 4) declining reproduction in conditions of the same economy; 5) equilibrium with expanded reproduction in the economy of the USSR.

I intend to deal with the first four questions only in the most general terms, making no claim to be addressing the numerous interesting problems that this involves, because the ultimate purpose of the investigation remains a purely concrete analysis of the living and developing Soviet economy with all of the relevant concrete facts and figures.

CHAPTER 1

Economic Equilibrium under Capitalism

1 Simple Reproduction with a Mixed Economy of Capitalism and Simple Commodity Production

Before turning to an investigation of this problem, let us make a few methodological observations.

When analysing the problem of proportionality with simple reproduction in pure capitalism, Marx operated with two Departments: Department I for the production of means of production and Department II for the production of means of consumption. Is it necessary, for an analysis of proportionality under a mixed form, to introduce new Departments, i.e., sub-departments for the sector of simple commodity production?

This question must be answered in the affirmative, and here is why. If it were possible simply to add the production of means of production in the petty-bourgeois economy to Department I of the capitalist sector, and the production of means of consumption to Department II of that sector, that would involve presupposing that the entire mixed form, from the viewpoint of the conditions of equilibrium, involves nothing new compared to the conditions of equilibrium already analysed by Marx. We would then be dealing with a simple arithmetic expansion of both Departments while preserving the conditions of equilibrium required for simple capitalist reproduction. However, such a presupposition is incorrect.

In the first place, with simple capitalist reproduction, the gross annual product is divided into $C + V + S$, i.e., into the constant capital being replaced, wages and surplus value, whereas in the petty-bourgeois sector, with simple reproduction, the annual product is divided only into constant capital and the income consumed by petty producers. This income can be called V only conditionally, because it is not completely regulated by the law of the value of labour power. Thus, the surplus value consumed by capitalists is not matched by any corresponding sum in the schemes of simple reproduction, and a counterposing of V in the capitalist sector to the consumed revenues of petty producers is also conditional. This circumstance, together with the previously noted peculiarities of the consumption fund of petty producers, has an essential effect on the entire set of conditions of equilibrium in the mixed form of economy as a whole. We are not yet referring to changes that are connected with the circumstance that petty production is not usually a matter entirely of commodity production; in its concrete form, the latter often has not yet separated from the umbilical cord of the natural economy. For a concrete investigation, this is enormously important, although here, at the present stage of this investigation, we begin with the assumption that what is involved is petty production that works entirely for the market, with subordination of the process of production and exchange to the law of value because it is connected with the market.

It is also necessary to keep in mind the dramatic difference between the organic composition of capital in the capitalist sector and the relation between constant capital (in a provisional sense) and V (also in a provisional sense) in simple commodity production. Given the dominant role of large-scale production in competitive spheres, this makes non-equivalent exchange inevitable from the viewpoint of the expenditure of labour in petty production.

Furthermore, it is only with the construction of parallel schemes for capitalist production on the one hand, and simple commodity production on the other, that we are better able to clarify for ourselves all of the processes connected with expanded reproduction of the mixed system, the dynamic of the displacement of petty by large-scale production, while preserving a moving equilibrium in the economy as a whole and also ascertaining more easily the fundamental patterns of contracting reproduction.

It would appear to simplify the whole investigation if the analysis included only that portion of small-scale commodity production that is involved in an exchange of values with the capitalist sector of the economy, leaving aside consumption in natural form and internal exchange within the sector of petty production. But this simplification, which is awkward for analysis of a mixed system with an overwhelming preponderance of petty production, in all other respects would mean failure to investigate the most immediate causes that determine the growth or weakening of the connection between petty production and capitalism; it would mean failure to explore more thoroughly the conditions of proportionality in the whole economic system, particularly the preconditions of disproportion that come to the surface in a real economy only as the result of new phenomena, not just in the capitalist but also in the petty-bourgeois sector of the economy.

Finally, in the analysis of equilibrium under real capitalism, in conditions of both simple and expanded reproduction, the following essential circumstance must also be kept in mind. In his analysis of this process, Marx started with the assumption that

> In as much as prices diverge from values, this circumstance cannot exert any influence on the movement of the social capital. The same mass of

products is exchanged afterwards as before, even though the value relationships in which the individual capitalists are involved are no longer proportionate to their respective advances and to the quantities of surplus-value produced by each of them.[1]

This assumption by Marx is totally correct insofar as what is involved is a closed circle of pure capitalism; to the contrary, when the issue involves material exchange between the capitalist and petty-bourgeois sectors of the economy, then the question of the deviation of prices from values, and above all the question of a systematic lagging of prices for small-scale production compared to the real labour expenditures they involve, as well as the question of conjunctural changes in this sphere, are enormously important. Here, the issue is not one of redistribution within a single sector but rather redistribution between two sectors, which historically and economically represent two distinct types of organisation of human labour. Here we cannot, in a concrete analysis, do without an investigation of the deviation of prices from values. This is what is new and different in the method of analysis of equilibrium with concrete capitalism as distinct from abstract capitalism.

• • •

Let us begin with the Marxist scheme of simple reproduction under pure capitalism and then transform it into the scheme of reproduction under concrete capitalism.

In Volume 2 of *Capital* Marx says:

> The society's total product, and thus its total production process, breaks down into two great departments:
> I.   *Means of production*: commodities that possess a form in which they either have to enter productive consumption, or at least can enter this.
> II. *Means of consumption*: commodities that possess a form in which they enter the individual consumption of the capitalist and working classes.
> In each of these departments, all the various branches of production belonging to it form a single great branch of production, one of these being that of means of production, the other that of means of consump-

---

1 Marx 1978, p. 469.

tion. The total capital applied in each of these two branches of production forms a separate major department of the social capital.[2]

As a numerical example, Marx takes the following magnitudes of the capital being applied and of the annual reproduction:

1) $4000c + 1000v + 1000s = 6000$ means of production
2) $2000c + 500v + 500s = 3000$ means of consumption

Consequently, in this scheme the applied capital in Department I is $4000c$ – i.e., the constant capital – plus $1000v$, which is the variable capital going to wages. In Department II, the applied capital is $2000c + 500v$.

From the viewpoint of the capitalist class, the new product equals the whole of the surplus value, i.e., $1000 + 500$.

From the point of view of society, the new product equals 3000 and comprises the capitalists' accumulation fund of 1500 plus the workers' consumption fund of 1500.

The basic pattern that Marx reveals in the analysis of simple reproduction, which represents his greatest theoretical contribution, is that equilibrium under simple reproduction, i.e., with the entire new product being completely consumed and no accumulation occurring, requires an equality of $v + s$ in Department I with c of Department II. This means that the portion of the annual product of Department I that in value terms equals $v + s$ of this Department, and which in material form consists of different types of means of production (the machines, materials and fuel entering into productive consumption, etc.), must invariably be equal to c of Department II, that is, the value of those means of consumption that the second Department sells to the first, thereby enabling Department I to sell the same sum of means of production to Department II to replace IIc.

Now, suppose that we are dealing not with pure capitalism but with concrete capitalism, i.e., suppose that some of the commodities in society are produced in conditions of simple commodity economy. Let us further assume that the gross product in the sector of petty production is equal to the gross product of the capitalist sector, although the value relation between the means of production being reproduced here and the consumed portion of the gross product will of course be different, because what we have conditionally called constant capital will here be relatively smaller (and in terms of the figures we use, also absolutely smaller) than in the capitalist sector due to the lower technical level. We must finally, of course, assume that the sector of simple

---

2   Marx 1978, p. 471.

commodity production is involved in continuous material exchange with the
capitalist sector through the exchange of means of consumption, a situation
that corresponds, as a rule, to the typical inner economic relations of real capitalism in which petty production is completely subordinated to market relations.

Under these conditions Marx's numerical scheme, reduced to a sum of 8250
for annual production, will look something like the following. (For the sake of
brevity we designate the subdivisions of the capitalist sector with the letter K
and those of the pre-capitalist sector with the letter P; likewise, the values that
sector K acquires by means of exchange from sector P are designated by p and
the reverse.)

KI. $4000c\ (3750k^3 + 250p) + 1000v + 1000s = 6000$
$(1000p + 1000k = KI\ v + s)$ $\Big\}$ 8250
KII. $1500c\ (1000k + 500p) + 375v + 375s = 2250$

PI. $750c\ (500p + 250k) + 1500\ (1000p + 500k) = 2250^4$
PII. $2000c\ (1000p + 1000k) + 4000\ (\text{consumption fund}) = 6000$ $\Big\}$ 8250

Here we have a scheme of economic equilibrium under simple reproduction
in the conditions of concrete capitalism, i.e., with the existence of simple commodity production alongside capitalist production. We leave aside the question of the inequality of actual labour expenditures in the equal values being
exchanged. Likewise, for the sake of simplicity we do not include any exchange
of consumer goods between the two Departments II.[5]

What conclusions can be drawn from analysing this scheme?

The most striking fact is that with concrete capitalism the equilibrium of
the whole system, in conditions of simple reproduction, does not require that
within the capitalist sector $s + v$ of Department I be equal to c of Department
II. On the contrary, they will as a rule never be equal.

The second conclusion is that, *taking the economy as a whole*, $v + s$ of Department I in the capitalist sector, plus the income consumed in Department I of
the petty-bourgeois sector (in our example $1000v + 1000s$ in KI, plus 1500 in sec-

---

3 [There is an error in the Russian text, which gives the figure of 3725k rather than 3750k.]
4 In this example, as distinct from those that follow, we use the identical ratio of 1:2 between
   the consumption fund and constant capital in both Departments of the pre-capitalist sector.
5 [Consumer goods produced within the capitalist sector are consumed within that sector, and
   consumer goods produced in the pre-capitalist sector are consumed within that sector.]

tor P), is equal to the constant capital c of Department II in the capitalist sector (1500) plus the value of the reproduced means of production in [Department II of] the petty-bourgeois sector (2000). Thus the equality established by Marx in the proportions of exchange between Departments I and II for pure capitalism (I $(v + s)$ = IIc) is no longer necessary for the capitalist sector and *takes the form of an analogous equation for the economy as a whole* if the production of means of production in both sectors is treated as one Department and production of means of consumption as a second Department.

Let us now consider why we get these two outcomes.

In the capitalist sector the equality of KI $(v + s)$ with KIIc would only be possible in one circumstance; namely, if exchange between the petty-bourgeois sector and the capitalist sector occurred on the basis of an exchange of equal values within the production of means of production on the one hand, and, on the other hand, also within the production of means of consumption in the two sectors. In other words: KI sells 100c or 200c to PIc and receives in return the same sum of means of production of a different type. The same must occur in the case of exchange between the second Departments of both sectors. It is quite obvious in this case that the equation I $(v + s)$ = IIc must correspond to an equality of values within the petty-bourgeois sector between the consumed income in Department I and the value of means of production in Department II.[6] But such a correspondence of proportions can only be purely coincidental and is completely uncharacteristic for the economy of real capitalism. And conversely, it is by no means coincidental that as soon as we have to construct proportions for real capitalism, i.e., for a mixed capitalist and petty-bourgeois economy, if we retain the arithmetical sums of Marx's scheme for Department I, we invariably must change them for Department II. If we retain the sums for Department II, we must change the volume of production in Department I, which corresponds, as we shall see below, to a different technical structure for the economy of society as a whole.

But if the sum KI $(v + s)$, representing means of production in material terms, cannot be fully exchanged for KIIc, i.e., for means of consumption from the second Department of the capitalist sector in order to replace constant capital in KII, then equilibrium can only be established by drawing PII into exchange. In other words, Department I of the capitalist sector sells means of production not only to Department II of its own sector but also to PII – in this case, for example, to the peasant economy, which is producing means of consumption. In return, the peasant economy receives that part of the means of production –

---

6 [That is, PI $(v + s)$ = PIIc.]

for instance agricultural machinery and artificial fertilisers etc. – with which it cannot be fully supplied from the petty-bourgeois Department of means of production.

As we shall see below, exactly the same will occur, in the sense of establishing equilibrium, if the reverse happens and KIIc cannot be fully exchanged for KI $(v + s)$: the deficit of means of production [in KII] will be covered from the realised income of PI, taking the natural form of means of production of petty-bourgeois origin (say, peasant materials such as flax, cotton, leather, small-scale artisan repairs, etc.), [with KII] providing factory-produced means of consumption (textiles, sugar etc.) in exchange.

As for the inevitability of an equality, *for the economy as a whole*, of the exchange proportions between that part of the means of production of both sectors that is exchanged for the means of consumption of both of the second Departments, and the value of the constant capital of both of the second Departments that is being reproduced – that equality, in the conditions of simple reproduction, is obligatory for any economy with a market system of exchange, whether it is a petty-bourgeois-capitalist economic system or a mixed commodity-socialist one such as ours. A disruption of equality in the exchange of these sums will inevitably mean either under-consumption or incomplete reproduction of the constant capital, i.e., an interruption of the fundamental condition of simple reproduction.

With a mixed economy, however, special importance attaches to that part of the petty-bourgeois sector that is least of all fixed in the iron vice of proportionality of the society's entire economy; we are speaking of the consumption fund in Department II of the petty-bourgeois sector. The specific feature of this part of the product, in terms of its weaker dependence on material exchange within the whole economy, is already apparent in Marx's scheme of simple reproduction, but it is only in Department II of the petty-bourgeois sector that it becomes most noticeable.

Indeed, $500v + 500s$, in Department II of Marx's scheme, is that part of the means of consumption that is created and consumed in this Department. If we assume, with the same magnitude of IIc (i.e., 2000) that due to a harvest failure in capitalist agriculture the total sum of the year's production of means of consumption declines from 3000 to 2800, then this must lead either to a reduction of $500s$ to $300s$, or else to a reduction of both s and v, either in that proportion or in some other proportion. In that case the proportional linkage between Department II and Department I will not be ruptured, since the value of commodities from Department II will be determined by the value of production for a typical average year, not by the labour expended on a unit of output for this particular exceptional year. However, to reduce $500v$ to $400v$ is extremely difficult because in capitalist production the wages fund tends to fluctuate around the value of labour power in the economy as a whole, and a reduction, other conditions remaining the same, has a pronounced effect on s. Conversely, in the case of a decline of $v + s$ in Department I, with an unchanged magnitude of Ic, we shall have not just a reduction in consumption in Department I but also the impossibility of fully reproducing IIc, i.e., the constant capital of Department II, which can be exchanged only for v and the surplus value consumed by capitalists of Department I.

If we take the consumption fund PII, i.e., Department II of the petty-bourgeois sector, then in the case of under-production in PII as a whole, but with preservation of the former sums of reproduction of means of production, the consumption fund can contract without disrupting the equilibrium of the entire system, just as it can increase if production expands due to, let us say, a good harvest from peasant fields. In both cases the divergence, under certain conditions, can be eliminated or moderated through a regrouping between personal and productive consumption within Department II itself.[7]

The situation is completely different with under-production in Departments I of *both the capitalist and petty-bourgeois* sectors if we assume, as in the first case, that the reproduction of constant capital in KI and PI remains unchanged. In that case, if instead of $1000v + 1000s$ we have, say, $900v + 900s$ or $1000v + 800s$, then the deficit of 200, in material terms a deficit of means of production, makes it impossible to reproduce 200 of constant capital in Department II.

The same will happen with a reduction of the consumption fund in Department I of the petty-bourgeois sector. In this case, the disproportion cannot be eliminated within the given Department; it will inevitably affect IIc of both sectors and must thereby be a shock to the entire economic system. We shall then have not just under-consumption in Department I for the given year but also automatic under-production in Departments II of both sectors due to a reduction of their constant capital. In practice this can be easily avoided with regard to the part of IIc that consists of fixed capital, because fixed capital can often be fully utilised without the corresponding depreciation expenditures applying to the current year, provided that the deficit will be made up in subsequent years (a form of borrowing from one's own fund of fixed capital). But with regard to that part of c that enters into circulating capital, such as fuel and materials, such an operation is impossible. Moreover, even in the case of carrying over depre-

---

7 [Peasant consumption in Department II will either rise or fall.]

ciation expenses to subsequent years, the disproportion will be moderated but the conditions of simple reproduction, strictly speaking, will all the same be disrupted.

The reader can therefore see, among other things, why economic disproportions are much more easily overcome with a rapid rate of expanded reproduction and are very slowly and painfully alleviated in the event that the economy approaches the level of simple reproduction (as, for instance, in England today). But we shall return to this extremely important question in an analysis of expanding and contracting reproduction in concrete capitalism.

The unevenness that we have pointed out concerning the connection of Department I with the whole, as compared to Department II, and the fact that the fundamental pivot of proportional dependence in the economy lies in the area of the exchange of means of production for means of consumption, and not in the internal exchange within each Department, explains the circumstances that caused Marx to construct his analysis of capitalist reproduction by beginning with division of the total social capital in use and the output of annual production into the two Departments described above. Of course, the method that Marx used in his analysis of equilibrium does not exhaust the entire problem. But it is the only appropriate one and the *foundation* of any further and more detailed study of the problem of equilibrium in commodity economy. Such a detailed analysis, involving investigation of the value equilibrium in exchange accompanied by a study of the material side of commodity exchange, is particularly necessary when studying equilibrium in the economy of concrete capitalism and/or in relation to the world economy at a particular stage of its development.

The reader can see from our scheme that exchange within Departments I of both sectors, and within Departments II of both sectors, changes nothing in the proportionality of the entire economic complex if what is involved is the exchange of equal values – in one case consisting of the natural form of means of production, and in the other of means of consumption. If Department I of the capitalist sector exchanges, shall we say, 250 of its machinery for 250 of material from Department I of the petty-bourgeois sector, then the value proportionality of exchange in the complex as a whole will not be disrupted. The same applies if 300 is exchanged for 300 or 350 for 350. This also holds for mutual exchange of means of consumption of the same value between Departments II of the capitalist and petty-bourgeois sectors. Here we have approximately the case that Marx analysed in passing, dealing with the problem of the distribution of means of consumption between capitalists and workers of Departments I and II from the viewpoint of division of the entire consumption fund into necessary means of consumption and items of luxury. That analysis showed that different proportions of exchange within the general consumption fund have no influence on the proportionality of the whole economy as far as the exchange of values between Departments I and II is concerned. The situation changes only in the event that the exchange may not be equivalent, and the difference in the balance of exchange must alter the proportion in the exchange of values between the two Departments.

But that is how matters stand with a *value* analysis of proportionality. When we are involved with analysis of the natural composition of the commodities entering into exchange, even in the first case a different type of proportionality will emerge, namely, proportionality of the *material* composition of exchange. This must extremely complicate a study of the concrete economy of a given country or of the entire world economy, yet it is impossible to avoid such a detailed analysis at some stage of investigating them.

Finally, among the most obvious patterns of exchange between the capitalist and petty-bourgeois sectors in conditions of simple reproduction is the fact that the total sums of value, moving from the first sector to the second and back again, must be equal. In the present case, 1750 equals 1750. In this case, an inequality in the balance of exchange would inevitably mean the impossibility of fully exchanging for each other all of the elements subject to exchange, which would lead in future to under-production and under-consumption, and thus to disruption of the very principle of simple reproduction.

In our scheme of concrete capitalism outlined above, we had under-production of 750 means of consumption in the capitalist sector, which, in the presence of the petty-bourgeois sector, meant the possibility of achieving proportionality by exchanging excess means of production in Department I of the capitalist sector for a corresponding sum of means of consumption from Department II of the petty-bourgeois sector, and a corresponding expansion of this second Department beyond the limits necessary for the petty-bourgeois sector itself. Exactly the opposite position arises if we have in the capitalist sector not over-production of means of production with a deficit of means of consumption, but instead under-production of means of production with over-production of means of consumption. In this case, the constant capital of Department II of the capitalist sector cannot be fully replaced from $v + s$ of Department I, and the deficit must be covered from Department I of the petty-bourgeois sector. This means there must also be a change in the distribution of productive forces within the petty-bourgeois sector. Production in Department I must expand while it must contract in Department II.

To illustrate this process, we provide here a scheme in which, as compared to Marx's scheme, production in KI is smaller while production in KII remains unchanged. Here is that scheme, along with our first scheme, but without any internal exchange between the corresponding Departments of the two sectors.

The New Scheme
KI. $3500c + 875v + 875s = 5250$
KII. $2000c + 500v + 500s = 3000$ $\quad\Big\}\; 8250$

PI. $1000c + 2000$ consumption fund $= 3000$
PII. $1750c + 3500$ consumption fund $= 5250$ $\quad\Big\}\; 8250$

The Earlier Scheme
KI. $4000c + 1000v + 1000s = 6000$
KII. $1500c + 375v + 375s = 2250$ $\quad\Big\}\; 8250$

PI. $750c + 1500$ consumption fund $= 2250$
PII. $2000c + 4000$ consumption fund $= 6000$ $\quad\Big\}\; 8250$

Comparing the upper scheme with the second scheme, we see how growth of production of means of production and reduction of production of means of consumption in the capitalist sector causes, other conditions being equal, reduction of production of means of consumption in the petty-bourgeois sector and expansion of its first Department.[8]

Historically, as we shall see below, the real development of capitalism occurred differently; to be specific, growth of Department I in the capitalist sector, i.e., the capitalist production of machinery, materials, etc., occurs together with development of capitalist production of means of consumption, although in this context Department I, due to the rise of the organic composition of capital, grows more quickly than II, while at the same time accumulation in II has a tendency to grow more quickly. In this context, the role of petty-bourgeois production in the society's economy declines steadily, partly in absolute terms but much more so in relative terms.[9]

---

8 [There is clearly a misprint here. The schemes show that when capitalist production of means of production *increases* (from 5250 to 6000), production of means of production in the non-capitalist sector *declines* (from 3000 to 2250). Similarly, when production of consumer items *falls* in the capitalist sector (from 3000 to 2250), production of those items in the non-capitalist sector *rises* (from 5250 to 6000). The principle is that changes in the capitalist sector are offset in the non-capitalist sector.]

9 [The obvious parallel is that in the Soviet economy the socialist sector will likewise displace the non-socialist sector, which is exactly the import of the law of primitive socialist accumulation.]

Indeed, if we take the uppermost scheme of the capitalist sector and compare it to the corresponding scheme of pure capitalism, in which Department II remains the same while production of means of production increases, i.e., if we compare it with the following scheme

    I. 4000c + 1000v + 1000s
    II. 2000c + 500v + 500s

then we shall see that a deficit here of 500c in II is covered by development of capitalist production of means of production, i.e., capitalism manages without an exchange of means of consumption from its Department II for constant capital produced in Department I of the petty-bourgeois sector. This means that the capitalist sector covers its own deficit of means of production, eliminating its economic dependence upon the petty-bourgeois sector.[10]

And conversely, when we compare the lower scheme, which has a deficit of means of consumption, with Marx's scheme, we see that in Marx's scheme capitalism achieves self-contained equilibrium through a development of capitalist production of means of consumption that ensures that Department I has both the necessary volume of means of consumption and a market for the sale of means of production within capitalism itself.

Historically, of course, these processes occurred by way of a simultaneous development of both tendencies. Capitalist production's annexation of the sphere of manufacturing means of consumption increases capitalist supply of these means of consumption and, in this context, the development of IIc creates a market for Department I, above all for capitalist heavy industry.

2   Expanded Reproduction with Pure Capitalism

Let us now turn to a more complex but at the same time more interesting theme, i.e., the problem of proportionality with expanded reproduction. Before turning directly to the analysis of proportionality under real capitalism, we must pause to investigate expanded reproduction under pure capitalism, since with Marx the whole exploration of this problem was interrupted at just the point where its continuation is absolutely imperative for understanding equilibrium in the economy of real capitalism.

---

10   Here we do not consider the issue of proportionality in terms of the *material composition* of exchange.

With Marx, the analysis of expanded reproduction under pure capitalism was completed in its essentials but not fully, because all of his schemes of reproduction begin with an unchanging organic composition of capital in Departments I and II, i.e., they begin with a constant level of technology. Meanwhile, even the most abstract analysis of pure capitalism requires the process of a rising level of technique to be reflected in the schemes of equilibrium, which means continuous change in the organic composition of capital in Departments I and II, i.e., a relative reduction of variable capital compared to constant capital, along with an absolute increase of both variable and constant capital.

In order to demonstrate why, when analysing the equilibrium of concrete capitalism as it develops, we cannot begin with only two Departments of the capitalist sector, we introduced above the scheme of mixed petty-bourgeois-capitalist production. Now we must show why it is necessary to build the same schemes on different foundations, which refer to the problem of the equilibrium of pure capitalism with expanded reproduction but in conditions of a continuously changing organic composition of capital.

Here is the scheme of expanded reproduction over five years that was elaborated most thoroughly by Marx.[11]

The initial scheme of accumulation is characterised by the following figures:

$$
\begin{array}{ll}
\text{I.} & 4000c + 1000v + 1000s = 6000 \\
\text{II.} & 1000c + 750v + 750s = 3000
\end{array} \Big\} \ 9000
$$

As a result of regrouping for the sake of expanded reproduction, Marx constructs the following scheme for the beginning of the first operational year:

Beginning of Year 1
$$
\begin{array}{ll}
\text{I.} & 4400c + 1100v + 500 \ (\text{consumption fund}) = 6000 \\
\text{II.} & 1600c + 800v + 600 \ (\text{consumption fund}) = 3000
\end{array} \Big\} \ 9000
$$

End of Year 1
$$
\begin{array}{ll}
\text{I.} & 4400c + 1100v + 1100c = 6600 \\
\text{II.} & 1600c + 800v + 800s = 3200
\end{array} \Big\} \ 9,800
$$

End of Year 2
$$
\begin{array}{ll}
\text{I.} & 4840c + 1210v + 1210s = 7260 \\
\text{II.} & 1760c + 880v + 880s = 3520
\end{array} \Big\} \ 10,780
$$

---

11   [Marx 1978, pp. 587–9. Marx's explanation of the process that follows is included as an appendix at the end of this document.]

End of Year 3

$\left.\begin{array}{ll}\text{I.} & 5324c + 1331v + 1331s = 7986 \\ \text{II.} & 1936c + 968v + 968s = 3872\end{array}\right\}$ 11,858

End of Year 4

$\left.\begin{array}{ll}\text{I.} & 5856c + 1464v + 1464s = 8784 \\ \text{II.} & 2129c + 1065v + 1065s = 4259^{12}\end{array}\right\}$ 13,043

End of Year 5

$\left.\begin{array}{ll}\text{I.} & 6442c + 1610v + 1610s = 9662 \\ \text{II.} & 2342c + 1172v + 1172s = 4686\end{array}\right\}$ 14,348

With a quick glance at this scheme the reader will see that equilibrium in Marx's schemes is achieved as follows. For both Departments, Marx leaves the relation between variable and constant capital unchanged, i.e., he does not alter the organic composition of capital. Furthermore, he leaves unchanged the level of accumulation in Department I at one-half of that Department's total surplus value. Then, to achieve equilibrium in exchange, in circumstances of a growing v and a growing $s/2$ of Department I, the latter going to consumption by the capitalist class, he requires the accumulation of IIc to adjust to these sums. He must therefore manipulate the surplus value of Department II, leaving the capitalists of this Department to consume each time a sum that exactly allows the other part of s, going to accumulation, to secure proportional exchange of a growing IIc for the growing $v + s/2$ [in Department I], plus the annual increase of IIv. It is quite clear that with this distribution of sums, Marx's numerical scheme discloses not only the basic patterns of expanded reproduction under pure capitalism, in conditions of a constant organic composition of capital, but also, if one may put it this way, the regular arithmetical patterns of the numerical example itself.

The fact is that equilibrium, while preserving at the outset the same sums of all the capital applied, and preserving also the same organic composition of capital, can also be achieved with exactly the opposite method. The fixed axis can be Department II rather than I. Department II can be the one in which a constant percentage of capital is set aside for accumulation, in this case one-half of the surplus value, with the surplus value of Department I serving as the fund for manipulation. This can be seen with the same initial numerical

---

12   [The Russian text mistakenly gives the figure 4249 for II and a total product for the fourth year of 13,033.]

scheme used by Marx if, for the regrouping of capital at the start of the first year of operation, we take as the basis the accumulation of one-half of the surplus value not in Department I but in II. The capital at the beginning of the year's operation will then be distributed this way:

> I. $4250c + 1062v + 688$ (consumption fund)[13]
> II. $1750c + 875v + 375$ (consumption fund)

The result at the end of the year will be:

> I. $4250c + 1062v + 1062s$
> II. $1750c + 875v + 875s$

And so forth.

We see here that equilibrium, on the basis of constant accumulation of one-half of the surplus value in II, is achieved because the capitalists of Department I are compelled to consume more and accumulate less in order for Department II to have a market in which to sell items of consumption and the opportunity to accumulate IIc on the scale required by the proportions of accumulation in II. The situation that emerges here is the opposite of the one that we have in Marx's scheme. In the latter, the capitalists of Department II accumulate less than they consume and thus make it possible to accumulate one-half of s in Department I. In our scheme the opposite is the case, and the capitalists of Department I consume more in order to secure the accumulation of one-half of IIs.

It is quite clear why Marx, with his numerical examples, takes Department I as the fixed axis and not II. If the scheme that we have given here should develop for several more years, the systematic under-accumulation in I and more rapid accumulation in II must impose a limit for accumulation in II due to its lower organic composition of capital, whereas in Marx's schemes equilibrium can prevail over the course of a longer period of years. But then Marx must accept a different rate of consumption in Department I by comparison with II, with the result that over five years the consumed surplus value in Department I grows by 46.4%, while in Department II it grows by 79%. In both cases, Departments I and II will consume and accumulate in different proportions, which, generally speaking, cannot occur under capitalism with its tendencies towards equalisation.

---

13   Here and in what follows concerning the capitalist sector, the 'consumption fund' refers to consumption by the class of capitalists.

But neither of these schemes serves to illustrate capitalist reproduction in conditions of a rising organic composition of capital, involving systematic displacement of workers by machines, when v may grow in absolute terms in both Departments but with constant capital building up continuously in both Departments at a more rapid tempo.

Indeed, if we take Marx's scheme for the first year and assume that, due to a rising organic composition of capital, $Ic = 4450$ and $Iv = 1050$, that is, machines displace some of the workers who would have been employed with a constant organic composition of capital, this must immediately cause a disruption of equilibrium in exactly the sense that the relative demand of Department I for means of consumption will decline to an extent equal to the part of the additional capital that would have gone to increasing v by 100 with a stable organic composition of capital, but will now serve to increase IIc only by 50. The result is, first, that Department II faces a curtailment of its market in Department I, and secondly, it is not in a position to acquire from Department I, in adequate proportions, the additional means of production that it needs. If Department I uses its surplus value to increase its constant capital by 50, then Department II receives correspondingly fewer means of production for the increase of its own constant capital.

If the organic composition of capital in Department I remains constant, while it changes in II, i.e., the ratio c/v grows in II, that will mean, other conditions being equal, an increase of IIc beyond the limits of possibility for a proportional exchange of IIc for $v + s/2$ of the first Department. Consequently, II's demand for means of production from I will not be fully met, which at the same time means the impossibility of a proportional increase of the market's absorptive capacity in I for the means of consumption that II sells to I.

Finally, if the organic composition of capital rises in both Departments at once, i.e., demand for means of production grows in both of them, that will mean the immediate destruction of equilibrium from two directions. In Department I, $v + s/2$ will grow, but it will do so more slowly than in Marx's schemes, which proceed from an unchanging organic composition of capital, while at the same time IIc will grow more rapidly due to systematic acceleration of the rate of increase of c compared to the rate of increase of v, if the level of consumption by the capitalists in Departments I and II is the same. In other words, the channel of proportionality, the passageway between Scylla and Charybdis, through which IIc must pass into Department I, will become relatively narrower in terms of $v + s/2$ in Department I (although it may expand absolutely), while the cargo of IIc will grow both relatively and absolutely along with a simultaneous relative and absolute growth of Ic.

Marx did not complete his investigation of expanded reproduction with pure capitalism. After establishing the law of proportionality for simple reproduction, he made it possible to analyse expanded reproduction. But he considered expanded reproduction only in conditions of an unchanging organic composition of capital and without any transfer of capital from one Department into the other. Had he continued his work, he inevitably would have had to introduce this complicating condition, without which a scientific analysis of the problem remains incomplete even though all of the requirements for solving it are already at hand.[14]

We can see, therefore, that the numerical example of expanded reproduction that Marx took as his starting point cannot serve to illustrate this process in conditions of an increase of the organic composition of capital. From what has been said, however, we can already see how it is necessary to change both the arrangement of the individual portions of capital as well as the other conditions involved in such a task.

If we begin with the fact that the organic composition of capital is rising in both Departments, that will mean: 1) a relative and absolute expansion of IIc, i.e., a greater demand from II for the means of production created in I than would be the case with a constant composition of capital; 2) a relative reduction of $v + s/x$ in I ($s/2$ with Marx). Consequently, the growth of IIc, which results from both accumulation and the additional sum connected with improved technology and the growth of c relative to v, must be ensured by a corresponding growth in I of $v + s/x$. That is, there must be an increase of the consumption fund in I, which prior to the exchange with IIc has the natural form of means of production (machines, fuel, materials) and exchanges for the growing IIc, which prior to exchange has the natural form of means of consumption produced in Department II. With a general growth of production in both Departments, and a general increase of newly attracted labour power, this can be accomplished only if $v + s/x$ in I, which is contracting in relative terms, grows absolutely and does so exactly in proportion to the absolute growth of IIc. A numerical example can also be constructed from the opposite direction, namely, with the increase of IIc adjusting to $v + s/x$ in I. Translating this into real economic relations, in the first case we would start from the fact that growth in Department I is determined by the growth of IIc, as its basis in the market, and the production of machines by more efficient machines occurs in

---

14   It is possible that in the photographs that comrade Ryazanov has acquired of all the manuscripts for *Capital* we will find something on this theme, since the second and third volumes of *Capital*, as they were published by Engels, did not reproduce *Marx's entire* heritage in this area.

the final analysis for the expansion and technical rationalisation of IIc, i.e., to reduce the expenditure of labour power in producing items for consumption. In the second case, the other aspect of the process is emphasised, namely, that Department II is adjusting to I, to the scale of accumulation in I, and it cannot acquire for the growth of IIc more than is assured at any given moment on the basis of the growth of Ic; in other words, the rationalisation of IIc must presuppose the rationalisation of Ic, which creates the need for a specific relative reduction of v.

But whatever direction is taken in approaching the problem, a contraction of IIc, apart from short-term fluctuations and crises, is impossible because such a contraction would contradict the very conditions of the problem: IIc must grow as the result both of the expansion of reproduction and of the rise in the organic composition of capital. We are left with the absolute increase of $v + s/x$ in I, which, with the relative contraction of v compared to the rate of growth of Ic, is possible only on the basis of an annual growth of the whole sum of social capital invested in means of production, and that growth must occur more rapidly than growth of the whole social capital, and especially of the capital invested in production of means of consumption.

We can easily persuade ourselves that this is the case if we analyse all possible variants of a change of $v + s/x$ in I. First of all, it must be noted that a rearrangement of the figures between v and s/x changes nothing for the given year[15] insofar as the sum remains the same, and it is precisely the increase of the entire sum that is at issue. If we assume the possibility of changing the magnitude of the sum going to accumulation, with the same amount of capital invested in Department I, which also means a change in the sum going to consumption, then it is quite clear that an increase in accumulation not only fails to solve the problem but, on the contrary, creates a still greater rupture of equilibrium, for more of the sum deducted from s/x in a given year goes to the expansion of Ic than to that of Iv.

In that case the solution, as it were, will consist of increasing s/x at the cost of accumulation. In other words, every year the capitalists of Department I consume more and more in relative terms compared to the capitalists in Department II, and every year the division of Is involves cutting back the share of accumulation. But it is perfectly clear that equilibrium on this basis, which may be possible for one, two or three years, must subsequently lead to a situation in which slower growth and eventually a cessation of growth in Iv must also

---

15   We refer to the given year because generally an increase of v at the expense of the share consumed by the capitalists during the following years must increase the expanded reproduction of means of production.

cause a slowdown and cessation in growth of the entire surplus value of Department I, i.e., a drying up of the spring from which the capitalists draw both an increase of their consumption fund and the reserves for raising the organic composition of capital in Department I. Consequently, this method does not solve the task over the long run, because it destroys the very precondition for solving the entire problem.

There remains, therefore, only one possible way out, namely, the absolute growth of the whole capital in I at a faster rate than in II, provided that there is no change in the relation between the capitalists' accumulation and consumption. But once the initial magnitudes of capital are given in Departments I and II, this is possible only on the basis of regrouping, which occurs at the expense of II. And this, in turn, leads us to conclude that with preservation of the same relation between the consumed and accumulated portions of surplus value, and with a lower organic composition of capital in II as compared with I, a solution of the whole problem cannot be found on the basis of an arrangement of capital in I and II that would lead from year to year to the automatic establishment of proportionality. Therefore, the very premise of the task requires a systematic transfer of capital from Department II into Department I.

But are we, perhaps, slaves to our own arithmetical examples? Can there really be no arrangement of capital from the very outset between Departments I and II, such that the numerical superiority of capital in I over that in II is so great that equilibrium will be accomplished not by way of the transfer of capital from II into I but in the reverse direction? From this viewpoint, among the other arithmetical examples with which Marx illustrates his positions on expanded reproduction under pure capitalism, the one of special interest to us is the numerical example that he provides in the chapter of the second volume of *Capital* that is devoted to accumulation and expanded reproduction. This example differs from his previous schemes in that the organic composition of capital in Department II is *just as high* as in Department I. At the end of the third year Marx gets the following numerical scheme:

I. $5869c + 1173v + 1173s$
II. $1715c + 342v + 342s$

The reader will see that in this scheme $v + s/2$ equals 1760, which is 45 more than IIc. Here, equilibrium can be achieved only by the transfer of means of production from Department I into II. But if we also include a new condition in this scheme, i.e., a rise of the organic composition of capital in both Departments, then this excess of 45 can be resolved either by an increase of IIc or by a relative reduction of Iv, associated with an increase of Ic, by comparison with Marx's scheme. But after a certain period of time, with this numerical example, we would probably face the same situation as we did in analysing Marx's first scheme, i.e., the necessity once again to transfer part of the excess capital from Department II into Department I. This is especially the case since it is very difficult to imagine such proportions in the arrangement of capital during expanded reproduction with which, from the very beginning, there is a marked increase of reproduction in I as compared with II.[16]

Consequently, we must look for a solution to this task by establishing for each year new proportions that guarantee equilibrium. If we take one Department as the starting point and centre of gravity, and adapt to it the distribution of capital in the other Department, this cannot provide a lasting solution to the problem. For that reason, at the end of each year we must allocate from the surplus value of both Departments the sum needed to support the previous year's level of production, and then distribute the remaining surplus value of both Departments, as a whole, on the basis of the conditions for proportionality of the next year. In the real conditions of capitalist development (if we exclude, of course, periods of crises), things will proceed something like this. Allowing for 'normal' bankruptcies in both Departments, the main framework of the distribution of capital will remain as it was formed in the previous year, and the new capital, accumulated during the previous year by way of currency emissions and the issue of stocks and bonds, is distributed unsystematically and spontaneously between various branches on the basis of taking into account the market conjuncture in each case between Departments I and II, and this new distribution of capital is eventually corrected once again through the market mechanism of the whole system's regulation.

The objection that may be raised to this proposal is that the transfer of capital from one Department to the other is impossible, because this capital already exists as different types of commodities *in natura*, and one cannot, for example, transfer means of consumption from Department II into I if I requires not means of consumption but rather means of production.

It can be shown that this objection is important in relation to those types of fixed capital that are already functioning in production. It is nearly impossible to transfer capital that is already invested in a railway, but has now become redundant, into the production of gasoline engines or into textile equipment, unless one is merely transferring scrap metal, the bricks of demolished buildings, etc. But this difficulty also exists for the transfer of capital *within* each

---

16   Of course, with a higher organic composition of capital in II than in I, a rise in the organic
      composition of capital cannot outstrip the growth of over-production in I. But such a
      scheme does not correspond to the real conditions of capitalist production.

Department. For example, it is even more difficult to convert soap that has been produced in excess into textiles, butter and so on, or coal into wool. However, the economy of capitalism is quite elastic, and at the cost of some loss of value it achieves a solution for all of these problems not by converting soap into butter but above all through a new distribution of labour power different from the one that exists, and through using commodity inventories and reserves of fixed capital that are not fully utilised in normal times and without which no social economy can function normally. From this point of view, the problem of transferring new capital from Department II into I is no more complex, since the economy as a whole operates with alternately expanding and contracting commodity inventories, together with the increasing and diminishing usage of existing fixed capital. What is involved in the present case is only the technique of relocating capitals, which are embodied in particular commodities, through the mechanism of the circulation of money. In this respect the investigator is not bound by the fixed time periods, years for example, which he himself establishes for his schemes. These schemes only have to illustrate the process as a whole, and they must not make the investigator a victim of his own arithmetical examples. In the analysis of value proportions, what is involved is merely the loss of a certain sum of these values due to the process of transferring capital from one branch into another.

Indeed, let us look at how it would be technically possible to transfer an excess of new capital from II into I to establish new proportions for the next working period, whether it be six months or a new operating year. Suppose that, at the end of the given year, the new capital going into expanding production and subject to distribution on the basis of new proportions between I and II is equal to 800 in Department I and 350 in II. Assume that, in conditions of a rising organic composition of capital and under the old proportion of the growth of consumption, absorption of all the new capital in I ensures the absorption of 200 IIc. In this case IIv grows by 90, and 60 remain to be allocated. Not all of the 60 are transferred into I, but only 60 minus a certain sum that is connected with a corresponding increase of production, and thus also of consumption in Department II. If the deduction equals 10, then the entire problem reduces to the absorption in Department I of 50 units of capital that are in excess in Department II and take the natural form of means of consumption. If we assume the presence of alternately expanding and contracting inventories in the normal conditions of capitalist development, i.e., during a period of non-crisis reduction of turnover and production, we can then assume that means of consumption to the sum of 50 are sold for replenishment of supplies for the social consumption fund; the money received for them does not return to Department II but instead, in the form of new [share] issues, increases the money capital of I. These stored up means of consumption, together with means of production taken from the reserves of I and more intensive usage of fixed capital, make it possible to proceed with additional expansion of production of means of production in Department I. This additional production creates a new supplementary fund of means of production, one part of which will go to replenish the decreased inventories of Department I and to augment the means of production already functioning in I as a result of the previous expansion. On the other hand, this entire process leads in Department II to a relative slowdown of the expansion of production of means of consumption and to a lower rate of replacement of IIc compared to the running start of the previous year. On the whole, we shall have a relative contraction of both the applied capital and the means of consumption being produced in Department II and a relative increase of the applied capital and the labour power being exploited in Department I, with an absolute and relative increase in the production of means of production.

Of course, not all the means of consumption can go into reserves: those that perish quickly will either go to waste or be sold below their value. Such loss of part of the newly created values continually occurs with unorganised production even during non-crisis periods, just as the so-called moral wear[17] of means of production also continually occurs with technical progress.

In the exact same way, the process of transferring capital from Department I into II can take place, although in that case there will be much less difficulty and the whole process requires from capitalism the loss of a smaller sum of value.

In fact, if we have over-production of means of production, this means that $v + s/x$ in I is greater than IIc. The transfer of capital from I to II, in terms of the natural composition of capital, means a transfer of means of production. But a transfer of means of production is exactly what II requires, because any increase of production in II implies, first and foremost, an increase of IIc. Department II then receives from I exactly the means of production that it lacks, which are purchased by II with the money capital that flows, in the final analysis, from I into II. The problem of expanding production in II then involves an increase of v from its own resources, i.e., at the cost of curtailing the surplus value consumed by capitalists in II. Since, with developed capitalism, c is always greater than v in Department II, the transfer of capital from I in the natural form of means of production already resolves, for the most part, the problem of expanding production in II. Additional workers, setting the added

---

17   [That is, technical obsolescence.]

means of production in motion, create a supplementary fund of means of consumption both for replenishing commodity reserves that were diminished at the beginning of the production process and for the future, while also increasing the fund of means of consumption that must serve to exchange for the additional means of production from Department I, bringing IIc to the normal level. In the case that we are considering, the expansion of production on just this scale solves the problem of proportionality.

We have considered the problem of a transfer of capital in the case that is most difficult in technical terms and most unfavourable economically. Meanwhile, apart from the most acute periods of crises, this problem is resolved under capitalism in a much simpler way. The equipment of enterprises in I and II is rarely utilised to the full. This is especially true with regard to heavy industry (one need only consider the average number of inactive blast furnaces in Europe and America over a decade, etc.). With the existence of a constant reserve of fixed capital in I, the problem of a transfer of capital from II into I essentially amounts to a transfer of circulating capital, particularly capital advanced for v, i.e., means of consumption for the added workers in I. In general terms, we must note that the incomplete utilisation of fixed capital is a very important instrument for achieving proportionality of production under capitalism – no less important, for example, than the reserve army of industry.

In investigating concrete capitalism, and especially in a study of capitalist crises, we continually encounter not just over-production in II but even more frequent over-production of means of production. A crisis frequently begins precisely with over-production in Department I. This means that in the present case, if we leave aside conditions for the distribution of effective consumer demand, the apportionment of social capital has a spontaneous bias towards over-development in Department I. But even if eight out of every ten concrete capitalist crises began with over-production in I, that would by no means contradict the general tendency in the distribution of productive forces that exists in a capitalist economy with a rising organic composition of capital. If we plot the average growth curve of the capital being applied in both Departments, together with the average growth of the entire social capital, the growth curve of II will be lowest, that of I highest, and the curve of the entire social capital will be somewhere in between. Here, we must never confuse the general line of development, the general tendency in the movement of the social capital being applied, in the sense of the growth of I at the expense of II, with the external forms in which this entire process occurs. The external form in which one or another tendency is expressed in capitalist society often has the appearance of exactly the opposite process. In this case, we are evidently dealing with such a situation. Precisely the constant tendency towards not only absolute

but also relative growth of I – given the technical difficulty of relocating capital from II to I and the easier and less painful transfer of capital from I to II –
must always entail the expansion of production running ahead in I, after which
the alignment of proportions occurs on the basis of a partial outflow of capital
from I into II. Apparently, with the spontaneous development of the capitalist
mode of production, it is mechanically easier to achieve a sharp expansion of
the first Department and then to accomplish a corrective transfer of a certain
portion of the capital into II, than it would be to leap every half year or every
year over the barricades of technical difficulties and the loss of value associated with a transfer of capital from II into I. This is all the more the case since
the overwhelming majority of means of production – for example, all mechanical equipment, construction materials, and many types of fuel and materials –
can be stored as growing inventories over a long period of time, whereas a significant part of the means of consumption, to the contrary, consists of food
items that cannot be stored for very long. For this reason, it will not be paradoxical to claim that the difficulties of transferring capital from II to I, given the
continuously growing economic need for such transfers, can lead precisely to
more frequent over-production in I. In this connection, one must simply point
out that this fact throws light only upon one and not all of the conditions in
which the process of aligning proportions occurs concretely in the capitalist
economy.

In addition, one further circumstance has to be kept in mind. In our analysis
we have always started with all commodities selling at their values. In terms of
the long-term process of development, during which fluctuations are evened
out, and since the only issue is to explain the movement of the average curve,
this is quite proper in methodological terms. However, to undertake a more
detailed analysis of the whole process, it would also be necessary to consider
the operation of the mechanism of deviation of prices from values, which regulates the entire system of the distribution of productive forces. In that case,
a more or less prolonged deficit of means of production can lead to a certain
portion of money capital being pumped out of Department II into I due to a
rise in prices for means of production, with a more or less prolonged departure of prices from values. We shall not dwell on that process here in order to
avoid complicating our analysis of the general conditions of equilibrium with a
rise of the organic composition of capital. Such an analysis is only necessary in
order to investigate the concrete economy of one or another individual country, or when analysing the separate components of the world economy at some
specific moment.

Thus, with a rise of the organic composition of capital, and in conditions
of a broader capital structure in II, the transfer of part of the surplus capital

from Department II into I is a general law of development of the productive forces. It operates quite independently of the fact that crises can more often be resolved precisely on the basis of temporary over-production in Department I, whether for reasons that we have pointed out or for other reasons that have been established by investigations of capitalist crises.

It now remains for us to illustrate this whole process by a numerical example. In order for the difference in the distribution of social capital – i.e., with inclusion of this new condition of a rise in the organic composition of capital – to be more obvious by comparison with Marx's schemes, we shall analyse Marx's own initial scheme of accumulation and begin with a year that produces the following sums:

I. $4000c + 1000v + 1000s = 6000$
II. $1500c + 750v + 750s = 3000$

As we have already mentioned, to achieve equilibrium Marx takes accumulation in Department I to be equal to one-half of the surplus value, and the scale of accumulation and consumption in II is adjusted to I. As a result, the capitalists in II must consume a great deal more in relative terms than the capitalists in I and accumulate less, which, strictly speaking, cannot as a rule occur either in real or in pure capitalism over a long period.

After rearranging the sums, Marx gets this scheme for the start of the new operating year:

I. $4400c + 1100v + 500$ (consumption fund)
II. $1600c + 800v + 600$ (consumption fund)

In other words, here it is not one-half of the surplus value in II that goes to accumulation – not one-half of 750 but only 150 – while the capitalists consume significantly more than the norm that prevails for capitalists in Department I. In this context, the organic composition of capital remains unchanged.

Consequently, our scheme must introduce changes at these two points. First of all, the rate of consumption must be the same in both Departments, and all of society's remaining accumulated capital must go to the expansion of production. Secondly, the scheme must reflect a rise of the organic composition of capital. From everything said previously, it is quite clear that these two tasks, other things being equal, cannot be completed without a transfer of excess capital from Department II into I, which then must always develop more rapidly than II. Otherwise, technical progress would not find its economic expression in an analysis of values.

In order to construct a scheme that satisfies these two conditions and reproduces both growth of the productively employed working population and also technical progress, we proceed as follows with Marx's initial scheme. First of all, as in Marx's case, we use the whole accumulated capital of Department I for expansion of production within I itself. This is by no means an arbitrary approach. With a rise of the technical level, Department I cannot develop solely on the basis of its own resources, and it is therefore all the more imperative that it utilise all of its own reserves of accumulation. In this case, the whole 500 must be distributed between c and v of Department I. A first approximation to the required scheme will thus give us the same distribution of capital as in Marx's scheme, i.e., $4400c + 1100v + 500$ (consumption fund).

Now let us turn to Department II.

As in Department I, the part of the year's surplus value created here and going to accumulation must equal one-half of the whole surplus value, i.e., in our example this figure will be 375. This new capital must 1) support a level of development in II that ensures equilibrium with the accumulation in I on the basis of its own resources, meaning that IIc must equal $1100 + 500$, i.e., Iv + the consumption fund of capitalists in Department I; 2) guarantee a rise in the organic composition of capital in I and II, which means a supplementary expansion in all of I; 3) ensure an additional increase of production at the expense of the remaining surplus value in II.

As a result of all these causal factors, from the new capital in II, which equals 375, 100 go to increase IIc in order to match the growth of v + the capitalists' consumption fund in I; 50 are thus used to increase the variable capital of II, which now, with this new approximation to the desired scheme, must be equal to $750 + 50 = 800$. This leaves undistributed surplus value of 225 in II. Taking the growth of the organic composition of capital to be 1% of the constant capital of the previous year, we shall then have an increase of IIc by 15 and of Ic by 40. Furthermore, due to the increase of IIc by 15, the existing distribution of productive forces requires that Iv increase by 15 and, finally, constant capital in I must grow by $15 \times 4 = 60$, which means an increase by 15 of the constant capital in II through development of the entire productive mechanism of I within the necessary proportions. In total, 130 out of the surplus value of 225 has been absorbed, and the remaining 95 is distributed throughout the production mechanism as follows: 7.3 to increase variable capital in II, 14.6 to increase constant capital also in II, 14.6 to increase variable capital in I, and, finally, 58.4 to increase constant capital in I. Adding up, we see that the total excess capital to transfer from Department II into I is 188. The whole scheme will appear this way:

I. $4558.4c + 1129.6v + 500$ (consumption fund) = 6188 $\big\}$ 9000 (after
II. $1629.6c + 807.3v + 375$ (consumption fund) = 2811.9 $\big/$ rounding off)

Compared to Marx's scheme that we looked at earlier, we shall have the following differences. Both the functioning capital and the whole level of production in Department I will be greater than in Marx's scheme due to the transfer into I of part of the capital from II. They will also be greater in Department II, but only because in Marx's scheme the capitalists in II consume significantly more than those in I, insofar as such an arrangement of sums in his scheme secures the arithmetic equilibrium of expanded reproduction. In our scheme, the capitalists of II, as in I, consume one-half of their surplus value, i.e., the conditions of consumption are identical in Departments I and II. Compared to Marx's scheme, this leads to an increase in II of both c and v, while IIc also grows due to the rise in the organic composition of capital.

But compared to Department I, Department II grows more slowly, and this expresses the fact of the rising level of technique in both Departments.

Thus, at the end of the first year of operation, the way that we have arranged capital will give us the following result:

I. $4558.4c + 1129.6v + 1129.6s = 6817.6$
II. $1629.6c + 807.3v + 807.3s = 3244.2$

We see from these figures that instead of the 6600 in Marx's scheme, Department I is larger by 217.6. Department II, compared to 3200 in Marx's scheme, yields an increase of 44.2.[18]

The ensuing years must likewise give a continuous increase of accumulation in II that exceeds what is needed in this Department, along with a systematic deficit of capital in Department I. There is nothing inexplicable in all of this, because in our scheme (as in Marx's) the organic composition of capital in Department II is lower than in Department I. Here v, when compared to its constant capital, is greater than in I, and for that reason, with other conditions being equal, accumulation proceeds more rapidly. If, to the contrary, the organic composition of capital in Department I were lower than in II, then with the same initial figures for the whole social capital we would have at the end of the first year and in following years *a systematic over-accumulation in Department I and under-accumulation in Department II.* This could easily be shown in

18   [The Russian text mistakenly gives the figure of 42.4.]

a concrete numerical example. Likewise, if we raised the organic composition of capital in Department II to a level that would be only slightly lower than in I, then the sum of excess capital subject to reallocation from Department II into I would in our example be significantly less than 188. Here it might have been possible to find a numerical example in which the entire process of transferring capital from Department II into I would serve the sole process of raising the organic composition of capital in society.

But it is perfectly clear that it was by no means a coincidence for Marx, in most of his schemes, to take the organic composition of capital in Department I to be higher than in II. Such is the real tendency of development for capitalism itself, a tendency that will also carry over to the socialist economy unless in future the exhaustion of the earth's fertile land leads to a condition in which the further development of social production causes a change in this respect. But a more detailed investigation of this problem is not part of our task.

Taking our scheme as the starting point, we could have portrayed the process of production's further development differently: to be precise, we could have made the volume of the transfer of capital from Department II into I greater at the outset than we actually did and then introduced correctives by transferring part of the capital from I back into Department II. Under real capitalism, this is seen quite often. But, as we have already remarked, such a development of social production does nothing to change the general tendency that we have established, which includes not only absolute but also relative growth in the size of the capital applied in Department I if the organic composition of capital in society grows and if, in the initial schemes, the organic composition of capital in Department I is higher than in Department II.

3   Expanded Reproduction under Concrete Capitalism

The analysis of expanded reproduction under pure capitalism, and also the analysis of simple reproduction under concrete capitalism, already provide us with all the necessary premises for an abstract-theoretical investigation of the conditions for equilibrium under concrete capitalism, i.e., for a mixed economy of capitalism and petty commodity production. As in the investigation of simple reproduction under concrete capitalism, we shall have to deal here with two sectors of the economy, with two Departments in each sector, and with the same provisional terminology. We shall consequently have the following algebraic scheme:

KI. $c + v + s$
KII. $c + v + s$
PI. c + the consumption fund
PII. c + the consumption fund[19]

In an investigation of expanded reproduction in such a system, we have a great many theoretically (and practically) possible cases that deserve to be analysed. In our study we shall deal only with three of them that are typical and most characteristic for the development of concrete capitalism and most important for the further study of equilibrium in the Soviet economic system.

The first case involves development of the capitalist sector with a relative and absolute contraction of the scale of production in the petty-bourgeois sector but with a growth of social production as a whole. The second case includes development of the capitalist sector with a stable scale of production in the petty-bourgeois sector of the economy. Finally, the third case has simultaneous growth of production in both sectors. All of these cases occur in conditions of a rising organic composition of capital in the capitalist sector.

There is no need to dwell for long upon the second case. If the dimensions of production in the petty-bourgeois sector are stable, and if development occurs only in the capitalist sector, then all of the changes in the system of proportionality will begin mainly in the capitalist sector. If not only the dimensions of production remain stable in the petty-bourgeois sector as a whole, but the proportions in the distribution of productive forces between its two Departments also remain constant, then this case cannot reveal anything new for the investigation because the entire analysis is then transferred to the capitalist sector, whence all changes in the system's equilibrium must also emerge. Only the third situation can be of interest, when the scale of production in the petty-bourgeois sector is stable in terms of its general sum of values but there is simultaneously a change in the distribution of productive forces between its Departments. In other words, if Department I grows, then II contracts by the same sum or vice versa. In the first case, the growth of production of means of production in the petty-bourgeois sector at the expense of the production of means of consumption must inevitably lead to growth of the consumption fund in PI, which takes the natural form of means of production and is subject to exchange for means of consumption, which, with a contraction of PIIc, must lead to an increase of demand in PI for means of consumption coming

---

19   With expanded reproduction in the petty-bourgeois sector we must have: C + the consumption fund + the accumulation fund.

from capitalist production. And this, in turn, requires that additional means of production from Department I of the petty-bourgeois sector find a supplementary market in the capitalist sector. In practice this means, shall we say, that an additional quantity of flax, cotton, leather, wool and so forth, coming from peasant production, must find a supplementary market in the capitalist sector, and Department II of the capitalist sector must ensure additional means of consumption for Department I of the petty-bourgeois sector.

In the reverse situation, i.e., with growth of PII at the expense of PI, Department II of the pretty-bourgeois sector must increase its constant capital by some additional sum. If it does not find this constant capital in Department I of the petty-bourgeois sector, PII must purchase these means of production from Department I of the capitalist sector and also find in the capitalist sector a supplementary market for its additional means of consumption.

Let us turn now to another situation, i.e. to our first case, which is of most interest for understanding the process of expanded reproduction under real capitalism, when the capitalist sector finds itself in a state of more or less rapid development and is displacing petty-bourgeois production both in the sphere of production of means of production and in the sphere of production of means of consumption. What this might mean in fact is that in the agricultural sphere large-scale capitalist production squeezes out small-scale production, and in the sphere of industry the large-scale capitalist factory squeezes out handicraft and artisan production.

For an initial scheme, let us take an economic year that finishes with the following numerical results in terms of the general sum of annual production.

The Capitalist Sector

$$2000c + 500v + 500s = 3000 \atop 1200c + 400v + 400s = 2000 \Bigg\} \ 5000$$

The Petty-bourgeois Sector

$$1500c + 1500 \ (\text{consumption fund}) = 3000 \atop 1050c + 2100 \ (\text{consumption fund}) = 3150 \Bigg\} \ 6150$$

In this scheme, the general dimensions of production for the capitalist sector are less than the dimensions of production for the petty-bourgeois sector. The organic composition of capital in Department I of the capitalist sector is higher than in Department II.

The dimensions of production in Department I of the pre-capitalist sector are about the same as in Department II, but the relation between constant capital and the consumption fund in the two Departments of the petty-bourgeois sector is different. This is connected with the fact that petty artisan and petty agricultural production of means of production usually require the application of a greater quantity of constant capital, mainly involving materials, than is the case with petty-bourgeois production of means of consumption. In our example, of course, this relation is chosen quite arbitrarily, using proportions in PII that approximate the conditions of non-intensive small-scale peasant farming.

For the sake of simplicity, we do not include in this scheme an exchange of values between the corresponding Departments of both sectors; for example, materials produced by the peasants exchanging for machinery from the capitalist sector, or peasant production of grain, butter etc. being exchanged for textiles, shoes etc. from the capitalist sector. Thus the scheme, as it is constructed, is characterised only by proportionality of exchange between *the different Departments of the two sectors*. As we have pointed out earlier, in the scheme of simple reproduction, internal exchange between the same Departments of the two sectors, if it involves the exchange of identical values, does not have any influence on the proportionality of the entire system *once we abstract from any analysis of the natural makeup of the commodities subject to exchange and deal exclusively with an analysis of values.*

With a brief glance at the scheme, the reader will see that the capitalist sector has a deficit of means of production. For replacement of 1200 IIc, Department I has at its disposal only the sum of 750. The deficit is covered by Department I of the petty-bourgeois sector, as 1500 means of production of petty-bourgeois origin exchange for means of consumption. Of these, 1050 cover the constant capital of Department II in the petty-bourgeois sector, and 450 cover the deficit of means of production in KII. On the other hand, PII receives 1050 means of consumption from its own sector and 450 from Department II of the capitalist sector.

In this connection, one must not forget for a moment that reducing the entire proportionality of exchange between the capitalist and petty-bourgeois sectors simply to the exchange of 450 means of consumption of capitalist origin for 450 means of production from the petty-bourgeois sector is only an abstraction for purposes of a value analysis, to which we are limiting ourselves for the moment. The fact is that KI purchases both means of consumption and means of production from P, i.e., not only cotton and leather of peasant origin, for instance, but also grain. On the other hand, KII not only purchases means of production from P but also exchanges, within certain proportions, means of consumption with PII. PI and PII also make purchases from both capitalist Departments. But when we omit the mutually offsetting exchange of values between the same Departments from different sectors of the economy, the problem of proportionality is reduced to what is shown in the scheme, i.e., the exchange of 450 means of consumption from KII for 450 means of production from PI.

Let us now look at the whole scheme in motion. We assume that: 1) one-half of the surplus value is accumulated each year in the capitalist sector; 2) the organic composition of capital rises in both Departments of the capitalist sector by 1% of the previous year's constant capital; 3) in the petty-bourgeois sector, to the contrary, reproduction contracts by 2% per year.

With these initial conditions, the regrouping of the applied social capital before the start of a new year of operation will be as follows:

The Capitalist Sector

I. $2204c + 546v + 250$ (consumption fund)
II. $1353c + 447v + 200$ (consumption fund)

If the capital applied in the petty-bourgeois sector has declined by 2% in both Departments due to a general fall in production, and if a number of enterprises have thus reduced or halted production under the influence of capitalist competition, we shall then have the following figures:

The Pre-capitalist Sector

I. $1470c + 1470$ (consumption fund) = 2940 $\left.\right\}$ 6027
II. $1029c + 2058$ (consumption fund) = 3087^{20}

If we now compare these two schemes from the viewpoint of proportionality, we see that Department II of the capitalist sector, in order to replace its c, has to exchange 557 of its means of consumption with the petty-bourgeois sector, whereas the petty-bourgeois sector can provide only $1470 - 1029 = 441$.

The result is 1) a deficit of means of production for replacement of KIIc in the amount of 116, and 2) a lack of markets in which to sell the same sum of means of consumption of capitalist origin.

There are three possible ways out of this situation: 1) a transfer of capital from KII into KI, i.e., the most difficult and costly option for capitalism, which in this case does not fully achieve the goal because to restore proportionality in Department I requires transfer of significantly more than KII can provide; 2) adjustment of the petty-bourgeois sector to the needs of capitalist development by way of an internal regrouping between PI and PII; or 3) recourse

---

20   [There is an error in the text, which gives the figure of 3187 rather than 3087.]

to both methods simultaneously. Given the leading role of the capitalist economy and the subordinate role of the petty-bourgeois sector, adjustment of the petty-bourgeois sector to the capitalist sector is generally easier to achieve. This adjustment, provided that we keep to our basic assumption that the petty-bourgeois sector is reducing its total sum of annual reproduction, can generally be accomplished in two ways: either the whole reduction falls upon PII while PI preserves its former scale of production, or else PII not only contracts by the entire 2% of production in the petty-bourgeois sector but there is also a regrouping within P, with the result that PI expands at the expense of PII, which is already contracting.

In our example, the first method will not achieve the objective because the disproportion is too great: it cannot be eliminated simply by a halt to the contraction of production in PI and a transfer of the whole contraction in the pre-capitalist sector to PII.

Suppose that production in the capitalist sector further expands at the old tempo despite the disproportion of the previous year. We are assuming that the disproportion has somehow or other been temporarily solved. If it is not the world economy as a whole that is involved but, let us say, the economy of an individual country, this can be accomplished in the case that we are considering through exporting the excess means of consumption and importing the same sum of means of production.

The end of the year will look like this in the capitalist sector:

$$
\left.
\begin{array}{l}
\text{I.} \quad 2204c + 546v + 546s = 3296 \\
\text{II.} \quad 1353c + 447v + 447s = 2247
\end{array}
\right\} \quad 5543
$$

The arrangement of capital for a new year (in this case the third year since the initial scheme) gives us the following result:

I. $2426c + 596v + 273$ (consumption fund)[21]
II. $1524c + 499.5v + 223.5$ (consumption fund)

If we now reduce the general dimensions of production in the petty-bourgeois sector by 2%, with all of the reduction falling on Department II, this is what we get:

---

21   I differs from the previous scheme due to the rounding off of fractions.

$$\left.\begin{array}{ll} \text{I.} & 1470c + 1470 \text{ (consumption fund)} = 2940^{22} \\ \text{II.} & 989c + 1978 \text{ (consumption fund)} = 2967 \end{array}\right\} \quad 5907$$

This means that the deficit of means of production in KII will be 655 − 481 = 174.[23]

It is true that this deficit will be less than the one that would have resulted if both Departments of the P sector had reduced production in the same proportion, but the deficit remains quite substantial nevertheless. To re-establish equilibrium requires a regrouping within P. If the regrouping for that purpose is on such a scale that PI increases the total sum of its production by 210, and PII cuts back production by the same amount, then with the previous relation between c and the consumption fund in P, we shall have the following scheme for petty-bourgeois production:

$$\left.\begin{array}{ll} \text{I.} & 1575c + 1575 \text{ (consumption fund)} = 3150 \\ \text{II.} & 919c + 1838 \text{ (consumption fund)} = 2757 \end{array}\right\} \quad 5907$$

As we see, the dimensions of production in the second variant remain the same in the P sector as in the first variant, i.e., with a contraction of 2 % compared to the previous year, but then the internal regrouping of productive forces within the petty-bourgeois sector leads to a reduction of production of means of consumption and an increase of production of means of production on such a scale that the remaining means of production for exchange with KII already come to 656, whereas KII needs to sell its own production and purchase means of production in the amount of 655.

Here we have restored the equilibrium that was disrupted by the too rapid growth of KII, given a relatively slower growth of KI in terms of proportionality within the capitalist sector and a contraction of PI from the previous year.

What might this whole process mean in practice?

1) Insofar as an absolute decline of 2 % in PII is involved, this means displacement of peasant production of means of consumption by capitalist production of means of consumption, i.e., reduced sowing of grain crops by the peasants for their individual consumption, a reduction of eggs, butter etc.

2) As far as the rearrangement of productive forces between PII and PI is concerned, this might mean increased sowing of flax, hemp or cotton at the expense of grain crops, an increased use of feed for commercial live-

---

22   [The Russian text mistakenly gives the figure of 2490.]
23   [The Russian text mistakenly gives a deficit of 173 for KII.]

stock to provide leather, wool etc. for KII, expanded cultivation of potatoes
for subsequent processing and so forth. During the development of capitalism, we observed this process in places where the development of urban
industry increases demand for peasant materials, and peasant production of
grain decreases to give way to capitalist grain factories or large-scale capitalist
farming.

It is quite clear that for capitalism a regrouping within the petty-bourgeois
sector is a very important means of achieving proportionality in the whole
system, if such a regrouping corresponds simultaneously to achieving proportionality in terms of the material elements of commodity exchange as well. If
we were dealing with over-production in KII under pure capitalism, i.e., within
a self-contained equilibrium, there would be no other way for the society's
economy to achieve proportionality except, in the worst case, by an industrial
crisis, or in the best case by a transfer of capital from KII into KI, which is often
accompanied by losses of value and a temporary slowing of the whole tempo
of expanded reproduction.

But beyond that, our example clearly proves the incorrectness of Rosa Luxemburg's theory concerning the role of the petty-bourgeois environment for
capitalism. In our scheme the petty-bourgeois sector is drawn into the capitalist turnover but not only does it not expand – it contracts. However, this
in no way prevents the whole of social production from growing.[24] Indeed,
the initial scheme gives a scale of annual production of 5000 for the capitalist sector and 6150 for the petty-bourgeois sector, for a total of 11,150. At the
end of the first year, despite the fact that the petty-bourgeois sector reduces
production by 2%, the intensity of accumulation in the capitalist sector out-
weighs this process and the result is that the annual production already comes
to 11,570.[25] In the final scheme, if we take its result for the end of the year, the
capitalist sector already surpasses the petty-bourgeois sector in the sense of the
general value magnitude of its production; specifically, it produces 6141 compared to 5907 from the petty-bourgeois sector, and society's total production is
12,048.

Accordingly, the development of capitalist reproduction is entirely possible
even with a contraction of the pre-capitalist form of economy. It is entirely possible in these circumstances, without any transfer of capital from one Depart-

---

24   [Luxemburg thought that when capitalism displaced small-scale non-capitalist produc-
      tion, it would deprive itself of 'third-party' markets in which to realise its surplus
      value.]
25   [The Russian text mistakenly gives the figure 11,874.]

ment of the capitalist sector to the other, provided that the requisite rearrangement of productive forces occurs in the petty-bourgeois sector. We might add that there would be no great difficulty in constructing a scheme in which contraction of the petty-bourgeois sector would occur with such internal proportions that the capitalist sector could expand its Departments without requiring any significant rearrangements in the petty-bourgeois sector. In that case, a deficit in the capitalist sector's exchange with the petty-bourgeois sector would be offset by a corresponding additional expansion of production within the capitalist sector itself.

It must also be noted that a regrouping within sector P is generally much easier than in the capitalist sector and involves fewer losses in value if, for instance, the peasant economy increases production of technical crops at the expense of grains, using the same working livestock and in most cases the same equipment, only changing the seed and spending more on fertiliser while also increasing the consumption of feed for the intensification of livestock production.

The extent to which such a regrouping of the productive forces is possible in terms of the natural composition of the commodities whose production is to be increased is an entirely different question. In the present case, if the deficit κ_{IIc} involves not only cotton, flax, hemp, leather, oil seeds for industry, sugar beets and potatoes to be processed into alcohol and syrup etc., but also machines, coal and oil, then a regrouping in the petty-bourgeois sector alone cannot fully solve the problem of proportionality. In that case the deficit of 174[26] in means of production, which we mentioned earlier, must be eliminated when capital is redistributed for the next year's production, partly by a regrouping in the P sector and partly by a transfer of capital from κ_{II} into κ_{I}. But this is already a different question, which does not concern a value analysis of proportionality and leads the investigation to the task of a combined value-natural analysis of the problem of equilibrium, which already implies transition to the study of a concrete economy.

Now let us take our numerical examples, but this time not in the conditions of contraction but instead of an annual growth of production by 2% in the P sector. Then we shall have the following arrangement of sums for the first year:

The Capitalist Sector

I. $2204c + 546v + 250$ (consumption fund)

II. $1353c + 447v + 200$ (consumption fund)

---

26   [The Russian text mistakenly gives the figure 173. See footnote 23 above.]

The Petty-bourgeois Sector

I. $1530c + 1530$ (consumption fund)
II. $1071c + 2142$ (consumption fund)

In this case, the deficit of KII in means of production and the shortfall of demand for means of consumption of capitalist origin will equal 98. This means that, from the viewpoint of the market, the disproportion is relatively smaller, because demand from PI for means of consumption, as the result of its general expansion, grows more quickly than their supply. PI's unfulfilled demand increases PI's purchases in KII, i.e., the growth of handicraft production and of peasant production of technical crops is accompanied by growth of the demand for textiles, shoes, sugar etc. of capitalist origin.

From the viewpoint of satisfying KII with means of production, all of this means increased supply of these means of production from PI, i.e., an increased supply for KII of cotton, leader, flax etc. from petty-bourgeois production.

As for the achievement of proportionality, it is accomplished in the same way as we showed in the previous scheme, i.e., either by a transfer of capital from KII into KI, by a rearrangement between PI and PII in the sense of expanding PI, or by a combination of both methods. The difference, by comparison with our first scheme, will be that if the whole burden of regrouping is transferred to the petty-bourgeois sector, then proportionality can be achieved with a smaller redeployment of productive forces from PII into PI, i.e., with much greater ease.

Consider now a scheme of equilibrium of real capitalism in conditions not of over-production of means of consumption and a deficit of constant capital, but instead in conditions of over-production of means of production in the capitalist sector with a deficit of means of consumption, which, as we shall see in what follows, will automatically lead us again to a deficit of means of production.

In order to set up a suitable numerical example, while introducing minimal changes in the figures already used, we can retain the same dimensions of social production and either 1) reduce the sum of capital applied in Department II of the capitalist sector and increase production by the same amount in KI; or 2) sharply increase the organic composition of capital in KII while not altering the total capital applied in the capitalist sector as a whole. In the latter case, the disproportion will be *even greater at the beginning* due to the sharp increase of IIc, but then it will quickly disappear as a result of the relatively sharp decline of accumulation in KII. Indeed, if we take the ratio of variable capital to constant capital in KII to be 1:6,[27] we shall have $1500c + 250v + 250s$. This means

---

27   [The Russian text mistakenly gives the ratio of 1:5.]

that as accumulation continues, it will not only rely from the outset upon the smaller sum IIv, i.e., 250 instead of 400, but also the annual deductions from accumulated surplus value to increase c will yield a relatively much smaller increase in v, which in turn will affect IIc. This will mean that KIIc will in future grow more slowly than $v + s/x$ in KI, and thus each year the pressure of the supply of excess means of production from KI in the petty-bourgeois market will increase. Equilibrium will then be achieved either by a transfer of capital into KII or by a contraction of PI along with growth in PII. We shall not consider this case in more detail here, because it is only theoretically conceivable and has no significance for illustrating the development of real capitalism, in which the organic composition of capital in Department II is normally lower than in I, not higher.

We shall turn therefore to the first method, i.e., keeping as our basis the same scale of annual production in the capitalist sector and rounding off the figure for annual production in the petty-bourgeois sector. While leaving the organic composition of capital in KII lower than in KI, we simply increase the quantity of capital applied in KI at the expense of KII. After reducing annual production in KII by 600, and increasing the volume of annual production in KI by the same amount, we shall have the following initial scheme:

$$\left.\begin{array}{ll} \text{I.} & 2400c + 600v + 600s = 3600 \\ \text{II.} & 840c + 280v + 280s = 1400 \end{array}\right\} \ 5000$$

Correspondingly, in the petty-bourgeois sector we shall have a quite significant rearrangement between Departments I and II in the sense of an expansion of PII at the expense of PI. The new arrangement, which entails annual production of 6100 and the equalisation of exchange proportions with the capitalist sector, with all other conditions remaining constant, will be:

$$\left.\begin{array}{ll} \text{I.} & 1184c + 1184 \ (\text{consumption fund}) = 2368^{28} \\ \text{II.} & 1244c + 2488 \ (\text{consumption fund}) = 3732 \end{array}\right\} \ 6100$$

In the capitalist sector, therefore, we now have over-production of means of production in the amount of 60. These 60 means of production, which are redundant in the capitalist sector, go to correct the deficit in PIIc that cannot be covered in the petty-bourgeois sector, while PII provides a supplementary

---

28   [The Russian text mistakenly gives the figure 2378.]

market for placement of these 60 units. In turn, KI uses this sum to purchase from PII the 60 means of consumption that it is lacking.

Now let us consider how the conditions of proportionality will change if in the capitalist sector, at the beginning of a new year of operation, the usual rearrangement of surplus value occurs, with one-half of it going to accumulation, while the petty-bourgeois sector begins the year with an expansion of production by 2% in each of its Departments.

If we capitalise one-half of the surplus value in both Departments – i.e., 300 in I and 140 in II – deduct an amount equal to 1% of the constant capital of the previous year to raise the organic composition of capital – 24 in Department I and 8.4 in II – and then divide what remains of the surplus value in both Departments in proportion to their organic composition of capital, we shall then get an increase of Iv by 55.2 and of IIv by 32.9. The whole scheme will then appear as follows:

I. $2644.8c + 655.2v + 300$ (consumption fund)
II. $947c + 312.9v + 140$ (consumption fund)

We therefore have a surplus of means of production in the capitalist sector in the amount of $655.2 + 300 - 947$, or 8.2.

With an increase of production by 2%, the figures in the petty-bourgeois sector will be:[29]

I. $1207c + 1207$ (consumption fund)
II. $1269c + 2538$ (consumption fund)

In the petty-bourgeois sector we shall have a deficit of 62 means of production. This deficit is slightly higher than the deficit in the P sector in the original scheme because PIIc, being initially larger than the consumption fund in PI, grows somewhat more quickly than the latter. However, whereas the entire

---

29 For the sake of brevity, we shall not provide the schemes of the petty-bourgeois sector for the end of the year, i.e., with the addition of the accumulation fund to c + the consumption fund. As in Marx's schemes of expanded reproduction, here we only establish the proportionality between constant capital replaced for the year and the consumption fund (in Marx's case $c + v + s/x$), and at the start of the operating year we distribute the accumulation fund in setting out the scheme of reproduction for this new year. At the end of the year, the petty-bourgeois sector in this case has the form:
I. $1184 c + 1184$ consumption fund + 47 accumulation fund (rounded off).
II. $1244 c + 2488$ consumption fund + 74 accumulation fund.

,deficit of means of production in PII was previously covered from the capitalist sector, i.e., from the balance left over in the exchange of KI's $v + s/2$ for KIIc, now this balance comes only to 8.2. Here we see a case in which development of KII is replacing PII both as a market for sales of production from KI and as a supplier of means of consumption to KI. As a result, PII cannot replace its constant capital in the amount of 62 – 8.2, that is, 53.8 units. It is lacking a market for this sum on the one hand, and on the other hand means of production in material form.

Equilibrium can only be re-established either by a reduction of production in all of PII or else by a transfer of productive forces from PII into PI in the following year.

All the conditions of proportionality in this case are even more obvious to us if we ignore the fact of the disproportion and continue with development of all the sums during the following year, i.e., if we let this disproportion develop further.

In that case, when we construct the scheme for the following year on the basis of the production results of the year just completed, we shall get the following figures for the distribution of productive forces:

The Year's Results in the Capitalist Sector

I. $2644.8c + 655.2v + 655.2s$
II. $947c + 312.9v + 312.9s$

On this basis, the new regrouping for production in the following year will be:

I. $2912.2c + 715v + 327.6$ (consumption fund)
II. $1066.7c + 349.5v + 156.4$ (consumption fund)

The Petty-bourgeois Sector

I. $1231c + 1231$ (consumption fund)
II. $1294c + 2588$ (consumption fund)

Analysing this result, we shall see that this year the capitalist sector not only has no excess of means of production for sale to the petty-bourgeois sector but rather itself has a deficit of 24.1 means of production. Nor can KII acquire these means of production from PI in order to replace its c, because in the petty-bourgeois sector we also have a deficit of means of production and overproduction of means of consumption. Here, too, Department II cannot find a market for 63 of its means of consumption, which must reproduce its missing constant capital, nor can it find means of production in the same sum. Consequently, for the whole of social production we have a goods famine involving means of production amounting to $63 + 24.1 = 87.1$

This situation (if we leave aside a slight difference between the rates of growth of PIIc and the consumption fund PI) results from two causes: in the first place, from the rise in the organic composition of capital in both Departments of the capitalist sector; and secondly, from the more rapid rate of accumulation in KII, which is connected with a lower organic composition of capital in this Department compared to KI. Consequently, with a mechanical development of the process of expanded reproduction, a previously mentioned tendency of the capitalist economy forces its way through, consisting of systematic over-accumulation in spheres with a low organic composition of capital, in this case in the area of capitalist production of means of consumption. And that, in turn, leads to the imperative need for society, more or less flexibly or else through a crisis, to effect a redistribution of the productive forces in the direction of increasing the capital applied in the areas of production of means of production.

This last example, which is characteristic of capitalist economy during its period of development, is also of special interest for us, because it partially reproduces (although in a form that is too general and abstract) the very same processes that we, *mutatis mutandis*, are seeing at present in the economy of the USSR, insofar as we study it from the viewpoint of the economic equilibrium of the system as a whole.

Before finishing with this part of our investigation, which has to do with accumulation and expanded reproduction under real capitalism, we would like to mention one other problem. Having considered the question of the transfer of capital from KII into KI, we should say a few words about the problem of transferring elements of production from the petty-bourgeois sector into the capitalist sector. If we leave aside all sorts of measures of non-economic pressure by large-scale capital and its state upon petty-bourgeois production (for example, the tax system etc.), and remain strictly within the sphere of purely economic relations and processes, then the most interesting and most essential form of the transfer of capital from the petty-bourgeois sector into the capitalist sector is use by the capitalist sector of petty-bourgeois monetary accumulation.

This monetary accumulation, from the viewpoint of the exchange of values, is a series of sales without corresponding purchases, in which the money from this operation will subsequently be at the disposal of capitalist production. Suppose that we do not have any growth of the capital used in the petty-bourgeois sector but there is a systematic excess of consumption beyond the consumption fund, or else we have an expansion of production but not on a scale that absorbs the whole surplus product. The result, let us say, is that each year 2% of the whole consumption fund (in our last initial scheme 2% of 1184 + 2488 = 73.4) represents partly sales of means of production of petty-bourgeois origin and partly sales of means of consumption without any corresponding purchases. If the proceeds from these sales are deposited in banks and savings banks or go to purchasing industrial securities etc., then all these resources in money form, either through the banking system or directly through purchases of industrial shares, are at the disposal of the capitalist sector of the economy and serve as a source of additional purchases from the petty-bourgeois sector without matching sales to it. If we exclude a partial return of values in the form of interest, what we have here from the economic viewpoint, under the veil of financial-monetary relations, is a one-sided stream of values from the petty-bourgeois sector into the capitalist sector. If PI sells means of production to the capitalist sector, for example cotton, leather etc. without making any purchases from the latter, and if PII sells grain, meat and butter without making purchases, while the money that is received from the sales serves the capitalist sector as a source of new purchases without sales, the result of this whole process is that the capitalist sector receives additional resources for its expansion: in this case, it increases its constant and variable capital but not on the basis of its own accumulation. Both Departments of K receive additional means of consumption for the increase of variable capital, along with additional means of production for the increase of constant capital. This reinforcement of the resources for capitalist accumulation from without, i.e., from sources that lie beyond the capitalist sector, is extremely important both for surmounting disproportions that occur when the capitalists lack resources for increasing variable capital and also when the expansion of production, which is required by the whole course of accumulation in the previous year, encounters a shortage of new capital in the material form of means of production that can be produced in the petty-bourgeois sector.

Accordingly, if a regrouping of productive forces within the petty-bourgeois sector, which is dictated to it by the mechanism of the capitalist market, serves within certain limits as an essential element for achieving equilibrium in the capitalist sector of the economy, on the other hand petty-bourgeois accumulation, being a most essential factor in facilitating capitalist expanded reproduction, also increases the elasticity of the whole mechanism for achieving economic equilibrium.

After this brief investigation of the conditions of economic equilibrium under concrete capitalism, we can now turn to a value analysis of equilibrium when the economy has stopped developing, when there is a decline of society's productive forces, and also when there is a turn back to reconstruction, i.e., we can begin a general examination of the process of declining reproduction. A clear example of this type of economy can presently be seen in some of the countries of post-war Western Europe. But given the very nature of the topic, in this context we must also consider the consequences of changes in conditions that we treated as constant in our foregoing analysis, i.e., we have to examine the effect of changes in the sphere of labour productivity and the rate of exploitation, and in the relation between the consumed and accumulated surplus value, along with several other aspects of the problem.

4   Declining Reproduction

An investigation of the problem of proportionality with declining capitalist reproduction is of more than theoretical interest. We are certainly not undertaking this study for the sake of pedantically augmenting the analysis of simple and expanded capitalist reproduction and to cover all the so-called 'possible cases'. Since capitalism entered its period of decay, several capitalist countries have lived for years (following the outbreak of imperialist war) in circumstances of declining reproduction. Some, such as England, to this day find themselves in this economic situation. Ever since one or another part of the world economy might at any moment take the path of rapid economic regression, an analysis of declining reproduction and its consequences has been of enormous practical interest. In particular, in view of the growing links between our economy and the world economy, such a study is also required in order to understand certain specific conditions of our survival and economic development. The unfortunate part is that I must limit my analysis of this problem only to the bare essentials in order not to deviate too far from my basic theme.

In theoretical terms, the following conceivable instances of declining reproduction are most typical: 1) a case where the non-productive consumption of capitalist society is at a constant level and there is either a steady reduction in numbers of the productively employed working population, a fall in labour productivity on the part of a stable workforce with the same level of wages, or a decline in numbers of those productively employed together with a drop in labour productivity; 2) a case where the number of those productively employed is stable or even temporarily rising, and where labour productivity is also stable or rising, but the non-productive expenditures of capitalist society are increasing with such enormous speed that they consume not just that part of the annual surplus value that goes to accumulation but also part of the annually produced fixed and circulating capital used in production. This must inevitably lead to a decline of the variable capital from year to year and thus to a fall in the surplus value being created from year to year.

The difference between the first and second cases lies in the fact that in the first case surplus value contracts due to a reduction of v but with a constant rate of exploitation. With a constant rate of non-productive consumption, there comes a moment when non-productive consumption exceeds the entire sum of s, and then depletion of the country's fixed capital begins. In the second case, non-productive consumption grows more rapidly than v and the newly created surplus value, and after a certain period the country, experiencing a reduced rate of accumulation, encounters the same result, i.e., the dis-accumulation of fixed capital, a drop in circulating capital, a reduction of v, and a growing excess of consumption compared to accumulation.

In both cases the time may come when disintegration of the economy is so great that the 'normal' dimensions of non-productive consumption, which existed before the decline began, will exceed the annual surplus value created in conditions of 'normal' exploitation of a given number of workers, and the disintegration will automatically advance further. At that point, if there is not a decisive curtailment of non-productive consumption and a significant rise in the rate of exploitation, any return to conditions of expanded capitalist repro-duction will already be completely impossible.

Following the outbreak of the imperialist war, we saw a combination of these two cases in the economies of the belligerent European countries, namely: 1) a general drop in numbers of workers employed in production due to repeated mobilisations; 2) a decline of labour productivity due to mobilisation of skilled workers and their partial replacement by unskilled workers, women, young-sters, etc.; 3) a fall in labour productivity due to the deteriorating quality of materials and the curtailment of capital expenditures on re-equipping, i.e., deterioration of the instruments of production; 4) depletion, without any replacement *in natura*, first of fixed and then of circulating capital, including insufficient supplies of materials, the exhaustion of normal inventories, and so forth.

In our analysis, for purposes of simplification, we shall consider the value equilibrium of reproduction in conditions where there is an enormous growth of non-productive consumption that consumes the entire surplus value of soci-ety and necessarily leads to systematic depletion of fixed and circulating cap-ital. We begin with the assumption that the customary non-productive con-sumption remains the same in absolute figures as it was before the economic regression began, the rate of exploitation and labour productivity remain con-stant, and all changes in the economy are connected with a sudden increase of non-productive consumption beyond the limits of what is customary for the

society in question. This case simplifies the situation and is not completely typical for the economy of Europe during the war, but it provides a basic outline
for understanding the processes that occurred in the wartime European economy and created the post-war conditions prevalent in the West. What we saw
in Europe was a curtailment of v, but that was due not so much to less capital being applied in production as to the mobilisation. However, the results
are the same. The decline of v and s – resulting from the deteriorating quality
of labour power with reduced wages for this less skilled labour – both point
in the same direction. The depletion of fixed and circulating capital, resulting
from a sudden rise in non-productive expenditures beyond the sums of annually created s, also occurred on a dramatic scale. However, what was unique
about this depletion was not simply that non-productive consumption took
the character of expenditure of the created values; there was also an increase
of production and of the apparatus for producing values, but this was for the
purpose of non-productive expenditures. Here we have in mind the armaments
industry. It would be no great difficulty for us to introduce, alongside Marx's two
basic Departments, a military-industrial sector in wartime Europe, i.e., the specific form in which most of the waste of society's productive forces occurred.
However, there is no real need for this provided that we make advance provision for the fate of fixed capital in the armaments industry when we come to
speak of the conditions of post-war reconstruction of the European economy.
In fact, if we suppose that, beyond the normal non-productive consumption,
society must cover a new and extraordinary sum of non-productive consumption caused by the war, then the questions that arise are: 1) Where will this sum
come from?, and 2) What is the form in which it will be squandered? The first
source for covering this extraordinary social expenditure, in conditions where
the usual level of non-productive consumption and of labour exploitation continue, will be the part of surplus value that previously was accumulated and
went to expanded reproduction. The second source, if we leave aside the depletion of inventories, is the squandering without replacement of the constant
capital in production. In concrete terms, if production of a value of 1 million in
some branch of production involves 300 thousand depreciation of fixed capital
and 500 thousand in materials, then a halt to the depreciation of fixed capital
frees up these 300 thousand either fully or for the most part, and they become
spoils for non-productive consumption. If the circulating capital of industry
also contracts in conditions of declining reproduction, then a certain portion
of those 500 thousand can also be transferred into the fund of non-productive
consumption. With a real fall in reproduction, part of the capital that is set
aside in advance for the wages fund is also freed up. This is why, when constructing a scheme of declining reproduction, we can simply deduct from the

value of annual production the sums that exceed the accumulation fund and correspondingly reduce the constant and variable capital of both Departments of the capitalist economy.

It is here that the extremely complex question arises concerning the relation between the whole of a country's fixed capital and the part that annually wears out. If, let us suppose, only $900c$ are replaced with declining reproduction compared to $1000c$ in conditions of simple or expanded reproduction, this does not always mean that a new cycle must begin with the whole of (capital) C^{30} diminished by the entire 10%, i.e., with a reduction by that amount of the actually functioning fixed capital. In reality, the issue is much more complicated. If a machine has six years of working-life left, and for 1–2 years there is no depreciation deduction in the economic as opposed to the bookkeeping sense – i.e., it cannot be replaced with a corresponding level of machine production in the country – or if a machine that would be replaced in normal conditions now operates for another 1, 2 or 3 years, this creates the temporary possibility of somewhat more fixed capital operating than would be reflected in numerical schemes for the actual reproduction of fixed capital. Here we will have a case of a unique kind of loan from the society's total stock of fixed capital. However, this is not significant over a long interval of time, only for a period shorter than the average time involved in wearing out the country's fixed capital. This is why, by ignoring this fact, which is of great practical significance, we deliberately simplify the problem in a *theoretical* analysis of the conditions of declining reproduction and deduct from the fixed capital that is active in production the whole of the portion of functioning capital that is not restored in a given year. Over a long period of time, this will be the correct way to understand the tendencies of the process that we are examining. But we shall return to this issue later, for the whole problem will be clearer when we have an outline of numerical schemes that illustrate declining reproduction.

Now another question arises. What will happen in the sphere of the distribution of society's labour when a definite part of the general mass of previously functioning fixed capital is not replaced in each successive year?

If, in our example, $100c$ of the $1000c$ are not replaced, and these 100 include 70 fixed capital and 30 that circulate in material form, i.e., raw materials, fuel and so forth, this means that the number of workers who used to replace $70c$ in the sphere of machinery production, erecting buildings etc., are now no longer employed in Department I, and there is also a reduction in the number of workers who replaced the $30c$ in materials, fuel, etc.[31] In other words, growth of non-

---

30   [The total fixed capital of society.]

31   If it is a question of the economy of a separate country, then the issue is more complex.

productive consumption at the expense of the depletion of society's capital means, in this case, reduction of the number of productively employed workers and expansion of the non-productive army of labour. In this case, there might be growing unemployment, or in wartime mainly an increase in the numbers mobilised at the front, and finally an increase in the number of workers in the armaments industry producing the instruments of war.

The latter condition must be clarified in somewhat more detail. It may seem strange to equate workers in the armaments industry with the army of the unemployed or with those mobilised at the front, since these workers were employed in production, even if it was – to borrow Comrade Bukharin's term – 'negative expanded reproduction'.[32] Nevertheless, such was the case. Workers in the armaments industry do produce values, but they are values headed for destruction. They do not produce the means of individual consumption, the means for productive consumption, or the means of production for items of consumption. Workers in the armaments industry also produce surplus value, but this surplus value, in its material form, continues to be the instruments of warfare, i.e., values that are headed directly for destruction. The surplus value of the capitalists, prior to its realisation, has the natural form of artillery, machine guns, rifles, shells, engineering equipment, ammunition etc., and its realisation consists of the exchange of all this for money or various securities with different maturity dates acquired from the state, i.e., for cash or titles to income. Purchases of means of production for the armaments industry, together with means of consumption for is workers and capitalists, are one-sided withdrawals from the country's resources in terms of values that are not replaced in natural form either by means of production or by means of consumption for the other areas of social production and consumption. In such conditions, the surplus value of workers in the armaments industry plays the following role: the machines, metals, fuel and workers' means of consumption, which are assigned to arms manufacturing, are not simply destroyed, but they are destroyed after being augmented by the surplus labour of the workers. Calculation of this surplus value is very important for a book-keeping record of the expenditures for war, but it has no significance whatever in an analysis of the conditions of proportionality for the whole of social reproduction: the surplus value of the armaments industry plays absolutely no part in this reproduction, and all the expenditures of material, of the wear incurred by fixed capital, and

---

In particular, the 30 units of circulating capital that are not replaced in natural form may involve a reduction of imports that may be due to reduced exports.

32 [Bukharin used this term in his book *The Economics of the Transition Period* (1920). See Bukharin 1982, pp. 52–3.]

of consumption by the workers must be entered into the column of society's non-productive expenditures.

Having said that, we must also mention what happens to these material values that are deducted from society's capital with declining reproduction, and to the surplus value of all branches other than the armaments industry. Values in the natural form of means of consumption go to maintaining various types of armies and to the consumption fund of workers and capitalists in the armaments industry. Values having the natural form of means of production, whether machines for the production of weapons and ammunition, metal or fuel, participate as constant capital in reproduction of the instruments of war and of military supplies, and once they pass through this stage of processing they are subject to destruction. In cases when the armaments industry itself creates means of production that might serve in their natural form for production in a normal period, these means of production appear among society's expenditures, measured in terms of their actual wear or consumption.

From all that we have been saying, the reader will see why, in a study of the conditions of equilibrium with declining reproduction, and of the actual occurrence of such reproduction that we are familiar with during the world war, we do not consider it necessary to add to Marx's customary two schemes of social reproduction a third scheme for the armaments industry. This type of non-productive consumption, taking the form of non-productive reproduction, can be taken into account in the schemes of society's reproduction as a whole only as a direct waste of means of production and means of consumption. It would be a different matter if we were studying the war economy of some concrete country: a value analysis would be quite inadequate, and we would also have to explore the proportionality of the material elements of exchange. The curtailment of reproduction in Departments I and II, in that case, would never turn out to be even approximately the same.

Now let us turn to arithmetical schemes to illustrate more clearly the process of declining reproduction expressed in terms of values.

For our initial scheme we take the summary of production for a normal pre-war year that gave, shall we say, the following results for Departments I and II:

$$\left.\begin{array}{ll} \text{I.} & 5000c + 1000v + 1000s = 7000 \\ \text{II.} & 1500c + 375v + 375s = 2250 \end{array}\right\} \; 9250$$

We can see from this summary of the gross income of society that its net income (from society's point of view, not that of the class of capitalists) equals $v + s$ in both Departments, i.e., 2750. The organic composition of capital is higher in the first Department than in the second: 5:1 compared to 4:1. During the entire period of declining reproduction we keep the organic composition of capital constant. We also leave constant the absolute figure of consumption by the capitalist class, i.e., 500 in Department I and 375/2, or 187.5 in Department II. We make this assumption not only for the sake of simplification, but also because the experience of Europe, both during and after the war, shows that the non-productive expenditures of capitalist countries are very difficult to reduce. While they fall as a result of the drop in salaries going to state employees, they increase due to other causes that are directly or indirectly connected with the war; for instance, growth of the state apparatus, splitting up the territories of former large states, etc. In addition, we leave unchanged the rate of exploitation of the working class, which we take to be 100% as in Marx's schemes. What this means economically is that in the variant of declining reproduction with which we begin our investigation, the fall of production occurs not as a consequence of declining labour productivity and reduced accumulation per productively employed worker, but instead for a different reason, i.e., in this case due to reduction in the numbers of productively employed workers (who are being diverted to the front and the armaments industry) and as a result of the simultaneous withdrawal each year of a certain part of the capital that functioned in production during the pre-war period.

Now, let us suppose that from the general sum of society's national income, which in our initial pre-war scheme is 2750, 40% is withdrawn in the first year, i.e., 1100. Assume that this sum is withdrawn in proportion to the net income of each Department, which means 800 from the income of Department I and 300 from Department II. Both sums exceed the surplus value of the respective Departments,[33] and consequently this deduction from the national income inevitably requires a reduction of part of the resources of functioning capital in the two Departments. In fact, of the 1000 units of surplus value in Department I, 500 go to normal expenditures by the capitalist class and all those whom they support at the expense of their consumption fund. As we have already stipulated, we take this sum to be constant throughout the whole period of declining reproduction. The remaining 500, which in the previous period of expanded reproduction served as the accumulation fund, are now also totally eaten up by non-productive consumption, and this still leaves 800–500, i.e., 300 to be covered. These 300 are taken from the capital of Department I in proportion to the distribution of constant and variable capital, while removal of part of the variable capital, from the viewpoint of the distribution of labour in society,

---

33   [There appears to be a misprint here. As he explains in the lines that follow, what Preobrazhensky intended to say is that the sums withdrawn are greater than $s/2$ in the respective Departments, that is, the surplus value left after capitalist consumption.]

means a corresponding transfer of a part of the workers into the army of the non-productive. Thus Iv, which in the original scheme was 1000, is reduced by 50 to now give 950, and Ic falls proportionately from 5000 to 4750.

The exact same thing happens also in Department II, where the sum deducted from income is 300 rather than 800, and the sum withdrawn from *capital* is 300–187.5, i.e., 300 minus the surplus value that previously went into accumulation but now becomes extraordinary non-productive consumption for the period of the war. Hence, 112.5 are withdrawn from capital, which means a reduction of IIv by $22.5v$ (leaving $352.5v$), while 90 are withdrawn from IIc, leaving $1410c$ of constant capital in Department II.

Following all of these withdrawals, the distribution of social capital in the first year of declining reproduction will be:

I. $4750c + 950v + 500$ (capitalists' consumption fund)
II. $1410c + 352.5v + 187.5$ (capitalists' consumption fund)

Comparing the figures of variable capital plus the consumption fund of I with the constant capital of II, i.e., the value magnitudes that must be equal in the economy to preserve proportionality, we see here that they are not proportional. To be precise: $950 + 500 = 1450$, which exceeds 1410 by 40. The cause of the disproportion, in the given conditions of curtailed reproduction, is quite obvious. Department II has a lower organic composition of capital and thus its constant capital is relatively smaller in relation to variable capital than in Department I, while its net income is also relatively larger. Thus, with a uniform rate of 'war tax' on revenues, the withdrawal from the capital of II is more burdensome and has a greater effect on its constant capital, while the 'normal' consumption fund of the capitalists in I always remains constant at 500. We shall see later that this is not a random disproportion for a single year but a continuous process that characterises a gradual transition to the proportions of simple reproduction. Therefore, with the conditions of declining reproduction that we have in the variant under consideration, a disproportion is lodged in the very foundation of the process. What we have here is the exact opposite of the law that we established for expanded reproduction in conditions of a rising organic composition of capital, when Department II had a lower organic composition and thus accumulation in that Department grew more quickly than in Department I. In that case, equilibrium was established by a transfer of capital from II into I, whereas now it can be achieved through the reverse operation, i.e., a more rapid withdrawal of capital from I and a slower withdrawal from II, provided that the total sum being withdrawn is a fixed quantity.

Let us now turn to the question of what this whole process that we have been describing means for the economy of society. A reduction of $1c$ by the sum of 250 means, first of all, that these 250, in the material form of machines, metal, fuel, raw materials etc., are withdrawn from the functioning capital of Department I and enter into non-productive consumption, i.e., are buried in the ground as artillery shells, converted into the constant capital of the armaments industry, burned up as fuel for troop transportation, etc. Secondly, it means that these 250 are not reproduced in the economy of society even in the future, which means a corresponding reduction of $1v$ by 50, or 5%. This 5%, in the form of money capital advanced for a corresponding 5% of v, is now released and in its natural form of means of production is likewise thrown into the pit of war. Among the workers themselves, 5% are either mobilised for the front or working in the armaments industry. Even if they are not directly producing the instruments of war, but instead means of production for the armaments industry, they are still cut off, as it were, from the productive apparatus of society and for a definite period of time cease to exist for it.

In bookkeeping terms of course – for instance, from the point of view of the depreciation of fixed capital in the individual enterprises of I – all of this can be viewed quite differently. It is a fact, as we have already shown, that the withdrawal of $250c$ (lower case) from Department I does not necessarily mean a decline of actually functioning fixed capital by the same amount; a smaller sum may be involved because it can come from reserves of C (upper case), i.e., from the fixed capital *of society as a whole*, since the non-reproduction of fixed capital can take the form of a temporary loan from the fixed-capital assets of the country.

As for Department II, the economic meaning of the withdrawal of 90 from $11c$ can be the following. These 90 have the natural form of means of consumption (manufactures, food products etc.). Normally they would have gone to Department I in exchange for a quantity of means of production of the same value that are needed by II, i.e., machinery, material and fuel. In the form of means of consumption, they are now at the disposal of a belligerent state and are non-productively consumed at the front. On the other hand, they also cannot be exchanged for means of production from I because I is curtailing its exchange fund insofar as it is reducing the number of workers; a part of the fund $1v$, in the natural form of means of production, is now not being reproduced. But it is possible that here, too, the *actual* reduction of functioning capital will not be the whole 90, even though those 90 have already been non-productively consumed. In fact, part of the $11c$, which consists of material and fuel, cannot be replaced from I, yet the *fixed* capital $11c$ can still provide reserves in the sense that it can be used for a certain period of time without being replaced. The crisis of fixed capital will be all the more serious at a later time, i.e., it will occur on a scale far exceeding the wear that is not compensated during the given year. The reduction of IIv signifies a lower production of new values in the form of means of consumption, corresponding to waste of part of the variable capital and a corresponding transfer of part of the workers into the army of the non-productive. However, if the production of means of consumption cannot be cut to the same degree dictated by the withdrawal of capital from II, then it would be possible to delay the curtailment of production, while preserving the same capital withdrawal, by a regrouping within II that would involve v declining by a smaller sum. This would increase the depletion of fixed capital from Department II's reserves. In that way, without any pressure on the exchange of $I(v + s/x)$ for IIc, it would be possible to minimise the inevitable curtailment of the gross production of means of consumption, which is enormously important precisely for a war economy.

European capitalism, despite expectations at the beginning of the war, turned out to be extremely flexible and elastic in overcoming the difficulties of war precisely because it drew very heavily from its fixed capital reserves that were not being reproduced. For example, it converted machines, buildings etc. into means of production and means of consumption to a much greater extent than would be possible in conditions of normal depreciation. In that way it freed up for the front and for the war industry the corresponding masses of labour power.

Let us now return to our scheme. At the end of the first year of declining reproduction, as a result of curtailing production but keeping the former level of exploitation, we shall have this outcome:

$$
\left.
\begin{array}{ll}
\text{I.} & 4750c + 950v + 950s = 6650 \\
\text{II.} & 1410c + 352.5v + 352.5s = 2115
\end{array}
\right\} \ 8765
$$

The dimensions of gross production have been reduced by comparison with the initial scheme, but the reduction is much less than if we compare the total [of 8765] with what would have resulted from the same initial scheme but in conditions of expanded reproduction.

Let us now further assume that the next year begins following a second withdrawal from national income of an even greater sum than previously, i.e., not 40% but 50% of the net income of the original pre-war scheme, which means a withdrawal of 1375 (as we know, the expenditures of belligerent Europe rose from year to year). Doing calculations similar to those that we already completed above, and making a withdrawal from Department II of 105 fewer than would be warranted by the net income of II, in order not just to eliminate the disproportion of the first year but also to forestall a disproportion for the second year, we shall then have the following distribution of capital in the second operational year of declining reproduction:

I. $4200c + 840v + 500$ (consumption fund)
II. $1348c + 337v + 187.5$ (consumption fund)

At the end of the year, with these figures for social capital, we shall have:

I. $4200c + 840v + 840s = 5880$ $\left.\right\}$ 7902
II. $1348c + 337v + 337s = 2022$

If we were to continue in subsequent years with a withdrawal from the gross income of a sum of values equal to that withdrawn in the current year or somewhat larger, we would soon have, after three-four years, such a decline of v in both Departments that the mass of surplus value created by all the workers in the country, with the same rate of exploitation, would approximate and then fall below the normal consumption fund of the capitalist class, i.e., in Department I below 500 and in II below 187.5. At that point, even with a full cessation of extraordinary military expenditures and of the squandering of social capital associated with the war, together with a halt to the declining number of productively employed workers, capitalist society would automatically collapse. If non-productive consumption by the capitalist class were not then reduced, or the level of exploitation increased, the productive forces would be destroyed even without any war simply due to the discrepancy between 'normal' non-productive consumption and the volume of surplus value being created. Capitalist society would automatically collapse.

The process of declining reproduction that we have portrayed has two important critical points that must be noted: the point of simple reproduction at the pre-war level of productive forces, and the point of simple reproduction at a significantly lower level. The conditions of equilibrium change in the course of this whole process in the following way: 1) first, we have the equilibrium of expanded reproduction in the original scheme; 2) then begins the growth of non-productive consumption, which at a certain stage leads to simple reproduction *on the level of the final year of expanded reproduction*. In our scheme, we began directly with a scale of declining reproduction such that not only was the whole accumulation fund used up in the first year, but the squandering of social capital also began. But if we return to our original scheme, we can reconstruct this first critical point by changing the condition of equilibrium. At the outset we have:

$$\text{I.} \quad 5000c + 1000v + 1000s$$
$$\text{II.} \quad 1500c + 375v + 375s$$

Suppose that non-productive consumption, which in a normal pre-war year and in conditions of expanded reproduction was equal to $1000/2 + 375/2$, or 687.5, now doubles due to causes associated with military expenditures or for some other reasons. The non-productive consumption will then eat up society's entire surplus value in the amount of 1375, and accumulation will come to a halt. But in this case it is not only expanded reproduction that will cease; there must also be a decisive change in the distribution of capital between Departments I and II. With simple reproduction, $v + s$ in Department I must equal c in Department II, but in our example, to the contrary, $1000v + 1000s$ in I exceeds $1500c$. If the economy of society lingers for a certain period at or close to the level of simple reproduction, this must inevitably entail an essential regrouping of productive forces. With the same volume of capital as we have in our scheme, the end of accumulation and transition to simple reproduction must lead to a decline of the capital used in Department I and an increase in II.

In fact, the whole capital of the two Departments, which equals 7875, will be distributed in the following way:

$$\text{I.} \quad 4632.6c + 926.4v$$
$$\text{II.} \quad 1852.8c + 463.2v$$

The result of a year of simple reproduction will be:

$$\text{I.} \quad 4632.6c + 926.4v + 926.4s$$
$$\text{II.} \quad 1852.8c + 463.2v + 463.2s$$

The surplus value, now being entirely consumed by capitalist society, will be 1389.6 instead of 1375 due to the lower organic composition of capital and faster accumulation in II, since the growth of IIv and accumulation in II exceed the fall in accumulation in I resulting from the reduction of Iv.

Two conclusions can be drawn from this example. The first is that if society, due to an increase of non-productive consumption, passes from expanded to simple reproduction, this changes the conditions of equilibrium for the entire economy and inevitably reduces the relative weight of the sector producing means of production. The second conclusion concerns the issue of new markets with the transition from expanded to simple reproduction. With expanded reproduction the problem of new markets can be very acute, involving over-accumulation in the sphere of production of means of consumption or else over-expansion of the production apparatus and over-production in Department I due to periodic changes in fixed capital that are associated especially with widespread technical improvements. But with simple reproduction, the problem of markets ceases to be acute and takes on a whole new meaning and significance. For an individual country, though, the question of markets can appear quite differently due to the dependence of its internal reproduction process on the world division of labour, which concretely means its need for certain imports that in turn require corresponding exports to foreign markets.

Thus the transition from expanded to simple reproduction, resulting from the growth of non-productive consumption with the same volume of capital as in the final year of expanded reproduction, is the first critical turning point in the regressive movement of capitalist reproduction that we are considering here. Beyond this point occurs such a growth of non-productive consumption that the consumption of society's capital begins. We have also established that at this stage, with proportionally equal deductions from the net income of both Departments, the conditions of equilibrium involve a more rapid depletion of capital in Department I if the organic composition of capital is lower in II than in I and if the normal non-productive consumption in I remains constant.

If the increase of non-productive consumption is exceptional and temporary, but it still continues so long that society's productive forces are degraded to the point where newly created surplus value can cover only society's customary non-productive expenditures, then the economy reaches a new critical point. Once this point is passed, even a halt to the exceptional non-productive consumption cannot protect the productive forces against further destruction unless there is a reduction of the normal non-productive consumption in bourgeois society, intensified exploitation of the working class, or a combination of the two.

We have examined one of the possible variants of declining reproduction, involving an increase of non-productive consumption as a result of enormous military expenditures, the depletion of society's capital, and a simultaneous reduction of productively employed labour power.

Now we shall examine briefly how the same results may occur due to other causes, operating either separately or together.

Let us return to our initial scheme.

The surplus value that is produced in a year in both Departments is $1375s$ with $1375v$ of variable capital. If we suppose that all of the conditions that involve an end to accumulation and declining reproduction are operative, then we may reach the condition of declining reproduction even without a sudden and acute growth of non-productive consumption with the military origins that we have been describing.

First of all, let the customary non-productive consumption grow, shall we say, by up to 10% compared to what is 'normal'. Such an increase may be connected, as we have seen in the example of post-war Europe, with increased spending on the army, with a post-war increase in the number of states and state apparatuses, with an increase in the number of invalids, with payment of war debts and reparations, and so forth. This will cause an increase of the consumption fund of the capitalist class from 687.5 to 824, or by 136.5.[34]

Let us further suppose that we have a drop in output by 15%, or 412.5, due to declining labour productivity associated with the irrational use of industry within new national frontiers, a deterioration of the raw materials, the wear of equipment, a decline in the quality of labour power, a lower intensity of labour, etc. If, in addition, the productively employed population falls by 15%, i.e., close to the scale of the actual chronic unemployment in Europe, then we shall have a situation in which society will either be on the brink of transition from expanded to simple reproduction or else it will enter the first stage of declining reproduction. If we add to this the difficulties encountered by individual countries, which are connected with the world division of labour in terms of their supply of materials from non-local sources, i.e., complications in reproduction of a part of the circulating capital, especially in the event of an unfavourable balance of payments with the material-producing countries, then in individual sections of the world economy we shall have even more conditions that create pressure in the direction of simple or even declining reproduction.

Our brief theoretical sketch of the conditions of declining reproduction, and of the new conditions of equilibrium in an economic system with such reproduction, may also be of practical significance. It can be applied, in one degree or another, to analysis of the European economy during and after the war. On the other hand, insofar as world capitalism generally finds itself in a stage of decline, in some parts or others it will inevitably pass from a retarded process of expanded reproduction to simple and declining reproduction for additional reasons that are not directly connected with the consequences of the war. In all of these instances, the theory of declining reproduction can serve as a helpful tool for studying the concrete economy of individual countries; it can also facilitate a better understanding of situations in the world economy when some parts are experiencing expanded reproduction at the same time as others are

---

34   [The Russian text mistakenly gives the figure 135.5.]

regressing or standing still in their economic development. In particular, it is only on the basis of a theoretical analysis of expanded reproduction with a continuously falling tempo of accumulation, and starting from an analysis of declining reproduction in separate parts of world capitalism during different periods, that we can understand the character of the current industrial crises.

Let us now try to apply the results of our theoretical analysis to an understanding of certain fundamental processes that we have observed in Europe's economy during and after the war. In the first place, all the belligerent countries had a reduction of productively employed labour power as a result of mass mobilisations of the proletariat for the front and for service in the armaments industry, along with a fall in labour productivity as women, youths and inadequately trained workers partially replaced those who were mobilised. This led everywhere to a reduction of variable capital and of the general mass of surplus value that was created in the belligerent countries.

In all of the warring countries, there were enormous losses of gross income that far exceeded the volumes of surplus value, and this inevitably led to destruction of the production reserves that existed in normal circumstances as well as the squandering, without replacement, of fixed capital and part of the circulating capital. The fact is that each of these causes, on its own, could lead to declining reproduction. The drop in productively employed labour power, at some stage, can render part of the social capital inoperative and lead to the stage of declining reproduction. And conversely, a rapid depletion of fixed capital – which is converted into means of consumption for the army, weapons of war or means of production for the war industry – is capable, at a certain stage in the development of this process, of paralysing a portion of labour power, even though the full usage of reserves of fixed capital may, generally speaking, significantly delay and limit the latter result. During the war both things happened in parallel. On the one hand, the diversion of labour power from production ran its course even in cases where the available volumes of capital would have enabled workers to be deployed in the production process. And simultaneously with the curtailment of the numbers who were productively employed, there was also depletion of the fixed and circulating capital of belligerent countries.

As for the production volumes of coal, pig iron and steel, one must simultaneously keep in view the scale of consumption of these means of production on the part of the war industry. Here, production was in large measure only the first phase of non-productive consumption. The production of coal, pig iron, steel, etc. for direct military requirements, could justifiably be excluded from the general production of the country as one of the forms of non-productive consumption, were it not for the fact that to some extent a number of other branches of production were in the same position and that the whole production apparatus of these branches, following the end of the war, was automatically included in the production apparatus of the peacetime economy.

Our scheme of declining reproduction, on the basis of a sharp increase of non-productive consumption, provides a general picture of the real process of destruction of the productive forces that we saw in the warring countries of Europe. But this picture is too generalised and does not capture several of the specific features of the European war economy. Here we also encounter a fact that always occurs when it is necessary to turn from a general theoretical analysis of reproduction to the study of reproduction in a concrete country or group of countries during a specific historical period. A theoretical analysis of equilibrium in value terms only provides the canvas for such an investigation, whereas now we must study equilibrium from the viewpoint of the natural makeup of reproduction, the balance of payments with other countries, currency relations, loans and indebtedness, and so forth.

In particular, even if our scheme accurately portrayed the year-to-year movement of gross production, investigation of an additional number of important processes would be required: 1) the extent to which fixed-capital reserves were used up; 2) changes in the conditions of raw material supply for the belligerent countries, which involved not only supply interruptions and a sharp jump in the prices of materials but also a halt to the supply of certain kinds of materials and a transition to processing related materials or surrogates (which inevitably changed the distribution of productive forces within the country compared to the situation before the war); 3) a reduction or almost complete cessation of exports for some countries, which, with war loans and foreign commercial debts also being incurred, meant a unilateral inflow of values from the outside at the expense of the nations' future revenues. All of these, taken together, powerfully altered the conditions of equilibrium that existed before the war, creating a unique economic regime that became extremely difficult to study on the basis of the law of value insofar as the operation of this economic regulator was itself extremely distorted due to the growing tendencies of state capitalism and a profound disorganisation of the world market.

But let us suppose that we have an ideal study of the European economy for the period of the world war, in which a value analysis, to the extent that it can be realistic, is accompanied by analysis of the natural composition of exchange and all the necessary corrections for the existence of state-capitalist tendencies. And suppose that the study provides us with an exhaustive description of the entire production apparatus of European capitalism as it emerged from the war, that it establishes the linkages of European capitalism with world capitalism in terms of markets and the supply of materials, and that it also takes into account the new obligations resulting from war debts, reparations and so forth. The question is whether we can examine the European economy, starting from 1919, as one of expanded capitalist reproduction. Or let us pose the question more concretely. If we take the quantitative figures for European production in 1919 and compare them with a previous year that most closely resembles the volume of gross production in 1919, will we see a process of reproduction that at all resembles the expanded reproduction of, say, 1890 or 1900?

The question can only be answered in the negative. The European economy since 1919, with its unstable equilibrium, its spasms associated with currency crises, insecurity of markets, interruptions in the supply of materials, profound disproportions between heavy and light industry, dramatic growth of non-productive consumption compared to the pre-war situation and so forth, cannot possibly be examined by starting from the conditions of equilibrium for capitalist expanded reproduction. In those cases where we do encounter a recovery process, it is not at all the normal type of expanded reproduction. In other cases, we see simple reproduction on the basis of curtailed production of surplus value and enormous growth of non-productive consumption, with fluctuations in the direction of declining reproduction. When the recovery process advances and the graph of gross production begins to rise towards the pre-war level and even surpasses it in individual countries, such as France, Italy or Belgium, the successes turn out to be extremely unstable, being connected with increased exploitation of labour power, with ruin of the petty bourgeoisie, and proving to be vulnerable in the event of currency stabilisation.

Let us first deal with the recovery process. Equilibrium in the recovery process is completely different from the equilibrium of expanded reproduction, and this is why: thanks to the enormous development of the armaments industry, the productive apparatus of heavy industry in Europe, consisting mainly of metallurgy and machine building, was seriously over-extended. When the recovery process began, the development of heavy and light industry occurred in differing circumstances from the viewpoint of economic equilibrium as a whole. We can explain this with an arbitrarily chosen scheme. Suppose that production in the capitalist countries of Europe, in place of the original scheme that we used previously, is characterised by the following figures for the beginning of the recovery and preserves the pre-war values for the consumption fund of the capitalists:

I. $3000c + 600v + 500$ (consumption fund)
II. $1100c + 275v + 187.5$ (consumption fund)

It is already apparent from this scheme that the approach of society's entire economy to simple reproduction, as a result of the contraction of c and preservation of the consumed portion of s on the pre-war scale, required an increase in the relative weight of the whole of Department II. Furthermore, if a recovery process begins, then Department I, with surplus value of 100 going to accumulation rather than the pre-war 500, is still in a position to develop reproduction on a much larger scale because it has larger reserves of fixed capital. If we had a normal process of expanded reproduction, and at the same time each Department developed only on the basis of its own accumulation fund, then given the fact that expansion would require creation of new constant capital, the 100 of new capital in Department I would be distributed between c and v in a ratio of 5:1, and we would then have for the new year $3083.6c$ and $616.4v$, that is, a very small increase of v. Now, if the additional c comes mostly from reserves of fixed capital, i.e., idle blast furnaces are fired up again and idle equipment is reactivated in engineering factories, etc., then the new capital of 100 now goes to increase that part of c that consists of circulating capital and to a much greater extent to the increase of v. If 80 out of 100 go in the current year to v, we shall already have a minor disproportion with IIc and a much greater one in the following year. Meanwhile, the reserves of fixed capital in light industry *declined* during the war, and the part of surplus value that previously would have gone to increasing IIv must now be siphoned off to plug the holes in IIc caused by the war, since no other capital exists for this purpose in monetary form. But this must further increase the disproportion between Departments I and II.

The unfavourable situation for light industry is compounded by the fact that it must purchase part of its material from outside of Europe if we are speaking of capitalist Europe as a whole, and from beyond its borders if it is a question of an individual European capitalist country. As a result, even if the development of production in I completely absorbed that part of the additional production of Department II that goes to cover the added IIc, this still would not by any means resolve the question of reproduction for Department II. It needs not just to sell, but to sell in a way that enables it to acquire the currency of countries that are supplying light industry with material. In conditions where heavy industry sells to the same countries, this problem is resolved simultaneously from both directions. Conversely, if light industry itself encounters difficulties in realising its production abroad, at the same time as heavy industry does not have adequate markets there, then the domestic exchange between Departments I and II, which is secured by definite proportions between IIc and $v + s/x$ in I, cannot be fully completed. Here, even if there is correspondence in terms of value between the magnitudes of the exchange, *which is possible when both Departments have normal ties with the world economy*, the exchange of values will be disrupted by the intervention of a new factor: a mismatch of the material elements of exchange. The result of all this is a situation in which light industry cannot restore its constant capital in a way that is proportional to its possibilities in the given conditions of accumulation (i.e., with the given $v + s/x$ in I), which is to say that it cannot sell products of consumption to I and abroad in an amount that corresponds to the increase of c. Department I then has overproduction for two reasons. First, because inclusion in the production process of the reserve of fixed capital means it already has over-production as a result of the excess of $I(v + s/x)$ over IIc. And besides that, it is unable to sell means of production in Department II even on a scale that is necessary for the growth of IIc, because the replacement of IIc involves a specific natural composition of the means of production, part of which, *under any circumstances*, must be purchased outside of Europe (cotton, rubber, wool, etc.).

Hence the chronic crisis of the recovery process in Europe that characterises the entire period of its economic life since the end of the war. This crisis of heavy industry, which also prevents development of light industry due to the cohesion involved in the movement of the two Departments of social production, finds its value expression, among other ways, in the continuously higher price index for products of light industry. It is enough to cite the prices for textile products: their relative increase cannot be explained solely by the price rise for material. As a result, for seven years the European economy has represented a whole tangle of glaring contradictions. Despite the enormous attrition of light industry's fixed capital during the war, machine building, with the temporary exception of France and Belgium, has not overcome a condition of permanent crisis. Despite the decline of per-capita consumption of products from light industry, the latter continues its extremely slow and painful growth. Chronic unemployment has thrown several million workers out of production. Exports have only developed in the countries with depreciating currencies, while in England, a country that has provisionally returned to the gold standard, foreign trade is falling from one year to the next. And all of this is happening while equipment in heavy industry is operating at little more than half of its capacity.

At the same time, it interesting to observe the specific forms that the recovery process has taken in the countries that have lived through a period of currency depreciation. Generally speaking, the depreciation of European currencies originated with the war. But once the conditions of currency depreciation are established, the reconstruction process follows its own completely unique patterns and itself becomes one of the conditions that have prolonged the currency chaos.

How does reproduction in the conditions of inflation differ from reproduction with a stable currency?

First of all, with inflation we do not have reproduction in the proper sense but rather the selloff below value of a country's labour power and fixed capital for production.[35] What occurs in this case can best be seen if we take the scheme just mentioned for the restoration process in Europe in conditions of inflation. If exchange is to occur on the basis of values, both Departments together will have gross production of $4100c + 875v + 875s = 5850$ for realisation.

If we suppose that the entire gross product is sold not according to values but for 10% less, then instead of 5850 only 5265 will be received in exchange for it. If the shortfall in receipts equally affects c, v and s, it will mean that 410 of constant capital will not be replaced, the wage fund will fall by 87.5, and the same will apply to the surplus value. If the surplus value is not affected, and the shortfall in replacing constant capital is 410, the result will be a reduction of real wages by 20% rather than 10%. On the other hand, if reproduction does not contract in conditions of inflation but instead there is a recovery process, the depletion of constant capital by 410 will not affect its circulating component (fuel, materials, etc.) but exclusively the fixed capital. The fact that the inflationary selloff of a country's labour power goes much further than selling it for 20% below value can be seen in the example of Germany, where in 1919 the real wage of skilled workers, taking the pre-war wage to be 100, was 75.4 in 1922 and 62.2 in 1922–23. In other words, during the years of the greatest inflation, i.e., in 1922 and 1923, the wage fund was reduced by 37.8% compared to the pre-war fund. At that time there was also a squandering of fixed capital in several branches (alongside accumulation in others).[36] In Italy the decline of wages, by way of contrast, was only a little more than 10% by 1925. In France, for the same year, it was even less, although here we must take into account the growth of relative surplus value due to a radical re-equipping of industry, with the result that comparison with the pre-war level would not be correct. The same also partly applies to Italy.

---

35 [As he explains below, by 'inflation' Preobrazhensky means currency depreciation and erosion of paper money's buying power. Nominal prices will rise, but if commodities are sold at paper-money prices, while gold is the world measure of value, commodities will typically be sold below their 'value'.]

36 The issue of whether Germany dissipated or accumulated fixed capital during the period of inflation can be resolved as follows. Take the gross product in gold prices of the world market; subtract the gross product in terms of domestic gold prices; take the share of wages in the gross product; calculate the under-payment in the wage fund; determine the amount of *individual* domestic consumption and exports. If the under-payment of wages is greater, that means that constant capital grew by the difference between the two figures. In the opposite case, it was depleted by the difference.

Now let us ask ourselves what the economic significance was and still is of the selloff below value of labour power and fixed capital during the inflationary period.

If we consider the part of reproduction that is limited to domestic exchange of values, in that context some branches take losses as sellers but profit as buyers, and only the workers lose in all cases. The balance of losses and benefits can vary widely for separate branches of production, but from the viewpoint of the national economy as a whole, the inflationary fall in prices[37] simply leads to a general fall in the gold index of domestic prices compared to world prices (with an increase of prices, naturally, in terms of paper money). Conversely, in the part of the economy that adjoins the world market, a hole develops through which there is an outflow into the world market of a mass of commodities below the value of production (taking the cost of v according to the pre-war index) and also below world prices, as products of national origin are squandered. However, with America's seizure of Europe's world markets and the advance of colonial industrialisation, such a selloff is the only serious way (leaving aside commercial loans) in which Europe can re-enter lost markets and, in particular, increase its trade with America in order to obtain the necessary currency resources and commence expanded reproduction of that portion of its circulating capital that consists of foreign materials. As we have already seen, European heavy industry has a hypertrophied production apparatus. When the expansion of production depends above all upon an increase of circulating capital, and especially an increase of the part that consists *in natura* of foreign materials, the sale of excess fixed capital, materialised in commodities, at prices significantly below production cost (not to mention the selloff of labour power, which never causes capital any grief) is clearly beneficial in the given conditions of operation once it becomes the only way to expand circulating capital. That was the significance of inflation for the reconstruction process in Germany, France, Belgium and Italy.

But there is still another side to this whole process. The selloff of fixed capital below value is enormously beneficial to capitalism when this capital is subject to moral wear in any event; squandering it, together with labour power, makes it possible to renovate fixed capital with the least losses. There can be no doubt that this was partly the cause for the inflationary selloff in Germany, where the low wage made it possible to commit considerable labour to reconstructing the means of production and adapting them to modern technical requirements. This process played an even greater role in France, where in post-war inflation-

---

37   [That is, in terms of real (gold) prices.]

ary conditions a rapid re-equipping of French industry and the selloff of old fixed capital simultaneously achieved two ends: re-inclusion in the world economy and the acquisition of resources with which to purchase materials, while disposing cheaply of things that would otherwise have had to be scrapped.

From this brief excursion into the area of the European economy, we see that not only during the war, when it was obvious, but also throughout the whole post-war period the economic equilibrium of Europe cannot be studied in terms of normal expanded reproduction and on the basis of the corresponding laws. Here the recovery process has its own laws of unstable equilibrium, which were most evident in the inflationary period and are continuing to find expression in the disproportion between heavy and light industry along with the impossibility of any re-inclusion in the world market that would correspond to Europe's level of industrialisation.

One of the most characteristic features of Europe's post-war economy is chronic unemployment, which results not from a normally protracted capitalist crisis but rather from a general crisis of the whole of European capitalism. England, whose impossibility of inclusion in the world division of labour on the basis of pre-war proportions became evident sooner than anywhere else, has already been living for seven years in conditions where about 1½ million of its workers have simply been thrown into the ranks of surplus population. Following the inflationary boom in German industry, the same process has begun there. In this case, now that the limits of the German economy's inclusion in the world market have been established with a stable currency, the number of unemployed workers fluctuates at about 2 million. We shall see exactly the same process in France following stabilisation of the franc, i.e., after France has been allotted its 'normal' share of ties with the world market. The process of throwing people into the army of the non-productive, which is apparently permanent for several million European workers, is intensifying all the more today, particularly in Germany, with the process of rationalising production. This rationalisation, contrary to what occurred in the conditions of capitalism's development, involves virtually no change in terms of access to the world market and will lead first and foremost to a growth of unemployment and a combination of American methods of exploiting workers with European wages. Unlike the earlier period of capitalist history, when the advance of technology and reduction of production costs and prices occurred together with a growing number of workers being drawn into production, with today's rationalisation the number of employed workers is falling without any drop in prices. A larger and larger part of Europe's working class is simply out of the picture. As if anticipating the theoretical possibility of such a blind alley for capitalism, Marx wrote the following in the third volume of *Capital*:

> A development in the productive forces that would reduce the absolute number of workers, and actually enable the whole nation to accomplish its entire production in a shorter period of time, would produce a revolution, since it would put the majority of the population out of action. Here we have once again the characteristic barrier to capitalist production, and we see how this is in no way an absolute form for the development of the productive forces and the creation of wealth, but rather comes into conflict with this at a certain point in its development.[38]

The European working population is clearly being put out of action, and it is happening precisely because the European sector of the world economy is running into 'the characteristic barrier to capitalist production' in general.

The second problem confronting European capitalism is to re-conquer some of the markets that were lost during the period of declining reproduction and are continuing to drift away from countries such as England, which already have one foot planted firmly in an economy of declining reproduction. But this is a very difficult task for old Europe to accomplish, given its enormous scale of non-productive consumption and its comparatively modest resources for accumulation, which are insufficient for the costly reconstruction of the entire economy that is required for successful competition in the world market.

Finally, it must be pointed out in conclusion that for an epoch of declining reproduction, or for an economy teetering about the level of simple reproduction, a fascist form of state appears in many countries to be better suited for resisting decline and, even more so, for attempting a transition to expanded reproduction at the expense of the working class. In terms of its social-economic foundation, fascism represents a new form of labour discipline that is added to the scorpions of hunger and the purchase and sale of labour power on the basis of the law of value, which drive the working class into the capitalist factory and subject it within determinate limits to bourgeois exploitation.

In the present context, we cannot deal with this theme at length. Likewise, we cannot undertake to answer the question of what must happen in the sphere of the capitalist economy in a period when the capitalist form has exhausted itself in terms of development of the productive forces but its replacement by an historically more advanced form has yet to occur. That sort of investigation would involve a movement from economics into sociology and politics, which is not part of our present task.

---

38   Marx 1981, p. 372.

E.A. Preobrazhensky, 'The Problem of Economic Equilibrium under Concrete Capitalism and in the Soviet System',
in *Vestnik Kommunisticheskoi akademii*,
Moscow, 1926, No. 17, pp. 35–76 and No. 18, pp. 63–84.

Appendix[39]

In Volume II of *Capital*, with which Preobrazhensky begins his exposition, Marx explains expanded reproduction in pure capitalism this way:

> The arrangement ... for the purpose of accumulation now stands as follows:
>
> I. $4,400c + 1,100v + 500$ (capitalists' consumption fund) = 6,000
> II $1,600c + 800v + 600$ (capitalists' consumption fund) = 3,000
>
> $$\text{Total} = 9000$$
>
> The capital in this is:
>
> I. $4,400c + 1,100v$ (money) = 5,500
> II. $1,600c + 800v$ (money) = 2,400
>
> $$\text{Total} = 7,900$$
>
> whereas production began with:
>
> I. $4,000c + 1,000v = 5,000$
> II. $1,500c + 750v = 2,250$
>
> $$\text{Total} = 7,250$$

If real accumulation now proceeds on this basis, i.e. if production actually takes place with this increased capital, then we have at the end of the following year:

> I $4,400c + 1,100v + 1,100s = 6,600$
> II. $1,600c + 800v + 800s = 3,200$
>
> $$\text{Total} = 9,800$$

---

39   [This appendix is quoted from Marx 1978, pp. 587–9.]

Let accumulation now continue in Department I in the same proportions; i.e. 550s is spent as revenue, and 550s accumulated. To start with, then, 1,100 Iv is replaced by 1,100 IIc, and 550 Is remains to be realized in an equal amount of commodities II; i.e. altogether 1,650 I$(v+s)$. But the constant capital in Department II that has to be exchanged is only 1,600, so that the remaining 50 must be supplemented from the 800 IIs. If we initially leave aside the money here, then the result of this transaction is:

I.   4,400c + 550s (to be capitalized); as well as 1,650$(v+s)$ in the consumption fund for capitalists and workers, realized in commodities IIc.

II.   1,650c (with 50 being added as above from IIs) + 800v + 750s (capitalists' consumption fund)

But if the former ratio of v to c in Department II remains unchanged, then a further 25v must be laid out for 50c; this has to be taken from the 750s; we therefore get:

II.   1,650c + 825v + 725s.

In Department I, 550s has to be capitalized; if the earlier ratio remains the same, then 440 of this forms constant capital and 110 variable capital. This 110 is ultimately obtained from the 725 IIs, so that means of consumption to the value of 110 are consumed by the workers in Department I instead of by the capitalists in Department II, the latter being forced to capitalize this 110s instead of consuming it. This leaves 615 IIs ... out of the 725 IIs. But if Department II transforms this 110 into additional constant capital, it needs a further additional variable capital of 55. This has again to come out of its surplus-value; deducted from the 615 IIs it leaves 560 for the consumption of the capitalists in Department II, and we now get, after the completion of all actual and potential transfers, the following capital value:

I. $(4,400c + 440c) + (1,100v + 110v) = 4,840c + 1,210v = 6,050$

II. $(1,600c + 50c + 110c) + (800v + 25v + 55v) = 1,760c + 880v = 2,640$; a total of 8,690.

If things are to proceed normally, accumulation in Department II must take place quicker than in Department I, since the part of I$(v+s)$ that has to be exchanged for commodities IIc would otherwise grow more quickly than IIc, which is all that it can be exchanged for.

If reproduction continues on this basis, and other conditions remain the same, then we get at the end of the following year:

$$\text{I.} \quad 4{,}840c + 1{,}210v + 1{,}210s = 7{,}260$$
$$\text{II.} \quad 1{,}760c + 880v + 880s = 3{,}520$$

$$\text{Total} = 10{,}780$$

If the surplus-value is partitioned in the same ratio, then Department I first has $1{,}210v$ plus half of s, $= 605$, to spend as revenue, a total of 1,815. This consumption fund is 55 greater again than IIc. The 55 has to be deducted from the 880s. The transformation of 55 IIs into Ic presupposes a further deduction from IIs for a corresponding variable capital of 27.5; there remains 797.5 IIs to be consumed.

There is now 605s to be capitalized in Department I, 484 of this for constant and 121 variable; the latter has to be deducted from IIs, which is still 797.5, leaving 676.5. Thus Department II transforms a further 121 into constant capital and needs for this purpose a further variable capital of 60.5; this similarly comes out of the 676.5, leaving 616 for consumption.

We then have in capital:

$$\text{I.} \quad \text{Constant } 4{,}840 + 484 = 5{,}324$$
$$\text{Variable } 1{,}210 + 121 = 1{,}331.$$
$$\text{II.} \quad \text{Constant } 1{,}760 + 55 + 121 = 1{,}936$$
$$\text{Variable } 880 + 27.5 + 60.5 = 968$$
$$\text{Together: I. } 5{,}324c + 1{,}331v = 6{,}655$$
$$\text{II. } 1{,}936c + 968v = 2{,}904$$

$$\text{Total} = 9559$$

and in products at the end of the year:

$$\text{I.} \quad 5{,}324c + 1{,}331v + 1{,}331s = 7{,}986$$
$$\text{II.} \quad 1{,}936c + 968v + 968s = 3{,}872$$

$$\text{Total} = 11{,}858$$

Repeating the same calculation and rounding off the fractions, we get at the end of the following year a product of:

I. $5,856c + 1,464v + 1,464s = 8,784$
II. $2,129c + 1,065v + 1,065s = 4,259$

_____

Total = 13,403

and at the close of the year after that:

I. $6,442c + 1,610v + 1,610s = 9,662$
II. $2,342c + 1,172sv + 1,172s = 4,686$

_____

Total = 14,348

In the course of five years' reproduction on an expanded scale, the total capital of Departments I and II has risen from $5,500c + 1,750v = 7,250$, to $8,784c + 2,782v = 11,566$, i.e. in a ratio of 100:160. The total surplus-value was originally 1,750, it is now 2,782. The surplus-value consumed was originally 500 for Department I and 600 for Department II, a total of 1,100; in the final year it is 732 for Department I and 745 for Department II, altogether 1,477. It has thus grown in the ratio of 100:134.

CHAPTER 2

Economic Equilibrium in the System of the USSR[1]

1   On the Economics of War Communism

Before we directly analyse the equilibrium of today's Soviet economy, making use of everything we have said about reproduction in concrete capitalism, let us first say a few words about the period of so-called War Communism. In terms of relations between the state economy and the private economy, we often under-estimate War Communism's legacy to the period of NEP. It will be useful, therefore, to re-establish the true scope of the changes that were made in relations between the private and state economies as a result of the transition to the New Economic Policy.

In terms of relations between the state and private sectors of the economy, the most characteristic feature of the period of War Communism was the separate existence, if we may put it that way, between small-scale, mainly peasant production and the state economy. There was no regular market exchange between these two sectors even though, generally speaking, an illegal and semi-legal market continued to exist throughout the entire period of War Communism. The actual exchange of items that did occur in the form of requisitions, on the one hand, and Narkomprod's supply to the countryside of products from the cities, on the other, had a highly specific character. To the extent that relations between town and country were regulated by the state, their particular character resulted from the general political and economic conditions during the period of War Communism, when the basic objective of all production and distribution (an objective that was externally imposed upon rural production) was not expanded reproduction in the state and private sector but production of a maximum volume of goods for consumption by the army, the urban proletariat and the rural poor, as well as production of weapons for defence – all of this with no concern for depreciation. Planned distribution of existing inventories, subordinated to the tasks of defence rather than expanded reproduction, played no less a role in the economy. This was the economy of a besieged city, whose goal was not normal reproduction in the economy but to survive as long as possible and win the war. Leaving aside the type of production relations, our

---

1   Published for discussion purposes in the journal *Vestnik Kommunisticheskoi Akademii*, No. 22, 1927.

economy during the period of War Communism was one of declining reproduction, which makes it similar to Europe's declining capitalist reproduction
during and after the world war, which we have already mentioned. But what
occurred in our country, if we take the state sector, was declining reproduction
in a *socialist type* of economy. That is what was unique about this stage of our
economic history.

Is it possible to illustrate this economy of declining reproduction and growing rupture between the state economy and the private economy in terms of
exchange, using the sort of arithmetical schemes that we employed in analysing capitalist and petty-bourgeois reproduction?

In principle, such an illustration is not possible. We have to remember that
in this case the issue by no means involves illustrating a process of reproduction in a commodity-capitalist society, in which all processes are subject to
the law of value, but rather an exchange of things on the basis of *other law-
governed patterns*, above all the requirements of defence, with the complete
elimination of any equivalence whatever both in the exchange of the total sum
of consumer items from the village for urban products and also in the distribution, within the village, of what came from the city in accordance with
Narkomprod's supply plans. Marx's schemes are not suitable for illustrating
reproduction in this type of economy. With his arithmetical examples, Marx
illustrated the conditions of equilibrium in an exchange of values under pure
capitalist reproduction. Those schemes are not appropriate when an economy
is becoming naturalised and ceasing in large part to be a money economy; when
it is not an equilibrium exchange of values that occurs but rather proportionality in the distribution of material elements of production in their natural forms;
when measurements of value are beginning to be replaced by measurements
of labour time or some other surrogate measurements; and finally, when production is subordinated not to the tasks of accumulation or even to those of
simple reproduction, but instead to the task of deliberate dis-accumulation of
constant capital as it is transformed into items for consumption and defence.
For this reason, a scientific analysis of the concrete economy of War Communism cannot be undertaken in terms of the categories of value.

At the same time, however, we know that our economy during the period
of War Communism, due to its extremely brief existence, did not succeed in
working out its own inherent methods of accounting, i.e., recording the economy's natural elements and means of consumption and reducing them ultimately to labour expenditures, or to labour time measured rationally and in a
socialist manner. During the period of War Communism, we used surrogates
for socialist accounting such as the pre-war rouble, the commodity rouble, or
bread and other rations (which are forms of natural accounting), starting from

a *quantitative* record of production in industry and what was acquired through requisitioning peasant production, etc. This natural kind of measurement did not occur in parallel with value measurements, as it does today, but was the actual basis for all calculations. If we were able to reproduce even an approximate balance of the national economy of Soviet Russia for each year of War Communism, i.e., for part of 1918 and mainly for 1919 and 1920, those annual balances would not represent reproduction and would establish the following fundamental economic facts:

1. As a result of the complete liquidation of capitalist production and capitalist trade, the economy comprised only two sectors: the state economy and petty production, in which the *commodity* character of production had been lost due to naturalisation of the peasant economy and the decline of handicrafts and artisan industry.

2. Only a very small percentage of the state sector's fixed capital, which was squandered during every year of War Communism, was restored, with the consequence that it was systematically dissipated. The consumption-oriented character of all production in the state economy was expressed in the fact that the fixed capital of light industry, which in the course of production assumed the material form of means of consumption, was not being restored, so that the volume of production of means of consumption grew at the expense of making no provision for the physical wear of equipment. Consequently, the relation between the part of constant capital in Department II that consisted of fixed capital, and the scale of reproduction in kind of this part of IIc in Department I, was fundamentally ruptured when compared to the production proportions not just of expanded but even of simple or slowly declining reproduction. On the other hand, the part of means of production in the small-scale economy that had previously been produced in Department I of the capitalist sector (or else was imported), was likewise expended without any replacement from Department I of the state sector. Finally, the means of production in Department I of the state sector, which consisted of fixed capital, were not replaced in that sector itself insofar as they were depleted in producing items for defence, including military transport, i.e., they were swallowed up by non-productive military consumption. All of this meant, above all, a paralysis of the heavy industry that works to replace fixed capital IIc of the state and private sectors.

3. The part of constant capital in the state sector that consisted of fuel, imported materials or materials from peasant production could not be reproduced in the required proportions because of protracted loss of the main fuel-producing regions (the Donbas, Baku), the blockade, the drop in production of technical crops in the peasant economy and the increased processing of such materials within the countryside itself.

4. As for material exchange between town and country, here the most significant fact, which explains the inevitability of the whole system of War Communism, was the following: even if normal market exchange had existed between town and country, the peasant economy, given a drop in its total output by 50% compared to the pre-war level, could not have provided the cities, *through exchange*, with the quantity of means of consumption, industrial materials and labour in natural form (transport by cart etc.) that the state required during a period of Civil War. And conversely, even if all these sums of value could have been provided by the countryside through normal market exchange, state production – taking into account the minimal levels of output and the enormous non-productive consumption caused by the war – objectively would not have been able to compensate for what it was receiving from peasant production even with extremely non-equivalent exchange and very high monetary taxation of the villages. This follows quite obviously from a calculation in pre-war roubles of the total production of means of consumption in state industry, subtracting consumption in the cities and at the front, and comparing what remained, again in pre-war roubles, with everything that was taken from the countryside through requisitions. Whereas in the first year of War Communism the disparity was still not so great, insofar as the Soviet government still had at its disposal the old pre-revolutionary inventories, by 1920, which was the most typical year of War Communism, peasant deliveries to the cities already enormously exceeded what the peasants received in return. This demonstrates that relations of market exchange between the state economy and petty production were generally impossible during this period.

The military-consumption character of the economy during this period also appeared in the fact that the industrial products that the countryside did receive through planned supply were distributed among the peasantry in a unique way by the committees of poor peasants. The rural strata that provided most to the state in requisitions did not receive the most in return, but precisely the opposite occurred: most of the supplies went first and foremost to the poorest stratum of the peasantry, who provided nothing material to the state but supported it in political and military terms during the Civil War. Consequently, the distribution of urban production was non-equivalent in two senses: in terms of the quantity going to the countryside compared to what came from it, and also in terms of the principle that controlled distribution within the villages. A corrective to this class-based distribution, which did not serve any reproduction in the peasant economy, occurred through illegal exchange between town and country in the form of the famous 'bag-trading'. In this way, the countryside took some measure of revenge for the system of distribution imposed upon it by the city, acquiring for a pittance textiles, clothing, furniture and other reserves left over in the cities from earlier years in exchange for grain, potatoes and other food products.

The contradiction between town and country grew. At the end of 1920 and the beginning of 1921, the countryside focused attention, in the form of peasant uprisings, on the critical issue of adjusting the system of exchange in the Soviet economy to the conditions of commodity production in agriculture. This adjustment was accomplished through transition to the New Economic Policy. But there were also reasons for the transition to the New Economic Policy that originated within the state economy itself as it began a peaceful period of existence. In a peasant country, the transition of the state economy from declining production in wartime to expanded socialist reproduction in peacetime required changes in the relations between proletarian industry and peasant farming that included the market system of exchange, incentives for peasant production of the materials needed for state industry, increasing exports, etc.

In this context, however, we must not confuse the changes of management methods in the state economy – resulting from the need to salvage everything from the customary capitalist methods of accounting and calculation that could be useful to the state economy itself at the existing level of socialist culture and during the initial stages of socialist construction – with those changes in the country's economy that were imposed upon the state economy by the predominance of small-scale commodity production. If it were a question of the first years or even the first decade of socialist construction in a country such as contemporary Germany, the general conditions for development of a socialist economy even there might have required preservation of the market system of exchange until, on the basis of experience, methods of distribution could be found that are inherent in the socialist form of production. And even there it is possible that petty and perhaps even medium-scale trade would have remained, operating at the junction of the state economy with a relatively unimportant private economy, although in this case there would not be conditions for *development* of commodity relations or private capital in its various forms.

In the USSR, however, and especially in agriculture, such a development is an inevitable fact that is imposed upon the country's economy by the enormous relative weight of petty commodity production and by the comparative weakness of the state sector. This fact places the state economy in conditions of uninterrupted economic warfare against tendencies of capitalist development and towards a capitalist restoration, which are supported from the outside by pressure on our economy from the world capitalist market. Thus, our economic system cannot achieve the internal stability that characterised the countries of capitalism when it was young and had just dissolved feudal relations and subordinated petty commodity production. This duel between the economy's socialist and capitalist elements, with the latter being supported by the vastness of petty commodity production, leads to dualism in the sphere of regulation and thus to unique conditions of equilibrium throughout the whole system.

2   Preliminary Observations

Analysis of the conditions of equilibrium in today's Soviet economic system requires division of the economy into three sectors: a) the state sector; b) the private capitalist sector; and c) the sector of simple commodity production. However, the nature of the investigation will often require a dichotomy between the first sector and the other two taken together, since those two sectors represent a unified sphere of the private economy as a whole, and the lack of necessary figures for the capitalist sector makes precisely a two-sector division the only possible way in which to undertake a concrete examination of reproduction.

Another peculiar feature in such an investigation, and a difficulty as well, is the fact that equilibrium of the system is achieved not on the basis of the law of value and equivalent exchange, but rather through a clash of the former law with the law of primitive socialist accumulation, which means that we cannot begin to analyse equilibrium with Marx's assumption that commodities sell, as a rule, according to their values. When, in Volume II of *Capital*, Marx poses the question of analysing reproduction, he makes the following reservation:

> ... [W]e assume not only that products are exchanged at their values, but also that no revolution in values [*keine Werthrevolution*] takes place in the components of the productive capital. In as much as prices diverge from values, this circumstance cannot exert any influence on the movement of the social capital. The same mass of products is exchanged afterwards as before, even though the value relationships in which the individual capitalists are involved are no longer proportionate to their respective advances and to the quantities of surplus-value produced by each of them.[2]

---

2   Marx 1978, p. 469.

As we pointed out earlier, Marx's assumption is quite proper when analysing a capitalist economy's equilibrium. In contrast, we begin the analysis of reproduction in our system with the deviation of prices from values, which is the general rule if we compare our domestic prices with world prices. As far as equilibrium is concerned, the peculiar feature of our economy during the period of primitive socialist accumulation is precisely the absence of equivalent exchange. Such exchange is the prevailing tendency towards which a capitalist economy inclines and which it achieves, with greater or lesser deviations, primarily on the basis of free competition and the free operation of the law of value in the distribution of social labour. Under capitalism, equivalent exchange may be considered the prevailing tendency, however numerous the departures from the general rule and however significant these departures have historically become with the development of monopolism. With the Soviet economy it is the opposite. Throughout the period of transforming the whole technical basis of the state economy, the rule is *non-equivalent* exchange. The entire existence of the state economy is connected with this non-equivalence, which is one of the most significant features of our system at the present stage of development.

War Communism meant first of all non-equivalence in the exchange (*razmen*)[3] of production from state industry for rural products that were alienated from the peasantry by means of requisitioning the output of the village, and secondly, the absence of any market-oriented commodity-money forms of such exchange, i.e., the lack of market exchange (*obmen*). During the period of War Communism, the level of development of the productive forces in both the state economy and the peasant economy was so low, and non-productive military consumption was so high, that a market form of exchange could not have prevailed and would have buckled under the pressure of the redistribution of national income that was imperative during the Civil War. Conversely, if the market system of exchange had held up, it would not have been possible to sustain the proportions of income distribution demanded by wartime conditions, and the chances for victory would have been eliminated.

As regards the period of NEP, or more accurately, the period of primitive socialist accumulation, development of the productive forces in both sectors not only allows for but even demands the market form of exchange, which is capable of securing for the state economy the necessary conditions for existence and development. But the exchange [*razmen*] of production between

---

3 I am using the term '*razmen*' instead of '*obmen*' in order to avoid applying a term, which has an established meaning and refers to a commodity economy, to a completely different kind of economy.

the state economy and the private economy, and above all between state industry and peasant agriculture, still cannot be equivalent either from the viewpoint of the relation between real labour expenditures on the products being exchanged or in terms of corresponding to the proportions of exchange that exist in the world economy. Our system could not withstand equivalent exchange controlled by the world market, and the whole process of reconstructing the state economy would have to come to a halt.

Accordingly, the economic equilibrium of the Soviet system during the period of primitive socialist accumulation is distinguished from the period of War Communism by the fact that the market form of linkage between the state and private economies has now been restored and the capitalist sector has also appeared on the scene. Non-equivalence of exchange continues in the present system and resembles War Communism, but in a significantly moderated form compared to 1919–20. This fact presents no obstacle to all those investigators who see an impassable abyss between War Communism and NEP and are incapable of scientifically establishing the historical continuity between the two forms of economic regulation. Besides the fact that NEP has changed precisely nothing in the property system of large-scale industry and transportation, which has remained constant since the epoch of War Communism, it has also preserved continuity with the epoch of War Communism by retaining non-equivalent exchange in this attenuated form. To uncritically hold War Communism to account for things that resulted from the general economic backwardness of the country represents childish thoughtlessness and a failure to comprehend causes and effects in our economic history on the part of those who have no idea of whom or what to blame for the fact that the level of development of the productive forces was and will remain backward for quite a long time. We must understand the consequences to which this leads at different stages in the Soviet system's existence.

But if we *hold to* non-equivalent exchange during the period of primitive socialist accumulation, using it for reconstructing our technical base, that does not mean we will *hold out* for very long in such an exceptional situation if, instead of catching up with capitalism, we lag behind it or simply preserve the gap in terms of technology and development of the productive forces. While one of the obligatory conditions of survival for the Soviet economy, with its state sector, is non-equivalent exchange together with all the protective apparatuses of such exchange – such as the foreign trade monopoly, planned imports and strict protectionism – the second obligatory condition of *continued* survival is gradually to move beyond this non-equivalence through steady convergence of the level of development of our productive forces with the level of the leading capitalist countries. These are the two conditions of equilibrium in our system insofar as they are connected with the expanded reproduction of precisely socialist relations – i.e., with what distinguishes us from a capitalist economy – and with the reproduction of capitalist relations in an economically backward country during a period when this backwardness in being surmounted.

Now we must make a few preliminary observations concerning the capitalist sector of the Soviet economy. It is completely incorrect to think that if survival of the state sector, during the period of its economic and technical backwardness in relation to capitalism, is the fundamental source of non-equivalent exchange – which essentially means a tax levied on the entire economy for the sake of socialist reconstruction – then the capitalist sector of the Soviet economy, *taken as a whole*, must be a territory for equivalent exchange, or that it is characterised by a general tendency towards more equivalent exchange even within the limits of the Soviet economic system. We have to remember that the commercial-industrial part of the capitalist sector on the one hand, and its agrarian part on the other, are differently situated in the sense of gravitation towards equivalent exchange. With regard to prices, the fundamental proportions within the country are formed between state industry and transport on the one hand, and the peasant economy on the other. *Private industry is in no position to alter these proportions* and has absolutely no interest in doing so. In this context, it plays a passive-parasitic role. While non-equivalent exchange, for the state economy, is the material source of technical reconstruction and the precondition for development of the productive forces in future years, *private industry simply adheres to the existing situation*. It situates itself within the pores of non-equivalent exchange between Soviet large-scale industry and the village for the purpose of accumulation that never becomes accumulation for industrial production. For that reason, it can neither contribute to reducing production costs nor become the starting point for positive competition with state industry. The places where private industry successfully competes with state industry are limited to certain branches of light industry, in which expensive mechanical equipment still plays no significant role or is inapplicable, and where the role of personal initiative and energy, of personal involvement, is relatively important. That is where it thrives, mainly through extraordinary exploitation of labour power and often of the labour power of one's own family. The bourgeoisie prefers to keep its accumulated resources in the form of money, considering it risky to convert them into the congealed form of new means of production. Private commercial capital is in exactly the same position. In the conditions of the goods famine and the lack of any rational setup for distribution through the state-co-operative network, especially during its early years, the private trade apparatus, in addition to the normal profit, is collecting conjunctural profit and generally trading at prices higher than those in the state-co-operative network. Private capital is playing a predominantly parasitic role in the sense that *while taking advantage of a conjuncture of non-equivalent exchange that it did not itself create, it is contributing nothing in terms of achieving greater equivalence.*

The agrarian half of the capitalist sector is in a different situation, represented by the kulaks and well-to-do peasants, who already have one foot planted in the systematic exploitation of other people's labour. We shall have more to say later concerning the relative weight of this part of the capitalist sector and its growing significance in the country's economy. Let us note for now that the basic strength of the capitalist sector, insofar as it will develop in general, will no doubt shift precisely to its agrarian component, where accumulation occurs directly in the form of accumulation of means of production and land parcels leased from the poor. Within the Soviet system, it is precisely agrarian capitalism that suffers first and foremost from non-equivalent exchange, because the kulak farm purchases more than the middle-peasant farm, which means that it overpays more on the basis of our domestic prices compared to world prices; it [also] sells more, and its expanded reproduction can only occur through the market exchange that enables it to realise its growing volume of production, including the part that constitutes surplus value. That is why the kulak economy is so passionately and deliberately hostile to the current economic system in the USSR, although the whole peasant economy generally suffers to some extent from non-equivalent exchange insofar as it is dependent upon the market and is not self-contained within the context of natural economy. The kulaks are attempting to remedy non-equivalent exchange with the city by holding back sales for months at a time, while the poor and middle peasant strata sell their grain at procurement prices. The kulak is trying to raise grain prices in the spring; he is trying to replace some crops with others that are more profitable; he is trying to accumulate in natural form and to by-pass the market, which he can only accomplish by increasing his own cattle and poultry production, erecting buildings, etc. But the opportunities for such economic manoeuvres are limited, and ultimately the kulak economy will clash with the entire Soviet system. The longer this situation prevails, the more the kulak will seek a solution to the problem not by economic means on the basis of the Soviet system, not by partially revising the balance to his own benefit, but by attempting to make his way to the world market through counter-revolution. At this point, the problem of economic equilibrium leads straight to the problem of social equilibrium and the relation of class forces for and against the Soviet system. There is an ongoing struggle between two systems of equilibrium: equilibrium on a capitalist basis, on the basis of inclusion in the world economy, regulated by the law of value, through liquidation of the Soviet system and crushing the proletariat; and equilibrium on the basis of temporarily non-equivalent exchange, which serves as the source for socialist reconstruction and *inevitably means suppression of capitalist tendencies of development, particularly in agriculture.*

From what has been said, it will be clear that whereas Marx's analysis of the proportional distribution of labour under pure capitalism began with equivalent exchange as a necessary assumption, and we likewise began with this assumption in our previous analysis of equilibrium in concrete capitalism, our present task of examining reproduction in the economy of the USSR must start from non-equivalent exchange, even though it is gradually and systematically being eliminated. *This means that at the basis of the entire process we always presuppose the existence of two different systems of property in the means of production and two different regulators of economic life, i.e., the law of value and the law of primitive socialist accumulation.*

3   An Algebraic Scheme of Reproduction in the USSR

If we provisionally apply Marx's terminology for a capitalist economy to the state economy and also the petty-bourgeois sector, an algebraic scheme of the three sectors of the economy will take the following form:

The State Sector
Department I. $c + v +$ surplus product
Department II. $c + v +$ surplus product $\quad + \quad \left\{ \begin{array}{l} \text{surplus product} \\ \text{from other sectors} \end{array} \right\}$

The Capitalist Sector
Department I. $c + v + s$
Department II. $c + v + s$

The Petty-Bourgeois Sector
Department I. $c +$ consumption fund $+$ surplus product
Department II. $c +$ consumption fund $+$ surplus product

The foregoing scheme is inadequate for our purposes, however, because it does not show how the individual sums break down from the viewpoint of their exchange with different Departments of the various sectors. A more detailed scheme, which we will use in what follows (even though we often take the two private sectors together), must take the following form:

The State Sector

		Constant capital reproduced annually on an expanding scale	The wage fund	The surplus product	
Department I	All of the fixed capital c				
		a) reproduced within the Department	a) the part replaced by exchange with IIc of the state sector	a) accumulation fund: 1) for expanding existing enterprises 2) for construction of new enterprises	Surplus fund for socialist accumulation[4]
		b) reproduced by exchange with the other Departments I	b) the part replaced by exchange with IIc of the other sectors	b) fund for non-productive consumption of the Soviet system, going to IIc of all sectors and to c of the military industry	
		c) reproduced by imports			
Department II	c	Constant capital reproduced annually on an expanding scale	The wage fund	The surplus product	
		a) by exchange with I of the state sector	a) the part replaced within this Department	a) the fund accumulated in this Department (additions to its own v and c)	
		b) by exchange with the consumption fund of Departments I of the other sectors	b) the part replaced by exchange with the consumption fund of other Departments II	b) the fund for non-productive consumption in the Soviet system	
		c) by exchange with part of the fund for non-productive consumption in Department I			
		d) by imports			

---

4 The movement of the natural composition of the socialist accumulation fund is clear from the whole scheme of expanded reproduction. More detail will be provided in a numerical analysis of Gosplan's control figures.

The Capitalist Sector

Depart-ment I c	c	$+v$	$+s$
	Same as in the state sector but without imports	Same as in the state sector	a) accumulation fund b) fund for capitalist consumption c) fund for non-productive consumption of the Soviet system d) alienated to the fund of socialist accumulation
Depart-ment II	Same as in the state sector but without imports	Same as in the state sector	Same as in Department I of the capitalist sector

The Petty-bourgeois Sector

Depart-ment I c	Means of production for production of means of production, annually reproduced on an expanding scale	Consumption fund	Surplus product
	a) reproduced within this Department	a) reproduced by exchange with IIc of the state sector	a) accumulation fund: 1) the part remaining in this Department 2) Exchanged for addition to the consumption fund 3) for additional means of production from other sectors
	b) exchanged with Ic of the state sector and Ic of the capitalist sector	b) exchanged with IIc of the capitalist sector	b) fund for non-productive consumption of the Soviet system
	d) by means of imports	c) exchanged with IIc of this sector	c) alienated to the fund of socialist accumulation

Depart-ment II	c	Means of produc-tion for production of means of con-sumption, annually reproduced on an expanding scale	Consumption fund	Surplus product
		a) created within this Department	a) produced (mainly) within this Depart-ment	a) accumulation fund: 1) additional consumption fund created in this Depart-ment 2) exchanged for additional means of production from other Departments in other sectors 3) own additional means of production
		b) reproduced by exchange with the con-sumption fund and with part of the fund for non-productive consumption within this sector	b) exchanged with part of IIv in the state sector and IIv of the capitalist sector	b) fund for non-productive consump-tion of Soviet society in natural form
		c) reproduced by exchange with v and with part of the fund for non-productive consumption in Department I of the state sector		c) alienated to the fund of socialist accu-mulation
		c) reproduced by exchange with part of v and s of Depart-ment I of the capitalist sector		

Let us now say a few words of explanation for this scheme, which even in this form far from exhausts all of the directions in which exchange occurs in our system with expanded reproduction.

From the viewpoint of exchange, the constant capital of Department I in the state sector divides into three components: the first, which is reproduced within the Department itself; a second that is reproduced through exchange with Departments I of the capitalist and petty-bourgeois sectors; and a third that is reproduced by importing means of production from abroad.

The wage payments of Department I in the state sector divide into two parts: one part is exchanged for means of consumption from Department II of the state sector; another part is reproduced through exchange with Departments II in both the capitalist and petty-bourgeois sectors.

The surplus product of this Department divides into: 1) the accumulation fund, which splits proportionally into c and v, with corresponding exchange of the additional v for means of consumption; and 2) the fund for non-productive consumption. The latter fund is consumed *in natura* within the Department itself only in the form of means of production for the military industry, while the remainder exchanges with the Departments II of all the sectors.

The constant capital of Department II in the state sector is reproduced: 1) by exchange of means of consumption for one part of the wage fund in Department I of the state sector; by exchange with the consumption fund in the capitalist and petty-bourgeois sectors (primarily for peasant materials); by importing means of production (in the form of machinery and materials such as cotton, wool, rubber, hides, etc.).

The wages of Department II of the state sector are partly reproduced within the Department itself, partly exchanged for the consumption fund of the petty-bourgeois sector, and partly for IIv of the capitalist sector.

The surplus product of Department II of the state sector is broken down in the same manner as the surplus product of Department I: it consists, therefore, of the accumulation fund and the fund for non-productive consumption. The latter is consumed *in natura*, and the former divides into two parts: one consists of additional v and is reproduced along the same lines as all of IIv in the state sector, while the other, which goes to purchase means of production, is reproduced in the same way as IIc of the state sector.

We are not providing any detailed examination of exchange by the capitalist sector with other sectors, because this process is clear from the analysis given above for the Departments of the state sector. The difference has to do with dividing the surplus value. Here, consumption by the capitalist class is added, introducing a modification in the exchange of means of production for means of consumption from the individual sectors, and a deduction from s is added for the fund of socialist accumulation, which also complicates the analysis of reproduction.[5]

---

5   For the time being, we are setting aside the question of how to calculate reproduction when it is complicated by alienation of surplus value from the capitalist sector and surplus product

The means of production of Department I in the petty-bourgeois sector, consisting of machinery, cattle, seeds, fertilisers, etc., which the peasant economy uses in the production of technical crops, as well as the equipment and materials of part of the artisan industry, divide into two parts: one part is reproduced within the Department itself, while the other part can be acquired through domestic exchange only for Ic of the state sector and partly by means of imports.

The consumption fund of Department I of the petty-bourgeois sector, having the natural form of means of production, exchanges in two directions: on the one hand for IIc of the state and capitalist sectors, and on the other hand for part of the fund of means of production of Department II within the petty-bourgeois sector itself.

The surplus product of Department I of the petty-bourgeois sector is divided into three basic parts: a) the accumulation fund; b) the fund for non-productive consumption to the extent that this Department is obliged to contribute; and c) the fund for socialist accumulation going to the state sector.

In turn, the accumulation fund [in Department I of the petty-bourgeois sector] consists of: a) additional means of production that it provides for itself, which go *in natura* to increase its own *c* through internal redistribution, i.e., without becoming involved in exchange with other sectors; b) means of production that are exchanged for means of production coming from Departments I of the state and capitalist sectors; c) means of production in natural form, which serve as a fund of additional consumption by new workers and must, therefore, in order to enter into consumption, be exchanged for means of consumption from Departments II of all three sectors in the same proportions as the overall consumption fund of this particular Department.

The fund for non-productive consumption, as in the case of the fund for non-productive consumption in Department I of the state sector (except for means of production for the military industry), must be converted into items for consumption by exchange in the corresponding proportions with *Departments II* in all three sectors, replacing their constant capital.

Alienation into the fund of socialist accumulation refers [first] to the part of taxes levied on small-scale production that goes not to non-productive consumption by agents of the state and the trading network but rather to increasing the capital funds of the state economy, including state funds for agricultural

---

from the petty-bourgeois sector into the fund of socialist accumulation. This is a very important methodological problem. Its solution raises the issue of the relation between domestic prices and world market prices.

credits. Secondly, this refers to the part of the fund for primitive socialist accumulation that is formed by exchanging the export fund – coming from small-scale and mainly peasant production and priced at the domestic level (which is lower than world prices) – for the import fund of means of production for the state sector, also priced at the domestic level (which is far higher than world prices). If we consider the entire process of reproduction in the USSR in terms of value relations on the world market, then this fund would have to include the whole balance coming from exchange of state production for private production, taking the output of the state and private sectors in terms of world market prices and deducting from that sum the part that is absorbed by nonproductive consumption.

The means of production of Department II of the petty-bourgeois sector consist of four parts: the first and largest part is reproduced within the same Department II since it is mainly a matter of peasant agriculture. This includes seeds set aside from the harvest and production of the peasant's own working livestock, his own feed for the livestock, his own fertilizer and buildings, and so forth. The second part is reproduced through exchange for the consumption fund of Department I of the petty-bourgeois sector or for part of IV of the capitalist sector. The third part is exchanged for part of the wage fund of Department I of the state sector, and the fourth part is reproduced through imports.

The consumption fund of Department II of the petty-bourgeois sector consists of two parts: the first and largest is reproduced within the Department itself; the second and significantly smaller part is exchanged for part of the wage fund of Departments II of the state and capitalist sectors.

As for the fund of surplus product in Department II of the petty-bourgeois sector, it is divided into the same four parts as the surplus product of this sector's Department I; the difference lies in all the changes to the system of exchange *associated with a different material form of the whole product.* The point is that the accumulation fund is first of all divided proportionally between a fund for additional consumption and a fund for additional means of production, with the additional consumption fund having the same composition as the basic consumption fund. The difference between reproducing this fund and reproducing the same fund in Department I of the petty-bourgeois sector is that in Department I, prior to exchange, this fund has the material form of means of production that must be exchanged as a whole for means of consumption, whereas in this case, i.e., in Department II, this fund has from the very outset the material form of means of consumption and is also consumed here for the most part. Only a small part is exchanged for means of consumption from the other Departments II. The fund for additional means of production, in turn, has the same composition as the means of production in general for this Department. This means that part of the fund of additional means of production is created within this same petty-bourgeois sector, while the other part is acquired through exchange with the other sectors.

As regards non-productive consumption, it includes, as we mentioned earlier, the part of the surplus product of this sector that goes to the income of those groups in Soviet society who represent non-productive consumption: expenditures on the state apparatus, the army, the non-productive part of expenditures on trade, etc. The difference, compared to Department I of this same sector, is that in this instance the fund of non-productive consumption has from the very outset the material form of means of consumption and is not subject to further exchange with other Departments, which inevitably does occur with the fund for non-productive consumption that has the material form of means of production.

As far as the surplus product going to the fund for socialist accumulation is concerned, everything that we have said concerning Department I of the petty-bourgeois sector applies without any change to Department II.

The scheme that we have provided for reproduction in the system of the USSR makes it possible to clarify the general conditions of proportionality in the type of economy we are considering during this particular period of its existence. We must explain these general conditions before we apply our scheme to analyse the data for individual years and attempt to replace the algebraic symbols with concrete arithmetical figures for economic years such as 1925/26 or 1926/27.

4   The First Condition of Equilibrium

Let us begin with the conditions of equilibrium between the state sector and the two sectors of the private economy, taken together, from the viewpoint of ensuring expanded reproduction in the state sector. We leave aside for now the material composition of the output being exchanged.

Suppose that the gross output of the state sector, at current prices in chervonets roubles, is 12 billion per year and is divided as follows: $8c + 2v + 2$ of surplus product. (In 1925/26 the gross output of the state economy in terms of producers' prices, together with the proceeds from transport, communications, municipal revenues and forestry, plus the gross output in construction, amounted to 14,350 million roubles, omitting various secondary items).

Suppose further that the exchange fund with the whole private sector comes to a sum of 3 billion, i.e., that the state sector sells means of production, means of consumption, and transport services to the private economy worth 3 billion chervonets roubles, and for this sum it receives from them means of production, primarily peasant materials, items for consumption and the export fund. The result is an even balance between the sectors, with no one-sided accumulation of unrealised commodity surpluses remaining in either of them. Now, assume that the whole economy of the USSR is included in the world economy on the basis of unhindered operation of the law of value, and world-market prices are imposed upon our industry while the volumes of exports and imports remain constant, i.e., abstracting from any possible changes in the dynamic of foreign trade. In that case the entire equilibrium will be upset, first and foremost the equilibrium in relations between the state sector as a whole and the private sector. In fact, suppose that the whole production of the state sector is now evaluated according to world-market prices, i.e., at one-half or less of the prices that prevail now. If, within the state sector, the part of Department I's production that replaces part of the constant capital of Department II (machinery and fuel for the production of means of consumption) is approximately equal to the part of Department II's production in the state sector that exchanges with I and consists of textiles, shoes, sugar and so forth, then the compulsory reduction of prices does not essentially alter the natural proportions of exchange within the state sector itself so long as the percentage rise in prices in heavy and light industry in the state sector does not significantly differ from the price indices for heavy and light industry in the world economy (if, for instance, our state-produced means of consumption are twice as expensive as the output of light industry in the world economy, and prices for machines are also twice as expensive as prices for foreign-produced machines). This would mean that if one of our engineering trusts sells machinery for half as much to our textile industry, the textile industry also sells its manufactures, which are going to consumption by the workers and employees of the engineering industry, for half as much. In short, since the change in the purchasing power of money is simultaneous for both sides, the material balance of exchange will remain the same as it would be if both sides valued their production not in 1927 chervonets roubles but in some other monetary unit, say in terms of the buying power of the pound sterling on the world market. Individual branches might benefit or suffer if the divergence of their prices from world prices is greater or less than two-fold. In that event, when exchanges between Departments I and II of the state sector do not balance and the remainder is covered by exchange for private production, a significant loss is incurred by the Department of the state sector that turns out to be more involved in material exchange with the private sectors.

In the case that we are considering, however, the most important change will occur in relations between *the state sector as a whole and the whole of private production.* The connection between the state sector and the whole of private production is by no means limited to the size of an imbalance that cannot be covered through exchange within the state sector. Department I of the state sector must always sell to private producers a quantity of means of production that is equal in price to the part of its workers' wages that go to purchase products for consumption from the peasants, plus a corresponding part of the means of production that account for Department I's share of non-productive consumption in the state sector after deducting means of production for the military industry. An even greater volume of exchange occurs between Department II of the state sector and the private economy, accounting for replacement of an important part of IIc in the state sector and also of the wage fund in this same Department. In our example, where the figure approximates the real one for exchange between the state sector and the private economy for the economic year 1925/26, the purchases of the private sector from the state sector and of the state sector from the private sector both come to the sum of 3 billion.

If the private economy sold these 3 billion of its output at world-market prices, then sales by the state sector to the private economy at world-market prices, i.e., at prices that are half as high, would enable the state sector to fetch only 1 ½ billion for its production instead of 3 billion, i.e., the state sector will receive only one-half of what it gets in an economic year when non-equivalent exchange prevails. The kind of disruption that this will bring to all the conditions of reproduction in the state sector is perfectly evident from a mere glance at our numerical example. A drop in receipts by 1½ billion will first of all eat up the entire accumulation fund. Secondly, it will affect part of the non-productive consumption. And thirdly, it must lead in future to the impossibility of properly depreciating fixed capital and replacing the part of circulating capital that consists of peasant materials. In total, this would mean complete disruption of the process of expanded reproduction, and if significant non-productive consumption continues, it could make even simple reproduction impossible on the level of the previous year.

The disturbance will be even greater if establishment of world-market prices for the materials and means of production that are produced in the private economy entailed an actual price increase compared to the current situation.

Thus we come to a first conclusion that is enormously significant. *With the present gap between world industrial prices and domestic industrial prices in the economy of the USSR, i.e., when the domestic prices of Soviet industry are far higher than world prices, an economic equilibrium that will secure expan-*

ded reproduction in the state sector can only exist on the basis of non-equivalent exchange with the sectors of private production.[6] This means that, in the conditions of price disparity that we have described above, the law of primitive socialist accumulation is the law that supports the equilibrium of the entire system, above all in its relation with the world economy. This law must inevitably operate until we overcome the economic and technical backwardness of the state economy of the proletariat by comparison with the leading capitalist countries.

5   The Second Condition of Equilibrium

Let us now turn to the next condition of the system's equilibrium, remaining for the time being in the same sphere of relations between the state sector as a whole and the private sector as a whole.

Let us take our numerical scheme for the state sector and assume that a new economic year is beginning on the basis of the accumulation sum acquired during the previous year. We assume, consequently, that with a surplus product in the state economy of 2 billion, half of which goes to non-productive consumption and the other half to productive accumulation, and with an increase of the exchange fund with private producers from 3 billion to 3 1/4 billion, the equilibrium of the whole economic system is secured. Now take the opposite case, namely, that actual accumulation, for whatever reasons – whether a sharp decline of wholesale prices that is not warranted by production costs, or a rise in non-productive consumption – amounts not to 1 billion but only 700 million. What will the inevitable consequences of this under-accumulation be in the state sector?

It is perfectly obvious that this will lead to a rupture of proportionality between the state and private sectors of the Soviet economy. Under-accumulation of 300 million will mean no possibility of expanding the reproduction of c in both Departments to the necessary extent, and the deficit of means of production will be 240 million. At the same time, we shall have an expansion of v in both Departments of the state sector that will be 60 million roubles below

6   This proposition, which is at the basis of how I frame the law of primitive socialist accumulation, has provoked numerous lamentations from my critics concerning 'collapse of the *smychka*, a policy of raising prices, etc.' But when I invite my critics to demonstrate that expanded socialist reproduction is compatible, at the current stage of the state economy's development, with equivalent exchange, no one has any response. The reason is perfectly obvious. The formulation that I am using merely acknowledges reality. I am simply trying to understand scientifically what actually exists. If equivalent exchange already existed in our country, the very problem of the *smychka* would no longer be an issue.

the norm, which, in addition to everything else, will mean a slower increase in the number of workers employed in production and thus a relative increase in unemployment. Finally, this will lead to a drop of 60 million in the surplus product of the state economy as a whole. With regard to the total production of the state sector, at the end of the year we shall have a shortfall of 360 million by comparison with the first example. If the share of the private sector in realising the state sector's production amounts, as we said, to 3 1/4 billion, i.e., about 1/4 of the entire gross output of the state sector, then a shortfall of output worth 360 million can signify a shortfall in the supply of commodities for the private sector of about 90 million at a minimum.[7] And this will mean the familiar phenomenon that we call the goods famine. If 2/3 of these 90 million involve state-produced means of consumption, then the unsatisfied demand of the private economy, mainly of the peasant economy, will lead to a compulsory reduction in personal consumption of light industry's products in the countryside and their replacement by handicraft and artisan production, i.e., increased processing of materials (leather, wool, flax and hemp) by primitive domestic methods, which will delay economic development in this sector. Secondly, this will lead to the peasantry consuming more of their own food production and abstaining from selling for export. Thirdly, the disproportion that we have mentioned will reinforce the disparity between retail and wholesale prices in trade, above all in private trade. As for the remaining 1/3, consisting of unsatisfied demand for means of production, given the impossibility of artisans smelting metal or producing complex agricultural machinery etc., the disproportion will have even more injurious consequences, depriving the peasant economy of the opportunity to increase, in conditions of expanded reproduction, the amount of machinery, equipment and other means of production that it requires.

In both Departments of the petty-bourgeois sector, repeated occurrences of goods famine will inevitably lead to a part of peasant output being withheld from sale – since these sales could not be followed by purchases – and to a phenomenon already familiar to all of us, which is the accumulation of unsold natural inventories in the peasant economy. This disproportion can be alleviated only by accumulation of money in the peasant economy, which is generally possible only with a stable currency or with an increase of the purchasing power of money because of a reduction in prices. However, it is self-evident that

---

7 I say at a minimum because the urban demand for commodities coming from state production is naturally satisfied first of all, and in this case the deficit, *for the most part*, is transferred to demand from the private economy.

such accumulation, insofar as it corresponds to the part of reserves in the peasant economy that should have been converted into means of production from the state sector, inevitably means an artificial delay in the process of expanded reproduction in the peasant economy compared to the opportunities within the peasant economy itself.

From what we have been saying, it obviously follows that the volume of accumulation in state industry, with the existing level of prices, is not something arbitrary but is subordinated to iron laws of proportionality. To determine this volume is one of the most important tasks for the theory of the Soviet economy and for the practice of the planned management of economic life. Secondly, any violation of the necessary minimum of accumulation not only strikes a blow at the state economy and the working class but also delays development of the peasant economy and artificially slows the rate of expanded reproduction in agriculture.

Now, let us examine the same question but from a different perspective. We have to consider what some economists – making an uncritical analogy between the Soviet system and capitalism and thus falling into petty-bourgeois philistinism – were inclined at one time to call over-accumulation in state industry, or causing it to rush too far ahead. At the outset, we have to agree on just what we take the term 'over-accumulation' to mean. If we understand over-accumulation to mean the sort of relation between overall social production and consumption in which the new means of production, being set in motion in both Departments, lead ultimately to such a dramatic increase in the output of means of consumption that they cannot be absorbed by the consumer market at the given price level – in which case the corresponding accumulation in Department I turns out to be pointless – then such a phenomenon is perfectly familiar in a capitalist economy and must inevitably provoke a sales crisis and the ruin of several enterprises in both Departments together with a drop in prices and a falling rate of profit. If we take a case that is theoretically possible, in which our state economy, on the basis of the previous year's accumulation, produces means of consumption in excess of the effective demand of both workers and the whole private economy with the given planned prices, the situation that results is much less serious than in capitalist society. The reason is that the dynamic equilibrium of our system presupposes, among other things: 1) rising wages for workers, 2) gradual reduction of industrial prices, and 3) re-equipment and expansion of the entire technical base in the state economy. In these circumstances, a sales crisis can mean one of three things.

1) One is that we incorrectly timed the implementation of our programme concerning the first two points, in which case equilibrium can be achieved either by accelerating the rise of workers' wages beyond what the programme

called for or else by a more radical measure, i.e., a general price reduction for means of consumption coming from the state sector that would be more rapid than our programme anticipated. In that event, the disproportion would be overcome by the swiftest route and with the fewest disruptions, since 'over-accumulation' would turn out to be merely a crisis in part of our production plan and would involve a timing error in terms of fulfilling the first two tasks. Furthermore, given our general lack of reserves in terms of credits, production capacity and trade, we must remember that *this disproportion could not exist for long without becoming evident*, and unlike capitalism we would begin to sur-mount it long before the process went too far. The harmful consequences of this sort of planning error would become apparent later in the sense that our fulfilment of the third task noted above would be postponed.

2) Another possibility would be that we miscalculated the time needed for the third task; that is, we expanded production of means of consumption too quickly *with the prevailing prices*, and the technical basis of the state economy, together with the measures taken thus far to rationalise labour, cannot sup-port our effort to reduce costs and selling prices or, in the worst case, even just to raise wages. In that situation, 'over-accumulation' results from incorrectly distributing productive forces within the state sector and from the fact that the process of technically re-equipping industry is lagging behind the general development of the economy as a whole. This will mean an internal dispropor-tion within the state sphere but not over-accumulation in terms of the relation between the state economy and private production. To seek a solution to such a crisis by implementing a price reduction, for which we are not prepared in terms of reducing production costs, can end up temporarily delaying the entire process of expanded reproduction. The same applies to a response to the prob-lem that would involve temporarily keeping a part of production in the form of a non-liquid fund while maintaining the existing prices. This lack of corres-pondence will continue until reallocation of the productive forces can restore equilibrium.

3) A third possibility is that an abrupt renovation of fixed capital diverts so many means of production into production of means of production, which are only able to expand output after several years, that any increase of the pop-ulation's consumption fund is delayed and, given the existence of the goods famine, the process of reducing prices comes to a halt. In this case we would have *not general over-accumulation* in the state sector (otherwise there could be a goods famine, even if only for means of consumption), but a disproportional-ity in terms of timing the individual requirements for expanded reproduction. We would then be confronted not so much with an error in plan construc-tion as with the natural result of passing from the so-called recovery process

to that of reconstruction. We would face the natural consequences of a situation in which the country's fixed capital, significantly curtailed by losses in depreciation during previous years, is being recreated with limited connection to the world economy and generally inadequate domestic accumulation in the material form of means of production. *What appears on the surface to be over-accumulation in heavy industry is merely a unique form of under-accumulation throughout the state economy as a whole.*

The very nature of the reconstruction of fixed capital, in the conditions we have described, is such that the process cannot but assume an uneven character. In order, shall we say, to expand the production of means of consumption in light industry by 100 million roubles a year, it is first necessary to increase production of means of production by 400–500 million. This can temporarily prevent the necessary tempo of production of consumer items, cause a special kind of goods famine, and delay a reduction in prices, especially in the event that a change in the structure of the peasant budget leads to growth in demand for means of consumption compared to the situation before the war. After a few years, however, it will become possible to reduce production costs rapidly, to lower selling prices and quickly increase the consumption fund. Instead of systematically reducing prices by, say, 2–3% per year, and systematically increasing the output of means of production by, say, 6–7% per year, it will be possible to realise the same programme over three-four years but in a more uneven way.

If we leave aside political difficulties during this period, the harmful consequences of such a development of the state economy amount primarily to the fact that production of export crops in the peasant economy will be delayed, and production of technical crops will be lower than the requirements resulting from rapid development of the state's light industry. This latter difficulty still lies ahead of us for the most part, although the artificial curtailment of peasant exports is already evident.

From the viewpoint of a general advance by the state economy, the case that we are considering will not mean a crisis of over-accumulation and over-production in the real sense, but simply the material impossibility of harmoniously co-ordinating the development of all aspects of expanded reproduction *in terms of time.* This impossibility is generally inevitable in the transition from the recovery process to reconstruction, because the transition itself, as we shall later see in more detail, means a decisive change in the general proportions of distributing the country's productive forces. The fact that new factories only begin to provide output three or four years after construction begins is a result more of technical than economic necessity. Here an initial delay, followed by a leap, is unavoidable. Partial amelioration of this leap would only be possible with higher exports and foreign credits. The impossibility of the latter altern-atives results precisely from the fact that it is not simply expanded production that is occurring in our country but expanded *socialist* production in industry, which world capitalism has no intention of assisting.

Consequently, we come to the conclusion that the dimensions of accumu-lation in the state economy, during any given year, are not arbitrary sums. A definite minimum of accumulation is forcibly dictated by the general pro-portions of the distribution of productive forces between the state economy and the private economy, and also by the extent of our ties with the world economy. Secondly, we conclude that over-accumulation in the state sector, given the enormous task of rapidly re-equipping and expanding the fixed capital of industry (which will require decades to complete) is completely impossible. This re-equipping essentially represents a domestic market with colossal absorptive capacity, not to mention the growth of the domestic mar-ket that is already occurring due to rising demand from the private sectors of our economy. Instead of talking about a crisis of over-accumulation in the state economy, whose objective is not to increase production of surplus value, we should be discussing the colossal under-accumulation that also affects the peasant economy and is holding back its development. We can also talk about insufficient accumulation in the sphere of peasant production of industrial material. We shall deal with that sort of disproportion when we analyse the material composition of the exchange between state and private production.

We must also note here that the two conditions of equilibrium that we have examined differ from each other in the following respect. The equilibrium of non-equivalent exchange in circumstances of a disparity between domestic and world prices, i.e., the equilibrium of an economy that is regulated by the law of primitive socialist accumulation in a struggle with the law of value, is the specific property of our economy and the law of our existence as a Soviet system during the entire period of overcoming our economic backwardness relative to advanced capitalism. Here, equilibrium is achieved as a result of the constant struggle of still backward collective production, in the sole country with a pro-letarian dictatorship, against both the capitalist world and the capitalist and petty-bourgeois elements within our own economy. This sort of equilibrium is an unstable balance in the struggle between two systems, which is achieved on the basis not of the world law of value but through constant violation of this law, constant violation of the world market, and complete or partial withdrawal of an enormous economic area from the world market's sphere of regulation.

It is quite a different issue when we speak of the second condition of equilib-rium, i.e., of the proportions of accumulation in the state economy needed to support equilibrium in the economic organism once the first condition of equilibrium has been secured for a certain period. The maintenance of domestic equilibrium, within an economic organism that is divided into a system of collective and private production, *brings state planning policy, led by the law of primitive socialist accumulation, into a different kind of confrontation with the law of value.* If, with the existing indices of domestic and world prices, we do not attain the necessary proportions in distribution of the productive forces and do so in a planned way, the law of value spontaneously breaks into the sphere of regulation of economic processes, forces the planning principle to retreat in disorder, and encroaches upon the specific proportions of the distribution of labour and means of production that result from the presence of a collective economic sector – that is, the specific proportions that guarantee not merely expanded reproduction but expanded reproduction of the Soviet type of system.

6   The Third Condition of Equilibrium

Let us now turn to the third condition of equilibrium, which involves the extent of our participation in the world division of labour and the specific conditions of realising this connection.

Let us take our former example referring to reproduction in the state sector. Now, however, in accordance with the question that we have to clarify, the annual production of the state sector must be divided into the two Departments. Suppose that the distribution of productive forces and of production between the two Departments is 40% in I and 60% in II.[8] In order not to stray from reality, let us further suppose that the organic composition of capital in I is lower than in II (as distinct from Marx's scheme, of which we shall have more to say later), so that the ratio of c to v in Department I is 3:2 and in Department II, 2:1. Let us also assume that the surplus product is 100% of wages and that this surplus product is divided in both Departments into two equal parts: one part goes to accumulation within the given Department and the other goes to Soviet society's fund for non-productive consumption. The whole scheme will then appear as follows:

---

8   In 1925/26 means of production represented 58.8% of the total output from our industry, and means of consumption, 41.2% (*Perspektivy razvertyvaniya narodnovo khozyaistva SSSR na 1926/27–1930/31*, Gosplan SSSR, pp. 123–4. See also the table on pp. 54–8). The corresponding data for 1913 and 1924/25, which are included in the 'Control Figures' for 1926/27 on p. 163, appear to me to be incorrect, an issue about which I shall have more to say later.

I. $2100c + 1400v + 1400$ surplus product (700 to the accumulation
          fund + 700 to the non-productive consumption fund) = 4900
II. $3350c + 1775v + 1775$ surplus product (887.5 to the accumulation
          fund + 887.5 to the non-productive consumption fund) = 7100

A quick glance at this scheme reveals a significant difference from the corresponding schemes that Marx used for capitalist production: IIc is not only significantly larger than wages and non-productive consumption in Department I of the state sector, but is also larger than wages plus the entire surplus product of Department I. All of this is perfectly natural in a peasant country, where a very large part of IIc in the state sector is reproduced through exchange with the petty-bourgeois economy, which provides our light industry with such means of production as cotton, flax, hemp, hides, wool, sugar beets, seeds for the oil-extracting industry, grain for the mills and potatoes for the alcohol industry. Let us suppose that half of IIc in the state sector, i.e., $1775c$, is reproduced through exchange with private production, i.e., we choose in advance a figure that exceeds the actual size of what IIc reproduces through exchange with the petty-bourgeois economy. Now we must ask: How can the other half of IIc be reproduced?

For reproduction of this half we have first of all the fund of 1400 for wages in Department I. However, this sum cannot go entirely to replace the half of IIc, because a part of the wage payments in Department I must be exchanged for peasant means of consumption. We shall assume that the latter exchange requires $1/3$[9] of the 1400, or 466.6. A fund of 933.4, in the natural form of means of production, then remains for exchange with IIc. Furthermore, since 700 of the surplus product in Department I will go to accumulation, the non-productive consumption fund of 700 remains from the surplus product for exchange with Departments II in other sectors. If we take the same proportion for exchange of this fund with Department II in the state sector and with the private economy [as we did with IV] – i.e., we assume that $2/3$, or 467, goes to the former and the remaining 233 to the latter – then the total exchange fund of Department I of the state sector that goes to replace half of c in Department II will equal $933.4 + 467 = 1,400.4$,[10] or 1400 when rounded off, whereas the sum

---

9   A study of workers' budgets gives a figure of more than 40 %, i.e., more than the proportion we are using, but when we take into account the processing of grain into flour and bread in state mills, the scale of state and factory woodcutting, etc., the figure that we are using will not be far from the truth.
10   [The text mistakenly gives the figure 1300.4.]

that must be replaced is 1775. There is, therefore, a deficit of means of production in the state economy equal to 375[11] million.

If we further assume that this deficit is covered in one way or another, then all we have to do is construct a scheme of expanded reproduction for the following year, based upon the figures for the original scheme, in order to see how the disproportion that we have noted will continue, decreasing slightly in some conditions and increasing in others. To be precise, of the 887.5 of surplus product in II that is committed to accumulation, 295.8 will go to increase v and 591.7 to increase c. Thus IIc will now equal 4141.7, and the part of it that must be covered by exchange with Department I will equal 2070.8. At the same time, the exchange fund in Department I grows proportionally due to the increase of v and of non-productive consumption, so that the part of it that must go to replace IIc will now be 1680 instead of 1400.[12] This means that in the following year the deficit of means of production will be 2070.8 – 1680 = 390.8 million instead of 375[13] – *with the same rate of growth of non-productive consumption*. And conversely, retaining the same absolute volume of non-productive consumption must increase the disproportion, because preserving the former sum or reducing its rate of growth means the exchange fund of Department I in the state sector is diminished at the same time as IIc of the state sector grows in relative terms. The question then arises as to whether the disproportion that we have discovered is a result of the numerical relations that we have selected for our example (even though the proportions are close to reality) or whether they represent an actual disproportion in our economy.

There can scarcely be any doubt that our example illustrates precisely the real disproportion that exists in our economy and is caused by: 1) the end of foreign capital investment in our industry; 2) a drop in non-productive consumption by the bourgeois class; 3) the failures in depreciation of fixed capital during previous years; 4) diversion of some of the means of production into construction of new factories that have yet to provide output; and 5) the general imperative for more rapid accumulation in Department I during the country's industrialisation.

What we observe, therefore, is an acute and continuously expanding deficit of means of production in our state economy. The question that we must now incorporate into our analysis concerns the role that foreign trade might play in overcoming this disproportion. This role is extremely important. Suppose

---

11   [The text mistakenly gives the figure 455 million.]
12   [The text again gives the mistaken figure of 1300 instead of 1400.]
13   [The text again gives the mistaken figure of 455 million.]

that the deficit of means of production in Department II involves a shortage of machinery for light industry, electrical energy, production from the basic chemical industry etc., while the deficit in heavy industry shows up as a shortage of equipment for the fuel industry, engineering factories, high-capacity turbogenerators, air compressors and other equipment for ferrous and non-ferrous metallurgy, etc. What can be accomplished by introducing foreign trade into the issue?

The introduction of imports accomplishes the following.

1) Light industry, instead of coming to a halt in its development and waiting for the time when Department I, on the basis of its own development, is able to provide it with the elements of c that are in short supply, can cover its deficit immediately from abroad. The problem is then resolved in good time, whereas dealing with it in a protracted and roundabout way, through development of our own Department I, would mean a growing crisis and the piling up of one problem after another, including in the sphere of exchange between the state economy and private production. In this regard, we must bear in mind one other extremely important circumstance, namely the following. If light industry, in order to increase its production by 100 units, requires a corresponding expansion of its constant capital, in this case of the part that is reproduced in Department I of the state sector, while there is a general deficit in the latter in terms of the means of the production needed by light industry, then the additional demand from light industry can only be satisfied through building new enterprises in heavy industry. But while construction is underway, it must each year divert far larger resources from the state economy's general accumulation fund than the value of the means of production needed to supply light industry with additional elements of fixed capital. The addition of $100c$ to Department II's fixed capital might require simultaneous investments in Department I of 400–500 elements of new capital. In the meantime, by turning to the world market we can resolve this problem directly and without delay through importing the means of production that II requires in the necessary amounts.

2) Heavy industry, instead of waiting for its deficit of means of production to be covered by its own internal development, and instead of equipping new factories with machines it has produced for itself – which would cause extreme delay in making new enterprises operational and prolong the crisis both within Department I itself and in the sphere of its exchange ties with Department II – can cut through the contradictions by importing equipment whose domestic production would intensify the crisis by diverting already inadequate accumulation into enterprises whose construction, given ties with the world economy, is by no means of primary importance.

3) Both light and heavy industry not only solve the problem of developing their production in a timely manner; to some extent they also solve the enormously important problem of accumulation at the expense of the private economy. The point is that the state sector, in our example, has a shortage of 400 million roubles in terms of means of production at domestic prices with which to replace fixed capital. In order to cover this deficit, it is enough for our state to export, shall we say, consumer products from the peasant economy worth 200 million roubles, or 100 million dollars, and to buy foreign equipment worth the same amount. This foreign equipment, costing 100 million dollars or 200 million chervonets roubles at world prices, would cost 400 million within our own country if we take into account the difference between domestic and foreign industrial prices. Consequently, thanks to the import of means of production, we make use of the difference between world prices and domestic prices and automatically accumulate fixed capital for our developing industry.

Thus, the relationship with the world market, which in a timely way resolves the problem of reconstructing and expanding the fixed capital of both Departments in the state sector, also resolves in some measure the problem of accumulation in material terms and does so specifically by the methods of primitive socialist accumulation.

But in addition to the case that we have considered, there is still another disproportion that can be resolved by imports. The issue involves replacement in natural form of certain elements of IIc to the extent that domestic production of material is inadequate in certain branches. We would probably delay the normal development of our textile industry by a decade if we waited for our own cotton production to develop to the point of fully satisfying this industry's demand for material.

Besides the cases that we have mentioned, imports are also absolutely necessary when, due to natural conditions, we do not produce at all one or another material (such as rubber) or means of consumption (coffee, for example). But I deliberately omitted this aspect of our relation with the world economy because in this case participation in the world division of labour is beneficial and necessary for us *in general, regardless of the structure of the economy and the level of its development*. What I have in mind is the import of means of production that we are generally able to produce for ourselves and whose production we will expand, but which we must import at the present stage of the state economy's development, first of in order all to maintain equilibrium in the system of expanded socialist reproduction and secondly in the interest of accumulating fixed capital.

Accordingly, we come to the conclusion that the third precondition for the equilibrium of our system is maximal contact with the world economy, taking into account the completely unique character of our exports and imports. In conditions where we have a general shortage in terms of our own production of means of production, and especially in conditions that involve the relative under-development of heavy industry compared to the demands from our own state and private markets and the necessary general tempo of the country's industrialisation, *our planned imports of means of production must be of such a volume and must be so constructed in material terms that they can serve, so to speak, as an automatic regulator of the entire process of expanded reproduction without ceasing to be a source of accumulation.*[14]

7   The Fourth Condition of Equilibrium

Let us continue. The fourth condition of equilibrium in our economic system is proportionality in the distribution of labour, and especially proportionality in exchange between the state economy and the whole domestic private economy with regard both to sums of value with the given prices and the natural composition of this exchange. In this context we assume that equilibrium in terms of value exchange is understood conditionally, i.e., in the sense of an equilibrium of non-equivalent exchange, or exchange as a mechanism of socialist accumulation. For the sake of greater clarity when investigating this fourth condition of equilibrium, we shall take our provisional numerical example, referring to the state sector, and add to it an arithmetical scheme of reproduction in the private economy, which, for simplification, we shall not for the time being divide into two sectors – capitalist and petty-bourgeois – as we would have to do in a more detailed analysis. As in the state sector, we divide the surplus product of the private economy into two parts: a fund of actual accumulation in each Department and a fund of non-productive consumption.

---

14   Of course, from the viewpoint of private production and its interests, the disproportion shown above can also be solved by the direct import of means of consumption from abroad, but it is perfectly obvious that such a solution to the problem entails a serious delay, if not the elimination, of expanded socialist reproduction. Many problems of the private economy, generally speaking, can be solved by the elimination of socialist industry or even just by elimination of the monopoly of foreign trade. The whole struggle between the state and private sectors of the Soviet economy leads directly to the issue of the basis upon which equilibrium in the Soviet economy can be established: on the basis of inclusion in the world economy under 'normal conditions', i.e., on the basis of the law of value, or by way of something new and unprecedented in economic history – planned imports that are subordinated to the task of primitive socialist accumulation.

Let us take the total sum of annual production for the whole private economy to be 17.5 billion.[15] We shall assume that this gross production is divided between the two Departments of the private economy in the following way:

I. $2200c + 2200$ consumption fund $+ 1100$ surplus product $= 5500$

II. $3300c + 6600$ consumption fund $+ 2100$ surplus product $= 12000$

The first Department produces technical crops in the peasant economy and generally all materials. It includes artisanal and handicraft industry: enterprises that produce means of production such as private blacksmith shops, repair shops, and handicraft production of equipment, wheels, carts and horse-drawn transport to transfer products for further processing, etc.

All production of means of consumption in the peasant economy takes place in Department II and constitutes the overwhelming share of all production in this Department: arable farming, the part of animal husbandry that provides products for consumption such as milk, butter and meat, and then there is market gardening, fishing, the domestic production of clothing etc. Department II also includes the production of fabrics and clothing in handicraft and private capitalist industry, the private leather industry, the private food industry, etc.

When making this division of the peasant economy into two Departments, we must always remember that such a division is a methodological abstraction. One and the same indivisible peasant farm almost always figures in both Departments simultaneously, because no matter how many means of consumption it produces, it must also produce a certainty quantity of means of production; conversely, the peasant farm that specialises in technical crops always produces means of consumption in some quantity or other.

Reproduction in Department I occurs in such a way that part of the means of production for the peasant economy, which include the materials it produces as well as means of production for the handicraft and artisanal industry, are created within Department I of the private sector itself. This includes production of seeds for the cultivation of flax, cotton, beets, hemp, etc. that are used for further cultivation of those same crops. The same sector of the economy produces working livestock and animal feed on cultivated or natural meadows, and also the livestock involved in producing materials (the sheep that provide wool are means of production for wool, and the breeding of sheep for wool is the

---

15   For the economic year 1925/26, the output of the whole private economy, according to Gosplan's control figures, was 16,397 million in terms of producer prices. [The text mistakenly gives the total as 17 billion, which does not correspond to the scheme that follows.]

production of means of production for wool). But there remains another part of the means of production that can only be acquired from Department I of the state sector. This includes metal and coal for blacksmiths and small repair shops, agricultural machinery for peasant production of materials, artificial fertiliser, railway and water transport to serve the replacement of $1c$ in the private sector, etc. In this regard the following question arises: Department I of the state sector, represented by machine building, the fuel industry, metallurgy, the construction and supply of electrical power, etc., has very little to purchase from Department I of the private economy, in any event less than this Department must purchase from heavy industry. Yet everything that heavy industry sells to replace its wage fund requires the sale by other sectors of the means of consumption that Department I of the private economy cannot provide. This creates an extremely complex web throughout the whole system of reproduction that Marx did not examine in his famous chapters in Volume II of *Capital* dealing with accumulation. Marx was operating with the conditions of reproduction in pure capitalism, where the whole equilibrium of exchange was concentrated on the size of $11c$ and its rate of growth in relation to $1(v + s/x)$ and its rate of growth. The part of $1c$ in the private sector that is not covered by its own production of means of production or domestic exchange with $1c$ of the state sector, might still end up in Department I of the private sector through realisation of the fund of non-productive consumption in Department I of the state sector. This problem can also be partially resolved by way of foreign trade: flax, hemp, raw wool, bristles etc. are exported in exchange for the necessary quantity of means of production.

We see, therefore, that reproduction of one part of $1c$ in the private sector represents a rather complex task that is resolved by drawing into exchange all the Departments of all sectors, and mainly through the channel of non-productive consumption plus foreign trade. It is not enough for this portion of $1c$ in the private sector, whose natural from is industrial material or means of production for private industry, to be sold. It is also necessary that the money received can be used to buy a sufficient quantity of exactly the means of production required. The systematic deficit of means of production that we described above, mainly in the form of fixed capital, characterises the period of reconstructing the technical base of the state sector and must increase still further as a result of the disproportionality that we have just been discussing in the exchange of $1c$ of the state sector for $1c$ of the private sector.

Prior to exchange, the consumption fund of Department I of the private sector consists of the same elements, i.e. industrial materials of all types that are created in the peasant economy plus means of production coming from handicraftsmen and artisans: the output from blacksmiths, repair shops, wagon

shops, production of various implements, harvesting wood for further processing, etc. One part of these means of production is realised within the
private sector itself and goes to reproduce IIc of the private sector, as represented in our example by the figure $3300c$.[16] In return, Department II of the private
sector provides Department I of the same sector with means of consumption.
The other part of the means of production from Department I of the private
sector, which replaces its consumption fund, goes to Department II of the state
sector as materials for the textile, leather, sugar, food oil and alcohol industry,
etc., and exchanges for textiles, boots, sugar and so forth.

The surplus product of Department I of the private sector, in terms of the
part that is most important and interesting for us, i.e., the surplus product
from production of technical crops in the peasant economy, consists of three
basic components: first, the fund of non-productive consumption that remains
in this Department and is used to pay a corresponding share of state taxes,
expenditures on the trade apparatus etc.; second, the fund of productive accumulation within the Department; and third, the fund going to socialist accumulation in the state sector. In our example, the whole of the surplus product
of Department I of the private sector comes to 1.1 billion, of which we shall suppose that 500 million go to accumulation, 400 to the fund of non-productive
consumption, and 200 to the fund of socialist accumulation.

As regards the fund of non-productive consumption, an enormous portion
of it must be exchanged for means of consumption from Departments II of
the state and private sectors, because means of production are not individually
consumed. The channel for such exchange is the reproduction of c in Departments II of all three sectors of the economy. As far as the accumulation fund of
500 million is concerned, this must also divide into two distinctive parts: 1) a
fund of additional means of consumption for expanded reproduction, i.e., the
portion of these 500 million that must be exchanged for means of consumption and serve as a consumption fund for new workers who will be employed
in production, and 2) the fund of additional means of production in the strict
sense. If we assume that the division between the consumption fund and the
fund for means of production occurs in the same proportions as in the previous year, then the accumulation fund for means of production will be 250
million. Now, let us consider the elements that make up the latter figure. The
smaller component of the 250 million will consist of means of production that
Department I of the private sector must purchase from Department I of the
state sector, i.e., from state heavy industry. The major part of these 250 million

---

16   [The text mistakenly gives the figure of $3500c$.]

consists of means of production that are created within the peasant economy itself and are added, to use the term imprecisely, to the capital of production. This includes: 1) seeds for technical crops, which are acquired within the same Department and go to *expansion* of the sown area; 2) expanded reproduction of cattle, fodder and manure fertiliser; 3) land improvements of all sorts aimed at expanding the area under technical crops and raising harvest yields; 4) farm buildings constructed with the peasants' own timber and tools; and 5) additional means of production that are acquired within the same Department but through exchange with private and handicraft industry.

Since expanded reproduction of technical crops requires means of production from the state sector, it is perfectly obvious that its development is most closely tied to the conditions of reproduction and accumulation in state heavy industry. On the other hand, Department II of the state sector is closely tied, as far as its expanded reproduction is concerned, to successes in the expansion of technical crops in the peasant economy that constitute its raw material base. Accordingly, expanded reproduction of Department II of the state sector requires a *prior* expanded reproduction in the part of Department I of the private sector that produces technical crops, and the expanded reproduction of technical crops requires a *prior* expanded reproduction in the part of Department I of the state sector that provides the necessary addition to means of production. This means that both state light industry and peasant producers of technical crops have a common interest in more rapid accumulation in heavy industry, which must always occur *prior* to expanded reproduction in these branches.

Let us consider one more particular example that we must often face in practice in a peasant country and that is related to the question we have been discussing. As we know, in our peasant economy the process of accumulation occurs unevenly in years of good harvests. With a single year of good harvest, hundreds of thousands of peasant households manage to 'mend their finances', having expanded their means of production to an extent that they may not be able to repeat for another five years. Suppose that we have a better than average harvest of flax, cotton, oilseeds etc. As a result, the peasant economy can put aside a sum for the accumulation fund that exceeds the normal average annual growth of accumulation. This means greater demand, among other things, for means of production coming from state industry and also for means of production produced by craftsmen. But since there are no good harvest years for machinery or metal in heavy industry, the demand for additional means of production coming from the peasant economy will not be met unless accumulation in heavy industry is systematically running ahead of accumulation in all other branches of the economy and, in particular, unless it can ensure the existence of necessary commodity inventories. If this is not the case, then in the best of all situations the accumulation fund that is intended for purchasing means of production from heavy industry congeals for a time in the form of money, and with a developed credit system this makes it possible to expand lending by redistributing the country's monetary accumulation, which, in turn, permits additional production in the corresponding branches of heavy industry. In the worst case, this accumulation fund is exchanged for means of consumption and will simply be devoured in the peasant economy, having increased the consumer budget of the peasant Department that produces technical crops. And we have yet to mention that the disproportion will be even larger in the event that heavy industry has already exhausted its own reserves of old equipment, so that any new additional demand can be satisfied only as a result of new investments in fixed capital that far exceed the total commodity deficit of the year in question.

Let us turn now to Department II of the private sector. If we exclude private industrial production of means of consumption (production by craftsmen and artisans of boots, clothing and textiles, along with the private food industry),[17] we shall then be dealing mainly with peasant production of means of consumption. The reproduction of constant capital, equal to a sum of $3300c$ in our example, takes place as follows. The larger portion consists of means of production acquired through peasant production of the means of consumption themselves. This includes seeds for grain crops, feed for cattle, manure for fertiliser, the reproduction of livestock, buildings that peasants erect with their own timber and tools, land improvement, clearing forests for new arable land, cultivating virgin soil, etc. The second part of the means of production is acquired by exchanging means of consumption from the given Department for means of production purchased in Department I of the private sector of the economy. Finally, the third part of the means of consumption of Department II of the private sector, which replace its c, involves sales to workers in the heavy industry of the state sector, in exchange for which heavy industry provides means of production in the form of agricultural machinery, equipment, nails, roofing iron and other types of iron, freight transportation, etc.

The consumption fund of Department II of the private sector is mainly produced and consumed within the same Department, with the result that the greatest portion does not enter at all into the so-called commodity part of production in the peasant economy. In addition, only a small part of it is involved in

---

17   The whole of private production – capitalist, artisanal and handicraft – amounted to 2,165 million chervonets roubles in the economic year 1925/26, including the production of both means of production and means of consumption.

internal exchange with the wage fund of Department II of the state sector, i.e., with the state's light industry. In other words, if we take the wage fund of state light industry to be 1,000, and the part of this fund that consists of consumer items coming from the peasantry and other private production to be 400, then with this sum the worker in light industry, depending upon the composition of his budget, will buy what he requires from the consumption fund of the private sector's Department II (bread, butter etc.), while the peasantry and artisans of Department II will buy consumer items from state production.

But this by no means implies that there must exist here a relation of complete or approximate arithmetical equality, such as Marx established in his analysis of capitalist reproduction for the exchange of IIc for I($v + s/x$). In our analysis of exchange between Department I of the private sector and Department I of the state sector, we have already established that Department I of the private sector, given the natural composition of the commodities being exchanged, must acquire more from heavy industry than heavy industry can purchase in return. But this means that Department I of the private sector must sell its means of production somewhere else in an amount equal to the balance, and then use the money that it receives to buy means of production from heavy industry. It is perfectly clear that this problem might be resolved by means of foreign trade. Part of the flax, hemp etc. is exported, and heavy industry acquires, through imports, what it needs in terms of equipment. Those selling the flax, hemp and so forth use chervonets roubles to purchase the means of production they need from Soviet heavy industry. In this way, the disproportion in terms of the natural composition of exchange between Department I of the private sector and Department I of the state sector is surmounted by bringing in the foreign market, which allows Department I itself to regroup the elements of production, thus freeing the resources needed for exchange with Department I of the private sector. The question can be resolved in an even simpler and more direct way, i.e., by importing from abroad the machines and other means of production for Department I of the private sector. If this problem cannot be resolved in the quantitative terms required, either because of the under-development of our own machine-building industry or of artificial fertilisers, etc., or because of the limited import quota allotted for the private economy, we shall have a goods famine involving heavy industry's means of production, i.e., another form of the rupture of equilibrium between the state and private economies due to the under-development of our heavy industry.

In exactly the same way, let us assume that the peasant economy, having produced means of consumption, must exchange more of its products for industrially produced means of consumption than can be provided through the wage fund of light industry, as we mentioned earlier. Generally speaking, this problem can also be resolved by bringing foreign trade into the picture. Whether it is possible to turn to the foreign market in practice, given the existing conditions, is a different question. In fact, let us assume that the workers and employees of the state's light industry buy 400 million means of consumption from the private sector, whereas Department II of the private sector needs to receive in exchange for its consumption fund not 400 but instead 600 million, i.e., its effective demand, accompanied by sales, is 600 million, and this sum represents its demand for the products of state light industry. In concrete terms, the peasantry has another 200 million roubles worth of marketable grain, butter, eggs and so forth, and it wants to use these 200 million to buy an additional quantity of clothing, boots, sugar and other manufactured products for consumption. But suppose that Department II of the state sector, i.e., state light industry, provides only 400 million and cannot provide any more. There is also a way out here along the path of foreign trade. It would involve exporting an additional 200 million worth of products coming from the peasantry and using the money received to import foreign factory-produced consumer items for the peasantry. In practical terms, however, given the shortage of export resources even for importing the most important means of production, this turns out to be impossible for the Soviet state during the early years of the reconstruction process. In order to draw these 200 million of additional export resources into circulation, it would first be necessary to purchase the products of light industry abroad at a cost to this year's import fund, i.e., at the expense of curtailing the import of means of production that are already in short supply. Due to the impossibility of such an operation, and given the inadequate development of our own state light industry, the economy of the USSR must also find itself facing a protracted goods famine of industrially produced means of consumption. The consequence is that a portion of the liquid resources from the fund of means of consumption produced by the peasantry is not drawn into commodity circulation, and the Soviet countryside begins the familiar process of increasing its own consumption of eggs, butter and so on, increasing its stocks of grain beyond the levels required for insurance against a bad harvest along with a number of related phenomena. *The result is that the agricultural economy, as a whole, is producing less for the market than would be objectively possible with a more rapid development of Soviet industry even with the existing very high prices*, not to mention the potential for an even faster growth of market-oriented production that would result from a faster reduction of production costs and industrial prices. This means another disproportion between state industry and the peasant economy, and there is no way of getting around it in present circumstances apart from a more rapid development of state industry.

Theoretically, this question could be resolved differently. From the additional export fund of means of consumption, which comes to the 200 million that we have already mentioned, let only 100 million go to purchasing means of consumption and then sell these products within the country, taking advantage of the difference between internal and external prices, for an amount perhaps equal to the 200 million. At the same time, the other 100 million in the export fund might be used to purchase foreign means of production, with the result of simultaneously satisfying the peasantry's consumer demand and partially resolving the question of accelerating the development of our own industry. Although such a solution to the problem is fully possible in theory, it is perfectly obvious that in practice, given our existing conditions, it would only alleviate the difficulty we have described but not eliminate it. The point is that even in this case we would have *to advance* 100 million roubles from the import fund for the purchase of means of consumption.

Our investigation of this question would be incomplete if we did not point out that the disproportion we have been observing has one positive aspect: an accumulation of unsold surpluses of means of consumption in the countryside makes it possible to hold prices for agricultural products stable at a low level. This outcome appears to be wholly a consequence of the planning principle in our economic life and proof of that principle's vitality, but in fact it is much more the result of the disproportion we have pointed out, i.e., a phenomenon that is well known to any commodity economy. The fact that we are keeping prices more or less stable is a product of the planning principle; the fact that we are keeping them stable *at a low level* is very much the result of a blockage of agriculture's development in the sphere of production of means of consumption, a blockage caused by the under-development of our industry and a real inadequacy of accumulation within it.

In analysing the domestic conditions of equilibrium between state industry and the private economy, we have thus far omitted the changes that are imparted to this whole process by existence of the non-productive consumption fund. We shall come back to this question later in a concrete examination of the economy of the USSR in 1925/26, only touching upon it in this theoretical part. This question cannot be considered without examining certain new questions that have no direct bearing on the theme that we are presently considering.

After everything we have said, we can formulate the following extremely important conclusion concerning the law of proportional exchange between the state sector of our economy and the two sectors of the private economy.

If, in the Soviet economy, IIc of the state sector plus IIc of the private sector, minus the means of production that Department II of the whole private sector acquires within itself, equals v plus the non-productive consumption of Department I of the state sector, plus the consumption fund and the fund of non-productive consumption of the whole of Department I of the private sector,[18] then: 1) with a deficit in Department I of the combined private sector, involving means of production from Department I of the state sector, the disproportion can be eliminated only on the basis of ties with the world economy; 2) the part of the consumption fund of Department II of the combined private sector that consists of means of consumption from state light industry must be equal to a part of IIv in state industry, i.e., that part of the wage fund of Department II in the state sector that consists of means of consumption purchased from Department II of the private sector with wages, which overwhelmingly involves means of consumption of peasant origin; 3) if internal exchange of the consumption fund of Department II of the combined private sector for the corresponding part of IIv in the state sector reveals an excess of demand from the private sector, the disproportion can be resolved either with the help of ties with the external market or else by such a redistribution of the national income as would provide resources for the further development of Department II of the state sector, which presupposes, however, a still more rapid development of heavy industry; 4) if it is impossible to resolve the disproportion in the economy in the ways we have indicated, then a goods famine develops throughout the entire private economy for both the means of production and the means of consumption coming from the state economy.

Throughout our analysis we have begun with a division of the peasant economy into two Departments according to the principle that Marx adopted for the capitalist economy. Is such a method correct in view of the peasant economy's extreme lack of differentiation in terms of an internal division of labour between the different branches of agriculture? Is it not the case that one and the same medium-sized peasant farm, committed mainly to grain crops, produces materials such as wool, hides and so forth at the same time as it produces means of consumption such as bread, butter, meat etc.? Do the cotton- and flax-producing regions not simultaneously produce meat, butter, eggs, grain and so forth?

All of that is true. Nevertheless, the method of dividing peasant production into Departments I and II, which we adopt from Marx, remains the most appropriate. In the first place, we must not forget that both Departments in Marx's analysis included capitalist agriculture, which, although it is more dif-

---

18   Minus means of production for the military industry, as will be clear from everything said thus far.

ferentiated in the sense of specialised crops, nevertheless always involves a close intertwining of production of means of consumption with production of means of production. A modern large-scale capitalist farm in Germany combines, for instance, livestock and cultivation of field crops with production of sugar beets and so forth. And secondly, if we began our analysis from a different direction, taking the peasant economy of the USSR as a whole in its relation to state industry, we still would find it necessary to apply the very same method. To be precise, suppose we are figuring out how much peasant agriculture can provide in the way of materials for our industry and exports; unless we determine this, resolving the issue of proportional development of the peasant economy and industry is inconceivable. In clarifying the total raw-material potential of the peasant economy, we thereby inevitably distinguish the part of its output that represents production in Department I. In determining the marketable surpluses of food production, we likewise distinguish a so-called Department II. In Marx's analysis, one part of the production of every large-scale capitalist farm figures in Department I, while the other part figures in Department II. It is the same in our calculations: each separate peasant farm provides a mixed output and thus figures partly in Department I and partly in Department II. The fact that one and the same plough, one and the same horse, etc., figure simultaneously as both means of production for means of production and means of production for consumer items, adds complexity to the general analysis of reproduction but is not sufficient reason for rejecting Marx's method of investigation, since replacing it with any other is impossible. When undertaking a detailed analysis of reproduction in agriculture, all that we require is further investigation of what percentage of these means of production belongs in Department I or Department II.

At this point, we still have to consider the role of non-productive consumption in the USSR's economy and how this consumption influences the conditions of equilibrium between the combined state and private economies.

To deal better with this question, let us adopt one of Marx's schemes referring to expanded capitalist reproduction, the following scheme for example:

I. $4000c + 1000v + 1000s$ (500 accumulation fund + 500 capitalists' consumption fund)

II. $1500c + 500v + 500s$ ($500/x + 500/y$)

In this case, 1500 IIc exchanges for $1000v + 500$ in the capitalists' consumption fund of Department I. Assume now that non-productive consumption falls by half in Department I with the same level of production. We shall then have the following:

I. $4000c + 1000v + 1000s$ (750 accumulation fund + 250 capitalists' consumption fund)

In this case Department I, thanks to the increase of accumulation at the expense of non-productive consumption, reduces its exchange fund with Department II from 1500 to 1250, while the reproduction of IIc, if there are no changes in Department II, requires 1500 means of production from Department I. Even if this reduction of non-productive consumption is merely relative rather than absolute – i.e., I's non-productive consumption fund either remains unchanged at 500 while the accumulation fund increases, or both figures increase but the accumulation fund grows more rapidly than the non-productive consumption fund, in which case the change will not be so abrupt as in the previous example – the same tendency remains and will involve a growing deficit of means of production for Department II. This is explained by the fact that the exchange fund of Department I will systematically lag behind the demand coming from Department II for means of production.

Should a corresponding reduction occur in Department II's non-productive consumption fund, we need only repeat the same numerical operation in Department II as in I in order to see where it must lead. In that event the additional accumulation fund, resulting from the reduction of non-productive consumption, is distributed between c and v in Department II in proportion to the organic composition of capital, and II will demand considerably more than 1500 means of production from I. That means the disproportion will grow from two directions simultaneously: due to both the relative reduction of I's exchange fund and also the absolute and relative growth of IIc. How this disproportion in the economy might subsequently be eliminated is another question. (Obviously it involves a general redistribution of productive forces between I and II on the basis of new proportions.) But when we simply move to a lower level of non-productive consumption and a higher level of accumulation, this inevitably changes the proportions of exchange between I and II, increasing II's demand for means of production and temporarily reducing the supply. *In this case the country's economy becomes more progressive from the viewpoint of developing the productive forces, the surplus product grows for society as a whole, there is a more rapid increase of society's aggregate gross and net production, and accumulation grows more rapidly – but the actual transition to the new path, which involves an increase of the relative weight of Department I, must cause a temporary disproportion throughout the economy.* This general-theoretical proposition means that we must draw the following important conclusion concerning the economy of the USSR. If, due to reduced non-productive consumption by the industrial bourgeoisie, the accumulation fund increases throughout the whole economic domain in which the state sector has replaced pre-war private capitalist production,[19] this must inevitably mean a reduction of the exchange fund of Department I in the state sector, together with a simultaneous *increase* of accumulation in Department II, which means a relative growth of IIc and an increase in IIc's demand for means of production. But since the means of production in Department II of the state sector consist not simply of machines, fuel and other means of production acquired from Department I of the state sector, but also of an enormous quantity of peasant material, this means that the actual transition to a system of reduced non-productive consumption and more rapid accumulation – once the pre-war level of production has been reached in Department II of the state sector and in the production of materials in the peasant economy – must inevitably cause a *chronic crisis in the supply of materials to state light industry*. Thus, even aside from the change in composition of the peasant budget, which is associated with the Revolution (we shall discuss this later), on its own the reduction in non-productive consumption within industry itself must have the consequence of more rapid accumulation and more rapid growth of the deficit in means of production.

But the state economy of the USSR eliminates only *part* of the non-productive consumption that existed with the bourgeois economic system. For example, suppose that out of every 100 units of the surplus product of pre-war capitalist industry 40 went to accumulation, 20 of the remaining 60 were non-productively consumed by the capitalists, and 40 went to non-productive consumption by the capitalist system as a whole, i.e., representing industry's share in supporting the bureaucratic apparatus, the army, interest payments on foreign debts, the non-productive expenditures of the trade apparatus and so forth. Our state industry can use this 20 % of the surplus value for additional accumulation, but in place of non-productive consumption by the capitalists it has its own Soviet non-productive consumption: there is still an army, a state apparatus, expenditures on non-productive consumption by the trade apparatus etc. Moreover, if our non-productive consumption expenditures of this type were to be higher than under capitalism, they would devour this whole saving of 20 % and even reduce the accumulation fund compared to the pre-war period, especially if the fund of surplus product in Soviet industry proved to be less than before the war.

I shall not deal here with how things actually stand in terms of figures. It should be mentioned that some non-productive expenditures have increased for us (the trade apparatus) while others have been reduced (the state budget).

---

19   We assume here that the production of surplus product remains at the same level.

For now, it is only important to establish two facts. First, if the part of surplus product that is spent non-productively is declining for us or has declined compared to the pre-war period, this must inevitably change proportions in the distribution of productive forces and cause a greater demand for means of production. The second fact is that non-productive[20] consumption in our economy, to some degree or other, inevitably continues to exist. And that fact, in turn, means different proportions in the distribution of productive forces compared to a scheme of the Soviet economy that we might construct if we ignored non-productive consumption. The point is that given the existence of non-productive consumption in the Soviet system, some part of the country's general consumption fund must be set aside to support the non-productively employed strata of the population. In order to produce this fund of non-productive consumption, the corresponding means of production must be produced somewhere. And this means that all Departments of all sectors of the economy must be involved to some degree in serving non-productive consumption. However, it by no means implies that distribution of the burden of non-productive consumption between the individual sectors of the economy, and between the individual Departments of these sectors, must be proportional to changes in the equations of exchange between the individual Departments that are caused by the very existence of non-productive consumption.

In concrete terms, this is how matters stand in the individual Departments. The fund of non-productive consumption in Department I of the state sector consists of means of production in material form. One part of this fund, which goes directly to non-productive consumption in the form of means of production, involves everything consumed by the military industry: equipment for weapons factories, metal for the production of means of defence, fuel burned up in production, etc. Another part of the fund of non-productive consumption in Department I must enter into exchange with Departments II of both the state and private sectors. The same will generally apply to the fund of non-productive consumption in Department I of the private sector, the difference being that the role of the military industry in absorbing means of production will in this case be very much less significant, with the exception of horses for the cavalry and so on. As far as the Departments producing means of consumption are concerned, their fund of non-productive consumption enters in material form into the consumer budget of all groups of the population who are not employed in productive labour. It is quite obvious that, in value terms,

---

20   The term 'non-productive' is used here in a social-economic sense, certainly not in a moral sense. After all, there is also *necessary* non-productive consumption.

the entire fund of individual non-productive consumption will be less than the share in which Departments II of both sectors will participate in the total burden of non-productive consumption, because part of this non-productive consumption will be covered by Departments I in the form of supplying Departments II with their means of production minus the means of production going to the military industry. And this means that the existence of non-productive consumption in Soviet society slows accumulation and the growth rate of society's gross and net production on the one hand, while on the other hand this non-productive consumption, albeit by purely negative methods, decreases the disproportion between Departments I and II of both sectors, which we discussed above and which means a deficit in means of production. With regard specifically to exchange of part of the consumption fund of Department II of the private sector for a certain part of the wage fund of workers in Department II of the state sector, the relative decline in the growth of IIv in the state sector reduces the exchange fund with this Department, and the reduced accumulation in Department II of the private sector reduces its demand for additional means of consumption from Department II of the state sector as well as its demand for means of production from Department I of the state sector.

Conversely, when there is a drop in non-productive consumption, the gross and net incomes of society grow along with accumulation, while there is also an increase of the goods famine for means of production. As we have already mentioned, however, development of the whole economy on a broader foundation subsequently creates, within the economy itself, the means for overcoming the disproportion, particularly on the basis of exports and imports.

To finish up with the question of non-productive consumption, it remains for us to deal with one critically important methodological question whose practical significance will be more obvious to us later.

How can we correctly determine the scale of non-productive consumption in the USSR and the influence that this consumption has on the whole process of reproduction?

There are two possible methods. First, there is the method that Marx applied when analysing capitalist reproduction in Volume II of *Capital*, where he understood v to represent that part of the advanced capital that is *really* spent as income by the working class. Marx thereby treated all taxes on wages as surplus value. The advantages of such a methodological approach lie in the fact that the whole of v is then fully involved in exchange, uncomplicated by the fact that part of v, which *formally* represents wages, essentially goes to pay for part of bourgeois society's non-productive consumption. A detailed examination of any actual country then only requires, in addition, a study of exchange within the fund of non-productive consumption, which is particularly necessary in order to take into account the role of the military industry in this consumption as well as the role of non-productive expenditures on the trade apparatus. This will also require a supplementary investigation of the monetary savings of the working class. With regard to the petty-bourgeois sector, this method requires that we take into account *only the real consumption fund of independent producers who are engaged in production*, while all of their real accumulation in the economy, plus the non-productive consumption of the social system, insofar as it falls on this particular sector, must be regarded as surplus product. This by no means precludes analysis of the exchange of real volumes of means of production from Departments I, which, in exchange for means of consumption, go to replace the constant capital of the Departments II. The difficulty here, generally speaking, is that it is never possible to clarify precisely what must be understood as the necessary consumption of the class of small-scale producers, since their consumption fund, as we have already noted, is not regulated by the law of value even in concrete capitalism. In our own case, moreover, it is also regulated to some extent by the law of primitive socialist accumulation. Furthermore, we must remember in this regard that the concept of productive labour is acquiring a different meaning compared to what it meant for Marx.[21]

The second method would consist of simultaneously deriving two balances: one for production and the other for consumption. This second method does not exclude the first, although in our opinion it must follow the first, because to begin immediately with a double balance would mean beginning not with a simpler general balance but instead with a complicated concrete one, not to mention the fact that this double balance, without a preliminary general one, might simply hide an *inability* to derive a single general balance.[22]

Furthermore, we must emphasise here the great practical difficulty of separating out, from the expenses incurred in trade, the amount that goes to paying productive labour as distinct from the part that pays for non-productive consumption by the apparatus. Trade mark-ups to cover transport expenses are easy to take into account and include in the production balance for transport, considered as one of the branches of *production*. In the same way, all taxes on

---

21   One of several concepts in Marxist political economy that must be defined differently when discussing our economy is that of productive labour as labour that creates surplus value. Without dealing with this question in detail, let us simply note that what we mean by the term productive labour in the *social* economy of the USSR is the social labour of workers and independent petty commodity producers who are creating means of production and consumption for Soviet society as a whole.

22   The derivation of a general balance on a methodologically correct basis is, among other things, one of the most important ways of verifying all of the data in our industrial and general statistics.

trade, apart from what returns to production through the state budget, must be included in the fund of non-productive consumption. Conversely, it is much more difficult to distinguish productive labour, used to move a commodity to the place where it is individually consumed, or expenditures on storage and so forth, from a number of other expenses connected not with this physical labour but rather with the general cost to society of the existing *system* of distribution, including above all non-productive consumption by the agents of private commercial capital and by the worthless agents of the state and co-operative trading network, along with all the pedagogical expenses incurred in propagating the science of 'civilised trading'.

Another very important methodological question concerns the general issue of what indices to take as the basis for calculating social production and consumption. It is quite clear that we shall have to use a dual system of accounting, one account involving pre-war prices as a form of natural accounting, and another involving real wholesale and retail prices in chervonets roubles as a way of measuring values.

At this point we can conclude for now our general investigation of the conditions for equilibrium between the state and private sectors of the economy. We temporarily set aside the question of how the conditions of equilibrium, and particularly the rate of expanded reproduction in the state sector, are affected by quantitative changes in the way society's burden of non-productive consumption is distributed between the socialised sector of the economy and the private economy as a whole.

8 The Fifth Condition of Equilibrium

The fifth condition of equilibrium in the overall economic system of the USSR is a systematic rise in wages. We have in mind not natural growth of the total wage fund in the state sector, which comes from rising numbers being employed, but rather growth of the wage fund also due to a rise of the average wage paid to the individual worker. The social structure of our state economy is such that, with a systematic rise in the level of productive forces, the price of labour power must systematically deviate from its value, and this means the very concept of labour as a commodity must gradually be eliminated. The growth of wages is also inevitable due to the very fact of the country's industrialisation, because change in the state economy's whole technical base, the increased rationalisation of work and so forth, inevitably entail more highly skilled workers. The collective character of property in the means of production in the state economy necessarily involves an advance of the proletariat's cultural level and creation of the elements of a new socialist culture. Should the growth of socialist culture lag behind development of the productive forces in the collective sector of the economy, that lag can itself become an impediment to further development of the productive forces. As it advances, every system of social production develops a characteristic form of labour discipline that is suited to its own structure, its own work incentives, and the type of average worker that it requires. Socialist industry must also create its own type of worker and its own incentives for work. This sort of worker can only emerge with a sufficiently high material standard of life for the working class, which must be significantly higher than what capitalism can provide to workers using the same technology.[23]

The enormous non-productive expenditures of the state and the co-operative trade-industrial apparatus, which has yet to develop even rudimentary methods of working that would correspond to the collective mode of production, are connected not just with a generally low level of development of the productive forces in the state sector but also with *a rudimentary level of socialist culture among the working class itself*. The culture of all social organs always aligns with that of the ruling class. To elevate the culture of Soviet society means, first and foremost, elevating the culture of the working class. An uninterrupted rise in the material standard of life for the proletariat is necessary not just for social reasons but also for economic ones.

Furthermore, we must not forget a fact that we established earlier, namely, that given the impossibility of the country importing a substantial amount of industrially produced means of consumption for the peasantry, who are producing means of consumption, the expansion of domestic exchange of means of consumption between state light industry and Department II of the petty-bourgeois economy is limited to the part of IIv in the state sector that goes to purchasing peasant means of consumption and those coming from private production in general. Even if we allow for the possible expansion of such

---

23 It must be clearly understood that a peasant protest against the growth of wages, against better measures for the protection of labour and general improvement of workers' lives, is profoundly reactionary from both a social-class and a narrowly economic viewpoint. Socialism knows only one kind of equalisation of the material conditions of town and country, and what this equalisation involves, leaving aside temporary improvement in the position of petty producers, is elimination of the very foundations of individual small-scale production. A highly developed collective economy in agriculture is capable of providing its workers with the same material welfare as socialist industry provides in the cities. Overcoming the contradiction between town and country, which is one of the historic tasks of socialism, cannot be accomplished by converting the urban worker into something like a rural blacksmith, who plays a subordinate role in the small-scale economy.

exchange as a result of occasionally adding imports of means of consumption produced abroad, the basic fund for exchange continues to be the part of $\mathrm{II}\nu$ in the state sector that we have just mentioned. With a given level of prices, this means that expansion of the wage fund for workers in light industry – which can occur due to an increase of the number of workers and also to a rise in the average wage level for workers in light industry – *must precede* increased satisfaction of peasant demand for the means of consumption produced in state light industry. The leading role of state industry is also evident in this part of the economic field. Together with a general reduction in prices, a rise in wages emerges as a factor that facilitates reduction of the disproportion in exchange between the rural economy and industry, and in this case reduction of the disproportion occurs not in a negative but rather in a socially and economically positive form.

9   The Sixth Condition of Equilibrium

The sixth condition for dynamic equilibrium in the economy of the USSR is a systematic reduction in prices for production coming from the state economy. This type of equilibrium is simultaneously economic and social.

   To start with, let us consider the economic side of this equilibrium.

   We pointed out earlier that one of today's so-called 'bottlenecks' in the development of state light industry is partly – and it will be even more so in future – the lag of peasant production of technical crops behind the demand for materials coming from industry. But what increased production of technical crops requires above all is increased accumulation in this branch of the economy. An increase of accumulation in this Department, with the same level of individual consumption, requires: 1) a general reduction in non-productive consumption, including reduction in this Department; 2) a price increase for technical crops; 3) a price reduction for consumer items; 4) a price reduction for means of production that Department I of the peasant economy acquires from Department I of the state sector; 5) a reduction of individual consumption in Department I of the peasant economy itself; and 6) increased labour using the available means of production. Some of these options are purely theoretical. A reduction of individual consumption is impossible or nearly impossible in the Department that we are considering, since it is already quite low. A reduction in prices on means of consumption produced by the peasants is likewise impossible; compared to prices for industrial products they are considerably lower than pre-war prices, which were already quite low. The only possibility is for the selling prices of grain, in regions producing technical crops, to approach the

procurement prices in grain-producing regions, i.e., essentially for a curtailment of non-productive consumption in the trade network, for transport costs
to be reduced and the transport facilities to be improved, especially on the main
and local roads. Apart from rectifying one or another incorrect calculation on
the part of the procurement organs, a systematic increase in prices for technical
crops is also impossible, for such an increase in prices would also be a factor
contributing to rising prices in state light industry. What remains, therefore,
is greater intensity[24] and productivity of labour along with better yields from
the land used for peasant production of technical crops, curtailment of non-
productive consumption throughout the whole political-economic system of
the USSR, cheaper means of production coming from Department I of the state
sector, and cheaper means of consumption coming from state light industry.
With regard to the latter, what is required is not artificial reduction of accumulation in these branches but a reduction of real production costs as a result
of re-equipping the technical base and rationalising production. On this point,
the interests of state industry align with the interests of peasant producers of
materials, and reduction of industrial prices is a stimulus for expanded reproduction in Department I of the peasant economy. Moreover, on the basis of
increased accumulation in this Department of the peasant economy, it will be
easier to achieve decisive successes in the matter of improving soil cultivation,
increasing livestock production, and generally improving labour productivity,
which will increase the total annual production of technical crops.[25]

As far as peasant production of means of consumption is concerned, the
situation here is rather different in the following way. The domestic market in
the USSR is not absorbing the whole output of consumer items from the peasant economy, and their export is obviously required in order to support general
equilibrium of the whole system. But the import fund that the state acquires
through these exports – given the conditions of production in state industry
that we have already mentioned – cannot to any significant extent be com-

---

24   It must be emphasised here that peasant agriculture in the USSR, even with the exist-
      ing means of production, could significantly raise its gross output by means of a greater
      expenditure of physical labour, and particularly by implementing a number of simple
      agronomic improvements. The struggle against fear of work in the countryside and the
      traditional laziness is one of the most important problems in the industrialisation of the
      country.

25   This is why the policy of the Soviet state is absolutely correct in selling agricultural
      machinery at artificially low prices. In future this must be turned into a system: given
      identical production costs, the means of production must always be sold at a price lower
      than production costs and the means of consumption at a price higher than production
      costs.

mitted to imports of peasant means of consumption and can only partly be used for the import of agricultural means of production. This contradiction, given the unfavourable coefficients in the exchange of peasant production for the products of state industry, together with the material shortage of the latter, has the effect of holding back the whole process of expanding production of peasant means of consumption and reduces the economic effectiveness of accumulation as well as the purchasing power of that part of the consumption fund that exchanges for the part of IIv in light industry that we have already mentioned. All of this impedes development of the marketed share of peasant production of means of consumption, reinforces the non-productive consumption of the peasant masses themselves, and hinders growth of the export fund. However, even when we have achieved the pre-war level of agricultural production, and when the volume of exchange of agricultural production of means of consumption is approaching that of pre-war Russia, the reduction of non-productive consumption by the bourgeoisie, the elimination of land ownership by the nobility, and the repudiation of foreign debts create the precondition for a very significant growth of the agricultural surplus product, which can contribute to the fund of expanded reproduction. The way out of the blind alley and disproportion, in this case too, lies in faster re-equipping of industry, curtailment of production costs, a systematic reduction of prices, and finally, a rise of labour productivity within the peasant economy itself. For every 100 units of its output that the peasant Department of means of consumption exchanges for part of Iv in the state sector in order to replace its means of production, it will receive more of these means of production in natural form. On the other hand, every 100 units of the consumption fund will make it possible to acquire more means of consumption in exchange for part of IIv of the state sector.

But a systematic reduction of industrial prices is important from the viewpoint of supporting not only the economic but also *the social equilibrium of the entire Soviet system*. The acute discrepancy between domestic industrial prices and world-market prices, i.e., the regime of far-reaching non-equivalent exchange, is exceptional and by its very nature temporary. It corresponds to the period of infancy in the development of a state economy in a backward, peasant country. Its historical purpose is to provide state industry with the resources needed to recast its technical basis and the opportunity to accumulate on the basis of modern advanced technology instead of old and worn-out technology. Only after completion of this process will the state economy be in a position, as we have already repeated several times, to develop all of the advantages that collective production ensures by comparison with capitalist production. However, the peasant economy must also develop during this period. It is not concerned with what stage of development socialist reproduction is passing through; what it requires are cheaper industrial commodities in the necessary amounts and of appropriate quality. This economic contradiction grows over into a social one: the growth of peasant discontent with the foreign trade monopoly, the striving to liquidate compulsory attachment of the peasant market to Soviet industry, and an effort to break through to the value relations of the world market without paying millions in taxes to the fund of primitive socialist accumulation. This social contradiction is the whip that is driving the state economy to make the domestic industrial prices of the state economy approach the prices of the world market. Speedy successes in this direction, accompanied by growth of state credit to organise the economy of middle and especially poor peasants, and to provide them with additional means of production, will alleviate this social contradiction. A delay on this path will make it more acute, threatening an uprising against the socialist sector mainly by the most developed and capitalistic elements of the peasant economy, along with the corresponding groups of the peasant population who are most constrained in their bourgeois development by the process of expanded socialist reproduction.[26]

10   The Seventh Condition of Equilibrium

Finally, the seventh condition of equilibrium of the Soviet system is gradual absorption, by a developing state economy and intensifying agriculture, of the country's excess population, an absorption that includes both the overt and the disguised unemployment that the Soviet system has inherited mainly from the agrarian relations of the old regime. This is where the situation is most dire and contradictory. Improvement of the state sector's technology and rationalisation of labour, as the natural preconditions for reducing production costs and selling prices, essentially mean a reduction of expenditures on labour power per unit of output. Even in the best equipped Soviet enterprises, these expenditures are far higher than in advanced European industry, not to mention America. The whole process of labour rationalisation will avoid leading to stagnation in terms of expanding the work force employed in state industry if it coincides with a sufficiently rapid expansion, in absolute terms, of the

---

26   Here we have come to the most important question of the relation between socialist development of the city and capitalist development of the countryside. The Soviet system, in the present difficult period, can only survive on the basis of proportionality between their rates of growth. A higher rate of socialist development makes it possible also to have a bigger dose of capitalist development without posing significant danger to the overall system.

country's industrial base. But this rapid expansion presupposes significantly faster industrial accumulation than we see presently (in 1927). The fact that the Soviet economy is now developing in breadth and not at the level of leading capitalist technology, that it is only catching up to that level, must have the inevitable result of a relative weakening in the rate of growth of the work force and a relative slowing in the tempo of absorbing the army of the unemployed. In the history of the Soviet economy, we can see an analogous process to some extent in the transition to NEP, when more rational use of labour power and means of production in 1921/22, together with a sharp rise in the general level of production compared to 1920, led to a reduction of the work force in state enterprises compared to the final year of War Communism. According to the five-year plan of development for the economy of the USSR that Gosplan has worked out, in the economic year 1930/31, i.e., by the end of the five-year plan, the overall production of state industry must increase by 70.4% whereas the number of employed workers will grow during the same period only by 27.9%, or by 2,053,000 people.[27] As for the volume of unemployment associated with migration from the countryside to the city and with growth of the work force within the city itself, its possible size is determined by the five-year plan to be 1,189,000 in 1926/27, with a slow, incremental and almost unnoticeable decline to 1,146,000 by the end of the five-year plan. Meanwhile, during the first half of 1927, unemployment has already exceeded Gosplan's projected figure by several hundred thousand. This shows that Gosplan's calculations, which in themselves are extremely pessimistic, are proving in fact to be too optimistic. And from the viewpoint of the relation between the work force employed in the socialised sector compared to the capitalist and petty-bourgeois sectors, any expected successes are exceedingly modest: the relative weight of the socialised sector rises in total from 11.2% to 12.6%, i.e., by a total of 1.4%. The situation in terms of agrarian over-population is even more severe: Gosplan's figure is 6.8 million people.[28] This figure, according to Gosplan's calculations, will at best not decline. There are numerous indications that it will increase and thereby also significantly increase the numbers of the urban unemployed.

On the other hand, intensification of agriculture, *the potential for which is directly proportional to the backwardness of our agriculture compared to the foreign peasant economy,* will on the one hand mean the absorption of new workers into agriculture, and on the other hand, a rise of agricultural labour productivity, i.e., a relative reduction in the expenditure of labour power per

---

27   See *Perspektivy*, pp. 2 and 21 of the appendix.
28   These are the figures from the People's Commissariat of Agriculture.

unit of output. But agricultural intensification requires an increase of agricultural accumulation. At the same time, if this accumulation were to occur at the expense of that part of the fund of surplus production that the countryside provides to the city for socialist reconstruction, it would lead to a slowdown in the tempo of expanded reproduction in state industry, i.e., in precisely the area that is decisive in the sense of overcoming in future all the fundamental contradictions of the transition period.

We have only had to outline the foundations of dynamic equilibrium in the economic system of the USSR in the most general terms in order to see the whole sum of economic and social contradictions that are inevitably revealed by our development towards socialism in the conditions of our isolation:

1) Accumulation on the basis of non-equivalent exchange – and the need to overcome this non-equivalence, two processes that do not coincide temporally.

2) Accumulation at the expense of the workers' surplus product – and the inevitability of a systematic growth of wages.

3) The need, in order to shorten the 'birth pangs of industrialisation' and for the fastest possible expansion of ties with the world division of labour and an increase of foreign credits – and the growing hostility of the entire capitalist world towards the USSR.

4) Accumulation at the expense of the peasants who are producing raw materials and of the whole peasantry in general – and the need to stimulate to the maximum the expanded reproduction of these materials.

5) Accumulation at the expense of exporting peasant means of consumption – and the need to stimulate these exports in conditions of an extremely slow reduction of industrial prices.

6) The economic imperative for the growth of market-oriented production by the peasant economy – and the social need to provide material support to the least market-oriented parts of that economy, the poor and weak groups in the countryside.

7) The need for price reduction on the basis of the rationalisation of production – and the struggle against growing unemployment.

This whole sum of contradictions demonstrates how closely our development towards socialism is bound up with the need to make a breach in our socialist isolation not just for political but also for economic reasons, and to rely in future on the material resources of other socialist countries.

This concludes our general outline of the conditions of equilibrium in the economy of the USSR. This essay is far from comprehensive even in its purely theoretical part. No doubt, it is inadequate in many respects, as with any such first attempt. On the basis of everything we have set out, however, we are already able to turn to an investigation of the concrete figures for our economy in specific years. From now onwards, on the basis of the algebraic schemes of reproduction in the USSR that we have sketched out here, our task will be to construct concrete arithmetical schemes of reproduction with the detailed figures that our statisticians will provide, beginning with Gosplan's control figures. Our focus in this concrete investigation will be on the economic years 1925/26 and 1926/27, as the most typical years for the end of the recovery period and the beginning of the so-called reconstruction process. In this concrete inquiry we must also touch upon certain theoretical questions, which, in the interest of abbreviating this purely methodological part of our study, we prefer to illustrate with numerical data from today's living Soviet economy.

E.A. Preobrazhensky, 'Khozyaistvennoe ravnovesie
v sisteme SSSR', in Vestnik Kommunisticheskoi akademii, No. 22,
(Moscow, 1927), pp. 19–71.

PART 2

[Concrete Analysis of the Soviet Economy]

∵

Results of the New Economic Policy in Soviet Russia[1]

The Russian Communist Party completed its move to the New Economic Policy at its Party congress in March of 1921. The change affected commerce first of all, because allowing freedom to trade increased the absorptive capacity of the free market quickly and brought an inflow of latent commodity values. All of this affected prices and the exchange rate of the rouble, whose decline temporarily slowed and within weeks even came to a halt in some places. Replacement of requisitions by the tax in kind promptly influenced the peasantry's political mood and had a calming effect on the countryside. In terms of the peasant economy, this measure could have only a modest impact during the first few months and was limited to the fact that it certainly contributed in some measure to expansion of the sown acreage. The political influence of the policy change was rapid and strongly felt amongst all strata of the population, although we shall have to leave that aspect of the question aside, since in this article we intend to discuss only the economic outcome of the new course. The policy change seriously affected the economy of the country as a whole only much later. It will be no mistake to say that reconstruction along the entire economic front only occurred by the summer and autumn of 1921, which leaves us with just a short interval of time, 7–8 months at most, from which to draw conclusions. Nevertheless, sufficient data have been collected for this period, from all branches of the economy, to allow us to provide preliminary summaries.

Before turning to those summaries, I think it necessary to offer a few remarks concerning the type of economy that either developed or was developing during the Civil War – I have difficulty deciding which expression to use, but in any case it assumed well-known features – as well as the type that is taking shape presently. It is not easy to provide this sort of characterisation, especially for the period of the New Economic Policy. Whereas our political order can be definitively characterised as the dictatorship of the proletariat in a peasant country – and this designation, in general and on the whole, remains correct both for the period of the Civil War and for the post-war period – neither the socialist nor the general economic literature provides ready-made terms to apply

---

1 Published in *Kommunisticheskii Internatsional*, No. 20, 1922.

to our previous economic system or to the present one. We are dealing with novel formations that not only have never before existed in history but also have never even been anticipated theoretically in any concrete terms. While it is easy enough to give an economic outline of the wartime period, since that is largely a question of the past, it is an extremely difficult task to do so for the new period that is still forming, in which everything is being reconstructed, everything is *im Werden*, and the economic materials are a soft as wax.

The principal features of Soviet Russia's economic organism during the war were the following. All large- and medium-scale industry, and all the large and medium estates that remained undivided, were in the hands of the state. The whole capitalist superstructure, which overlay the country's petty-bourgeois base, became a socialist superstructure if we take socialisation to mean simply socialisation of the means of production. If socialist production is understood as collective production, not for profit but for planned distribution through the workers' state, then within the socialist sphere we had both socialist production and socialist distribution in extremely primitive and crude forms. But there is more to it than that. The most distinctive feature of our economy in the wartime period was the attempt by the proletariat to dictate its methods of distribution also to the small-peasant economy. The Soviet authority took this path out of necessity. Given the enormous need of the city and the army for agricultural products; the impossibility of the state acquiring them through trade with the countryside, due to the inevitably passive trade balance between town and country caused by industry's disintegration; and the impossibility of acquiring the necessary resources through use of a falling currency, the proletarian state was compelled to introduce compulsory seizures of agricultural surpluses. In order to acquire supplies, it was often necessary to seize not only surpluses but also part of the fund for direct peasant consumption. Requisitioning was not a socialist method, in the proper sense of the word, for distributing grain in the country, but it might have developed into socialist distribution between the proletariat and the peasantry had there been the material wherewithal in the cities, i.e., had the city been able quickly to provide an equivalent volume of industrial products for peasant grain.

To do that was impossible. On the other hand, the distribution of city products in the villages had to adjust to the petty-bourgeois type of economy, i.e., each proprietor, through co-operation, should acquire more in return for providing more grain. But that did not happen either. What happened was requisitioning, with no equivalent transfer of commodities from town to country, while even the few commodities that were transferred to the country were distributed on an equalising basis. In its initial stage, requisitioning was a natural tax with grave and extremely harmful consequences for development of a petty-bourgeois economy. It could not grow into socialist distribution because of our poverty, the disorder in industry, and the delay of the workers' world revolution. If the latter had come to the assistance of our proletariat in 1918, 1919 and 1920, the situation would have changed fundamentally. Our proletariat could have consolidated its position and, on the basis of the compulsory distribution of agricultural products already underway, it would have been materially possible to make this compulsory distribution voluntary and acceptable to the peasantry in the form of co-operative distribution.

That was the position we had to retreat from when adopting market distribution, whose extent is presently limited by the tax in kind and the planned economy in the sphere of state industry. This is exactly the point that constitutes the fundamental difference between the old economic policy and the new one; the organisational reconstruction of the whole of socialist industry is connected with precisely this about-turn.

The difference is not that we have leased most medium-size nationalised enterprises to private employers or artels, but that the proletarian state has been forced to enter into a relation of market purchase and sale with the peasantry, selling part of its output to buy the agricultural products it needs. On the basis of large- and medium-scale socialist production, we previously tried to subordinate the small-scale economy to socialist distribution. Now, to the contrary, we are compelled to restructure socialist production according to the requirements of petty-bourgeois, commodity-money distribution. From our offensive against petty-bourgeois production, we have gone over to the defensive and preparation for a new offensive on a different basis – on the basis of market distribution (apart from the tax in kind) and a market struggle of large-scale state production with petty production.

Of course, once involved in a struggle in this sort of arena and with these kinds of weapons, our state industry can succeed only if it is reconstructed in a different way, if it acquires the necessary flexibility, and if the forms of its relation with the state are fundamentally changed.

A development of the productive forces in industry, based on socialist distribution or a socialist type of distribution, as distinct from a development that relies fully or partially on the market, demands entirely different organisational forms. Our economic leadership had no need to dream up these forms; they have adopted the highest form of market-based industrial organisation that capitalism has managed to reach – the system of organisation through trusts.

Leaving aside individual enterprises that are in the hands of local Soviet organs or are not subject to trustification by the Supreme Council of the National Economy, the major portion of state enterprises are now organised in a system of state socialist trusts. Our state industry simultaneously includes elements of both a socialist and a capitalist type of economy. The basic elements of socialism are socialisation of the instruments of production and transport in the hands of the workers' state; the state economic plan, which facilitates productivity in the development of individual branches of production; state provision of consumer products to workers and employees according to a special plan that is co-ordinated with the production plan (in 1921–22 about 4 million people continue to receive state provisions); the supply to industry of instruments of production, fuel and raw materials from the resources of the socialist state through its own internal redistribution; and the establishment of wage categories by the trade unions on the basis of a fund that accounts for 50–60% of all products involved in budgetary expenditures. The capitalist elements are seen in the following facts: 1) some state enterprises work wholly and others partially for the free market, and without exception they must all make purchases in the free market, even though for some groups these purchases are minimal and incidental; 2) calculations in monetary form are now being introduced between state enterprises themselves and between them and the state, and there are reasons to think this will become the prevalent form of accounting despite the shakiness of our declining currency; 3) there have been some preliminary and completely successful experiments in state wholesale trade and the use of co-operatives for market distribution alongside of the older forms of provision in kind for workers and employees; 4) the state has moved from the role of organising production to leasing some of the medium enterprises that for now are not profitable, in most cases taking 8–10% of gross output in the form of rent. There are also other less important socialist and capitalist features, but we cannot deal with them here since space is limited.

On the basis of what we have said, we can now attempt to characterise the type of economy that is taking shape in our industry and for which there are no ready designations in Marxist literature. Throughout the territory of Russia, almost all the forms of economy known to nature now exist and co-exist, and in this respect Russia represents a museum of visual aids for the history of economic life. We have: 1) the patriarchal type of natural economy among nomads and in parts of the North; 2) the petty-bourgeois commodity-money economy; 3) commercial and industrial capitalism in the form of private enterprises with hired labour in the cities and further afield in the villages; 4) state and cooperative capitalism, although state capitalism, if we understand that term to mean a coalescence of the proletarian state with some of the capitalist enterprises, exists more in projects than in reality; and 5) socialism, if we consider the trusts of the workers' state, operating within the limits of a state plan and partly within the limits of market distribution, to be a socialist form of economy. If we wish to characterise the state economy on its own, there are equal grounds for calling it a commodity-capitalist or a socialist-commodity economy. In any case, if we communists have agreed to call the transitional stage from capitalism to communism 'socialism', since classes still exist under socialism (even though there are only two of them, workers and petty independent producers), a state persists, and the system of distribution satisfies the principle 'to each according to his needs, from each according to his abilities', then the present type of state economy in Soviet Russia can be called transitional from capitalism to socialism. At best, this is one of the most primitive and backward forms of socialist economy: it is compelled to implement its production plan partly and perhaps even mostly by using the free market; it has to clothe the distribution process even within the socialist sphere in the form of paper money; it must subordinate the petty producer by way of the market; and it has to acquire surplus value from petty production only partly in kind but mainly in the form of commercial profit from the sale of its output, as monetary taxes, and in the form of a barbaric tax levied by issuing paper money.

But with all the backwardness of our type of socialist industry – whose head alone breathes the pure and clear atmosphere of socialist accounting and planned management, while its legs and body are submerged in the swamp of the free market – this industry has one great advantage over our wartime industry. That advantage is the following.

During the period of so-called War Communism, we advanced quite far in terms of the socialist form of production and distribution, but in terms of development of the economy's productive forces things went very badly. Centralisation in managing the state economy was less a matter of serving production goals than a consequence of our poverty, helping to calculate and consume as economically as possible (especially at the front) all of the available supplies and resources in the country. An incredibly rapid pace of development would have been needed in industry in order for the economy's productive forces to adapt to the socialist framework that was created following the October Revolution and during the Civil War. But such rapid development did not and could not take place. It was impossible not just because the war devoured all the main energies and stores, leaving industry with no circulating resources, but also because the low cultural level of the proletariat prevented us from finding the incentives to raise labour productivity and economise in the use of resources that would correspond to the socialist structure of the economy. Though it may sound paradoxical, it is an indisputable fact that the productive forces of industry could not develop, among other reasons, because the form of industrial organisation, regardless of needless bureaucratic distortions, was too socialist in character.

Conversely, the current form of industrial organisation is lower, in terms of its type, than during the war, but better adapted to development of the productive forces in the context of a petty-bourgeois peasant market. Not only is it easier for industry to function and for individual branches to manage better with inadequate resources, compared to the time when there was a single state supply plan that was never completely fulfilled, but the peasant economy for the first time is also directly attracted by this change in industry, since an increase in the quantity of products going to the peasant market motivates the peasant to expand his sown acreage and increase the amount of the grain surplus that can be offered for sale. None of this stimulus is part of the socialist order, but it is the only possible way to lift the economy at the current stage of development.

In conclusion, I shall try to substantiate my conclusions with some generalised statistical data.

The central economic bottleneck for Russia's heavy industry and for operation of all the southern railways is the Donets Basin. Here are the monthly output figures for the Donets Basin for the second half of 1921: July, 9.1 million poods; August, 11.3; September, 18.5; October, 34.3; November, 43; December, 53 million. If we add the output from smaller mines, the figure for November is 52 million; for December, 63 million; for the first third of 1921, 116 million poods; for the second third, 63 million; and for the final third (including the small mines), 180 million. The miners' productivity is returning to peacetime levels, and in some mines it is higher than before the war. In 1919 the productivity of a miner reached 3358 poods per month; in November 1921 it was 3400. The extraction of coal is also increasing in nearly all the other coal districts. In Siberia it has increased from 4 million per month to more than 7 million. In the area around Moscow, output in July rose to 5.6 million, i.e., an all-time record for that basin. The growth of output is also exceeding projections for the biggest mines in the Urals, at Kizel. Peat output in 1920 came to 92 million, with 126 million in 1921. Although it is occurring more slowly, there is also growth in the smelting of iron and steel, which declined the most catastrophically of all the main branches of industry compared to pre-war output.

The annual production programme for metal has been set at 20 million poods, that is, 2.5 times more than was actually achieved in the previous year.

The output of oil in Baku, which fell to 11.6 million in September, has since continued to expand. October saw 12.6 million poods, November 13.5, and December 15.2. We are seeing a significant increase of production throughout all the other main branches of industry; engineering, manufacturing, leatherworking, chemicals and salt. The newspapers are full of information every day about one or another factory that has exceeded its production programme, sometimes by up to 200%, and once the pre-war level of productivity was reached, we began to hear reports even of exceeding the pre-war output.

Compared to the summer months, we are witnessing a sharp increase in productivity throughout our industry as a whole. True, there was also improvement in the second half of 1920 once harvesting began and food supplies started to arrive at the factories. But the improvement in 1920 was much less significant, and then it was interrupted and replaced by a crisis in the spring and summer due to food and fuel shortages. The expansion that we have seen in the autumn and winter of 1921 is much more stable for the following reasons, several of which are connected with the circumstances of the New Economic Policy: 1) the existence of peacetime conditions; 2) development only in enterprises that are assured or can assure themselves of supplies of food and fuel all year round; 3) improvement in the fuel industry; 4) the opportunity, if state supplies are inadequate or interrupted, to use the free market as an alternative; 5) payment of workers according to their productivity, together with the transition of every enterprise to economic accounting in all operations, which was altogether too rare in our enterprises during wartime.

In any event, even if transport problems have affected the delivery of grain from 2,000 versts away in Siberia, causing a disruption of supply and a decline in the output graph, the decline will be less than in 1921, just as the recovery at the end of 1921 was far greater than during the second half of 1920.

It will be clear from what we have said that development of our large-scale industry depends entirely upon food supplies. The importance of surpluses from the peasant economy is what sets the limit for possible industrial expansion. Because of the contraction of sown area, the drop in livestock numbers and the wearing out of agricultural equipment, Russian agriculture is now providing only one-half of the pre-war output. A country that at one time fully supplied its own urban population and exported up to 500 million poods of grain is now unable to satisfy its own domestic needs. It is clear, therefore, that the fate of large-scale Soviet industry is far more closely connected with the fate of the peasant economy than people have sometimes thought.

Let us consider the tendencies that can be observed in the peasant economy under the New Economic Policy. Starting with the outbreak of war, agriculture saw a continual reduction of the sown area year after year. During the Revolution and Civil war, this process continued unabated. The turning point came in the winter of 1921: in the hunger-afflicted provinces, the sown area fell to 75% of the year before.

In the areas of poor harvest, sowing has now already reached 102%; in the producing provinces, 123%; in the consuming provinces, 126%. Were it not for a natural disaster in the Volga region, we would be speaking of progress in the peasant economy all along the line. In any case, the turning point has come, and in most districts the decline of the sown area has been reversed.

The handicraft and artisan industries, whose production before the war was about 900 million gold roubles, suffered far less from the war and revolution than large-scale industry, and free trade has greatly influenced the increase of production in those industries. We have no general statistics for a period as short as 10 months, but some surveys in individual provinces (Kiev, for example) definitely note an increase in the number of enterprises involving both single individuals and artels.

Before the transition to the New Economic Policy, the majority of medium-sized enterprises were idle due to a lack of materials, fuel and circulating resources. During the past six months, some of those idle enterprises have been re-activated by local Soviet economic organs, and a large number have been leased to private individuals, co-operatives and workers' artels.

Altogether, about 3,000 enterprises have been leased. As a result, in this area too there has been an expansion of production and an increase of the country's commodity fund.

Thus, in the whole economy of the USSR, including large-scale and small-scale undertakings, both in the city and in the countryside, there is a quite obvious tendency towards development of the productive forces following their uninterrupted decline over the past seven years. This fact is enormously important in principle when considering the general position of Soviet Russia and scarcely needs further emphasis.

As for trade, it is of colossal importance to the workers' state during this new period, for it is precisely through trade that the main economic link between the proletariat and peasantry is being established, and especially because it is through trade that state industry is acquiring that portion of its food resources that has to be added to returns from the tax in kind (about half of the total). At the present time, a large part of the products distributed by the anarchic route of the market pass through the hands of private trade, a smaller part through co-operatives, and an even smaller part through state organs for domestic wholesale trade (foreign trade is almost entirely controlled by the state). Large state wholesale stores and warehouses are only beginning to be organised. The task of the state in this area consists of using state credits to help cooperatives and the state wholesale trading network, plus mixed companies with state participation, to master the trading apparatus and convert private commercial capital into a subordinate apparatus of the state and of the large-scale producer in their relations of commodity exchange with the peasant economy.

That is how the lowest form of socialist industry looks in an enormous, backward country. Our entire future depends upon the development of large-scale industry and electrification, which must change the technical basis not simply of industry but also, gradually, of agriculture. With the survival of capitalism in the world's leading industrial countries, this process will be quite difficult and slow. The proletarian revolution in the West could vastly accelerate the process, converting it from a matter of decades into a matter of years.

E.A. Preobrazhensky, 'Rezul'taty novoi ekonomicheskoi politiki Sovet-skoi Rossii',
in *Kommunisticheskii internatsional*, No. 20,
(Moscow and Petrograd, 1922), pp. 5301–10.

CHAPTER 2

The Economic Policy of the Proletariat in a Peasant Country[1]

A vast majority of comrades in the Comintern regard Soviet Russia's New Economic Policy as simply a limited tactical manoeuvre on the economic front, which the Soviet authority had to undertake due to pressure from the peasantry and in order to maintain power in the hands of the proletariat.

Such a viewpoint is incorrect, although it must be acknowledged that Russian Communists have done very little to provide a more appropriate interpretation of NEP.

There is no doubt that NEP is the tactic of a slow flanking movement on the part of the proletarian government in a country that is not supported by proletarian revolution in other countries and is compelled to build socialism in isolation within a hostile capitalist encirclement.

But it is also the economic policy of the proletariat in a *peasant* country that finds itself in this kind of position. Any analysis of NEP, of what it offers today and what it promises, must therefore pay attention to both of these circumstances.

If an industrial rather than an agrarian petty-bourgeois country found itself in this position of socialist isolation, it would still have to manoeuvre and tack. But, assuming that such a country could hold out during a long period of capitalist encirclement without an adequate internal agricultural base, its economic policy would obviously be different. We can come to this same idea from a different perspective if we assume that a proletarian revolution has occurred in Germany and the smaller countries of central Europe (Czechoslovakia, Austria, Hungary), and ask whether we might then completely eliminate our New Economic Policy and replace our present economic system with a 'genuine' socialist organisation of labour in state industry and the socialist distribution of urban and rural production. It is enough just to pose the question in order to answer it in the negative. A revolution in Germany would fundamentally alter the international political and economic circumstances of Soviet Russia and would open up enormous opportunities for much more rapid socialisation of

---

1 This article by E.A. Preobrazhensky was published in issue 23 of the journal *Kommunisticheskii internatsional*, 1923.

the entire economy. It would eliminate all the elements of tactics and man-oeuvring from NEP, but not NEP in its entirety.

What would remain of NEP is the *organic part*, the economic policy of the proletariat in a peasant country.

These elements of NEP require proper clarification, for in this respect the Soviet power is following a route that every economically backward country will have to traverse when the proletariat comes to power.

Let us consider the relations in which large-scale state industry finds itself with regard to the non-socialised part of the economy, above all the peasant economy, and the direction in which these economic relations will inevitably develop.

During the period of so-called War communism, the Soviet authority made a grandiose attempt to subject its petty-bourgeois environment to a compuls-ory system of planned *distribution* at a time when this environment remained committed to the small-scale, individual mode of *production*. There is room for debate about what to call the system of distribution that we had during the period of War Communism: semi-socialist, pre-capitalist, a planned nat-ural economy, and so on. But the label is not the point. Our requisitioning was essentially a system of compulsory loans in kind, imposed upon the peas-antry because it was impossible for the state to fulfil its promise to pay for agricultural products with industrial products. The peasantry rejected this sys-tem not only because, *as a class*, it did not receive from the city any equival-ent for the products surrendered through requisitioning, but also because the system of alienation through requisitions, and the egalitarian distribution of products from urban industry, extinguished every incentive for small, inde-pendent proprietors to expand production. We realised during the period of War Communism that such a system of levelling in distribution was not appro-priate for the workers, i.e., for the class that had to implement socialisation (see below). What could we expect then from the mass of small-scale independ-ent producers? This whole system of compulsory distribution was abolished at the end of the Civil War, which had necessitated at least the basic features of such a system in a country with a falling currency and a scarcity of bread. The peasantry has compelled the state to return to the former system of market distribution.

Given these conditions, the task of the Soviet state also evolved and can be formulated as follows:

1) How can the output of large-scale industry be increased on the basis of an allocation system that ensures maximal labour productivity *with the existing level of culture and socialist consciousness on the part of the work-ing class?*

2)   How can the country's agricultural output be increased using the forces of petty production itself, while simultaneously taking control of that production from the same direction as capital always did previously, i.e., with the use of trade and credit?

3)   How can we move to the next step, which must be a period of transforming the technical foundations of small-scale peasant production?

With regard to the first task, the way to accomplish it has already been outlined in full. The existing level of culture and socialist consciousness among the working class is such that there can be no talk of egalitarian distribution in the state sphere. During the period of [War] Communism, we conducted an experiment in distribution through egalitarian rationing. It yielded the most abysmal results. That was the period when the working class as a whole demonstrated the greatest heroism and self-sacrifice, which history will never forget. Hungry, and with hungry children behind him, the worker stood at the machine, often fainting from exhaustion but not abandoning his work. Individual detachments of workers and different factories and plants performed miracles on the economic front. But all of this was accomplished in the general rush of a surging revolution, not because of egalitarian distribution – even, perhaps despite it – at a time when it was a feat simply to work and when not even half of the pre-war productivity could be expected from the working class. When it became urgently necessary to raise labour productivity at any cost, especially in some of the most important branches, we had to bid farewell to levelling and to pay wages on a monthly basis: piecework payments spread more and more widely. It was typical, in fact, for the Soviet government and the trade unions partially to reject levelling even before the transition to the New Economic Policy.

NEP accelerated the process of moving to the new system of payments for labour, and presently such payments, for the most part, are based on the same principle that applies to wages under capitalism: the greater the individual's output, the greater the pay. If levelling through rations during War Communism is regarded as a 'step forward' compared to the wage system under capitalism, then the form of wages under NEP is a step backward compared to the years of War Communism. However, there are good reasons to doubt that egalitarian distribution by rationing was a real – even if imperfect – element of socialism. The new form of wages has brought positive results. It has served everywhere as the most powerful stimulus for raising labour productivity, which in a number of factories has regained the pre-war level. And if we recall that these achievements occurred with an extremely low wage level (2–3 times lower than before the war), then this success speaks for itself.

Socialism in the sphere of distribution means greater equality on the basis of higher productivity. Where productivity is falling or stagnating, levelling is a poor consolation. In this case, the upsurge in labour was largely (although not completely) connected with the elimination of egalitarianism in distribution. That is the obvious answer to the question of whether Soviet Russia has travelled very far on the road of socialist distribution within the state sector. It has hardly moved beyond capitalism. But it would be a mistake to deny that some advance has occurred. On the one hand, this advance involves a more or less planned distribution of the wage fund for state workers and employees (there is a special central organ for setting wage levels), which already represents the nucleus of better planned distribution in the future. On the other hand, this step forward involves elements of collectivism that have already taken root. In a number of enterprises, the worker receives payment on the basis not only of his individual output but also based upon the output of the enterprise as a whole. What direction might development take from here?

Is has never been established with any precision in the socialist literature just what form of distribution in a socialised economy is characteristic of *socialism as such*, or even whether there is any difference in this respect between capitalism and socialism. For example, we know that in his essay 'The Day after the Socialist Revolution',[2] Karl Kautsky allowed not only for the existence of a capitalist type of wage but also for wage variations in different branches depending upon the supply and demand for workers with varying sets of skills. Yet between the wage system under capitalism, with which we are all familiar, and the system of purely communist distribution, which is founded on the principle 'to each according to his needs and from each according to his ability', there must be an historically transitional stage of distribution just as socialism itself is the transitional stage from capitalism to communism.

It is wrong to think that socialist distribution must differ from capitalist distribution only because, with socialism, the entire product of the socialised part of the economy is distributed according to plan, while distribution of the wage fund (whose size is determined in capitalism by the balance of forces between workers and capitalists, whereas in socialism it is established on the basis of taking stock of all resources in the economy) will occur in approximately the same way as under capitalism. That would mean that the worker, under socialism as well, will receive remuneration depending not only on his skills but also the size of his individual output (when it can be calculated). If that were the case, it would mean that the stimulus for production under socialism remains

---

2   [The reference is to Part II of Kautsky 1910, pp. 103–89.]

the same as under capitalism, and it would then be incomprehensible how humankind might leap from individual work incentives into a communist system of labour organisation.

In reality, there must be a whole series of gradual transitions, which will yield incomplete, imperfect and logically flawed forms of rewards and incentives just as socialism itself, as unfinished communism, can be incomplete and illogical. Socialism must begin where capitalism leaves off: with individual payment for the labour of workers plus some instances of sharing in the enterprise profit, i.e., in the present case bonuses for excelling in terms of output. But socialism creates the conditions for gradually replacing individual payment for labour with collective payment. With piece-work, the worker says to himself: 'the more I produce, the more I will receive'. With collective payment, he says: 'the more my factory or trust produces, the more I will receive'. From here, the next step leads to the slogan: 'the more the whole social collective produces, the more *everyone* will receive'. Collective payment will initially be combined with individual payment: the worker will receive more, the greater is 1) the individual output and 2) the collective output of the whole enterprise. Gradually, the part of the individual worker's earnings that comes from the fund for collective bonuses will grow, together with the percentage of the wage fund that will be set aside for collective bonuses. The moment when the majority of workers in a socialist regime transcend individual work incentives in favour of collective incentives will perhaps be no less important in the struggle for communism than socialisation of the instruments of production. This transition will be completed because individual incentives are already proving to be *inadequate* for socialist production – too backward and conservative – especially since the development of technology does not increase but rather *decreases* the possibility and the usefulness of keeping a separate account of each individual's work (electrification, transport, etc.). On this basis, the re-education of young people will also proceed more rapidly in the spirit of demands that the new mode makes upon the mass psychology of workers, their collective instincts, their socialist consciousness and their habits.

The Soviet authority has already made a minor advance in this direction under NEP with the experiment in so-called collective supply, which was undertaken in a number of the largest enterprises and produced satisfactory results from the point of view of production. It is true that this form is not presently compulsory, but it can be adopted through voluntary agreements between the trade unions and economic organs. In one form or another, collective payment (after a fit of capitalist reaction under NEP) will develop and in future become the predominant form of pay under the dictatorship of the proletariat. Of course in a peasant country, where the petty-bourgeois psychology is strong even amongst the proletariat, we have not been able to progress significantly beyond the methods of the capitalist wage system. But advanced industrial countries, with the dictatorship of the proletariat, will be able from the very beginning to progress further along the road to socialist distribution.

Following seizure of power by the proletariat, one of its most important tasks consists of promoting its own vanguard for mastering science, the commanding posts of industry and the entire state apparatus. If, during the first decade, it does not surpass its defeated enemy in the sphere of culture, it must at least become its equal. That is the fundamental difference between a bourgeois and a proletarian revolution. During the period of its struggle for power, the bourgeoisie was not an oppressed class but a class that was competing for power with the nobility. As an exploiting class and a minority with all the blessings of life at its disposal, including resources and leisure, the bourgeoisie could and did reach a higher cultural level than its opponent – the landed aristocracy and the priesthood. Not so with the proletariat. The proletariat turns out to be capable of seizing state power sooner than it can take possession of the culture of the epoch and begin to create its own culture. In this respect, it catches up with the defeated bourgeoisie only *after the conquest of power*. And wherever the proletariat, as in Russia, occupies a lower level even by comparison with the proletariat of other countries, this problem is all the more important, not to say threatening, and involves the very survival of workers' power.

This problem confronts Soviet power under NEP just as it did during the period of War Communism. Indeed, under NEP the danger threatening the proletariat due to the cultural superiority of the defeated bourgeoisie and the bourgeois intelligentsia is even more serious. That is why the Soviet authority is now making even greater efforts than before to proletarianise higher education and assist the proletariat in its endeavour to master science. Our achievements in this respect are still not that great, but they surpass everything that the proletariat could accomplish during an entire century of the bourgeois regime. We have a network of workers' faculties with 50,000 proletarian students. The first courses in the higher schools have already been significantly proletarianised last year and this year. Within 3–4 years the majority of students in all the higher schools (save perhaps the arts) will be student-proletarians and socialist-minded peasant youths. And I have yet to mention our communist schools, our party schools, beginning at the county level and extending to the highest level, Sverdlovsk University for example, together with the military schools, whose students have already come exclusively from the workers and peasants for some time.

As far as raising labour productivity and increasing the supply of commodities and the corresponding wage level are concerned, in this regard things are much worse for the moment than under capitalism. Industrial production is reaching only about 1/5 of the pre-war level. Productivity per worker is generally below the pre-war level, which still remains the ideal. At the same time, though, we can note an increase in the absolute volume of output and in per-worker output during the last year and a half. But the destruction in industry, due to war and revolution, is so great that in the general opinion of most economic workers Soviet industry will not reach the pre-war level for at least 4–5 years, and only after that will it be possible to advance beyond the limits where capitalism left off. The only major branch in which we have surpassed capitalism is electrification. The situation with wages is much the same. During the years of the Civil War, wages fell to a level where no normal production was possible. Now, however, wages are steadily rising, even if only very slowly. In coming years this growth does not promise to be rapid, because following the accumulation of circulating capital (which is still terribly inadequate) industry will turn to the reconstruction of fixed capital and other construction in the cities, for which 'primitive socialist accumulation' will be necessary at the expense not just of the petty-bourgeois classes, upon whom taxes are levied, but also at the expense of wages.

The task of restoring industry and wages to pre-war levels, and then of going beyond, is common to every proletarian state. For now, we cannot even say whether the victorious European proletariat will begin its industrial reconstruction from as favourable position as ours, compared to the pre-war level, because no one can predict the scale of devastation that the European economy will experience as the result of inevitable civil war.

In contrast, the task of economically subordinating a peasant economy to large-scale state industry is quite peculiar to Russia, as an agrarian country, and will not arise in the same way in Germany, Austria or Czechoslovakia.

Only the Balkan countries and Poland will find themselves in a somewhat analogous position with a proletarian regime. In order to understand the organic rather than the tactical aspect of NEP, i.e., the aspect that is really involved in the expression 'seriously and for a long time',[3] it is necessary to understand the existing economic relations between state industry and the peasant economy and how they will develop in the near future.

If the peasant economy is to be subordinated to state heavy industry and the state banking centres, it is first and foremost imperative – in fact, it is an obligatory precondition – for state industry itself to be sufficiently powerful.

How do matters currently stand in that respect?

---

3   [See Lenin, 'Tenth All-Russian Conference of the RCP(B)', in Lenin 1965b, p. 429.]

According to estimates from S.N. Prokopovich,[4] the entire national income of European Russia in 1913 came to 11,805 million roubles (rounded off to the nearest million) from the following sources:

Agriculture	5630
Forestry and Fishing	729
Industry	2566
Transport	1055
Construction	842
Trade	980

If we add the income from trade in industrial products to that from industry, transport and construction – since it is best regarded, in methodological terms, as part of industrial income that has been attributed to trade – and if we also add the income from trade in agricultural products to agriculture, then we must acknowledge that before the war Russia was not so much an agrarian country as was commonly supposed.

If we want to establish the relation between *large-scale* industry and agriculture, we have to subtract from the total industrial income that going to crafts (611 million) and to artisans (289) along with part of the income of small producers in fishing and forestry. Even then, however, the ratio between large-scale capitalist production and agricultural production was approximately 4:7, and with the addition of small-scale industrial incomes to those in agriculture, it was 4:8.

Generally speaking, the pre-war economy was dominated by industrial, banking and especially commercial capital, which occupied the commanding positions in the economy as a whole and thus subordinated agriculture. If the *pre-war economic proportions* still existed, and the proletariat occupied *all the positions in the Russian economy once held by capital*, it would have undivided economic control over the whole of petty, non-socialised production. Unfortunately, however, during the years of war and revolution the balance of forces between the small- and large-scale economy, particularly between large-scale industry and the peasant economy, changed dramatically to the benefit of small-scale production. Large- and small-scale production did not suffer to the same extent during the war and revolution. In 1921 the net national income of the whole country, as a very rough calculation, came to 5 billion gold roubles

---

4   Prokpovich 1918. [See S.N. Prokopovich (ed) *Opyt ischisleniya narodnovo dokhoda 50 gub. Evropeiskoi Rossii v 1900–1913*, Moscow, 1918.

at pre-war prices, while the net industrial income, according to our economic workers, was 500 million (gross income being about 1 billion). The net income in transport was about one-quarter of the pre-war level, or roughly 350 million. Even these figures are probably exaggerated. As for peasant income, it came to more than 3.5 billion, while that of craftsmen and artisans fell to about half of the pre-war level. In any case, the ratio of net production in large-scale industry and transport to the peasant income was approximately 1:5, representing a disastrous step backwards compared to the pre-war proportions. True, industrial production has increased this year (along with a drop in production costs), but production in the peasant economy has increased *even more* thanks to a good harvest, and the income balance between industry and agriculture has become even less favourable for the former.

These are the conditions in which the proletariat of Russia faces the task of economically subordinating the peasant economy to state industry. This is an extremely difficult task with the existing proportions in the economy, although it is certainly possible with the restoration of industry. Peasant production can be subordinated to large-scale production in two ways: through exchange, using trade and credit; and through production, which means transforming the foundations of the peasant economy with electrification and mechanisation. The second alternative is a future prospect for us, but we have already begun to implement the first one even though our achievements in this direction remain quite negligible.

In the area of trade with the countryside, our task consists of gradually eliminating private middle-men and private merchant capital from the relation between large-scale industry and the peasantry by relying upon cooperatives and making the state a monopolist not only in trading the products of large-scale industry with the countryside, but also in controlling a major portion of the agricultural products entering the market at large. In some places we have been successful. For example, in the province of Orel 60% of all trade now passes through the state trading organs, and in some factory centres workers' cooperatives dominate the market. Thanks to the monopoly of foreign trade, the state is able to control the country's entire trade with foreign capital in grain and agricultural materials.

As far as credits are concerned, the basic forms must be long-term credits for land improvement; commercial credits for the purchase of agricultural machines, improved seeds and artificial fertilisers; and cash loans from Gosbank for the purchase of horses and for the general reconstruction of agriculture. Long-term agricultural credits will play an enormous role in Russia's future. They are the easiest way for the proletariat to subordinate agriculture to the dictatorship of large-scale industry. Gosbank can extend credits to the peasantry not only in the form of money, but mainly in the natural form of factory-made agricultural machinery and all the other commodities that the countryside requires. Receiving loan repayments and interest in kind, i.e., in the form of grain and materials for export, Gosbank can gradually secure for the state a significant portion of all the agricultural surpluses being produced, which, together with proceeds from the tax in kind, will constitute a fund of food and materials both for Soviet industry and for foreign trade. In future, the state will be able to move easily from the role of principal buyer and sole creditor for the peasantry to a role involving advance orders and general control over peasant production. With the corresponding pricing and statements of policy, Gosbank's role as creditor (accepting some products in payment for loans and not others) will allow it to influence the expansion of one crop, encourage the development of another and prevent a third, thus using a capitalist form to subordinate the individual peasant economy to the demands of a general economic plan. Moreover, in these ways it will be able to assemble a reasonably accurate account of total production in the countryside, since a creditor must be aware of all the economic resources of a debtor, and socialism means accounting above all.

If we keep in mind that the state also has enormous opportunities to redistribute the national income in other ways, i.e., by levying taxes, which must increasingly fall on the more well-to-do strata in the village and on private merchant capital, then the combination of all these means make it possible for the Soviet authority to divert a growing volume of water from the canals of primitive (or more accurately, secondary) NEP accumulation into the mill of primitive socialist accumulation, transforming the newly reviving capitalist relations into a lower and subordinate form compared to the forms of the large-scale socialist economy.

E.A. Preobrazhensky, 'Ekonomicheskaya politika proletariata v krest'yanskoi strane,'
in Kommunisticheskii internatsional
(Moscow and Leningrad, 1922), No. 23, pp. 6275–90.

CHAPTER 3

Economic Crises under NEP[1]

Comrades, the economic crisis that has struck our economy since approximately the month of August is attracting close scrutiny from all sides: from our economic managers, who are directly affected by the crisis in their practical work, and also from all those economists who are interested in theoretically comprehending what is happening.

But I must say that until very recently we did not have any detailed discussions about economic crises under NEP either in our literature or at our conferences. It seemed that with an economic system in which the commanding heights, as we call them, are in state hands – when the state has a monopoly over large-scale industry, transport and foreign trade and also controls the banking system and the largest part of wholesale trade – in that kind of system, economic crises can hardly be of any serious consequence. That is what many people thought, although far from everyone. And those who did not think that way have proven to be correct. Indeed, this crisis is an early warning to those optimists who assumed either that there could be no crises in the conditions of NEP or that they would be so moderate and fleeting that they need not be discussed. A typical illustration can be seen in the way even very knowledgeable economists have treated the issue. A few days ago Comrade Milyutin's book appeared with the title *The New Period in the World Economy*. This is a very informative book, and I recommend it for your attention. But I did not find a word in it concerning the question that presently concerns us. Meanwhile, a system of embryonic socialism, in a peasant country with the dictatorship of the proletariat, must inevitably give rise to internal disproportions in the economy, and the question of how to alleviate these disproportions and surmount their harmful consequences with an appropriate economic policy must be one of the central issues for any economic study that aims to analyse the economic forms of the transition period, especially in our economy, which, for the time being, provides the only real illustration of such forms. We find nothing of the sort in Comrade Milyutin's short book. I cite this example to show how, until very recently, until the lesson of this crisis, we were quite optimistic concerning the ques-

---

tion of whether such crises were possible. Now we must focus a great deal more attention, albeit belatedly, on this issue and analyse all the specific features of our economy from the point of view of realising the output of state industry and in terms of material exchange between the city and the countryside.

Before I turn to consider the relative weights of the different components of our economy as a whole, using production data for 1922/23, I wish to say a few words about our economic structure. On the initiative of Vladimir Il'ich, we have taken to speaking of the form of economy that we have established as one of state capitalism. It is true that in his last article, 'On Co-operation', which he published in *Pravda*, he explained to us that he used this word in a quite provisional sense, having mainly in mind, for the most part, purely practical purposes and counting on large-scale concessions involving foreign capital, thus appearing to suggest that he was using the term more for tactical reasons in relation to world capital than in the interests of a strictly scientific definition of our economic system. In any event, this definition is not sufficiently accurate from the scientific-theoretical point of view, nor does it provide sufficient clarity in the area of practice. It is a good thing, therefore, that while Vladimir Il'ich continued to use this term in his last article, he at least emphasised its very conditional meaning.

It will be much more correct to call our economic system a mixed commodity-socialist form of economy. On the one side, we have state industry and transport in the hands of the state – although these elements of socialism must operate economically in the circumstances of a commodity economy and make their way using commodity methods – and on the other side we have the surrounding petty-bourgeois economy, which, in terms of the size of its output, plays the predominant role in our economy as a whole. The forms that may be called state-capitalist play quite a modest role. These include mixed companies, i.e., a partial coalescence, if we may use that expression, between our socialist capital and foreign capital, or in some cases with domestic private capital. We might also conditionally include cooperative enterprises if we regard all of our cooperatives in their current form as a type of coalescence between cooperative and state capital, for which there are certain practical and theoretical grounds. Next, state capitalism would include a small number of concessionary enterprises. Their number is growing, but their relative weight in our economy is for now insignificant. Then there is private merchant capital. As you will see from an analysis of the figures that I shall provide, it plays an enormous role throughout our economy in the sphere of distribution. However, this is not state capital but rather anti-state capital. Then there is petty-bourgeois production in town and country, which is the basic form of our economy. I leave aside patriarchal economic forms because they do not play a significant role. Such is the highly diverse picture of all the economic forms that are interwoven with each other through trade on the one hand and bank credits on the other.

In general and on the whole, all of these forms are in direct contact with one another, and there are already grounds for speaking of a single economic organism if we abstract from the rural-urban economic gap and the incipient boycott of the town by the country, which has increased recently but will no doubt be temporary. This is the complex economic system that we have. As I mentioned, it is more correct to call it a mixed commodity-socialist form of economy in which the leading role – the role of the locomotive that is pulling behind it the commodity freight cars – belongs and will increasingly belong to our state industry, our transport, and also our banking system.

The extraordinary complexity of the question we now face, when we have to address the problem of realisation within the context of a commodity economy, is due first to the fact that it is extremely difficult for us to take into consideration all the elements of proportionality at each particular moment during any given year. On the other hand, we also have difficulties of another kind. We do not have suitable statistics for manipulating the state economy in this extremely complex conglomeration of different economic systems. And even if we had such statistics concerning the state part of the economy, we would never be able accurately to take into account the absorptive capacity of our petty-bourgeois environment or, given fluctuating prices for products of the peasant economy, the influence of the external market on our whole economic system. But be that as it may, and however difficult the task of this analysis may be, we cannot understand anything about the current crisis – neither its causes, nor how it is presently developing, nor its prospects in the near future – unless we address this problem of realisation and clarify both the basic elements of proportionality in the present economic system and when material exchange between city and village can proceed normally, without any further threat of a rupture in the link between them.

To make clear the sort of figures with which we have to operate here, I shall provide you with all the necessary materials and calculations that have a bearing upon this question, beginning with the relative weights of all the individual components of our economy. I begin with the output of industry. According to calculations by our economists and statisticians – which are open to debate but are ultimately the last statistical word that we have – the net pre-war production of our industry in 1913 (excluding material and fuel) was 2,300 million gold roubles. Now, the *gross* output of our industry, in pre-war prices, is 1,650 million gold roubles for 1922/23. The gross output of our industry in today's inflated prices, according to the average index for industrial products in 1922/23 up to 1 October, is 2,315 million gold roubles. The value of our industry's net output – which we reach by taking 38% of the gross on the basis of the data available for such calculations – is 877[2] million gold roubles.

I must tell you that these figures have been reached as follows. When the calculations by TsSU[3] failed to satisfy economic workers at Gosplan, the latter undertook its own calculations through the work of comrades Groman[4] and Strumilin.[5] Comrade Groman's figures are higher than the ones I use here, but these are the data that we on the commission received. The commission was especially appointed by Gosplan to take account of production and consisted of Strumilin, Groman and me. These are the commission's data. We used the following method to do the calculations. On the basis of existing labour statistics, we took the number of workers at state enterprises. Then, using statistics from VSNKh,[6] we took the total annual output per individual worker, as derived by VSNKh's calculation of the value of production from 1 million workers. Then we multiplied the number of employed workers, as given in the labour statistics, by the output per worker, thereby reaching the sum that we consider to be most accurate. There were also other calculations done to verify this output; some of the results were a little higher and some a little lower than our own. We therefore consider this figure of 877 million for the gross output of state industry, over the past year and at current prices, to be quite accurate and if anything perhaps a slight under-estimation.

Now, let us consider the data for the pre-war and current output of rail and water transport. For rail the figure was 607 million, and for water it was about 91 million, excluding sea-borne transport, which we omitted because the sum is inconsequential. Therefore, transport's output was 698 million. Today, taking shipments to be about 40% of the pre-war figure, the value of our transport will be approximately 280, or if we round off, about 300 million gold roubles

---

2 [Preobrazhensky uses the sum of 877 throughout this essay, although .38 × 2,315 is actually 879.7. The difference results from using the rounded figure of 38% in place of the actual figure, which is 37.88%. The figure of 2,315 multiplied by .3788 gives 876.9, or 877.]
3 [Central Statistical Directorate.]
4 [Groman, Vladimir Gustavovich (1874–1932), an economist with Gosplan until 1928, purged as a Menshevik in the spring of 1931.]
5 [Strumilin, Stanislav Gustavovich (1877–1974), economist, statistician and a leading figure in Gosplan.]
6 [Supreme Council of the National Economy.]

per year. If we then add these figures for the output in state industry and transport, we get 1,177[7] [million gold roubles] as the estimate, in value terms, of our state economy.

Let us now consider the output of craftsmen, artisans, and leased and cooperative enterprises. The pre-war net output, according to some statisticians, was 700 million gold roubles, which is the figure that Comrade Groman considers to be correct. According to the data from Prokopovich, the figure is 900 million. Thus the pre-war figure for the net output of crafts and artisanal industry was between 700 and 900 million. That is the value of the net production from the artisan and handicraft industry. What is the value of production from these branches today? We have made the following calculations. We have data from the latest urban census, conducted by TsSU in the month of December. On the basis of these data for December, which we multiply by 11 and add to the total on the basis of the pre-war relation between industrial output and artisanal and craft production in the countryside, we get a figure of 452 million gold roubles for the gross output of industrial goods by artisans at current prices. We tried to derive this figure by a different route and came up with 405 million gold roubles. This second figure is less accurate because we multiplied the number of artisans and the workers they employed by the value of the average output per worker. As a result, we arrived at this figure of 405 million gold roubles, which is lower than the actual figure because the number for artisans and the workers they employ came from the 1920 census. Since 1920 the number of artisans and their workers has increased, and the same applies to the number of small private factories that have been leased and to cooperative enterprises. This explains the fact that the first figure is larger than the second, which was reached by a different method.

We then came to the conclusion that it would be best to increase this sum by 20% to compensate for any under-estimation of both the number of facilities and their output. We consider this addition of 20% to be the minimal necessary. The result is a total of 564 million gold roubles for gross production, and for net production (omitting materials provided by artisans' customers), 400 million gold roubles in round numbers. We therefore have two figures; 1177 million on the one side and 400 million gold roubles of net output from artisanal industry on the other.

I now turn to agriculture. The net pre-war output in agriculture, according to Prokopovich and the sources that he used for his calculation, was 5,630 mil-

---

7   [There is a misprint in the text giving the figure 1,117, but 877 + 300 = 1,177.]

lion gold roubles. Our net output for 1922/23, if we consider it in pre-war prices as calculated by Groman, comes to 4,200 million, while the net output from agriculture at current prices is 3,100 million. These are the sums with which we must operate in our subsequent analysis. Consequently, these sums for output give us 3,100 million for agricultural production at current prices at one pole; at the other pole we have 1,277 million gold roubles for handicrafts and production from state industry, or 1,577 million roubles when transport is included.[8]

This figure cannot be properly evaluated and used to answer the question before us unless we take the analysis in another direction. We must determine how much of agricultural production is commodity production, i.e., how much of its output the peasantry consumes in natural form and what portion it sends to market. In this connection, we have widely differing estimates. I shall introduce you to the available data, beginning with the situation before the war. As I have already mentioned, before the war agricultural production came to 5,630 million gold roubles. Consumption in natural form took 3,797 million. Thus the commodity portion of agricultural production, i.e., the portion that appeared in the market, was 1,833 million gold roubles,[9] and the share of commodity production was 32.6 percent[10] (according to data from Prokopovich), i.e., 1/3 of all pre-war agricultural production went to the market. And what is the situation now? This is a question of colossal importance when it comes to answering a whole array of other questions and ultimately the entire problem that I have posed. I shall deal, therefore, with three methods of calculation that generate different results. The first method: if we deduct what was fully consumed before the war from [today's] net agricultural output at pre-war prices – which came to 4,200 million – i.e., if we begin with the assumption that today our peasantry maintains the same level of consumption as before the war, we are left with a balance of 403 million gold roubles.[11] If we then deduct the tax in kind that the peasantry has paid,[12] and the tax rate is 70 kopecks per rye unit, then we must subtract 263 million gold roubles from the 403 million gold roubles, and the total output from the peasantry that could be disposed of in the market is only 140 million gold roubles.

Here is how the value of the tax in kind is calculated. The latest data from Narkomprod, concerning receipts from the tax in kind for 1922–1923, give the

---

8   [877 for industry + 400 crafts = 1,277 + 300 transport = 1,577.]

9   [5630 – 3797 = 1833.]

10   [1,833/5,630 × 100 = 32.56.]

11   [The text says 402, but 4,200 – 3,797 = 403.]

12   [i.e. the taxed portion was paid to the state and not marketed.]

figure of 377,400 million rye units. I multiply by .70[13] – which approximately corresponds to the pre-war figure[14] – and get the sum of 263 million.[15] Since the whole calculation is in pre-war prices, we get comparable values. Thus, with this method of calculation, which clearly exaggerates the volume of peasant consumption [assumed to be the same as before the war], we get a balance of 140 million[16] – which is completely insignificant in terms of providing a market base for our industry.

Other methods, which are more precise and come closer to the truth, are the following. We take the pre-war marketed output to be 32.6 % of the total, but we make a proportional correction: marketed output before the war must be larger than it is presently, in the same proportion as pre-war production [5,630] exceeds current production [4,200].[17] From these proportions we get 24.3 % as the marketed share for the agricultural economy as a whole. This means that out of the whole sum of today's peasant production at pre-war prices, 1,020[18] could enter into commodity circulation. Deducting the tax in kind [263] and converting pre-war prices into today's prices, we get a sum of 522 million gold roubles. That is the sum of what the peasantry can sell and with which it can proportionally make purchases.

If we take the percentage representing the marketed surplus of net output in terms of today's prices, which, of course, is methodologically more correct, because peasant consumption can hardly change much due to a movement in prices, we shall then have the following sum: 755 [million] free surpluses minus the tax in kind of 263 [million], and the result that we get is 492 million roubles. Thus, the latter two calculations give approximately the same sum [522 and 492].

Now I turn to other calculations that approximate these ones. The data provided by comrades Strumilin and Groman give a figure of about 700 million;[19] those from TsSU give 306 million. Thus my sum falls between these fig-

---

13   [i.e. 70 kopeks or .7 of a rouble. .7 × 377.4 = 264.18.]

14   [100 – 32.6 = 68.4.]

15   [.7 × 377 = 264.18. The figure of 70 % represents the pre-war level of peasant consumption. The assumption is that 70 % of the tax proceeds would otherwise have been consumed.]

16   [403 – 263 = 140 million roubles worth of grain being marketed.]

17   [Pre-war agricultural production was 5,630, the current figure is 4,200. 5,630/4,200 = 1.34. 32.6 = 1.34x; x = 32.6/1.34 = 24.3 %.]

18   [The text gives the figure 1,200, but 24.3 × 4,200 = 1,020.]

19   The scientific value calculations from Strumilin, made on the basis of budget studies in the cities, are the ones that I regard as more justifiable [as opposed to those from TsSU]. But it seems mistaken to me to apply the budgetary average to everyone, especially the petty-bourgeois population of the small cities of Russia. The result of doing so is to overestimate urban buying power for the products of agriculture.

ures. I believe the average of these two figures is quite probably correct and can be taken as an approximate measure of output marketed by the peasant economy. The result of our calculations, therefore, gives us a pair of fundamental sums. At one pole we have 1,277 million of output from state industry along with output from private artisans and craftsmen plus cooperative output. And at the agricultural pole we see 500–700 million. These are the key data for calculating both proportionality and the disproportions in our economy.

I shall now proceed with the analysis. Consider this question: What was the relation between the pre-war value of marketed agricultural surpluses and the pre-war value of production marketed by large- and small-scale industry? It was the following. As I mentioned, before the war agriculture sent products worth 1,833[20] gold roubles to market. We shall take the percentage marketed by industry to be 100, giving us 2,300 million for large-scale industry and 900 million for small-scale. Timber and fisheries, using a different figure to determine marketed share, accounted for 220 million, and construction for 408 million. I take the figures given by Prokopovich, but I add them up differently because he adds housing rent for flats to the output of the construction industry, which is methodologically incorrect. The income of a *given* year cannot include part of the previous year's production, which is what he does. As a result, we get marketed industrial output of 3,828 million. Agriculture marketed 1,832 million before the war. And the relation between the two sums was 48%.

What is the relation today?

Here we come to the most critical point of our whole investigation, where two methods of calculation are possible. Since we do not have data for forestry and fishing in 1922/23, one option is to reduce the pre-war figure by approximately one-half – in line with the reduction of all products coming from small-scale industry and crafts – and then add this sum to the value of the current output of our large- and small-scale industry. Alternatively, we can exclude both pre-war and post-war estimates for fisheries and forestry. I have used both methods, and here are the results of my calculations. If we take it that construction, fisheries and forestry are providing 50% of pre-war output, then the current relation will be 500 million of agricultural output compared to 1,591 million of urban output, which in percentage terms means 31.5% compared to 48% before the war.[21] With the second method of calculating the pre-war situation we get 57%, while the figure for today is 38%.

---

20   [The text mistakenly gives the figure 1,832.]
21   [Marketed agricultural products are 31.5% of marketed industrial products, compared to a pre-war figure of 48%.]

These are dry figures, comrades, and it is not immediately possible to grasp what is going on. But these figures characterise the very heart of the question we are facing. In a purely spontaneous way, our pre-war economy reached the proportional relation between marketed output in agriculture and industry that is reflected in these figures. In this case, equilibrium was reached over a period of decades and all of the relations became more or less settled as the norm.

The first question that we must raise in order to understand the current situation is how close we are to these pre-war relations. Generally speaking, we are no fans of the past, but when it is a question of how to ascertain the proportionality of a vast economic organism, from which we cannot stray very far even with a fundamental change of the political regime, since we are using the same technique as before the war and all the fundamental economic elements are generally identical, the pre-war figures and proportions must tell us a great deal. And here is the point: if the pre-war proportionality prevailed, these figures would be 48% by one calculation and 57% by the other. But today we have figures of 31.5% and 38.3%, meaning the disproportionality between industry and agriculture with the first method of calculation is 16.5%, and with the second method, 18.7%.[22] These are the magnitudes that immediately reveal to us the roots of the current crisis, for if the disproportion here were not 16% or 18%, but even just 5%, this would still be the source of a significant crisis throughout the whole economic system. That is something every economist understands. After all, 5% of numbers in the billions is quite a large sum.

I believe that the most significant cause of the current crisis, which has been further intensified due to mistaken policies in the sphere of credit and prices (of which I shall have more to say in the second part of my report), is this disproportionality in the production base of the system, which strikingly emerges from a comparison with the pre-war relations. What does this disproportion mean from the viewpoint of realisation? Here is what it means. At one pole we have 1,277[23] million worth of production from urban industry. At the other pole, we have 500 million worth of agricultural output that can be exchanged in the market. Proportionality will only occur here in the event that the demand from the urban population for agricultural products, plus industry's requirements in terms of peasant materials, corresponds to the value of agricultural surpluses entering the market. Consequently, a crisis can arise either from an insufficient

---

22   [The text mistakenly gives the figure 18.9%.]
23   [This is the figure given earlier for output from handicrafts and state industry, omitting transport.]

demand for the surplus of agricultural products or from an insufficient demand from industry for peasant materials.

The first element of proportionality, therefore, is proportionality in terms of food products. Here I must point out that although I have been working purely with value relations, I have now come to the point where the natural form of the values being exchanged takes on enormous significance.

If we assume that the peasantry, when buying things in the market, has unlimited purchasing power, then it can move without limit from element-ary to more cultivated needs. To the contrary, when the city is buying things from the countryside, or more accurately when the countryside is selling to the city, the situation is quite different. There is a definite physiological limit to urban consumption, beyond which the city cannot consume any further signi-ficant amount of bread, animal feed, meat and so forth. If the city's purchasing power for agricultural products triples, the consumption of bread cannot do likewise. The countryside is in a less favourable position than the city in the event of over-production of food products relative to the domestic market. Conversely, if its purchasing power permits, the peasantry can move from one level of demand for urban products to another. Thus, the peasantry would sell 500 million gold roubles worth of output to the city if the city, at the other pole, had a corresponding demand for that output. But if the city is not in a position to absorb that sum – and the statistics indicate that it is not – then the peas-antry faces over-production mainly in the area of grain crops. This is the first obstacle to material exchange.

Now let us look further. If the peasantry is not in a position to realise its sur-pluses fully, how do things stand for industry's realisation of the 1,277 million produced in 1922/23? I must point out here that my analysis of the city's pur-chasing power for industrial products has not yet been completed because I have encountered extraordinary difficulties in making any precise estimates. The problem is that our statistics are not fully adjusted in a way that would allow the data to be used in a state that is trying to establish a socialist eco-nomy. We need to calculate the size of the market for consumer products, both agricultural and urban, if we wish to proceed further.

We know the number of workers and employees who are on state supply or work in state enterprises, trusts, etc., plus the number in the army. They include approximately 4 million people. We know their average budget because we more or less know their wages. Consequently, we can find the annual total of all wage payments in all lines of work for workers, employees, the army, etc. At a rough estimate, the sum is 600 million gold roubles per year. Next, we know from budget studies what percentage of wages goes to food products and what percentage goes to other items (food takes up about 48%). In this context we have to determine the value of food products coming from the city, such as sugar and the like, and for this purpose we can come to reasonably precise figures.

Next, on the basis of budget studies we can do some calculations concerning the 400 million gold roubles that represent the income of craftsmen, artisans and private industry, and we can establish the sum that craftsmen and artisans spend on consumption of agricultural products on the one hand and the products of urban industry on the other. It is a great deal more difficult to clarify the market capacity represented by Nepmen and the petty-bourgeois population of the cities, who are not engaged in productive labour or who are engaged but not in a way that allows their output to appear in any statistics.

It is also necessary to clarify the sum of values that goes to means of production for industry itself, i.e., how much our state enterprises buy from each other in the way of machinery, fuel, etc. This sum must further include the depreciation of equipment and what is being capitalised, i.e., serving the goal of expanded reproduction, above all the increase of fixed capital in Marx's so-called Department I.

I repeat that I have attempted to make such calculations but have not completed them. Insofar as certain basic data are available, the figures for material exchange do not balance out in my estimates. I am postponing publication of any results of my work until it can be completed. I only want to point out here the methodologically correct approach to the question. I do not doubt for a moment that the analysis will establish the following facts. First, that our city is in no position to purchase all of the surpluses from the peasant economy, while the peasantry, having these surpluses in hand, is in no position to absorb the surpluses of urban production that can only be realised on the peasant market. This clarifies the enormous importance for us of exporting agricultural products to eliminate the blockage that has formed throughout our economy.

True, it is theoretically conceivable that industry, if assured sufficient supplies of materials, could further develop production on the basis of a continued rise in wages. In that way we might partially achieve, within the confines of commodity relations, a socialist distribution in the cities and thus substitute the effective demand from our own workers for an additional peasant market. This variant requires a separate investigation because it confronts us with the enormously important problem of transitional economic forms at a time when market distribution and market realisation are supplemented by socialist distribution within the working class, even though it occurs through the capitalist form of increasing wages. I shall return to this theme on another occasion and attempt to explore the question in more detail.

In general terms, in order for us to undertake the necessary analysis of all the conditions for material exchange in our commodity-socialist economic system, we shall need three schemes rather than the two with which Marx worked. A third scheme has to be introduced that will characterise material exchange and its numerical patterns and proportions between state industry and the peasant economy. I doubt that we will ever get perfectly accurate data, but I am convinced that if a number of economists took up this issue they would be able, even given the inadequacy of current statistics, to establish the approximate basic magnitudes and thus arrive in practice at the most important and interesting question of all, which concerns the possibility of keeping real accounts and thus in future actually regulating the whole economy during the period of NEP.

Now I turn to the question of our economy's trading apparatus – its size and how much it is costing our economy, i.e., how much NEP costs from this perspective.

First of all, how do things stand with the cost of the trading apparatus? Here are the facts for pre-war relations. The pre-war turnover of new values, created during a particular year and newly entering into circulation, after deducting what was consumed in kind and for transport, was 5,650 million gold roubles. Data from the Ministry of Finance for 1912 give a total trade turnover of 7,920 million. The fact that these two figures differ is understandable because the annual trade turnover includes not only values that are newly created during a given year but also older values, some of which often circulate two or three times. But for our calculations the principal importance attaches to values that have entered into commodity circulation from production and represent what labour has newly created within the country during the year. How many times they are subsequently transferred is also of interest, although from a different viewpoint, i.e., mainly in terms of society's non-productive expenditures on the type of distribution apparatus that trade represents, but that is already a different question. Trade income before the war, in other words the whole revenue from trade, including both wage costs for sales clerks etc., and also what was capitalised in trade – and you know that before the war an enormous sum was capitalised in our country by just this route – came to 980 million gold roubles according to data provided by Prokopovich. In percentage terms, this represents 17.3 % of the whole net product that entered into commodity circulation. Thus, before the war the country spent 17.3 % of the whole sum of new values entering into the channels of commercial circulation for the pleasure of the Kolupaevs, the Razuvayevs and the whole trading apparatus.

What is the current situation in this regard? This is an extremely important and tragic question for our national economy, as you will presently see. At this

Printed Cottons: The Mark-up on the Wholesale Price (In State, Co-operative and Private Trade and the Average Mark-up)

	January	February	March	April	May	June	July	August	September
State Trade	–	31	24	25	39	43	32	42	–
Co-operatives	–	25	27	29	31	31	24	27	–
Free-Market Trade	–	39	28	36	44	40	44	42	–
Average	–	33	24	29	40	37	34	36	–

Note: According to data from the Statistical-Economic Secretariat of the Commissariat of Domestic Trade

point I must demonstrate how I get a figure that at first sight appears to be perfectly mad. I shall begin by citing the tables collected and compiled in order to calculate the costs added by retail trade to the wholesale price of the trusts. Here is the mark-up that is added in retail trade to state industry's wholesale price of printed cottons in Moscow.

These figures are perfectly straightforward, and we also have the following data for all commodities sold in Moscow.

The Average Margin of Moscow Retail Prices over Wholesale Prices as a %

No	Name of commodity	January	February	March	April	May	June	July	August
1	Rye Grain	9	4	8	4	7	11	32	11
2	Rye Flour	17	14	11	13	7	16	21	25
3	Wheat Flour	18	45	34	21	62	51	32	41
4	Oats	37	27	30	41	19	21	41	16
5	Millet	34	26	19	49	50	15	39	43
6	Buckwheat	30	15	18	36	31	34	43	29
7	Rice	45	31	54	25	27	38	6	16
8	Butter	19	13	16	11	18	13	26	16
9	Melted Butter	15	22	17	13	8	13	11	11
10	Sunflower Oil	32	24	32	33	34	24	19	15
11	Beef	12	17	15	10	18	31	12	67
	Agricultural average	**24**	**22**	**23**	**23**	**26**	**24**	**27**	**28**
12	Herring	66	70	75	104	104	89	74	46
13	Lump sugar	7	7	13	11	12	18	20	26
14	Granulated Sugar	7	23	16	18	16	21	20	18
15	Confectioner's Sugar	70	39	31	24	21	25	17	3
16	Chinese Tea	14	17	16	17	25	17	17	17
17	Table Salt	68	76	39	62	61	61	58	41

The Average Margin of Moscow Retail Prices over Wholesale Prices as a % (*cont.*)

No	Name of commodity	January	February	March	April	May	June	July	August
	Average for processed foods	39	39	32	39	40	39	34	25
18	Matches	42	49	24	14	18	46	28	27
19	Kerosene	44	73	41	35	27	32	21	19
20	Soap	126	41	33	14	26	45	17	3
21	Nails	105	58	27	11	30	26	25	27
22	Calico	45	33	24	29	40	37	34	36
23	Thread	93	50	30	48	36	26	26	17
24	Linen Bag	66	58	18	3	15	15	15	–
25	Firewood (mixed)	13	–	11	5	21	35	9	9
	Average for Non-processed Industrial Commodities	67	45	26	19	27	33	22	20
	Average for all Commodities	41	35	26	27	29	32	27	25

note: According to data from the Statistical-Economic Secretariat of the Commissariat of Domestic Trade

The Average for all months and all commodities is 30.25%

I also have numerous similar materials and graphs for the situation in the provinces, referring not just to cotton prints but also to other products of mass consumption such as salt, kerosene and sugar, along with figures for individual commodities in specific regions of the country. Here the situation differs widely. There are two tables that are quite amazing, showing prices for cotton cloth and refined sugar, as approved by our Commissariat of Domestic Trade, i.e. wholesale prices, list prices, and actual prices for the provinces of Vladimir and Kursk, for the Kubano-Chernomorskaya region and for Saratov province.

The price in the Kubano-Chernomorskaya region is more than double what the Commissariat approves. That was at the beginning of 1923. In April the Commissariat's price was little changed, but in Kursk province, not that far from Moscow, the price exceeded the Commissariat's by 120%. The picture is the same for other regions. Then there is salt. In this case the average retail prices for all of Russia are more than 60% higher than wholesale prices.

For sugar, wholesale prices throughout the USSR were 50% higher than those listed by the Commissariat; and for June, July, and August they were more than 110% higher. The base price for kerosene in Baku (including excise) is one-half the all-Russia retail price, i.e., the retail price involves a 100% mark-up and is 80% higher than the Samara delivery price. An enormous number of cases have occurred when prices for manufactures in the provinces were more than

200 % of wholesale prices. It would be tiresome to continue, but this is enough to illustrate what it means to live in a period of primitive socialist and secondary NEP accumulation. It will be no exaggeration if we take the general mark-up over the initial price, the factory wholesale price, to be 60 %. For the past year at least, with its wild relation between the wholesale and retail price, this estimate will be on the low side.

If we take the total of all industrial products sold on the market to be 1,277 [million], and for agricultural products 500 [million] – or, 700 [million] according to Groman and Strumilin – this would mean either 1,777 million or 1,977 million [roubles]. Assume that 1,500 million pass through the trade apparatus and the rest are sold directly by producers to consumers (the peasant trade at bazaars, goods ordered from craftsmen, etc.). Take 60 % of this sum and we get 900 million. Subtract from that the shipping expenses of the trade apparatus, say, one-half of all transport costs (which is clearly an over-estimate). Also subtract 100 million for taxes paid to the state and 50 million for losses due to currency depreciation, in other words, a tax in the form of currency emissions. We then have the income of our trade apparatus – including private trade, state trade and the cooperatives – which amounts to 600 million roubles for the past year. This sum exceeds the income of the whole of the artisanal and craft industries and approaches the total sum of production in the whole of state industry. These are atrocious figures, and the estimates leave little room for dispute. One part of this sum goes to expenses of the apparatus, to wages, etc., and the other is the NEP accumulation fund. The relation between the two is difficult to judge, but no matter how much we exaggerate the number of people employed in trade, I consider the figure for accumulation that emerges here to be quite threatening.

What kind of staffing is involved in trade? Unfortunately, the data provided by our statisticians are completely unsatisfactory and can provide no guidance whatever. According to the data from TsSU, the last census figures showed 150 thousand trading enterprises. This is an extremely low number. If we begin with the assumption that each shop, on average, has approximately three employees, then we have an army of nearly half a million who live exclusively through trade. But the figure is an understatement because before the war about a million trading licenses were taken out. Accordingly, before the war we did not have an army of a million but a million just of the trading establishments alone. Of course, only one or two people are employed by the great majority of small trading establishments, but this still means we had a colossal pre-war trading army. Trading incomes of 600 million now hang on the distribution of real values amounting to 1,500 million! These figures remind us of Persia, Turkey and China! When it is a question of the most appropriate economic policy, our first blow must be struck here. In our struggle against the [price] scissors[24] and the high cost of living, this is the first place where pressure must be exerted in order to plug the hole through which such a massive sum of values is leaking out of our economy.

In the second part of my report, I shall examine how the current crisis, which is occurring on the basis of disproportionalities in production, has developed in the area of trade and been intensified by mistakes in terms of credit policy and the pricing policy of our trusts.

• • •

Comrades, here on the blackboard we have a drawing of the price scissors. It is a summary of the disproportionality that I addressed with the other figures and comes at it from another direction. It is a photograph of our conjuncture, which I mentioned when I analysed production relations within the Soviet Union. You can see that up to a certain moment in the autumn of last year, the relation between [prices for] agricultural and industrial products was the reverse of what it is now. The lines intersect in the autumn, and we have a a fleeting equilibrium from the pre-war perspective. Then the picture is one of industrial prices climbing (calculated in commodity roubles and in banknotes), followed by a certain decline in the summer and then a sharp leap upwards.

Let us cite figures that characterise the discrepancy between agricultural prices and prices for manufactured goods in comparison with pre-war proportions.

Dates for the data	Percentage divergence of the scissors	
	Retail prices	Wholesale prices
1 August 1922	99	74
1 September 1922	119	94
1 October 1922	138	111
1 November 1922	165	127
1 December 1922	158	134
1 January 1923	170	152
1 February 1923	171	169
1 March 1923	187	176

---

24   [The 'price scissors' referred to a graph showing the indices for industrial and agricultural prices. From the autumn of 1922 onwards the index for industrial prices rose while that for agricultural prices fell, representing the two blades of the 'scissors'.]

(*cont.*)

Dates for the data	Percentage divergence of the scissors	
	Retail prices	Wholesale prices
1 April 1923	186	199
1 May 1923	199	227
1 June 1923	214	232
1 July 1923	220	206
1 August 1923	238	242
1 September 1923	287	312
1 October 1923	315	320
8 October 1923	303	320
11 October 1923	303	301
15 October 1923	250	–
21 October 1923	–	295
22 October 1923	236	–

I have a few words to say about the reduction and the fluctuations of the scissors that can be seen over two-three weeks. First of all, it follows from what I have said about the disproportionality between agriculture and industry – which in terms of value relations intensifies all the more as industrial products rise in price and the value of agricultural products falls – that this lack of correspondence had to become all the more obvious when the greatest volume of agricultural products comes to market without being met by sufficient domestic demand. This had to be expected precisely in the autumn, when the peasantry, in order to pay their tax in kind with cash,[25] had to throw a significant part of their surpluses into the market in a very short time. If this production is not bought up, prices will fall for agricultural products, the [agricultural blade of the] scissors will fall, and the countryside will have a reduction rather than an increase of purchasing power for urban commodities. Hence, on the basis of the most elementary logic of economic policy and knowledge of the facts, only one conclusion can follow: if the peasants, by means of their sales, do not acquire the money needed both to pay the tax and to buy more urban products than usual, the result will be that low grain prices will not increase the absorpt-

---

25   [In March 1923 the XII Party Congress allowed part of the food tax to be paid in cash and amalgamated some other minor taxes into a single agricultural tax. By January 1924 the tax in kind was entirely replaced by cash payments as a means of increasing the demand for money to help stabilise the chervonets rouble.]

ive capacity of the peasant market in early autumn, as the trusts and trade organs expected, but, to the contrary, *the level will fall even lower than usual* because it is precisely during this season that the monetary tax must be paid. In such conditions, a policy of raising prices for urban commodities is economically (and thus commercially) illiterate and intensifies the crisis rather than alleviating it.

What were the reasons for the widening gap between industrial and agricultural prices to the extent that *it was not caused by a downward movement of agricultural prices* and therefore depended upon state policy? First of all, our industrialists reasoned this way. Autumn is on its way and will energise trade after the summer lull, requiring the greatest supply of commodities in the market since that is when the peasantry will be making purchases. If that is the case, we must store up these commodities and increase production on the one hand, and on the other hand raise wholesale prices when the moment is convenient. If there is ever a time to skim the cream off the 'conjuncture', this is it. The trade organs thought to themselves: the time is coming to trade with the peasants and we must procure the maximum supply of goods for autumn sales. We need to continue buying, even at a higher price, because we will sell it all in any event. That is what our industrialists and state traders were thinking.

In order for industry to expand accordingly, further credits had to be provided. Thus the people responsible for credit policies reasoned in unison with industrialists and traders: maximum credits must be extended to industry during the summer. As a result, all the credit resources of our Gosbank were distributed as follows. On 1 August, i.e., at the beginning of the crisis, trade received 9% of the total sum of banknotes issued for credit purposes, transport 0.5%, agriculture 8%, and industry received 70.4%. In other words, an enormous part of Gosbank's credit resources was handed to industry. This led to increased production on the one hand and a rush of credit in the sphere of commodity exchange on the other. In terms of available credit, therefore, all of the preconditions existed for industrial expansion; altogether 140 million chervonets roubles (including those issued previously) were invested in industry, which, after receiving the loans, expanded output. The traders bought up these products in the hope that when the peasant began to buy, everything would be sold. Trade based on credit rose by almost 2 ½ times compared to the spring. This often meant that one person re-sold to another, and he sold to a third, etc., all in the hope of selling everything come the autumn. They all overlooked one minor issue, one link in the chain of material exchange: they forgot that if the peasant cannot sell, neither can he buy. They forgot that this link is the initial basis for the whole expansion of industry and commercial credit. Should things misfire here, all the excitement will lead to an acute crisis since it is not funded by consumer demand. Even if prices had not soared, there would still have been a crisis, although it would not have been so acute. The rise in prices had to intensify it all the more. Meanwhile, there need not have been such a problem with the fundamental link in exchange had people thought of how to purchase, in a timely manner, everything that the peasant would be bringing to market. Consideration should have been given to providing credits for grain procurements in order to prevent an Achilles' heel in the whole problem of realisation. This is precisely where an error of timing occurred and aggravated the crisis, which had developed spontaneously and could have been moderated by a correct credit policy. But we shall come back to this later.

Everyone asks how we explain the surge in prices that occurred precisely in the autumn and reached such extremes. After all, there was no increase of consumer demand. In the first place, urban demand was a stable sum proportional to wages, and wages did not noticeably rise during these months. The fact is that the increase did not result from a growth of consumer demand that was overtaken in a purely spontaneous way by the growth of production, as happens in practically all crises; it was the result of speculative demand from the trade apparatus itself, which was counting on doing a brisk trade and miscalculated. Any other explanation, as we determined in Gosplan, does not stand up to scrutiny. For example, we hear complaints that taxes and excise duties seized everything up. But the evidence totally refutes this explanation. In the first place, throughout the entire year our industry paid a sum equal to 14.6% of net output if we calculate all taxes and excises using Gosplan's index, and somewhat less than 12% if we use the average monthly index. But that refers to the entire year. The essential issue is whether any increase of taxes and duties occurred precisely during the quarter than concerns us, i.e., in July, August and September. According to information from Tsentronalog,[26] these are the facts: there was an insignificant increase of 6–7%, which involved other forms of tax but not excise duties; as far as excises are concerned, there was even a small decline for the quarter. Consequently, there is absolutely no possibility of explaining a price rise coming from this source. In terms of price formation, neither excises nor taxes were a factor responsible for the *increase in prices*.

Consider the other complaints, namely, that transport inflated the fee schedule for shipments. A study done at Gosplan determined that there were no significant changes here and transport likewise cannot be blamed. Now people are saying that production costs rose in general due to a rise in the prices for materials. Here, too, Gosplan's investigation provides no support for the complaint: although the prices of some materials did rise, light industry had purchased its most important material – cotton – before the period that concerns us.

---

26   [The central taxation authority.]

In the final analysis, only one explanation remains; namely, that industry tried to put pressure on the market by way of a price increase in order to extract maximal revenge for the period when it squandered the state's fixed capital and 'sold off' production at low prices when grain prices were high. According to Gosplan's estimates, the fact is that during the year industry accumulated 300 million roubles of circulating capital. It attempted to increase accumulation during the autumn, but at this point it ran into the crisis. The trade apparatus followed the same policy of accumulation; it also raised prices and ran into the same crisis. Prices rose and surpassed prices established by Komvnutorg.[27] A special name even emerged for this operation. At the Nizhny Novgorod fair, even Tsentrosoyuz[28] contrived to buy fabrics from the textile syndicate at prices above those set by Komvnutorg. The result was a general inflation that carried these figures to absurd levels.

It soon turned out that the whole inflation was not funded by consumer demand. There was no expansion of consumer demand. On the contrary, wages, which had gradually risen during the year and thus spurred demand for industry, stabilised. The countryside rushed to pay its taxes with the use of money and was not up to making purchases, because the price of grain fell and it would have been foolish to buy anything in such conditions rather than wait for a rise in grain prices. The result was eruption of the crisis, for which all the signs were evident, ranging from a blockage in the commodity turnover to contested bills of exchange. The clearest manifestation of a crisis is bankruptcy. It is premature to speak of bankruptcies, but many solid organisations came very close to the precipice and were only saved by state support. One of the clearest conjunctural indicators is the volume of trade on the bourse. On the Moscow and provincial bourses, beginning from October of last year, there was a gradual increase of volume involving millions of roubles. The turnover in Moscow for October was 20 million, for November 28, for December 45, for February 80, for March 98. In April there was a certain decline to 65, followed by 73 in May, 123 in June, and 126 in July. Then the crisis began, with a fall to 99 in August and 89 in September. The abrupt rise in prices was followed, therefore, by a drop of nearly 40%. That was the situation in commodity trade.

Looking further, this crisis was intensified because Gosbank, after dispensing most of its loans to industry, shut down credits and counted on industry's repayments to provide part of the capital needed for grain procurements. But that was not so simple because industry was expected to pay at a time when

---

27   [The Commissariat of Domestic Trade.]
28   [The Central Union of Consumer Societies (or consumer co-operatives).]

commodities were not selling and everyone had to request postponement of payment. Consequently, the shutdown of credits was just as much of a mistake as the issuing of more loans at a time when adequate resources had to be committed in a timely manner to grain procurements in order to avoid driving the peasantry into the clutches of private buyers. The error in both the timing and volume of credits for grain procurement left the peasants with no cash at a time when all of the calculations for realisation of industrial products were based on peasant demand. Cutting off credits, however useful it might have been in the sense of forcing the trusts to lower prices, threatened even healthy enterprises with bankruptcy and the impossibility of paying wages. And that is not just politically dangerous – the effects are already evident – but also impedes realisation through expenditures from the wage fund and inter-enterprise purchases (fuel, instruments of production).

Now, comrades, on the basis of all the figures and connections that we have considered, it is perfectly clear what the correct policy would have been in the area of both credits and prices.

Let us now turn to grain prices. On this question we have a long history of debate. Let me remind you of one moment that it will be very helpful to recall just now. This question was raised during the spring at Gosplan. A certain Professor Kondrat'ev[29] spoke in favour of a policy of raising grain prices. His argument was by no means impeccable, and we were quite justified in suspecting him of framing the essential question in Narodnik terms. But this was not simply a stereotypical conflict between the Narodnik and Marxist viewpoints. Of all the Marxists present, I was the only one who, for a variety of reasons, called for a complete change of policy on this matter. Comrade Larin was there and spoke more forcefully than anyone else against a policy of raising grain prices. He assured us that everything was fine: the lower the grain prices, the better it is for industry, for the working class, and even for the peasants themselves.

(Reply from Sh.M. Dvolaitsky: Larin is a well-known authority on peasants.)

At the time, I argued in Gosplan that it would be a mistake to consider a general increase of grain prices in the domestic market; instead, we should look to exports, which would automatically lead to an increase while simultaneously expanding our economy on the basis of exchange. The problem was not properly understood at the time, and although comrades did not disagree with my view, there was no decision taken according to the arguments that I set out.

---

29   [N.D. Kondrat'ev was an agricultural economist and also author of the theory of 'long cycles'.]

Time passed, and the issue became obvious. If we want to eliminate the disproportionality in our economy, we must deal directly with the question of grain prices. The view that we are better off the more cheaply we buy grain from the peasant is completely incorrect and false. This view has been refuted by the entire situation in which we find ourselves. It is a crude simplification and represents vulgar Marxism because it does not take into account the situation of the economy as a whole.

The next question is how these scissors might be closed. There are two possibilities. One is to reduce the production costs of industrial goods at the factory level. It is not possible to go very far in the direction of reducing costs at the factory and plant level until the technical conditions of production have changed, concentration has occurred, etc. Pressure has already been applied here, and hardly anything can be achieved that will actually have an effect on selling prices. As for the intermediate apparatus of distribution and the possibility of curtailing its expenditures, which I have described for you, in this area there is great potential for cost reduction. Finally, there is one other point where closing the scissors might be possible from another direction, and that is an increase of prices on agricultural products through exports. If the peasants, who currently have surpluses of more than 200 million poods (beyond what they sell domestically), are in a position to sell these surpluses, particularly if they do so at prices higher than we have now, this will mean an increase of the countryside's buying power for industrial products and will also help to close the scissors.

The next question is whether, on the other hand, this might be disadvantageous to the state. The opposite is true: with high grain prices, the state profits from a grain price increase when it has part of the tax proceeds available in natural form. When grain prices decline, so does the value of the portion of the tax paid in kind, and we lose out. Here is a numerical example for the recent period. In the first quarter of 1922, the state distributed 50 million rye units through the budget at a value of 108 million roubles, i.e., a rye unit was worth about 2 roubles. In the second quarter, the respective figures were 56 and 97 as prices fell; in the third quarter 61 million were distributed at a value of 63 million, making the rye unit worth about 1 rouble; in the fourth quarter the figures were 121 and 97. In the first quarter of 1923, 121 million were distributed, and the value was 85 million. The same pattern continued in the following quarters. As you can see the state, having the tax in kind at its disposal, loses out when market prices for grain decline. It is true that it also loses when it is a question of exports and export revenues, since the purchase price of grain rises. However, the state cannot chase after profit at the expense of extremely low grain prices, not only because that means greater losses due to devaluation of the tax in kind but also because a policy that is damaging to the whole process of material exchange in the national economy is unacceptable and unprofitable from the general economic point of view. And that is leaving aside the fact that low prices corrupt the grain procurement apparatus without promoting any speedy reduction of overhead expenses. To the extent that may be appropriate for public discussion, Comrade Frumkin could tell us how things stand in that connection. In any event, there is a very great potential here for reductions. Buying grain for 35 kopecks, we sell it for a price of 1 rouble 7 kopecks to 1 rouble 10 kopecks. That is a huge difference, but our profit is meagre and sometimes we have a loss. You can see that there is abundant room here for closing the scissors.

Now, let us consider what a rise in grain prices means for us in terms of redistribution of the national income and purchasing power. Our industry, including large-scale and small-scale, brings to market about 1,277 million in new values annually, while the commodity portion of the peasant income is about 500–700 million. Suppose this involves 500 million rye units. If the price increases by 50%, not only does the peasantry increase its income by 250 million roubles, but its purchasing power for urban products also rises to 750 million roubles. This means that a completely different proportionality begins to form, i.e., one in which the peasant's yoke can be balanced in a way that was not previously possible. How does this bode for the city? An increase of the grain price means the worker must spend more on agricultural products. We have the economic means to deal with this, because wage payments are indexed and we also have a certain portion of the tax proceeds in kind. Insofar as we have craftsmen and artisans who purchase grain, there will be a partial income transfer from these strata to the producing element of the peasantry. In exactly the same way, the remaining urban population will be giving up part of their income to the countryside if grain prices rise. And that will not be a bad thing; it can only be beneficial from the viewpoint of providing a stimulus for expansion of the sown acreage.

But an increase in today's extremely low grain prices, while beneficial and expedient in terms of a more appropriate distribution of national income, will not increase the possibility of realising industrial products if all that is involved is a shifting of domestic purchasing power from the pocket of one class into the pocket of another, with no accompanying rapid expansion of exports. The more the peasants buy, the less will urban dwellers buy; all that changes is the character of demand for commodity one or another, not the potential total demand, which is fairly constant at any given moment. Therefore, what is important for the national economy is not merely a rising price of grain as such, but rather a price rise on the basis of exports. A rise in the grain price can also have another positive result. The peasantry will then decrease the pointless consumption of that portion of the surpluses that is now lost mainly due to the low price of grain. The most damaging aspect of this type of consumption today is home-made liquor. Thus, an expansion of the outlets for our grain to flow abroad, together with greater procurements, will mean an increase in the elements contributing to equilibrium and a reduction of disproportionality.

If we look back, from this perspective, at the whole period when the current crisis was maturing, it becomes perfectly clear what the correct policy would have been in terms of credits. It should have been one of providing the necessary credits for grain procurements and *providing them in a timely manner*. The peasantry could have paid its taxes to the state without driving down the price of grain, without paying a tax to private buyers, and perhaps would have had more resources to purchase commodities from the city. Then the state would also not lose so much per unit of taxation due to the low equivalents. In my opinion, therefore, the basic mistake, as far as credit policy is concerned, occurred in the system for distributing credits; rather than alleviating the coming crisis it did the opposite and aggravated it because all resources were committed to industry and then could not be freed up when grain procurements had to be expanded. On the other hand, industry itself used the shower of credits to expand production beyond the limits of real effective demand on the part of consumers.

Now consider the policy of the trusts themselves. The trusts behaved like chicks that wandered from the hen and had no hand to guide them. They behaved according to the standard methods of bourgeois competition; they randomly probed the market but with one difference, namely, that in the capitalist countries there is an organised market whereas in our country it is not yet properly developed and established. As a result, we had neither the spontaneous regulator of the capitalist market nor organised leadership coming from the state. And this is happening when the state has a monopoly over all large-scale industry and there cannot even be any genuine competition! The policy of the trusts, who blindly raised prices to the breaking point, was severely harmful, dangerous and ultimately unprofitable for both the state and the trusts themselves. Its result was to intensify the crisis that was simmering deep within the base of production and could have been anticipated and partially alleviated even with the most elementary attempt at planned regulation and the most cursory analysis of the conjuncture. Once the crisis erupted, our economic organs proceeded to curtail prices, in some cases voluntarily and in others under pressure from Narkomfin and its head offices. But this sort of price reduction can only go so far. The cotton fabric that we have in Moscow is three-four times more costly than agricultural products, and even if sold at a 30% discount it will hardly reach the countryside when grain is selling for 12 kopecks in Poltava province. And any further reduction in prices for our industry will be directly ruinous. This is why the focus, for the moment, must be mainly on raising prices for agricultural products by means of a maximal development of grain purchases and exports. Unfortunately, very little has thus far been accomplished in this direction. All of our grain procurements for export come to about 80 million poods, a sum that represents only 1/3 of the disposable surplus in the peasant economy. These procurements have still not had any essential effect on grain prices, although the conjuncture will of course change with time.

To summarise, I shall draw the conclusions that flow from everything I have said and speak for themselves. First and foremost, we must consider all the elements of our economy in dynamic terms, at least to the extent needed in order to foresee fundamental changes in the conjuncture, especially those that have a seasonal character in an agricultural economy such as ours. Furthermore, we need a steady, planned policy in the area of economic regulation, beginning, of course, with the state economy. Next, we need a single centre for keeping track of the conjuncture and regulating it in place of the five centres we currently have. The fact is that our production programmes are confirmed by Gosplan; Narkomfin assigns loans to industry; Gosbank provides industry with the credits; VSNKh is to manage and regulate the activity of the trusts; and state trade is not properly managed by anyone. Prices, as the most important lever for regulation – which must not be detached from all the other elements of the economy and an economic plan – are to be regulated by Komvnutorg. And then there is still the STO.[30] If we become better organised for the general regulation of economic life, which is already overdue, then even if we cannot free ourselves entirely from economic crises under NEP we shall still be able to foresee them and consequently moderate their damaging consequences for the national economy.

I have attempted in this report to give a thorough analysis of the causes and consequences of the first economic crisis under NEP. This crisis, i.e., a crisis on the basis of disproportionality between industry and agriculture, is the most fundamental of all the sorts of crises that we are fated to experience. But in order to remain true to the theme of my report, I would also have to analyse the crises that are possible on the basis of other disproportions, for example, within the state sphere proper and so forth. I shall return to this subject at another time. [...][31]

---

30   [The Council of Labour and Defence.]

31   [Contributions to the debate from M.A. Larin and M.I. Frumkin have been omitted. What follows is Preobrazhensky's conclusion to the report and his responses to the questions that were raised.]

• • •

Comrades, I shall try to be brief because there is very little that requires a response from me. There were actually no real objections. I shall begin with comrade Larin. He reproached me for forgetting the connection between our pre-war economy and the world market. This is the only part of his speech, the sole observation, that I acknowledge to be correct. But I deliberately left this out of my analysis because it would have required me to look much further to determine the percentage of the marketable surplus in relation to industry. Before the war, we exported about 1,500 million roubles and imported a smaller sum because we had to maintain an active trade balance in order to pay the interest on foreign loans. But we were not only a country that imported foreign industrial products, which supplemented and accompanied those from domestic industrial production, which weakens comrade Larin's objection – we were also a country that imported foreign capital. This new capital flowed to us in the form of fixed capital and subsequently was thrown into the market as one of the components of products produced domestically. The result of all this was to decrease the share of our own production that went to fixed capital and to increase the share going to products of mass consumption. That sort of economy led to very complex relations and proportions in the distribution of productive forces, which are difficult to capture in the kind of rough percentages that I have provided here. For that reason, I accept Comrade Larin's suggestion to extend the analysis further, and I shall do so elsewhere. I doubt, however, that the results of such an analysis, once everything is summed up, will make any essential difference to my conclusions.

Comrade Larin also said that I forgot about the demand originating from the state itself. I spoke of commodity production in industry in the amount of 1,277 million, or 1,577 million when transport is added, and 500 million in agriculture. But I did not think it was necessary to add that a balance requires adding 777[32] million or 1,077 million to the 500.[33] I did mention in my report that I was not dealing with the question of the scale of capitalisation and the demand that originates within industry itself. I analysed only the consumed portion of what is produced, because it is precisely the disproportion in this area that is the cause of our current crisis. Comrade Larin furthermore says that I forgot about strat-

---

32   [The text mistakenly gives the figure of 700 million.]

33   [A balance between industry and agriculture would require an additional 777 million in agriculture if the figure for industry is 1,277 and 1,077 million if the figure for industry is 1,577.]

ification among the peasantry. If I did not discuss that issue, it does not mean that I forgot it. I can say, however, that when it is a question of rising grain prices, poor peasants who are buyers do suffer, but there are also elements among the peasantry who benefit when grain prices are low, as well as those groups living in provinces with developed technical crops. For one thing, peasants in the North-West are making a fortune from flax because it is selling at the pre-war price while grain can be bought for a pittance. The peasantry in regions with technical crops are profiting at the expense of the regions with grain crops, and if we were to do the sums, it is still not clear what the final outcome would be. I certainly did not forget stratification among the peasantry, but we are dealing here with aggregate numbers, and in those terms my conclusions are beyond dispute.

Comrade Larin arrived 15 minutes late, but he did not miss anything because during those 15 minutes I said nothing about the stupidity of our trust managers. In my earlier analysis, I showed that the crisis developed spontaneously on the basis of disproportionality in the economy. Specific factors might have intensified or weakened it. If we had implemented a correct credit and pricing policy, on the basis of a general economic plan, the crisis would have been less painful. But the crisis itself came spontaneously. I am convinced that my analysis and my conclusions are better justified economically than those of Comrade Larin, who attributes the whole evil to one thing: an unplanned economy. That is too superficial ... we had no planned economy, and the result was the scissors. This is not the way to approach the question. The scissors developed on the basis of relations that formed in the economy spontaneously and could only be partially altered with a planned economy. A plan can and will alleviate crises – and the more planning we have, the better – but it cannot eliminate them entirely.

Comrade Larin was factually incorrect when he said that agricultural acreage has been growing for two years. This is the first year of expansion. Last year we had a contraction, although it is true that it was due to a sowing shortfall in the famine-stricken areas. Comrade Larin cited Lenin to the effect that the main reason for introducing NEP was the lack of revolution in the West. There is a big difference, as they say in Odessa, between the main cause and one of the causes. However the revolution unfolds in the West, none of us will deny that we shall not be returning to the form of economy we had during War Communism. That will not happen. No one will claim that a revolution in the West could justify today, in 1923, the methods of requisitioning that we adopted in 1918. Since we are compelled to live for decades with the petty-bourgeois economy, any methods that make it impossible for such an economy to develop on the basis of its own incentives are unsuitable and must be replaced by other methods. From this perspective, no revolution anywhere in the world will lead us back to requisitioning, and no successes of a German revolution will lead us back to requisitioning.

There are much more sophisticated methods available to us for mastering the peasant economy. They are feasible, and I dealt with them in my book *From NEP to Socialism*. These methods, which must include an enormous role for long-term credits to the countryside, can provide us with everything we need in economic terms for achieving socialist regulation of the economy as a whole. But this is not the sort of regulation we had during War Communism. Comrade Larin says that if we join with the future Soviet Germany in a single union, that fact will assure us of the opportunity to re-group the productive forces very quickly on a new basis, which will inevitably compel us to deepen and reinforce the planning principle in our economy. I agree with that. However, I think the question is posed incorrectly. After all, if it is true, then we must also accept the opposite conclusion: in the event of a defeat for the German revolution, we would have to strengthen the NEP element in our economy. That would mean that the elements of free competition etc. would have to be strengthened at the expense of a planned state economy. I do not agree with that. I believe that we are moving towards a planned economy regardless of the successes of the German revolution. Joining with Germany in an economic union can merely accelerate this process.

Now I have a few criticisms to offer in response to comrade Larin since he accused me of *Narodnichestvo*.[34] I must repeat categorically that I have no sympathy for *Narodnichestvo*, but in response to vulgar Marxism I do think it necessary to speak up for a proper formulation of the pricing question. I have to remind comrade Larin that during the period when the scissors were widening and it was urgent to raise the question of changing our pricing policy, of developing exports etc. – during that period he spoke about everything being just fine, and today he regards that as his contribution. During that period I was already saying the opposite, that nothing was fine and we must adopt a course towards raising grain prices on the basis of exports. At the time, he thought my way of framing the question – which today has been confirmed as totally correct – was that of a Narodnik and could not be taken seriously. Instead of thinking the question through, he and a number of other comrades simply brushed the issue aside by recalling our old stereotypes from the struggle against the Narodniks in totally different circumstances. My position has nothing to do with *Narodnichestvo*; to the contrary, it is Comrade Larin's position that does

---

34   [*Narodnichestvo* refers to the doctrine of the Narodniks, or Russian agrarian populists.]

have a definite relation to vulgar Marxism. I must also point out that he did not balance his attacks at the start of his speech with his conclusion. At the start he said that I am a Narodnik, but at the end he mercifully added that in the body of my talk there were merely inclinations towards *Narodnichestvo*.

I now turn to the final question. I do not completely agree with Comrade Frumkin that we have to see another cause of the crisis in the fact that our agricultural production this year is somewhat lower than it was last year. If Comrade Frumkin thought this through more fully, he would see where it leads. If, with production of 2,800 million poods, we have a surplus of 200–250 million that is not absorbed in the domestic market but instead lies idle and puts downward pressure on the market, this means that the graph of grain prices will not rise if, in place of the current surplus, we have one of 300 or 400 million poods weighing upon the market. A shortage or a surplus means something entirely different if we have an export adjustment that absorbs *all* surpluses. Then any increase in the harvest is also an equivalent increase in rural purchasing power (*caeteris paribus*).[35]

We are now entering a period when the question of grain exports is becoming the central problem for development of our economy. We have come up against the problem of the external market. In particular, the question of whether Poland permits free transit of our grain under favourable conditions, in order that we face no barrier there, is profoundly important to our economy. At the current stage of development, it is a question of whether our agriculture and our entire economy stands still and decays or makes rapid progress. I do not agree that the crisis would be less severe if we had a good harvest. The crisis would be more profound, the inflow of products from the countryside into the cities would be greater, peasant discontent would grow, and the disproportionality throughout the whole economy would be even more acute than it is now.

E.A. Preobrazhensky,
Ekonomicheskie krizisy pri nepe.
Moscow, 1924, pp. 3–33, 47–51.

---

35   [All other things being equal.]

CHAPTER 4

Economic Notes: On the Goods Famine[1]

It is clear to everyone that the goods famine results from effective demand exceeding supply. It is also clear that the excess signifies inadequate production, *at least for the present moment,* compared to demand. i.e., that the goods famine is a function of inadequate accumulation in industry, which is also obvious. But apparently it is not obvious to everyone that the goods famine is not a seasonal phenomenon. The fact is that it has actually lasted a year and a half; its latest acute attack began before the harvest, and it has stubbornly persisted for four months since the harvest, despite limited shipments of peasant grain to the market that do not correspond to the size of the harvest. In fact, this view of the goods famine as seasonal cannot survive for long because it will soon be exposed to the inevitable test: once the current outbreak of the goods famine has lasted for a year, that explanation will be worthless. But since refutation of the 'seasonal theory' in practice will by no means put an end to the season for theories that tend, in the final analysis, to regard the current volume of industrial production and its rate of expansion as normal, we believe it is worthwhile to share with readers certain data from an investigation that deals with this whole problem.

According to Gosplan's control figures, the gross product of the agricultural economy in 1924/25 was 9,150 million roubles, or 71% of the pre-war level. For the whole of industry it was 5,000 million, or 71.4% of the pre-war figure. Apparently, there is a superficial arithmetic proportionality.

Let us examine the relationship between the volumes of production that are entering the market for sale, i.e., the percentages of commodity production in agriculture and industry. In this connection, Gosplan's control figures provide the following data. In 1924/25 the commodity portion of agricultural production was 2,857 million pre-war roubles compared to 4,498 million in 1913, or 63.7% of the pre-war figure. The commodity portion of industrial production is taken to be 7,011 million in 1913, with 4,450 million in 1924/25, or 63.5% of the figure for 1913. Here, too, there seems to be complete arithmetic proportionality in terms of commodity production.

---

1 Article by E.A. Preobrazhensky, published in *Pravda* on 15 December 1925.

The question is: *Why was there no goods famine in tsarist Russia during any pre-war year that corresponded to the level of production and the marketed share in 1925*, i.e. during any of the years from the decade of 1900–10?

Just posing the question this way is enough to prompt us to seek an explanation primarily (although not solely) in the different composition of budgetary expenditures in the countryside and among workers, and perhaps also in a different distribution between the country's productive and consumer demand. I shall deal here only with the first issue, which is the basic and decisive one.

From the viewpoint of the conditions of realisation and distribution, the commodity portion of the pre-war countryside can be divided into two components: 1) the mass of commodities subject to *compulsory sale* and bringing no equivalent to the peasantry; and 2) the commodity mass that provided money in exchange, which was used (after deducting monetary accumulation) to acquire industrial commodities or commodities exchanged between the peasants themselves.

Let us take a closer look at the first item, i.e., the portion of peasant agricultural production realised on a compulsory basis. It had to cover three basic sums: 1) central and local taxes; 2) the rent that peasants paid for use of land in addition to their own allotments; 3) usurious rates of interest to the kulaks, buyers-up and landowners, as well as maintenance of the clergy and other smaller items. To some extent, the latter expenditure still exists today, although one would think it must be less than before the war. We shall not be examining it here, only the first two items. If we take all the revenues in the tsarist budget for 1913, including direct taxes, indirect taxes, tariffs and royal monopolies, and divide them by a population of 175 million, the per-capita revenue going to the state will be 12 roubles 78 kopecks, or 11.2 % of the country's gross income. The budget for 1924/25, from the same sources as in the pre-war case (thus omitting, in particular, the revenues from transport and Narkompochtel[2]), when divided by the population, gives a per-capita figure of 7 roubles 66 kopecks, or 7.7 % of the country's gross income. Taking 1912/13 in particular, the peasantry paid 10 roubles 54 kopecks per capita in direct and indirect taxes in the 50 provinces of European Russia, compared to 3 roubles 56 kopecks in pre-war roubles for 1924/25.[3] Consequently, in 1924/25 they paid a total of 815 million less in pre-war roubles or 1,400 million less in chervonets roubles (taking the agricultural population in 1924/25 to be 116.8 million). Compared to the pre-war situation, today's payments of state taxes by the peasantry have fallen much

---

2   [The People's Commissariat for Postal and Telegraph Service.]

3   According to preliminary calculations from TsSU for 1925/26, the peasantry will pay 4 roubles 64 kopeks per capita in pre-war roubles, or just 44 % of the taxes levied in 1912/13.

further than today's agricultural income. What that means is that *a signific-ant portion of rural commodity production is no longer subject to compulsory sales.*

As far as rental payments are concerned, according to the well-known study by Karyshev,[4] by the late 1880s a total of about 49.8 million desyatins were ren-ted to peasants in addition to their own allotments (i.e., landlord holdings, royal estates, treasury lands, church and monasterial lands, and urban land – which were cultivated and used as pastures and hayfields). The average rent in the 1880s was 6.3 roubles per desyatin. Subsequent to that, the number of peasant freeholds grew significantly, but so did the rental payments on a smaller volume of rented land, especially in the Central Black Earth zone and in Ukraine. If we take into account the three-field farming system, in which there was no charge for fallow land, but then add rental payments for all the pastures and hayfields, the peasants' annual rental payments before the war came to *at least* 200 mil-lion pre-war roubles, or about 360 million in terms of our chervonets rouble. If we recall that the whole of the single agricultural tax planned for the budget of 1925/26 comes to 235 million, then the reader will understand the significance for the peasant budget of the elimination of rental payments to landlords. But this question presently interests us from another perspective, namely, mater-ial exchange and the exchange of commodity production between town and country. The abolition of rental payments amounting to 200 million pre-war roubles, or 360 million chervonets roubles, means elimination of another large portion of compulsory sales of peasant commodity output with all of the ensu-ing consequences.

What are the consequences of the figures we have provided for the reduction in taxes and the removal of rents in terms of urban-rural material exchange for 1924/25, and thus also for 1925/26?

The first conclusion is that, due to the reduction of compulsory sales, the peasantry has much greater discretion compared to the pre-war period in choosing the time and conditions for disposing of surpluses and in making economic calculations in general. This applies not only to the well-off element of the peasantry, who always enjoyed a certain freedom in making economic decisions, but even more to the main mass of the countryside. This fact has enormous significance in explaining why the peasantry is in no rush to sell grain.

---

4 Karyshev, *Krest'yanskie vnenadel'nye arendy* (Dorpat, 1893). A.I. Chuprev takes the area of rented non-allotment land to be 40 million desyatins. See: *Melkoe zemledelie v Rossii i evo osnovnye nuzhdy* (Moscow, 1906), p. 17.

The second conclusion is that a reduction in compulsory sales, given the same agricultural income as before the war, must lead to increased rural consumption of food products.

Finally, the third and most important conclusion is that a much smaller part of this sum of commodity production – i.e., of 2,857 million for the past economic year and 3,639 million for 1925/26 (or any other numbers if Gosplan's data on commodity production should be inaccurate) – goes to compulsory sales without any equivalent than was the case before the war, meaning that, in the same conditions of realisation, peasant effective demand for industrial commodities and for products exchanged between the peasants themselves must grow by a corresponding sum.

The enormous significance for our theme of this latter conclusion is perfectly obvious. *Maintaining the equilibrium between the commodity mass coming from industry and from agricultural production, on the basis of pre-war proportions for last year and this year, entails an acute disruption of the equilibrium between the effective demand of the countryside and the commodity production of the cities.* And this is the key for explaining why we now have such a persistent goods famine. Our current goods famine is the result of all the positive changes in the peasant budget that came with our October Revolution. While the Civil War and requisitions were continuing, and the general level of peasant production was much lower than before the war, these consequences of October were not apparent for perfectly obvious reasons. But the closer we come to the pre-war proportions of production in industry and agriculture (for this year the figure is 90%), the more obvious will *the specific conditions of Soviet agriculture* become, and the more forcefully must the apparent arithmetic proportionality, as compared to the pre-war situation, be transformed before our eyes – and it is already being transformed – into a significant, protracted, and by no means seasonal disproportionality in the distribution of productive forces between industry and agriculture.

But there is more to it than that. Disproportionality also awaits us from another direction even though it is not yet fully evident. I have in mind the progressive change in the very character of wages in the Soviet system on the one hand, and the changing way in which the former surplus value is spent on the other. Since wages, to the benefit of the working class, are currently less regulated by the law of value than before the war and will be even less so in future (this refers especially to the wages of unskilled workers), this fact, together with lower tax deductions from wages, must mean a relatively greater consumer demand from the working class from one year to the next and thus the need for a more rapid rate of expanded reproduction on this account. As far as the changing use of surplus value is concerned, here we must keep in view both *the pre-war bourgeoisie's non-productive consumption through the import of foreign consumer goods* and also the fact that an important part of the dividends, received by foreign capital from foreign-owned industrial enterprises in Russia, also went abroad. (According to calculations by P.V. Ol', a total sum of 2,243 million in capital was invested in our country. If we take the average dividend to be 8 %, the profit paid to imported capital must have been about 180 million per year.)

All of this must lead to expansion of the domestic market for industrial products. From the viewpoint of the national economy, the importance of this increase of worker-peasant demand, as the stimulus for a totally different rate of expanded reproduction in industry from that before the war, currently results not from a different level of development in the economy as a whole but rather from a different system of national income distribution and a change in the balance of foreign payments. The state is taking less for non-productive purposes; less is going to non-productive classes as far as expenditures abroad or consumer imports are concerned; and *nothing* is going to payments on foreign debts or profits on foreign capital invested in our industry. If we add together all of these sums, minus the increased consumption in natural form, we get the increased fund of effective demand within the country that has resulted from the October Revolution.

The reader will probably have noticed already that I am referring to an increase of domestic effective demand that by no means equals the entire reduction of parasitic consumption or of revenues going to the state budget. The point is that the country's consumption budget – the budget for the exchange of commodities within the country – and the expenditure budgets of individual classes, are two quite different things from the viewpoint of the distribution of national income. If, shall we say, the peasant does not pay rent to the landlords, and if the entire country pays much less into the budget of parasitic classes or for maintenance of the state, this does not mean that elimination of these non-productive expenditures involves an equivalent increase of the country's domestic effective demand. It is true that the nobility, the bourgeoisie and the state bureaucracy also consumed, but they did so only at the expense of workers and peasants. When one and the same sum of domestic effective demand, which is being satisfied by domestic production, is divided one day between five classes and the next day between three, the demand of the three increases but the entire country's demand can remain unchanged. In terms of the material exchange between town and country, in terms of the proportionality of the commodity volumes of industry and agriculture and the proportions in distribution of the productive forces, what is important is not simply the removal of parasitic incomes but rather elimination of the part of those incomes spent either outside the country *or else within the country but on consumer goods imported from abroad.*

In order to make especially clear, in terms of the issue under consideration, all the specific features of this precise moment in our economy's development, I shall summarise and clarify with a numerical example; the figures may be arbitrary, but they are generally close to reality.

Let us take a pre-war year when gross output was close to today's, say a year with production worth 18 billion pre-war roubles. Of these 18 billion, suppose that 6 billion go to restore constant capital; 1 billion goes to accumulation, and 250 million of this accumulation sum flow abroad; 1.5 billion go to the state apparatus (after deducting the personal consumption of state employees) and to payments abroad; the peasants consume 7 billion; workers and craftsmen consume 1.5 billion; and the non-productive classes consume 1.5 billion.[5] Now, consider the same volume of production under Soviet conditions. What will the difference be in terms of the exchange of this mass of commodities? 1) Of the 2 billion worth of consumption by the parasitic classes, the part spent to import consumer items from abroad, or what the bourgeoisie and nobility spent abroad, will be freed up; 2) another sum will be freed up that was connected with the state's payments on foreign debts and with a number of other expenditures by the old state apparatus that no longer exist for the new system of the Soviet state; 3) and finally, there is the surplus value of foreign capitalists. If we suppose that all of these released sums come to 1.5 billion, then the peasantry increases its consumption in natural form by this amount, and the country's exports of agricultural products decrease accordingly. The workers, since they have more to spend, increase their demand for both rural and urban products. The peasantry, given normal conditions for realising their production, increase their demand for industrial commodities with the same proportions of industrial and agricultural production as prevailed before the war. And that is the source of the prolonged goods famine that results even when exports of rural products are significantly reduced compared to the pre-war figure.

Accordingly, even if all other economic conditions were the same as before the war, i.e., if we first and foremost still had the pre-war import of capital being invested each year in industry and transport, even then, given the changed character of the national income distribution and a halt to the flow of values out of the country, we would still have the goods famine due to the inadequate

---

5   [These figures in fact add up to 18.5 billion rather than 18, but that discrepancy does not affect the point that Preobrazhensky is making in this example.]

development of industry. And what can we say about the current situation, when there is almost no import of foreign capital into the country apart from an extremely insignificant inflow of concessions capital? If, therefore, we add this second cause – i.e., the liquidation of capital imports – to the previously mentioned cause of the goods famine, the disproportionality between industry and agriculture will be all the more striking.

It is true that the reduction of parasitic demand has been partly offset in recent years by an accumulation of circulating resources by the trading apparatus, and this has relatively decreased the intensity of the additional worker-peasant demand. But this increased accumulation of circulating capital in trade must eventually return to normal limits.

In the most abbreviated terms, these are the considerations that lead us to claim that the current tempo of accumulation in industry, that is, the tempo of expanded reproduction, is completely inadequate compared to the additional domestic market that the October Revolution created for us in circumstances where the import of foreign capital has ceased. The realisation of this domestic market is becoming all the more noticeable the closer the entire economy approaches to the level of pre-war production with the pre-war proportions between industry and agriculture. *This additional demand now has and will continue to have the same effect as if before the war, say, tsarist Russia had acquired an extensive new agrarian territory that represented additional demand for products coming from the industry of that time.*

The conclusions from what I have been saying are clear. If we do not follow the line of least resistance, i.e., an abrupt increase in the import of means of consumption from abroad (which, by the way, can be done without upsetting the equilibrium of our trade balance, but only to the detriment of importing means of production), if we do not convert the line of the greatest NEP pressure into the line of the least socialist resistance, then we have to acknowledge that 1) the projected expansion of industry is inadequate; 2) the budget allocations for industry are inadequate and, I would say, even scandalously meagre for a socialist state; 3) the financial plan for the renovation of fixed capital, and especially the financial plan for construction of new factories, is inadequate and lagging behind the tempo of development of the whole national economy.

On the basis of everything I have said, I can firmly predict that the inadequacy of our industrial development, the inadequacy of its accumulation of new capital, and its lack of correspondence to the development of agriculture, will be recognised by everyone as a perfectly obvious fact. And I very much fear that when this fact is universally recognised, there will be people among us who will recommend a way out of the situation precisely *along the line of least resistance*; they will not propose more intensive accumulation in our industry at the expense of the country's whole economy, or satisfying domestic demand with the output of our own industry, but instead an abrupt increase in the import of means of consumption from abroad in the form of a permanent system of relations between our economy and world capitalism. Every worker will understand that this will definitely be a system for undermining socialist industry.

E.A. Preobrazhensky,
'Ekonomicheskie zametki: O tovarnom golode', in *Pravda*, 1925, 15 December.

CHAPTER 5

Economic Notes: On the Consequences of the Goods Famine[1]

In my [previous] article on the goods famine,[2] I discussed the long-term causes that bring about the goods famine. Now we shall focus on the consequences of the goods famine, the problem of equilibrium in our economy, and the question of what economic course is dictated to us by the present economic situation.

In an economy with commodity-money exchange, a disruption of equilibrium in the distribution of productive forces is first of all apparent in the sphere of prices. With the goods famine, which we are now experiencing for a second year, this disproportion in the economy is likewise expressed in the sphere of prices, although in our economic system the price movement has its own unique features. Before dealing with these unique features in the movement of prices, which are connected with the distinctive structure of this economy, we ask ourselves the following question. Suppose we did not have the socialisation of industry and transport in our country – how would equilibrium [then] be reached in an economic system with a goods famine for industrial commodities, i.e., with insufficient industrialisation of the country?

On the basis of the law of value's operation, equilibrium would be reached as follows. A long-term price rise for industrial commodities would have to lead to increased imports of the necessary commodities on the one hand, and to a redistribution of the productive forces between town and country on the other hand, including an inflow of new capital into the branches with insufficient production of commodities. Thus, on the basis of the law of value's operation, there would be a purely spontaneous adjustment of production to the country's increased effective demand.

But in our conditions, with our nationalised industry, achievement of equilibrium in the foregoing manner is impossible. We ourselves are the managers of our own industry, and if we do not ensure the necessary scale of accumula-

---

1 Article by E.A. Preobrazhensky published in the journal *Bol'shevik*, No. 6, 1926.

2 *Pravda*, 15 December, 1925. By the way, in a feuilleton published in *Pravda* as his own opinions, comrade Guloyan presented to readers all the main conclusions of my first article without mentioning the source; most importantly, he presented them as a polemic against the main point of my feuilleton. I invite comrade Guloyan to ask someone with literary experience what we normally call such behavior.

tion within it in a planned way, we ourselves sustain the goods famine. On the one hand, by nationalising industry we limit the operation of the law of value in the state economy; on the other hand, we are not replacing the operation of this law with the required rate of planned socialist accumulation, i.e., we are not ensuring, on the basis of a consciously planned policy, the kind of distribution of labour power and material resources within the country that can secure economic equilibrium. In such circumstances, we do not eliminate the activity of the law of value but instead create conditions in which this law assumes the most misshapen and ruinous form for us. In the sphere of private trade, i.e., first and foremost in the sphere of retail and wholesale-retail trade, the prices on scarce commodities rise sharply, but this price rise does not spontaneously lead to a redistribution of the country's productive forces in the interest of its industrialisation, only to rapid accumulation in the sphere of private capital. Private capital raises prices to the limits of effective demand and flourishes from the economic disproportion.

Consequently, inadequate accumulation in industry and a tempo of expanded reproduction that is too slow inevitably lead to a fall in the purchasing power of our money in a particular sphere of commodity circulation. But the decline of the currency, apart from this cause, is also associated with two other causes that must be analysed, for otherwise it is extremely difficult to understand the economic difficulties that we are experiencing. These causes are the following.

By reducing the single agricultural tax, we disrupted the balance of payments between town and country to the benefit of the latter. On its own, this reduction was bound to have noticeable consequences in the sense of a relative increase of monetary resources being left within the peasant economy. Added to this are the circumstances, first, that 1925 was a year of good harvest; second, that during this year we had a general expansion of the sown acreage; third, that the peasantry continued to increase production of technical crops and industrial raw materials in general; fourth and finally, that prices began to rise in the private economy. As a result, the countryside, given the inadequate supply of industrial commodities in the market, received more money than it could spend. The balance of payments between town and country turned out to be an imbalance. With normal currency conditions, this would necessarily lead to increased paper-money accumulation in the countryside. The peasantry would accumulate money for future purchases, deposit its excess cash in state savings banks, etc. But with a falling currency and even one that is merely fluctuating, they resist accumulating money for reasons that are quite understandable. To sell 100 poods of grain for 100 roubles, put the 100 roubles in the savings bank and after a year have 104 roubles, including the interest, means – if grain prices are rising – that after a year the 104 roubles will possibly buy only 90 or 80 poods of grain. In that sort of market situation, it is better for the peasant to sacrifice some percentage of the grain to the mice and rats than to be tempted by 4% on their cash deposits in a savings bank.

Moreover, grain prices last spring were sharply higher than in the autumn of 1924. The peasant who sold grain at limited prices in the autumn clearly lost out compared to his neighbour who hung on to the grain and sold it for twice the price in the spring. All year long the poor man's wife nagged at him for his 'mismanagement' and 'inability to trade', pointing out how his neighbour withheld the grain and sold it for twice as much. There is no doubt that the memory of all that left a strong imprint on the peasant psychology, and this year the countryside will be very cautious in trading grain, expecting that prices will be higher in the spring. All of this reduced the peasants' accumulation of paper money to a minimum. The village understands perfectly well that when prices are climbing it is more profitable to hold surpluses in commodities than in money, and that cash surpluses are only better when prices are falling and the 100 roubles set aside in January 1925 will buy more commodities in January 1926. It is quite obvious that with the current conditions, i.e., with the halt to paper-money accumulation in the villages, all of the plans for using this accumulation in the interest of industry are also crumbling for at least a year.

The second cause of our currency's instability is the mistake committed by Narkomfin in the issue of paper money. If we take the volume of currency circulation at the end of 1924 and compare it with the end of 1925, we see that the increase in overall circulation was 70%, while during the same time period production by our state industry hardly increased by 40%, and the entire commodity circulation by even less. Obviously, this also led to inflation. And if the exchange rate of the chervonets fell by only 8% during this period, in terms of the average wholesale and retail indices, that only demonstrates how stable our currency is in general and how slowly it responds to the experiments being done with it.

It is clear from what I have been saying that there was more than enough reason for the decline of our currency. Now we have to consider what was unique about the price movement that we mentioned earlier. Assume, as a result of all the reasons mentioned, that we have 15% more money in circulation than the minimum required. In that case, how can currency equilibrium be achieved without taking artificial measures to reduce the quantity of money circulating within the country? Following a spontaneous route, this usually happens on the basis of a price increase for all commodities *at every* stage of commodity circulation. If the commodity turnover in the country remains unchanged, then an increase of all prices by 15%, and thus a fall in the purchas-

ing power of all the money in circulation, will result exactly in the establishment of currency equilibrium. The whole money supply is devalued to exactly
the extent by which it exceeds the minimum required for circulation. But with
us this whole process occurs through unique forms that are exceedingly costly
for the state economy. The wholesale prices of our trusts remain fixed, with
the consequence that on the territory of the state economy no spontaneous
establishment of currency equilibrium occurs. *But the entire process is thereby
transferred artificially to the private economy,* where the movement of prices
remains beyond our regulation or else we regulate those prices only to a negligible extent. The private economy is thereby left to achieve currency equilibrium through raising prices; in other words, *we give the private economy an
exclusive monopoly on these increases.* In the private economy, prices rise for
grain and for those types of industrial materials over which we have little regu-
latory control, and the private economy receives more in terms of paper money
for its entire output. Conversely, the state economy sells its whole output at
fixed prices, i.e., for a fixed total sum. This means that the balance of payments
between the state economy and the private economy sharply changes to the
benefit of the private economy and to the disadvantage of the state economy.

It is also perfectly obvious that with this sort of market conjuncture, not only
does the state economy as such lose out, but the workers and state employees do so as well insofar as they buy food products on the free market. Consequently real wages decline, and when we implement planned wage increases
they in fact succeed only in preserving the former minimum real wage.

· · ·

What are the conclusions that follow from these circumstances for our economic policy?

Here we must distinguish between measures of a *purely conjunctural character* that we must take in the very near future, and measures that involve the
general line of our economic policy calculated over a long period of time.

As far as current measures are concerned, we must first of all take care to
compensate the state economy for all its losses due to the falling currency. We
must correct the payments imbalance in the interest of the state economy,
return to it what it has lost, and secure it against future losses. Realistically,
we can imagine two basic methods by which to accomplish this goal: first,
a tax increase on the private economy, which, of course, is most difficult to
implement; and secondly, an increase of our trusts' wholesale prices for the
commodities of mass consumption that involve the most severe shortages and
provide the greatest profit to private capital. However undesirable the latter

operation may be, it is the only way out of the situation if we wish to limit the accumulation of private capital and stop the outflow of values from the state economy into the private economy. Of course, this means a price increase that cannot be reflected in a further increase of retail prices. On the other hand, this is the only way we shall be able to acquire the necessary resources to compensate the working class for what it has lost due to price increases in private trade and to guarantee it a definite real wage level for the future.

As for measures of a long-term character, here we must clearly and firmly take up the task of reaching a level of accumulation in state industry that guarantees equilibrium throughout the entire economic system. For the coming economic year, we must construct our state budget so that industry is *first and foremost* assured the necessary resources for the portion of new construction that it cannot guarantee with its own resources. Our budget must be the budget of a *socialist* state, i.e., the interests of socialist accumulation must be in the forefront.

Secondly, we have to implement a policy of wholesale pricing by the trusts that will guarantee socialist accumulation from this direction. With a stable currency, this will initially mean stabilisation of wholesale prices, followed by cautious reductions that must not under any circumstances impede establishment of the necessary proportion of accumulation or the growth of wages.

Third, we must revise the taxation system in the direction of increasing it and, above all, increase taxes on the well-to-do elements in the countryside. From this point of view, the level of direct taxes proposed by Narkomfin is clearly inadequate.

Fourth, we must begin working at once on an import plan that will fully and completely guarantee the import of all the equipment that industry requires for the current year together with all necessary materials. *Only after all the demands of industry are totally satisfied* can we talk about fulfilling other claims through the import plan.

If we do not guarantee all of these urgent measures – and the crying need for them is evident in the goods famine – we shall not only fail to eliminate shortages next year, but 1926 will also prepare the elements of a goods famine for 1930. We must understand that we are lagging terribly in terms of new construction. Within a year we shall already be unable to increase our metallurgical output by using the equipment of the old factories. Meanwhile, new factories will not be able to generate output for at least three years if we begin their construction immediately. The socialisation of industry and transport is not something to joke about. If we restrict or eliminate the law of value as the spontaneous regulator of capitalist production, we must replace it with planned socialist accumulation *in proportions that are dictated to us by the whole eco-*

nomy of the country. The idea that we might restrict our capital expenditures and develop light industry more intensively is a reactionary utopia. This idea is mainly nourished by analogy with 1921, i.e., with a period when our industry had hardly begun to recover from an unprecedented breakdown. When a man is lying on the ground and has to get up, the question of whether he should lean first on one hand or one foot makes some sense. But once he is up and moving at full speed, you do not recommend to him that he move the left foot more quickly than the right one unless he is lame or paralytic. Yet people are recommending that today's industry, which is moving at full speed, should move one foot, i.e., light industry, more quickly than the other, i.e., more quickly than heavy industry. That kind of advice is either economic illiteracy – which is easier to ridicule than refute – or else it conceals some other kind of secret thoughts. Such secret thoughts can only be the following.

If our agriculture is posing effective demand that exceeds the productive capacity of our industry, then with the given level of accumulation it is only possible to achieve equilibrium by increasing the import of finished consumer goods, i.e., by following the line of least resistance. This is not a path for industrialising the country; it is *the path of linking our effective demand for consumer goods to foreign industry.* If we accept long-term postponement of any sufficiently rapid industrialisation of the country; if we are prepared to accept prolonged and systematic under-development of our heavy industry; if we are going to be content with a long-term deficit in the area of socialist accumulation; if we are stubbornly going to close our eyes to the economic and political danger of such a position – then it makes sense to talk about a more rapid development of light industry and a moderate rate of capital construction. But in that case we must have the courage to foresee all of the consequences that follow from such a path of development for our economy.

With the growth of our harvests and export potential, we shall inevitably face such pressure from the private economy on our customs system and our monopoly of foreign trade (i.e., on the barriers that we erect to paralyse the operation of the world economy's law of value) that our artificial obstacles will be completely shattered and our import plan will be constructed not in accordance with a plan for industrialising the country but instead like Trishkin's caftan,[3] so that patches in the form of imports of consumer goods will grow from year to year.[4] We concede that such a line in economic policy has its own

---

3   [In a popular fable by I.A. Krylov, Trishkin repairs a hole in his caftan by cutting off material from another part of the caftan, creating another hole to be repaired. A comparable English expression would be 'robbing Peter to pay Paul'.]

4   [There is an obvious misprint here in the text, which says 'patches in the form of *exports* of

rationale, but it bears no relation to decisions by the XIV Party Congress concerning the programme for industrialisation. It is dictated by petty-bourgeois pressure on the economic policy of the proletarian state. This line is leading us in exactly the direction that the capitalist countries want from us: it means liquidation of the foreign trade monopoly, liquidation of socialist protectionism, inclusion of the USSR in the system of the world division of labour on the basis of the operation of the world law of value, and *preservation of Europe's existing level of industrialisation through increasing the relative agrarianisation of our country*. The party must resolutely and categorically reject not only this kind of economic policy – should anyone quite consciously propose it – but also any policy of wavering from side to side and of opportunism on the issue of industrialisation, which *unconsciously* leads to the same objectively inevitable result.

At this point I would like to turn to my objections to comrade Stetsky's feuilleton on 'Economic Difficulties', which was published in *Pravda* on 6 February of this year. There are many valuable points in comrade Stetsky's feuilleton, but there is no clear distinction made between today's conjunctural tasks and the central problem of our economic policy over a long period of time. Likewise, in his explanation of the causes for the economic difficulties that we are experiencing, comrade Stetsky makes no clear distinction between the consequences of economic disproportions and those resulting from currency fluctuations. At the same time, comrade Stetsky's article is a typical example of the policy of balancing between two stools.

Comrade Stetsky thinks the fundamental cause for the emergence of today's economic difficulties is 'the complexity of the task of establishing and groping for the correct relations between the socialist nucleus of our economy and the petty-bourgeois environment, between large-scale state industry and the peasant economy'.

Exactly what concrete mistake did we make in the matter of 'groping for the correct relations between large-scale state industry and the peasant economy'? To that question, comrade Stetsky answers as follows:

> In our analysis of the current situation we cannot possibly ignore our autumn, or more accurately, our summer 'miscalculation', since it played no small role in the emergence of the difficulties that we now face .... There is no denying that at the basis of the current difficulties is the dis-

---

consumer goods will play a growing role from year to year'. What Preobrazhensky clearly has in mind is that *imports* of consumer goods would be increasing from year to year.]

proportion between industry and agriculture. But we also must not forget the role that our grain procurement policy has played in intensifying this disproportion ....*Any attempt to circumvent this fact is an attempt to evade recognition and analysis of our errors by reverting to generalised and pointless discussions about the disproportion between industry and agriculture.*

There is no question that our autumn blunder had a very damaging effect on our economic construction, particularly in terms of weakening the currency, since the volume of currency issues was calculated on the basis of an unwarranted assumption concerning the commodity turnover. One of the conclusions that must be drawn from this is that Narkomfin's policy on currency issuance must be discussed five times more carefully by all the planning organs than has been the case to date. But all of this refers to only one aspect of the problem, which does not happen to be the most important. The goods famine in our country was already obvious *before the autumn blunder*, which means that diverting the focus of attention to this recent concrete miscalculation amounts to an attempt at 'evading recognition' of some other mistake that *preceded* the one in the autumn. And this brings us to the general need for a strict distinction between conjunctural miscalculations and more fundamental blunders that have more protracted and profound consequences. Under-estimation of the growth of effective demand from the peasantry and the cities was that sort of error. This under-estimation occurred as early as 1923/24, and in the area of economic policy it led to the slogan 'Industry, do not rush ahead', which in practice entailed systematic under-accumulation in industry. Consequently, the fundamental miscalculation, with which all of our economic difficulties are mainly connected, was made not in the autumn of 1925 but throughout 1924. In 1925 we simply reaped the harvest of this initial miscalculation, which still persists and for which, apparently, there are no volunteers willing to accept any responsibility. And this means that in the debates of 1923–24, and in subsequent arguments on the same topics within the planning organs, it was the 'industrialists' who proved to be absolutely correct – not those who dreamed of achieving a *smychka* with the peasantry through industrial under-production.

It is true that comrade Stetsky does not deny the role of the disproportion between industry and agriculture. In the passage that I have quoted, he writes in one place that we must not 'deny' and in another that we must not 'forget'. Two 'must nots': we must not fail to recognise, and we must not fail to own up. But does that not mean, comrade Stetsky, that you yourself must confess that you were mistaken in the fundamental debate with the industrialists in 1923–24? Is it not obvious that if we had prepared in 1924 the elements for increased production of commodities to meet peasant demand in 1925, even if only in the amount of 70 or 80 million roubles more than we now have, we could have bought 70 million more poods of grain from the peasants and shipped 100 million more poods abroad? Is it not obvious that we might have avoided being compelled to reduce our imports of industrial equipment, to curtail production and to lay off workers in branches connected with imports of foreign materials?

Comrade Stetsky formulates one of our impending tasks in the area of economic policy as follows: '*The only correct and acceptable course for us is to aim for a general reduction of domestic prices and stabilisation of the chervonets*', I agree completely with this line of economic policy insofar as it is a question of formulating our programmatic tasks in the area of the economy. But comrade Stetsky's formulation, while it is generally true, provides no answer whatever to the concrete question of the present day: If the state economy has already lost, as I suspect, at least 100 million roubles through the decline of the currency, and if the real wage level has fallen due to the rise of prices in the private economy, from what sources does comrade Stetsky propose to cover the payments imbalance between the state economy and the private economy, a deficit *that is already a fact*? In comrade Stetsky's article we find no answer to this question. Meanwhile, it is not a question of speaking out in favour of a stable currency and a price reduction, but of *practically demonstrating how, with inadequate socialist accumulation, we can have a stable currency and a normal retail markup on the wholesale prices of the trusts.*

After some delay, comrade Stetsky discovers America: we can make use of peasant accumulation not through issuing currency but instead through the development of peasants' savings deposits, using these peasant savings to provide credits to industry. The author of these lines wrote about that theme as early as 1922. There is absolutely no dispute about using peasant accumulation. But instead of telling us about marvellous possibilities for the future, let comrade Stetsky tell us how to ensure, with a fluctuating currency and in the absence of peasant accumulation in the form of paper, the necessary accumulation in industry for expansion of production and for the required capital expenditures. After all, it is quite clear to everyone that any plan to supply industry with the necessary resources on the basis of using peasant accumulation and new currency issues, *for this year at least, has collapsed* insofar as it meant reverting to these methods of financing industry at the cost of reducing budgetary allocations and accumulation within industry itself. But even a failed plan, which was based on great optimism regarding the private economy and great pessimism regarding the state economy – however rotten a plan it might have been – was at least a plan. That plan must be replaced by something; it must be replaced by a suggestion of fully concrete measures, not by dreams of how well we will use peasant accumulation, at some future time, to provide credits for industry.

I must also deal with the part of comrade Stetsky's article where he talks about the development of heavy industry. Today, there is a rather widespread opinion among us to the effect that greater allocations to capital expenditures for state industry are an important cause of the country's intensifying goods famine. In place of empty comments on this theme, I tried to calculate how much in the way of tradeable commodities our industry has withdrawn from the market for its capital expenditures. It turned out that in fulfilling the plan for capital expenditures of 800 million roubles, during 1925/26 we would have taken tradeable commodities from the market amounting in total to about 5 % of the general commodity turnover. That is what the whole force of the argument amounts to concerning the unsustainability of our capital construction. On this question comrade Stetsky writes: 'Development of heavy industry is the precondition for development of light industry. But we cannot squander all of our resources on the development of heavy industry'. No one is suggesting such economic ignorance as 'squandering all our resources' on heavy industry. *What we need is proportional development of both heavy and light industry.* At the same time, however, we urgently need capital construction for the struggle against a future goods famine and for reducing prices on the basis of technically re-equipping our industry. The point is that we must reconcile these two tasks, not slide into a position of opportunism and marking time in the matter of industrialising the country. For the sake of clarity, it would have been much better if comrade Stetsky had directly answered the question: What figure does he support for capital construction? Is it one that anticipates future liquidation of the goods famine or one that perpetuates and intensifies it?

Allow me to summarise. In comrade Stetsky's article there are many true ideas of a mainly academic character, but they are not accompanied by any understanding – or more accurately, even any acknowledgement – of the fundamental error of our economic policy, which has resulted in the inadequate scale of socialist accumulation and therefore also an inevitable aggravation of the goods famine. In this connection, the line of economic policy recommended by comrade Stetsky, as well as his damaging suggestions on specific issues, represents *continuation of the policy of inadequate accumulation* (which becomes more dangerous for us the longer it continues), and it means the beginning of a policy of cautious retreat from the decision of the XIV party congress on the industrialisation of the country.

Without wishing to be a prophet, I am tempted by way of conclusion to offer a prediction. The author of these lines, to judge from past example, will probably be accused of under-estimating one thing, over-estimating another, and again under-estimating a third, in short, of a deviation. In present circumstances that is inevitable. By way of justification, however, I want to say the following. For economic policy makers such as comrade Stetsky, my 'deviation' is desperately necessary. They are always seeking a refuge for their line between the stools. But in order to sit between stools, there must be at least two stools, which means at least two deviations. One deviation is the agrarian one, which has more or less been provided for them both formally and in fact. Now they need to find a second one in fact or else dream it up. Then everything will be in order: their overalls will be ready for them, sewn out of two deviations that obscure the truth of the Golden Mean. Then they will be ready to formulate and justify an arithmetical average and to distribute an appropriate number of kicks to the right and the left.

The only trouble is that the goods famine in the country will continue ....

E.A. Preobrazhensky,
'Ekonomicheskie zametki [O posledstviyakh tovarnovo goloda]'
in Bol'shevik, 1926, No. 6, 31 March, pp. 60–9.

CHAPTER 6

Address from E.A. Preobrazhensky in Debates on the Report from V.P. Milyutin on 'Perspectives of Economic Development in the USSR (Gosplan's Control Figures)'[1]

Comrade Preobrazhensky. First a personal question. Comrade Dvolaitsky cited a book whose author, he said, is a utopian and he did not want to name him. Some of those present think that I am the author. I assure you that I am not the author of that book.

Comrades, I shall begin with what comrade Dvolaitsky had to say here. He framed the question as follows: of course, it would be desirable to tax the well-to-do strata in the countryside, and perhaps something can be done in that regard, but in the first place it would be very, very little, and the main thing is that this is dangerous because such a measure will immediately affect the attitude of the middle peasant to Soviet power. This operation can only be more or less thoroughly implemented after we have firmly won the middle peasants to the side of Soviet power. My answer to comrade Dvolaitsky is the following. By the time the Soviet authority has finally won over the middle peasant, we shall no longer be having today's sort of debates. Consequently, comrade Dvolaitsky in fact spoke against any additional taxation of well-to-do elements in the countryside.

We must not forget that our state economy is presently experiencing major difficulties due to its shortage of the resources necessary for capital expenditures. When, instead of providing an answer, comrade Dvolaitsky asks: 'What about the middle peasant, what will his attitude be?' – he forgets, comrades, that we are in fact waging a struggle to win over the middle peasant, to win his sympathy. Which would he prefer? Would he prefer additional taxation of the village upper stratum, or instead that the middle peasant, being dissatisfied with the goods famine, joined with the rural upper stratum and found a different system and some other economic policy that would be more satisfactory? We must decide which of these routes is better. Is it the route that involves

---

1 Published in the section headed 'Transcript of reports delivered at the Communist Academy' in the journal *Vestnik Kommunisticheskoi akademii*, No. 17, 1926.

struggle against the goods famine and solving the problem of the middle peasant's discontent, particularly by means of taxing the propertied strata of the village or, to the contrary, a route that refuses this additional accumulation and increases the goods famine from one year to the next to the extent, of course, that it is a consequence of not implementing this measure? The fact is that we face the danger of a discontented middle-peasantry uniting with the well-to-do rural upper strata even as things currently stand. Which is to be preferred?

We also start from a position that is completely beyond dispute and has been confirmed many times by party congresses and by all the research that has been done – that Soviet power is based upon the bloc of the working class with the majority in the countryside. Should this bloc be disrupted by the pressure exerted upon us by world capital, we shall not hold out. To return to this question in its general form amounts simply to chatter over things that are perfectly indisputable. We are concerned with a more immediate question: what *concrete* form must the bloc of workers and peasants assume today? What concrete relation with the different strata of the countryside will allow for the development of industry? What are the necessary capital expenditures, and how much agricultural credit should be extended to whom? That is how the question stands.

Comrade Dvolaitsky provided no answer to this concrete question and simply pointed out how dangerous the situation is when the middle peasant stands up for the interests of the well-to-do in the countryside. (*Comrade Dvolaitsky*: No, he will not be happy himself, be assured.) Comrade Dvolaitsky, you have to answer directly: are you in favour of additional taxation on the rural upper strata or opposed? My answer is straightforward – I am in favour. And I shall prove that it is both possible and necessary. (*From the audience*: What amount are you proposing?) This is not Narkomfin or the tax department of Narkomfin; we are determining the general line of economic policy and must decide whether to adopt a particular approach or not. The question of what figures are involved will be decided in another institution. That is why I am establishing that comrade Dvolaitsky gave no clear and specific answer to the question. I regard his answer as an evasion or, if you prefer, a deviation (*Laughter*) rather than an answer to a clearly posed question.

Furthermore, comrade Dvolaitsky talked about how we must not, in any case, abandon the countryside to plunder by private capital, saying that cooperative trade is less costly and must be supported. Whether cooperatives conduct trade more economically is not the issue: the issue is whether we can afford the luxury of extending a huge volume of resources to the cooperatives in the form of commodities on credit, which means taking resources from production at a time of acute goods famine. That is the question we must answer. We cannot continue with this policy of taking capital from production. Given the inadequate volume of commodities in the country, we gain no advantage by eliminating private capital entirely from commodity circulation. That time will come, comrades, but it will come later.

The sector of private capital in trade, thanks to its relatively lower turnover costs, operates much less expensively than cooperatives when there is an over-supply or saturation of commodities. Lenin said that we must allow capitalist forms in order that they might spur our socialist enterprises. With a sufficient supply of commodities, the ideal situation for us would be to allow the sector of private capital to play a subordinate role that would pose no threat. But how do things stand just now? At the present moment our task is to have the state with-draw from year to year a part of what it has invested in cooperative trade and replace it with private contributions from the peasantry. Cooperation works with contributions from the peasantry. We currently have a situation here that is completely abnormal. If you take Gosplan's figures and other official data on the question of whose resources the cooperatives work with when serving the countryside, whether they are agricultural or consumer cooperatives, you will see that up to now they work mainly with our state resources. The resources actually provided by the population are negligible. At the same time, we have more and more grain supplies and money being set aside in the villages from year to year. Grain supplies that we need for exports are being set aside. Can anyone object to having the well-to-do elements of the countryside, who use our cooperatives and make purchases in cooperative shops at the expense of the circulating resources that the state has invested in cooperative trade, make a contribution of their own? No, our programme is to mobilise those resources, and we must act much more energetically in this sphere than we do today. Replacement of state resources by the resources of peasants who use our state cooperatives is a clear programme. Anyone who objects to it does not under-stand our fundamental interests in terms of relations with the peasantry and the private economy in general. (*Comrade Dvolaitsky*: Where can they invest? At what interest rate?) Comrade Dvolaitsky, if you want to devote the next ses-sion to more concrete figures, let us do so: you bring yours and I'll provide my own calculations.

Comrade Dvolaitsky said here that we presently take a great deal from the countryside in the form of non-equivalent exchange, and we must not take any more. No one is suggesting that we take more in this form. Our programme aims to reduce this non-equivalence, to reduce prices and bring them closer to the world level. The question is how, at the present time, to distribute the resources available in the country, as registered in all of our statistical data, in such a way as to overcome the goods famine as quickly as possible. All I have to say is that the defect in comrade Dvolaitsky's calculations is that he did not mention how much this non-equivalent exchange is being diminished thanks to reduced taxation by comparison with the pre-war period. (*Comrade Dvolait-sky*: The tax payments are lower by 600 million chervonets roubles. I forgot to mention that.) You said that they overpay by 800 million, but we have forgone 600 million due to overthrowing tsarism and eliminating rent. That means the village overpays by 200 million. And that is not so strange. Generally speaking, though, one should not offer up calculations that overlook a sum of 600 million (*Applause.*)

Now, comrades, I turn to the fundamental issue. Indeed, the whole point is to formulate the problem in a way that is fundamentally correct. Unfortunately, I cannot analyse all of the individual positions taken by comrade Milyutin because his report knocked on the doors of a great many important problems. But he considered those problems very briefly and quite inadequately. And the political conclusions that he ended up with, and which I must answer today, were not substantiated by his previous statements. There are some structures that collapse if you begin to refute them, but they also collapse if you begin to support them. And if other comrades are going to support comrade Milyutin's report, it must still collapse because the economic section of that report in no way confirms his political conclusions.

Take the question of industrialisation. What is industrialisation? In the first place, industrialisation means an increase of industry's share in the total output of the country. In this case we shall be talking about state industry, not industry in general. Secondly, a more rapid increase of the working population employed in state industry compared to overall growth of the employed population. Third, an increase of accumulation in state industry that is more rapid than in the private sector of the economy. Fourth and finally, a capital structure in state industry that ensures from year to year the growing importance of production of means of production and the reproduction of fixed capital. Those, comrades, are the four basic points that must be considered. How does our industrialisation measure up in terms of these four points?

In this context we are not concerned with expressions of belief – that I believe in socialism, I believe in victory and so forth – we all believe in such things, and the working class believes just as much as we do. If we say to the middle peasant: 'Yes, we believe in socialism', he will say: 'Go to hell with your socialism and your beliefs and just give me more commodities'. If we turn to the worker, he will say: 'I believe no less than you do, but manage the economy better'. The issue is [first of all] to provide a concrete answer to all the basic questions about how matters stand with us, and to do so not from a viewpoint of fideism, that is, of beliefs, but from the viewpoint of knowledge and facts. Secondly, we must have a quite definite perspective and a clear view of where a threat might emerge and of what link, as Lenin said, we must take hold of first of all. So, how do matters stand with us in terms of industrialisation? Point one. The share of industry in the whole country's output is growing. That is an indisputable fact. But it also perfectly true that the past year, which was one of utilising old fixed capital, is no indicator of the process of industrialisation. When we reach the pre-war level of production, when all of the old fixed capital has been re-activated, when any increase of production will be based upon the creation of new fixed capital – only then shall we be in a position to say whether industrialisation is advancing and at what speed.

There are comrades here who have gone through Marx's *Capital* and know perfectly well what reproduction means when old fixed capital is being brought back into production and only circulating capital needs to be accumulated, as compared to the time when additional *C* must be freshly accumulated. In the previous period, we were dealing with re-activating old means of production. We accumulated circulating capital, but we did so with enormous disruptions and difficulties. Comrade Smilga correctly pointed out that the period we have been passing through involves the small affairs of the Revolution. That is true. We can only speak of great work in the sense that, with the greatest self-sacrifice and heroism, and in conditions much worse than before the war as far as wages are concerned, our working class has completed this process so that we are now on the verge of the pre-war level. *This heroism* can be regarded as part of the great work of the Revolution. However, from the economic point of view, this period was simply one of bringing old capital into operation, i.e., it was a period of the Revolution's small economic affairs.

Now we face the fundamental problem of a more rapid growth of the share of state production in the country's overall output. It is a plus for us that in the forthcoming first year of reconstruction our output is growing more rapidly than that of the private economy. Then there is the question of attracting labour power. Comrade Pyatakov has already mentioned that during the past year more than 400 thousand people were brought into large-scale industry; yet the five-year plan of VSNKh, which comrade Dvolaitsky thinks is utopian, anticipates recruiting a total of 500 thousand over the whole of the next five years, whereas we recruited almost that number during the past year alone. Why is that? It is because last year was still part of the period of recovery and therefore was not typical of the new period. Relative to the growth of the whole population, such a slow rate of increase will already be dangerous. Then there is the question of the relation between Departments I and II, to use Marx's terms, i.e., between production of means of production and production of means of consumption. Gosplan's statistics show that in American industry the ratio of production of means of production to production of means of consumption is

61:39. We are making progress in this direction, but it is slow, and in 1924/25 the ratio was 53:47 compared to 56.8:43.2 before the war.

Now I turn to the final question concerning capital expenditures. The situation here is the worst of all. I shall give you figures from Gosplan that no previous speaker has mentioned. A very important fact for us concerns the relative pace of development of private capital accumulation and state capital accumulation. Comrade Trotsky has frequently emphasised that this fact has decisive significance. We cannot close our eyes to what our opponent has accomplished both within the country and abroad. When we compare the tempo of our development with the development of capitalism on a world scale, and with the domestic private economy, this is what we get. During the past year we had an increase of capital investment. If we turn to the table from Gosplan, which shows the percentage increase of the country's capital investment *compared to the existing fixed funds* of the private and state sectors, we see the following picture: on the part of the state, a growth of 1,025 million in the funds for 1925/26 and 1,235.4 million projected for 1926/27; in the private economy, 626.8 million and 764.4 million. Compared to the past year, this means that next year will bring a 20% increase of fixed capital funds in the state sector and 21.9% in the private sector. In absolute figures, our funds in 1925/26 were 25,816 million, while the private funds were 26,033 million. For the past three years, however, growth in the private sector was so great that our growth in 1926/27 will only partially make up for the lag of the past three years (*Control Figures*, pp. 311–13 and 120). This is precisely why comrade Pyatakov paid such serious attention to this part of his speech. This is where the greatest threat lies.

Summarising, we can see how matters stand with industrialisation. We have only begun to industrialise, and the most important point – the point of capital expenditures – is the weakest. If we allow ourselves to fall behind at this point, it means the goods famine will carry over and accumulate from one year to the next; in fact, it means closing our eyes to all the dangers and difficulties that lie ahead of us rather than being fully conscious of these dangers and discussing the measures that we need to implement. We are not protesting against belief in the success of socialism but against a frivolous attitude towards the problem of capital expenditures. We must protest against cheap and childish or bureaucratic optimism and demand the most serious evidence that things are going well in this respect.

Now, comrades, I turn to the next point. We have an extremely unfavourable relation between our economy and the world economy. If you look at the section of Gosplan's booklet entitled 'The USSR and the World Economy', you will find there a table of world prices compared to our own average prices (p. 158). Look at the table that deals with the relation of industrial prices. The result, according to the overall index, is that our goods are 30% more expensive (29% to be exact). But when we discuss the *smychka*, we have to address the question of our *industrial prices*. The pre-war coefficient was such that one had to pay 64 roubles abroad for the same quantity of production that cost 100 roubles in our country. The ratio was 64:100. Now the ratio is 42:100. Here, comrades, is where the greatest danger of our whole situation is to be found, a danger that increases every year as our contact with the world economy increases. There is danger here for all of our plans. We are becoming included in the world economy. Every year, comrades, we are experiencing more and more pressure from world prices.

On the other hand, we currently have emergence in the countryside of the kulak stratum and a stratum of capitalist farmers, of the well-to-do peasantry, who exercise a very strong influence on the rural masses when it comes to judging our relations with the world economy. These strata are the non-commissioned officers of capitalism, and they now have a better understanding of international economic relations. This well-to-do peasant, who is cultivating his plot better by hiring seasonal rather than permanent labour etc., has already made himself an object of considerable attention from our Narkomzem.[2] These elements, comrades, understand the situation very well – better than the middle peasants. They are the ones calling first for a peasants' union, and secondly for abolition of the monopoly of foreign trade.

We must keep in mind that for the moment we have fenced ourselves off from the world economy; we have artificially fenced off our territory. We have tied our domestic market to our own industry, which trades very expensively. That is where the danger lies. We must gradually get out of this situation. But how? With a victory, not a capitulation. This is our whole problem at the present moment. If we are slow to industrialise, to alleviate the goods famine, to reduce the difference between our prices and world prices, we shall accumulate peasant discontent from year to year, and the more cultured and conscious strata in the countryside will give it ideological expression. We are approaching the moment when this wall that we have built to fence ourselves off from the world economy will be under pressure not just from world capital, whose effects we feel every day, but also from the other direction. Pressure will increase from the upper strata in the village, who will drag the middle peasants along as well. The wall may be breached: that is the danger that threatens our survival.

When the ratio of foreign prices to our prices is 42:100; when we take into account that our ruling proletariat numbers 5–6 million compared to 22 mil-

---

2 [Commissariat of Agriculture.]

lion peasant households; when we remember that every point up for discussion in foreign trade agreements is more difficult to defend than it was before; if we remember that it was comparatively easy for us to complete the recovery process in circumstances that were politically much more favourable for us than they are now, i.e., when world capital was covered with unhealed wounds from the world war and temporarily left us in peace, when the sort of situation prevailed that Lenin spoke of when he said that the struggle between the capitalist countries temporarily gives us the opportunity to survive until we gather our internal strength – when we recall all of this, it is time to think about what particular features a new period will bring. The period that I have been talking about is coming to an end. We are entering a period when we shall face new difficulties and when industrialisation is becoming the problem of our struggle to survive.

Such is the world situation in which we must solve the problem, including elimination of our goods famine. To think, in such a situation, that we can somehow solve all of these domestic questions without looking abroad at our main enemy means failure to understand the most important aspect of our situation, failure to understand the new phase of our relation with the peasantry. With every passing year, the survival of the USSR becomes more and more unbearable to foreign capitalists. Anyone who has been abroad knows how the capitalists' attitude towards us has changed. That is the context in which we must solve the problem of industrialisation. Hence also the problem of tempo.

In this context we cannot say that we will build socialism at a snail's pace.[3] That is a fool's approach to the issue, a fool's theory of our development (*Applause*). The seriousness of the situation demands our resolute determination in the area of economic policy. We cannot afford to have a peaceful tea party at the current stage of the revolution. Our enemies will not allow it. We must keep in mind that we are entering a period of grave difficulties. (*From the hall*: You are the one who wants to do something stupid). The question of doing or not doing something stupid is exactly what our entire debate amounts to. Commit fewer stupidities? Right! But if an objective account were drawn up of all the stupidities committed, the results would be very interesting. And I am quite certain, comrades, that such an account would show a surplus in the balance of stupidities for our opponents in today's debate! (*Comrade Dvolaitsky*: Is 10% growth a snail's pace?)

Comrade Dvolaitsky, why are your badgering me with numbers? First of all we must ensure that the 10% happens. After all, you know VSNKh's five-year

---

3   [This was a term used by Bukharin.]

plan, and what does it prove? To double production over five years will require investment through the budget of 400 million roubles a year, not the 107 million projected for the coming year. 107 million – that is the net benefit to industry in terms of the budget. If you deduct what industry pays to the state, that is the ready money that industry is to receive. You can see that even according to the data of this five-year plan, which contributes extremely little in the sense of struggling with the goods famine, we must secure 400 million for industry from the budget. What this means is that in 1926 we already accumulating an enormous deficit of capital expenditures. And what does the five-year plan offer in terms of struggling with the goods famine? Its response to this question will hardly get us beyond the pre-war norm of per-capita consumption. And according to comrade Dvolaitsky, even this five-year plan is a utopia. What realism! But why is there so little growth of the consumption fund? Because our production of means of production must grow more rapidly than production of means of consumption; because we must spend more on capital; because we are importing less and the population is growing. Everyone knows what Marx meant by expanded reproduction. To increase production from 9 thousand (or 9 billion), as in Marx's reproduction schemes, to 10–11 thousand requires an enormous increase in the production of means of production even with a constant level of technology – and more still if the technology is advancing. According to VSNKh's five-year plan, which comrade Dvolaitsky calls utopian, we are making extremely little progress in the sense of raising consumption. Comrade Dvolaitsky asks: what does this figure show, a snail's pace or a quick march?

I don't know. I think the response to this question has to come from the consumer himself, and above all from the working class; let them answer whether they think it is a snail's pace or a rapid tempo if, after five years (including the past year), their consumption of industrial commodities will only be slightly higher than the pre-war level.

Consequently, the question of industrialisation has to be treated with a great deal more seriousness than the way it is presented here by comrades who have tried to defend the position that everything is more or less fine with us and everything that can be done is already being done.

On pp. 124–5 of Gosplan's control figures, you will find that Gosplan has tried to calculate the balance between town and country for last year and for the coming years. What is that balance? We read:

> The difference between total incomes and total expenditures yields a balance that must determine the extent of monetary accumulation in the countryside.

The balance-sheet that we have constructed (see Table 1)[4] shows this balance rising from year to year by a figure in the order of 180–260 million roubles. The continuous growth of this balance indicates the growing shortage of commodities.

Here you see, comrades, the origin of the accumulation that is occurring in the upper strata of the village but not showing up in our savings banks. This is explained by the fact that in terms of the redistribution of national income, what has happened here, to put it mildly, is a misunderstanding; we have made some kind of error. Under capitalism this would be corrected spontaneously. Suppose there is a shortage of industrial commodities under capitalism. That means their prices rise, selling prices rise at the factories and plants, while retail sales cannot expand. Prices for industrial goods would rise to the breaking point – and an inflow[5] of capital into industry would begin, industry's role would grow, which requires new expenditures from the entire national income on the expansion of existing enterprises – and the very fact of such redistribution would permit this growing demand to be satisfied.

We are currently seeing a rise of retail prices for industrial goods. But only we – our nationalised state industry – we alone are able to implement the expansion that can establish a proper relation between all sides in the economic life of the country.

We have to cover the deficit of commodities by increasing production. Yet we are not doing so to the extent required. And insofar as we fail to do so, we ourselves are the factor that is intensifying the goods famine. We are sitting at precisely the point where the law of value would spontaneously lead to a transfer of resources into industry, and we are not implementing a planned redistribution of the national income; we are in fact acting as a brake on the necessary redistribution. As a result, we live in a condition of growing goods famine. This year we have a commodity deficit of 380 million roubles, and Gosplan's figures predict a deficit of 500 million roubles next year. And what will that mean for the growth of retail prices? Once that kind of deficit occurs, there will also be deterioration in the area of value relations. That is why our alarm over this question is so understandable.

Every system exists so long as it satisfies the minimum of social needs. If this system does not satisfy those minimal needs, if we are going to have systematic under-production and inadequate fulfilment of effective demand, this can

---

4   [This refers to the table given by Gosplan in the Control Figures.]
5   [The text speaks of an outflow (*otliv*), but this is clearly a misprint.]

affect the mass mood and lead to what Comrade Lenin often warned us about: the masses will begin to think of a better system that will better satisfy their needs. That is the greatest danger, which accounts for our alarm concerning the size of capital expenditures. In order to avoid being overthrown, and once we have fenced ourselves off from the world economy, we must endeavour first and foremost to close the difference between our prices and world prices. If this dam is breached because of the slow pace of industrialisation, if the monopoly of foreign trade is breached, we will no longer find ourselves included in the world economy on the basis of planned imports, as we are today, and in that case 3/4 of our heavy industry will be eliminated. That is why we are raising all of these problems.

Permit me now, comrades, to turn to the question of what must be done. I have already given a partial response. But I shall begin by quoting something that was put very well in Gosplan's control figures, where we read the following: 'Mistakes made in the sphere of economic policy are often transformed into economic necessity' (p. 9).

So, comrades, since the mistakes that have already made have become an economic necessity, don't ask us for a cure. The issue now is partially to correct the consequences of the mistakes of the past. What can be done in the conjuncture that has formed today? Here we have to say: let us agree on the first and fundamental point, that the level of industrialisation is inadequate if we compare the ratio of our prices to world prices and take into account the accumulation of discontent on the basis of the goods famine and prices. That is the first proposition. Anyone who says the pace of industrialisation is adequate should be expelled from our meeting as a chatterbox. (*Laughter*).

Given inadequate industrialisation, what resources can we find and where might we look for them? To that question we reply as follows. First: a different budget structure for the coming year, different from what we have had previously, so that what industry requires for planned capital expenditures will be worked out not on an annual basis (because our economy has outgrown that kind of formulation) but instead for five years in order that these resources will be guaranteed to industry first of all. Industry comes first, and then everything else. That is the kind of approach to our budget that is required of a socialist state. Any other approach is inconceivable and would contradict the whole situation in which we find ourselves. It would simply mean swimming with the current. When departments demand a certain sum for themselves before everything else, and say that there will be a disaster otherwise, we must not give in. It is impossible now to construct a budget that way. The budget must be compiled so that industry's needs for capital expenditures are the first paragraph on the expenditure side of the budget. In this respect, we have already lost a good deal of time. I am not saying that we can correct this in six months. We have to look ahead several years. According to VSNKh's five-year plan, 400 million roubles is the minimum in terms of budget allocations for new construction. The first point, therefore, is that the state budget must make maximal provision for capital expenditures.

Second: increased taxation of the well-to-do elements in the countryside, to be raised in step with the growing income of these strata. Who will object to this on grounds of principle? No one will object, and if anyone does, he will simply be forgetting what meeting he is attending and the circumstances in which he is speaking. This proposition is also indisputable in principle, i.e., speaking in terms not of figures but of general policy. We know that capitalist accumulation is proceeding in the countryside, that this is a result of the weak influence of our state industry on agriculture and of limited cooperation in production among the rural poor. This means that a thread of economic development that was disrupted by the Revolution, involving the upper strata of our countryside moving towards becoming a stratum of capitalist farmers – this thread has been taken up again by history and is being woven once more. And to the extent that development occurs in this direction – i.e. along a road that is not ours, that is not collective but is also clearly prevalent for the time being – our task is to convert capitalist into socialist accumulation to whatever extent possible.

That, among other things, is what Lenin considered to be necessary when he wrote that we must limit the exploitative tendencies of these prosperous kulak elements and build our own accumulation fund at the expense of theirs. We must implement this programme systematically and on the basis of a well thought-out plan. As long as we cannot eliminate capitalist accumulation in the village, we can still restrict it. But we must not forget for a moment that the elements that are currently improving the economy on a capitalist basis are the elements that are our class enemies. They will try to overthrow us at a favourable moment, but they will not grow into socialism. They will try to over-throw us. As Lenin said, they are dreaming of Cavaignacs and Galliffets,[6] as we have seen in analogous situations in Europe. We know who these people are; they are our enemies. For the present, we cannot replace this type of develop-ment in the countryside with our own socialist type, but within the limits of what is possible we must squeeze out the maximum for industry. That is bey-ond debate. Comrade Dvolaitsky asks for taxation figures. Let's sit down and

---

6   [Louis-Eugène Cavaignac (1802–1857) was the French general who put down a massive rebel-lion by workers in Paris in 1848, known as the June Days Uprising. Gaston Alexandre Auguste, Marquis de Galliffet (1830–1909) was a French general involved in crushing the Paris Com-mune in 1871.]

we will count, but I have no confidence in your calculation of the tax percentage for the wealthy strata. They are masters at hiding their incomes. What will
this measure provide for us? If it yields another 50 million a year, with further
increases, I can show you what these figures will mean for our industry over five
years.

The third point: a gradual withdrawal of industry's circulating capital from
the cooperatives and its replacement with peasant capital. There are difficulties
here. They lie in the fact that the prosperous peasant has no wish to be involved
with our cooperatives because they are not his. He can do without cooperatives.
The difficulty is that the strata who do need cooperatives have no significant
resources, and those who do have resources do not want to join, although they
buy from the cooperative store. Consequently, these strata must be forced to
pay for cooperative services. And as for accumulation by the middle peasant,
the main thing is to try to get this accumulation flowing into the cooperative
channel so that state capital will be replaced mainly by capital from the middle
peasants' own farms. I do not know how much we can acquire from this source
and from the struggle against mismanagement in cooperatives. Our cooperatives are neither state nor social, and neither society nor the state controls
them – they are in a position where the flowers that bloom best are their overhead expenses. In that respect we have a struggle ahead of us. By taking this
route we can squeeze out tens of millions for industry.

The fourth source is pressure on private capital. Comrade Dvolaitsky spoke
here and said that our taxation of the private trader will be shifted onto the
consumer. There are taxes that are transferable comrade Dvolaitsky, but there
are also taxes that are not. If someone present here should call for measures
that will enable us to shave this profit without any risk to the consumer, everyone would sign up. We have no definite policy concerning private capital as
far as curtailing conjunctural profit is concerned. Narkomfin will impose tax
pressure, but that is not enough. That is why we must find another approach
to this question. You say: to put pressure on the kulak is a danger in relation to
the middle peasant; to put pressure on the private trader means he will pass it
on to the consumer. What is to be done? To mark time and manoeuvre, then
make concessions to the petty-bourgeoisie, and then capitulate to their pressure – that, comrade Dvolaitsky, is what I call a *memento mori*[7] for Soviet power!
(*Applause.*)

(*Comrade Dvolaitsky from his seat*: Isn't a law being drafted to increase the
taxation of private capital?)

---

7   [A reminder of inevitable death.]

I think that this law, if it is actually implemented, will give us 20–30 million roubles. But we must not forget that during the past year private capital has reaped a harvest of 300–400 million.

Now for our regime of austerity, or more correctly, the mistakes of our leadership. First of all, we must find savings that will yield tens of millions. We have to demand economies not just from the worker, the employee or the economic administrators. The regime of austerity can yield significant sums for us in comrade Dvolaitsky's opinion – even up to 300 million, which is clearly an exaggeration. But there will, in any event, be certain sums for us.

Now I come to our capital expenditures. We now face the phase in our economic development when we must build new factories and plants, creating a new basis for industry. For the next year we have allocated a little more than 100 million roubles for completely new construction. We have an acute shortage of cast iron. I have made enquiries about three metallurgical plants whose construction is vitally necessary for us since they will help us to overcome the iron shortage that the country is experiencing. How do things stand in this regard? It turns out that construction of these factories was not even begun this year. The resources for them were not allocated. During this year and the coming years we shall be experiencing a cast iron famine. When we speak of 200–300 million roubles for capital construction, this seems to be a trifle in relation to our budget, while in terms of the capital expenditures that would solve the problem of metal, the cart is standing still due to the lack of 30 million for this year. Meanwhile, due to the shortage and in circumstances of scarce foreign currency, we have to import cast iron from abroad.

The measures that we are proposing demand a familiar struggle – a class struggle – first of all with the upper strata in the village that we want to tax. We must make this decision before those elements become politically stronger. In exactly the same way, we must resolve upon a struggle with private capital involving the utmost in resourcefulness and manoeuvring. If we do not agree upon these and other necessary measures, we shall be following the line of least resistance, in other words, the line of inflation. There will be a great temptation to turn to this source, given budget shortages and all the other shortcomings. We have to declare categorically that there is not and cannot be any place for inflation. Inflation for us means a tax on wages – that is the first point; and secondly, inflation in our conditions means a shock to our entire system. It will mean that instead of really struggling with our difficulties, particularly with those strata that are accumulating in the countryside and disrupting our export policy – instead of that struggle we would be taking the line of least resistance and reverting to a measure that is 10 times more dangerous.

Now for the final question concerning the building of socialism in one country. I do not know, comrades, why comrade Milyutin raised this issue or how it is
connected with Gosplan's control figures. But if pleased him to touch upon the
question, allow me to address it in my conclusion. If we have an army in which
the commander-in-chief and the general staff tell the soldiers before a battle
that they may win – but perhaps they will not – such a commander must at the
least be removed and possibly shot. It is another matter if the staff discusses
the difficulties of winning and the possibility of losing, which it is both admissible and necessary for us to do. But that is as far as it goes. It does not involve
sowing doubts among the masses that have to do the building, any more than
among the soldiers before a battle.

We must not close our eyes to the difficulties we face in constructing socialism or behave in practice as if victory were 100 % guaranteed. Posing the issue
that way just sweeps the whole problem aside: each of us knows perfectly well
that we must build, we are building, and we will build socialism. What we do
need to know is that we do not have a long time in which to do so. The well-
to-do peasantry may rise up against us in alliance with world capital, which is
going over to the offensive both economically and in military-political terms.
All we must do in such circumstances is remember that the danger threatening us is great, very great! Are we building socialism in such circumstances?
Our situation is one in which construction can always be interrupted by hostile forces. Consequently, we are building socialism in one country at a definite
historical stage and with the expectation of support from the entire world proletariat (*Applause.*)

I see no contradiction at all between what comrade Sokol'nikov said and
what I have said. We are building socialism now in the circumstances of a
breathing space between two battles. I refer anyone who does not understand
this to the inhabitants of the city of Glupov.[8] (*Applause.*) Our construction is
occurring between two battles, and this must determine our general policy,
our economic policy and the policy of the Comintern. There are some people
who do not understand this. But those who do understand adopt a different
approach to every problem, coming from the view that we are living in a period
before a new battle and that we had better coordinate our struggle to realise
socialism with at least the decisive countries of the West. We must regard this
interval of time, during which we exist in isolation, as the preparatory period
before the next battle. This must have an effect upon every question. Do you

---

8 [In 1870 Mikhail Saltykov-Shchedrin satirised tsarist Russia in *The History of a City*. He named
the city 'Glupov'. The adjective 'glupyi' means 'foolish' or 'stupid'. Glupov was a city of idle and
hypocritical fools.]

really not understand something so elementary? While we are building socialism in our country and arguing over whether it will take 30, possibly 40 or even
all of 50 years, is it worth risking the whole construction effort because of a
quarrel with the well-to-do [peasantry] in the ninth year of [proletarian] dictatorship? Whether we complete the construction five years sooner or later makes
little difference. When people are building socialism with that kind of attitude,
I say: that is the attitude that can destroy Soviet power. That, comrades, is what
we must ultimately understand! (*Applause*). We must be aware that we are living through a particular historical interval that history has allotted to us and
that separates one great October battle and our Civil War from another battle
that will be much greater and much more decisive for the fate of the working
class. Anyone who approaches every problem from this viewpoint will think
differently about many of the questions that have been discussed here so cas-
ually.

To conclude, while I was seated here [in the auditorium] and tossed out a
remark about mental reconstruction in connection with the reconstruction
of our industry, comrade Strumilin replied to me from this rostrum: 'Aren't
you proposing a reconstruction of Leninism'. (*From the hall*: That's right.) In
the first place, I was quite astonished to see comrade Strumilin speaking from
this rostrum as a Leninist.[9] (*A voice*: Correct). (*Applause.*) I was surprised and
delighted because for at least 15 years we have not seen comrade Strumilin in
our ranks. What did we expect from comrade Strumilin? What did this whole
audience expect from him? We expected that he, as a Gosplan worker, would
come and discuss where he disagrees with previous speakers on the cardinal
questions that have been addressed from this platform. But instead he busied
himself with proving that he is a believer and that there are others of little faith.
Really, is that what we wanted to hear from comrade Strumilin? As a member
of the Bolshevik party for 22 years, do I really need to be reminded of Leninism,
especially by comrade Strumilin?

As far as mental reconstruction is concerned, that is something that is absolutely necessary. Comrades, we have entered a new period. Without this mental
reconstruction, the reconstruction of our economy will proceed more slowly
than is objectively possible due to the potential inherent in our system. I regard
our meeting here in the Academy as an attempt by the collective reason of all
members of our party to think through this new period. On the one hand, it
threatens us with grave dangers. At the same time, however, the victory that can
be won in this second battle, in a wider arena than our own country, will be a

---

9   [S.G. Strumilin was a former Menshevik.]

decisive victory for the fate of humankind. In the course of today's discussion,
I believe we must set out and concentrate our attention on the fundamental
problems of a new period for our economy; we must put aside political attacks
and sorties (*From the hall*: Correct) apart from those that arise from the material of the discussion itself. As far as the political attacks made against me are
concerned, I shall respond to them elsewhere, not here.

Vestnik Kommunisticheskoi akademii
Moscow, 1926, No. 17, pp. 223–36.

CHAPTER 7

Economic Notes: Gosplan's Control Figures and Our Economic Tasks (Written during or after October 1926)

Gosplan's control figures for 1926/27, as well as the discussion of economic issues, have placed before the party and the working class a number of fundamental questions concerning our economic reality on the one hand, and a number of the most important questions concerning the economic policy of the state [on the other]. All of these problems must be considered and resolved in one manner or another at the forthcoming all-Union Party Congress. It will be useful, therefore, to bring together all of these fundamental questions that we are currently struggling with and to summarise some results of the discussions concerning them.

1   The Goods Famine

The gross output of all our industry – large and small, state and private – increased from 9,996 million in 1925 to 14,015 million in 1925/26 and is expected to be 15,858 million chervonets roubles in 1926/27. The corresponding commodity components of production for these three years are the following:

	1924/25	1925/26	1926/27
Industry	5,530 million roubles	8,000 million roubles[a]	9,200 million roubles
Agriculture	4,658 million roubles	5,741 million roubles	6,197 million roubles

a   [There is a misprint in the text, which gives the figure 8,600.]
CONTROL FIGURES, PP. 234–5

At the same time, the goods famine during the economic year 1925/26 amounted to a commodity deficit of 380 million, and in 1926/27, if the current year's price relations remain constant, will grow to 500 million roubles.[1] In other words, growth of the commodity portion of industrial produc-

---

1 *Kontrol'nye tsifry*, p. 79.

tion in 1925/26 by 2,470 million – or about 45% beyond the previous year – together with an increase of commodity production in agriculture by more than 23%, produced a commodity deficit of 380 million roubles. This year's growth of the commodity portion in industry is expected to be 15%, with a total growth of commodity production in agriculture of about 8%, and the goods famine will grow to as much as 500 million roubles.[2] Our goods famine means that industrial production is inadequate compared to effective demand. And this shortfall, in turn, means a shortage of fixed and circulating capital in industry together with inadequate opportunities for imports. Accordingly, the guidance provided by the industrialisers on this point – mainly concerning the inadequate accumulation in industry with the inevitable consequence of industry lagging behind agriculture – has been fully confirmed by this year's experience and by the results expected for 1926/27.

2   Retail Prices

The level of retail mark-ups over the selling prices of the trusts is character-ised by two basic phenomena: first, the extent of rationalisation of the trade apparatus, and second, its level of accumulation. With an excess supply of com-modities over demand, and given adequate circulating capital in trade, retail accumulation occurs within normal limits determined by competition, and the trading apparatus becomes more rational. Conversely, a systematic shortage of industrial commodities, such as we have had and still do have in our country, corrupts the trading apparatus and the co-operatives, does not provide suffi-cient stimulus for rationalisation of the trade turnover, and permits private retail to raise prices to the limit, i.e., to the point of exhausting effective demand or a buyers' strike by consumers. To all of this must be added the enormous expenditure of resources connected with secondary buying and selling, which always flourishes in the circumstances of a goods famine and commodity spec-ulation. The result is that we have a swollen and extremely costly apparatus of state trade and cooperatives, which is extremely slow in rationalising, along with very rapid accumulation in private retail. In these conditions, the retail mark-up over the trusts' wholesale prices was 8% on 1 October 1923, 35% on 1 August 1924, and rose to 62% by 1 April of this year (compared to an average mark-up of 20% before the war).

---

2   We have yet to mention that the average per-capita consumption of industrial commodities lags far behind the pre-war level.

In the meantime, the selling prices of our trusts were reduced several times and by 28% as a whole over the two years from 1923–25.[3] Thus our industry lost hundreds of millions that were expropriated in trade and did not reduce prices for consumers. While this situation still had some limited justification during the period when circulating capital was being accumulated in trade, it is now intolerable. An administratively imposed reduction of retail mark-ups in the cooperatives has not brought the expected results. Private capital took full advantage of the resulting market conditions; our trusts continued to trade at fixed prices; and materials were procured at fixed prices, which meant that the general price increase in the private economy threatened peasant production of technical crops. This year we experienced a dangerous process of interruption in growth and even a reduction of acreage sown to flax, oilseeds and sugar beets along with a shortage of cotton.

The result is that we again arrive at the sole economic means for overcoming the rise of retail prices and for reducing the costs of commodity circulation, or the problem of expanding the production of scarce commodities, i.e., everything still turns on the inadequate accumulation in industry. Every other means of struggle with this curse can at best play a secondary role, and to offer them up as a serious cure is sheer charlatanism. On this issue the industrialisers have turned out to be absolutely right. They opposed reducing prices for commodities in short supply and suggested using all of the additional profits to expand production of those same commodities. This was not done in a timely way, and the state paid heavily for repeated experiments in cutting delivery prices, which produced no results in retail. Then everyone finally understood that the industrialisers were proposing the sole economically literate pricing policy, and people stopped talking about reducing wholesale prices. Next, a general price rise began in the private economy while the trusts' selling prices were held constant, i.e., they remained fixed in conditions where a number of other factors in price formation began to move in an upward direction. This meant that the production costs of state industry inevitably had to rise. We then proposed an increase of the trusts' wholesale prices[4] in order to avoid a situation in which maintenance of the old level of wholesale prices in new circumstances, with private prices rising, would become a general tax on state industry. That suggestion was rejected and interpreted as an attempt to raise *retail prices* (which would not necessarily follow at all), and then several months passed and a number of the major

---

3   See Grintser, 'O promyshkennykh tsenakh', in *Ekonomicheskoe obozrenie*, May 1926, pp. 50–2.
4   'Ekonomicheskie zametki', in *Bol'shevik*, No. 6, March 1926.

trusts spoke up about rising production costs, which means their selling prices must also rise. But this will only be done after a delay, and industry will bear the costs of that delay. At the same time, the decision taken to raise railway rates means *a rise in wholesale prices for all the trusts from another direction.* Thus, the stubborn logic of the situation is imposing upon our economy a measure whose inevitability we predicted nine months ago, after listening in a stupid polemic to everything that people who foresee things too early must endure.

3   Wages

In recent years wages have risen rapidly in our country for three reasons: first, because they were at an unprecedentedly low level of only 67.1% in 1923/24, compared to pre-war wages; second, due to the use of old equipment, which changed the focus of accumulation to circulating capital in industry; third, due to the rising intensity and productivity of labour. As a result, the average wage was 82.6% of the pre-war level in 1924/25, 91.3% in 1925/26, and is expected to be 99% in 1926/27. Consequently, during the current economic year the average annual wage will equal the pre-war level, while output in industry and transport will also, apparently, be somewhat above the pre-war level. The greatest lag in wages has been among metal workers, whose wages in 1925/26 were 75.7% of the pre-war level and are expected in 1926/27 to reach 82.5%; among miners, for whom the figures are 65.3% and 73.7% (while output in 1926/27 exceeds the pre-war level); and among transport workers at 73.3% and 77.5% (while shipments are at the pre-war level).

A comparison of the pre-war and current wages of foreign workers with the wages for our workers reveals that in 1925/26 we had 87% of the pre-war wage, while in America the figure was 128.1%, in England 99.3%, in France 99.7%, in Germany 95% (for skilled workers), and in Italy 89.7%. Consequently, this year's wage level lags behind the pre-war level compared to what is happening abroad, but the wage dynamic is better in our case because wages are steadily rising whereas abroad, apart from America and Germany, they are falling: for England in 1921 they were 111% of the pre-war level; for France in 1923, 107.3%; for Italy 102.4% in 1922.[5] Conversely, the relation between the pay of skilled and unskilled workers abroad has moved in the direction of an increase for

5   *Kontrol'nye tsifry*, p. 154.

unskilled workers,[6] while in our country the gap between these two categories continues to be enormous.

What are the prospects for further wage increases, without which any movement towards socialism is inconceivable?

In terms of long-term prospects, there are two fundamental ways of raising the [real] wage level: a general reduction in prices and an increase in labour productivity. As far as prices are concerned, a significant reduction compared to the present level would be possible – without any reduction of wholesale prices – if we managed to eliminate commodity shortages in the market, i.e., just by an increase of production. Meanwhile, our lack of fixed capital that is even tolerably up to date in technical terms has compelled us to bring into operation plants that should have been levelled 30 years ago. The question of raising labour productivity, therefore, is one of new technology, of renovating fixed capital and new construction. The question of raising wages thereby becomes a question of the size of capital expenditures in industry. That is the question of all questions for our economy.

Now a few words about vodka. One-half of all vodka in 1925/26 was consumed in the cities, which means that no less than 40 % was consumed by workers. As we have seen, though, this whole problem is connected with the problem of accumulation in industry. From one direction, this means that the question of raising wages is one of increasing the share of industry in the country's national income, and secondly it involves raising labour productivity. We have regained the pre-war intensity of labour, and any further movement in that direction will only be possible with a better organisation of work, elimination of periodic material shortages, improvement in the quality of materials etc. The main thing is to improve labour on the basis of re-equipping the whole technical basis of industry. The highest paid worker in the world, i.e. the American worker, operates in conditions of the world's most advanced technique of mass production.

According to the budget for 1925/26, the income from the excise on vodka was 301 million roubles, and the total proceeds from vodka sales came to about 440 million roubles. The annual sum of all wages paid to workers in industry, transport and construction was 2,630 million roubles. If we assume that workers consumed 40 % of the total quantity of vodka, this represents a reduction of real wages by 6–7 %. Any health-minded public figure with an economic edu-

---

6   In France, for example, the wage of unskilled workers, if the wages of skilled workers are taken as 1, increased compared to the pre-war period by 25 %. See my book *Ekonomika i finansy sovremennoi Frantsii* (Moscow, 1926), p. 71.

cation would take stock of the workers' vodka consumption from a medical, social and economic point of view. From the economic point of view, there is scarcely any doubt that the state budget gains significantly less from workers' vodka consumption than the state economy loses, not to mention the decline of culture and general social interests, the corruption of everyday life and so forth. Vodka consumption by the workers amounts to the state borrowing from the physical resources of the working class. It is time to take up the task of gradually replacing the state budget's vodka revenues from workers with other sources and gradually, from year to year, to do this to the best of our ability.

4   Housing Conditions and Unemployment

The control figures summarise the position with regard to the housing question as follows. According to data from the TsSU, at the end of 1923 the average housing space per person in the USSR was 12.8 square arshins.[7] If we subtract just the three largest cities, which had average per-capita living space above or equal to the sanitary norm of 16 square arshins (Leningrad, Odessa and Kiev), we get 11.8 square arshins per person. Today, when we would expect housing space to be rising in absolute figures rather than falling, the average space per person turns out to be much lower than in 1923/24, not exceeding 11.5 square arshins per person for the whole of the USSR; and if we leave out the three previously mentioned cities (in which, by the way, apartment conditions are also improving), the total comes to 10.1 square arshins in 1926.[8] All of the largest industrial centres – such as Kharkov, Rostov, Nizhny Novgorod, Ivanovo-Voznesensk, Sverdlovsk, Tula and Baku – show a reduction in per-capita living space, with a small increase only for the Don Coal trust. In terms of arshins per person, the living space for workers doing physical labour has changed over the years as follows: it was 10 square arshins per person in 1923/24; 9.5 in 1924/25; 9.2 in 1925/26; and for this year, 1926/27, the figure is expected to be 9 square arshins. Consequently, housing conditions for workers continue to deteriorate. Construction in the cities this year will be 521 million roubles in place of 448 million in 1925/26. That means growth will be quite modest and the scale of construction will be significantly lower than in pre-war years. Furthermore, we must also take into account the fact that only 86–90 % of the demand for construction materials will be met in 1926/27. And yet there are still people, even

---

7   [1 square arshin = 0.5058 square metres.]
8   *Kontrol'nye tsifry*, pp. 62–3.

in these circumstances, who are so flippant as to raise an outcry over super-industrialisers!

The figures for unemployment are even more ominous. In 1924/25 we had 1,300 thousand unemployed in our country. In 1925/26 the figure dropped to 1,230 thousand, that is, only by 70 thousand, despite the fact that during this year the total number of workers in all of industry rose by 736 thousand, in construction by 165 thousand, and in transport by 126 thousand – i.e., by 1,027 thousand just in these groups. What will happen in 1926/27, when the combined growth in these three basic branches is expected to be 524 thousand, i.e., one-half of the current year's growth, and the increase in the number of office workers, state and private, is also expected to be far less than during the past year? The control figures project 1,200 thousand unemployed in 1926/27, but this figure is clearly an under-estimate that is not warranted either by the data mentioned or by the annual movement of labour from the countryside to the cities, even though the projected figure is threatening enough in itself for a period of economic growth. It goes without saying that the only real way to struggle with urban unemployment is through more rapid industrial development, particularly new industrial and residential construction.

5   Capital Expenditures

Everything that we have said leads us to the fundamental question of our economic life, with which all the problems of our development and all our current ills are connected – the question of capital expenditures in industry and transport, and particularly the question of new construction. The struggle with the goods famine, the struggle for lower prices, the struggle to raise wages and reduce unemployment – all of them compel us relentlessly to follow the main barometer, i.e. the figure for annual capital expenditures.

Let is begin with the basic funds of the national economy of the USSR. In 1923 the state sector consumed 204.6 million roubles of fixed funds while the private sector saw growth of 538.8 million. In 1924/25 the state sector had growth of only 126.3 million, compared to 587.5 million in the private sector. In 1925/26 the state sector had growth of 1,025 million, with 626.8 million in the private sector. In 1926/27 the expectation is for growth of 1,235.4 million in the state sector and 764.4 million in the private sector.[9] Thus, the growth of fixed funds in the state sector over the past three years, after deducting losses, was 946.7

---

9   *Kontrol'nye tsifry*, pp. 312–13.

million, compared to 1,753.1 million in the private sector. Compared to the past year, the growth of state funds in 1926/27 will produce an increase by 20%, compared to 21.9% in the private sector.

Generally speaking, we took a big step forward during the past year, but we still did not exceed the growth that had occurred over three years in the private sector.

Specifically, 'in industry during the first two years we see an insignificant increase of the fixed funds or near stability (and this after consuming fixed capital during the entire period since the war and revolution! – E.P.). And it is only during the current year of 1925/26 that a turning point comes, with a significant immediate increase of approximately 500 million, which represents about 9% of the total funds in industry'.[10] This growth of new capital must not be confused with the gross sum of capital expenditures in industry, which includes depreciation, i.e., the replacement of worn-out capital. These gross capital expenditures in 1925/26 amounted to approximately 800 million, and for 1926/27 Gosplan projects them to be 845 million while the STO figure is up to 900 million.

Is this a great deal or very little?

From the viewpoint of the growth of new capital compared to pre-war times, it is a considerable amount. Viewed in terms of the consumption of fixed capital from previous years and its growing technical backwardness (moral wear), it is not very much; and from the viewpoint of overcoming the goods famine, it is very little. We must not forget that the 800 million of capital expenditures in the past year coincided with a goods famine of 380 million and predatory retail prices. According to Gosplan's data, capital expenditures of 840 million will correspond to a goods famine of 500 million. According to the five-year plan of necessary capital investments worked out by VSNKh, we need average capital expenditures in industry of 1,200 million per year. Thus, even the figure of 900 million in capital expenditures represents a deficit of 300 million compared to the minimally necessary investments that would ensure overcoming the goods famine in the future, and even then not very quickly.

Things are even worse in transport. The fixed capital of transport has been ruthlessly depleted throughout the entire period of war, revolution, Civil War and NEP, with the sole exception of the past year. In 1923/24 the consumption of fixed capital in transport was 64.7 million roubles; in 1924/25 the figure was 96.8 million; and growth in 1925/26 was only 117.4 million, which is equal to 1.1% of

---

10   *Kontrol'nye tsifry*, p. 120.

the total capital, whereas the increase of funds in agriculture was about 3% for the total period. For 1926/27 the proposed increase of fixed funds in transport is the petty sum of 181.6 million, i.e., the equivalent of 1.7% of the total capital. Transport is the weakest link in our entire system. Meanwhile, every advance in other areas depends upon it.

Such are the data, and what do they indicate?

They show that despite our economic successes in recent years as we re-activated reserves of older fixed capital, and despite the projected progress in 1926/27, which will be much slower, the fundamental indicator of our development – capital investments – was totally inadequate last year and will continue to be even more inadequate with the sum of 900 million for the current year (that figure that does not include transport and electrification). Yet there are people who regard this figure for capital expenditures as sufficient and have no aversion to calling themselves 'economists', apparently because they have specialised in the regime of economy[11] with regard to our entire development.

The party conference must make a judgement concerning all these fundamental problems of our economy and address the issue of finding further resources for the development of our industry and transport and for increasing the fixed funds of the state economy.

Where can these resources come from?

The most important sources are the following: 1) further reduction of budgetary expenses for the sake of industry and transport; 2) an increase of factory prices for commodities that are in short supply without any increase of retail prices,[12] i.e., at the expense of mark-ups by the trade apparatus; 3) additional taxation of the bourgeoisie and the village kulaks together with a number of credit operations, including perhaps a grain loan from the well-to-do rural strata; 4) a gradual reduction of the industrial resources tied up in trade operations by the cooperatives and their replacement both from the cooperatives' own profits (which in the past year were more than 100 million) and by attracting the peasantry's own resources; 5) use of some of the savings from the regime of economy for capital investments.

---

11   [The 'regime of economy' was the term for what is commonly called 'austerity'.]

12   Specifically, thanks to the unprecedented cotton harvest in America, the inevitable fall of cotton prices and the possibility of increased credits, we have a good opportunity to expand production significantly of a commodity in short supply and thus reduce the retail price.

These are not the only possible resources for achieving the objective. The important thing is for the party's thinking always to begin with the fact of the absolute inadequacy of accumulation in industry and transport and to look relentlessly for a way out of the current situation.

E.A. Preobrazhensky, *Ekonomicheskie zametki:*
kontrol'nye tsifry Gosplana i nashi khozyaistvennye zadachi,
RGASPI. F. 589. Op. 3. D. 1853. L. 183–92 (Typescript)

CHAPTER 8

Economic Notes: What Is New in the Economic Situation[1]

Our press has often announced recently that we are seeing a notable reduction of the goods famine.

In his article in the December [1926] issue of *Bol'shevik*, comrade Mikoyan also reports this news and attempts to show how it has happened and what the evidence is to confirm it. At the Moscow provincial conference, comrade Bukharin declared: 'We are not seeing an intensification of the goods famine but its easing. I say again: on the whole, the goods famine has not intensified but is noticeably easing'.

People are saying that Gosplan's assumption of a worsening goods famine in 1926/27 has turned out to be unfounded, and the prediction itself is being attributed to 'pessimism and lack of confidence' on Comrade Smilga's part when he presided over compiling the control figures. The present author took no part in compiling those figures and thus bears no formal responsibility for them. However, I must say that neither the method of 'easing' the goods famine on the pages of newspapers and journals nor the current way the control figures are being criticised is likely to contribute any proper awareness and understanding of what is actually happening just now in our economy.

Studying the problem of the goods famine on the basis of factual data, I have come to conclusions that I would like to share with readers in this article. But let us first refresh our memory of how Gosplan framed the problem. The control figures say that if prices for agricultural and industrial products remain unchanged from what they were in 1925/26, we can expect growth of the goods famine from 380 million in 1925/26 to 500 million this year.[2] In methodological terms, this is a perfectly correct way of posing the question. Any increase or decrease of the goods famine during a new year, by comparison with the year just completed, can be most clearly seen only by comparing prices. Only in that way can we get a snapshot of the disparity between effective demand and supply, and the dynamic of that disparity compared to the previous year, in terms of a change in the volume of commodities that is not being obscured by price movements.

---

1 Article by E.A. Preobrazhensky published in the journal *Bol'shevik*, No. 6, 1927.
2 See *Kontrol'nye tsifry*, p. 79.

From that perspective, what has transpired in these terms during the first quarter of this economic year, i.e., from 1 October 1926 to 1 January 1927? Is it true that a so-called partial moderation on the commodity market and a certain weakening of the demand for commodities has resulted from a large increase in the supply of industrial commodities, implying an unexpectedly large increase of output?

Let us sort this out.

First, we turn to the question of how effective demand has been developing. Gosplan's projection of the scale of the goods famine, as we have noted, began with an assumption of price stability compared to 1925/26. What has been happening with the prices for agricultural products?

For all the cereal grains, prices fell sharply compared to weighted average prices for the USSR during the corresponding months of the previous year. For example, the procurement price in kopecks for a tsentner[3] of wheat in October–November was:

	October	November
1925/26	726	748
1926/27	624	614

In other words, during the months when procurements were at their peak, a pood of wheat sold for 20 kopecks less that it did last year.[4] We see the same picture for other grains; only rye had a less significant price decline.

The result is that for wheat alone, with 243.6 million poods procured up to 1 January, the peasantry was paid about 50 million roubles less. For all the grains, the sum will be about 70 million roubles. Since at least 250–300 million poods have yet to be purchased, and the prices compared to 1925/26 are not likely to change dramatically after 1 January, the decline of grain prices alone will reduce the peasants' effective demand by at least 100 million roubles compared to what it would have been with 1925/26 prices. The price increase on certain technical crops cannot essentially change the situation, since the sown area or the commodity portion of output for several crops, such as oil seeds, flax, and sugar beet has contracted.

---

3 [Here Preobrazhensky refers to the price of 1 tsentner = 100 kilograms or 1 quintal, although he subsequently speaks of the price per pood. 1 pood = 16.3807 kg.]

4 [The price for a tsentner of wheat was 748 kopecks in November 1925, or approximately 122 kopecks per pood. The price in November 1926 was 614 kopecks per tsentner or 101 kopecks per pood, meaning approximately 20 % less.]

Therefore, the decline of the peasantry's purchasing power for the year by 100 million roubles, due to lower agricultural prices and a rise in industrial retail prices, means a growth of the disproportion between agriculture and industry – not an abatement of the goods famine.

But could it be that the goods famine eased due to a previous contraction of urban effective demand? That is not what happened, nor was there a previous contraction of rural effective demand. If, say, wages in the country had declined, causing a reduction of workers' demand for industrial commodities, that would have to be described as a cut in wages, not as an easing of the goods famine.

Moreover, in calculating working-class demand, it is time we paid attention to the increase of vodka consumption and the role of this expenditure in the budget of the working class. In 1924/25 the cities, i.e., mainly workers and employees, consumed 70% of all vodka compared to 30% in the countryside. In 1925/26 the figure was 49% for the cities and 51% for the countryside. But if we include in the first figure all of the factory towns outside of the cities, the urban total would be higher. If we assume that 70% of all vodka poured in the cities was consumed by workers, then of a total of 440 million roubles earned from vodka sales (of which excise accounts for 301 million) the workers account for 154 million. With wages of 2,630 million roubles, vodka took about 6%. Approximately half of the entire increase in real wages for 1925/26 was eaten up by the vodka tax.[5] And in 1926/27 vodka sales and revenues are expected to be significantly higher than in 1925/26; to be more precise, up to 500 million roubles. We have to surmise that during the first quarter the population has already paid more in vodka tax than during the corresponding quarter of last year and thereby reduced its resources for purchasing other commodities.

Now let us turn to the other side of the coin, the supply of industrial commodities. Changes in the situation from this direction can occur in two ways: a growth of production and increased supply of industrial commodities with constant prices, i.e., movement in the direction of a real easing of the goods famine, or else a rise in prices for industrial commodities, i.e., an increase of the disproportion and a masking of the goods famine with the aid of high prices. In other words, if for each 100 roubles of effective demand we have a supply of 100 at the same prices, instead of the former 95, we shall then have a lessening of the goods famine. If we provide the former volume of commodities for 100 roubles of demand, but instead of 95 roubles they now cost, say,

---

5   In 1924/25 the real wage was 82.6% of the pre-war level. In 1925/26 the figure was 91.3%.

102–103 roubles due to a rise in prices, then we shall have masked the goods famine and increased the disproportion merely by a change in its value expression.

What was the actual state of affairs compared to the same months last year and to Gosplan's estimates, which assumed constant prices?

According to data from Narkomfin's Conjuncture Institute, the USSR index for retail industrial prices in private trade during the final quarter of 1925 was 2.24; for the year it was 2.29; for the most recent quarter it was 2.63; and for 1925/26 it was 2.57. Simply put, this means that for a given quantity of commodities, which cost the consumer an average of 2.24[6] kopecks at the end of 1925, he paid 2.63 kopecks during the same months of 1926, i.e., .39[7] kopecks or 17% more. The index of labour statistics shows a price increase of 14% for this period. In December the situation did not improve. In Moscow, for instance, the price of the budgetary basket of goods rose, and in Ukraine the price increase for December ate up everything that was achieved by the campaign to reduce prices. True, there was somewhat less of an increase in cooperative prices, but they still increased. If we take into account that the total of industrial production to be provided to the market this year is 7 1/3 billion, or a little less than 2 billion per quarter, then the price increase in just one quarter, compared to the same quarter of the previous year, must devour, in private sector trade alone, up to 100 million of effective demand with the same quantity of goods being purchased that is projected in the plan.[8] A curtailment of demand for this reason, in the parlance of economically literate people, is attributed to a rise in prices, not to an easing of the goods famine.

Now calculate these over-payments by consumers that result from rising prices not just in the private sector but in the whole of retail trade, plus what the peasantry did not receive from grain sales compared to Gosplan's projection (which was based on the same procurement prices as in 1925); divide the deficit of 500 million roubles that Gosplan projected by one quarter; allow for the higher excise taxes this year – and then tell us where there is an over-estimation of the goods famine or whether Gosplan's figure is more likely to be too low. It is true that the general output of industrial products this year is supposed to be greater than Gosplan expected, and this increase will provide real resources for

---

6 [The text mistakenly gives the figure 2 kopecks.]

7 [The text mistakenly gives the figure 39 kopecks rather than .39 kopecks.]

8 [.39 × 2 billion = 78 million, but Preobrazhensky is perhaps including in this rough estimate an expectation of continuing retail price increases in 1927.]

reducing the goods famine. In this regard the under-estimate in the figures is apparently a fact. But the influence of this increase, compared to the planned output of industrial commodities for the market, is 'music of the future'. During this quarter, for example, the increased output of the fuel industry for the broad consumer market will not have any obvious impact, and the increased production of other branches, textiles for example, will only be felt later.

Meanwhile, a number of comrades have already announced and are still declaring that there has been an 'easing of the goods famine' during the current quarter, taking the rise in prices, the reduction of effective demand due to the fall in grain prices, the increased vodka tax, the higher excise taxes and a certain weakening of demand connected with all of this – to be an easing of the goods famine. They are often forgetting that at some point the rise in prices, with a given level of demand for commodities, begins to discourage buying even before the effective demand is exhausted. Concretely, if effective demand with existing prices absorbs 100 units of commodities, but prices are beyond the reach of consumers, then a price rise from 100 to 105 will perhaps allow for up to 90 units of the commodity to be sold and 10 units of demand will not be utilised. The reverse picture is often seen with a drop in prices. Finally, to those who support the view that we are experiencing an easing of the goods famine, every consumer may pose the natural question: if we are seeing an easing of the goods famine, why are retail prices not only failing to come down but during the past month have even risen somewhat? What is going on?

What is going on is that we have no easing of the goods famine but its suppression within the economic organism: all we have is movement from one form of crisis to another. Thus far we have no easing of the goods famine but instead a more acute disproportion between industry and agriculture, an increased disparity between higher retail prices for industrial commodities and a drop in the procurement prices for grain, and simply a movement of the crisis into a new phase. The economic organism is spontaneously beginning to correct the disparity by retching over the high prices and convulsively curtailing demand, while reducing the production of crops in the private economy that have become unprofitable in current market conditions from the viewpoint of labour expenditures. The first harbinger of this is the slower growth or halt to the growth of technical crops. This is where the law of value makes itself felt as the spontaneous result of commodity economy, which is competing with our planning principle in terms of establishing the proportions of the economic system. The most crucial part of the peasant economy, the one that is most closely tied to our industry and sustains it with raw materials, faces the threat of a halt to its development.

As for the sphere of supply and demand for industrial commodities, what we are approaching here, apparently, is a situation analogous to the autumn of 1923. Only now the centre of gravity is first and foremost the wholesale-retail prices scissors. A reduction of retail prices is the central challenge, which, if it could be accomplished, could at least partially restore relative equilibrium to the market. But this nut is far more difficult to crack than many people have supposed. The campaign to reduce retail prices by externally imposed administrative pressure on the cooperatives has generally failed except for one positive result: it has delayed the possibility of an even greater price rise in connection with the general revival of trade during the autumn. *The economy's trade apparatus – not just the private part but also the cooperatives – is slipping away from planned management by the state.* We must first of all recognise that fact and then understand it in order to have any hope of success in deciding the issue of what practical measures must be taken in order to reduce prices.

Our trading apparatus is cumbersome, clumsy and 'over-populated' as a result of becoming bloated with the spontaneous growth of the previous period. It works badly and is incredibly costly.

Moreover, during the previous period trading mark-ups included some percentage for the creation of circulating capital.

Our trading apparatus was pampered and spoiled from its very birth by the fact that it developed in the corrupting circumstances of the goods famine, which prevented any rational approach to the issue of trade. As far as many commodities are concerned, especially those in short supply, there was even no trade in our country in the proper sense but only distribution, with any kind of mark-up for hungry consumers who eagerly snapped up whatever they could find. Where is there any adequate incentive here for minimal mark-ups, for rationalisation of the apparatus, for a struggle against added charges? The very best rod to use, for educating a trade apparatus in the spirit of reducing circulation costs, is a market sufficiently stocked with commodities, making it imperative to seek out purchasers rather than distributing in a manner resembling the Food Commissariat [during War Communism]. For that reason, it remains true for the current period that the very best means for reducing the wholesale-retail scissors is *expanded production of the commodities in short supply*. Nothing can replace this fundamental factor in the rationalisation of trade. Any other means can at best rectify the situation somewhat but can never reduce the costs of the trading apparatus even to the pre-war level. A different motive [is required]. The attempt to reduce trading costs in the cooperatives has shown that the easiest way to effect this reduction is by increasing the volume of the commodity turnover and the workload of the apparatus, not by its physical contraction.[9] Here, too, the solution is to increase the volume of commodities on the market, including the commodities that pass through cooperative trade.

Finally, it is only saturation of the market that can seriously hurt the accumulation of private capital. Private capital, which is not its own enemy, is now fleecing the consumer first of everything that the cooperatives take from him; secondly, it adds further charges; and thirdly, it gains from the fact that its greater resourcefulness means lower trading costs than in the cooperatives. Only with saturation of the market and even a degree of over-saturation will private capital, with its greater flexibility, be compelled to reduce its prices in order to avoid being left without any buyers.

Summarising all of our efforts to reduce retail prices over several years, we have to conclude that we have not found any solution to this problem. At the Moscow party conference, comrade Bukharin already emphasised that we have reduced the wholesale prices of our state industry by 36%, while retail prices during the same period have only fallen by 3%. I shall return to this sad conclusion below in connection with the question of the selling prices of our trusts. For present purposes, we simply have to recognise this fact.

Why have we failed in reducing retail prices? Above all, of course, it is because the state, in the struggle to reduce prices in commodity circulation, has had to work against spontaneous forces, against the law of demand and supply, and against a 'delayed reflex of the law of value' in our economy, which leads to a rise in prices without a corresponding spontaneous influx of labour and means of production into the sphere of production where there is a deficit of commodities. In this area the physical force of our regulation, if we may put it that way, has a much weaker effect than in the sector of nationalised industry. Despite the fact that state trade and the cooperatives embrace two-thirds of the commodity turnover, the spontaneous laws of the market also overpower planned regulation even in these two-thirds of the territory that either belongs to the state or is under state control.

If we want to take a rough summary of the results of our regulation of trade during the period of NEP, two basic figures come up: first, a comparison of pre-war mark-ups with the average trade mark-up of the cooperatives and private traders, and second, a comparison of cooperative mark-ups with those of private capital. The pre-war mark-ups were about 20%. The current mark-ups in private trade are about 50%. In cooperative trade they are 15–20% less,

---

9 I do not mean to say here that a physical contraction is not necessary or possible, only that it meets with the strongest opposition.

but there are no accurate data, no weighted data for the whole of exports. If we take the pre-war mark-ups of the trading apparatus and the average mark-up of for all types of trade in the country, the overall balance from regulating trade is still negative.[10] Conversely, in state and cooperative trade, prices are lower than in the private trade sector in the following terms: the same quantity of commodities that cost 100 kopecks before the war [now] costs 265 in private retail trade and 225–230 in cooperative trade, i.e., 18 % less (these figures for the cooperatives need to be verified). Here regulation is having a positive effect.

How can we reduce the trading expenses of the cooperatives, of state trade and of private trade?

As far as the latter is concerned, it is difficult to achieve any serious results until the goods famine is overcome and sales of handicraft industry are included in the cooperative turnover, although everything possible must be done here. As for state and cooperative trade, a reduction of their retail prices is urgently needed. Our entire economy and its development are currently running into the problem of the wholesale-retail scissors, which puts our system of exchange under fire.

By how much and at whose expense is it possible to cut trade mark-ups in the cooperatives and state trade?

If the question is: can we? – we must reply 'yes'. Prices are so inflated that we might soon have a glut in the market along with the goods famine and partial strikes by consumers who want to make purchases but either cannot or do not wish to do so with the existing prices (we also must not forget the class composition of our consumers, a question that, unfortunately, is not adequately studied, just as in the case of the whole dynamic of mass demand and supply in Soviet conditions). At this point the state, faced with the market's spontaneous opposition in the matter of reducing prices, will momentarily be supported by those spontaneous forces. In a situation of market glut, the trade apparatus, pressured by both consumers and the government, will have to give in: it will now be possible to squeeze out of it a reduction of some percentage in the mark-ups.

But what will the percentage be? How can mark-ups be cut? All that can be cut are the so-called 'dependent' elements of the added charges.

The cooperatives and state trade have profits, which they themselves claim come to about 120 million. The rule should be that neither cooperatives nor

---

10   For 1925/26 the total of all mark-ups for the entire trading network was 4.7 billion roubles, and for 1926/27 Gosplan projects 5 billion. Since retail prices are higher than they were last year, the mark-ups for this year will no doubt be significantly higher than 5 billion. That is where pressure must be applied!

state trade should have profits, at least in the coming years, during any period when retail prices are rising or stabilising. You would think that profits perform a great service with the present mark-ups, which, from the viewpoint of the mark-ups in the well organised capitalist trade of Europe, are fantastic, or more accurately, beyond scandalous. People tell us: after all, the profits are modest, just 120 million in all. But if profits are so modest with the present mark-ups, this is proof precisely of bad management. Although some of the cooperatives' profits also go to the members, we should take the general view that profits are inadmissible during a period when prices are rising or stabilising; we should be establishing records of exemplary work in terms of reducing prices compared to other cooperatives, not in terms of the graph of profits.

Secondly, the current profits include an increase in the circulating capital of state and co-operative trade. While this was natural in the first years of trading, when state and cooperative trade were released shirtless into the free market and had to acquire circulating capital on the run, it is intolerable now to 'calculate' with the expectation of increasing capital. What is needed is a more rapid turnover of the capital that already exists plus credit.

The third and perhaps most reliable way to cut mark-ups is to accelerate the turnover with the existing trade apparatus. If the swelling of our trade apparatus is to come to a halt, an increase of the commodity turnover will automatically decrease the costs of trade relative to the volume.

Next we must consider, wherever necessary, a compression of the existing apparatus of state trade and the cooperatives. No proper rationalisation has yet occurred here. With the same volume, private trade requires fewer people and spends less on labour power, not just because we have better measures of labour protection, accountability and control (accountability and control, incidentally, are not always an absolute benefit – often they are costly bureaucratic outgrowths), but because *we are less efficient in using labour power and have not yet found the incentive inherent in a collective system to replace the positive aspects of bourgeois competition.*[11] We must not forget that large-scale cooperative trade, along with the advantages of all large-scale production, has the disadvantage that the balances from enterprises that function well go to save those that are bankrupt – but without replacing the positive aspect of

---

11   Not everyone in our country yet realises that our persistent failures in reducing retail prices are connected, among several other causes, with an organisational crisis of the Soviet system of exchange, and this crisis, this inability to 'trade in a cultured way' (of which Lenin spoke) is connected with the problem of our general cultural development. No shock-work campaign will help us against that sort of problem: what this requires, as Lenin said, is a 'cultural revolution'.

any bankruptcy insofar as bankruptcy removes rotten organisms from the system. Whereas competition in bourgeois trade mechanically eliminates the rot, with us the rot becomes a companion of the system itself at least until we have mastered the new system and its distinctive features.

Finally, we should be thinking whether, over the next two-three years, we might transfer part of the labour costs in cooperative and state trade, which are too high, to the actual consumer. Time, unfortunately, is not something that we currently treat as an expensive or scarce commodity. Instead of bringing the commodity to the consumer, should we not be encouraging the consumer's approach to the commodity? To be concise: should we not be liquidating those enterprises in the state and co-operative network that fail to reach some minimum ratio of turnover to labour power? And obviously, we must categorically put a halt to expanding the network to places where there is no possibility of fully utilising the apparatus.

These are the resources for reducing retail prices in cooperative and state trade. What might the results be? With 3,808 million roubles of cooperative turnover last year and significantly more in 1926/27, and in the corrupting circumstances of the goods famine yet at a moment when trade is threatening to seize up, the result could be a 6–7 % reduction in prices, i.e., enough to eliminate most of the price increase for the past year. That would be an essential success for this year.

Now we have to consider the possibility of reducing wholesale prices in order to stimulate the reduction of retail prices. I think these are the sort of cartridges that we always know how to fire. The whole point is to reach the consumer. Otherwise, hundreds of millions of roubles, intended to improve the situation of consumers, will be intercepted by the trading network. In general and on the whole, the reduction of output prices over the past three years has almost entirely failed to reach consumers. The same thing could happen this year. At the same time, a reduction of output prices for just the portion of industrial production that goes to rural and urban consumers, even by just 3–4 %, represents an enormous sum – 1 and a half million roubles at least – and that will be a direct deduction from the fund for expanded reproduction. *Since the expansion and technical re-equipping of industry is the fundamental factor in reducing prices*, the real process of easing the goods famine will be delayed, along with any genuine and lasting change to the market conjuncture that would benefit the consumer, all for the sake of a temporary effect on the market that may easily be eaten up by the trading apparatus.[12]

---

12   In particular, it would be terrible bungling on our part if we did not take full advantage of
       the exceptionally favourable conditions in the world cotton market and failed this year to

There is no doubt that in certain branches of industry a reduction of output prices is possible and necessary, especially in the conditions that have currently formed in the market. The challenge is to avoid any blanket price reduction and to implement any reduction at the moment when it will totally and completely reach the consumer and when we can be assured that everything possible has been squeezed from the trading network to reduce retail prices. We must, however, be wary of any indiscriminate and panicky reduction of output prices in the event of a crisis in trade. That would strike a blow at industry, giving the trading apparatus an opportunity to shift to industry some of the consequences of a crisis that is caused by the inflation of retail prices and for which industry has no responsibility whatever. Finally, these sacrifices on the part of proletarian industry are not likely to benefit the strata of rural consumers that concern us. *The poor and middle peasants, having sold their grain surpluses at lower prices by 1 January, purchased industrial products at inflated retail prices.* But the kulaks and the well-to-do, who held out in the expectation of a spring price rise and are now selling their grain more profitably, will purchase industrial commodities at reduced prices. For the sake of poor- and middle-peasant buyers, we are interested in choosing a different season for price reductions, the summer and especially the autumn, when these strata are more likely to be able to buy. Meanwhile, in the past year the attempt to reduce prices in precisely this season has to be recognised as a failure.

I am not proposing any systematic, concrete measures in this article. I only wish to convince comrades to begin a discussion of the economic situation before an interruption of trade occurs. If we correctly sort out what is happening in our economy now, at the beginning of 1927, it will be easier for us to outline all the practical measures that will have to be undertaken in the sphere of the state's economic policy.

• • •

Postscript. This article had already been written and sent to the editors of 'Pravda' when I was told that at the last plenum of the Central Committee certain comrades called my book *The New Economics* the 'gospel of the opposition' and the theoretical justification for a policy of raising prices. I must remind readers that on the question of pricing policy my book defends the following

produce sufficient textiles. Since development of the textile industry encounters obstacles from the equipment side as well, we must ensure that it quickly receives imports of new equipment. The expansion of production in the textile industry that is already planned is clearly inadequate.

programmatic thesis, whose validity has been sufficiently proven by our economic experience: 'A correct pricing policy for the products of state industry must pursue the following three goals: accumulation for expanded reproduction and for technically re-equipping industry, a rise in wages, and a reduction in prices' (*Novaya Ekonomika*, 1st edn, p. 237; 2nd edn, p. 276).[13] Furthermore, let me point out once and for all that I alone, as the author, am responsible for my book, which is not an article of faith for the opposition. It is well known that the views of the opposition on pricing policy have been set out in several official documents and addresses, for instance, in declarations to the July 1926 plenum of the Central Committee, at the xv Party Congress, and at the Seventh expanded plenum of the Executive Committee of the Communist International.

E.A. Preobrazhensky,
'*Ekonomicheskie zametki: Novoe v khozyaistvennoi situatsii*',
Bol'shevik, No. 6, 1927, 15 March, pp. 57–65.

---

13   [See Volume II of *The Preobrazhensky* Papers, Part 2, Appendix 2.]

CHAPTER 9

Notes of an Economist on 'Notes of an Economist'

Ural'sk, 5 November 1928

N.I. Bukharin's voluminous article, published in *Pravda* on 30 September, deserves serious attention both from those whom he bombards without mentioning their name or giving an accurate address and also, of course, from those he does name, including the author of this article.[1] Among the long list of enormous problems that Bukharin raises, for now I shall deal primarily with the problem of reproduction and only from the point of view of equilibrium in our economic system.

For the sake of convenience, I shall begin by providing a very brief sketch of the core ideas of Bukharin's theory of slowing the pace of industrialisation, sticking as much as possible to his own text.

The introduction to the article has this to say:

> ... [W]e ourselves have not been sufficiently aware of the really novel conditions of the reconstruction period. It is for precisely this reason that we have 'lagged behind': we raised the problem of our specialists only after the Shakhty affair;[2] we began to deal practically with the problem of collective and state farms only after the crisis in grain procurements and the associated disturbances, etc. In brief, we have acted largely in accordance with the good old Russian proverb 'Unless it thunders, the peasant doesn't cross himself'.[3]

Since I have no objection to this conclusion and am truly delighted that disagreements over this question have ended, I shall now turn to the advice that the author, having now 'crossed himself' after the thunder, offers us concerning the basic theme.

1) The reconstruction period is essentially different from our previous period of construction, i.e., the recovery period: 'There is a tremendous difference, let

---

1 [Preobrazhensky had been expelled from the Communist Party in October 1927 and was working with a local planning commission in the Urals when he typed this essay.]

2 [In May 1928 fity-three engineers and managers from Shakhty, in the Northern Caucasus, were tried for allegedly sabotaging the Soviet economy. This was a major 'show trial' and a prelude to Stalin's use of purges as a method of 'class struggle'.]

3 [Bukharin 1982, p. 302.]

us say, between simply repairing a bridge and *building* a new one'.[4] 2) During the three years of the reconstruction period, the state economy and the whole socialised sector have achieved great successes in expanding fixed capital.

3) However, despite all the *decisive* differences between our pattern of development and the capitalist pattern, these successes have been accompanied by 'unique "crises"'[5] that seem to 'repeat', as if in a concave mirror, the crises of capitalism.[6]

4) The goods famine is not a law of our development.

> From the fact that a 'goods famine' is not an absolute law of development in the transitional economy, that 'critical' disruptions of the basic economic proportions are not inevitable, the following conclusion results.
>
> *In order to attain the most favorable (or most crisis-free) course of social reproduction possible, together with systematic growth of socialism and, therefore, the most advantageous possible relation of class forces within the country for the proletariat, it is necessary to attain the best possible combination of the basic elements of the national economy (to 'balance' them, to arrange them in the most useful manner, actively influencing the course of economic life and the class struggle).*
>
> Every denial of this most important and most essential task represents *capitulation in face of petty bourgeois spontaneity ....*[7]

5) We have a simultaneous shortage in our national economy both of grain and of some materials, as well as an insufficient supply of industrial commodities in the countryside.

The view of the 'Trotskyists' – that industry is lagging behind the country's demand, including demand from agriculture – is not true. The data show that it is lagging behind itself as it were, i.e., it cannot satisfy its own production demands. On the other hand, one-half of the demand from the countryside is coming from the non-agricultural earnings of people who in one way or another are involved in the state economy. Rather than satisfying the demand for industrial commodities, from this perspective industrialisation creates such demand.[8]

---

4 [Bukharin 1982, p. 302.]
5 [Bukharin 1982, p. 305.]
6 [Ibid.]
7 [Bukharin 1982, p. 308.]
8 [See Bukharin 1982, p. 318.]

6) We do not plan properly. Grain farming lags far behind market demands, and pricing policy does not ensure sufficient productive accumulation in agriculture to meet the goals of expanded reproduction. On the other hand, we also construct plans of capital expenditures that cannot be fulfilled due to deficits of construction materials, even though the prices may be realistic from a financial viewpoint. Since agriculture 'limits' our industrial expansion in terms of both grain and materials, it is primarily from this direction that we must think about beginning to eliminate the disproportion. To summarise in general terms: a) with regard to fixed funds, gross production and commodity production, the tempo of industry's development is running far ahead of the tempo of agricultural development; b) grain farming, which faces extremely unfavourable conditions, threatens to lag behind the minimal tempos necessary; c) half of the demand from the rural population is non-agricultural demand and to a significant extent[9] originates with the development of large-scale industry itself and the socialist economy; d) a further increase of industry's tempos of development is largely determined by agricultural materials and export limitations.

7) In addition to proper planning, 'we must learn to be cultured administrators' and avoid the 'thousand follies, big and small' that we are committing. Furthermore, 'we did not reconstruct our own ranks in the manner required by the reconstruction period'.[10]

On the first point, as well as the introductory part, I am in complete agreement with the author. And yet there were so many arguments at one time concerning the difference between the recovery period and the reconstruction period, and so many 'terms' (alarmists, defeatists etc.) were aimed at those who demonstrated that the reconstruction period will not proceed as smoothly as clockwork and will create a mass of difficulties for which we must prepare in advance. But, now that the optimists are beginning 'to cross themselves after the thunder', it only remains for us not to stand in the way of their becoming

---

9   [There is a misprint in the text, which refers to an 'insignificant' (*незначительный*) extent rather than a 'significant' (*значительный*) extent. The passage by Bukharin to which Preobrazhensky is referring reads this way:

   ... *almost half of the income of the peasantry* (and consequently *almost half of rural demand*) is the result not of agriculture, but of other earnings, of earnings connected, for the most part, with *industry itself* (construction work, etc.). Hence, to reach a conclusion concerning the lag [of industry] behind agriculture on the basis of the single fact that rural demand is not covered would be absurd.

   (Bukharin 1982, p. 314).]

10   [Bukharin 1982, p. 328.]

wiser; we just modestly note that during these two-three years, as they were coming to all these sacred truths, life moved on little-by-little and managed to create new tasks or to complicate the old ones, which have now been multiplied by the coefficient of the delay in resolving them.

There is no need to argue about the great successes of the state economy in terms of expanding the fixed capital of our industry during these three years. But it would be a grave mistake and an obviously tendentious approach to the matter to refuse to analyse the importance of these figures. After all, the growth of fixed capital in state industry by 2 billion roubles over three years hardly covers or 'only just covers' the so-called depreciation gap of past years, which, according to various calculations, comes to about 2 billion roubles. It we take the fixed capital of the whole state economy together with the cooperatives – including transport, where the losses of fixed capital have been especially serious and recovery is occurring slowly – the growth amounts to only 14%. These figures are striking when it comes to refuting the White-Guard lie that we are continuing to eat up our fixed capital left from bourgeois-landlord Russia, but it would be false to use these figures, without mentioning the depreciation failures of past years, to prove that 'industry's rate of development greatly exceeds that of agriculture'.[11] Nothing that 'great' has happened because agriculture did not decline as much during the years of war and revolution as industry did in terms of both production and its fixed funds.

Here is what the dry figures tell us about the movement of fixed funds in state industry and the private economy, i.e., peasant agriculture, during the past 4 years (in millions of roubles):

| | 924/25 | | 1925/26 | | 1926/27 | | 1927/28 | |
	Annual wear	Investment	Annual wear	Investment	Annual wear	Investment	Annual wear	Investment
Agriculture (Private)	859.1	1,437	6,863.5	1,368.4	889.5	1,454.8	978.1	1.554.0
State Industry	330.6	353.5	331.6	790.2	344.9	1,011.0	381.5	1,284.1

DATA ARE FROM *CONTROL FIGURES OF THE NATIONAL ECONOMY OF THE USSR FOR 1927/28*, PUBLISHED BY 'PLANOVOE KHOZYAISTVO', PP. 520–1.

---

11   [Bukharin 1982, p. 319.]

This means that industry barely halted the consumption of fixed capital only in 1924/25, while the peasant economy continuously increased its accumulation. Railway transport continued to consume fixed capital even in 1924/25 (the wear for the year was 286.7 million with investment of 255.4), and the state housing fund in the cities continued to consume capital even in 1925/26 (with wear of 189.2 million and investment of 157.8).

The total of fixed funds in the peasant economy grew from 16,230.7 million at the beginning of 1924/25 to 18,518.3 at the end of 1927/28, i.e., an increase of 2,287.6 million, compared to an increase in industry from 5,726.6 million to 7,776.8, or 2,050[12] million. This two million hardly covers the wear of previous years.

But consider how things stand in another respect. When industry covers its current wear of fixed capital along with that of previous years, this represents success in terms of covering the wear but not a rapid increase of new fixed capital. It is true that this involves replacing old equipment with new, so that production efficiency increases, but it is not the sort of growth that goes, on the whole, to increasing production compared to pre-war times.

The most serious mistake by VSNKh[13] has always been that in its reports for the general public it has never clearly emphasised the difference between actual new construction and capital investments in new construction that simply cover the current depreciation and that of previous years. In this way it has simply helped to breed the light-headed, dilettantish and deceitful optimism of those who have preferred to busy themselves with this 'useful' business rather than seriously investigating the actual state of affairs. From this viewpoint, it is helpful to examine first how much we spend on new construction compared to capital investments in existing enterprises, and second, what portion of the surplus product being created by workers in state industry is going to new industrial construction.

Of 861[14] million in capital investments during 1925/26, only 100 million or 12% went to new factory construction; in 1926/27, only 275 million of 975 million, or 21%;[15] and in 1927/28, only 230 million of 1,066 million, or 24%.[16]

---

12   [The text mistakenly gives the figure 2,750. The next sentence makes the error clear.]
13   [Supreme Council of the National Economy.]
14   [Preobrazhensky does not give a source for this figure. It clearly does not come from the Table that he provided. Later in this document he gives the figure 863.1. The source for the latter figure appears to be data from the annual survey of industry compiled by the Central Statistical Department (TsSU).]
15   [275 is actually 28% of 975.]
16   [230 is actually 21.6% of 1066.]

Not long ago the TsSU[17] published an interesting work on state industry for 1925/26 and made a first attempt, so far as I am aware, to calculate the 'surplus value' – or more accurately the surplus product – received by the state from state industry.

Marx began his arithmetical examples of the process of capitalist [re]production, as we know, with a 'norm of exploitation' of 100 %, i.e., he assumed that, on the scale of capitalist production as a whole, 100 roubles, pounds, or marks is appropriated by the capitalist class as surplus value for every 100 roubles, pounds or marks paid out in wages The concrete statistical data for the total national profit and the total wage fund in individual countries were in fact close to this proportion; for example, in England during the '90s of the last century and in Germany before the world war.

In those same schemes, Marx further assumed that out of the whole surplus value, one-half is consumed by the capitalists, i.e., by the whole of capitalist society apart from the workers, and the other half goes to accumulation, i.e., becomes part of society's functioning fixed capital.[18]

Of course, this half, this 50 %, does not include depreciation expenses for equipment that is wearing out.

Now let us consider the corresponding proportions in our economy. According to work from the TsSU in the annual survey of industry for 1925/26,[19] the whole of net production – i.e., the whole of the newly created product plus the excise – was 4,850.3 million, and the 'elements of surplus value', as the authors of the book called it, came to 2,691.3 million; that is, according to Marx's terminology for a capitalist economy, the 'norm of exploitation' – or as we say, the norm for the alienation of surplus product – was 125 %.[20] The authors of the book made a methodological mistake by adding the entire sum of the excise to the surplus value, whereas the excise is a tax on all consumers and not just on workers. To compare the wage fund with 'elements of surplus value' acquired specifically from the workers, we have to calculate the total excise for net production, subtract from wages the excise that workers paid to the state, and then compare the real consumption fund of wages with the surplus product. After doing that calculation on the basis of the amount of excise paid by workers

---

17   [Central Statistical Department.]

18   How closely these figures depict reality could be partly seen if there were published data for the sum of all profits in a capitalist country plus the total of all new securities issued together with investments in existing enterprises.

19   *Fabrichno-zavodskaya promyshlennost' SSSR*. Izd. TsSU, 1926.

20   [$v + s = 4,850.3 - 2,691.3\ s = 2,159\ v$. $2,159\ v\ /\ 2,691.3\ s$ gives the figure of 125 % as the wage fund.]

during the year in question, when the excise was 185.8 million, if we take the proportion on the basis of budget studies, we will get a real wage fund going to consumption in the amount of 1,673.1 million roubles. The sum of alienated surplus product without the excise was 1,962.6 million roubles, and consequently the norm of alienation was 117.3% or somewhat lower than in the work by the TsSU.[21]

But in the present context we are not interested in the norm of alienation – we shall come back to that question in connection with the problem of non-productive consumption in the Soviet system – what is important for us here is to clarify what portion of this surplus product is going to accumulation within industry itself, which, in normal conditions – i.e., covering the depreciation failure of previous years – entails another question: What portion of this surplus product is going to actual new construction?

The enterprises that are financed by emissions can be traced with the balance sheets.[22]

In the year that we are considering, 100 million roubles went to *construction* of new factories, 447 million to expansion and reconstruction of existing enterprises, and 157 million to capital repairs. In the area of housing construction, only the wear of previous years was replaced in most cases, and capital repair does not involve new construction. Consequently, 100 million has to be attributed to new construction, plus investment in electrical construction minus annual wear, or 57.9 million, plus a part of the 447 million, because another part of this sum also went to depreciation expenses. According to the table of fixed funds,[23] capital investments plus electrification came to 863.1 million for the year; wear in industry came to 331.6 million plus 14.2 million in electrification; and the total, minus wear and housing construction, will be 409.9 million roubles. In relation to a surplus product of 1,962.6 (omitting the excise), this represents 20.9%[24] accumulation, i.e., a level of accumula-

---

21   In my own studies of this question, which I undertook using material from VSNKh for *The New Economics*, the 'norm of alienation' for the same year, 1925/26, was about 120%. I did not use these conclusions because they still needed to be verified.

22   [The text refers to 'Предприятия которые *фиксируются*', but the intended word is clearly 'финансируются'. This is a reference to the financing of some investments by issuing new currency.]

23   [The text says 'По вине приведенной таблицы …'. The literal translation would be 'Due to the fault of the above table …', which makes no sense. If the intended wording were 'по виду', the literal translation would be 'by appearance'. Whatever the case, these data do not come from the table that Preobrazhensky provided earlier; the source seems to be the data from the Central Statistical Department.]

24   [The text mistakenly gives the figure 30.9%. 409.9/1,962.6 gives 20.9%.]

tion that is two and one-half times less than what Marx thought was possible[25] to use as a numerical example of capitalist accumulation in the economy.[26]

Where is there any 'extraordinary' tempo of accumulation in state industry? Whatever may be extraordinary here – for example, the level of non-productive consumption by the Soviet state at the expense of the workers' surplus product – it is by no means the tempo of real accumulation in industry.

Looking further, what is the essence of the current crisis of the Soviet economy? There are two striking issues here that leap from Bukharin's article. On the one hand, he throws up his hands helplessly before the unique bilateral [dis]proportion of our economy; we are short of grain and materials brought to market by the countryside, while we are simultaneously short of industrial commodities provided by the city for the countryside. However, the idea also emerges, though it is cautiously expressed and imperfectly developed, that the goods famine is the result of incorrect planning, that the disproportion is connected with too rapid a rate of industrialisation, that we have not managed to achieve *'the best possible combinations of the basic elements of the national economy'*,[27] that rural capital accumulation is inadequate and the plan for capital expenditures in industry is excessive, in a word, that we are rushing ahead of what is objectively possible for the country in terms of the rate of industrialisation. Hence, the reader of the article of concludes, of course, that industry must hold back and not rush ahead of agriculture.

First of all, without any explanation from Bukharin, we know and have long known what role spontaneity and the planning principle play in our economy. The only debate was over which policy would reduce and which would increase these elements of spontaneity. We also knew, long before Bukharin's 'explanation', that the major part of our economy is the state economy, and thus any 'analysis of the laws of the transition period' must include an analysis of the laws of development of the state economy. The only argument concerned: 1) what these laws are and just what is imperatively dictated in the economy of the state sector by its entire structure and by the existing level of development of this sector in its relations with the private economy (i.e. what is dictated above all by the law of primitive socialist accumulation; there were sages who denied the existence of any such law, or if you wish, any such objective norm);

---

25 [The text mistakenly says 'was impossible'.]
26 [The text says 30.9%, but $409.9/1962.6 = .2088 \times 100 = 20.885$ or 20.9%. Marx assumed 50% of surplus value was reinvested; 20% is 'two and one-half times less' than 50%.]
27 [Bukharin 1982, p. 508.]

and 2) what part of economic policy is the product of passing conjunctures and results from errors, lack of planning, and the spontaneous influence coming from non-proletarian interests.

In order to take a correct methodological approach to analysis of the Soviet economy, it is necessary to begin with the fact that this is not just an economic but also a social crisis; i.e., besides expressing specific disproportions in economic relations, it also results from the struggle of two implacably hostile economic forms (and the corresponding classes), which are forced together into the single economy of the country. Consequently, all the conclusions must be drawn from the fact that the kulak has no desire to grow into socialism even within one country, despite all the optimistic predictions on that account from Bukharin and his 'school'.

Secondly, when analysing economic disproportions we must separate the elements of long-term and objective lack of correspondence from the latest mistaken economic policy and again highlight the sort of errors that have quickly congealed and become economic necessity.

Let us begin with the economic questions.

Do we have a disproportion in our country between agriculture and industry?

There is a pronounced disproportion, and it consists of the fact that industry systematically fails to satisfy the demand from the countryside for commodities, thus blocking the process of development and the increase of agricultural production for sale in the market. Indeed, the idea is elementary and perfectly clear to any economist that if the existing and potential commodity fund in the countryside cannot be fully converted into industrial commodities from the city, then the very process of increasing commodity production becomes pointless for the countryside.

Where did this disproportion originate?

It has a dual origin. The historical disproportion, which is independent of state policy, consists of the fact that the revolution: 1) destroyed the landlord economy and part of the kulak economy, i.e., curtailed commodity production in agriculture, which was already reduced by enormous over-population; 2) caused an upheaval in the peasant budget – the peasant economy no longer pays rent, pays less in taxes and consumes more agricultural products, while demand for industrial products has increased relative to the level of commodity production in agriculture, with the result that commodity production is lower and consumption higher than before the war; 3) the population of the USSR has increased compared to the pre-war population on the same territory; 4) average crop yields are still lower than before the war; 5) the smaller scale of farming, due to partitioning of the land, causes a deterioration of soil cultivation and reduces production for the market; and 6) the sown area is still somewhat smaller than before the war.

However, the latter cause is also partly a consequence of an insufficiently rapid development of industry and its supply of commodities to the countryside.

All of these factors – some of which are historically progressive, such as liquidation of landlord agriculture and the altered composition of the peasant budget, while others are regressive – are objective in character. The same character and weakness applies to industry, since it is connected with backward technology acquired from the old regime, with failure to provide for depreciation of old capital, and with our socialist isolation in the world.

But conversely, we must not lump together with objective causes the current relative weakness of industry insofar as it is connected with past errors in the area of economic policy. Among the striking errors of this sort is the slogan and the associated practice of 'slowing the pace in industry, not rushing ahead of agriculture, down with the super-industrialisers' etc. This includes failure to understand, over a period of several years, the sources of industrial accumulation and its objectively inevitable dimensions (people have now begun to think a little more clearly about this question); errors in the area of national income distribution (which have now been partially acknowledged and corrected); criminal complicity in the growth of non-productive consumption in the Soviet system, particularly the 'over-population' and costliness of the bureaucratic apparatus of the state, cooperatives, trade unions and the party; stupidity and bureaucratism in economic management at all levels of the state economy; losses stemming from an office-holder's attitude towards socialist matters, i.e., attempts to accomplish historically progressive tasks with historically reactionary methods and unsuitable personnel; waste of the most vital and scarce material values in inept capital construction; the assignment of people to manage production not according to the principle of talent, socialist responsibility and independence but instead on the basis of the greatest servility and subservience to officialdom on the part of people who often understand nothing of the task entrusted to them; and the rapid and spontaneous increase among cadres of the sort of people who replace constructive socialist enthusiasm and pride in work, which is so vital to the country (in this respect the late Dzerzhinsky, for example, was a model), with debauchery, alcoholism and preferential treatment.

People may say: all of this exists, but it is all trivial compared to the historically formed disproportion between industry and agriculture.

No, this is not trivial. Every economic historian knows the role of these 'trivia', for example, in the history of Puritanism and the development of English and

American industry. Has anyone summed up these 'trivia', has anyone taken the trouble to calculate their cost when multiplied over several years? If industry lost just 150 million roubles every year due to an inappropriate distribution of the national income, and an equivalent amount due to the 'over-production' of bureaucracy, plus a hundred million from economic mismanagement and blunders stemming from the improper assignment of people (which Lenin considered to be extremely important), these 400 million roubles a year, multiplied over four years and adding in the surplus product that would have resulted from productive consumption of these resources, will come to more than 2 billion in losses to industry of fixed and circulating capital, which would have meant the possibility of reducing unemployment by several hundred thousand people instead of losing hundreds of millions in the commodity fund for the countryside. If, despite all of these ulcers, holes and gaps, we are moving forward and ultimately have a more rational and rapidly developing economy than would have been the case under capitalism, that is solely because we have parasitically attached ourselves, together with our 'bureaucratic flare-ups', to the advanced organisational structure of nationalised industry and are drawing upon its resources of structural-socialist rationalisation to cover all of these insane expenses.

Our bureaucratism and economic mismanagement have fastened upon the conquests of October and are feeding upon this historically most important organic source of socialist accumulation. From the same source we are covering the material consequences of our miscalculations, our mistakes in economic policy and our losses springing from lack of culture.

I can only welcome the fact that Bukharin's article also recognised everything just mentioned, and I particularly agree with his assertion that 'we *did not reconstruct our own ranks in the manner required by the reconstruction period*'. He should have added that the way our ranks have been 'reconstructed' from Moscow to Alma-Ata and Tobol'sk[28] does nothing for socialist construction and is typically associated only with a reconstruction for the sake of restoration.[29]

Now, let us turn to the issue of disproportion insofar as it also has its source in the social crisis of the Soviet system.

When we adopted NEP, the country became more peaceful and the economy began to recover. When comrades commented that everything was going well, Lenin often warned in private conversations that 'When everything is going well, that is also a bad thing', What Lenin meant by those words is that given the

---

28   [The reference is to the expulsion of oppositionists.]
29   [Preobrazhensky is referring to the prospect of counter-revolution.]

whole set of circumstances involved in building socialism in a peasant country encircled by capitalism, the class enemy must be an ever-present and serious enemy, lurking about even if not yet visible. But over time the new enemy did appear, and its name is – agrarian capitalism.

During the first years of industrialisation, at least during the first dozen years, while the technical level of our industry does not compare to that of an advanced capitalist country, we can only industrialise through exchange with the countryside. The law of primitive socialist accumulation is the law of our survival and development during this interval of time. The clearest expression of this type of accumulation in the state economy at the expense of the private economy, and above all at the expense of the commodity-producing private economy in agriculture, is the discrepancy between prices for grain and industrial commodities even compared to pre-war proportions. These prices for industrial commodities serve first recovery and then reconstruction, which in present conditions means systematic over-payment by the private economy to the benefit of the state economy. And since the private economy in our country is concentrated primarily in agriculture and the state economy in industry, the entire contradiction of development following this general line must inevitably take the form of a more or less pronounced antagonism between industry and commodity-producing agriculture, and primarily between industry and field cultivation (because the state is compelled to begin equalising prices sooner in relation to technical crops from branches that produce directly for the state). To take what can and must be taken from the private economy to support industrialisation – that is the historic task of Soviet power during this period on the economic front. To avoid a break with the middle peasant – which means with the mass of the countryside – is the central task that we currently face.

During the first five years, when capitalist elements in the villages had not yet gained in strength, rural commodity producers, including the kulak, quietly accepted the prices being dictated to them. But now these capitalist elements are rebelling against our policy. While the recovery in agriculture takes the form of conversion of modest farms into middle-peasant farms, and of some poor-peasant farms into middle-peasant farms; while an enormous portion of the increased output is consumed in natural form or accumulated and the commodity supply for the city grows comparatively slowly; and while capitalist elements were experiencing their own 'recovery' period, our pricing policy was accepted by the countryside. Just how systematically – or better, how stupidly and simplistically – our planning organs appraised the dynamic of our relations with the villages, having stubbornly erased from all their multi-year plans any account of the inevitable sharpening of class struggle with the rural upper strata, can be seen from all the various five-year plans of the past two years.

Look at any of them and you will see how everything worked smoothly on paper, without any 'hills and valleys' or complications of class struggle; prices for agricultural products would remain stable, while our own state economy and state agriculture would develop at a completely insignificant rate. Such plans could only be conceived as a result of forcibly erasing from the party's consciousness any thought of the threatening dangers from capitalist development in agriculture, against which the opposition so persistently warned. But then all of these five-year plans were wiped out in a single day as soon as procurement prices rose for grain.[30]

It is perfectly understandable why the development of capitalist relations in agriculture must provoke a rebellion against our pricing policy, which, in turn, is vitally necessary for us for a certain historical period. If the middle-peasant farm consumes 80 % of its field crops and sends only 20 % to market, to receive less for that 20 % is a far less significant issue than receiving less for the commodity output of a kulak farm, which consumes 20 % and sends 80 % to market. On the other hand, the relative weight of kulak opposition to our pricing policy is far from proportional to the relative weight of kulak production as a whole in the country's total grain production. If, out of a gross field-crop output of 4.5 billion poods, the state requires 600 million poods for the cities, the army, the lumber industry and regions that produce technical crops, and if only 100 of these 600 million come from kulak and well-to-do farms, it is enough for the latter to keep these 100 million in their barns in anticipation of receiving a higher price, or to sell their grain in the spring at twice the price on the free market, in order to topple the state's entire economic plan for the year. What limits us in that case is not simply agriculture, but also a definite social group within the agricultural economy.

What conclusion must we draw?

Above all, the conclusion is that the state economy must have its own agrarian base. If the private commodity production of field crops cannot be reconciled with our pricing policy, then the state cannot be reconciled with

---

30   All of these five-year plans were constructed with the assumption of stable agricultural prices and a systematic reduction of industrial prices. This author has frequently proven – while drawing a storm of indignation from astute optimists – that what is important, given intensification of the goods famine, is not a reduction of industrial prices but a more rapid increase of productivity with the same prices. Ask any urban or rural consumer today which he prefers: a reduction of the price for commodities by, say, 10 % or a 10 % increase in the supply of commodities at the same price. Everyone prefers the latter. The planning organs have also finally recognised the situation: projecting a 6 % reduction in costs next year, they are expecting to reduce delivery prices by a little more than 1 %. Finally, they understand.

the private economy's monopoly in the production of field crops. Nowadays it is quite often recognised that there has been much delay in constructing state farms and in collectivisation. We have already cited the relevant passage from Bukharin's article. S. Kosior, in his speech at the general meeting of bureaux of party cells in Kharkov ('Pravda', 7 October), also declared: 'We should have decisively raised the question of the state farm and collectivisation[31] two years ago in order to increase the supply of grain', True, it should have happened, but why didn't it? For the simple reason, obviously, that delayed construction of state farms is a direct consequence – or more accurately, the flip side – of delayed recognition of the kulak threat. Why build state farms, why needlessly take 100 million from the budget for these state farms when the countryside is using grain for moonshine and there are only a few kulaks – and those kulaks that we do have are selling their grain at prices dictated by us and not demanding any investment of state resources in their 'sector'? The kulak threat is a fantasy of the opposition for its own factional purposes. The outcome: they *delayed* state farms and recognition of the kulak threat, while *hastening* the expulsion and exile of the oppositionists who warned of this threat in good time and called for the construction of state farms.

And what is the total result of all this?

The result is that the disproportion between commodity-producing agriculture and industry is being complicated by the social antagonism with capitalist elements in the countryside. This antagonism and the associated elements of economic crisis are not temporary and passing phenomena but rather enduring nails driven into our economy insofar as the prevalence of petty production in agriculture is not something transitory; and this 'small-scale production *engenders* capitalism and the bourgeoisie continuously, daily, hourly, spontaneously, and on a mass scale' (Lenin).[32] This leads us directly to the question of two general lines of our economic development, which we shall discuss later when we come to general conclusions.

Now, let us turn to the causes of the disproportion and crisis.

Many good economists, upon observing our market, shrugged their shoulders and openly declared: we don't understand it – with almost the same grain production as in the pre-war period, the country is not only failing to export the nearly half a billion poods that were exported before the war but also has a grain crisis. Industry has already surpassed the pre-war level and is expand-

---

31   [When Preobrazhensky speaks of collectivisation, it is important to remember that no one in the Left Opposition contemplated *forced* collectivisation or immediate elimination of the kulaks as a social class.]

32   [Lenin 1966a, p. 24.]

ing production each year more rapidly than population growth, yet the goods famine is actually growing rather than diminishing.

A goods famine that affects only industrial commodities, in the presence of an adequate supply of agricultural products, is a perfectly comprehensible phenomenon and signifies industrial under-production; in a capitalist economy it is spontaneously overcome by rising prices for industrial commodities and an influx of capital, together with expansion of production in the deficit branches. Likewise, a one-sided deficit of agricultural products is overcome with a sufficient supply of industrial commodities. But what is the meaning of a simultaneous deficit involving both industrial commodities and agricultural products? What does it mean to have this two-pronged failure to satisfy effective demand, and how can it occur with a stable currency? If there is a unilateral deficit of industrial commodities for the agricultural economy, then agriculture sells but is not in a position to spend all of the money it earns, i.e., it accumulates monetary reserves. Likewise, monetary reserves are set aside by industry if it is not in a position to purchase all of the agricultural commodities it requires. When monetary reserves are also being set aside here, what that means is not a disproportion between sectors of the economy but instead a disproportion between aggregate production and the country's aggregate demand. And as a conjunctural phenomenon, i.e., until such time as production expands or demand falls, it is surmounted in the conditions of world exchange by imports (which are often accompanied by the export of gold). Our current bilateral disproportion signifies a disproportion between total production and total demand, but all of this is further complicated and obscured by inflation.

The source of the disproportion between production and consumption in our country is above all the non-productive consumption of the state apparatus. When the state apparatus non-productively consumes at the cost of limiting worker and peasant consumption to their [effective] demand, there is a corresponding decline of demand from the commodity-producing classes that is not usually the source of a disproportion (unless it has some other cause).[33] When the existence of enormous non-productive consumption is also accom-

---

33   [This is a confusing paragraph. Preobrazhensky is suggesting that the incomes of working people will almost always be spent to satisfy recurrent needs. The need for commodities persists, but if industrial commodities are unavailable in the countryside or prices are too high, peasants may consume or accumulate more of their output rather than sending it to market. The point appears to be that buyers' resistance can be the effect and not the cause of the kind of disproportion he is addressing. As an example of 'some other cause', he may have in mind a boycott by purchasers in the form of middle peasants consuming more of their output and kulaks withholding agricultural commodities from the market. See pp. 261–62 of this article.]

panied by and partly fed by inflation, and when certain organs throw new paper
money into circulation to make purchases without sales, i.e., when this money
does not signify any increase of production and of the supply of commodities in one or another part of the economy, the inevitable result is that demand
swells compared to supply. The situation becomes even more complicated and
confusing when credit inflation is added; when the issue of new chervonets
roubles to the economic organs, according to the credit plan, is not accompanied by any corresponding increase of production and commodity supplies in
the country's economy; and when more and more attempts are made to borrow
from a circulation that was already inflated in the previous production cycle. In
that case, the economic organs formally represent effective demand for materials, building supplies and other means of production, while their workers also
represent demand for means of consumption – but in fact, and on the scale of
the economy as a whole, their demand is not grounded in any real increase of
commodity production and commodity supply.

The way out of this situation has to be sought in three directions: 1) in expansion of production, above all industrial production, because, as we have already
pointed out, the backwardness of agriculture is delaying the development of
industry since agriculture itself has *previously* been held back – even with its
currently miserable technology – by the inadequate development of industrial
production; 2) in a reduction of non-productive consumption within the Soviet
system (the first step here must be a study of the scale of this non-productive
consumption, which no one has thus far undertaken); 3) in a return to a correct monetary and credit policy, eschewing 'easy' and fraudulent successes by
way of inflation. We must not forget that with a strict policy of output delivery
prices and partly fixed cooperative retail prices, we are postponing all the consequences of inflation but simultaneously preventing the spontaneous market
from correcting the disparity between production and consumption through a
general rise of all prices; we are driving the inflationary abscess inward, creating
an uncertain and anxious condition throughout the whole economic organism
of the country and, in the final analysis, giving a monopoly over price increases
to the private market, especially to its basic component – the market for agricultural commodities. And this means that we are permitting a spontaneous
redistribution of national income that is bad for the state economy, while also
frustrating all of our accomplishments in terms of a more appropriate policy
of class taxation of the well-to-do strata in the countryside and the NEP-men.
The current rise in grain prices, which has overturned all of the five-year plans
and fallen like snow upon our heads, is unobjectionable as a measure aimed at
correcting the unreasonably low prices for grain crops. Much of what Comrade
Bukharin says on this theme is correct, although he also makes a raid here, to

the benefit of neither the village nor the city, upon those who believe, and do so correctly, that the law of socialist accumulation limits the law of value.[34]

But we must not forget one thing: a rise of grain prices, accompanied by a reduction of industrial prices in conditions of adequate industrial accumulation and an adequate prior reduction of costs, would be a positive measure prepared by previous real successes in the economic sphere and would signify some closing of the scissors between prices for agricultural and industrial commodities. But since current economic conditions make it folly to think of lowering industrial output prices, a unilateral rise in grain prices inevitably diminishes the buying power of the rouble and from that viewpoint is the first penalty from inflation. I very much fear that this penalty will not be the last one. We have accumulated such a tide of inflation in the canals of circulation, and have so bloated the expenditure part of the budget, that this tide will still break through the dam of fixed prices somewhere.

There is great danger of a general rise in prices. It is best to approach that danger with eyes wide open and to resolve, quickly and firmly, to halt any further expansion of chervonets roubles and treasury circulation until the inflationary situation ends. We must categorically refuse, once and for all, to use loans to cover the budget deficit and inflation for the purpose of credits, since we achieve nothing but an illusion of rapid progress and merely intensify and further confuse the crisis situation that already exists. The general retail index in September of this year, compared to September of last year, rose from 2.26

---

34 Bukharin points out that counterposing the law of value to the law of primitive socialist accumulation is foolish because 'under capitalism there was a law of accumulation, which operated on the *basis* of the law of value'.* This expression from Bukharin is remarkable because accumulation in a pure capitalist economy follows from the relation of distribution between capitalists and workers, not between one group of commodity producers and another. In our country, this accumulation results not just from the relation of distribution between the state, as a commodity producer, and all the commodity producers in the private economy. Consequently, the counterposing that Bukharin thinks is foolish results from the difference between capitalism and socialism (at the initial stage of the latter's development in a backward country). I very much regret that limits of space prevent me here from considering other theoretical questions touched upon by Bukharin.

In any event, the law of primitive socialist accumulation does not cancel or restrict the law of the proportional distribution of labour and means of production, which is obligatory for every society's economic system, although it does restrict and gradually replace the form in which this law is manifested in a commodity economy, i.e., the law of value. We can therefore say that the law of socialist accumulation is the specific historical form of manifestation of the law of proportional labour distribution in the transitional economy. But we must not forget that this law is not the sole regulator; and not being a law in the sense of a spontaneous pattern, it is becoming a conscious norm.

*[Bukharin 1982, p. 316.]

to 2.63. Despite this ominous warning, the credit plan for 1928/29 projects a growth of [currency] emissions by no less than 300 million roubles. We must put an end to this policy of inflation. And once we are clear on this score and have resolved to end it, we must firmly put into practice this principle: more productive consumption, less non-productive consumption, and especially more output and fewer bosses (especially stupid ones).

It is true that N.I. Bukharin made the reservation that he had no intention to deal with questions of monetary circulation. If he did so because he has sinned at times by supporting inflation and does not want to criticise himself, that is his own private matter. But the substance of the issue requires that this vitally important problem be raised with the utmost clarity. We must not forget that in some branches industry can 'lag behind itself' precisely because we have 'over-industrialised'. Our author ruminates at length over an elementary truth for any economist (and not just for an economist) – namely, that any financial plan for industry and its individual branches must be consistent with the availability and corresponding movement of the elements of production in natural form, otherwise the money intended for reproduction will not be able to buy anything. As a member of the politburo and its major economist, Bukharin has approved many things besides a five-year plan and Gosplan's control figures for the current year. Is it possible that he has only just discovered at the end of 1928, for completely non-progressive reasons, the simple truth that any economic plan, in which the circulation of money is not coordinated with the circulation of natural values, has not taken even the first steps towards drafting a complete and coherent balance of all the parts of the national economy, and that he has until now been approving not a scientifically established planning balance but simply scraps of paper and a 'system' of figures that are nicely bound together but do not correctly capture any of the details of proportionality in the national economy? I have no wish to suggest that all of Gosplan's work has been so hopelessly bad. It is true that it has been far from perfect and has not yet resolved the methodological issue of compiling a correct balance, which is an extremely complex task in general[35] and has simply exceeded the capacities of several of the leading planning workers who became involved in this project because of

---

35   A chapter from the third volume of *The New Economics* was published in No. 21 of the 'Vestnik Kommunisticheskoi akademii', where I attempted in general algebraic form to resolve the problem of drawing up a single and comprehensive balance of all parts of the national economy in conditions of non-equivalent exchange and with the existence of three economic sectors: the state, the private capitalist, and the petty-bourgeois. My ideological opponents [have been silent] apart from some silly student's scribbling by a certain Karmalitov in No. 10 of 'Bol'shevik' for this year. [In this Volume, see Part 1, Chapter 1.]

their talents in other areas. Nevertheless, a great deal of work has been done, and the main elements are already completed. I am not the one, therefore, who is making such a negative assessment of all our work in planning – that is the assessment that follows from Bukharin's 'discovery'.

It is quite obvious that if individual branches of production have financial resources for their development that exceed the market supply of necessary elements of production coming from other branches, that would only mean a partial and easily correctible disproportion within industry itself. But if the disparity assumes a general character, in that case we are looking at the product of a credit-driven and general inflation. What else could explain the fact that over long periods of time industry has monetary resources that are not matched by material values previously created during the economic year or currently being created?

This is where inflation becomes confused with over-industrialisation.

Bukharin points out that the intended scale of expanded reproduction, including capital construction, exceeds the volume of construction materials – bricks, cement, glass and construction steel. As for steel, so far as I know metallurgy is one of the most fundamental parts of heavy industry. Bukharin himself acknowledges the deficit, and it would be odd not to do so because this is the branch of production that lags furthest behind the pre-war level. But that only means that our heavy industry is lagging behind, not that we are racing ahead with it (cast iron is at 82% of the pre-war level, while cotton fabrics are at 112%). As far as the deficit of bricks and other construction materials is concerned, does Bukharin really suggest that we adjust the rate of industrialisation to the number of brick factories we have? Is that his answer to the questions of industrialisation? Just think what a compelling economic imperative that is. Bricks and cement factories, together with production of almost all other building materials apart from metals, require the least investment in fixed capital and the shortest time for construction compared to other branches; all of the necessary materials are available in unlimited quantity, and the fundamental expense involves labour power, which, if we are talking about a deficit in terms of the food supply, still consumes agricultural food products even if unemployed. This means that of all the commodities in short supply, including lumber, a shortage of building material is the easiest of all to overcome. Apart from random accidents in the factories, is it not simpler to explain the deficit of construction materials in terms of planning percentages? In fact, what we are dealing with here is simply a planning percentage,[36] i.e, one of those

---

36   [That is, the planned rate of growth for production of construction materials.]

'follies, big and small'[37] (in this case an extraordinary folly) 'that cost a pretty penny'.

The plan for expanding production of construction materials over the past year was obviously inadequate; our planners did not yet grasp the proposition that with industrialisation of the country it is necessary for construction in general, and for production of building materials in particular – in the absence of imports – to grow in completely different proportions from those in industry as a whole; specifically, to grow much more rapidly than the overall average rate. Construction is also the main site for absorption of the new labour power that is being drawn into production. During the past two years, the number of new workers in the whole of large-scale census industry grew by just a little over 200 thousand, while in construction alone the number was about 350 thousand. The plan has to be revised sharply upwards for production of building materials, and it must always begin with a special rate of development for this branch. And this is completely achievable from the viewpoint of Bukharin – who previously argued that the goods famine in our country results from an historical disproportion and did not want to blame anything on errors of economic policy, but who now has also 'crossed himself' on this issue and argues that the goods famine and the crisis situation can also result from poor planning. How is it that poor planning, on its own, can account only for a partial crisis in the supply of building materials and not for a general crisis? The only pity is that as far as the influence of economic policy in intensifying the goods famine is concerned, Bukharin recognised this common and correct proposition only to provide a better motive for reducing the planned rate of industrialisation; that is to say, he is using a true proposition to support extremely frantic and terribly harmful conclusions.

A very important part of Bukharin's argument involves pointing out that the predominant part of demand for industrial products comes from industry itself, and that a large part of rural demand is connected with the peasant's non-agricultural[38] earnings, i.e., essentially originates with industrialisation. The fact that developing industry itself creates an additional market and additional demand for industrial products is something every economist knows. But all that follows is that this demand must be taken into account and that covering

---

37   [Bukharin 1982, p. 328.]
38   [The text says 'agricultural' earnings, but this is clearly an error. Bukharin argued that:
        In reality, ... almost half of the income of the peasantry (and consequently almost half
        of rural demand) is the result not of agriculture, but of other earnings, of earnings con-
        nected, for the most part, with industry itself (construction work, etc.).
        (Bukharin 1982, p. 314).]

previously created urban and rural demand can be [...][39] not only of the closest branches but of all the unfinished construction in so-called 'Department I', i.e., production of means of production. If the deficit extends all the way up the production ladder, then, in addition to inflation this simply demonstrates a very significant lag on the part of industry in satisfying total demand and a delay in co-ordinating heavy industry with light industry – the kind of lag and delay that has accumulated not just this year but over several years and is manifested in the incorrect proportions between production and consumption. While over-emphasising the question of reserves in general, Bukharin forgets to mention that the most severe and formidable difficulties can result precisely from a lack of reserves of fixed capital, above all of fixed capital in heavy industry, where the only thing currently saving us from running into a dead-end is our mismanagement of the accumulation of scrap iron in previous years.

As far as the non-agricultural demand of the rural population is concerned, we are also fortunate that our construction workers are mainly peasants from Yaroslavl, Kostroma and Kaluga, who live and maintain themselves for half of the year in agriculture. If our construction relied upon strictly proletarian construction workers, their demand would be twice as high and the housing crisis in the cities would be much more acute.

But the focus of Bukharin's conclusions is the old position of G.Ya. Sokol'nikov[40] and Shanin[41] that the development of industry is limited by a backward agriculture that produces little for the market, and that the disproportion must be resolved from that direction, i.e., by first stimulating a more rapid development in agriculture, without which it would not be possible to move ahead quickly enough in industry. Bukharin talks about insufficient accumulation in agriculture and claims that in order to develop agriculture, and especially the production of grain and materials, we must guarantee greater capital accumulation for expanded reproduction.

This is a very serious and quite crucial question. With regard to such questions, diplomacy is either political cowardice or involves impermissible contempt for the party and the working class. In Bukharin's article there is also not a word about curtailing the non-productive consumption of the Soviet system and a great deal about excessive plans of capital construction, so that we have to ask him this question, to which he must reply directly and without any equivocation: Whom are we to take from, how much, and to whom are we to make a

---

39   [Part of the text is illegible.]
40   [The Commissar of Finance from 6 July 1923 to 16 January 1926.]
41   [L. Shanin was a former Menshevik and a theoretical advisor to the Commissariat of Finance.]

transfer? Needless to say, he suggests transferring to agriculture and taking from the existing funds for industrialisation. If Bukharin is really convinced that this is the only way to address the problem, let him suggest a different distribution of the national income and undertake to defend such a measure. After piling up so many figures, let him specify a single number and explain its purpose, for the sake of which he erected a whole pyramid of numerical data in his article.

Since we have no answer to that question in Bukharin's article, we shall try ourselves to draw all of the conclusions that follow from his position and analyse them.

If Bukharin is displeased with the current distribution of national income and the rate of capital construction, and if he reduces the issue to greater benefits for agriculture when it comes to carrying the burden of industrialisation, this can be accomplished in four ways: 1) a reduction in taxes on the commodity-producing countryside, since most of the poor are already exempt from taxation, or at least from the agricultural tax, and we cannot seriously expect much in the way of expanded production and capital investment from this stratum;[42] 2) a rise in prices for grain and raw materials; 3) a transfer of agricultural credit away from the poor and the collective farms to individual commodity-producing farms; 4) a reduction of industrial prices.

Without accusing Bukharin of such a horrendous proposal as adopting the first three possibilities, the final measure could only be implemented in the current circumstances at the expense of the already inadequate accumulation in industry or else by cutting workers' wages.

It is difficult to be an enthusiastic supporter of our rather crude and technically barbaric single tax on agriculture, which creates much anxiety in the villages with its bureaucratic levy and is not even decisive in financial terms for our seven-billion rouble budget. But, in terms of economic regulation, this tax is of paramount importance to us as a method of *compulsory commodification of the peasant economy*. It is absolutely imperative from this point of view until such time as a natural commodification of agriculture will be assured as a result of the development of industry and the complete satisfaction of peasant demand. Such natural commodification is presently far from sufficient to support economic equilibrium between town and country; it is far from sufficient even when encouraged by means of compulsory commodification through direct taxation. What will be the outcome if we weaken the operation of this regulator?

---

42 [The poor produce for consumption, not commodities for the market.]

We must not even think of reducing the agricultural tax. If it is adequate and not excessive this year, we still have to improve the method of collection, because our quarrel with taxpayers involves not the sum of taxation in general but rather the uneven way in which it is apportioned and the bureaucratic indifference of officials to the economic interests of individual households and even entire regions.

The second route is an increase of procurement prices. Bukharin's article was written after the July plenum's decision to raise grain prices. Let him tell us whether he proposes to raise them further and by how much, and let him also tell us his secret as to how, while sticking to the anti-kulak course now being conducted by the party and recognised as correct by Bukharin, it is possible to implement by a market route and through pricing policy any sort of redistribution of national income and accumulation that would not be of greatest benefit to the major commodity producers, i.e., the biggest kulak farms.

It is not even necessary to discuss the unacceptability of the third route. The party line, aimed at strengthening collectivisation and extending credit to collective farms, is a most fundamental economic and social necessity.[43] If Soviet agricultural credit, given its stupid bureaucratic implementation, often turns into a redistribution of resources from those who know how to manage to those who do not, what is needed is to improve the methods of practical work, not to destroy an approach that is generally correct.

But let us assume that, through some miracle of redistribution, these resources are guaranteed only to middle-peasant farms in the countryside. It is 100% certain that this whole redistribution would quickly be reflected in a weakening of the tempo of industrialisation and a reduction of the commodity supply coming from industry. But where is the guarantee that on those same peasant farms such redistribution will lead to expanded reproduction and increased production for the market rather than simply to growth of the peasantry's own consumption, which will already be increased as a result of the curtailment of commodity exchange with industry? There is no such guarantee at the moment, given the failure to satisfy effective demand from the countryside for industrial commodities; in fact, precisely the opposite is guar-

---

43   [It is worth noting here that whenever Preobrazhensky discussed collective farms, in any of his writings, he always linked their development with the provision of state loans to support the mechanisation of agriculture and related agronomical improvements. He believed that voluntary, state-supported collectivisation would benefit the peasants themselves while also promoting industrialisation.]

anteed. Really, what sense does it make for a peasant – who has received an exemption from the agricultural tax or sold the same quantity of his products for a higher return, due to a rise of procurement prices – to try to increase commodity production and supply, if even before that price rise he returns from the market with an unsold piglet, chicken or butter because the shops do not have the industrial commodities he needs to purchase, even at inflated prices, with the money he receives? What sense does it make to exchange a real product, whose price is rising, for paper money that is declining? A redistribution of the national income to the benefit of agriculture, when its development is being blocked by the under-development of industry and insufficient supply, will inevitably lead merely to growth of the peasants' own consumption, which all the comparative budget studies show is already bloated for a number of products, i.e., it will further aggravate the disproportion between town and country and between production and consumption on a country-wide scale. I very much recommend to our 'peasant philosophers' that they think all of this over. Their grumbling, of course, meets with heated applause from the petty-bourgeoisie and philistines, but in view of the social character of that applause, I emphasise that their proposed 'improvements' will only intensify the crisis, making today's city and tomorrow's countryside even less prosperous. There are never easy remedies to difficult situations.

At present, two general lines of development are emerging, and they are more sharply defined than ever before for the party, the working class and the country. The first line: we are compelled by the struggle against the kulaks to restrain [development of] the productive forces in the countryside in a capitalist direction, which up to now has remained prevalent among those rural elements who are most responsible for commodity production. We are forced to curtail commodification of agriculture in its capitalist forms. But then we must struggle with all our energy to construct our own agrarian basis and place our wager on a gradual replacement of commodity surpluses from capitalist elements with our own production and with commodity surpluses from the middle peasantry, while stimulating their commodity output with a steady increase of commodities supplied from rapidly developing industry. This will require several years, perhaps another six or seven, during which time we will meet with more than one crisis, more than one wave of petty-bourgeois protest, and more than one upsurge of indecision within the party and even among the working class if we keep them up to date on all the prospects and dangers, hiding nothing from them and rebuilding the relation of the party to the working class in the sense of strengthening workers' control over party policy. If we maintain our endurance, composure and firmness, we will prevail by following this line – and it will be our greatest victory since

October and the Civil War. State industry will emerge from this struggle [as the victor] and will be surrounded by an environment of socialist agriculture.

The second line: we open the floodgates for capitalist development of the countryside, we open up the prospect for every robust farmer in the village to become a kulak and to paddle his way to capitalist commodity production, and we base ourselves more and more upon this growth of capitalist commodity production, upon commodification that costs us nothing in terms of our own resources and is secured to us as if it were a gift from history. But along with this comes uncontrollable agrarian over-population and poverty; the state economy becomes more and more dependent upon agrarian capitalism, which, given the extensive petty-bourgeois basis of our countryside, conceals within itself an enormous potential for a spontaneously developing spiral; and the state economy, under spontaneous pressure from this capitalism, degenerates in terms of its social fabric and loses any prospect of socialist development.

Those are the two general lines. Each of these two lines, and none other, is actually inherent in our circumstances. Serious policies can be divided only along the watershed of these two general lines. The muddle-headed position taken by Bukharin, who cannot even tell us exactly what he stands for, is confused and leads to no practical conclusions of any sort, yet it simultaneously drags us towards the next [...][44] we have resolutely rejected.

When we decided at the party's Tenth Congress to make the transition to NEP, guided by Lenin and under the roar of Kronstadt's guns, N.I. Bukharin (according to Rosengol'ts, who was a witness) commented at a backroom meeting of Old Bolsheviks: 'Now we are creating a situation in which one might wake up some fine morning as the editor of a petty-bourgeois newspaper', At the time, many people laughed at the joke. When, one fine morning, N.I. Bukharin read his article 'Notes of an Economist' in No. 228 of *Pravda*, he hardly suspected that he had woken up as the author of a petty-bourgeois article. Yet here is a trivial but also typical fact: one fine morning, several days after the appearance of that issue of *Pravda*, I went to the Ural'sk district planning commission, where I am working as an economist with Timofeev, a member of the party's Central Committee who is well known both here abroad, and he greeted me with an enthusiastic question: 'Have you read the article by Bukharin? I agree with it completely and absolutely',

---

44   [Part of the text is illegible.]

I very much hope that my own article, which essentially aims to persuade people on its merits and not to be a polemic, will help others, and even N.I. Bukharin himself, to understand how far he has gone along the wrong road.

E.A. Preobrazhensky
RGASPI. F. 17. Op. 71. D. 108. L. 4–16.
Copy. Typewritten.

PART 3

[*Socialist Culture and Morality*]

∵

[CHAPTER 1]

On the Material Basis of Culture in Socialist Society[1]

I must from the outset limit my theme somewhat more narrowly than the title itself suggests. I shall be discussing the material prerequisites of culture in socialist society, understanding the word 'culture' to mean science and art. I confine myself to this area in advance. I shall also touch upon the incentives for labour and creativity in such a society. As for the entire sphere of culture, including material culture, that is something I shall not fully discuss here because it would lead me too far astray from the part of the topic that I would like most of all to highlight.

I must also limit another concept in advance – the concept of socialism and what we understand by the words 'socialism' and 'socialist society'. This restriction is extremely important because, on the question of what socialism means, we unfortunately still do not have firmly established systematic and, most importantly, concretised concepts. We have general formulae and general definitions of what a socialist society means, but their concrete content is not yet adequately determined.

I shall understand a socialist society to be one in which classes still exist, at any rate two basic classes: the class of workers in the state socialist economy on the one hand, and on the other hand the petty-bourgeois strata of the population, who in economic terms are already completely subordinated to the planned economy but nevertheless still exist as a separate class. Petty-bourgeois production will thus continue to exist in a more or less modified form, and specific groups of the population will be materially dependent upon this mode of production and will not be directly included among the workers who are unified by socialist industry and agriculture. In such a society, the state will also naturally exist as some sort of remnant of today's state. Consequently, we must imagine a society that has more or less completed the struggle against capitalist classes and done so victoriously, one that still has a state that is curtailed and contracted by comparison with the existing one; a state in which a whole series of functions have died out yet certain state functions still remain (naturally, they must remain until such time as the entire labour collective of the future society constitutes a single whole, a collective that is no longer divided by the conditions of production and the sources for acquiring a mater-

---

1   A report delivered by E.A. Preobrazhensky at the central club of the Moscow *Proletkult*.

ial income). And insofar as the issue will involve the material prerequisites of culture for such a socialist society, I shall have in mind primarily the ruling class, which will be united around state production and will not simply predominate economically over the remnants of petty-bourgeois classes but will also simultaneously be the main creator of the culture of socialist society.

I shall begin with the first point, which is also the most important. That is the question concerning the quantity of the surplus product that socialist society can expect, which will significantly determine the scope and dimensions of a new culture. From the previous history of all human culture we know perfectly well that culture – in the narrow sense of the word, as I have specified and defined it here – culture, in this sense, only began to emerge when a surplus product began to appear within society. Accordingly, the quantity of the surplus product is extremely important in determining the actual material basis of culture. It is true that in a society not yet divided into classes, and where there did not yet exist any surplus product – in this original society, whose specific stage we call primitive communism – certain *psychological* preconditions for the creation of culture did exist. The stimuli came from the severity of nature, which forced humankind to apply brains and inventiveness in the struggle for existence. But at that time there did not exist, in the first place, sufficient leisure time to enable all members of society to engage in work not directly connected with the acquisition of food. And secondly, since there was no surplus product, there could also be no specific groups of people, differentiated from the general collective, who could devote themselves, as a specific group of people do in societies with a large surplus product, to specialisation within particular branches of ideological production such as science, literature and so on.

When we look further at the history of cultural development in the period of class society, we shall see that this development of culture was closely connected with the dimensions of the surplus product that was at society's disposal and could be distributed mainly by the ruling classes, as stewards of this surplus product, to the tables of science and art and to those groups that engaged and specialised in such matters. If we look at ancient culture from this point of view, in Greece and Rome, we shall see that both Greek and Roman culture were created on the backs of slaves, who far more than the actual creators of this culture produced all the material preconditions that made possible ancient art and literature along with the embryos of science that existed in Greece and Rome. These material facts, on the other hand, gave the Athenian citizen the opportunity to engage in the arts and sciences, having nearly the whole day as free time, and made it possible for him to participate actively in the creation of Greek culture. If we may put it this way, the extravagance of the propertied classes, in terms of subsidising those groups of the population who were able to and actually did live to a large extent from such occupations, depended very much upon the quantity of this surplus product. With regard to the Roman citizen and Roman culture, the latter was likewise created on the basis of the surplus product that, with the slave system, was squeezed out of the slaves and without which the flourishing of ancient culture would have been impossible.

If we recall the period that replaced ancient culture, if we recall the first period of the early Middle Ages, a period when the enormous cities that arose during the epoch of ancient trading capitalism and the slave-holding economy fell into decay, we shall see a simultaneous decay of the culture that had blossomed in quite magnificent colour in the period when slavery prevailed, i.e., the period when a large surplus product existed and allowed this culture to develop. I am not concerned with the question of this culture's ideological content, only with the formal and quantitative aspect.

If we look further to the period of capitalism's flourishing, and if we recall the enormous quantity of surplus value that the bourgeois class acquires and acquired from exploitation of the proletariat, a significant part of which it was able commit to creating its own bourgeois culture mainly through the brains of the third element, the intelligentsia, the relationship between the quantity of bourgeois society's surplus product and the scope of its culture will then be perfectly clear to us.

From that point of view, we must now look at the preconditions of culture in socialist society. How will socialist society differ from capitalist society in this respect? Compared to earlier epochs, we see in capitalist society a colossal development of technology, a colossal accumulator of surplus product, enormous possibilities for the development of culture, yet at the same time we see certain limitations. I shall not presently discuss these limitations insofar as they are connected with the fact that only a certain part of society participates in the creation of this culture – we can turn to that later. I am speaking of the material limitations connected with the economy of capitalist society itself. What do they consist of? The surplus product, which the class of capitalists acquires as the aggregate owner of the means of production, is divided into two basic parts. One part must go to expanded reproduction; accordingly, this part is naturally deducted from the surplus product and cannot go to subsidising bourgeois culture. This part must go to expanding the material basis of capitalist production. The second part constitutes the so-called capitalist consumption fund, as Marx calls it, and here we have in mind not only a consumption fund in the narrow sense, i.e., what is consumed by the capitalists as articles of luxury and so forth, but also the part that is at the disposal of groups of the population that are sustained at the expense of surplus value. This includes the whole section of the intelligentsia that lives at the expense of surplus value, including all those groups in bourgeois society that merely consume without creating any cultural values and are not producers even in the field of ideological creativity. Thus, the dimensions of the surplus value that can be consumed in subsidising culture are naturally limited by the size of the entire surplus product, which in capitalist society, if we take the wage to be constant, depends on the successes of technology and the rational organisation of the economy.

If we look at socialist society from this point of view and compare it to capitalist society, what might the changes be? We are all accustomed – and quite rightly so – to regarding the socialist mode of production as a higher form of economy compared to capitalism. What is meant by the fact that the socialist mode of production is a higher form? For now I am not considering any other aspects of socialism compared to capitalism. I am taking just one aspect – the material basis. Under socialism, how does production differ in this regard from capitalist production? First of all, it will differ because with socialist production science will serve production to a much greater extent. Under socialism we expect a much greater development of technology, and from this point of view socialist society will be the next step in the progressive movement of humanity in general at the point where man comes into contact with nature.

Moreover, we know that with a socialist economic system the enormous benefits ensured by a planned economy will be utilised. It is not my task to discuss all the potential advantages, for us almost tangible, that a socialist economy has and must have compared to a capitalist economy. I shall deal only with the most important ones: much greater efficiency, much more flexibility of the whole production organism in terms of its internal distribution of functions, much more centralisation, and much less expenditure on all the apparatuses that used to serve each private enterprise separately. If we take transport, for example, there will be none of the cross hauls that today result from competition between separate enterprises. If we take tariffs and national frontiers, with a more expedient regional organisation of Europe a whole series of separate and decaying local industries will have to shut down, and those branches of industry must develop that can grow more efficiently, not from the viewpoint of the mercenary interests of a particular country's bourgeoisie but rather from the viewpoint of a planned socialist economy on the whole territory of Europe, and so forth. Here the advantage of a socialist economy is beyond any doubt. I shall say no more on this point. What has been written in this regard in the socialist literature, both scientific and utopian, is sufficient to highlight this aspect of the question.

Other questions are much more difficult for us. To be precise, how, in concrete terms, will the entire production activity and the entire organisation of the economy take shape organically with a socialist society? There is no doubt that these questions are more pressing for us. Here we have encountered thousands of obstacles when we have only begun to embark upon state organisation of the economy. The most immediate, the most difficult and the most important questions for us are precisely organisational questions.

And now the next issue, which is partly associated with development of a much higher level of technique in socialist society, is the question concerning what mass of people will participate in creating the future culture. This is an extremely important question to which an answer must also be provided here. We usually respond to this question as follows: A socialist society will be a society in which all the toilers, all the workers of society, will participate in and be creators of the future culture. As a broad formula, not yet filled in with any concrete content, that is generally correct. But when the issue involves its concretisation, we encounter a whole series of difficulties. All of these difficulties are not part of my theme, but I must say a few words concerning the most important.

All of the cultures that have thus far existed were cultures of the ruling class. There is absolutely no debate among us on that issue. Only a few representatives of the oppressed classes were involved as creators of the culture of the exploiters: they were attracted as persons who were detached from their own class. Marx once said that the most dangerous ruling classes are those that know how, in timely fashion, to select and attract the minds of the working class into serving them and then to rule the masses of the proletariat through this stratum. And this is what all ruling classes have very skilfully done throughout the whole history of culture. The exploiters were able to find, caress, bribe and then transform the best elements that made their way up from below and stood out for their abilities and talents. Those whom they were unable to convert they persecuted, drove them into a blind alley, deprived them of the possibility of advancement or physically eliminated them. Thus, all previous culture up to the present day was the culture of the ruling classes.

But what does this mean, in terms of numbers, for the participation of distinct groups in this culture? If, for example, we take France prior to the Great Revolution, the France that we customarily regard as a country in which intellectual life seethed and boiled, in which the encyclopaedia was published several decades before the Revolution, in which free thinkers clamoured and materialist philosophy was developed – how numerous was the population that in fact participated in creating this culture? We can say without any exaggeration that hardly 1/50 to 1/100 of the whole population took part in the creation of this culture if we think in terms not only of the active participants, the active workers in the field of ideological creativity, but also of the audience who were capable of listening and understanding. Consequently, if it is a question of the actual subjects of cultural creativity, an even greater restriction is involved. We are dealing, therefore, with an extremely narrow social stratum in whose circle new cultural values were created. On the basis of my reckoning in another context, which dealt with ingenious and talented people from the thirteenth century onwards, I can say just how few these people were who directly participated in the creative process. I calculated about 2,000 persons. Of course, this circle of the most outstanding and most prominent was followed by a periphery of the less talented and less well known, who still more or less take part in intellectual life. Increase this number by ten times over – and it will still be insignificantly small by comparison with the whole population of this period.

Consequently, looking from below, we have the 99 % of the toiling masses who are absolutely not involved in cultural life or else participate in the persons of their more or less gifted individuals, who are making their way upwards and are then absorbed by the ruling classes; the next stratum is an audience who understand what is going on and what is being created for them; and finally there is an extremely narrow, almost guild-like circle of people, who in fact are the creators of this culture. Thus, the entire organisation is quite hierarchical even in the sphere of culture, and in a sense it duplicates what prevails in the social-political field. The analogy can be taken even further if we include the organisation of the bourgeois scientific workshop. How is everything formed there? How does the head of a school function? He has an institute of scientific journeymen who are obliged to fulfil his assignments. Here a definite caste spirit develops, all kinds of restrictions are created for new elements, etc.

Thus, in capitalist society – which up to now has created maximal opportunities for the development of culture compared to all social formations that preceded it – bourgeois culture, although it is ultimately quite well funded in the sense that it develops on the backs of millions of workers and peasants who serve the capitalist elite, in fact depends upon a very narrow class basis. From this point of view, it cannot be compared to the culture of a society in which the relations between people in the process of production and distribution fundamentally change, creating a basis that must be incomparably wider.

Our general idea of socialism as a society in which the masses will be drawn into the creation of culture is perfectly correct. But now we have to look beyond the general formula. The question we face is this: In what form will culture in a socialist society be organically and directly connected with the very structure of production and distribution? How will it be connected with the labour incentives that will replace those typical of capitalist society? In this respect we can imagine things in a couple of ways: one is that socialist society copies bourgeois society in the sense that it makes the field of ideological creativity into a specialty of a certain group of people, although the group is numerically much wider than was the case in bourgeois society. On the other hand, the free time that remains to the workers of socialist society after their 5–6 hour working day (the numbers I am using are arbitrary) – this leisure time will allow almost the entire mass of workers in socialist society to be same class audience for the group of cultural creators that the bourgeois class, comprising a minority of society, was in relation to the active creators of bourgeois culture. We can imagine the expansion of this basis as follows: the basis and the audience itself expand, and the group of active cultural workers grows, but these workers are specialised; they have no connection with physical labour and only work in a certain area of ideological and non-material labour.

But we can also imagine a different answer to the question: material labour is an obligation for everyone without exception, and cultural work is for each individual an ideological superstructure over his material production. Five hours of material work, through participation in material production, and during the remaining time each participates in all of the work and activity that grows out of material work and continues it in other directions (this superstructural work will in part facilitate reduction in the amount of time necessary for reproduction in the sphere of material labour). That sort of answer to the problem is also conceivable. Which variant can we think of as more correct? I think that they should not be regarded as opposites, for in this area the issue depends upon the stage of socialist society that we are considering.

All of the questions connected with socialist society are extremely difficult to examine concretely unless we agree in advance on what we take the period and conditions of development of this socialist society to be. We have it now in a quite embryonic condition. We can imagine the situation after 15–20 years, when our state economy creates 70% of the national income and is the basis of the country's entire economy. We can also imagine the ensuing stages, when the petty bourgeois strata, who are only historical remnants of pre-capitalist forms, will be an appendage of the socialist state economy and will be fully included in this economic system. Of course, in each of these stages of development of our state planned economy there will be corresponding relations in all other spheres, including completely different relations between people. Take the relations of subordination in the field of industry between the technical commanding stratum and those who do the implementation, i.e., between the engineers and technicians on the one side and workers on the other. Throughout all the stages of socialist society these relations will be changing. And if we remember that socialist society is the transitional stage from capitalism to full communism, it will be difficult for us to consider one or another formation of socialist society unless we specify more or less accurately what moment we are considering and in which historical period. From this point of view, it is theoretically much easier for us to draw a parallel between capitalist society, taken in pure form, and communist society, than to compare the situation in capitalist society with that in socialism. Socialism is the undeveloped form of communism, or communism in the process of development, communism at the crossroads, *im Werden*. And when we consider the questions of how culture will develop, which hands and brains will be involved, how numerous the participants will be and how people will relate to each other, and what free time and surplus product there will be (which mean essentially the same thing), it will be difficult for us to answer all of these questions at once for an entire period that will possibly last a century. What happens in 1940 will be different from what happens in 1960, while socialism will exist in both 1940 and 1960.

Take, for example, the question of whether we shall copy bourgeois society in the first stages of socialism, and if so, to what extent. I find it difficult to answer that question. I do not believe that we shall have any dramatic leaps here. It seems to me that what will occur is a gradual attraction of new strata of the working class into science along with a general rise in the level of culture in accordance with the material achievements of production in the state economy and its material accomplishments compared to all the other backward forms of production. I do not think that any very rapid cultural revolution is possible over a period of a few years, or any sharp leap from the stage in which socialism is only beginning to emerge from the capitalist integument to one in which all of the masses begin to take part in cultural life or become active creators or a responsive audience for this culture. In any event, if we take socialist society at the stage where the socialist mode of production is predominant and petty-bourgeois forms are merely its appendages, tolerated for the time being and eking out a rather miserable existence, all of this presupposes a sufficient change in the very nature of Soviet man, a change that involves at least two-three generations. A generation will emerge who will not have known capitalist relations and will not be corrupted by capitalism in the way ours has been, as we drag behind us all the rubbish from bourgeois society, often without even noticing this charming inheritance. The historical task of our generation is to break through the doorway to socialism and to be succeeded by generations who will be raised on the basis of socialist relations and will possess, almost as a social instinct, a certain collective discipline and conscientiousness at work that is required for socialist production.

Now consider the participation of the masses. We must expect that at the outset, at the very first stages of socialist society, the whole of the masses will participate at least to the extent of constituting the audience for the new culture. We can also imagine a certain collective participation of all workers of socialist society in the creation of this culture, although it cannot be ruled out that initially we shall replicate bourgeois relations. Only later can we imagine a situation in which *everyone* will take part in the process of creating material goods and will use all of their time freed up from material production for work in the sphere of culture.

What social groups and specialisations will then be possible? (Their existence cannot be doubted, for without specialisation any future development of culture is impossible.) We can imagine a completely new type of specialisation that presupposes everyone's familiarity with the fundamentals of science and art. What this will all mean concretely we cannot presently say. But here we must note one fact that is extremely important for the future culture: everything depends upon an increase of the national income in general and of free time in particular, which can be devoted to culture. How can we conceive this symbiosis between the material base and the future culture?

In this respect we have one remarkable example to prove the enormous significance for this entire gradual improvement of the actual human being who must make this step-by-step advance. We have the period of so-called War Communism. In 1918–20 we attempted to apply forms of distribution and production on the basis of incentives that were not typical of a capitalist and petty-bourgeois economy: the factory works, and everyone receives as much in the way of rations as the state can provide for all workers more or less equally. In the area of distribution, each worker at Narkomprod, who was engaged in the distribution of herring, textiles and so forth, worked on the basis of some sort of incentives. We assumed that he works for the benefit of society, that he is distributing social assets, and that he consequently has sufficient incentive to work in a new way and – on the basis of the collective interest and the incentive of understanding the common proletarian, governmental and social tasks – to do no worse than capitalism. Those were our illusions.

It is true that this entire period of War Communism was inevitable and necessary for a whole number of other reasons more fundamental than our illusions concerning the preparedness of the working class for collective distribution. Here we had an experiment of transferring present-day man, with all of his incentives for labour cultivated by capitalism and petty-bourgeois economy, to another arena that demanded from him other motivations and where the old incentives were an obstacle to success in the work that had to be accomplished under War Communism. And what happened? It turned out that at this point we encountered the fiercest resistance. Capitalism resisted us most vigorously exactly on the front of the old psychology of the worker, the psychology of the employee, of the shop clerk etc. The individual incentive for participation in labour disappeared, and we saw the extremely gloomy consequences. You all remember the incredible dirt and indifference to the consumer that prevailed at the Narkomprod shop to which people came to receive their due. What we saw there was plundering of state property, i.e., absence of the collective motivation necessary for success, and the operation of incentives that dragged the masses backwards to the customary ways of private interest – more for me and let others go hang. During War Communism there were many instances when this heritage from capitalism, on its own, accounted for a whole series of setbacks that we experienced.

Now we have NEP, and the same shop clerk who so rudely and neglectfully issued some product to you at Narkomprod – how he has changed, how he cringes before you when cutting a piece of sausage in some private store where he works for a NEP-man. Now we see 'bourgeois' cleanliness where previously we had 'socialist' dirt. How quickly Moscow took on a new appearance! What happened? Of course, there are many economic reasons explaining the change, but by no means the least important reason is to be found in the people themselves; in the fact that these people, who had certain incentives for work in the routine machine of capitalist or petty-bourgeois production, lost these incentives and turned out to be fish out of water when we tried to move forward in certain respects and to break out of capitalist relations during the period of War Communism. And conversely, when these people found themselves in a position where individual incentives could begin to operate under NEP – things worked as smoothly as butter. This shows us what enormous importance the incentives for work have for the successes of production – incentives that continue to operate with the current level of production and the given level of consciousness. The incentive for work, developed by capitalist and petty-bourgeois society, is grafted onto the oppressed classes, and on that basis they can also work as if they were fulfilling the usual and normal tasks for which they are totally prepared. They cannot suddenly dissociate themselves from those incentives. They have to transfer to new ways and take what is within them, particularly what they have learned in the period of struggle against capital, and on that basis create collective incentives for work.

The next question is how, from this perspective, things will be in socialist society. Here we must ascertain the connection between the material preconditions of culture – a higher technique, a much larger surplus product, and much more free time during which the whole of the masses will be drawn into the cultural process in an orderly economic system – and the incentives for work in socialist society. This question is extremely important. It involves our entire system of education, which we must even now create in preparing a new generation who will have to continue our effort.

I see the matter this way. Socialist society, insofar as it is the transition stage on the way to full communism, cannot give us anything that is perfectly complete in terms of the incentives for work. Here, too, we shall have a certain transition period from individual incentives, cultivated by capitalism, towards collective incentives that will become instinctive under communism. We can imagine an initial combination of the two. At the present moment, to some degree, we already have a certain tendency to move in this direction, and in future it will be much stronger.

What might such a combination of individual and collective incentives for work consist of? At the least it involves the following. Certain foreign comrades who have visited our factories have been struck by the devotion to the enterprise and by the conscientious attitude towards the affairs of the particular enterprise as a whole that our workers already have. They were quite amazed by this, and in this respect the difference between capitalist Europe, where the worker is completely disinterested in how things are going at the enterprise – when the work is done and the pay has been pocketed, good-bye – and what now prevails in Russia. We see an enormous interest of workers in their factory; they are interested in whether their factory is in the black or the red, whether or not it is working at a loss, whether it has fulfilled the production programme, uses fuel economically, etc. These questions interest the worker, and as time passes an ever-increasing mass of them begins to share that interest. And that is natural because we are witnessing the beginning of a process that can be called day one of the birth of completely new incentives for work. This is a question of colossal importance for the entire future of socialism, because if we are able to replace individual incentive with the incentive that organically characterises the socialist mode of production, we shall then have resolved the question of the tie that exists between the economy we now have and a human psychology that lags behind, still has not adjusted to these economic relations, and will otherwise be a heavy burden that impedes our gradual progress.

In our factories a certain collective interest is already emerging among the workers, although it is true that it is a rather narrow interest on the scale of the factory. But the factory, all the same, is a collective. And when the individual worker is interested in the output of the factory as a whole, he is already moving from the point of view of a purely individual interest, interest in his own earnings, to the beginning of a collective incentive for work. We can imagine other transitional stages as we move, perhaps, to workers of whole branches and trusts being interested in the affairs of the trust as a whole, and to competition between the individual branches of industry. On the other side, the forms of distribution will also adjust to this collective stimulus to work, which has already begun to happen on the new economic base and will continue to develop. The further we advance, the more wages will represent distribution of a bonus fund, if we may put it that way. One can imagine the kind of wage that the individual worker is interested in and that he receives according to his individual output. That is a tribute to the past. What we have at present is our concession to the petty-bourgeois instinct, our concession to capitalism, but it is still something we are struggling against. On the other hand, the worker receives a certain portion of his pay from the bonus fund of his enterprise, trust, or a branch of industry that fulfils its production programme. In that manner the wage begins to consist of two basic sums: one that is connected with the individual output of the worker and is associated with the incentives of the old world, and on the other hand a portion in which we already see the breath of new life in a distribution where there is no difference between the lathe operator Ivanov and the metal worker Petrov, and it is completely inconsequential who produced more since the distribution is more collective. If we think on the scale of the state as a whole, then we shall have a wage fund consisting of two sums – a capitalist type of payment and one that is more appropriate to socialism, a collective payment.

In this way development will occur at the cost of the withering of individual incentives and individual remuneration of labour in favour of the triumph of collective compensation for the collective accomplishments of labour. If we take the further development of technique, electrification for example, we see that the further it proceeds the more an individual accounting of the results of labour becomes increasingly difficult. If you take a vast system, a regional electrical station for instance, that serves tens and hundreds of enterprises, it becomes exceedingly difficult to individualise payment. It will be even more difficult if we organically join the station with another enterprise, transport for example. It is extraordinarily difficult in transport to produce an individual accounting of labour and of the processing done by each individual worker. The development of technique makes keeping an individual record increasingly difficult. On the other hand, the social structure of the whole state encourages the development of collective incentives and the changeover to collective wages; and the further it proceeds the more the role of individual incentives diminishes along with individual payment for work, which at a certain moment is transformed into a backward relic that is already incompatible with the economic structure of society.

What will the significance be for culture? Above all, this will mean an expansion of its basis. If it is not a narrow group of engineers but rather the mass of workers who participate in improving the conditions of production and new inventions, when millions of eyes will be fixed on whether something might somewhere be improved, or whether new improvements might be applied to a machine that has some imperfection or other, and if in place of tens and hundreds of eyes looking into this there should be a million eyes, then we can imagine what a colossal difference there will be in the results. In this regard, we can cite an example in the data that we have for workers' inventions during the four years of revolution. Today there is a colossal growth of the number of workers' innovations compared to those before the war, and here we have a complete revolution. Meanwhile, 25% of our workers are illiterate and only a small percentage of them have completed introductory technical school. The basic conditions that would enable the mass of workers to take part in innovative creativity are extremely unfavourable. However, even with these conditions there has been an enormous leap forward. You can imagine what the results will be when millions, not only of literate people but also those who have completed major training, will be participating in such effort. From this point of view, technique in socialist society will develop incomparably more quickly than in capitalist society, and tens of millions rather than tens of thousands will be involved in its improvement.

Now I turn to the relation between these collective incentives for work and those who manage work. In capitalist society there is certainly a need for an overseer. In a new society that emerges from the capitalist one and still retains 90% of its basis – take Soviet Russia in our own period – overseers are necessary but they are becoming much less so than under capitalism. For now, however, the overseer is necessary. This is most unfortunate and very sad, yet it remains a fact. Each of you who is associated with production knows this very well. But in future, when the collective incentives for work are predominant, this institution of the exploiting stratum will become extinct. Through a specified system of labour training, all the necessary habits and discipline of collective labour will become social instincts and will be manifested in the same way as any physiological instinct. When we have a new man in a new economic system, then, of course, the material consequences of such labour, of such collectively conscious labour, will be incomparably greater than under the capitalist system. Technique will advance much more rapidly because it will be driven by millions, and there will be no such obstacles to the use of inventions as there are under capitalism. (You know that a whole series of machines are not put to use under capitalism because, although they save labour, they do not yield a profit and are not useful when labour power is cheap.)

Those are the main points upon which I wanted to focus attention. I have only touched upon the most basic and essential questions connected with the material base. I have not dealt at all with questions as to how we might concretely envision, in numerical terms, the surplus product of socialist society, what share of it must inevitably go to reproduction or what can be devoted to enabling society to develop its cultural activity and raise a young generation in the spirit of a socialist epoch of enlightenment. Then there is the issue of the degree to which technique and its successes will economise on labour time, leaving more time for cultural and mental activity, etc. I cannot answer such questions because I have no wish to make unfounded predictions. I openly admit to you that I cannot quite clearly envisage the technical basis of socialist society. At the moment it is still difficult to say how socialist society will look in this regard. Many of our utopias, including the very brief utopia that I wrote myself,[2] are justifiably criticised for crudely forecasting the technical changes that might occur in the course of an entire century. I consider those reproaches to be quite well-founded. That is something that must be left to communist-engineers with sufficient technical imagination. But the greatest revolution that is expected in production technique in general will be the revolution in agricultural technique. Unfortunately, I cannot say anything about this aspect of the matter. I still have to highlight the question of cultural relations between town and country. But my report has already become too long, so I shall end it here.

[...][3]

Concluding Remarks by Comrade Preobrazhensky

First of all, despite what has been said here, I categorically insist that Proletkult suggested that I give a report 'On the Material Preconditions of Culture in Socialist Society' – not in 'capitalist' society.

One of the comrades who spoke here endorsed a completely inaccurate criticism that was aimed at a book by comrade Bukharin (see the objection to comrade Bukharin in the article in the journal 'Under the Banner of Marxism'). The point that he referred to is utterly mistaken. In the first place, comrade Bukharin never denied that the whole social complex takes part in the creation of culture in the sense that if the toiling masses did not create a surplus product there would be no culture. But the style of this culture, its character, is determined by the class that usurps power for itself, puts its own stamp upon this culture, and uses everything created in this area in the interests of sup-

---

2 [Preobrazhensky apparently has in mind *From NEP to Socialism.*]
3 [The debate on Preobrazhensky's report has been omitted.]

porting its own domination. There is pressure in the technical field, the wish to develop the particular society's productive forces, but this occurs in such a way that the material consequences are also usurped by the dominant class. That is what I was discussing. But does this mean that the backs of the slaves, upon which the whole culture arose – in Athens or Rome – that the backs of these slaves, their muscles, blood and brains did not participate in the creation of this culture? If, instead of noting the exploitative character of these cultures, instead of emphasising their inevitable collapse, we formulated the question to suggest that these cultures were created by the unqualified masses, then we would be taking the Narodnik point of view and glossing over the true state of affairs. For that reason, the rebukes made here against comrade Bukharin were completely unfounded.

Now I turn to what comrade Zander said. Several times he turned to the issue that it would be desirable to have a theory of the crash of capitalist society from the economic point of view. I completely agree with him that such a work is desirable, but for my own part I refuse to speak on that question. I have no ready-made design, and if did I would be the first to write about it. There are different points of view on this question. Perhaps it could be shown how, at a certain stage, the mechanism of the capitalist economy creates greater contradictions than its progressive aspects can smooth over. As for the fact that the bourgeoisie appears gradually to be emerging from the crisis, we cannot foresee how long the current improvement will last. For example, the revival of American industry is beyond question, but, on the other hand, there is also no doubt concerning the colossal collapse of America's agriculture. England has recently begun to surmount the crisis, France and Belgium have almost done so, but a financial crash has yet to come in France.

Speaking of incentives, comrade Zander pointed out that when technique progresses and the scale of enterprises is vast, the great wheels of enterprise spin in such a way that the human individual's role is reduced to that of an insignificant screw. Once he begins to work he cannot stop, and there is no point here in talking about incentive; the technique itself embraces the man and compels him do what it requires. But the worker can still not turn up at work at all. If 50 or 60 people do not turn up, then it may be necessary to bring an entire electrical station to a halt. That is the first point. And secondly, it is not true that, even in the enormous mechanism of the factory, poor work by individuals or groups of workers is of no consequence.

Now consider the extremely important question concerning distribution of the surplus product and its role in the successes of culture in general. Comrade Zander poses the question this way: it has not been proven whether per capita production was greater when Athenian culture flourished or in the period of the Middle Ages. Take the early centuries of the Middle Ages, when there was not yet a major class differentiation or especially marked inequality in terms of property. I do not have the relevant statistics, but let us assume that on average the surplus product was greater than in the ancient world. This would prove nothing. We know that slaves were underfed, but free citizens had a surplus and were in a position to create their culture. This means that culture can develop even when there are not sufficient products for everyone, provided that incomes are arranged in such a way that a part of society has free time and all the material requirements for creation of culture.

Now I want to turn to a very complex question concerning creativity in the future and the considerations that came to my mind under the influence of what comrade Kan said here. First of all, I must object to a certain addiction on the part of comrade Kan and other comrades to the word 'proletarian', which they use much too frequently. I think that even in the hall of Proletkult this excess is completely uncalled for, and comrade Kan has overdone it a bit. For him, technique turns out to be proletarian simply by the fact of becoming the standard. But the origin of that standardisation lies in the distant past. Comrade Merezhin correctly pointed out that standardisation begins from the moment when mass demand emerges, when industry no longer works to order, when attempts are begun to simplify the products being turned out and to reduce the variety of product types. Already under capitalism, standardisation applies not simply to the manufacture of tools but also to the methods of work and ultimately the psychology, etc. The tendency towards standardisation is as old as the machine. It is even older than the machine because it is evident even in the age of the manufactory. These processes of standardisation cannot be regarded as specific characteristics of socialist society – they also refer to capitalist society, and there is consequently no basis for indiscriminately calling them the proletarian tendencies of technique. That would be historically incorrect.

It is too bad that comrade Kan, as an engineer, did not fantasise a bit here. I expected that he would tell us something new, that he would give a picture of future technique, when we shall have mass usage, for example, of energy from splitting the atom and so forth. Take the technique associated with the acceleration of growth by using and concentrating solar energy. What will that mean for the structure of agriculture? Not long ago a Bulgarian professor discovered a more perfected way of stimulating seeds, i.e., soaking them in a solution that stimulates them to grow more rapidly. With seed stimulation the productivity of the soil increases almost ten times over compared to use of ordinary seeds. If this will be applied on a massive scale, what will our agriculture look like then? Of course, it would cause a complete transformation. The conclusion is this: we do not know what technique will be thirty years from now, and for that reason we do not know what our future society will look like. The big general question is whether it will involve standardisation going as far as comrade Kan imagines. I think that we can envisage a completely different situation: millions of brains earnestly searching in different directions, millions of inquiring eyes focusing on the most diverse aspects of nature, and millions of experiments, planned and unplanned, in order to probe nature in all directions. In this respect standardisation will be more of an obstacle that a stimulus for progress. If we conceive a picture of the future in the most optimistic terms, we might imagine a structure something like this. There will be maximal diversity in this creative work, both individual and collective. There will be entire 'factories of invention', whole regiments of inventors, all connected by a single plan. There will also be loners. Maximal diversity in creative work and maximal standardisation in using the results achieved.

But we also face another question – that relating to incentives for the whole society to develop. This is an extremely important question. Capitalist society is internally contradictory: it advances along the line of expanded reproduction, while the subjective incentive of the leaders of production is the quest for profit. Only individual incentives are utilised at the given stage of development as a whole. The same question naturally arises for a socialist and perhaps even more for a communist society. The internal equilibrium of communist society may not appear to be conducive to progress. That sometimes appears to be the case when making a comparison with the antagonistic capitalist system. But we have to say that we all actually know why Morgan strives to accumulate, since he only consumes 1/10,000 of his revenues. In this case it is more a matter of description than of explanation. But if the stimulus for progress in capitalist society is class struggle, it follows that this struggle is itself something productive. The absence of equilibrium in society, manifested in the class struggle, results from the absence of equilibrium between human society and nature. Of course, there will also be no such equilibrium under communism. And that disproportionality will be the stimulus for progress. It merely takes a different form in an antagonistic class society, the form of struggle between people themselves.

In conclusion, I want to say a few words concerning one comment from comrade Kan regarding incentives. He says that in capitalist society everything is aimed at 'taking', as compared to 'giving' in socialist society. This example, however, reminds us of Sergei Petrovich-Andreev[4] or the type portrayed by

---

4 [Preobrazhensky has in mind the story of 'Sergei Petrovich' by L. Andreev, in which the hero ends his life by suicide.]

Dostoevsky – the arch-failure. Some people believe that a person who fails in bourgeois society ends his life because he has nothing to give to society on account of his lack of talent. Would it not be more correct to suggest that they end their lives precisely because they are unable to take anything? But that is just a passing thought.

In socialist society the social instinct can be utilised on a much wider scale than under capitalism. Everything that is socially necessary and socially useful will be done spontaneously. A member of society will instinctively do what is in society's interest without even considering the origin and genesis of motives for his activity. As for cases of deviation from the common norms, they will be regarded as abnormal. Thanks to the fact that the fundamentals of socially useful activity will become instinctive, much greater energy will be preserved for the direct struggle with nature.

> E.A. Preobrazhensky, *O material'noi baze kul'tury*
> *v sotsialisticheskom obshchestve*
> (A Report delivered to the Central Club of Moscow Proletkult).
> Moscow, 1923, pp. 3–26, 45–51.

CHAPTER 2

On Morals and Class Norms[1]

1 In Place of a Preface

At the present time we have a need for a short popular book or brochure on morality. This need is not only theoretical, or more accurately, not so much theoretical as practical in nature. The emerging worker-reader and our young students not only wish to know what morality is but are also asking the question: 'Am I living the right way?' While answering the first question from the point of view of the Marxist theory of society involves no difficulties, especially since the answer is essentially given by Marx and Engels, a response to the second question is incomparably more difficult. This question is being raised as a totally concrete one, in a specific historical period and by representatives of a specific class. It is so broad and imprecise that it must appear to be rather naïve, yet it is nevertheless vitally important. The exploiting classes, who ruled the economic and political sphere before the revolution, supported their system of domination not just with the state, as an apparatus of class oppression, but also with certain moral restraints. They imposed their morality upon the oppressed classes. The Revolution overturned the economic and political domination of the bourgeois-landlord bloc and brought disgrace to the exploiters' morality. But some of the questions that were answered according to the dictates of the exploiters' interests and the morality of the classes that were overthrown – some of those questions are now being raised from the viewpoint of the working class in conditions of proletarian rule, and they are not always being phrased in some vague, mystical, moral form.

The task of this brochure is not to provide concrete answers to all of these questions, but rather to pose correctly the general question of morality in principle. In this context, some questions will disappear because they turn out to be stated incorrectly. As far as the necessary and vital questions are concerned, to whom they should be addressed and where the answers should be sought will become clearer. At the same time, an assessment will be made of the peculiar *practical* amorality that extends the principle 'everything is allowed' into areas where, in terms of the interests of the proletariat and its future, far from everything is permissible. This vagabond philosophy has nothing in common,

---

1 E.A. Preobrazhensky, *О морали и классовых нормах*, 1923.

of course, with communist amorality; it is a product of a certain ideological-organisational interregnum and the inertia of the final phase of disintegration of the morality of the overthrown classes. The old norms have disappeared, and meanwhile the methods of the collective's influence on its individual members, which are typical for the proletariat in a socialist system, together with the limits of such influence in different contexts, have not yet been fully worked out or assumed final form. The proletariat's public opinion has not yet developed with respect to a number of questions that go beyond the limits of Soviet law and the tactics and organisational methods of party and trade-union organisations. At the same time, though, these questions are vitally important to the proletariat in terms of its class cohesion and internal solidarity as well as for the future of a society in which the proletariat must play the decisive role in every area. We have in mind, of course, the immediate future of our Soviet society, not a society of the future.

There is very little Marxist literature on the question of morality. Apart from the places that everyone knows in the works and correspondence by Marx and Engels, as well as brief excursions into the field of morality in the Marxist literature on the theory of historical materialism, we can point to the famous book by K. Kautsky on *Ethics and the Materialist Conception of History*;[2] a few places in works by G.B. Plekhanov, especially concerning the French materialists; some places in works by A. Bogdanov; a couple of pages in the book by N. Bukharin in *The Theory of Historical Materialism*;[3] and some work of rather poor quality from a Marxist viewpoint by Dietzgen. And that is about all.

As for distortions of the Marxist position on the question of morality, or sentimental-philistine 'corrections' and 'additions' to Marx, along with attempts to 'reconcile' him with Kant, etc., that sort of literature is much more common. To polemicise with its authors in the sixth year of the proletarian revolution is absolutely pointless. It would be like debating with Milyukov and Struve concerning the advantages of Soviet democracy over a bourgeois republic. In practical terms, our argument with Marx's ethical critics has long been resolved by the fact that during the Civil War all of those gentlemen turned out to be on the side of the Whites and thereby clearly revealed the social roots of their moral inspiration. Stanislav Volsky, with his pompous book *The Philosophy of Struggle* (Volsky himself was also in the camp of the counter-revolution), should likewise be included among those narrow-minded intelligentsia idlers in the field of morality. Another petty-bourgeois falsification of

---

2 [Kautsky 1918].
3 [Bukharin 1969.]

Marxism on the question of morality is the brochure by N.N. *On Proletarian Ethics*.[4]

I specifically mention the latter brochure because of its attention-grabbing subtitle. However, one can already tell from the title itself just how deeply the author got to the bottom of ethics in general. There is as much 'proletarian' in his ultra-intelligentsia ethics as there is ethical in the contemporary proletariat, i.e., both of them amount to zero.

2   Morality and Law

In our exposition we shall begin with the customary, so to speak philistine, ideas of morality (even if philosophically grounded) and then gradually move towards a way of framing the question that we consider to be correct and consistent with Marxism.

When a revolutionary, sitting in prison, begs the tsar for a pardon or turns in his party comrades for interrogation, we are talking about a crime against revolutionary ethics. When a group of workers at some capitalist enterprise do not submit to the collective decision during a strike, return to work and begin to play the role of strike-breakers, we are talking about a violation of the principles of proletarian morality.[5] When a doctor reveals secrets of his patient's illness, that is usually referred to as a violation of medical ethics etc. Based on these examples, we can already give what is regarded as the customary definition of morality. Morality is said to be a system of norms or rules determining the behaviour of people in certain areas of their activity.

In place of the Latin word 'moral', the word 'ethics' is used in almost the same sense.[6] But in conventional speech the word 'ethics' has acquired a different shade and a somewhat different content. While we usually understand morality to mean practical norms of behaviour, by ethics we more often mean general concepts of morality or the theory of morality. As far as the words moral and ethical are concerned, they mean conforming to the demands of morality; immoral and unethical refer to violating the principles of morality. We know that the actions of people in society are also regulated by laws, enactments by

---

4   [Koshkarev 1918. The brochure was republished in 1918 by VTsIK. Its subtitle was 'Proletarian Creativity from the Point of View of Realistic Philosophy'.]

5   We shall consider below whether this term is suitable.

6   [The Latin *moralis* is a translation of the Greek *ethikos*.]

the organs of state power, etc. The question is: Which actions are regulated by legislation and which by moral legislation?

The dividing line here is roughly as follows. In the first place, the laws forbid a society's citizens from committing one or another act that violates the interests of the ruling class and the whole existing social order. Morality forbids or encourages behaviour from the viewpoint of a particular class, and thus not necessarily from the viewpoint of the ruling class. Secondly, the body that is responsible for the court and punishment is the state. Conversely, legislation in the sphere of morality takes the form of so-called public opinion, and thus in class society the public opinion of a given class. This public opinion does not have the capacities for repression or the repressive organs that are at the state's disposal, especially if we are dealing with the public opinion of a *non*-ruling class. The instrument that a society or class uses to influence its individual members is public censure or approval, which, it is true, can sometimes take such tangible forms as the severance of relations, denial of help and support, boycott, etc. The laws of the state forbid one behaviour or another, but they have nothing to say about which behaviour is recommended. Moral norms not only censure some activities but also encourage moral acceptance of others. Moreover, the law may not forbid some acts that are condemned by morality. Moral judgement, to the contrary, is also passed upon acts that are prohibited by laws, and it does not always conform to the spirit of those laws. We can see, therefore, that the spheres of human behaviour that have normally been and continue to be subject to moral assessment (in a class society) is wider than the sphere regulated by legislation. But it is still confined within certain limits. What are those limits?

3   Subjective Goals and Objective Consequences

Not every act is normally subject to moral assessment. If some tourist strolls on a hill in an unpopulated area and throws stones down for amusement, this activity will not be called either moral or immoral. But that instantly changes if there is a person standing at the foot of the hill. The tourist can cause him harm if he continues his activity, and now this activity may be looked at from the standpoint of morality or immorality. It is clear, therefore, that only those acts that bring benefit or harm to people are subject to moral assessment. Consequently, an act cannot be considered, on its own, to be moral or immoral if it is taken apart from time, space, a person's social relationships and the interests of other people: it depends on how it affects other members of society (or the actor himself if we consider him as an individual in a society of people such as himself). Therefore, only certain kinds of activity immediately stand out from the infinite number of human activities.

But even these will be significantly curtailed if we bring into the discussion the consciousness and will of the person committing the act, which is what the old morality used to do all the time. Let us return to our example. Suppose our tourist continues to throw stones from the hill, fully convinced that there is no one at the bottom, and then the stone that he throws down injures or kills someone. In this case, the behaviour of the murderer may not be subject to moral assessment, for what happened contravened the will and intention of the guilty party. Take the opposite case. In an area where the population suffers from a water shortage, a member of the community accidentally discovers a spring while burying something that he stole or in some other manner. Nobody will think of calling the act of this citizen highly moral. On the contrary, another member of the community, who put in considerable time and effort unsuccessfully looking for a source of water for the community, will be considered a moral person (in this regard), and his activity will be considered to deserve moral approval.

Of course, if all the good intentions in the world ended the way the service of Krylov's bear did,[7] and all the acts committed with wicked intentions opened up wells of happiness for humanity, then the concepts of moral and immoral, as applied to a person who is acting consciously, would change entirely. If an intention involving some benefit for other people is usually approved and encouraged as moral, it is only because this intention has, so to speak, the fragrance of a positive result. It is not the intention itself that is encouraged by moral approval (because an intention on its own, which is not acted upon and is fated never to be acted upon, does not have any value, either positive or negative); what is encouraged is the consequence, or more accurately, what is often associated with it in reality. In exactly the same way, so-called 'evil' intentions are censured because they are usually precursors of harmful acts that a society or class strives in advance to prevent, forestall, or interrupt at the stage of intention.

---

7   [In Krylov's fable *The Hermit and the Bear*, a lonely man becomes friends with a lonely bear. The bear is supposed to keep flies off his friend while he sleeps, but when he becomes frustrated by a persistent fly he uses a stone to kill it and ends up killing his friend as well. The bear failed to recognise the difference between the immediate good (driving off the fly) and the enduring good (his friend's long-term welfare).]

4   Moral as Useful; Immoral as harmful

But do not the words 'moral' and 'immoral' always mean 'useful' or 'harmful' to people?

If we leave aside the goals and intentions of people doing some act or other, and speak only about real activities and their consequences, that will be exactly the case. 'Moral', translated from the obscure language of morality into normal speech, always means good for people or a certain group of people, useful, and expedient; 'immoral' means harmful, destructive, and inexpedient. There is not a single system of morality in the world whose demands are not rooted in the needs and requirements of certain societies or classes. Strike-breaking is considered one of the most grievous crimes against proletarian morality because it does enormous damage to the fighting proletariat. Cowardice and betrayal in war are considered the most serious crimes against military ethics in full proportion to the harm they cause to one side in the fight. Theft is considered immoral among property owners, whose mode of production requires support for the forms of private property. On the contrary, amongst a group of people whose occupation consists of violating the rights of property, and therefore also property-owners' morality, i.e., among thieves, not to steal something that is left exposed (except for what belongs to members of the gang themselves) is considered immoral or the height of negligence. Medical ethics forbid revealing the secrets of patients' illnesses because such disclosure materially harms doctors as a specific profession. (Or, if we accept the doctors' own version, because disclosure forces sick people to avoid medical assistance, i.e., medical morality safeguards the interests of public health).

Moreover, an action might be more or less moral based on that old scale. Translated from moral into material language, this means that some action or other is more useful or less useful to a society or a class. Strike-breakers would have committed a more serious crime against proletarian morality if they did not simply try to sabotage a strike but also called upon the police for help against the strikers, i.e., if they caused even greater damage to the people on strike, etc.

In short, it is always and everywhere the case that in a given society, class, or group of people, what is beneficial, good, and necessary for this society, class, or group is considered moral; everything that is unfavourable for this society, class, or group is immoral. The harm may, of course, be direct or indirect, just as the benefits may occur in the present or in the future.

5   The Evolution of Moral Norms

But, after all, what is beneficial today might be harmful tomorrow and vice versa. How do matters then stand with morality?

Morality also changes. History gives us countless examples of this kind. In fact, the entire history of morality, first and foremost practical morality, is one continuous example of this kind.

When the labour of a single individual was not very productive and the average person could not normally create a surplus product – since whatever he created was barely enough to sustain his own life – in that period warring tribes took no captives but killed them instead. A captive could not provide any surplus product for his master. The morality of these tribes considered it both permissible and necessary to exterminate those who were defeated. When labour productivity increased, so that a captive could not just provide for himself but also yield a surplus product to the master, then the extermination of captives came to a halt and they were taken as slaves and forced to work for the victors. The morality of the victors trailed along behind their changed interests and began to condemn the killing of captives as immoral.

Trade in human beings and slavery is considered immoral in a developed bourgeois society. In contrast, the Greeks and Romans, who created ancient culture on the backs of slaves, did not think to consider slavery immoral as long as slave labour played an important role in their economy. But slave labour, in a certain period of society's development, turned out to be less profitable compared to serfdom or hired labour – and morality did not hesitate to pass sentence upon it.

Exactly the same history was repeated with serf labour. The first 'discovery' that serfdom is 'immoral' and 'an affront to human dignity' was made by those groups of serf owners who had already discovered in their own economic practice that hired labour is economically more profitable than serf labour. Particularly here in Russia, industrialists and a part of the nobility began to advocate emancipation of the peasants based on 'moral' motives when hired labour, being more profitable, started to displace serf labour not only in industry but also on the estates of landlords who were producing for the market, especially in the south of Russia.

The murder of old people, based solely on their inability to work, is considered deeply immoral in all societies and all economic systems where surplus product exists, particularly in agricultural communities, where the aged additionally play the role of 'elders', i.e., the organisers of production. On the contrary, among many tribes of wild savages, the killing of old people past a certain age is an ordinary event and does not contradict moral views. The reason is clear. Tribes that have this custom possess such miserable means of subsistence that the upkeep of old people would deprive a corresponding number of the able-bodied and their children of survival. The lesser of two evils is chosen. Killing old people, in this case, is considered moral because it is a means of preserving the group as a whole.

Let us also consider suicide. The Chukchi[8] consider it miserable cowardice if an old person past a certain age does not commit suicide. The reason is clear from what we have said. In communities where the means of subsistence are sufficient for all members, and where population growth is beneficial, especially among agricultural peoples, suicide is considered immoral. For example, Christian morality, having become established in a society already possessing systematically significant volumes of surplus product, considers suicide a sin. Among the proletariat of capitalist countries, where the great majority of suicides are committed on the basis of penury and unemployment, moral indignation is directed against the actual killer of these suicide victims, i.e., against a system that murders the hungry with their own hands in front of warehouses full of goods (suicides among workers rise precisely during periods of unemployment and crises, i.e., at the time when there is the greatest excess of unsold goods). The suicide of a revolutionary, ending his life because of disappointment and failures in the fight against an exploitative system, i.e., deserting the battlefield, arouses no particular sense of admiration because the strength of this person committing suicide would have been helpful for the struggling class in the future. Revolutionaries hold a completely different view of their fellows who commit suicide in order not to betray their comrades during torture and interrogation, or who commit suicide after flogging in a penitentiary. In this case, suicide either forestalls damage to the revolutionary party or else a protest-death ensures better conditions of prison life for the living.

On some issues, moral attitudes have changed several times over the course of history. For example, infanticide was and to some extent still is considered acceptable in many tribes with a nomadic way of life. Such systematic killings are necessary in those conditions because they enable mothers to move with the tribe and consequently to escape death in the severe conditions of a hunting life. Among settled agricultural peoples, where this motive disappears and population growth is beneficial from a production point of view, infanticide is considered a serious moral (and not only moral) crime. But once again, in ancient Sparta, where the first motive did not matter but raising only the strongest citizen-soldiers was imperative from the military standpoint, there

---

8 [The Chukchi are an indigenous people in the far northeast of Russia.]

was a custom of killing physically weak children. In a modern society, where the surplus product is sufficient to provide for all living adults, children and old people, and where only relative rather than absolute overpopulation exists, killing live children is considered a crime, although various viewpoints exist on abortions, depending on class interests and the material circumstances of different groups of the population.

6   Morals in Class Society

In a society such as the modern one, i.e., in a class society, some groups of people are interested in one thing, others in something else; what benefits some groups may be precisely what is harmful to others. What happens with morality in class society? How does it change?

In class society morality follows class interest, which forces it to strut about in vague, mythological garb, i.e., it is simply class morality. Every class that is established and has particular interests either creates its own morality suitable for itself, or else it revises the old morality to suit its needs, making amendments to it, expanding or curtailing its demands, and interpreting one point or another in its own interests.

Let us return to our example with strike-breakers. The striking workers try to shame strike-breakers and to compel them by some means or other to join the majority. That is totally consistent with the interests of the workers and consequently with their proletarian morality, which requires class solidarity of all toilers in the struggle. But then the factory owner appears on the scene and addresses a thunderous speech to the strikers. We would expect him to say: 'Swindlers, you want to deprive me of my last group of workers, you are preventing me from disrupting the strike, you are swindling me for a loss of tens of thousands of gold roubles'. But the reality is completely different: our factory owner prefers the language of morality. 'Why are you preventing people who want to work from doing so?' the factory owner says. 'You are violating human freedom; you are committing violence against the person. Do you really not want freedom? Why are you infringing upon the freedom of others who do not agree with you?', etc. This is one of millions of examples in which two classes can have completely opposing views on one and the same question if their interests are diametrically opposed. The morality of one class prescribes to its members something forbidden by the morality of the enemy class. That is the first point.

Secondly, we can see from the example provided how a violation of the material interest of a single person or an entire class is perceived or con-

sciously portrayed by that person or class as a violation of human morality in general. This happens because certain groups or classes have *already*
managed, *through an unconscious process*, to adjust their moral beliefs and
all the content and forms of their class consciousness to their class interests.
Whatever does not undermine their system of thought, established on the
grounds of a particular system of production and distribution, is true for them;
whatever complies with their class interests and strengthens their chances for
victory in the class struggle is moral for them. Let the reader now imagine the
entire class of capitalists instead of our factory owner; instead of a question
of strike-breakers at a single factory, imagine the key interests of the bourgeois class, which it is defending in a struggle with opposing classes; instead
of the speech-making factory owner, let all of his specialised deputies in such
matters come forth, i.e., the *litterateurs*, professors, religious preachers, and
lawyers who are defending the exploiters of labour power. Then he will get
the picture of what is really happening in contemporary society. Whatever
is beneficial to the bourgeois class is preached as being moral, as morally
obligatory, as natural and necessary *for everyone*. Whatever is directed against
this class, against its domination, its system of ownership, the state, the family etc., is regarded or presented as a violation of human morality in general.

But there were and still are other social classes apart from the bourgeoisie.
What do they do in this case? They do exactly the same as our factory owner
and the entire bourgeoisie. Whatever is beneficial to these classes, whatever
supports and strengthens their power, increases their incomes in the present
and ensures they will receive them in the future; whatever accords with established class psychology and contributes to internal class cohesion – all under
the banner of eternal verities of goodness, truth, beauty, justice, freedom etc. –
is defended by their *litterateurs* and religious representatives and manifested in
real life as the public opinion of the entire class, which condemns some actions
by its members and condones others.

When the interests of these classes, as owners of all sorts of eternal truths,
clash with one another, this conflict of interests is turned into an argument over
eternal truths. And when an attack is sufficiently prepared by this spiritual artillery, when the ranks of each class are closed under the banner of these truths
and their allies from other social groups join in, then 'criticism with weapons'
begins. And even though eternal truths, in themselves, have neither excessive
appetites nor ambition, it is in their name that one class grabs incomes and
power from the other one. If we remain at the level of the bourgeois or feudal
outlook, it may seem that over the course of history no classes ever fought others for their interests; it was just that one 'eternal' truth grabbed another by the

throat with millions of inspired hands – that one morality declaimed morality to another with the volleys of cannon and machine guns.

But if the current morality of every class is always class morality, then the first question is: Why does this delusion and self-delusion exist and endure, and what point is there in passing off class morality as universal and eternally true? When these clashes occurred, the representatives of different classes could see very well that the morality of their opponents was far from universal. Yet their sight betrayed them concerning themselves. How does it happen that people of a certain class are truly convinced that the truths they are defending are eternal and universal, and at the same time there is everywhere and always a striking harmony between the attributes of these truths and class interests? In short, how does consciousness imperceptibly adjust to material interests? That is a question that concerns the theory of class consciousness. As for the question of why such self-delusion persists, the answer is not difficult. When class morality is passed off as universal and eternal, it is not only people from that class who will adhere to it, which is natural, but also other social groups who might temporarily be drawn to side with that class. If our factory owner had spoken directly about the interests of his own pocket, the only people who might have sympathised with him would be other factory owners who had also been, or might yet find themselves, in such an unpleasant position. The only thing the workers might have said is: 'What's good for you is not good for us, and that's all there is to it'. But when our orator speaks about freedom in general and how violence is inadmissible, any simpleton from the workers' midst might think: 'Indeed, it may be true that I am mistaken'. And there is no doubt that on this issue a great majority of people from other classes will support the factory owner, who is standing up for 'freedom' against those who are 'violating' it. Generally speaking, disguising one's class morality in the costume of universal truth and justice has played an enormous role in history and continues to do so. That is how the ruling class imposes its morality upon other dependent classes and on occasion compels them to serve its own interests so long as they do not free themselves from an alien morality and develop their own. Thus, even if there is no universal morality in class society, such an illusion was well worth inventing.[9]

Not only does every class have its own morality in class society, but in different periods of its historical existence the same class also changes its morality

---

9   Intermediate classes, especially the petty-bourgeoisie, have always nibbled eagerly at the bait of eternal truths and still do so, especially the petty bourgeoisie; attracting the petty bourgeoisie to its side has always played an important role in the strategy of big capital. Capital needs the commodity of 'eternal truths' first and foremost for this consumer.

to a greater or lesser extent. And that is fully understandable if we recall that the social circumstances and interests of a class change, just as everything else does in this world. For example, when the bourgeoisie was represented in the first stages of its existence by mercantile capital, it had yet to make a break with the morality of the social class that dominated society at the time, i.e., the morality of the landed aristocracy and the clergy. And the official morality of those classes was generally Christian morality. (Mercantile capital simply adjusted that morality to suit the interests of primitive accumulation, for the benefit of which it allowed ample scope.[10]) As the bourgeoisie began to grow stronger, and its interests began to clash with the interests of the aristocracy and clergy, it began to liberate itself from their morality, at first by supporting different reform movements within Christianity that more closely expressed its goals (Lutheranism, Calvinism etc.). When it grew even stronger and made ready to oust the aristocracy and clergy from power in society, it promoted writers, scholars and moralists who set out to prove that religion in general is an illusion of the human mind and sheer superstition, that only reason can reveal the truth to us. And 'reason' did not hesitate to disclose a whole number of such truths that justified the bourgeoisie's rejection of the old morality and opened the way for it to fight for power. Wherever (for example, in France) the antagonism of interests between the bourgeoisie and the aristocracy were deep and acute, the rupture in the sphere of morality was absolute and the bourgeoisie sent Catholicism into retirement. Wherever the antagonism of interests between these classes was less profound (in England for example), religion likewise turned out to be not so profound an 'illusion', and a compromise was reached between the bourgeoisie and the old morality.

And now the bourgeoisie is in power. The slogan 'Enrich yourself' is promoted. And the bourgeois begins to enrich himself with the hands of the proletariat as individual capitalists develop furious competition with each other. Freedom of action for capital and the representatives of capital is the main moral demand of the bourgeoisie: everything is good, everything is permissible, everything is moral that gives capital an opportunity to grow unchecked, using the toil of the workers. And to wipe out all of the obstacles on the way to self-aggrandising capital, the slogan that is promoted is 'Down with all moral-

---

10   It is interesting that while the nobleman, in his day, took from Christian morality the principle 'Let tomorrow look after itself' and squandered his fortune, the representative of the priesthood emphasised in his sermons the renunciation of earthly goods (in favour of the Church), whereas the Kolupayevs and Razuvayevs [i.e., kulaks and merchants in *Haven of Mon Repos*, written by the satirist M.Y. Saltykov-Shchedrin] advocated abstinence in the interests of primitive accumulation.

ity'. The freely acting individual, completely following his own egoistic desires, will best of all provide for the common good, because the interests of the individual and the interests of society coincide. However, if anyone encroached on the inviolability of the private property or incomes of the bourgeois, the guilty party would suddenly find that the slogan 'Down with all morality' must be understood wisely and carefully; that this slogan, in the language of reality, only means 'Down with any morality that is preventing the development of capital'.

But while enriching themselves, the bourgeoisie become more convinced with each passing day that growth of capital is accompanied by growth of the proletariat, by clarification of its consciousness, and by its increased activity in the battle for its demands. The proletariat also demands a place for itself at the feast of life, and more and more it threatens bourgeois domination. Bourgeois morality begins to undergo a new cycle of changes. The bourgeois recalls his old acquaintance, the Christian morality that reined in the popular masses so well during the dominance of the aristocracy and that he so thoughtlessly declared to be useless and harmful. On the wrinkled face of that old lady he begins to discover new merits that he never noticed in the heated days of his historical youth. And now we witness this morality's resurrection from the dead. In America and England, where hypocrisy and sanctimony among the upper classes is especially developed, we can observe the following situation: the millionaire, the factory owner and the stock gambler step forth as preachers, with the Gospel in their hands, and they tell the working masses who have assembled to listen: 'Brothers, do not worry about the joys of your life, act as Christ commanded. Do not follow our sinful example. We have accumulated wealth, but there is eternal torture awaiting us in the next world. On the contrary, your lot is better, because it is easier for the poor man than it is for a rich man to enter the kingdom of God. And be grateful that we are preparing a Heaven for you by depriving you of the blessings of this life and are ready to accept eternal damnation for doing so'. Thus, under the influence of the proletariat's growing strength, the bourgeoisie begins to reject its own morality and is forced into a contradiction with it, resorting to moral hypocrisy. (This is a common trait of decomposing classes that are facing inevitable loss of their dominance.) On the other hand, the growing solidarity of the proletariat also unites the bourgeoisie in the face of common danger. The old slogan, 'Everyone act at your own risk', begins to lose its value in capitalist society. More and more frequently, whenever it is indispensable in the interests of the entire bourgeois class, 'violence against the person' begins to be practised among the patented defenders of freedom of competition. Any contemporary European bourgeois is an incomparably more timid liberal with regard to morality than his grandfather and great grandfather were in the revolutionary epoch. And although in practical life, in pursuit of pleasures of all kinds, no morality really exists for him, he cannot find the words to say, as his grandfather did, 'Down with all morality'.

But the old morality is not always thrown away entirely by a new class as useless junk. Like a thrifty housewife, cutting a new dress out of old clothes when her measurements change, the human psyche strives to manage with the old truths adjusted to its new needs. In human history, new wine is much more often poured into old wineskins. A vivid example of how one and the same system of morality can serve different classes comes from Christian morality. Priests, the petty bourgeois and the repented bourgeois see that as its supreme virtue: they attribute it to the fact that Christian morality is the only universal morality capable of serving as life's leading principle for all times, peoples and classes. In reality this prostitute, always trying to look younger, has served many gentlemen only because she is replete with contradictions and can be interpreted in any manner. Every class took from her only what suited its own interests; every class interpreted different aspects of Christian morality in its own way, reading its own thoughts into it as suggested by its own interests.

We can see hundreds of examples from history and modern life of how Christian morality was torn into pieces by different classes, and how the most opposed interests were justified by references to the teaching of Christ.

'Our land is so small, there is no space for a chicken to run, we would like to have a little more land' – said the peasant to the landowner before the revolution.

'Do not covet something that belongs to your neighbour' – didactically replies the landowner who has not forgotten Holy Scripture.

'Be merciful, father, the land is God's. Christ told to us to share even a shirt. Are we asking for much? Just what we need to live on'.

The Christian landlord replies: 'Man shall not live by bread alone. Be patient and you will inherit the kingdom of God in heaven'.

When the peasants became too persistent, the evangelical discourses ended and the police, gendarmerie and army appeared on the scene. Peasants were mercilessly beaten and shot, and the peasantry in turn killed the landowners. And all of that occurred within the confines of one and the same Christian morality, to which nobility, peasants, priests, policemen, Orthodox believers, and sectarians all swore. Patience, resignation to fate, submission to the established authorities – all of these moral precepts of Christianity were excellently used by the exploiters in different countries to justify their dominance over the masses. Conversely, everything in the Gospel that is democratic and directed against wealth and inequality of any kind was used by the masses in their struggle with the oppressors, because they had not yet managed to create their own new morality and could not finally emancipate themselves from the chains of religion. Even the proletariat, during the initial stages of its class struggle, still tries to toe the line of Christian morality, and at that stage Christ is seen by many leaders of the workers' movement as some sort of original socialist. But further development of class conflict corrects these mistakes of the proletarian movement's childhood, and the proletarian avant-garde severs all connection with religious fetters.

7 The So-called Eternal Moral Truths

But is humanity really unable, over the course of its centuries-old history, to produce such moral demands as would be mandatory for all people despite existing contradictions between their interests, demands that would reflect the commonality of interests of all humanity as a species in the struggle with nature? After all, there are such questions as the value of human life itself; the question of the integrity of the whole human race; and such qualities as conscience, honesty and courage on the one hand, and lies, betrayal and cowardice on the other.

Let us start with the first question and conduct a survey among different classes on the well-known Gospel commandment 'Thou shalt not kill'.

Let us address the clergy first, as those most competent in the Scriptures. 'Of course murder is a sin – the Father replies – but ... but Christ himself, after all, did drive merchants from the temple'. And based on the fact that Christ drove merchants from the temple with a whip, under the tsar the servants of the Church 'bade farewell' to those who were expelled 'to a better world' with a rope around their neck for their struggle against capital. They also 'bade farewell' to millions of people who were sent by the ruling classes to be killed in wars.

The pious petty bourgeois replies, 'Murder is a sin but ... but if someone climbs into my barn and I shoot him while protecting my property, who would say that I am a dishonest person?'

Ask a big bourgeois. He will respond 'How shall I put it, murder is a bad thing, but ... but how do you not shoot such wretches who are ruining industry with their strikes?'

The Orthodox landowner already gave us his answer previously. If we now weigh up all of these restricting 'buts', then the translation of 'Thou shalt not kill' from [Church] Slavonic into the Russian language will mean: shoot whenever you need to. Therefore, in response to one of the most fundamental questions concerning human life, the operative morality gives an answer completely in the spirit of class interests.

But if not a single human life, then perhaps the interests of the whole of humanity, of the survival of humankind, will be dear to everyone despite differences of class interests, i.e., temporary, transitory and changing interests? No, not at all.

'France is degenerating, look at our peasant, whom you have tortured with unbearable extortion and reduced to poverty and physical decline. Spare the future of our country and our race' – says the French bourgeois to the aristocrat before the revolution.

'After us the deluge' – he replies, cheerfully finishing a bottle of champagne.

'Look, the nation is becoming weaker every year under the influence of exhausting labour in your factories', says the English aristocrat to the new gentleman, the capitalist who just recently grieved soulfully for the French nation. 'We need to implement factory legislation, protecting the nation from the plundering of workers and degeneration'.

'What's that? Are you trying to kill industry?' – the indignant capitalist replies, and he continues to suck the lifeblood not only out of grown men and women but also from children as young as five years of age, so long as degeneration of the population does not begin to threaten the military might of the state and, in a word, the same bourgeois pocket.

Similar examples come from every country during every epoch as soon as the division of society into classes is well underway. The interests of humanity are only protected if they coincide with class interests. And when the latter come into conflict with the interests of the species, or with the interests of social development, the representatives of different classes never consider putting their common interests first; their morality stands guard, above all, for their own class interests.[11]

Let us look further. Maybe, although classes differ in the goals of their activities and their definitions of good and evil, they can reach moral consensus in the realisation of their goals and the means for achieving them? Perhaps they agree that some means are good and morally acceptable and others are not? Perhaps they all agree in their understanding of truthfulness, honesty and faithfulness to one's word?

History replies that there is nothing in the world that is absolutely moral or immoral in terms either of ends or means; there is neither absolute truth nor

---

11   Generally speaking, the interests of humankind as a species are usually protected (in fact, not just in words) by society's most advanced class, for their class interests correspond with those of social development and humankind's future. Therefore, the interests of the species do not, so to speak, have permanent lodgings in class society but move about as one class replaces another in power.

absolute falsehood. Different classes favour truth and honesty differently. For example, the feudal knight strives to hold high the banner of honesty and loyalty to his word, given to his master and his peers. But he differentiates between someone from his own circle and the common people. To deceive the former is to him a great moral crime, but when it comes to the latter – any means to an end. But a competent merchant says directly that if you don't deceive, you won't sell. Another does not deceive, but only because, in his own words, honesty in trade has become more profitable. In general, the share-price of truth and honesty on the one hand, and lies on the other, rises and falls in the history of every class. When a class is strong, striving for power and has a future ahead of it – it raises the share-price of truthfulness. It is more truthful and objective in both its practical life and in science and art. On the contrary, when a class is tending towards decline and loss of its power and dominance, it resorts to any means to save the situation, just as a bankrupt does when trapped by his affairs. Truth is unprofitable – the share-price of lying climbs, and there will never be any shortage of talented people who will prove that a lie can do very honourable service to humanity. If a member of a particular class employs a lie and slander in the interests of his class and not for his own purposes, and if he is successful, he will always remain an honest and respected member of his class and will be considered a person of higher morality than his colleague, who kept silent while he was lying in the name of his class.

Decaying Catholicism brought forth the Jesuits, examples of whose methods are well known. But Catholicism would not have tolerated this order for a single day, nor the order its own members, if the order or its individual members employed lying merely for their own ends.

Ruling classes use lying for the deception and unrestricted exploitation of oppressed classes. All morality is essentially based upon the class lie: one class passes off its class interests, successfully varnished with 'non-class' moral and other truths, as the universal interests of humankind. And conversely, oppressed classes very often resort to the instrument of the lie as a weapon of defence against their oppressors. Any underground work, any conspiracy, any secret preparation of an uprising etc. – all of these require lying. Whereas for everyday life in a classless society a lie is detrimental to everyone in general, because it forces members of society to expend extra energy in finding the truth, things are different in class society. The lie is rejected or not put to use only in cases when using it would be detrimental to class interests.

Maybe courage is a quality we look for?

Yes, courage is a quality valued by people of all classes, because no one has thought of a way to win a struggle by means of cowardice. But – alas! – differences are also possible in assessing this quality. 'The insanity of the brave is the wisdom of life', sings the bourgeois, raring for action before the revolution. 'A million in your pocket and a "whist"[12] party in a peaceful and quiet setting – that is the wisdom of life' – says the same bourgeois a century later. Generally speaking, courage is valued more highly among peoples and social groups whose existence is tied to warfare. Conversely, peoples and social classes who can achieve more not through courage but by means of resourcefulness, for example, or by cunning and intellect, never think of putting courage before the latter qualities. And that is quite understandable. Whatever is more useful for a class in its struggle, whatever provides it with the best outcome for the least effort, is more moral for that class. Indeed, morality itself is nothing but a means for binding all members of a class more closely in order to protect their interests as a whole and to employ all members of the class most effectively to this end.

How about betrayal? Is it not morally disgusting for all classes? Alas! – whoever is a traitor to a particular army, class, or people is only a 'useful co-worker' for the opposing side. Every class, army, etc., taking advantage of betrayal and rewarding traitors from the opposite side, thereby proves that they do not hate traitors in general but only their own traitors. And that is all there is to it.

What about conscience? Is it not the voice of human morality in its purest form – the voice that is foreign to all narrow egoistic considerations and resounds precisely in opposition to them? Let us have a look.

It often happens among Samoyedic[13] peoples that a member of the tribe who has grown rich will one fine day, influenced by the voice of conscience, give away all of his accumulated wealth to his kinsmen. Then he resumes his customary occupations until once again, ashamed of his material superiority over his neighbours, he divides his property. Although a Russian merchant of the old school was not so susceptible to distributional endeavours, even he would have felt his conscience disturbed if he did not provide shelter to holy fools, did not include a certain amount in his will for the poorhouse, did not give alms, did not contribute to the monastery and did not hang a hundred-pood bell at a church, etc. But already our merchant's son, who has studied at university and is generally an eminent person, is not at all disposed to feed fools, contribute to monasteries, donate church bells, etc. And what his father considered a matter of conscience and a most moral undertaking, the son considers immoral and at the very least stupid. He thinks it immoral and irrational to feed parasitic monks and holy fools, to spend money in support of superstitions, and he

---

12   [The card game 'whist' was widely played in the eighteenth and nineteenth centuries.]
13   [The term 'Samoyed' was traditionally used to refer to a number of indigenous peoples in Siberia.]

prefers to use those resources to 'provide work' to the toilers, i.e. to expand the scale of exploitation. How about the feeling of remorse? Is the son completely unfamiliar with it? No, quite the contrary. Only recently he avoided contributing to a fund that was organised by the commercial-industrial class to seek an increase in import duties by means of agitation. And then, in spite of a resolution by all the factory owners not to increase wage rates in response to workers' demands, a decision for which he himself voted, he violated that resolution in order not to lose lucrative orders because of strikes during the busy season. As a result of all that, the son of our devout merchant does feel remorse. Furthermore, at a factory nearby that of our merchant's son, where a strike was underway, some of the workers returned to work prematurely and the success [of the strike] turned out to be incomplete. Now these workers feel pangs of conscience and are ashamed to meet their comrades. A Dragoon captain from a punitive squad stayed late playing a game of 'vint'[14] at the home of the marshal of the nobility. He failed to perform an execution in a village where the peasants, meanwhile, burned down the landowner's estate house. The captain feels very uncomfortable. And then there is the terrorist who was late in intercepting the train of a dignitary, into which he was supposed to toss a bomb. He feels guilty before his party comrades and the class whose interests the party serves in its struggle.

In all of these cases we see remorse, a good deal of remorse. What is common to all of these examples is that people commit certain deeds, carried away by personal interests, and then feel guilty. But towards whom? The terrorist feels guilty towards his class, the peasantry shall we say; the captain, towards the nobility; the factory owner, towards other factory owners; the workers, towards other workers; the Samoyed, towards his kinsmen. Each feels guilty towards his class, to which he has done harm. True, the Samoyed has no such class. Classes have not developed among the Samoyeds, and he feels responsibility towards the community of his kinfolk, i.e., the social environment in which he lives and to which he is connected materially and psychologically (the Samoyeds have strong remnants of primitive communism). Our pious merchant is much less sensitive about his sins before society (whether imagined or real is of no consequence) than the Samoyed does. But he also remembers the time when he was a simple man, and his donations to benefit the beggars, the holy fools and the almshouse are only a more modest version of what the Samoyed does with his division [of personal belongings]. And even his spending on the bell and the monastery, insofar as this is not an act of compromise with the Church as a

---

14   [Vint was a popular card game in nineteenth-century Russia.]

social institution, is merely a misshapen form of the same act, whose pure form we saw in the case of the Samoyed. But the son of the merchant already operates in an environment that has come with the commercial-industrial class, and he feels remorse only to the extent that his actions cause injury to his class. The thought could never occur to him that he might feel moral responsibility[15] to the indigent for his wealth, such as the Samoyed feels so acutely, nor even the foggy reflections of such a sense that troubled the conscience of his father. On the contrary, he considers his use of his capital in the production of surplus value to be a moral affair because he thereby 'feeds' the poor. As far as the captain, the terrorist and the proletarians are concerned, everything is self-evident.

As a general rule, the following can be said. In societies that have not decomposed into classes, the individual person feels responsible for his actions before the entire community. Where the original community is dividing into classes but they have not taken final economic form, and where the members of these emerging classes have not yet worked out a class ideology, there is either responsibility to the community within which the classes are forming or else there are unique forms of responsibility that correspond to the transitional status of the emerging class itself. When a class or classes are fully formed, responsibility exists, as a rule, in relation to the class. The voice of conscience is the voice of one's own kind resonating within the individual; it is a thread pulled by one's kin in order to remind the individual member of his bond with the whole. In a class society, this voice already resounds as the voice of class. The 'voice of one's class' likewise compels all moralists to obscure, conceal and distort this truth – whether willingly or unwillingly, consciously or unconsciously. And the class of proletarians alone has an interest in bringing this truth to light in all its magnitude.

8   Social Instinct and Class Interest

But have we not forgotten something? In the life of our factory owner, the merchant's son, there was one occasion when the remorse that he experienced could not be called the voice of class. The fact is that once upon a time there was a worker drowning in a river, and our factory owner could have saved him since he swims well, but he did not want to risk his life and the worker drowned. Thinking of it from time to time does make him feel not quite at ease with himself, especially since one of the factory owners whom he knows did res-

---

15   I am speaking, of course, of a typical representative of the class and not the exceptions.

cue a drowning worker in a similar situation. He also knows of an opposite case, when a worker rescued a factory owner. It is also remarkable that this [latter] factory owner is not a man of kindly soul at all, and workers at his dyeing and bleaching factory are dropping like flies. After being rescued, he forced over a hundred workers to die from backbreaking toil in a suffocating atmosphere. Even the worker who saved the life of that factory owner had no tender affection for him; and during a strike, when everyone's children were dying of hunger, he and his wife more than once wished he were dead. How can we explain all this?

At this point we have to make a small digression.

Man is a communal and social animal. All social animals are characterised by the fact that they live in groups, not by themselves, and in their struggle for existence they help each other. It often happens that this help to others, to the entire group, goes so far that a single member of a flock of birds, a herd of animals, or a swarm of insects perishes while saving the species. When, for example, a lion attacks a herd of buffalos on the steppe, an old male, the leader of the herd, enters into single combat with the lion and usually dies, but he allows the herd to escape. The buffalo acts unconsciously, involuntarily, as any other social animal does in similar situations; he cannot act differently, just as a falling person cannot help trying to grab something in order to avoid injury, or as anyone involuntarily dodges a threatening blow to the head. (In this case the species also dodges a blow by exposing one of its members to it.) If the buffalo could reason, and reason in the way that a bourgeois usually does when he is in danger, he probably would have decided: my legs are strong, let others become the lion's lunch, not me – and run away. But the strength of the buffalo, the strength of all social animals, lies in the fact that they do not reason as our bourgeois-individualist does (with the exception of human beings, they do not reason at all). This wonderful capacity for self-sacrifice is the result of a long development. Those species in which it developed most highly turned out to be better adjusted for the struggle with nature and with their enemies, and they survived; those species in which it was weaker, and each was more inclined to act alone and save himself – perished. Thus, by force of natural selection, the capacity for self-sacrifice for the benefit of the species developed and became stronger. It is the same sort of useful acquisition for social animals as claws and teeth are for the lion, sharp vision for birds, tusks for an elephant etc. Of course, it is not outwardly visible but remains hidden in every member of the species as the capacity to act. If man, with his physical weakness, ultimately prevailed as a species in the struggle with nature and reached his current position, it is to a significant (if not greater) extent due to his capacity for self-sacrifice, or more accurately, his ability always to deal with his fellow members (unconsciously and for the sake of the species itself and for his fellows) in the interests of preserving the whole.

But let us take man in the period when people are divided into different tribes at war with each other. Social instinct now takes the form of tribal instinct. It operates in the interests of kinship and against hostile tribes. When different classes form among one people, social instinct begins to serve class interest. In itself, instinct is blind like any involuntary movement or aspiration. Class interest opens its eyes, and [instinct] begins to look at the world, so to speak, through the eyes of class interest. Having developed on the basis of mutual assistance and preservation of the species, which was conducive to the rescue of other members of the group in the struggle with wild animals and every sort of danger, in class society [instinct] is directed towards protecting the interests of members of a specific class and doing the most damage to enemy classes. On the barricades, where an insurgent people and a defending dominant class work miracles of bravery, *the social instinct of one part of society confronts the social instinct of another*. And although it is of common origin amongst all people, it is now directed towards their mutual extermination. The more frequently classes go into battle the more frequently this instinct, now governed by class interest, is revealed. The more peaceful is the internal environment of society, the more concealed and dormant it is within many people. This instinct is most intense among oppressed classes who are rising up for their emancipation. It is weakest where the conditions of class existence suppress it. For example, the usual competition in capitalist society, the readiness of every bourgeois to devour the capital and incomes of his fellows, the aspiration solely for personal benefit, the competition that is dictated by the interests of developing production at the capitalist stage – all of this drowns out and suppresses social instinct. But let the entire bourgeois class be threatened with the danger of being stripped of power and property, and the picture changes dramatically. Some Ivan Ivanovich Ivanov, who is known to society simply as a stock-market gambler and is indiscriminate in profiting at the expense of his class brothers, now suddenly turns up in the forefront of those who are fighting for the salvation of bourgeois rule and perhaps loses his life and power in saving the interests of the whole. And Petr Petrovich Petrov, who in normal times usually interpreted much in the interests of the whole, may end up in the front ranks of deserters. 'They are beating up our people!' sweeps through the workers' districts – and thousands of proletarians rush to the place where the action is in order to help their own.

What is it that moves masses to act so impulsively when everything is happening so quickly that no one has an opportunity to consider the situation and make a conscious decision? It is the social instinct, being urged in the required direction and directed by class interest, or simply, if one may put it this way, class intuition. Frequently among our wild ancestors, over a period of tens and hundreds of thousands of years, this concern that 'They are beating up our people' was expressed in different languages even when there was no articulate speech and some semi-animal shout expressed that thought. And with the uncontrollability of the elements, people strove to assist their own. When that cry resounds in class society, everyone rushes to assist those whom he regards as his own, i.e., people of his own class.[16]

But no matter how strong class interests are, or how fiercely social groups fight each other in moments of conflict, in the normal course of life the social instinct, when it does not encounter class interests, can also appear as the instinct of kinship. With this entire digression, we can now explain a similar example. The factory owner is not saving worker but a human being in general terms, an abstract person so to speak. And for the worker who is saving the factory owner, what matters is not that he is a factory owner and a rather unimportant one at that, but that he is a man, a member of the species *homo sapiens*, exposed to mortal danger from external nature, before which, as in the face of wild animals, all people are members of one species.

But change the social environment, let the action occur during a civil war, and take a look now at the actors involved. Once both sides are mercilessly exterminating each other, the drowning bourgeois will not be rescued by the worker, nor will the factory owner clamber to rescue a communard. He would be more likely to shove him back into the water. Otherwise he would have to rescue the drowning man as a human being and, without even letting him get dressed, shoot him right there on the shore as a representative of the enemy side.

The social instinct could serve as an excellent motivating force on behalf of general social norms if society were not divided into classes. And although it is deeply rooted in human nature and sometimes acts like any other useful instinct with irresistible force, it is weak precisely because it is unconscious. Just as a timely, light push may deflect a terrible blow – not because the push is

---

16   In general terms the social instinct is of much more ancient origin than class interest. Where the latter does not yet take precedence, the social instinct may at times prevail in the form of the consciousness of another class and lead one to act contrary to one's own class interest. The transition of some people from the ruling class to the side of a revolutionary class, and the emigration of some individuals from the ranks of the aristocracy and bourgeoisie to the side of the proletariat, can be explained in large measure, if not completely, by the operation of the social instinct.

powerful but because it is skilfully directed – so class interest, strong with the force of consciousness, takes social instinct prisoner in exactly the same way because it is weak in its blindness and is transformed in fact into class instinct. Only a future society, emancipated from class struggle and from the very existence of classes, will manage to make full use of the social instinct of man, which is one of the most precious acquisitions of his long history.

• • •

Thus, in searching for universal human morality we have arrived at the unfortunate conclusion that such morality, i.e., a practically operating and universal morality, has never existed. And knowing the effect of class interest on people's consciousness and actions on the one hand, and that the search is occurring in class society [on the other hand], it is not even worth looking for. But if there is no universal morality, then anything at all can masquerade as morality.

But excuse me, someone might say to us, surely the famous moral rule 'Do not wish upon others what you do not wish for yourself' is just such a universal moral requirement? No doubt, this counsel is quite respectable in terms of its age and the good wishes it entails. And if its implementation depended upon a well formulated maxim, this one would leave nothing more to be desired. It would be fine, for example, if all the aristocrats and bourgeois did not wish upon the working class what they do not wish for themselves, i.e., unbearable toil, homelessness in old age, premature death, poverty, injustice etc., and if proletarians wished upon the bourgeois gentlemen and the aristocrats a working day of at least six hours, socialisation of the means of production etc., in a word, all the best that they could want for themselves and expect from socialism, then everything would have been settled to everyone's satisfaction. But our venerable rule, if it ever served as a guide, surely existed only for individuals of one and the same class. Even this purely formal rule either ignores the division of society into classes or else it considers this division to be as unavoidable as natural law and does not even propose to infringe upon it.

The same generally applies to the principles and moral law formulated by Kant: 'Act in a way that the maxim of your will could serve as the principle of universal law'.[17] This law is also purely formal in character. Let us see what will come out of it if we give it concrete content, which in contemporary society means class content. The bourgeois, as a typical representative of his own

---

17   [Immanuel Kant (1724–1804) was one of the most prolific and influential of liberal philosophers. Kant argued that all morality is subsumed under the 'categorical imperative' of universal moral law. Kant's moral philosophy played a significant part in the rise of Social-

class, will say: 'I hire workers, sell the product of their labour on the market, own private property and enrich myself, and I think everyone must be able to protect their own interest, etc. I not only allow for the possibility, but I demand that the principles of my activity be the basis of universal legislation'. The worker will reply: 'Everyone has to work, and he who does not work does not eat; the means of production must belong to society; exploitation of one person by another is inadmissible; and we have to strive for socialism. I demand that all of this serve as the basis for society's legislation'. Other classes would likewise speak out in the spirit of their own class goals and class interests. What would happen then to our poor 'universal law'? It would end up in the hands of the class that is stronger and able to turn all of its class legislation (under the threat of imprisonment and execution for those who disobey) into 'universal law'. And then the whole of Kant's vaunted universal law unravels at the seams, exposing merely the boundless petty-bourgeois utopianism and narrow-mindedness of its author.[18]

We see, therefore, that morality in class society is class morality. And that is absolutely inevitable. Within a certain sphere, morality regulates the behaviour of people of a given class or of those classes that are subject to the authority of the ruling class's morality. Morality is subordinate to the general law of the dependence of ideology upon the material conditions of class existence. It would be absolutely impossible and intolerable if the material interests of a given class, say the ruling class and its commanding role in production and distribution, were protected over any prolonged period by the state apparatus; fortified by a corresponding system of legislation; ideologically justified in religion, philosophy and science in general; expressed in a class-biased way in art – and, at the same time, they were in complete contradiction with morality. In other words, a condition cannot continue over any long period in which morality preaches that a class do what contradicts its own interests, what does not comply with its role in production, and what does not correspond to its

---

Democratic 'revisionism', which in practical terms meant abandoning class struggle in favour of social reforms that might be agreed with enlightened representatives of the bourgeoisie.]

18   However, none of this prevented the formal, dry and insubstantial Kantian morality from playing a progressive role in the feudal-philistine and provincial Germany of the time. Equality of all before the law, abolition of feudal privileges, individual rights, freedom, equality and fraternity – all these political demands put forward by the French bourgeoisie in an open struggle with absolutism and the Church – were formulated by the son of a Konigsberg saddler in the hazy language of morality, that is, in a form not particularly dangerous to the Prussian king and the landed nobility. But at the time this was a step forward.

historical role at the given stage of social development. That is why morality is included in the general system of ideology and all the norms that serve class interest. If, moreover, with regard to the uppermost elements of ideology, which are most remote from the economic foundation, we can establish their dependence upon that economic basis through analysis, then in the sphere of morality, i.e., in the sphere of norms of practical behaviour, that link must be all the more obvious and immediate. With regard to the ruling class, this is perfectly clear and obvious. For example, if the bourgeoisie, during the period of intensive accumulation and expanded reproduction of the capitalist economy, were guided by the Gospel rule about the shirt that you are urged to give to your 'neighbour', and instead of concentrating capital to expand production was giving out surplus value to the 'poor', this would have made capitalist production impossible. Such morality would have glaringly contradicted not just the narrow material interests of the class of capitalists, but also the interests of society's economic development at its capitalist stage. The same can be said about the landed nobility in the period when large landed property and an economy based upon serfdom were being created.

It is rather different with the morality of oppressed classes in the sense that here it is more difficult to trace the connection between the morality that actually prevails in the practice of a class and the interests of that class. This occurs because an oppressed class is not always aware of its class interests, and its operative morality can, therefore, at a certain stage in the development of the class, be at odds with its class interests. An oppressed class initially develops into a class 'in itself' (*an sich*), i.e., it occupies a particular place in the process of production and distribution and a particular social position in relation to the other classes of society, and only subsequently, sometimes by way of a prolonged formation of its class consciousness, does it become a class 'for itself' (*für sich*), i.e., a class that has become conscious of its interests and is self-determining in relation to other classes that surround it. So long as the oppressed class has not yet become self-determining in that way, for a certain period of its existence it is led not by its own inherent class norms, which answer to its class interests, but instead by the ruling morality, i.e., the morality of the economically and politically dominant class.

Take, for example, the working class at the dawn of development of the capitalist mode of production. As a class of wage workers, selling labour power to capital, it already exists. But it is still held captive by the morality of the bourgeois class. It relates to the institution of private property in the means of production as to something eternal and natural. Compelled by its economic position to use the strike in its struggle to improve its material position, it still regards it as something of a crime, and not merely because the law considers it a crime but also because it has yet to free itself from the thrall of bourgeois public opinion and remains frightened and timid. It is hounded during a strike like a beast that has broken out of its cage, and for its own part it sees the condition of a prolonged strike struggle as something unnatural and intolerable. It feels a kind of moral responsibility for the idle machines and the owner's losses. It has not yet got beyond the view, imposed upon it by its exploiters, that the owner who provides it with work also feeds it. During this period it seeks a compromise in every way possible with the morality of its masters; it attempts to excuse its struggle in terms of the customary moral ideas of the master and begs history's pardon, as it were, for the fact that it exists as a class. And it makes its first timid attempts to find ideological justification for its struggle, so to speak, from within the ideology of the exploiters: it comprehends its own class position and formulates its class interests in vague religious forms, using the contradictions of Christian doctrine and Christian morality. Later on, influenced by the practice of economic struggle, it gradually begins to construct its own class norms, but still within the confines of what is required for justification of the strike and its successful outcome. It already subjects strike-breakers to a moral and often a material boycott, but the strike is still justified in terms of the dominant ideas and the morality of a commodity economy: pay a 'just wage' for work, i.e., by and large the average market price of labour power. In this period the proletariat still does not lay claim to the entire surplus value, and that is very strikingly reflected in its customary morality of the period, for example, the morality of the average English trade unionist, which is essentially a special 'democratic' edition of the common bourgeois morality, adjusted for the workers' way of life. It is only during the following period of the struggle for power that the proletariat breaks away from the whole web of the exploiters' ideology and morality and begins to develop and realise its own class norms, which answer to the tasks of its class struggle.

We can see from this example that morality always remains class morality in a class society, but a class is often guided by the morality of another class to which it is economically subordinated and from whose ideology it has not yet broken away. *That is why oppressed classes must look for their specific class norms not during the period of their conception and the first steps of their class struggle, but in the period of forming a class 'for itself', in the period of acute class conflicts with enemy classes, and finally, in the period of dominance of a new class in the economy and politics of the country.*

After all that we have said, we can now give a more exact and scientific definition of morality compared to what we have contented ourselves with thus far.

• • •

9   Is There a Proletarian Morality?

If all morality is class morality, if even amorality, i.e., rejection of any morality, in the conditions of class society essentially means replacement of the old morality by a new one that simply is not called by that name, then naturally the following question now emerges: How do matters stand with proletarian class morality? In the first place, does it exist at all, and if it does exist, what is its material content in the period before as well as after the social revolution?

At the outset a few things must be said about terminology. When people previously used the word morality, in the great majority of cases they understood it – and in many cases still do understand it – to mean a system of norms and rules of conduct that are recognised as absolute and obligatory. Whatever is recommended by one or another morality was not just considered necessary, useful, and appropriate for the class but came draped in fog and mythology. In particular, the interests of the whole clan, collective, and class put pressure on the consciousness of an individual not as an openly formulated class interest and collective directive – do this in the interests of the collective, do not do that – but also in the mystical guise of the 'voice of conscience'. This was especially pronounced when the personal interests of a member of the collective collided with those of the whole, and the battlefield between personal and collective interests was the conscience of the individual. The question that the individual faced then took the form of whether or not to violate morality in general, whether or not to act against one's conscience, and not whether to act to the benefit of one's class or to do it harm. In the consciousness of the individual member of a class – of an oppressed class for example – the struggle against another class, which is imposing its ideology and morality, took the same mystical form. The release of a person from the increasingly foreign morality of another class (i.e., from a morality that is beginning sharply to contradict his own class interests), takes within his own consciousness the form of a struggle of one moral truth with another.

In these conditions, the question naturally arises as to whether it is appropriate to use the terms 'morality', 'ethics', 'moral', 'immoral' etc. among a class that not only does not fetishize its own or another class's norms but, to the contrary, is interested in every possible way in exposing the mythological attire of morality wherever it has disguised totally prosaic social interests and social processes.

There can be two answers to that question.

The first is that class norms have always existed in class society. They have played a very important role in social life, particularly in the processes of class struggle. These norms were draped in mythology, but that by no means prevented them (quite the contrary) from fulfilling a definite function in society. These norms appeared in mystical attire and were called moral norms. But the main point was not what they were called or how they appeared; most important was their social essence. Thus, while the terms 'morality', 'moral' and so forth are pointless to retain – even in the conditional sense of class norms – when speaking of proletarian class norms, the essence of past morality also must not be seen simply in terms of its mystical attire. The appearance and the essence of class norms were at the time inseparably linked, and they can only be distinguished logically, by way of abstract analysis.

The second answer is that class norms have always existed in class society and will exist until classes disappear. They are also necessary for the proletariat. But the essence of morality is not the fact that this is a pseudonym for class norms, but rather that these norms are fetishized. As soon as the mystical shell breaks apart, class norms remain but morality disappears. Morality, consequently, is not a system of class norms but the element of fetishism accompanying these norms. This second point of view is maintained by comrade Bukharin in his book *The Theory of Historical Materialism*. He writes:

The proletariat must not preach a capitalistic fetishism. For the proletariat, the standards of its conduct are technical rules in precisely the sense of the rules according to which a joiner constructs an arm chair. The latter, wishing to construct an armchair, will plane, saw, glue, etc., which acts are involved in the labor process itself. He will not interpret the rules of woodworking as something foreign to him, of supernatural origin, whose victim he is. The attitude of the proletariat in its social struggle is precisely the same. If it would attain communism, it must do this and that, as the joiner at work on his armchair. And everything required, from this point of view, must be done. 'Ethics' will ultimately, in the case of the proletariat, be transformed into simple and easily understood technical rules of conduct, such as are required for communism, and thus it will really cease to be ethics *at all*. For the essence of ethics is in the fact that it involves norms enveloped in a fetishistic raiment. Fetishism is the essence of ethics; where fetishism disappears, ethics also will disappear. For instance, no one would think of designating the constitution of a consumer's store or of a party as 'ethical' or 'moral', for anyone can see the human significance of these things. Ethics, on the other hand, presupposes a fetishistic mist, which turns the heads of many persons. The proletariat needs rules of conduct, and it needs to have them very clear, but it has no need of 'ethics', i.e., a fetishistic sauce to flavor the meal. Of course, it is obvious that the proletariat will not at once succeed in liberating itself from the fetishism of the commodity society in which it lives; but that is another question.[19]

I think there is no need for us to revise terminology with regard to the past. We may, of course, agree to understand morality in such a narrow sense as comrade Bukharin suggests. But that does not help us.[20] Quite the contrary. The term 'class morality' has been established in our Marxist literature since the time of the *Communist Manifesto* to refer to all morality, which is a system of norms in the interests of a given class, no matter how these norms may be attired. This terminology can be left alone. Otherwise we would have to understand class morality to mean not the very essence of norms, together with their ideological cloak, but only the cloaking itself. We would then have to say: class morality is the system of *cloaking* class norms, and not a system of *cloaked norms*.[21] As far as terminology for our own time is concerned, we acknowledge, together with comrade Bukharin, the unreasonableness of using the old manner of expression. Consequently, in reasoning strictly scientifically, we must not speak now of proletarian morality or proletarian ethics when only proletarian class norms are involved. From this point of view, the term 'proletarian morality' can only be used with reference to the period of the proletariat's development as a class when it was approximately at the level of Weitling's thinking,[22] i.e., when it began to recognise the contradiction between its fundamental class interests and the interests of the bourgeoisie, when it began to emancipate itself, in its practical life and struggle, from the morality of the exploiters but had not yet learned to formulate its own interests apart from religion and all the mystical formulae of the absolute and universal [morality] of class norms, because the proletariat is by no means moral.[23]

---

19   [Bukharin 1969, p. 239.]

20   [The point is that *class norms* involve expectations of appropriate behavior and cannot be equated with the merely *technical rules* mentioned by Bukharin.]

21   Also, we must not forget that the period of overt class norms, that is, approximately from Marx to communist society, will in historical terms be a mere episode compared to the period of cloaked norms that embraces thousands of years.

22   [Wilhelm Weitling (1808–1871) was a petty-bourgeois utopian socialist.]

23   An uncritical use of the words 'morality', 'ethics' and so on in relation to proletarian norms is essentially a relic if not of bourgeois ideology then of bourgeois-feudal terminology. Some Marxists commit the same error. [Preobrazhensky's point is that unlike the 'morality' of all other classes, proletarian class norms must be understood in historical terms and make no claim to universal validity. In a classless society they will be replaced by general social norms and ultimately absorbed into the instinct of human sociability.]

Thus, in the interests of precision in scientific terminology, we must not speak of proletarian morals if we define morality as a system of *cloaked* class norms, because the proletariat has absolutely no intention or interest in creating moral cloaks for its class norms. It is another matter if the old words – 'ethics', 'morality' etc. – are used in everyday speech due simply to habit, merely as a consequence of the usual conservatism of language, or because we have not conceived a new terminology. There is no need here to be particularly captious and to reveal our erudition at every step. We say in everyday speech that 'the sun rises and sets', although, as we know from astronomy, the sun does not rise and set. This terminology will probably persist for some time to come, especially since its indeterminacy and vagueness allows it to serve as a refuge for our language in cases when new norms are forming but their essence and boundaries are not yet clear and there are no new words for them. However, elimination of the old moral terminology among workers will happen more rapidly because it was never especially familiar to the workers' language. The words 'sin' and 'sinfully' are dying out together with religion, and the words 'immorally', 'unethically' etc. are rejected by proletarian science before this occurs in everyday class usage.

But before we turn to the question of the proletariat's class norms prior to the social revolution, we must demonstrate first that these norms can exist at all and that there exists a definite sphere within which they must apply.

When we remove the mystical element from morality – its supposed universality and absoluteness – and thus restrict everything to class norms, and finally, when we remember that all human behaviour is strictly conditioned and that freedom of the will is a myth, the question then arises as to whether these class norms and the so-called responsibility of a person for one's own acts is a myth, even if it has now been transformed into answerability not to the hidden voice of conscience but instead directly to one's class. We certainly have no intention, for example, to apply the class norms of the proletariat to the bourgeoisie. It is first of all pointless, and for that reason alone it would be foolish. The above-mentioned factory owner, who gave in to workers during the strike, did not do so under pressure from the public opinion of the proletariat but for personal material considerations. Not only does he derive no moral satisfaction from the fact that he shortened the suffering of the strikers, but, on the contrary, he feels remorse before members of his own class, who reproach him for cowardice and betrayal of common capitalist interests. To address moral exhortations to a bourgeois and expect him to act in ways that benefit workers but contradict his own class interests (which is what all utopian and petty-bourgeois socialism was engaged in) means pretty much the same as 'morally' exhorting a stone falling from a roof to spare the head of a person standing below. But here the fol-

lowing question arises. If the stone's fall occurs strictly on the basis of physical
laws governing falling bodies, is not every human act completed on the basis
of similar iron laws of physiology and society? If so – and it is undoubtedly so,
otherwise we would concede a breach in the law of causality – then what does
this have to do with any sort of responsibility to class or society, and in this case
class norms?

This is something we have to stop and think about. We cannot divert a falling
brick from its trajectory by means of moral exhortation. But can we alter its trajectory at all? Of course we can. In order to do so, we need to add a *new* physical
condition, a new factor, to all of the physical conditions that affect its fall and
its direction. In other words, with a suitable blow to the brick at the moment
of its fall or just before, we can alter its trajectory and thereby save the person
standing below from a skull fracture. It is exactly the same with the behaviour of
every single individual. *An act that would have occurred under certain given conditions may not occur if a new condition is introduced that will begin to operate
and be added to the conditions that have so far determined human behaviour.* All
that is required is for this new condition to be a factor of sufficient strength to
exert an influence in the necessary direction, as in the case of a purely physical
force. Can public opinion of the class, say, to which a particular person belongs,
be such a factor? The social experience of people shows that it can. If human
free will is a myth – a myth originating with the exploiters (and supported in
part by the conditions of a petty-bourgeois individualistic economy) – the letters from repentant strike-breakers, published by the hundreds in the pages of
'Pravda' in 1912–13, were no myth. Nor are the endless number of cases when
the public opinion of a class governs the acts of its members, when the expectation of censure from class comrades prevents commitment of an act harmful
to the class (the case of shame), or when the expectation of moral approval
from the class incites one to acts of heroism in the interests of the class, etc.,
etc. Thus, if we take a person who has to act somehow or other in the *absence*
of any factor of class approval or reproach, there will be one act. If we *include*
the effect of this factor – a different act might follow. All of this will be strictly
based upon the law of causality. When physiology of the brain advances beyond its current state, we shall be able to describe in purely physiological terms
the social reflexes of a person and what we call the moral weight of the public
opinion of a class upon a single individual.

But if the public opinion of a class, and the class norms that briefly and
exactly formulate what this public opinion requires, are themselves a real social
force, we must still establish the limits within which this force operates. A sceptical and humorous attitude towards morality, as a system of prescribed norms
to which no one adheres, commonly results from observing the facts of decom-

position of an old morality that no longer answers the interests of the class and is preserved out of habit, as with old clothes. But, at the same time, new class norms have usually formed already that possess actual significance. These norms serve class interest, unite a class in its struggle, bind individual class members as a rope binds a bundle of rods, and compel the individual member of the class to subordinate his social behaviour to the interests of the whole.

Whenever class norms are coordinated with class interests and are at their service, the entire class observes their fulfilment with thousands of eyes and supports its morality as the symbol of class unity. And if the personal interests of class members conflict with class norms, if these norms put pressure on an individual member in the manner of a physical force and turn out to be stronger than he is, it is only because the entire class is physically and socially stronger than each single person from this class. In those cases when a single person or a particular group from the class breaks free from the chains of class norms, and when the latter are powerless to keep them in line with the old generally accepted and approved behaviour, this happens because these protestors are either the first pioneers and defenders of new but already emerged class interests that are understood differently, or else they are simply breaking away from their class and moving to the side of a different class. This occurs most frequently when an old class is disintegrating and the deserters from this class join up with a new class that is entering the historical arena and has a future. Recall how certain strata of the nobility deserted to the side of the bourgeoisie in the period when the bourgeois revolutions were maturing, and how people deserted from the bourgeoisie and the bourgeois intelligentsia and adopted the proletariat's point of view. In both cases, what happened was not the emancipation of individuals and social groups from class norms in general, insofar as class society and class struggle still exist, but rather their transition to compliance with other class norms.

The proletariat is a special class. Its interests are changing. Up to the conquest of power they are one thing; after the conquest of power, another. But, both before and after the revolution, it wages a bitter struggle against its old enemies for survival, for victory, and for construction of a new economic and social system. Every struggle has its own rules of victory. One of the most important conditions for victory is the unity and organisation of the class, which magnifies its striking force and subordinates each individual human force to the interests of the whole. Among the bonds that transform a class into an organised army, class norms take a prominent place. They are necessary for the proletariat; they exist during the period when it is still an oppressed class; they change their content but still persist after it has defeated its enemies in the *first battle*, i.e., when it has seized power; and they will remain as long as it exists as a class – until the class division of society is completely overcome and class norms are transformed into general social norms (that will then become instinctive).

What is the content of these proletarian class norms before and after the proletarian revolution?

10   The Class Norms of the Proletariat before the Revolution

The working class begins the struggle against its exploiters mainly for improvement of its economic position: to curtail capital's share of the surplus value and correspondingly to increase the share of wages, to shorten the working day, to protect labour during production, to win the right from the bourgeois state to form free trade unions, etc. In cases when the proletariat must confront the bourgeois state during this period, its actions do not go beyond the limits of this very first and most elementary goal of its class struggle. They remain confined to that narrow objective. Its most important weapon of struggle during this period is the strike. Hence, the class norms of the proletariat are built around the strike above all, and they are dictated by the objectives of a successful strike struggle. The individual worker is powerless against his employer. But at certain moments all the workers of a factory together, especially at times of industrial buoyancy, often turn out to be stronger than the individual employer. In the case of a conflict, they can only realise their strength through harmonious and joint action. The linchpin of proletarian class norms, the main commandment of the strike struggle and of the workers' struggle in general – 'One for all, all for one' – emerges in precisely that period. And this principle already involves the characteristic difference from the bourgeois morality of this period. By this time, the bourgeois class is organised in the state or has subordinated absolutism to its own interests. It knows how to defend its class interests through the weapon of the state machine. But the very development of the bourgeois mode of production at this stage requires extensive freedom of competition. 'Everyone for himself' – that is the slogan of the individual bourgeois competing against his class brethren. This individualistic slogan represents the complete opposite of the previously mentioned principle of collective proletarian struggle. Hence the terrible hatred of the workers towards strike-breakers and the owner's pets, who play the role of spies; towards the masters and the factory slave-drivers; towards all who thwart a united proletarian front and go over to the class enemy. The public opinion of the working class condemns not just inveterate strike-breakers, but also all of those strikers who cannot tolerate the hunger and privation and agree to go back to work despite the common decision. Hence, on the contrary, it shows every sort of approval, encourage-ment and moral and material support to the most determined and persistent workers, who act as leaders of the strike, formulate their interests, 'slaughter' the owner on every point of the demands being made, then get fired from the enterprise as a result, go to jail, etc. The workers need such people; the public opinion of the working class supports them and inspires their heroism; and when they go to prison and exile, accompanied by contempt from phil-istine bourgeois public opinion, the workers see them as their very best people, provide support for their families, etc. And often a strike continues, after all the demands have been met, only because thousands of people demand the return to the factory of a few leaders who were sacked by the employer. 'One for all, all for one'.

Already at this stage of the struggle, the working class begins in practice to circumvent the existing rules of the owners and petty-bourgeois morality; it begins to use the instrument of lying and deceiving the owner to support class comrades. If an unemployed worker, with poor mastery of the necessary skills, needs to get a job and submit a sample [of his work], that sample is made behind the master's back by skilled workers, and this deception is considered perfectly legitimate and proper in the workers' everyday life. The same is true of all other occasions when it is possible to deceive the owner, such as passing off waste as good work, signing into the factory and then leaving before the shift ends, etc. Conversely, the attitude towards all of these acts begins to change only when the trade union itself begins, in the common interest, to answer for its members' work, and when such behaviour by individual workers may scuttle a general agreement that benefits them all.

That is the time when everyday proletarian mutual assistance emerges. In bourgeois circles, they say 'That-a-boy' about a factory owner who has ruined other factory owners with his competition. As for a worker who has person-ally benefited at the expense of his class comrades, they say in their circles that 'He's a rat'. Mutual assistance between competing bourgeois is an exception. Mutual assistance emerges in everyday proletarian life as the general rule. They provide assistance to the unemployed, they help them find work, they feed their families, etc. This mutual assistance takes organised forms. Different kinds of societies and mutual-aid funds are created and financed by wages when the working class is not yet strong enough to compel the state to transfer a part of these expenses to the owners.

The rules of proletarian struggle begin to form into a system of proletarian norms, the fixed capital of which is already created in this period. Trade-union and other economic organisations of the proletariat are created, and some of these class norms become written norms, incorporated into the charters of proletarian organisations and materialised, so to speak. Most remain unwritten, but they become firmly established in class consciousness, are handed down from childhood to the younger generation of teenagers, and enter into the flesh and blood of the working masses. This is the time when the prehistoric inheritance of mankind, the social instinct, also begins to serve the economic struggle. This capital and these hidden social reflexes are drawn from the depths and shore up the working mass in the most difficult moments of its struggle. This instinct still prevailed in the wild, when the ancestors of today's worker had to act as a group. It broke out as a natural force of unknown origin when the ancestors of British workers smashed the nobles under the leadership of Taylor; it fortified the courage and cohesion of the peasant masses whom landlords hanged during the Pugachev[24] rebellion; it rendered service during the bourgeois revolutions; it was awakened in moments of mass action during a war; but, like quiet gunpowder, separated from any spark, it lay under a bushel during the period of individual smallholders. And now, when millions of people are united in great masses within factory walls, when mass pressure, self-defence, and attacks by the masses are becoming all the more frequent and inevitable, this same human principle, originating in our animal past, is again being summoned to life and responding to the call.

Strikers have gathered for a meeting. They need to discuss the terms of capitulation. They have no more strength to hold out. Every single worker has decided for himself that it is impossible to endure any more, they must surrender. They gathered, began talking, felt the power, and then someone shouted: 'We will die but not give up!' And everyone felt a new wave of strength, a new impulse for the struggle, a new resolve: 'We will not give up!' the mass roars, and each returns home with a firm intention to hold out. The struggle continues ....

When the workers' movement grows beyond the limits of economic struggle, when new and wider goals appear on the horizon more frequently and more persistently, when the next stage of the struggle is not for a fragment of the surplus value but for its elimination, for elimination of the entire system of exploitation, a struggle for workers' power, for socialism – then the social content of the proletariat's class norms expands and becomes enriched. Class goals are formulated in the program of the workers' party. The methods of organisation and struggle are also partly formulated there. As before, however, much remains unwritten. Class norms begin to adjust over time to this central goal of

---

24   [E.I. Pugachev (1742–1775) was a pretender to the Russian throne who led a rebellion in 1773–74 against Catherine the Great.]

the struggle of the working class. It remains true that only a minority are active and conscious, and sometimes they lose touch with the mass as a whole, which has yet to catch up with its vanguard. But that does not change the essence of the matter. *Those norms that ensure the most complete success in the struggle for power of the whole are the most important norms of the proletariat, even if the entire mass of the class has not yet achieved a full understanding of its own class goals or risen to heroism in the struggle for their fulfilment.* But all of that comes in due course.

Until then, its vanguard and leading minority represent the class as a whole. Any assessment of the activity of individual members of the class and of the class itself as a whole, from the standpoint of its norms in the period of the struggle for power, is subordinate to the main goal of that period. A worker does well when he steadfastly upholds his demands in a strike together with all the others, but he does better if he does not confine himself only to an occasional struggle but becomes a member of a union. It is even more useful for the class if he is not just a member and pays his dues on time but also takes an active part in the trade-union movement, recruits new members for the organisation, etc. It is more useful still for the class if he is not only an active worker for the trade-union movement but also a member of the party. His services to the class are greater still if he does not hesitate to go to jail or into exile for the party cause, and even more lofty if he 'sacrifices' his own life on the barricades or in civil war for the common cause. But individual heroes from the working class and even entire strata of leaders cannot be victorious without the whole class. Only the mass can triumph in the decisive struggle. This is why the highest demand of the workers' class interests and class norms is that the entire class throw itself into achieving its goals, that it subordinate its entire activity to the interests of the struggle for total victory. This is what we see in moments of the greatest exertion of class will, in moments of mass proletarian revolution.

Such are the class norms of the proletariat during this period. These interests demand that an individual member of the class regard himself as an instrument of the struggle of the entire working class. These interests demand that, when necessary, entire groups of leaders perish in forcing a path for others, so that when the moment comes the entire proletariat will fearlessly throw the body of the class into storming the capitalist trenches.

Immanuel Kant, the celebrated theorist of petty-bourgeois morality, put forward in his day a moral imperative: never regard another person as means to an end but always as an end in himself. Sentimental philistines of all countries have shed many tears of emotion over this and other principles of Kant's morality, considering them to be the basic requirements of 'universal morality'. There have been some simpletons, considering themselves Marxists, who have attempted to connect Kant with Marx on this issue, to combine the theory and practice of scientific communism with this commandment of a petty bourgeois who turned the demand of an individualistic philistine – 'Don't touch me' – into moral dogma.[25] One can imagine how far the proletariat would have advanced in its struggle had it been guided by this demand and not by a completely opposite one in its own class interests.

The proletariat is cruel and merciless in its struggle for power. Not only does it not spare its enemies; when necessary for the cause, it does not spare even the finest representatives of its own class. The supreme wisdom of proletarian struggle is not that everyone should poke around inside one's own personality and recite one's rights, but that everyone – selflessly, almost spontaneously, without phrases and unnecessary gestures, and demanding nothing for oneself – must pour all of one's own energy and enthusiasm into the common stream and make one's way to the goal together with the class, possibly falling dead in the process.

In the North of Siberia a vast herd of deer is crossing a wide river. Reaching the other side is essential to save the entire herd from hunger. But the river is deep, and the social instinct of the herd creates a bridge with the corpses of those at the front. The proletariat only entirely realises its full class strength when every single member of the class is ready, when needed, to throw his body into building a bridge that the entire proletarian collective uses to cross over into the society of the future.

11   The Class Norms of the Proletariat after Winning Power

The proletariat is in power. It has fulfilled the goals to which its struggle and the class norms that were formed in the course of that struggle were subordinated. Now the situation has fundamentally changed. Since the purely political struggle is not over yet and has territorially moved to a different arena, all those norms and habits that are needed for class cohesion and further victories remain in force. But some of these norms are already enshrined in the legislation of the Soviet state and have become Soviet law. At the same time, the fighting class organisations it has created, the trade unions and the party, are also partly turned into pillars of the state structure. But in new conditions its norms take on new forms. What are these new forms?

25 [See the assessment of Kant by Marx and Engels in *The German Ideology* (Marx and Engels 1964, p. 207).]

Let us begin with labour discipline. In bourgeois society the worker has no interest in expanding production and increasing his output for the same wage. The more he produces, the more the employer gets to spend on luxuries; the more goes to the bourgeois state and its hangers-on; the more will rot during an industrial crisis of overproduction; and finally, the more people will be senselessly destroyed in the next imperialist war. Where would labour enthusiasm come from here? How and why would spontaneous labour norms emerge for the toiling proletariat in the capitalist system? Even in those rare cases when workers do feel a spontaneous enthusiasm for labour[26] – this harbinger of the future free labour of all for all – the practical futility of this impulse becomes even clearer in face of the exploiting leeches who invariably pocket all the fruits of selfless labour inspiration.

Instead of developing his own voluntary labour discipline, the worker must defend himself against a compulsory labour discipline that is externally imposed upon him. It is supported by the capitalist, by subjecting the worker to supervision by all sorts of overseers, by the wage system, by the interest in enterprise profits, by dismissal for negligent work, etc. But that does not satisfy capitalist society. It tries to penetrate into the worker's soul and to install there an internal overseer in the form of its own principles of morality, the principles of the master's views regarding the production process and the worker's duties. And capitalists abroad have been quite successful in this respect. One need only recall the psychology of the average English trade unionist or any member of the American Gomperite federation.[27] From this standpoint, the worker's consciousness in capitalist society is a permanent battlefield between the norms and ideas imposed upon the proletarian by bourgeois exploiters and the norms dictated to him by his class interest, regardless of how it affects production.

When the proletariat gains power; when, with a feeling of deep relief, it frees itself from capitalist norms and the entire bourgeois heritage in this sphere, it must quickly turn to establishing its own class norms that regulate the economic process in the factory and workshop. Its attitude towards the economic process now fundamentally changes. By means of the strike it was striving to acquire for itself a larger share of the product of its labour. Now it can acquire a larger share if it contributes more itself. The relation to the strike also changes. A workers' strike in the enterprises of a workers' state is now impermissible. The norms created around the strike, and the energy that went into this mode of

---

26   There is an excellent description of one such episode in Gorky's 'Autobiographical Tales' (*Krasnaya Nov'*, No. 2(12), p. 15).

27   [The reference is to the American Federation of Labor, led for many years by Samuel Gompers (1850–1924).]

struggle, are radically transformed. In place of the strike serving to improve the life of workers, now there is a new, voluntary, enlightened class consciousness and comradely labour discipline. With us, this discipline has already emerged and is developing and growing stronger. It must be extended not just to workers but also to all office workers, specialists, etc. These strata must be subject to the production norms of the working class. Also being transformed are all the worker's attitudes towards the factory's property, which is now the workers' property, towards accuracy and precision at work, towards absenteeism, etc. The relation of our worker in Soviet Russia to his factory and the results of his labour are already profoundly different from what is seen abroad in capitalist factories.

But this process of change, from the norms of a worker-slave to those of the worker-master, is not immediate and requires a certain period of time. Old habits and ideas will be with us for years after the victory of the proletarian revolution. Here is one vivid example of that sort. At one Moscow tailoring factory, the factory head required higher skills in one department for processing a new consignment of materials and replaced one worker with another who was more suitable. The latter was then called a strike-breaker by some of the workers. I am not going to recount here how this matter, which is quite interesting in terms of principles, ended, but one thing is already apparent from what has been said: how strong and automatic the old proletarian norms, ideas and modes of expression still are, and how sharply these ideas contradict the whole structure of our state industry. In fact, a strike-breaker now, from the standpoint of common proletarian interests, is the one who damages production; the strike-breaker, in conditions of proletarian power, has turned into a 'labour-breaker'. The second worker in our example does not fit that description at all.

Directly connected with this question is the more general question of formation of a new man for the new society. Soviet Russia has come face to face with this question. The experience of War Communism and NEP demonstrate what an enormous problem we confront here. As we have already mentioned, the incentive for labour in capitalist society, for the worker and employee, apart from general economic compulsion – if you don't go to the factory you will die of hunger – is the corresponding system of wages. The worker in a capitalist factory is usually of petty-bourgeois origin. If he is the son or grandson of a worker, his great-grandfather was almost always a former craftsman or ruined peasant. The capitalist encourages in him purely individualistic incentives for work – the more you work, the more you get – and to the extent that the development of technology is not an obstacle, he uses a piece-work wage as a basis for labour pressure on the worker. That is why, when the working class turns to revolution and begins construction of a new economy, it has been deeply corrupted by capitalism in this regard. In essence, capitalism itself did not so much create the individualistic incentives for work as use the petty-bourgeois heritage in the psyche of the worker himself. Moreover, these incentives harmonise with the entire social psychology and daily life of the capitalist period in general.

It was with just this heritage that we had to establish the economy during the period of War Communism. Many of our failures at the time were due to military and economic causes, but one of the main causes must also be seen in the fact that a new economy, on the basis of new principles, started with the old man. A great leap forward was taken all at once, and it was not possible in a year or two to adapt the psyche of the old worker to the new system. Moreover, as soon as the proletariat begins to build its state economy, it requires not simply a worker, not the old worker, but a worker of the state economy, an office worker and engineer of the state economy. Remember what happened when something completely new was required of the workers and employees – collective incentives to work – and all they could offer was the old garbage left behind from the old regime and the ruined relations of the past. Remember how uncomfortable and dirty it was in any of Narkomprod's distribution centres, how rudely the employees dealt with the public, how they plundered state supplies. But why? The old incentives for work were not used, they turned out to be unnecessary and damaging, yet new ones had not been created. The old owner was driven out, but a new collective owner had not yet fully emerged. Consciousness of the common interest was weak and could not overcome and replace the old habits and individualistic incentives in distribution, or the attitude at work that 'it is not my concern'. New forms of production and distribution proved to be in glaring contradiction with the old psychology and the old habits. It was as if there was no driver at the steering wheel of an automobile and instead a couple of oxen were harnessed to it.

But how everything later changed when NEP began! How polite the sales person is in a NEP-man's store or in the MPO,[28] though he was pushing you away with his rudeness and irresponsibility at the Narkomprod distribution point! How apathetic, lazy and arrogant he was at the latter and how attentively polite he is now. How quickly 'communist' dirt and dust was replaced by the bourgeois cleanliness and exactitude of NEP. What happened? Among other things, War Communism could not be based upon incentives to work that had not yet taken root among the working masses, and the old incentives were ruining everything

---

28   [The Moscow Consumer Society.]

and standing in the way. To the contrary, NEP established a *smychka* with these old incentives and put them to its own use. That is why the machine began to move so well even with the same human material. But does it not turn out that this machine is a bourgeois one?

Yes, it is old in many ways, but it is also new in many ways. Under NEP the state economy can rely to a certain extent upon the old incentives for work because in many respects it too works with capitalist methods. But already today, and to an even greater extent in the near future, the state economy will not be able to develop all the benefits inherent in an integrated economic ship of socialism; it will not be able to begin smothering the saplings of capitalism unless it has a cadre of new people who can run a state economy and work within it. Even today we cannot move ahead quickly in certain areas – in state trade for example, where we have all the economic advantages – mainly because we lack cadres of new workers who have not been corrupted by capitalism and are at the same time competent. Individual incentives, those backward and miserable incentives of the past, behind which there seems to be a petty bourgeois with eyes bulging out of fear for 'mine'; this enticement of pre-socialist man whom the Hegelian *'List der Vernunft'* (cunning of Absolute Reason) drove to work with a carrot in front of his nose, just as we lure a cow into the barn – these individual incentives must be replaced by consciousness of the common interest and by the worker's ability to absorb this consciousness as a nearly spontaneous collective stimulus to work according to new principles.

Of course, this will not be possible right away. Individualistic incentives will die out gradually. For a certain period there will be combined individual-collective incentives. This will also be reflected in the wage system. The worker will receive more for himself by producing more, but for collectively producing more, the whole factory will be paid from a supplementary bonus fund. In future the bonus fund, or some new payment in another form, will more and more displace the old form, and this will occur simultaneously with educating the working class in collective incentives for work. This entire process will occur more quickly the sooner our young workers develop a completely new attitude towards work in their own state, thanks to a new system of education and in step with consciousness of their historic tasks, and the sooner – to use an old word – they adopt a new production morality. The young people must understand that they are our main hope. The adult generation is too corrupted by capitalism and too accustomed to the old ways. It seems to me, for example, that even members of the Communist Party, regardless of how great the historical role they have played in the period of breaching the walls of capitalism, or how great their role will be in the coming three-four decades – even they are already deeply tainted by capitalism and do not represent suitable material for a pure communist system. (Their good fortune is that they will not live long enough to see communism and will therefore go to the grave as revolutionaries and heroes.)

But no matter how deeply we are mired in the past in terms of psychology, the new economic relations are doing their work. The outdated psyche of the worker, which is slowly hobbling along behind technology and economics, impeding their race ahead, is beginning gradually to catch up with the structure of state industry. The more this happens, the more the widest strata of the working masses are beginning with the utmost attention to monitor how their enterprise is working, whether it fulfils its production programme, etc. They are beginning to feel that they are the masters, and this is leading to a marked change in the social attitude of the working class concerning such issues as the unauthorised plundering of factory property, absenteeism, swindling by the administration for the sake of getting more, and finally, evaluation of the director's qualities (which are improving). Previously, the public opinion of the workers tolerated plundering, especially when the food situation deteriorated; everyone covered up for everyone else when labour discipline was violated. The best director was the one who would overlook it and indulge the masses in anything. Now, everything is fundamentally changing. The public opinion of the working class already condemns all disruptions of labour discipline, a careless or criminal attitude towards property, etc., because all of this can damage the entire enterprise. The best director is now considered to be the one who is the best manager and who best guides production and safeguards the factory.

This about-turn in public opinion, which is connected with a reversal in the norms of behaviour, is of colossal importance. The construction of communism, insofar as it concerns man, his habits, instincts and class norms – this construction starts precisely with the beginning of this reversal in the psychology of the mass of average workers. Now the industry of the workers' state is beginning to acquire the worker it deserves and without which it cannot be socialist industry. Of course, following the proletarian revolution in the West this process of adjusting the human material to a historically higher economic system will occur much more rapidly and naturally than in our peasant country, where the percentage of the purely hereditary proletariat is small compared to those who have recently migrated from the countryside.

The creation of a new man, for a new economic system in Russia, must also mean a simultaneous rebirth of the national character of the Russian man, at least among the proletariat. This refers not just to methods of work but also to the whole of everyday life. The current type of Russian worker is essentially a product of serfdom, partially reformed by Russian capitalism. Our miserable capitalism could not significantly transform the character of our worker – yesterday's peasant – so that he would correspond more closely to the demands of large-scale industry and its advanced technical base. At its very peak, this process was interrupted by the war and the revolution. This work must be completed by the new system. This change of character has to happen, above all, under the disciplining pressure of 'Her Majesty, the Machine'. In this respect, the Soviet period will just automatically continue the work of capitalism.

But whereas re-education previously occurred under the owners' supervision and pressure, which no longer exists, it is now being replaced by a special factor. The owner's pressure is being replaced by a process of re-educating the entire working mass under pressure from its leading vanguard, whose task is to attract the entire mass and who are also re-educating themselves on the basis of the conscious social necessity for such re-education. This re-education is already occurring, and not just as an invisible molecular process; on the contrary, open war has been declared on the 'old man'. A short time will pass, and the public opinion of the working class, as a result of this great shift, will harass – up to and including a boycott – anyone who dares, shall we say in the fifteenth or twentieth year of proletarian dictatorship, to give off the scent of the old Russian character at work or in social life: laziness, sloppiness, imprecision, carelessness about the future, failure to fulfil one's obligations, lying to class comrades, etc. All of these qualities are incompatible with electrification and the technical progress of large-scale production in general, and also with the social life of the new worker on the basis of a higher form of economy and more advanced technique.

Here we must say a few words about deception and lying. Lies and deception are often totally necessary weapons in the struggle of an oppressed class against its enemies. It is enough to recall that the entire underground work of revolutionary organisations depends upon deceiving the surrounding people and the governmental authorities. For a workers' state that is surrounded on all sides by hostile capitalist states, lying in foreign policy is often necessary and useful, etc. Thus, the working class and its party see lying and open acceptance of the right to lie quite differently from Mistress Snowden[29] and other pious petty bourgeois, who are systematically tricked and made fools of by the representatives of large-scale capital. These gentlefolk, like the rather widespread breed of petty-bourgeois 'socialists' who resemble them, always stand for 'truth' and 'honesty'. They just forget that you cannot deceive the working class and remain personally honest. To be honest with bourgeois swindlers and

---

29   [Ethel Annakin (1881–1951), later Viscountess Snowden, was a Christian socialist, a suffragette, a member of the Fabian Society and a harsh critic of the Bolshevik Revolution.]

scoundrels in politics, considering yourself a paragon of honesty while socially lying, i.e., exposing the class you represent to blows from the enemy – that is the height of social wisdom for these toffs, the price of their honesty and their aversion to lying. They avoid the historical truth about the lie and prefer to lie about the truth, thereby soothing their petty-bourgeois soul. We take a completely different position on this issue.

But lying becomes a very harmful habit in community life and all social work when it not only has no connection with the interests of class struggle but, on the contrary, causes the corruption of the working class. Of course, the future belongs to the truth insofar as it belongs to a classless and not a class society. Lying is a product of the enslavement of one human being by another, a product of class and group struggle. It will disappear along with society's class divisions. But even before that happens, lying must be driven out of relations within the working class, and especially from relations of communists with each other.

It is unacceptable to resort to lying within the party to serve group interests in the same way as we lie in the struggle with our class enemies; this corrupts the party from within and diminishes its fighting capacity. The damage to production from lying is so obvious that there is no need to dwell upon it. A state economy, one that is internally well organised, cannot be built unless this destructive grit, which inhibits the smooth motion of the machine's wheels, is removed from the entire mechanism. And since re-education of the whole working class must begin with its vanguard, i.e., with the Communist Party, the war against lies and deception in intra-class relations must begin with liquidation of such remnants within the Communist Party itself. It is one thing to throw sand and dust into the eyes of one's class opponent, but it is quite another to do so with one's comrades in the struggle.

Meanwhile, the lie and its outdated harmful manifestations have deeply penetrated our national character. Much has already been written in our literature about the fact that the Russian man lies too much, lies without personal cause and with great harm to others. For a Russian serf, the lie was an instrument of defence against the master and the tsarist police. The master, the tsar and bourgeois domination have all been buried, but the habit of lying, cultivated by our entire past, still remains in the national character. Here we need a lot of 'washing, scrubbing and cleaning up' as Lenin once said in a different context. Here is a small example from life. You are walking on a street and ask a pedestrian for directions. The person you are asking does not know for certain, but he pretends that he knows and sends you in the opposite direction without consciously intending to do you any harm. It is the same in a great many areas. That is how 'references', statistical tables and the like are dealt with in our state apparatus, etc. Such fabrication and deception, often without any selfish intentions, is a frequent occurrence related to the lack of any sense of responsibility for one's own words, promises, messages etc., and it causes incredible harm in all of our construction. It may seem monstrous, but it is a fact that if a special society were now formed in Soviet Russia, whose members made a commitment to telling the truth, to honestly fulfilling their obligations and cultivating these principles among the broad masses, such a society would find rich soil for its work and would greatly contribute to the task of bringing up the new Soviet man, who is presently in such colossal demand from the new system of economy.

If there were rapid successes in this direction, the rebirth of our worker, which is already under way, would lead, and *lead from below*, to a beneficial rebirth of our entire state apparatus. In particular, it is only the pressure of working-class public opinion upon the mass of officials, and simultaneously a broad movement in the same direction among the officials themselves, that can eliminate the whole Asiatic and tsarist legacy in our state apparatus, above all the most disgusting, disgraceful and degrading phenomenon for the whole Republic, that is, bribery. An administrative struggle with this evil will never lead to total success unless bribery, along with everything else inherited from a shameful past, is surrounded and squeezed from all sides and thrown out of the workers' state by the newly forming and strengthening proletarian public opinion, which is spreading its norms of behaviour throughout everything that operates under the roof of the Soviet state. Conscientiousness and precision at work, precision in mutual relations between workers of the new structure and towards their state, are *indispensable in terms of production*; a revolution is imperative here, and the time is ripe.

We can now measure directly, in gold currency and tens of millions of roubles, the losses suffered by every sector of the state economy due to the slow emergence and education of the new man.[30] Now it is for our young people to decide. They are the ones who have not been corrupted by capitalism: they have received their first lessons in social upbringing to the sound of the crashing Romanov throne and the roar of our Red artillery. With the same energy and enthusiasm as they showed when they attacked the White trenches, they will soon rush to the aid of our industry and our ship of state to drive out the legacy of the Romanovs and Kolupayevs.[31] Supporting and connecting with each

---

30   Comrade Trotsky has shown very clearly and convincingly how battles are lost due to minor inaccuracies and trifling neglect. It would be worth calculating how much our Republic loses each year due to our so-called 'negligence' and whether the sums involved might even cover our budget deficit and rouble stabilisation.

31   [Kolupayev was the name of a kulak in *Haven of Mon Repos*, written by the satirist

other according to the principles of socialist work and socialist incentives to work, they will immediately accelerate our delayed development. They must remember that many from the adult generation are already beyond hope and it is too late to re-educate them. They will take with them to the grave the precious relics from the exploiter system that they have been unable to renounce.

But the social bonds of the worker are not limited to his relations with his state, his industry, and his comrades in the labour process and social work. Within the bounds of the Soviet state he is already running into other classes, above all the class closest to his own – the peasantry. But, on the other hand, he is encountering questions of a social character such as the family, sexuality, and the issue of preserving the species. How must the issue of proletarian class norms relate to all these other spheres?

With regard to other classes, for example, we can quickly do away with the NEP-man. He can be at peace; the class norms of the proletariat do not extend to him. We must compel him to obey the proletarian state by means of external force, mercilessly suppress his resistance and make him work conscientiously, without hope of any alternative, for the workers' state. From his point of view, i.e., bourgeois norms, from the point of view of his morality, he is right when he robs the Soviet state and creates conditions for a capitalist restoration. To think of domesticating him is dangerous daydreaming and only enables him to steal more from us and deceive us. He is the enemy. We will ultimately deal with him as the enemy.

The hundred-million peasant mass is another matter. The worker will have to live side by side with this class for decades. Without cooperation in the peasant economy, large-scale socialisation of agriculture is impossible. With the growth of industry, peasant youth will be an inexhaustible reserve for the proletariat itself, as a class. On the other hand, due precisely to the long period of anticipated co-habitation of these two classes, there must be not only an economic tie between the peasant economy and the state economy (the *smychka*), but also a certain co-ordination in the area of social psychology. The working class is deeply interested in having the peasantry also regard the state apparatus as their own and participate actively in improving it. For this and other reasons, the re-education of the peasantry by the proletariat, as the more advanced class, acquires enormous significance. We need to detach all of the most talented, sensitive, socially progressive and vital elements among the

---

M.Y. Saltykov-Schedrin. Lenin spoke of 'Kolupayev capitalism' in 'The Agrarian Programme of Social-Democracy in the First Russian Revolution, 1905–1907', in Lenin 1962, pp. 422–3; see also Lenin, 'The Cadets on "Two Camps" and "Sensible Compromise"', in Lenin 1963, p. 86.]

peasant mass from petty-bourgeois production, with its backward and limited petty-bourgeois psychology. At the same time, the working class is interested in seeing the pressure of its public opinion, the educational and organising pressure of this public opinion, gradually spread also to the peasant masses. And although the spread of proletarian norms to the peasantry is hopeless where this will clearly contradict the class interests of the latter, it is nevertheless not hopeless *always and throughout the whole period of this class's existence.*

To the contrary, from the history of other classes we know that a ruling class can subordinate not only backward classes to its ideological influence, culture and morality, but even whole groups of a class that is more advanced but not yet awakened and socially self-determined. Remember how the class of the nobility, during the period of its splendour and energy, kept other social strata standing to attention, how perfect the life and culture of the nobility and aristocracy seemed to others, how what was achieved in face of this culture even seemed grimy, although historically it represented a higher mode of production.[32] Remember, too, how the most progressive elements of the nobility emigrated to the camp of the bourgeois freethinkers. All of this will also occur in our country, a peasant country with the dictatorship of the proletariat, only in other forms, of course, and on a giant scale because it will involve tens of millions. And in our case, with the rapid successes of industry, there will be a general flight to the cities by the best peasant youth; when proletarian culture has also triumphed *on the economic front*, the working class will attract the most mobile and socially responsible strata of the village, who will be ashamed of their barbarism and, with sickle in hand or having thrown it away completely, will catch up with the hammer, which has rushed far ahead. Then the working class will also become legislator for the village in the area of class norms, and on this site it will reap the fruits sown by its victorious industry.

That is what will happen in future. For now, the issue is to attract to the side of the proletariat only the advanced minority in the countryside. They are a mere streamlet, just the first precursors of the torrents that will flow into the proletarian river from the peasant fields once the peasantry as a class, together with the whole of today's peasant life, becomes detached at its roots by the new economy.

Let us now turn to the next question.

Are the family and sexuality the sort of questions that lie beyond class norms and exclusively involve private life? No, much of this pertains to what is called a 'private matter', but much of it also has a deeply social character. It is very

---

32   [Preobrazhensky has the achievements of the rising capitalist class in mind.]

important to understand how to separate these socially significant questions from what is a matter of indifference from the social point of view, and to be able to answer questions of the first sort by starting from the interests of the proletarian class as a whole and its future. In this context, we must note that questions of the family and reproduction assume special significance precisely when the proletariat comes to power and begins to be responsible for the physical condition and physical future of the species.

The forms of the family, which have long been established on the basis of peasant farming and small-scale handicraft production, automatically carry over to the family life of the working class as well. But capitalism very soon begins to dissolve the old forms of the family: it drives the working wife into the factory, tearing her away from the home pot, and thereby undermines the basis of the old family in the kitchen. However, after partly freeing women from dependence upon men and creating the first preconditions for more human conditions of marriage and the bond between men and women in general, capitalism could not stop there. Capital would not be capital if it decided to transfer maintenance of the worker's children from wages to surplus value. The process of the old family's dissolution, begun under capitalism, also came to a halt under capitalism because the question of social child-raising was not only impossible to solve in bourgeois society but could not even be raised as a practical problem for the masses to decide.

When the proletariat takes power, it is left to complete the enormous issue of creating conditions for the final simplification of a new form of family. This task is first and foremost one of the social upbringing of children. And the task of social child-raising, in today's Russia for example, is above all a financial question. When our industry begins to develop quickly, it will resolve a whole plethora of other problems and questions, almost all of which have to do with our poverty. The question will then be resolved as to whether the rudiments of social child-raising, preserved under NEP from the period of War Communism, will become the starting point for the transition to social nurturing, at least in the city, and will first of all provide social upbringing for a whole generation of proletarian children.

The question of the form of the family has been indisputably answered; there can be no doubts concerning further evolution, at least concerning the raising of children. It is also clear that only in this way is the emancipation of women possible, together with enormous savings for the whole society that is gradually disposing of all the pots of the individual kitchen. This is a programmatic question for the Communist Party, involving no disputes between communists. And, for that reason, the task of every communist and every conscious worker involves facilitating in every way the organisation of social child-raising

and rearrangement of the family along new lines. If, even when the preconditions for social nurturing are already available, some segments of working men
and women cling to the old family forms, they will probably be regarded in the
same way as those workers who today, instead of attending a rally or a meeting
of their union, go to evening prayers. The women will remain with the pots and
the children, deprived of the possibility of contributing to the struggle for the
fundamental interests of their class and its future, while their comrades, with
the faith and enthusiasm of mass pressure, will move the socialist ship forward.
And the big question is whether the future socialist state will permit some parents to spoil their children with home nurturing, distorting them in their own
image and likeness.

But in our day another question is more urgent, namely, the question of how
the burden of child-raising should be divided between men and women when
social nurturing has hardly begun to make its way and the overwhelming mass
of children remain dependent upon their parents. This question arises not just
in cases when husband and wife separate, but also when they live together. The
most appropriate decision here would be that the parents either have the same
responsibility for raising the children, or if it is there is a concern involving
the purely material side of the issue, more should be done by whichever one
is materially more secure. Above all, the public opinion of the proletariat must
defend here the elementary equality of women and men in fulfilling their obligations, which are essentially social but can only be handed over to society with
the establishment of a system of social child-raising as the prevailing form. It
cannot by any means be considered a normal situation in working life when all
or the major portion of the work of raising children falls to the working woman,
who also finds herself materially in much worse conditions compared to the
men of her class. The principle of comradely equality must be fully implemented here.

The next question concerns the form of sexual relations. With the organisation of social upbringing this question emerges in pure form, not obscured
by other conditions connected with the family. Specifically, is it possible from
the viewpoint of proletarian interests to pose and give an answer to the question of what forms of sexual relations are more compatible, if not with the
current social relations and social interests then with the relations of socialist
society: monogamy, short-term relationships, or so-called promiscuous sexual
intercourse? Up to now, the defenders of one or another point of view on this
question were more likely to justify their own personal tastes and habits in this
area with all sorts of arguments rather than providing a correct answer grounded in sociology and class. Some have preferred the rather philistine personal
family life of Marx and are inclined to favour monogamy; they have tried to raise

the monogamous form of marriage into a dogma and a norm, using medical and social arguments to that end. Those who incline in the opposite direction attempt to portray fleeting marriages and 'sexual communism' as the natural form of marriage in the future society; practicing this kind of relation between the sexes is sometimes proudly regarded as an 'act of protest' against the petty-bourgeois family morality of the present.

In reality, all such ways of posing the question can be reduced to the fact that people recommend to communist society their own personal tastes and pass off their own personal sympathies as objective necessity; meanwhile, the question of the forms of relations between the sexes, about which there is such an uproar from the moral point of view, becomes – when separated from its connections to the family – *a social question first and foremost, but only in terms of the physical health of the species.* It is hardly possible that anyone will be able to prove that one or another form of marriage within the working class, given the social rearing of children, can directly influence the success or failure of the proletariat's struggle for communism. The workers of a socialist society can, therefore, be quite indifferent from this perspective concerning one or another form of sexual relations. This entire problem becomes a social problem only in connection with the physical preservation and strengthening of the species, above all from the point of view of the healthiest and best offspring. Accordingly, answers to the question must be provided by medicine, not by the Communist programme and the associated militant class norms of the proletariat. But even medicine, apparently, is in no position to prescribe a standard and uniform recipe here.

If the best offspring occur most frequently, other conditions being equal, as the result of a sexual relation connected with love, and if love involves a long-term bond for some and a brief connection for others, which often depends upon the temperament of those involved, then in such conditions one and the same result (the best offspring) can be achieved through different forms of sexual relations. Obviously a medical, or more correctly a biological approach to the question requires taking into account other aspects of the problem: the prevention of physical exhaustion through sexual intercourse, the best combination of *physical* attributes of the parties who are entering into a sexual union and creating offspring, etc. And all of this proves once again that all of the questions arising here must find an answer in medicine; and socialist medicine, on the other hand, must provide such answers both for particular cases and in a general setting.

Now we have come to those norms that are dictated by the tasks of physically preserving and strengthening the species. We must note that the full scope of this problem can only be posed under socialism, for it is only under socialism that the interests of the toiling masses, who constitute the overwhelming majority of society, come to the forefront, which in turn also brings to the forefront the interests of the physical preservation and physical future of these masses. Capitalism cannot pose this problem, even for the bourgeoisie, in view of the comparatively fluid composition of the capitalist class (as opposed to the estates of feudal society) resulting from the deeply individualistic principles of bourgeois life in general, but mainly because the union of people (marriage) among the bourgeoisie is subordinate to the task of 'a union of capitals' and for that reason is not subject to any medical regulations. As regards the overwhelming majority of the population, i.e., the workers and poor peasants, the most rapid capitalist accumulation and unhindered extraction from the working population of the maximum surplus value is possible only when capitalism generally has no need to think about the health of the working masses. Nor does capital ever have any such concern, possessing an enormous reserve army that is continuously replenished with new cadres from craftsmen and peasants who are being ruined. In the conditions of bourgeois domination, the working class defends the interest of preserving the species only by fighting for better working conditions and, on the basis of the existing balance of forces, by securing the most favourable conditions for its own material existence.

When the working class is itself in power, it already becomes responsible for the physical health of the entire society. The basic condition for physical regeneration of the species, of course, is elimination of superfluous labour, improvement of the material situation and housing conditions, development of a system of physical education for the masses, etc. But beyond all this, enormous importance must attach in future to society's control over the offspring of its members. From the socialist point of view, it is totally absurd for an individual member of society to regard his own body as absolute personal property, because the individual is merely a single point in the transition of the species from the past to the future. But it is ten times more absurd to take the same view of 'their' offspring. There are millions of people with syphilis, who must categorically be prevented, in the interests of preserving the species, from having children and thereby poisoning the blood and bestowing parasyphilitic consequences upon a succession of future generations. But here we need not just legislative regulation. We need a categorical demand of proletarian public opinion to its members, pointing in the same direction. There must be a corresponding internal conviction on the part of the patients themselves, which is formed above all by the pressure of public opinion from the people around them. What applies to syphilitics is also applicable to a whole number of other sick people and other groups who, in the interests of preserving the species, should not have offspring. If either a woman or a man must not have offspring for biological reasons, then the potential maternal feelings of the woman and the man's wish to have children must be regarded as merely sentimental personal emotions to which society must make no concessions. They must themselves suppress these feelings in their own interests. We have yet to mention that there must be a most ruthless struggle with those who spread sexual diseases without even thinking of the crime they are committing against other members of society, often against their own class comrades.[33]

It is premature to pose the question of whether we can expect future intervention by the socialist state or, in its absence, the intervention of science in sexual life for the purpose of improving the species by way of artificial sexual selection. Here we need only point out the total and unconditional right of society to extend its regulation of sexual relations even to this extent. The same applies to the responsibility of each member of socialist society to implement voluntarily in one's own life whatever will be prescribed in this sphere by social-biological necessity,[34] as formulated by science.[35]

The most important substratum for all the class norms of the proletariat is not just a clear consciousness of class interests on the part of the working masses, but also a semi-conscious class cohesion, a kinship with all other members of the class and hostility towards the representatives of foreign classes. This psychological unity of the proletariat plays a very important role throughout its struggle both before and after the proletarian revolution. In particular, it is especially important and precious during the period of NEP, when the state economy interacts with capitalist forms of economy and the workers of state industry are forced to be involved in continuous business connections with representatives of the capitalist world and bourgeois specialists. In cases when this class cohesion between our communists and non-party workers weakens, they are easily influenced by the enemy class, which for the present is still (although not for long, it is true) more advanced in cultural terms than the proletarian milieu.[36] As a result, we have already seen and continue to see cases

---

33   I think there is no need to prove that proletarian interests demand a most energetic
       struggle against prostitution insofar as it is rooted not just in the social conditions that
       encourage it in terms of supply but also in the demand for it, including demand coming
       from among the working class itself.

34   Bourgeois individualism is horrified by the thought even of the possibility of such artifi-
       cial sexual selection in the interests of preserving and strengthening the species. And this
       happens at the same time as it considers it perfectly natural for forms of the family and
       sexual relations to be subordinated to the interests of private property.

35   [Interest in genetics during the 1920s was promoted by the People's Commissariat of
       Health with the aim of improving social hygiene and public health. See Krementsov 2011,
       pp. 61–92; also Paul 1984, pp. 567–90.]

36   This influence of a culture that is hostile to us can in some cases be noticed in our work-

of our economic workers being snared by bourgeois operators, as happened, for example, in the sad memory of the Orekhovo-Zuevsky trust.[37] Conversely, where the workers have a strong sense of class, it is much easier to resist the disintegrating influence of the NEP environment. Hence the practical conclusion: the strengthening of class cohesion between all workers in all branches of work and merciless condemnation of all deserters from the proletarian family who are attracted to bourgeois elements and prefer the company of our class enemies to the workers' environment.[38]

Let us consider one further pressing question – that of material equality among the proletariat and within the Communist Party under Soviet power. During the period of War Communism we went very far in carrying out the principle of equality, and doing so was both economically and politically necessary. When products were scarce and we had to maintain the defence capability of the entire working class during the period of the Civil War, this equality in poverty did not weaken but instead strengthened us in the face of the enemy. When we returned to peaceful conditions [under NEP] and had to increase production with the human material that was available, and with the same incentives for labour that the workers retained from the petty-bourgeois and capitalist period (i.e. primarily individualistic incentives), we were compelled

---

ers' faculties, where young workers often fall under the influence of elements hostile to us among the instructors. We shall have many more years of struggle against these ideological vacillations by young people.

37 [Orekhovo-Zuevo, an industrial city in Moscow oblast, was the site of the first and largest Russian strike, which occurred in 1885 against the textile factories. Despite brutal repression, the strike lasted several weeks and acquired legendary significance. When the leaders were arrested, they shouted: 'Remember, one for all and all for one!' In late 1922, however, just prior to this work by Preobrazhensky, the workers at these same factories joined spontaneous strikes elsewhere in protesting against rising prices and falling wages.]

38 There has recently been much discussion in communist circles about marriages between communists and people from other classes and debate over the extent to which they are admissible. Essentially, there is no problem here in terms of principle. This is an area of private affairs, although it is understandable that a bad marriage can have a harmful effect on the activity of a communist. But it can affect many other things that we do not normally treat as personal matters. In general terms, if a party member does not behave in a communist manner, he must be judged for objective actions without going into why they happened. But the socially important point in considering this question is the following. If a communist man marries a woman from a bourgeois background, attitudes will spontaneously and unconsciously be much more lenient than in the case where a communist woman marries a NEP-man. Such facts are the clearest measure of how deeply our 'morals' still involve the Asiatic inequality of women and a double-standard of morality. [There is an error in the text, which says '... attracted to bourgeois elements and prefer the workers' environment to the company of our class enemies ....']

to begin at the point where our capitalism ended. We had to resurrect much of the capitalist wage system, i.e., the system of wage inequality according to workers' skills and rates of output. To this was further added the inequality between individual enterprises and trusts, based on which of these enterprises proved more able and which were less able to connect with the market. At the given stage of development, and with the given human material, inequality turned out to be necessary for us in terms of production.

This inequality cut through the Communist Party along the same lines, provoking complaints among those who were 'lower down' against the better paid, so-called 'higher ups'. Thus, insofar as the position within the working class as a whole is concerned, this protest against inequality was, essentially speaking, a protest against the fact that socialism is growing out of capitalism. This is a reactionary protest if it is based on a striving for petty-bourgeois equalisation without taking into account the needs of production. It can be progressive to the extent that it represents a protest of socialist consciousness, which has grown up among the workers, against the remnants of capitalist relations, and if it is directed above all against forms of inequality that are not at all called for by the needs of production. This protest will be all the more progressive, the more rapidly the level of skills grows amongst the entire working class and any increase of inequality or any sort of privileges for any particular group of workers becomes unnecessary for production.

As far as the Communist Party is concerned, precisely because it is a mass party it would hardly be possible to separate it from the living conditions of the working class as a whole and transform it into a 'community of equals' in material terms. But since communists work and are obliged to work in the interests of the whole working class and not out of concern for material benefits, here the struggle against any forms of inequality that are due neither to political nor to economic considerations, and that simultaneously weaken the internal cohesion of the party, must be waged much more decisively than anywhere else. This inequality within the Communist Party and the privileged position of certain of its strata, which far exceeds the limits needed to prevent exhaustion of the most valuable party cadres in purely physical terms, is extremely harmful in the sense that it can lead to a struggle to preserve privileged positions, to numbing of the party's tissues, to careerism and bureaucratic degeneration of certain party strata. This process will be all the more dangerous, the more new and newly qualified young people enter into leading posts in the party and Soviet apparatus and meet with a resistance that is in no way dictated by the interests of socialist construction.

Generally speaking, our party has given in too often to the automatic movement and mechanical construction of the state apparatus. In terms of pay, the state apparatus has been equated with the bourgeois specialist, who had to be attracted by satisfying his needs and habits. But during the period of NEP such equation has also begun with the 'older generation' of skilled workers. This was historically inevitable for the state apparatus at a certain stage. But the more rapidly specialists are trained from among the workers and absorbed into production and the apparatus, and the more rapidly, on the other hand, the training of a new generation of skilled workers proceeds in factory schools and by other means (and *the majority* of the proletariat must be skilled in the future), the less justification there will be for the state to maintain the old system of payment and the associated material inequality, which in the state sphere is swollen out of all proportion and beyond all reason. This new stage will probably begin in half a dozen years. But even now it is time to speak up against such an extent of inequality in pay that is simply the result of aping bourgeois relations rather than serving any practical interests. There is no doubt that the near future belongs to equality in the area of material living conditions for state workers. And although equality as such, equality at any cost, is not some end in itself in our construction, it will nevertheless be gradually achieved on the basis of the needs of the developing economy itself and a new psychology among the young generation of workers.

In general terms, the question of equality in material conditions, and all other such questions, must be posed not from the viewpoint of some absolute and abstract socialist justice, but rather in terms of the interests of development and the advance of our entire socialist construction. And in each particular case it must be solved concretely. At the given stage, what is it that facilitates progress and increases the strength and solidarity of the fighting proletariat, what weakens it, and finally, what has no effect one way or the other? Inequality has been and for now remains necessary for production, and within the limits of production requirements we have to put up with it. We shall oppose inequality when development of new production relations and the presence of a new generation of workers will not only no longer require such inequality but will also find it to be an obstacle to further progress.

In conclusion, there is one further question that is seriously distressing the peasant strata of our party: How compatible is work on their own individual farm (and all the ensuing consequences) with work in the Communist Party? Is it not a question of either the independent farm or the Communist Party? There is absolutely no need for such an 'either-or'. The communist peasant only needs to bear in mind that once he has joined the party, he must thereby regard his individual farm not as an end but as a means for achieving our communist goals. In other words, if he can be a model proprietor and also wage propaganda by the *activity* of cultivating the soil in new ways, while remaining a good communist, then everything is fine. If he can be a model communist only at the cost of becoming a gaunt farmer, then he must prefer the latter outcome. For a rural communist, the farm must take second place and the party first place if he wants to remain a communist. In that case, the farm must be seen simply as a means for a living, nothing more. Paraphrasing a famous verse, we might say: you may not be a good proprietor, but you are obliged to be a good communist. In practical life, of course, it is extremely difficult to draw a line showing the moment when one's own economic interest begins clearly to interfere with communist duties, but in principle there is nothing insurmountable here. When they were in the underground, members of our party were able to combine the most diverse work for satisfying material needs with active work in the party as their main work, to which the former was subordinated as a means. A whole range of other problems that confront the rural communist can be solved from this point of view, including the permissible forms and extent of trade operations, etc.

The examples that we have given from the sphere of proletarian class norms demonstrate first that such norms really do exist, and second, that they will inevitably exist as long as classes exist. It would be completely improbable if, during the period of proletarian dictatorship and existence of the socialist state, these paramount attributes of class society continued to exist but class norms, which play such an important role in unifying the class, sustaining its internal ties, its militant cohesion and the influence of the whole upon the parts, for some unknown reason ceased to exist. We have given some examples. It is not our task to provide a systematic description of all the proletariat's class norms, since the main task of this work is *to pose* properly the actual question of morality and class norms. From what has been said, however, it is already clear what position has to be taken concerning the spontaneous 'amorality' that is quite widespread among a section of proletarian young people who do not know how far to carry it.

If we take this amorality to mean repudiation of the rules of bourgeois and petty-bourgeois morality in theory and practice, together with exposure of this 'non-class' smokescreen that conceals class norms, then such 'amorality' is essentially a Marxist and historical-materialist attitude towards the morality of other classes. If this amorality becomes a denial of all norms in general, and thus also of proletarian class norms, then such amorality, in conditions of a yet to be completed class struggle, is at best utopian-bourgeois and theoretical confusion and at worst a product of influence upon the proletarian coming from petty-bourgeois and anarchistic individualism. But it is more likely that what we have here is not some 'unhealthy' and 'dangerous' influence, but simply the fact that some of our young people are still at loose ends. Having freed them-

selves from the moral shackles imposed by exploiting and historically backward classes, they immediately lash out in words against morality in general,
although in practice the enormous majority of them faithfully comply with the
basic norms of their class.

12   The Future of Class Norms

As socialist relations develop, proletarian class norms will change in the sense
that they will be rationalised and become more simplified and flexible; they
will, if we may put it this way, become expedited. There is no need for a coercive
response from class public opinion in order for a worker of socialist society, in
some sphere or other that is regulated by class norms, to begin acting differently
and in the class interest. He will gradually become accustomed to automatically carrying over into his practical activity everything dictated by science and
the common interest. If medicine, let us say, determines that social harm results from some habit that has taken root, a struggle against this habit does not
have to begin with a stubborn effort to forge the public opinion of a majority of
the class on this question, followed by compulsory extension of this new norm
to all class members and supported by the pressure of that public opinion.

The general elevation of the cultural level and consciousness of workers in
socialist society will be expressed, among other things, in the fact that they will
learn to do everything that is socially necessary with much greater ease and
in a more natural way than was the case in stagnant social formations, where
achieving whatever was necessary in class terms required the spread of some
new morality. Take an example. Suppose that, at a certain stage of socialist society's development and for whatever reasons, the birth rate has dangerously
declined. Science need merely sound the alarm in order for all members of
society to draw practical conclusions quickly, consciously and voluntarily. In
such conditions the slogan 'Increase childbirths' will by no means have to be
transformed into some entrenched social norm for an entire period until the
necessary ratio is established in society between mortality and reproduction.

That is one side of the story. On the other hand, there is no doubt that as
class divisions are eliminated in society, class norms will themselves become
general social norms, all the more so as workers in the socialist sector of the
economy gradually become the overwhelming majority of the entire working
population. But there is another reason. With the end of class struggle, class
norms must either die out to the extent that they took the form of weapons in
that struggle, or else they must be transformed. In other words, they must serve
other purposes on a new social basis. The bonds of a class that is struggling with

other classes will become the bonds of the entire society in its struggle with nature. Class norms will turn into social norms. How long they will endure, and in what form future social norms may be genetically linked with class norms – the answer to these questions will very much depend on what stage in the development of the future society we have in mind. What will still be preserved in one stage as a social norm will already in subsequent stages be absorbed into instinct and will unfold in the activity of each individual in the form of a realisation of the capital inherited from previous generations. It is important here to emphasise just two circumstances. First, with the elimination of class society each and every norm will be freed from everything generated by society's class division. And second, we can state that law will be eliminated sooner than unwritten class norms and the universal social norms that follow. The most likely outcome is that legal norms will be gradually replaced during the transition period by general social norms, and the partial inclusion of the latter within social instinct will occur on a wide scale only during a later historical period.

Therefore, our answer to the question of the future of class norms is that these norms have the same sort of future as the army, police, court and state in general, i.e., they have no future. With regard to the future of general social norms, all we can do for now is guess. For whatever period of time is involved in the passage from socialism to communism, they must exist. They are the form in which mankind will psychologically bid farewell to the last remnants of the class period of human history.

E.A. Preobrazhensky,
O morali i klassovykh normakh,
Moscow, Petrograd, Gosudarstvennoe izdatel'stvo, 1923, pp. 3–114.

PART 4

Appendices

∵

From NEP to Socialism (A Glance into the Future of Russia and Europe)

In the first lecture hall of the Moscow Polytechnic Museum, according to long-established practice, lectures were given for workers who were not satisfied with the knowledge received in school and continued their education during their free time. In 1970 a series of lectures was given here concerning the history of the Great Russian Revolution. These lectures drew a considerable audience and were heard simultaneously by workers in other districts, who were linked to the first auditorium by radio. The lectures were delivered by Minayev, a professor of Russian history who also worked as a mechanic in the railway workshops.

Minayev's course began with the first Russian revolution of 1905 and ended with the epoch of civil war in Europe. The historian taught his audience how to employ the methods of historical materialism in the analysis of concrete historical facts and also conveyed to them considerable concrete historical information, mainly of an economic nature, drawn from the epoch under review. The fifth lecture, which Minayev delivered on 13 May, began with an outline of the political and economic situation that formed in Europe after the first wave of proletarian revolution in the years 1917–20. This volume includes the whole of the fifth lecture and those that followed.

Lecture No. 5

1   European Capitalism in a Blind Alley

Comrades! In my previous lecture I gave you a picture of the events that took place in the years 1918–20. From the facts that I presented, you could see that the first volcanic eruption of the proletarian revolution turned out to be too weak to penetrate the social crust of capitalism throughout Europe as a whole. I also attempted to explain why the revolution was unable to defeat bourgeois society in Europe with only a single blow. It would be a mistake, however, to underestimate the importance of the success that was achieved. The victory of the proletarian revolution in Russia meant that one-half of Europe and one-sixth of the world's surface passed under the power of the workers. From the standpoint of the winning side, a war does not begin badly when the first battle leaves it in possession of one-sixth of the enemy's territory. At the same time, it would also be improper to overestimate the material consequences of this first stage of the revolution. If we compare the number of people living in Soviet Russia at that time with the world's total population, we find that only 1/15 of mankind was under Soviet power. The material consequences of the revolution seem equally insignificant if we clarify the relative weight of Soviet Russia's economy in the world economy of the day. In the first years of the revolution, the country's net national income did not exceed five billion gold roubles in prewar prices. That sum represented less than 1/12 of the annual national income of Europe and America, and thus an even smaller percentage of world production.

Nevertheless, a breach had been made in the capitalist front. Within the body of world capitalism, a salient was formed where it was materially possible for the proletariat gradually to prepare the prerequisites for a socialist economy. The political and economic situation in Europe was unique during the 1920s in that capitalism, being unable to plug the hole resulting from the first stage of the revolution, was forced to adjust to the existence of the first Soviet state and to the new system of property – which meant social ownership (at least in large-scale industry). Being in no position to crush the Soviet Republic, capitalism agreed to tolerate its existence, although it naturally looked upon such a state of affairs as temporary and considered the existence of Soviet power in Russia to be a passing affair. As you know, history decided otherwise.

How did this situation come about, and what were the forces that led to a new outbreak of the workers' revolution in Europe?

Let us first consider the economic situation prevailing in Europe after the initial stage of the world revolution. Saving itself from collapse, yet torn by internal contradictions, capitalism began gradually to heal the wounds it had received during the world war. It was forced to undertake this work at a time when industrial production in Europe had fallen by almost one-half. Capitalist Europe would have been able to recover from this level of production in a short time had all the elements needed for expansion been at hand. These elements included an adequate supply of labour, the means of production, reliable sources of raw materials, and adequate markets whose absorptive capacity would have to expand more or less proportionately with the growth of production. As for labour power, during the 1920s there was a vast surplus relative to the existing level of production. Six million unemployed – that was the reserve army that existed when capitalism, having recovered politically, commenced a new cycle of its development. Similarly, an enormous surplus of means of production was on hand, and factories were working at half of their production capacity. Normally, new capital accumulation is necessary in order to create a fund from which resources can be drawn for the creation of fixed capital required in the expansion of production. But this was not the case. In the given circumstances this was a vitally important fact, for post-war Europe was in no condition to accumulate for the sake of expanded reproduction; on the contrary, it was forced even to dissipate part of the capital that had been accumulated in earlier decades.

Two other considerations remain, and here matters were most unfavourable for capitalism. During the war, the development of American industry had taken a gigantic step forward. At the same time, domestic industry experienced an important development in the colonies and semi-colonies, areas that before the war had served as sources of materials and markets for European industry. The result was that the market for European industry significantly contracted. The volume of materials that could be sent to Europe likewise declined, since now a significant portion of these materials began to be processed in America and in the colonies. In consequence of this new distribution of markets and material sources in the world economic system, European industry found itself curtailed and reduced to a much narrower basis for production compared to pre-war times. Before the war, of course, European industry had established a certain proportionality between the main elements of production. Now, when sources of raw materials as well as markets had contracted more quickly than the other elements of production, the old structure could not be restored without first restoring all the other previous proportions. And just as the strength of a chain is determined by its weakest link, so European industry was unable to develop beyond the limits dictated by the available markets and materials; industry was now forced to adjust to these limits. Russia's departure from the world economic system made the situation even more critical, for it entailed the loss of an enormous market and one of the richest sources of materials. European industry could expand its material sources and markets in three possible ways: 1) by drawing Russia back into the world economic system through a simultaneous increase of the country's agricultural productivity; 2) by increasing the purchasing power of the population within Europe proper; or 3) by way of a new war with America, which had squeezed Europe out of a number of regions that once served as its material sources and markets.

Added to these difficulties was the problem of food. Even before the war, European industry was based on a slowly developing agricultural sector, which caused food products to become increasingly expensive. The production of grain became relatively more costly at a time when industrial products were falling in price due to the rapid development of industrial technique. In turn, the lagging rate of technical progress in agriculture impeded the fall in prices of industrial products by raising the price of grain. Thus, from *this perspective*, European industry was already on the brink of crisis before the war began. The failure of the first Russian revolution [in 1905] – which, in the event of its success, would have ensured a rapid development of Russian agriculture – closed this doorway for Europe. The war shook up all the cards and overshadowed the grain crisis with all the other crises, but the problem was not resolved and it confronted Europe anew when the war was over. The problem became all the more serious because European agriculture had sharply reduced its output during the war, and Europe's dependence on foreign grain markets had further increased.

Europe was unable to find a way out of this situation through a war with America because it was incomparably weaker than America in every respect, not to mention the fact that a united European capitalist front against America was impossible. An increase in the purchasing power of Europe's own population, above all of the working class, was likewise impossible. Capital was actually forced to adopt the opposite policy of reducing wages in order to expand surplus value and thereby to finance increased purchases of more expensive materials. Trying to expand its access to markets and materials by peaceful means, Europe was driven to take advantage of every opportunity, both internally and in the colonies, in addition to restoring economic links with Russia. When the Russian grain market became detached from the European economic system, Europe found itself heavily dependent economically, and particularly with respect to food and currencies, on America. Conversely, restoration of the Russian grain trade would mean creation of a second, enormous rival centre for the world grain trade, including cheaper grain. The inclusion of Russia in the European economic system would make it possible for Europe to develop her industry without having to transfer a large amount of capital and other productive resources from industry into agriculture, which would have signified regression for the economic system as a whole and for culture in general. If one hundred million Russian peasants, who produced two billion poods of grain in 1920, began to produce five billion by 1930, this would represent a colossal extension of the basis of European industry as far as food was concerned. But the restoration of Russian agriculture, which recovered much more quickly than Russian industry, at least in the early years, dramatically increased Russia's demand for industrial products from Europe.

You can see then, comrades, that Soviet Russia's strength during the 1920s was primarily a consequence of Europe's weakness. The Achilles heel of European industry lay in Russia, and Russia was under the rule of the revolutionary proletariat. Without drawing Russia back into the world economic system, Europe could not possibly experience rapid growth. Bourgeois Europe failed to turn Russia into a colony of Europe by supporting the civil war and intervention. Now it was necessary to choose different, more peaceful means, and a first effort of this nature took place at the Genoa Conference. Here, capitalist Europe wished to ensure that Russia, in exchange for her return to the world economy (i.e. in exchange for something vitally necessary to Europe), would repay bourgeois Europe for all the tsarist debts and compensate the losses incurred by European capitalists as a result of industrial nationalisation. The Soviet government would not agree, and subsequent events proved that this was exactly the correct course. Moreover, events demonstrated that Soviet Russia itself under-estimated its own strength. Capitalist Europe was in far greater need of Soviet Russia than the bourgeois diplomats indicated or even realised at the time. In that sort of situation, the one who can wait the longer has the greatest strength. Russia was able to wait longer, and it turned out to be stronger than Europe.

It was a fact though, that development of Russia's own productive forces also required a close economic connection with Europe. In contrast with the industrial countries of Europe, and especially with England or Germany, Russia was a country that possessed everything needed to in order develop into a self-sufficient economic organism. The economic and geographical requirements, together with the required social character, were all present. In the first place, Russia possessed all the natural resources needed to create a powerful industrial-agricultural complex. Coal, oil, peat, timber, iron and other ores, cotton, all kinds of raw materials except rubber, unlimited possibilities for agricultural development and for increasing the output of materials from livestock production: all these were at hand. Thus, all the requirements were there for a rapid expansion after the American pattern. There was also one enormous difference from America though, a difference that did not hinder but rather promoted the creation of an integrated economic unit. Here I am speaking of the socialist regime. At a certain stage of industrial development, the economy of capitalist America required that its markets be expanded beyond the country's frontiers. In this way, American industry and agriculture were woven into the world economic system. American industry was always outgrowing the limits of domestic demand and inevitably burst into the external market. Since the economy's motive force was profit, production could only be distributed by means of sales; if goods could not be sold, then from the capitalist point of view it made no sense to expand production. To the contrary, in a country such as Russia, where the natural and social requirements existed side by side for a self-sufficient economy (until the victory of socialism in other countries), the situation was quite different from that in America. Industrial development did not require external markets, for as more was produced, more could be distributed by socialist means. 'The more the better' is not a saying that applies to capitalist production, because not all that is produced can be sold. In contrast, such a saying is more than appropriate for socialism; it is fundamental. The more that is produced, the more can go to each worker. It is true that a socialist economy, even more than a capitalist one, requires proportionality between its parts. But this proportionality is not reached through the market; instead, it results from calculating the possible limits of consumption. In any case, for Russian industry of that time, working for the sake of domestic consumption, there could be no talk of over-production.

True, this industry was not socialist in the full sense of the word, unlike our modern industry for example, since only part of the total production was subject to *socialist* distribution. Because the small, independent peasant farm was the prevailing form in agriculture, to a large degree industry still produced for the domestic peasant *market*. In order to purchase grain and materials, industry had to sell a portion of its output to those who produced the grain and materials. Over-production was only a danger to the extent that some individual branches might produce more than was needed by peasants and workers, while other products, which both needed, might suffer from under-production. But this is leading us to a different problem, which I shall turn to later when I tell you of Russia's economic development during the period of transition from capitalism to socialism. Here, I wish to clarify only one point: while our industry needed an increase of absorptive capacity in the *domestic* peasant market, its development did not depend upon *external* markets, because socialist distribution between state industries and among the state workers and employees provided an outlet that substituted for the safety valve represented by a new foreign market in the case of a developing capitalist industry.

While Soviet Russia possessed all of the natural requirements for a temporarily isolated economic existence (until the proletarian revolution came in other countries), the most rapid development of its productive forces did require economic contacts with capitalist Europe. The capitalist countries were driven towards Russia by the need to seek markets and materials for their developing industry; Russia was pushed towards Europe by the inadequacies of its industrial development, which were further aggravated, in turn, by the disorganisation of agriculture. Russia's pre-revolutionary capitalist industry could not survive without a sufficiently strong agriculture. Socialist industry, likewise, could not develop quickly without a strong agriculture. But in order for agriculture to recover quickly, it required outside assistance in the form not just of short-term commercial credit but mainly in the form of long-term credits for land improvements and restoration of the economy. Russia's socialist industry could not provide agriculture with this kind of help on a large scale. It could not guarantee the volume of credits required, since it needed assistance itself in the form of credits. It was short of circulating capital and had significantly depleted its equipment during the war and the revolution.

Only the wealthier industry of Europe could provide Russian agriculture with credits, and European industry had its own pressing interest in Russia's agricultural expansion. The resulting economic situation in Europe during the 1920s was such that both capitalist Europe and socialist Russia needed a mutual economic bond in order to develop their productive forces: a rapid, almost spasmodic development of Russian agriculture had to serve as the initial motive force for growth during this period of Europe's economic history. European industry, as I mentioned earlier, did not possess the domestic preconditions for a speedy reconstruction. New markets were required, and new sources of supply had to be found beyond Europe's boundaries. It followed that the economic development of Europe during this period turned on the Russian village. This was the line of least resistance if progress were to occur.

A simplified economic calculation will indicate how true this conclusion was. Each step forward in economic terms means an increase of new values being created within a country, by hundreds of millions or even billions of roubles annually, with all of the ensuing consequences: an expanded potential for productive accumulation and thus for construction of new factories and railways; greater production within existing factories; and increased opportunities for the personal consumption of both capitalists and the working class, etc. Imagine for a moment that the whole European economy in the 1920s consisted of a single entity (which was only partly true). Imagine further that the objective is to increase the annual sum of values being produced by European industry in the shortest possible time, say by two billion gold roubles. How would that be objectively possible, given the conditions we have described and assuming that the mechanics of the capitalist mode of production are preserved?

Let us suppose that European capitalism acquires the resources with which to buy an additional volume of materials and then locates and purchases the materials, which on its own would be almost impossibly difficult in a short period of time. Even then, however, it would still have to sell the additional output being produced. Capitalism would create within itself a market for a part of this new production, but the remaining part would require that a further market be found with all haste, for otherwise the value of the goods being produced could not be realised. Since neither the one nor the other could fall from the skies – in fact, both could only result from a gradual unfolding, step by step, of economic processes both within Europe and beyond its frontiers –

it is perfectly clear that a rapid leap forward by European industry, based only upon its own productive potential and existing markets, was impossible. If European industry rushed to expand and then produced an additional two billion in values that could not be completely realised, the result would be such a crisis and such a waste of scarce resources – causing a reaction against expansion throughout the entire industrial organism – that, in the wake of such an experience, industry would not even be able to maintain the limited volume of production that existed beforehand. The restoration of European capitalist industry would be a simple matter if every factory not only started to produce at the same level as before the war but also managed first to sell everything produced, and second to sell at prices that would ensure the continuation of production. But since the fabric of the world economy had been torn apart in consequence of the world war, any development of European industry turned out to presuppose a number of additional new economic processes.

Russia agriculture, by comparison, required very little in order to raise its annual production.

If Russian agriculture produced about two billion poods of grain during the first years of the revolution, by 1922 the average harvest was large enough to cause an expansion to approximately three billion. And in order to produce more than three billion, to raise production to four billion (the pre-war figure), all that was needed was first to till 25% more land, which was available and could readily be worked; second, to make a number of elementary improvements in the peasant economy, (such as early ploughing of the fallow, tillage of the autumn plough land, drill seeding, etc.); third, to round out the supply of agricultural equipment; and fourth, an increase of working stock and their deployment to districts that had suffered most from loss of cattle. None of these measures involved any change in the structure of the peasant economy, let alone in the structure of the European economy. But these measures, when they became a reality, fundamentally altered the entire economic conjuncture in Europe. Thanks to Russia, the European economy ceased marking time (although not for long, as we shall see below), whereas Russia, even if it had continued to be isolated within Europe, could have continued to move forward without capitalist Europe, albeit at a slower pace of course. Here we have a partial explanation of what appears – at first glance – to be a paradoxical phenomenon: namely, the fact that economically backward Russia played such a decisive role in the whole history of Europe. But at this point I must end my description of the general-economic situation in Europe. In my next lecture I shall outline the history of Russia's economic development during the period of the so-called New Economic Policy.

Lecture No. 6

2   Russia's Economic System after the End of War Communism: The
       Restoration of Russian Agriculture during the First Decade of NEP

During the period of so-called 'War Communism', which lasted until the spring
of 1921, the structure of Soviet Russia's economy was much simpler than it later
became. If we leave aside the nomads (the Kirghiz, Kalmyks, Buryats etc.), two
different types of economy existed within the country's economic organism:
socialist large-scale industry, with an orientation towards planned production
and a planned distribution of products, and the small-scale production of peasants and handicraftsmen, with the system of distribution through the market.
The Soviet state failed in its endeavour to introduce a system of compulsory
distribution for agricultural products without introducing changes in the system of petty-bourgeois production itself. In place of compulsory seizure of
surplus agricultural output from the countryside, and its planned distribution
along with the products of urban industry, i.e., instead of petty-bourgeois production adjusting to the system of large-scale socialist production, it was now
necessary, on the contrary, to adjust large-scale state production to the market distribution of the petty commodity economy. Now, socialist production
had to subordinate the small-scale peasant economy and crafts to itself on
the basis of distribution through the market, i.e., mainly by the methods of
large-scale capitalist economy. The inevitable result was a plethora of different forms throughout the entire economy of the country. To a great extent,
large-scale state industry began to work for the market. Even so, the entire
state economy continued in some measure to be a planned economy, although
planning now had to conform to the market and all planning projections were
necessarily approximate. The result was diversity throughout the whole economy. Together with organs of capitalist regulation, such as the State Bank and
its subordinate network of credit institutions; and alongside the bourses, syndicates, and so on, there also existed organs for the state's planned guidance
of the economy, such as Gosplan, the Supreme Council of the National Economy, Narkomprod, and organs for the planned administration of wages (the
Shop Fund and the Supreme Council for Wage Rates). The diversity increased
still further when, together with purely state enterprises, mixed state-capitalist
societies and enterprises also began to emerge and then cooperative societies,
which not only played an enormous role in the area of distribution but also controlled many producing enterprises. One after another, concessions enterprises
also sprang up with the investment of foreign capital. In trade, private capital
grew and became stronger, controlling mainly small and medium-scale retail
trade. Finally, the predominant form of economy was small-scale peasant production in the countryside and small-scale handicrafts in the cities. At the very

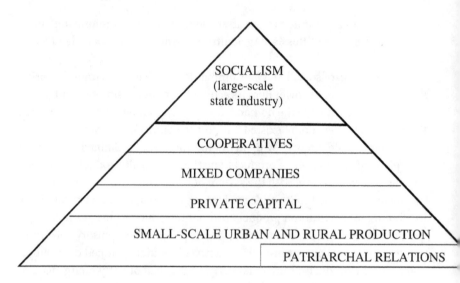

lowest level came the patriarchal economy of the nomads in the outlying areas. An unfortunate attempt was made at the time to label this diverse and mixed type of economy as state capitalism.[1] This description was unfortunate because it was totally unable to encompass the great variety of economic interrelations and was stolen from another form of economy, genuine state capitalism, i.e., the sort of system in which the capitalist state coalesces with private capitalist production, organised into trusts and headed by the banks.

The capitalism that then existed in Russia (and that grew up, for the most part, on the basis of private trade) was hardly of a state character, and the state had nothing in common with capitalism in the sense that it was an organisation of the proletariat for the purpose of crushing capitalism. This mixed type of economy can best be portrayed in the shape of a pyramid, divided into several bands, with the main band (4/5 of the value of annual production) consisting of roughly two dozen million petty-bourgeois undertakings with a stratum of patriarchal-tribal economy. Above this petty-bourgeois basis was a much narrower band of small and medium-sized capitalist enterprises in trade and industry that were not regulated by the state, and then a still narrower band of capitalist relations that were regulated by the state (mixed companies etc.). Higher still was a band of cooperative production and exchange; and finally,

---

1   [Lenin often used the term 'state capitalism' with reference to NEP, but the main proponent of state capitalism was the Finance Commissar Grigory Ya. Sokol'nikov. See his *Gosdartven-nyi kapitalizm in novaya finansovaya politika* (Redaktsiya izdanii Narodnovo Kommissariata Finansov, 1922).]

the whole upper part of the pyramid represented a solid unit of socialist relations that were not yet the dominant ones but were struggling for dominance.
This system as a whole, with its two main bands – an upper socialist band and
a lower band of small commodity production – could be called a commodity-
socialist system of economy.

At the outset, all of these diverse types of economy were unable to define
their respective spheres, determine their place in relation to one another, or
establish close economic links among themselves. But, as time passed, things
were settled quite quickly. Large-scale industry and transport remained almost
entirely in the hands of the proletarian state. Medium-sized industry was
divided into two halves: one remaining with the state and the other becoming
private, usually through enterprises being leased by the state either to private
individuals, artels, or cooperatives. Wholesale trade was primarily in the hands
of state trading organs, mixed trading companies and the cooperatives, and
only partly under the control of private commercial capital. In other words,
large-scale trade was in large measure socialised or subordinated to the state
directly or indirectly. In contrast, small-scale trade was mainly in the hands of
private capital and partly in the hands of cooperatives. Almost the whole of
agriculture and small-scale industry was controlled by independent commodity producers.

The connection between all these types of economy was initially formed
mainly through trade. During the epoch of War Communism, a sharp division
had existed between large-scale state industry and the peasant economy. A
textile or shoe factory would deliver its entire output to the state. By far the
major share of this output would go to the army or be distributed among the
workers as work clothes, etc., leaving only a small portion to reach the countryside. And even this portion was not distributed in such a way that those
who sent the most grain to the city received the most in the way of urban
products. The opposite was frequently the case: someone who was poor and
had been exempted from grain deliveries had a better chance of obtaining manufactured goods than the *kulak* who had sent his surplus to the city. This narrow link between industry and agriculture was brought into being through the
state. There was no more direct link between the peasant farm and large-scale
industry, unless one includes the sale by workers of a small part of production
that they received as wages, or a part that was embezzled and sold to the countryside illegally.

With the New Economic Policy, to the contrary, the same textile factory was
connected by a hundred different threads both to the peasant economy and to
individual state and private enterprises. In the first place, the factory became
part of the system of the state socialist economy upon joining a textile trust,

whose production programme was confirmed by Gosplan and received credits
from Gosbank. At the same time, it also had lively connections with the non-
socialised sector of the economy: it sold printed cottons to the peasantry by way
of the cooperatives and purchased grain or flax from them; it nurtured private
trade with these cottons and, through that trade and through the cooperatives, it was linked to all sorts of private enterprises; the factory received its
cotton from the peasant farmers of Turkestan, and so on. In the exact same way,
an entrepreneur with a leased soap works, who together with his enterprise
belonged to the private, non-socialised sector of the economy, was nevertheless drawn into the economic system as a whole. He sold his soap not just to
the peasants but to state institutions as well, and he purchased materials not
only from the peasant but also from a state wholesale shop. He also transpor-
ted his shipments on the state railways and received credits either from the
State Bank or from a credit institution connected with the State Bank. In these
various ways, an economic connection was established between different economic systems whose tendencies were mutually hostile.

You will certainly be interested in the further question of how the socialist form of economy, in the midst of this jumble of economic forms, became
predominant and first subordinated and then absorbed all the others. This
dominance was won through a long and stubborn struggle, and in the early days
victory by no means consisted of expanding the socialist form of economy as
such.

There was a time when large-scale production, having just emerged from
the stage of War Communism, floundered quite helplessly in the conditions of
money-based commodity exchange. At one time it was battered by small-scale
handicraft production, just as mongrel dogs can sometimes exhaust a strong
bear. They robbed and mocked it; some of the former capitalists, now sitting in
the organs of industrial administration, did everything possible to make things
difficult for industry and to profit from the workers' inability to guide the entire
economy, and particularly their unfamiliarity with trade. The workers in large-
scale production at one time earned less than workers in handicrafts, not to
mention independent craftsmen and artisans. Panicky and defeatist exclama-
tions could even be heard during this period among certain groups of Communists, although the latter, it is true, were few in number and confined to
elements from the intelligentsia: 'We should lease back more, if not everything,
to the capitalists, since we can't cope with it in any case'. But they did not write
such things so much as keep their thoughts to themselves, as memoirs from
that epoch demonstrated. Nevertheless, this critical period passed. Large-scale
industry regained its footing, and gradually the economic midgets respectfully
stepped aside – those who had been living by stealing from large-scale pro-

duction and by a rapacious waste of labour power, given their near-monopoly position on the free market.

During the first years of the New Economic Policy, the country's economy spontaneously struggled to regain its pre-war positions. The proportions of the pre-war economy were looked upon as the model for rebuilding the whole of economic life – with such differences, or course, as the fact that all the heights of production, i.e. large-scale industry and transport, the entire credit system and a large part of wholesale trade, were now in the hands of a new class, and the mode of economic regulation was historically superior to capitalism.

I have already mentioned to you the positions held by different economic types in the economy of the country, and it was from these initial positions that a gradual advance began. During the early years, economic changes tended to be quantitative in nature (only at a later point did quantity make the transition to quality). The economic forms that I have been describing, which had been established during the period of War Communism, now assumed their content. As for the forms themselves, they only began to change in the second phase of economic development, when they proved too restrictive for any further progress.

During the first year [of the New Economic Policy] it already became clear that industrial development depended upon successes in agriculture. There were months when large-scale industry, regardless of the terrible goods famine and exhaustion of all the country's commodity stocks, particularly in the rural areas, was unable to sell its production quickly because of the harvest failure. This problem could not possibly be attributed *entirely* to the ineffectiveness of the trading apparatus. Any future development of industry would be possible only if there were an expansion of its agricultural base. Experience had shown that when the country's entire agricultural sector produced two billion poods of grain, industry had one foot in the grave. True, the most important branches of industry and transport received most of their food products not so much by purchases from peasants as from returns from the tax in kind. But the return from the tax in kind also depended, first and foremost, upon the volume of production coming from the agricultural sector as a whole.

The favourable harvest of 1922 initiated a period of gradual improvement for the whole economy. Indeed, the elements of this improvement were discernible as early as 1921, but the famine interrupted the process. Otherwise, industry might quickly and without further stoppages have rounded the corner by the autumn of 1921. In 1922 the agricultural sector saw 800 million more poods of grain harvested than in the previous year. This meant that industry could achieve a substantial expansion over 1921 so long as growth was not hampered by other factors related to material and fuel supplies, etc.

The peasant economy began to recover quite rapidly. Having declined by about 30% compared to the pre-war level, the sown area now began to expand from year to year. In the northern provinces, land that had never before been cultivated was brought under the plough. The success brought about by the first elementary improvements in soil cultivation – which were promoted by the People's Commissariat of Agriculture – raised the peasantry's confidence in the science of agronomy and aroused enormous interest in further improvements. Moreover, by various streams and rivulets the first sprouts of newly introduced crops found their way into different farms and districts, aided by transition from the peasant *obshchina*[2] to separate farmsteads and settlements. Economic improvements also occurred in the communes and artels that survived the disintegrating influence of NEP. Following the success of the first major campaigns for early ploughing of the fallow, autumn ploughing, drill seeding and drought-resistant crops, efforts were mounted in the South and the South-East to bring about a widespread conversion from a three-field to a multi-field system. The cultivation of root crops was extended, promoting more cattle-raising, improving the milk yield from dairy cattle, and making more manure available for fertiliser. In some places and on some farms, intensive gardening and ribbon sowing took hold. By a thousand different routes, new information on improved land usage reached into the countryside. The agricultural campaigns of Narkomzem,[3] articles in the newspapers and agricultural journals, agricultural brochures, successful experiments on state farms, lectures by agronomists, annual agricultural exhibitions at both the local and national levels, initiatives by Red Army men who had attended agricultural lectures in the services, other initiatives taken by war prisoners, who saw and adopted the more advanced agriculture of Austria and Germany: from all these sources new and vital knowledge percolated into the rural areas.

This knowledge fell on fertile ground that had been ploughed in advance by the great worker-peasant revolution. The world war, the Revolution and the Civil War threw millions of people about, expanded their horizons, and fundamentally changed the stagnant, conservative psychology of the Russian peasant. The countryside awakened not merely to political life but also to a new kind of culture in agriculture. For whole centuries in the past, the methods whereby the vast majority of peasants worked the land had scarcely changed at all. Suddenly, in a single decade, a full-scale revolution took place. The peasantry was gripped by a desire to expand the sown acreage and to increase yield. The

---

2   [The *obshchina* was the traditional village commune, which farmed the land through periodic redistribution of strips among households.]

3   [The People's Commissariat of Agriculture.]

famine along the Volga had a positive significance in the sense that it greatly enhanced the interest of the peasant masses in any measures that might make the threat of drought less menacing to the rural economy.

The strongest stimulus for an expansion of sowing and higher yields came from rapid development of the urban commodity market and from foreign trade. During the period of War Communism, the peasant was forbidden to sell grain, since all surpluses were to be surrendered to the state. Moreover, in the majority of cases the peasant had no particular interest in such sales, because the urban market could not guarantee a selection of the commodities he required. The crop failure and economic dissolution brought hunger and led to a very different turn of events in the countryside: the peasantry sought to consume all that was produced, because selling grain and buying needed commodities was either impossible or made no sense. Now [with NEP] each extra pood of grain that was sold for cash made it possible for the peasant to purchase in the market more of all the things he needed. Each year the volume of foreign trade also grew, and the peasantry was now able to buy foreign goods, particularly agricultural machines. At the same time, both demand and prices rose for agricultural materials and technical crops, especially flax, hemp, wool, leather and so forth. This demand originated both with domestic industry, which was now growing, and also with foreign industry. This fact, in turn, provided enormous encouragement for the restoration of crops that had begun to fall into abeyance; that is, mainly the technical crops.

During the Civil War, these crops had been displaced by grains in the North and North-west. Flax and hemp could not fetch a price that would cover production costs, while it was very difficult to acquire grain. Instead of buying grain and selling technical crops, the peasantry of the North and North-west switched to grain cultivation. This could continue so long as industry was in a state of disarray, its functioning branches could make use of previous stocks of materials, and there was no foreign trade due to the blockade. Now, to the contrary, the processing and export of technical crops moved once again in the direction of pre-war proportions. As prices for these products rose, the peasants of the affected areas turned once more to growing technical crops. During the famine years, the sown acreage in these regions had been increased by comparison with pre-war times, so that it was now possible, given a stable supply of grain, not merely to achieve pre-war production levels for technical crops but to surpass them. This redistribution of agricultural crops, as compared with the period of War Communism, meant that the North and North-western provinces now produced economically more profitable technical crops, while the Central Black Earth zone, the South, and the South-East specialised exclusively in grain crops. Similarly, cotton cultivation was restored in Turkestan, where it had been driven out by bread grains during the famine years. On the whole, thanks to an unbroken expansion of the sown area together with continual improvements in methods, Russian agriculture began to increase its output each year by roughly 10%. The successful recovery in agriculture allowed industry to develop on this sound basis and also made it possible to begin exporting grain in substantial quantities.

The greatest impediments to agricultural development in the grain-growing areas were an inadequate cattle population and repeated crop failures in certain regions. The devastation of working livestock, due to the famine, was particularly serious along the Volga and in southern Ukraine. All of these factors created the need for extraordinary efforts by the Soviet authority to purchase and distribute working stock on a massive scale. Horses were purchased both in the nomadic herding regions, where numbers had also been depleted because of fodder shortages, and in other regions of the Republic. From an economic viewpoint, the shortage of livestock had two further, completely divergent consequences. On the one hand, it evoked a lively interest among the peasantry in motorised cultivation, which met with striking success when it was first applied in the fields of the South and South-East. The first large-scale agricultural concession enterprises sprang up here, involving mainly German capital and a colonial resettlement of unemployed European workers. On the other hand, the Soviet government increased its purchases of tractors for use on peasant farms where there were no horses. A large number of tractor detachments were created, which ploughed the peasant fields on the basis of terms agreed with the government. The shortage of drivers was overcome thanks to an inflow of skilled foreign workers, who emigrated to Russia partly because of unemployment, partly for class and ideological reasons, and thanks also to the expansion of professional and technical education within Russia itself. From the beginning there were circles of SR[4] and Narodnik agronomists and economists who took an ironic and pessimistic attitude towards the potential development of motorised agriculture in Russia, particularly when successes in this area buried all their reactionary and petty-bourgeois hopes concerning the vitality of the petty, individual economy. But years of intensive expansion revealed the full potential of mechanised cultivation, especially in the South-East of Russia, a region that was suited to mechanisation by virtue of local conditions and also because it lay on the main oil transport route from Baku up the Volga.

The shortage of livestock had another opposing influence upon agriculture, however, which warmed the hearts of all the petty-bourgeois utopians. In areas

---

4   [The reference is to the Socialist-Revolutionary party.]

with neither sufficient working stock nor tractors, the peasant economy temporarily leaned in the direction of a Chinese type of agriculture, or suburban market gardening. Wheat came to be sown in small beds, and the shortage of horsepower frequently caused the plough to be displaced by the shovel and hoe. In the rich black earth areas, this kind of cultivation yielded striking results in terms of crop yield per desyatin,[5] but it simultaneously caused a reduction of the sown area and the conversion of unworked land into waste. It was obvious that this type of agriculture could not last: just as soon as horses became available, the economy did away with this system, retaining only certain positive aspects of intensive cultivation on a small portion of the arable land.

We can see, therefore, that the first phase of agricultural development, which we have been describing, was concerned mainly with the return of peasant activity to the pre-war level and with a number of elementary improvements that had not been practised in the countryside before the war. The only real exception came in those districts where mechanised cultivation was introduced and where the peasantry successfully completed the transition to a multi-field system. In general and on the whole, the technical basis of the small-scale peasant economy remained unchanged.

But all of these advances required great efforts both by the peasants themselves and by the Soviet government. The most important assistance to the peasant economy from the Soviet government took the form of seed loans, especially for the areas affected by crop failure, along with long-term agricultural credit. This credit played an enormous role both in restoring agriculture, especially the poorer elements, and in establishing the closest economic links between the peasant economy and large-scale industry and the Soviet state's banking system. Initially the credit was not large, but it grew year by year, particularly when foreign capital became involved in the project. At first, long-term credit was administered by Gosbank's special department for long-term credit. Later, this department became a specialised joint-stock bank for agriculture, with the Commissariat of Agriculture playing the leading role after Gosbank. Other shareholders included the trusts that sold their products to the peasantry through use of long-term credits, above all trusts whose members included factories producing agricultural implements and artificial fertilisers.

The agricultural bank gave out loans both in cash and in kind, examples being agricultural machinery and artificial fertiliser. While the state currency remained unstable, it was absolutely imperative that the bank's loans be repaid not in depreciating currency but in real agricultural products equal in value to

---

5   [One desyatin was approximately equal to one hectare.]

the original loans plus interest. Otherwise, the bank would have experienced enormous losses due to the falling exchange rate of the rouble. This sort of loan made sense though, and not only because of the declining value of the currency. Beyond that, it had another fundamental economic importance. The system of loans and repayments in kind led to elimination of private merchants as middle-men between the peasantry and large-scale industry. Both sides benefited from the system, since the potential profit of the private middle-man now remained in the pockets of the state on the one side, and the peasant on the other.

This type of bond between the peasantry, state industry and the state bank was retained even after the paper currency was stabilised. The result was that the state, in addition to the tax in kind, began to acquire a growing volume of agricultural products without any intermediaries, and receipt of these products was dependable even if harvests should not be particularly good. Together with the tax in kind, this was a more or less stable fund upon which a developing industrial sector could confidently rely.

The agricultural products that the bank received were distributed, of course, not merely as payment for products from the factories working to supply the peasantry, but also between all the industrial enterprises that dealt with the bank either directly or indirectly through the Trade-Industrial Bank. The raw materials that the bank received from the peasantry in loan repayments were partly distributed amongst state enterprises and partly reserved as a foreign trade fund. From this source, the State Bank acquired foreign currency and was able to meet its foreign obligations. The point was that the State Bank, while extending credit to the peasant economy, was itself borrowing from large capitalist firms abroad – particularly from those who were selling to Russia the types of commodities needed by the peasant.

Foreign capital had originally attempted to establish direct links with the countryside; now it was forced, in the final analysis, to enter into a type of economic bond with peasant Russia that operated *through the organs of the Soviet state*, in this case through the bank for long-term credit. The resources of the state bank and those of industry, plus foreign credits and special loans, constituted a fund for long-term loans to the Russian countryside. This tie, which connected agriculture with industry via the banking system – the *smychka*, as Lenin called it in his day – emerged slowly at first and was initially insignificant compared to the volume of ordinary rural-urban trade with the villages through the cooperatives and the private trading apparatus. Even so, within a few years this tie became increasingly important and proved to be a more progressive form of distribution than any other kind of exchange within the commodity-socialist economic system. Trade on credit, and credit operations in general (including loans for land improvements), provided a most favourable vantage point from which to influence peasant production as a whole. During the epoch of War Communism, the socialist state's attempt to influence the peasant sector through *requisitions* had met with disaster; now it proved more viable in this new form, which was perfectly understandable and acceptable to the peasantry. *The recipient of loan repayments gradually became the controller of the quality of products received and the purchaser whose needs and requirements the peasant economy had to accommodate.*

You are wondering, no doubt, just what the intermediary links were between the bank for long-term credit and the peasant economy.

The role of intermediary at the lower level was performed by credit societies and by special credit organs, created by the State Bank and its local branches to help in the distribution of loans and to supervise repayments. At first, petty-bourgeois and reactionary Narodnik elements attempted to organise a more or less centralised network of credit cooperatives and to counterpose them to state organs. Practical work very quickly revealed, however, that the upper level of that sort of organisation, as of agricultural cooperatives in general, was perfectly useless ballast between the state as producer and the peasant as purchaser of agricultural machinery, fertiliser, and other industrial products. This was all the more true when the leadership began to engage in political intrigues, promoting division rather than unity between town and country. The existence of these upper levels contradicted the basic principle of all cooperatives; namely, to avoid all unnecessary intermediaries between producer and consumer. Moreover, in this case the credit cooperatives had no significant resources of their own and could not exist, especially while the currency was unstable, without credits from the state-producer and foreign capital.

Credit societies, associations of peasant borrowers and other types of co-operatives constituted the organisational mechanism that connected peasant agriculture and large-scale socialist production. Thanks to this apparatus and a far-flung system of bank inspectors, it was possible for the agricultural bank to reduce to a minimum any risk in its credit operations with the countryside.

In order to conclude our description of agriculture in this period, we must now say a few words about the social groupings that could be discerned in the countryside at the time. With the transition to the New Economic Policy, rural class contradictions naturally began to sharpen. Those *kulaks*, who were not totally ruined by committees of the poor in 1918, started now to revive. In addition, from the ranks of the middle peasantry a stratum of more well-to-do elements emerged. This group included the part of the middle peasantry that was strongest in economic terms, possessed an adequate supply of both livestock and implements and, most notably, took advantage of every opportunity afforded by the New Economic Policy.

Once trade in agricultural products was permitted, the *kulaks* and this section of the middle peasantry immediately threw themselves into expanding their sown area and became the first practitioners of commercial agriculture, which had almost disappeared after the October Revolution [...][6] of high prices for grain, precisely these strata utilised the favourable conjuncture on the grain market most successfully. At a time when the entire peasantry was seized by the desire to expand the sown area, this was the only rural group that had the maximum *material potential* for such expansion. Most notable among this group was the pull of the independent farmstead, the desire to have their own separate land, along with the greatest effort to improve land cultivation.

The weak or totally impoverished peasants, having no horse in most cases, were in an entirely different position. Wanting to retain their holdings no matter what, weak peasants had to rent a horse and borrow seed etc. from the first group, with the result that they fell into dire economic dependence upon the well-to-do elements. These same poor peasants, who were unable to cultivate their own strips of land, ended up leasing land to others who were cramped within their own allotments. These elements of the peasantry were partly or totally transformed into wage workers for the *kulaks*, or else they went to the cities[7] for various kinds of state jobs, such as logging, rafting firewood, repairing railway tracks and the like. With support from the agricultural bank, a large number of these weak peasants were able to regain their footing and even to become middle peasants. But another group slid down into the ranks of the poor and only began to recover economically during the ensuing period, when the mass development of complete producers' cooperatives began.

The main mass in the countryside consisted of middle-peasant farms. The economy of this fundamental rural stratum had been severely shaken during the period of civil war and repeated crop failures. But now, with the years of good harvests, they began to recover. The middle peasantry also benefited somewhat from high grain prices, even though they sold very little due to their meagre surpluses. This stratum had a great interest in cooperatives, yet when it came to improving methods of cultivation they mostly turned out to be more conservative and less flexible than the first, well-to-do group.

This stratification of the countryside and the clear emergence of economically strong and well-to-do elements, together with the development of rural hired labour, could not, however, assume such scale and forms as might have

---

6 [A line of text is missing here due to a typographical error that repeats an earlier line from the same paragraph.]

7 [The text refers to 'cities' (or towns), but Preobrazhensky clearly meant to say that poor peasants turned to the state sector of the economy.]

led to the emergence of large-scale or, at the least, medium-sized capitalist farms (we are excluding, or course, the large capitalist agricultural enterprises belonging to foreign concessionaires). The reasons were the following. On the one hand, there was the political rule of the proletariat in the cities, which supported poor rural elements against the wealthy and curtailed the degree of exploitation. The state organs used legal means to restrict exploitation of the poorest rural strata, annulled any oppressive agreements, and thereby inhibited the process of capitalist accumulation. The state also introduced a progressive income tax in town and country alike, so that capitalist accumulation at one of the poles in the countryside was utilised for so-called primitive socialist accumulation. Finally, a third reason was the natural slowness of such a process in general; even in conditions favourable for agricultural capitalism, it usually stretched out over several decades. In the present case, history did not leave adequate time for such a process. In the second phase of the period we are considering, large-scale urban production and electrification began to exert an organic influence over the whole of the small-scale peasant economy, initiating a process whereby the entire technical basis of the peasant economy was reconstructed. In these conditions, the process of capitalisation was driven into a blind alley due to a massive expansion of cooperative agricultural production. However, we are now running ahead of ourselves, so let us return to the period we are considering and note what happened with the Soviet farms and collectives.

The Soviet farms were transferred to so-called cost accounting, and after a few years of development in normalised conditions they very soon recovered and began to play a very important role, above all through assisting in improvement of the entire peasant economy. Almost all of them produced improved strains of seed, which they then exchanged for peasant grain, making possible a dramatic improvement in the peasants' yields. They acquired breeding facilities for better types of cattle and established a wide network of service points that significantly helped to increase peasant cattle-raising. This was also a period of high grain prices, both internally and on the world grain market, so that it was quite profitable for the state to invest capital in the development of large-scale grain farms. Proletarian agriculture also enjoyed great success; many Soviet farms, which the Agricultural Commissariat considered uneconomic, were assigned to various factories and plants and began to show a profit.

It was true that the spontaneous attempts by factories to acquire their own farms, whatever the cost, declined once the general grain shortage in the country was eliminated and prices for the products of large-scale industry approximated pre-war levels in relation to grain prices. Thereafter, proletarian state farms assumed more of a health function than an economic one, serving as points of contact between industry and agriculture and as resorts where city workers and their children might spend their summer vacations.

New Soviet farms became very important in the far reaches of the country, where the state began to cultivate a vast area of land that previously had been left idle. Several large-scale livestock farms were also created here, helping to increase the horse population of the peasant economy and producing a considerable volume of raw materials for foreign trade. The construction of large farms received a particular impetus when the successes of the first agricultural concessions became apparent in the South and South-East of Russia. After they paid from 10 % to 15 % of their production to the state – according to their contracts – the owners were still left with a very large return.

Of a total of 15,000 communes and artels at the beginning of the period we are considering, some were dissolved and a number of the former communards became very industrious, progressive, and well-to-do proprietors. Another group of collectives survived right up until the time when the mass tendency towards cooperation occurred throughout the peasant economy in response to the influence exerted by large-scale industry and electrification.

The general result was that the Russian peasant economy, during the first phase of this period, not only regained its pre-war level of production but surpassed it.

However, large-scale proletarian industry subordinated the agricultural sector during this first decade mainly through exchange (trade and long-term credits), and only to a modest degree on a production basis through the state farms. More substantial changes only began with the second decade. We shall postpone discussion of how they occurred until we have first considered what was being done in the area of state industry.

Lecture No. 7

3   The Industry of Soviet Russia during the Decade of NEP

In this lecture, our concern will be the development of industry in the Soviet Republic during the first decade of the so-called New Economic Policy. Among state industries, the main beneficiaries of the transition from War Communism to NEP were those with articles to sell on the free market. In contrast, the heavy industry of the Soviet state continued to find itself in a very difficult position since it sold only a small portion of its output on the free market and delivered – or sold, if you will – the major share of what it produced to the state and state enterprises, all of whom were quite unreliable when it came to making payment. Transport was in a particularly serious condition, with revenues far less than expenditures. Given the overall state budget deficit, the transport deficit was not fully covered and restoration of fixed capital was considerably delayed. With the population's meagre buying power, at one time even those industrial sectors that did resume trading began asking to return to the bosom of state supply, i.e., they bluntly pleaded for a share of the resources being acquired by the state through the tax in kind, monetary taxes and the issuance of paper currency. Industrial executives were wailing at the time over the so-called sales crisis. Then the 1922 harvest changed the picture. The harvest brought increased rural demand for industrial products, and the trading portion of state industry, which in fact comprised its largest part, increased its resources by tapping the free market. It was as if the sales crisis had never existed. Instead, there was an outcry about a goods famine – that the countryside was buying up everything available and that industry was short of raw materials.

On the other hand, there was greater success in collecting the tax in kind, and the state, having reduced its expenditures on the now curtailed army and bureaucracy, was fully able to satisfy industry's needs for agricultural products. Occasionally the agricultural sector experienced its own kind of 'sales crisis'.

During this period, the nationalisation of large-scale industry and transport played a colossal role in shaping the general development of the country's entire economy insofar as the government also used state resources to support such socially necessary branches as transport, the fuel industry and metallurgy, which, if left to the fate of the market, would have disintegrated completely and pulled the rest of industry along with them into the abyss. Support for the electrical industry and the construction of new power stations was also enormously important. State industry at the time acquired the materials, food and fuel resources that it needed from two sources: purchases on the free market, and purchases from state enterprises and the state itself, since the state had substantial resources from the tax in kind. Similarly, industrial production was distributed in two ways: one part was sold on the free market, another to the state and state enterprises.

Although these relations of buying and selling among state enterprises were superficially capitalist in appearance, in reality they were merely a special form of the distribution of values within the socialist sector. In order to understand both this period and the further evolution of socialist industry, it is imperative first of all to distinguish two different things: *large-scale industry's connection through the market with the non-socialised part of the economy, and the connection of state industries with one another on the basis of buying and selling.* In these terms, state industries were divided into two groups: those that acquired the *major portion* of the necessary elements of production by trading with the economy's non-nationalised sector in the private market, and those enterprises whose production remained mostly *within the socialist sphere*, where it was of no consequence whether the products went to the state free of charge or to state enterprises in return for payment.

An extreme example of one type was the textile factory that sold all or nearly all of its output on the free market and purchased its materials there as well, while its workers also bought all their food there; an extreme example of the other type was the factory producing military equipment or locomotives, in which case almost all of its output remained within the state sector and only quite insignificant sums were involved in purchases and sales on the free market. To ascertain the extent to which socialist industry as a whole was connected with the market, it would be necessary to add up all the purchases and sales between state enterprises and the non-socialist sector, and to compare those figures with the total of mutual transactions between state enterprises and with the state itself. This kind of analysis would reveal an enormous difference between the positions of enterprises of the first and second type, and also the duality in the position of some enterprises that were linked almost equally with both the state and the private sphere of the economy.

Enterprises that existed *mainly* through material exchange with the private economy were, of course, completely dependent on their markets for sales and materials, i.e., on conditions in the peasant economy, meaning the harvest. The second group depended primarily on the return from the tax in kind and on uncommitted state resources that might be used to support heavy industry and transport, whose market was either the state itself or state enterprises working for the market. Here, the state was the primary source for covering deficits, as with transport industry; or else it was the sole market for sales, as with the military industry; or it was the accumulator of capital for new construction, which was the case in the construction of new electrical stations. True, the return from the tax in kind also ultimately depended on the harvest, but not so directly as in the first case, because the tax in kind was also collected in poor harvest years when the peasants were left with scant resources to purchase the products of industries working for the market.

In any event, the position of industry during the 1920s was such that the burden of heavy industry and transport could not be shouldered by the part of industry that worked for the market. The weight of this burden would have collapsed and crushed light industry had the state not assisted heavy industry with the resources that it acquired from taxation, in kind and in cash, from the non-socialised sector of the economy, i.e., first and foremost from petty production. During this period, industry was producing at merely 1/5 of the pre-war level, whereas the revenues of the peasant economy, artisans and handicraftsmen had only declined by ½ compared to the pre-war level. Thus political power, in the hands of the proletariat, was a powerful factor in redistributing the whole national income and supporting large-scale production with resources from the less seriously damaged small-scale sector. During this period, the construction of such mighty power stations as the Kashira, Kizel, Utka and Volkhov hydro stations was completed as well as several smaller ones. Of course, such reconstruction of fixed capital in heavy industry would have been absolutely impossible without state support. Thus, with state support, heavy industry was helped to survive until better times. Light industry, working for the peasant market, simultaneously became more able to make its payments thanks to good harvests and the growth of peasant buying power. Now it could pay in full for transport shipments, fuel from the coal trusts, machines and equipment from the engineering works and electrical energy, thereby also supporting heavy industry.

Still, industry developed more slowly during the early years than might have been expected, given the enormous stimulus from successes in agriculture. In fact, if industry, thanks to successful collection of the tax in kind on the one hand, and expanded commodity exchange with the countryside on the other, had been able to process raw material worth 200–300 more gold roubles than in the previous years, this would have allowed it to expand not by that sum but by a much greater one, because in the process of working up and adding value these materials double and triple in value (a case in point: raw leather is purchased, say, for 10 gold roubles, but the leather goods made from it are worth, shall we say, 50 roubles, etc.). However, the development of industry was delayed, because once industry had created circulating capital it then had to restore its fixed capital as well and significantly raise wages from year to year. As for the increase in the number of functioning enterprises, here progress was even slower because the industry of the day, due to individual enterprises producing at much less than capacity, yielded a very costly product even despite a low wage. The goal of the economic organs was not so much to start up as many enterprises as possible as to ensure that the functioning ones operated at full capacity. This concentration of production led to lower prices on industrial products and greatly reinforced the exchange of commodities between town and country. A rapid increase in the number of functioning enterprises only began when the relative prices of grain started to decline.

Now, let us consider how different branches of industry developed during this decade in terms of the volume of production.

The branches that began to recover most rapidly, of course, were those working mainly for the peasant market and not requiring especially large expenditures on the restoration of fixed capital. Both the textile industry and the part of the metal-working industry that served the countryside were restored quite quickly. But the textile industry very soon ran into another obstacle – the shortage of cotton. Cotton-growing in Turkestan recovered much more slowly than the textile industry, and the state was forced to purchase enormous quantities of foreign cotton. These purchases consumed a large part of the Republic's gold reserves. The subsequent fate of the textile industry turned out to be totally dependent upon the success of our foreign trade. The problem was compounded by the fact that for several years our oil industry yielded only very small surpluses for shipment abroad, and the main export commodities were timber, furs, platinum, and a growing volume of grain. As far as flax, hemp and animal products were concerned, foreign trade in these commodities only started to grow when peasant production of these materials began to exceed the needs of domestic industry.

As for the fuel industry, within five years the Donets Basin reached the pre-war level of production, which was significantly exceeded in the mines of the Urals, Siberia, and around Moscow. The output of peat already surpassed the pre-war level at the beginning of this period; as a number of innovations were developed in peat extraction and combustion, this branch of industry did very well. The oil crisis of 1923 and 1924 was overcome thanks to an increase in production using our own resources and also with the assistance of foreign concessionaires. The increase in oil production was especially important In the Emba district. The metallurgical industry recovered in pace with successes in the coal industry. Metallurgy reached the pre-war level of activity more quickly in the South than in the Urals, where it found itself in a blind alley due to the previous predatory destruction of forests and only began to develop after it was connected by a main railway line to the Kuznetsk district and its coking coal. The first decade also saw the initial operations in newly uncovered copper deposits in the Bogoslovsk region, along with iron ore in the area of the Kursk [magnetic] anomaly.

The engineering industry developed in two directions, producing equipment for agriculture and also means of production for industry and transport. Since the main problem for factories producing agricultural implements was the great assortment of types, here the basic task was to standardise production. This was all the more difficult, for there had never been many factories in Russia that specialised in the manufacture of agricultural machinery; in most cases agricultural machine-building was only a supplementary concern of the engineering works. The construction of new plants required significant special resources that the state did not possess. During this period tractor production also improved.

The other sector of the engineering industry, which supplied both industry and transport, initially developed mainly at the expense of the state, from which it received continuous subsidies. Apart from the South, its main centres were in Petrograd and the Urals, the Petrograd fuel problem being resolved by construction of the Volkhov hydro station. Already during the first decade, the transport industry reached its pre-war level. Likewise, the building of water craft for inland navigation was resumed with the help of English capital. As for ocean-going transport, the low level of British freight rates and the opportunity to purchase new vessels abroad meant that it would have been economically irrational for Soviet Russia to build its own merchant marine. The Russian aeroplane industry, in contrast, achieved great successes and was developed with the assistance of German capital. In the area of the chemical industry, it should be noted that during this period there was a rapid increase in the production of artificial fertilisers. The phosphorus deposits of Vyatka, Kostroma, Tula, Orel, and Chernigov provinces were worked quite extensively. These operations began in a semi-handicraft way but were gradually transformed into one of industry's most important branches, producing both for domestic use and also for export. We should also mention the construction of oil presses in Siberia for the large-scale processing of cedar nuts.

The condition of transport at the beginning of this period was the most tragic. Transport is a branch that can only be sustained and developed if the whole economic organism is in robust good health, with a vigorous exchange of products; it survives and grows as the result of plump deposits of capital elsewhere in the economy. But, at the beginning of the period under review, the whole of industry was scarcely able to stand on its own feet, meaning things were all the worse in transport. The decay had already begun in the second year of the world war, and during the revolutionary years transport survived by consuming its own fixed capital and by a dreadful exploitation of labour power. Moreover, the length of track was vastly over-extended relative to the general level of the economy, with industry producing at only one-fifth and agriculture at one-half of the pre-war level. An improvement of the tax in kind and the state's financial resources increased revenues in light industry producing for the market, and the general development of trade and paid haulage increased the resources available to the transport industry. Some support for transport, mainly in the form of needed railway materials, also came from small railway loans floated abroad.

A complete restoration of transport proved impossible in the early years. At first the most important main lines had to be restored, leading to the ports and connecting the capital with the South, the Caucasus, and Siberia. The rest of the network began to revive only subsequently, and then at a slow pace. New railway construction was only undertaken in the fifth year of the New Economic Policy, when attention centred on the completion of lines and spurs that had been started earlier. At the same time, automotive and air transport began to develop gradually. At the start of the New Economic Policy, automobile travel was still accessible only to a narrow circle of people, above all to the so-called 'commissars', about whom you now read so much in the historical literature concerning the Great Revolution. These machines were beyond the reach of the average worker. As early as the middle of the decade, however, each factory and plant had motor vehicles not only for hauling loads and trips by administrators but also for use by the workers and their children. The automobile began gradually to displace coachmen, and by the end of the decade travel by horse became either a luxury or a sport in the major centres.

Now, I must say a few words regarding the successes of electrification during this period. If you only knew, comrades, the poverty that prevailed in the country at the time of the revolution! If I were to describe to you the daily diet of the average worker and his family, you would understand what heroism, what daring and courage the Republic showed in the struggle against devastation, by turning already during this period to implementing the plan for electrification. Any new construction project, which yields a productive result only after several years, can only be undertaken in a society where there is adequate accumulation and where a part of the surplus value (if we are speaking of capitalism) or of the surplus product (in the case of socialism) can be diverted from current expenditures on supporting labour power and the old scale of reproduction into new construction. In Soviet Russia during the 1920s such surpluses did not, of course, exist. On the contrary, the most elementary needs of the population, and especially of the working population, could not be met.

In these conditions, the construction of new regional electrical stations meant a deduction from the already inadequate income of the workers and peasants in the name of the future and was a great, mass surge of self-denial on the part of the people in their striving to progress. The plan for Soviet Russia's electrification was calculated for a period of ten years. In its original form, however, it was not implemented during that time, although, on the other hand, achievements were made in this area that had not been foreseen in the plan. In particular, after construction of the power stations at Shatura, Kashira, Utka, Kizel and the Volkhov hydro station (near Petrograd), regional electrical stations were then built in Donets, Nizhny Novgorod, Chelyabinsk and the newly electrified Baku region, a station was erected at the Dnepr rapids, etc. Moreover, a specially organised Russo-German transport company undertook to investigate the building of an electrical super mainline connecting Berlin, Moscow, Irkutsk and Vladivostok, which required construction of a number of hydro-electrical stations along the main route. Local electrification also developed rapidly. If it was not included in the network of the nearest regional electrical station, the central city of each district considered it a matter of honour to have a small electrical station serving the local countryside.

All of these new electrical stations began to have an enormous influence both on economic life and on the social and day-to-day relationships within the Republic. However modest the electrification of that period may appear by comparison with our own achievements, it led to: 1) enormous saving in the use of fuel for all those enterprises going over to electrical energy; 2) vast economies in transport, which was freed from shipments of tens of millions of poods of wood, coal and oil (the majority of power stations worked with local fuel such as coal, peat, shale, etc.); 3) and an enormous saving of labour power in enterprises where electrification was followed by the mechanisation of labour and the replacement of crude physical labour by machines (the cutting and sawing of timber, loading and unloading, and so forth). According to one rough estimate, the annual savings resulting from electrification in this period already exceeded the work of one million men.

Here, I must conclude my account of the condition of industry, and in our next lecture I shall deal with the position of the working class and the system of distribution in that period.

Lecture No. 8

4   The Wage System, the Training of Skilled Workers, Red Engineers

Under the New Economic Policy, the position of the working class improved in pace with the recovery of industry and agriculture. As early as the first year of NEP, when the number of factory workers was cut back and piece-work was introduced practically everywhere, workers' earnings rose and their positions improved somewhat compared to earlier years. The yardstick will mean nothing to you nowadays if I say that the average wage at the beginning of this period was the equivalent of 10–15 gold roubles (at that time calculations were done in gold roubles at pre-war prices, and the exchange rates for paper currency and ration coupons were translated into gold roubles). The problem was that wage payments were far from accurately calculated. When transport could not cope with shipments and the distribution department of the Food Commissariat made mistakes, or when paper money either was not shipped to the outlying areas or was in short supply – in these circumstances the workers did not receive even these miserly wages on a regular basis.

It is true that at the beginning of NEP the workers still received a number of services free of charge (apartment, water, lighting, travel, children's instruction, newspapers, books and occasional entertainment). But charges were subsequently introduced for all of these, with the exception of education for the children. Wages were also raised, although in most cases not proportionately. After the 1922 harvest, the position of the workers again improved somewhat, and this time the change was not just seasonal. I must add that during the years of civil war the workers' fortunes improved on a seasonal basis with the collection of the tax in kind in autumn and winter, and then deteriorated in spring and summer when the agricultural products that could be requisitioned were insufficient. Now, at least a certain regularity was established throughout the year in the distribution of state resources. At the same time, the most important products that workers had to acquire. i.e., food products first and foremost, relatively declined in price from the famine prices of the civil war years (with the exception of fats). In subsequent years, this improvement in the workers' position continued without interruption. Every new advance in industry meant not only an increase of circulating capital in the enterprises and an opportunity to expand operations and repair the equipment, but also resources with which to raise wages. On the whole, real wages grew each year by 10–15 per cent.

Moreover, during this period a characteristic difference became evident in the methods of distribution prevailing in the commodity-socialist economic system compared to a purely capitalist system. In the capitalist system, overproduction was usually followed by a pause and reduced production while commodities lying idle in the warehouses were absorbed into circulation. To the contrary, once large-scale industry was nationalised, this method of distribution ceased to be necessary. In addition to the purchasing power of the free market and that of state industry, there was the market among workers for consumer goods. In the case of over-production, for example, say in the textile industry, the state could take products that could not be sold on the free market and distribute them amongst the whole working class on credit charged to wages. Just as the credit system permits an enterprise to spend at the expense of future income, so in this case the state would give an advance to the worker-consumer out of the future income of the economy as a whole. Shifting from its 'socialist' foot to its 'bourgeois' foot, it could manoeuvre and solve the problem of a sales crisis as follows.

The output of industries manufacturing means of consumption was divided into one part, for which there was effective demand in the free market, and a second part that went to the state for expanding the real-wage fund. The enterprises that produced this 'surplus' – from a capitalist viewpoint – were paid by the state in accordance with its resources, either receiving the full value of the surplus or else simply being given a subsidy to continue producing at the same rate. These purchases of 'surpluses', or state subsidies, were undertaken with resources left to the state after deducting expenditures on the bureaucratic apparatus. From the economic viewpoint, this type of solution was also facilitated by the fact that the state's payments to its own enterprises – which had produced beyond the norm – went mainly to the acquisition of raw materials. And this portion, as I have already mentioned, is always less than the value of the finished product created from the materials. The main difficulty here lay not in finding a socialist method of solving a partial sales crisis by the sale of surpluses to the state, but rather in ensuring that the state always had a sufficient reserve fund for subsidies to developing industry. This problem was solved as the state increased the portion of the national income that it received from petty production. Thus, our grandfathers gradually learned how to use simultaneously both the advantages of socialist economic relations and those of capitalist forms that could not yet be eliminated.

The question of 'over-production' of means of production was solved in somewhat the same manner. During the period that we are considering, one group of state enterprises systematically manufactured more machines and metal than the other part could buy, due to the shortage of fixed and circulating capital. The state economy seemed to become entangled in the snare of capitalist forms of calculation. But since fixed and circulating capital does not fall from the skies, instead being created in industry's own production process, here too the state's task was to cut through this contradiction between capitalist forms of calculation and the real potential for expanding production by recourse to the state's own fund. In this case, the state also provided the necessary subsidies for purchases of means of production to those factories that did not have free resources for that purpose, or else it provided subsidies to the enterprises producing means of production according to their output. Here, we come to the question of how central guidance of the whole state economy emerged during this period. But we shall have more to say about that at a later time.

Thus, already at that time, large-scale socialist industry began directly to serve the goals of improving the workers' position and increasing their consumption. True, it was always very difficult to find a balance between what could and should be allocated to a consumption fund for the workers, and what had to be capitalised for the expansion of fixed and, in part, circulating capital. The state economy of this period struggled with the same Hamlet-like doubts as a man who owns neither boots nor trousers and only has the money to purchase either one or the other.

If the workers of Soviet Russia, already in the second part of the first decade of the New Economic Policy, began to eat and dress no worse than before the war, and if their real income was equal to and sometimes exceeded that of European workers, the situation was much worse in the area of housing. The process of rebuilding destroyed houses and constructing new ones lagged far behind the increase in urban population.[8] In capitalist society, a certain portion of capital always flowed into housing repairs and new construction. That was the case with us before the war. During the war and revolution, not only did all new construction come to a halt, but there were also no resources even for current and ordinary repairs. So great was the destruction of housing that, despite a drastic decline of the urban and particularly of the worker population during the years of famine, the buildings available and fit for habitation were not sufficient even for this greatly reduced number of urban inhabitants.

During the initial years, the restoration of housing began first of all with the repair of existing structures, and there was very little new construction. The new construction began mainly in Moscow, where for the first time and with great fanfare several vast new workers' apartment blocks were built according to the last word in housing technique. The completion of these first structures occasioned a great celebration not only among the Moscow proletariat who would live in them but also throughout the entire Republic. However, neither these relatively few structures nor the increased repair of older houses could resolve the housing crisis. As industry was restored, not only did workers who had fled to the countryside during the famine now return to the cities, but the cities also attracted the unemployed peasant population coming from those strata who failed to restore their farms. The pull from the countryside to the cities also increased due to the land hunger and overpopulation that began to make themselves felt in the countryside. Moreover, urban construction and repair work attracted a mass of construction workers from the rural areas.

Despite the fact that urban reconstruction was strongly helped by the organisation of special joint-stock building societies, whose shareholders were the workers and employees who hoped to acquire an apartment in the newly constructed buildings, and despite the fact, finally, that foreign capital was attracted into the construction industry, the crisis was still not overcome. You can judge its scale by the newspaper articles available in our archives. In the vicinity of the big cities, the government was then obliged to build a number of workers' housing estates of wooden construction, which have been preserved up to the present day, as you know, along with a number of tram lines for use by these settlements.

---

8 [There is an error in the text, which says 'The increase in urban population lagged far behind the process of rebuilding destroyed houses and new construction.']

In general terms, as you know, the question of the fate of big cities was by no means solved in the way outlined in the socialist literature of the capitalist period, which had much to say about the so-called urbanisation of the countryside. It was technically impossible and in many respects economically inexpedient to dissolve a large city and scatter it in village fields. Of course, all of the non-essential appendages of the large city were moved either to the outskirts or beyond, and you know that the past half century has witnessed quite a lot more such work. But you also know that we are far from having completed this task and still do not know when and how it will end.

For factories that cannot be relocated to the source of their materials, it is more profitable to continue working in the big city amongst an array of other factories that provide everything needed for production (except the materials) and produce things that are used precisely in the big city. The big city is actually a single giant workshop, and to break it up often proved to be economically damaging. Moreover, the big cities could only partly be replaced as cultural centres, notwithstanding all the successes of radio broadcasting. It was natural, therefore, that a solution for the problem began to be sought primarily in transport and not in the dissolution of large centres. During the decade that we are discussing, enormous attention was already devoted to the transport question. True, Moscow communicated at the time with its suburban districts mainly by railway, electrified suburban lines, and automobile; aeroplane communication did not occur on the mass scale that we know today. But this only facilitated travel in the periphery of Moscow and its environs, where tens of thousands of workers could live and enjoy all the benefits of cottage life during the summer.

While a worker can today live up to a hundred versts away from Moscow, flying there in the morning and back in the evening on a passenger aeroplane, at that time he lived at most within a thirty-verst distance from the city and commuted to Moscow by railway or tram. The workers of that day learned not to waste the time spent on travel and usually read the latest articles in the newspapers. You can judge the housing needs of those years from photographs that are preserved in the museum of the revolution and to some extent from the paintings by our historical artists in the Tretyakov Gallery.

Now, let us consider the origins at that time of the system of socialist distribution, which we still have and which, unfortunately, even for us does not yet correspond to the communist ideal of 'from each according to his ability, to each according to his needs'.

During the period of War Communism, a bold attempt was made (partly out of economic necessity) to leap over the low cultural level of the masses and to introduce a levelling system of rations. There was virtually no difference between the rations of the most highly skilled worker and those of the unskilled. At first there was very little difference between the remuneration of a worker and an engineer, or a worker and the most responsible Soviet official, even People's Commissars. Each enterprise received food in proportion to the number of workers it employed, quite independently of enterprise output. The enterprise received the same if it produced 100 % of its target or 10 %. As for distribution within the factory or plant, here the worker who produced the maximum output received exactly the same as the one who produced the minimum. It would be more correct to regard this experiment in distribution not as an attempted semi-socialist distribution but rather as a means to ensure the physical survival of the proletariat at a certain phase of the civil war. If we look at the question in these terms, the system of distribution during War Communism appears altogether different; from the viewpoint of providing physical maintenance for a class (and not of supporting and developing production) this system was probably quite justifiable. But it could not continue for long even in the period of War Communism.

In some branches it was imperative to increase production at any cost, in the war industry for example, which was feverishly working to supply the front. Given the shortage of resources, it was necessary to emphasise so-called shock-work branches and shock-work enterprises. This shock-work was then extended beyond industry to several other branches. Thus, the front of equality in wage distribution was breached even before the beginning of the New Economic Policy. Moreover, piece-work was gradually introduced, and payments to specialists were raised; the wage scale eventually included about two dozen different categories.

Even greater inequality was evident between unmarried workers and those with families. During the period of War Communism, there were free meals for children, which were also extended to bourgeois elements. With NEP these meals for children were almost completely abolished, and workers' children therefore had to be supported not by the state but by their parents. Consequently, there was a great difference between the position of a highly skilled bachelor and that of an unskilled worker with a family. And since payment for the work of specialists now surged upwards, the man earning the highest rate received an income several tens of times greater than the man earning the lowest.

Moreover, to inequality *within the enterprise* was added *inequality between enterprises*. The practice of selecting enterprises according to their importance to the economy as a whole, already initiated during War Communism, continued now but in a purely spontaneous way. The enterprises that turned out to be necessary from the standpoint of the free market were those producing the commodities for which demand was highest. Unless an essential enterprise was supported by the state, as one that was imperative whether or not it produced a deficit, the question of its importance was left to the discretion of the market. In the market, not all industries were judged by the same standard: there were favourites and stepchildren. Some enterprises earned significant profits; others either barely made ends meet or failed to do so entirely. The former were able to pay workers and technical personnel much more than the latter, which made use of the right they had been given to adjust wage scales downward.

Thus, if we consider distribution during War Communism egalitarian, the first years of NEP, in accordance with the Hegelian triad, were the total negation of equality and an extreme manifestation of inequality. If moral terms can be used, we would have to call this distribution extremely unjust. Yet the inequality was completely necessary at the given stage. True, the personal interest of every worker in increasing output was stimulated by a purely bourgeois method; but such a method of distribution did compel everyone to do better compared to the period when industry was socially secured by the state and labour discipline crumbled. The slogan of this period was: expansion of production above all else and with the lowest possible cost, and increase of the volume of products in the country by whatever means worked. Given the country's poverty, the low cultural level and unpreparedness for any other system of distribution that would have meant more equality, no other outcome was possible. The inequality of that period was justified by the fact that labour productivity really did rise and the most arduous period was overcome.

But these very successes in production, and the increase in state revenues, actually created the conditions in which unequal distribution began gradually to disappear. During the first decade this process did not advance very far, but its basic outlines were already quite clear. Let us now consider how all this happened.

When the resources of state industry began to grow and tax revenues increased, the first step was to guarantee a minimum wage. The growing resources of the state and state industry made it possible to raise wages in general. However, the Soviet authorities and the trade unions, while raising the wages of all categories, strove to increase the income of the lowest paid strata relatively more. Another influence on the decline of inequality within the working class came from the successes of electrification, which meant that there was generally less need for crude physical labour. This redistribution of labour between skilled and unskilled groups led to an ever-expanding number of the previously unskilled becoming machine workers and receiving a higher wage. In that way, successes in electrification automatically led to greater equality in the material position of workers. Next, the development of a system of technical education for the workers had an enormous influence. Every working youth who experienced technical instruction was familiar with the basics of several different occupations. Children of unskilled workers and of peasants who had immigrated from the villages were given the same training as those of highly skilled workers.

The skill levels of all workers became more equal, and young workers who had completed technical school could not be paid as if they were unskilled, even in cases where they were assigned to unskilled work.

As for the inequality of payment between workers and technical personnel, it also began to decline as the former technical schools were filled with students exclusively from the workers' faculties and later with young workers from the lower and middle-level technical schools. This gradually changed the fabric of the entire cadre of specialists in the country. The new Red worker-engineers regarded themselves merely as more highly skilled workers compared to the rest of the proletariat and did not expect the kind of pay demanded by bourgeois specialists. And when the state and the trade unions raised the wages above all of the lowest paid strata, it did not cause any protest from the cadre of worker-engineers. Inequality between individual enterprises was also gradually eliminated due to gradual establishment in practice of the necessary equilibrium and proportions between different branches of production, which brought with it the establishment of greater material equality in the position of individual enterprises.

Inequality between married men and bachelors, which had peaked during the period when children's meals were virtually abolished and there were mass closures of kindergartens, children's colonies, nurseries and so forth, now began to level out due to the new advances in social child-rearing. Having few resources for public education in the first years of NEP, the state was naturally unable either to subsidise new homes for children, orphanages, etc. or even to provide resources to those that had already emerged. With advances in industry and the growth of state taxes, a sharp turnabout occurred here. Each year a larger portion of the state budget went to popular education, first and foremost to the education of workers' children. The number of children's institutions multiplied quickly, and their conditions improved every year with the active support of trade unions and individual factories and plants. Children's meals were fully restored, and in addition to food the state provided teaching aids, clothing, toys, etc. All of this entailed progress not only in the sphere of social child-rearing, which during War Communism had been more of a dream than a reality, but also in terms of equalising the material position of married and single people. Now the worker with a family no longer had to spend a large part of his earnings on children, for the state itself provided children with almost everything they required.

Before turning to the organisational structure of the Soviet economy in this period, I still have to highlight one important fact from the history of the time, and that is the crisis of skilled labour power. When industry was rapidly disintegrating, and even when it had *just begun* to recover, no severe crisis of labour power was felt. True, there was a moment, particularly in the autumn of 1920, when there appeared to be a shortage of skilled workers. But that was merely a temporary difficulty because industry's expansion at the time was also quite temporary. After a few years of the New Economic Policy, a different situation was created when a systematic expansion of industry began. Then it became clear that our industry would not be able to reach pre-war levels for one very simple reason: more than half of the skilled workers had completely vanished. Some had died of natural causes, some had died at the front, some had taken responsible position in the state apparatus, and some had settled hopelessly in the countryside. On the other hand, there had been a significant general reduction in the skills of the entire work force. There was so little training of workers and young workers for skilled work that it did not even cover the natural loss. Yet it was now necessary not just to cover the natural yearly attrition but also to provide new cadres for expanding production.

The Republic was able to surmount this crisis in two ways. First, there was substantial immigration from Western Europe of cadres of skilled workers who were driven to Russia by raging unemployment. But the main solution was the energetic and rapid establishment during this period of an enormous network of schools of factory apprenticeship, in which the general-educational aspects of the programme were significantly expanded. Since there were not enough young workers from the cities to fill the newly organised schools, the state had to undertake several mobilisations among peasant youths and also include children from urban petty-bourgeois strata as well as those of the so-called intelligentsia-professionals. This was not accomplished without a struggle, because the children of the intelligentsia strove in great numbers to rush into the higher educational institutions even when, in terms of their abilities, they were not qualified compared to the best cadres of the proletariat. Several years were required in order to reach some equilibrium between the number of skilled workers turned out by the thousands from these schools, and the number who were needed to serve a developing industry. The need to fill this gap in the very body of the working class naturally delayed for a long time the realisation of the point in the Communist programme dealing with education, which demanded general and polytechnic education for all young people up to the age of 17. That programme only began to be fully implemented two decades later.

Lecture No. 9

5   The Organisation of State Industry

The question of the system of organisation and management of industry during this period is extremely interesting. First of all, we see here for the first
time in history a combination of two systems of economy, socialist and capitalist, a combination of socialist leadership with market-capitalist regulation.
Equilibrium in this economic system was achieved on the basis of both of
these principles simultaneously. Reviewing the economic literature of the day,
we can see that several firmly convinced Communists of that period did not
always realise either the inevitability or the advantages, under certain circumstances, of a combination of the two methods. There was a time when
many leading managers rejected the principle of socialist regulation, mistakenly supposing that this method and the capitalist method are mutually
exclusive *in any and all circumstances*. They reasoned as follows: once the
attempt at socialist management of industry failed during the period of War
Communism, exclusively capitalist regulation must take the stage and must
be given the right of way, with no interference, otherwise there would be no
regulation whatever. In reality, it turned out that this maximalist way of posing the question, while absolutely correct in politics – either a dictatorship
of the bourgeoisie or a dictatorship of the proletariat – could not in practice be justified in such a simplified form for the sphere of economic relations.

    Historically, what we had in Russia was a combination of socialism with cap-
italism in the economic sphere, together with the dictatorship of the proletariat
in the political sphere and gradual subordination of the lower capitalist form to
the higher socialist one, followed by the complete victory of the latter. True, this
was not simply an evolutionary process, because the capitalist form also tried
to mount a resistance in the political sphere and was smashed, as we shall see
later. But this defeat of the capitalist form also occurred because it came into
conflict with socialism after it had already become intertwined and interwoven
with the socialist system, in which it played the role of a lower economic formation.

    The period that we are considering was also interesting because this dec-
ade sufficiently clarified which capitalist forms and methods are most viable
and are only gradually replaced by more advanced socialist ones, and which of
them would simply drop away, like a snake shedding its skin, once proletarian
industry more or less established its footing. In any event, experience demonstrated that socialism could successfully utilise many capitalist forms (capitalist calculation) and categories of simple commodity production (money) long
after the political power of the class that represented these forms in the aggreg-

ate was eliminated. It also revealed something else. It demonstrated (as in the example of consistent democracy) that many problems of an economic character, posed by capitalism itself and even solvable with capitalist methods, could not be fully dealt with as long as the capitalist class retained power.

During the period that we are describing, economic construction proceeded to a significant extent by trial and error. That part of the heritage of War Communism that became a practical hindrance was rejected, and every aspect of capitalist forms that was clearly useful for the time was adopted. And that was a good thing. Thanks to such caution, no socialist methods were rejected that might later begin to play an important role. On the other hand, only the most necessary capitalist forms were adopted, so that the economy was not subordinated to all the winds and storms of market spontaneity.

Let us begin with the summit. What organs were responsible for regulating economic life in general and for directing large-scale state industry in particular?

At the peak of the economic system we find the State Planning Commission (Gosplan) and the State Bank. The former organ constitutes the brain of the socialist economy; the latter, if this analogy might be made, is the spinal cord in a world of capitalist spontaneity (a capitalist economy, as we know, does not have a brain). During this period, it seemed to some economic administrators that Gosbank must supersede Gosplan, converting it into a planning commission [within the bank]. This was at the height of socialism's adoption of those capitalist methods that were suited for the particular moment. Exaggerations were natural at the time. But Gosplan remained, and its role began to expand with each passing year. Gosbank remained too, and its role likewise expanded. The difference between them, however, can be seen in the fact that Gosplan still exists today, as you know, whereas Gosbank has already ceased to exist. When we today consider our economic past in a long historical context the role of this or that institution becomes clear. Gosbank had to organise and adapt capitalist relations to socialism, partly completing in new conditions what our undeveloped capitalism had not yet finished, and then subject capitalist elements to socialist leadership – in concrete terms, to leadership by Gosplan. The task of Gosbank, given the dictatorship of the proletariat, was that of a *provocateur*, using capitalist methods to betray capitalism to socialism. Gosplan's task was to adapt socialism, which it represented, to the capitalist and commodity relations operating within the country while attempting to master them. To characterise the role of these two organisations, which represented two historically different types of economy, one could use Plato's famous comparison of two horses, body and soul, harnessed to the same chariot. Gosbank and Gosplan, like a wheel-horse and a trace-horse, were harnessed to the same chariot, and whoever drove the wheel-horse thereby also controlled the trace-horse. But any good coachman knows that at times the horses must be allowed to race ahead until they are again reined in.

During this period, the capitalist trace-horse also impetuously raced ahead until it was restrained by the wheel-horse and its driver. One must keep in mind, of course, that I am not thinking so much of Gosplan as a specific institution, located at the time at No. 7 Vorontsovo Square, as of the entire socialist principle in the economy as a whole. In exactly the same way, Gosbank also serves us only as a collective concept of the organising principle in the sphere of capitalist spontaneity. Some time elapsed before Gosbank and Gosplan became properly separated and each took up the tasks for which it was suited. There was a period when many economic organs attempted to elude control by Gosplan and other organs of state regulation, and Gosplan itself was to some extent repudiated. Similarly, it was only several years after its creation, following stabilisation of the currency and acquiring the right to issue the state currency, that Gosbank took on a dictatorial role in terms of capitalist regulation of the economy.

Specifically, the whole picture now looks like this.

The state bank began its operations with resources that were completely inadequate for financing industry, which was half ruined, deprived of any circulating capital, and also confronted at the outset by the sales crisis. Likewise, the funds that the bank could allocate for financing the peasant economy, which required huge sums for long-term loans, were absolutely insignificant. In addition, because of the sharp and continuous decline of the currency, the bank's fixed capital rapidly depreciated, and thus the very financial lever that was to exert an active influence upon the economic life of the country was fundamentally undermined. Only continuous state support saved the bank from inevitable collapse. Naturally, in such conditions the bank could provide credit only to those enterprises that had a chance of surviving and promised to return the loans provided to them. The obviously hopeless enterprises, which during the period of War Communism were provided with resources to survive along with the healthy ones and at their expense, disguising the hole through which state resources uselessly drained away – these enterprises now died a natural death or were compelled to change their organisation fundamentally and make ends meet.

Replacing supply estimates with bank financing no doubt played an enormously positive role, accustoming enterprises to strict accountability, cost savings, avoidance of commercial loss and flexibility in managing their affairs. But this system also had negative consequences. With such a system, enterprises that were important for the whole economy but unprofitable from the capitalist point of view were pushed into the background and not regarded as particularly attractive clients of the bank. Only Gosplan's intervention, i.e., the intervention of socialist reason, enabled such enterprises to carry on, and the force of spontaneity was still so great that enterprises that were commercially profitable yet of little importance from the general economic point of view were in better condition than enterprises that were important to the state. In the newspapers of the time, throughout several years of the New Economic Policy, we encounter constant complaints that heavy industry is in a critical state while light industry is flourishing.

Trying to save itself from bankruptcy, and in the interest of the most effective distribution of state resources, Gosbank was not only compelled to make a natural selection of enterprises when financing them, but also, given the falling currency, tried to make its operations if not profitable then at least break-even. For that reason, it demanded payment of interest and part of the principal in kind, reserved to itself the right to share in the profits of enterprises that it financed, and itself became involved in trading on commission. The immediate source of these precautions was temporary and caused by the falling currency. However, the same system was subsequently retained for different reasons.

The point was that payments in kind, particularly in the sphere of agricultural credit, led gradually to elimination of the private intermediary between the state and the peasant, resulting in reduced costs for the country's distribution apparatus. Likewise, with economic development came the bank's participation in profits and its closer connection with the enterprises being financed. Such a connection helped the state, from its financial centre, to take up the reins that the Supreme Council of the National Economy had dropped during the period of NEP, leaving state industry adrift. Participation in trade was enormously important because, given the decline of large-scale industry's importance in the economy as a whole, there was an increase in the relative weight of petty production, which was linked up as a single entity with the entire economic organism chiefly through trade. Financing trade in all its forms, the bank acquired enormous economic influence over unorganised small-scale production. On the other hand, with an economic structure in which large-scale industry was still weak, trade was the most effective instrument for accumulating capital *at the expense of small-scale production*. Not only would it have been inappropriate for the bank to disengage from all of this, but it was also necessary for it to strengthen its role in trade by all possible means, subordinating it indirectly to 'socialist reason' and using a capitalist form of accumulation for the socialist treasury.

All of this organisational activity by the bank – within the private sector of the economy as well as in the state economy, which was now functioning in accordance with capitalist methods – quite naturally developed more fully with stabilisation of the currency and after the bank acquired the right of currency issue. Stabilisation of the rouble was accomplished in Soviet Russia much sooner that one might have expected, given the appalling condition of monetary circulation at the very beginning of the New Economic Policy. Stabilisation was accomplished thanks to eliminating the budget deficit. The budget began to make ends meet thanks to punctual receipt of the tax in kind and all the monetary taxes, a reduction in the number of loss-making enterprises and an increase of those making a profit, further curtailment of the bureaucratic apparatus and, finally, the resumption of grain and materials being exported abroad. Once the budget was in equilibrium, there was no great technical difficulty in organising a stable currency. Old notes were exchanged for new, full-valued paper roubles, with silver coins serving as small change. At the same time as this operation was taking place, the right of issue was transferred from the state treasury to the bank, which hitherto could only issue banknotes that were backed by gold and foreign currency. The right of issue allowed the state bank to become a powerful economic force throughout the country's entire economy, and it became the financial brain in the sphere of monetary circulation. This occurred in the following way.

When the currency was falling, accumulation in cash was impossible. Cash circulated rapidly, and even expansion of the commodity turnover could not, under these conditions, have any significant influence in increasing the total demand for money. With stabilisation of the currency, the speed of monetary circulation sharply decreased, which meant an increased demand for money throughout the country's entire economy. If, during the period of rapid currency depreciation, the value of the entire sum of paper currency in the country fell to less than forty million gold roubles due to money's speed of circulation, now the requirements of the turnover and of accumulation came to hundreds of millions of gold roubles. To satisfy these needs required an additional issue of hard currency, which simultaneously meant an enormous increase of the monetary resources of those responsible for this issue. The rich proceeds of this issue went to Gosbank and greatly increased its financial power. The country's commodity turnover, expanding from year to year, together with foreign demand for Soviet roubles as a result of the development of external trade, meant that despite an increase of all the means of non-monetary transactions, an expansion of the volume of means of circulation was required. The State Bank now provided this annual supplementary issue, skimming the cream from circulation without ever altering the rate of the rouble. In addition, so-called seasonal issues also increased the financial power of Gosbank. The fact is that Russia, as a predominantly agricultural country, experienced very large fluctuations in its need for money during the period of realising the harvest, and in this respect it differed significantly from industrial countries.

In industrial countries, the commodities that are being produced go to market more or less evenly throughout the whole year. Conversely, a vast agricultural country threw a much greater portion of its production into the market during the autumn than during other times of the year. During this period the need for means of circulation expanded greatly, agricultural products became less expensive, and money acquired greater purchasing power. On the other hand, spring and the first half of the summer saw the reverse phenomenon, i.e., a reduction of the means of circulation. Having acquired the right of issue, Gosbank brilliantly utilised these seasonal variations of the market and currency conjunctures for the accumulation of capital. In the autumn, when all the commodity producers in the village sought money and endeavoured to offload commodities, Gosbank, in order to meet this spontaneity, extensively used its right of issue within the limits of the required monetary circulation. Gosbank threw hundreds of millions of fully valued roubles into circulation, financing the grain trade and purchasing many tens of millions worth of various agricultural products. During spring and summer, when a currency hangover set in and the large volume of paper money issued in the autumn could lead to a decline in the rate of the rouble – during this period, when commodities were not looking for money but rather money was looking for commodities – Gosbank again responded to this spontaneity and in favourable market conditions sold off everything that it had bought cheaply during the autumn. Consequently, Gosbank provided commodities when spontaneous forces demanded them, taking excess sums of money out of circulation and leaving behind only the increase over the previous year that was required by the annual expansion of the turnover. This regulation of seasonal fluctuations on the money and commodity market secured an enormous profit for the bank, which every year expanded its working capital.

With a stable currency, the power of the bank also increased due to growth of its revenues from lending operations. At the same time, stable currency conditions also caused a rapid increase of deposits. The bank now relied upon both its own capital and the capital of all those who made deposits in its own branches and in subordinate credit institutions, becoming the centre for the whole monetary accumulation occurring throughout the country. Through its currency operations, commissions, its role as intermediary, its deposit and other operations, its participation in mixed branches with foreign capital and its share of the profits from state trusts, the bank became an enormous force during the first decades, and its importance increased even further during the period of so-called *gryunderstvo*, or the establishment of new enterprises.

Unlike the capitalist countries during capitalism's period of full-blooded development, Soviet Russia, in the period that we are examining, possessed very modest resources for new construction. While fatty growths of capital were always being formed in capitalist countries but not re-absorbed into production, resulting in an increased supply of surplus capital and a decline in the interest rate, in Russia, to the contrary, recovering industry and agriculture completely absorbed the whole increase of new values. Both industry and agriculture always suffered from insufficient capital for the expansion of production. This enormously increased the influence of the bank over each individual enterprise, which was tightly bound to the bank by the rope of credit. As for new enterprises, they were virtually impossible to set up without the bank's involvement unless, of course, they were established by foreign capital. The result was that the bank not only secured for itself a founder's profit but also acquired influence over the management of enterprises. At the same time, the fact that new enterprises could not be established without Gosbank's involvement made it possible for the state to implement its economic plan, encouraging the organisation only of such enterprises as were expedient from the plan's point of view.

Private commercial and industrial capital was at first only loosely connected with the bank. It was very difficult for a private individual to acquire a loan because Gosbank was short of resources even for the most important enterprises. At first this credit was extended to the private economy more out of principle than for any direct, practical results. Moreover, private entrepreneurs and traders were not yet creditworthy; they still did not have sufficient property that would serve as collateral for bank loans and had only just begun to sheer the sheep. However, a number of more stable enterprises also emerged here after a series of bankruptcies. These enterprises turned to Gosbank for credit, since the interest rate charged by money-lenders, given the general shortage of capital in the country, varied from one to three percent a day. These enterprises now received credit from Gosbank and were tied by financial strings into the general economic pyramid, headed by Gosplan.

As the actual power of Gosbank and the whole state credit system grew and its role expanded in the private economy, the bank gradually became not only an instrument for regulating this sphere of the economy but also occasionally an axe of the socialist state that chopped off within the private economy whatever was harmful to the state economy. The government had no need to publish an order for the closure of one or another private enterprise whose existence, for whatever reason, was undesirable for the state. The bank kills this enterprise through denying credit and kills it on lawful capitalist grounds, just as the biggest banks of the bourgeois countries kill hundreds of enterprises. In the great majority of cases, however, just the threat of denying credit was enough to make bank-financed enterprises begin to operate in the manner required by the state.

In capitalist countries, the banking system made those who commanded the banks into the commanders of the economic life of the country. During the epoch of finance capital, the banks dispose of not just their own capital but the whole surplus capital of the country. The result is that with the savings of a French peasant, a worker, a petty bourgeois and an official, a railway is being built in some other part of the world and new enterprises are being opened up, while the investors are not even asked whether or not they consider these projects to be necessary. The mighty state bank of the Soviet government, with its far-flung network of provincial branches and subordinate financial institutions, likewise acquired the actual capacity to dispose of all the free resources of the private economy that were deposited in credit institutions. Some kulak in Tula or Kursk province, who realised the senselessness of storing his money in his own 'land bank' – a cellar – would deposit it with a branch of Gosbank, a credit society, or a savings and loan office in order to receive interest. But these deposits, which amounted to hundreds of millions of gold roubles over Russia as a whole, were not left idle in the bank. They now passed through Gosbank as a loan to Soviet industry and transport, were used to construct the next district electrical station, increased the circulating capital of state trading organs, served as long-term agricultural credits, and so forth. In short, the capital of the kulaks now served the expansion of socialist production.

Thus, capitalist accumulation within the country became an instrument of socialist accumulation.

But this occurred not only through the bank, not only indirectly, but also directly. State taxes – in both cash and kind – levied on petty production and on the private sector in general, including concessions, served the same purpose. Furthermore, state industry and state trade extracted part of the surplus value from petty production in the form of commercial profit. This profit was mainly acquired from small-scale production not only through domestic trade but also through foreign trade, since state organs were the principal and monopolistic traders in grain and materials on the foreign market. And where private Russian or foreign capital was involved in trade, the state acquired income in the form of customs duties on exports and imports.

At first many people thought that once state industry regained its balance, and once state trade was improved and the state banking system was strengthened, taxes would be eliminated and replaced by a corresponding addition to the selling price of commodities. This would have been possible had there been only two remaining elements in the country's economy: state industry and small-scale peasant production. But that method was impracticable as long as private industry – artisans and craftsmen – still existed and were competing with large-scale state industry; as long as an important part of trade was in private hands; and finally, as long as concessions capital operated within the country. A surcharge on commodity prices would have enabled not only the state to acquire additional income, but also its capitalist attendants and competitors during the transition period. This measure could only have been implemented in the sphere of production that was exclusively in state hands. As a result, this system was only fully adopted much later, when all of the necessary social-economic preconditions for it had been created.

Thus, the values acquired by the state had two origins: income from state industry on the one hand, and extraction of a certain portion of the revenues from non-socialised production, above all from the peasant economy, on the other. Both of these items grew, but at different rates. The first grew more slowly than the second. Essentially, the income from industry at first consisted of excises, taxes, and interest payments on loans from the state bank. And since subsides to state industry exceeded the sum of these revenues, it followed that industry as a whole had a deficit according to capitalist methods of calculation. Industry recovered largely at the expense of petty production, although it simultaneously helped small-scale production to recover, especially as regards the peasant economy.

The portion of values that the state acquired from small-scale production served as the main source for the introduction of planning in the state economy. After deducting the costs of the army, the bureaucratic apparatus, education and culture, a certain sum was left each year to be spent on expanding production and on new construction. The task of Gosplan, VSNKh, Gosbank and the Trade-Industrial Bank was to use these resources most expediently (including foreign state loans, although these were not very large). The economic organs had to determine the proportions in which the different branches of production should expand, and then make corresponding decisions regarding the production programme of the trusts and of entire branches of industry. In this connection, the state had to overcome – if one may put it this way – the inertia of capitalist methods of calculation and a whole series of prejudices implicit in capitalist economic management.

Under a dual economic system, where combined methods of regulation were the most appropriate, the capitalist manner of thinking stubbornly impressed capitalist prejudices upon the economic administrators. So it was, for instance, with the so-called sales crisis, where the solution was prompted not by capitalist practice but by a socialist understanding of the total economic process and the interests of working class. Surplus production of consumer goods went to increasing the consumption of the working class and thus ensured higher labour productivity in the next phase. On the other hand, this sales crisis imposed a more or less accurate clarification of all the production and raw material requirements of the entire state economy, which prompted the state to undertake more rapid organisation of its own large-scale agriculture and required clarification of the direction in which the peasant economy must be regulated, which crops to develop and where, which ones to curtail, and so forth.

The crisis was also gradually resolved concerning industry's circulating capital and restoration of its fixed capital. When the capitalist method of keeping accounts between trusts and individual branches of production threatened at some points to retard the entire process of development in individual branches, the state intervened and broke through the log jam. It supported the branches in need from its own reserves and did not allow the fetishism of capitalist forms of accounting – which held separate enterprises or branches of production in its grip – to stand in the way of development of industry as a whole.

In the same way, the organisation of long-term agricultural credits, on a scale that would have been unthinkable for the capitalist system of economy, was implemented not merely and not so much out of consideration for the direct profitability of these operations in the immediate future, but rather to secure an agricultural basis for future large-scale production and actually to adjoin the whole agricultural economy to large-scale industry. This long-term credit, in turn, resolved the sales crisis, although from a different direction.

The fact that in certain branches the main or monopolistic producer of industrial products was the state, and that the major portion of the country's wholesale trade was in its hands and those of cooperatives and mixed societies, enabled the state to regulate prices to the same extent as if the state were managing a planned economy on the basis of the capitalist mode of distribution. The market, with its capriciousness and its spontaneous waves of rising and falling prices, gradually ceased to be a source of surprises for the planned economy. This was due partly to studying the needs of small-scale production and partly to the power resulting from the dual monopoly in the production and trade of products from large-scale industry. The market was gradually tamed for socialism. Limitation of the market's power occurred in two ways, through mastering it on the basis of its own laws and through distributing a part of the values in ways that by-passed it, including the collective payment of enterprise bonuses from the state wage fund; the extension of long-term loans independently of the market along with distribution of these loans in kind, without any middlemen; the sale of commodities to peasants in winter and spring on credit, pending the next harvest; and new, planned construction that was independent of any influence from the market conjuncture on the distribution of free state capital, etc.

As a result of such regulation of the non-socialised part of production and leadership of the other, socialised part – that is, on the basis of the combined methods of planned leadership on the one hand and capitalist calculation and market accounting on the other – the new commodity-socialist system of economy, which took shape in our country during the period of NEP, found a much greater equilibrium of its components than was ever possible for pure capitalism. This leadership and regulation were not yet socialist, but at the same time they were a higher economic and historical form compared to the predecessors. For instance, the strongest trusts and syndicates in America were able to regulate sales, prices, and partly production in individual branches, but the resultant for the economy as a whole emerged as the spontaneous product of their mutual struggle; the barriers to expansion of production, which are associated with existence of the profit institution and thus with the imperative for a particular level of effective demand, could not be eliminated. On the contrary, the mixed form of regulation and leadership of the economy in Soviet Russia internally combined all the potential of purely capitalist regulation with the methods of a planned economy, which ensured a wide opportunity for unimpeded and rapid development of the productive forces of the entire economy.

During the period that we have been considering, the country's private economy in general, and small-scale rural production in particular, were influenced by and brought into the orbit of large-scale industry and state regulation mainly through trade first of all, and secondly through credit; that is, from the direction of exchange. *A connection of this sort does not yet lead to an organic transformation of the small-scale peasant farm into another, higher form of production, although it does closely approach it.* The peasant sector begins an organic regeneration and is included as an integral component of the general economic system only when it is fastened to large-scale industry from the direction not simply of exchange but also of production.

This inclusion of the peasant economic system within the general system of the state economy could occur, on the one hand, through 'inclusion' of entire villages within the power lines of district electrical stations, which must lead to a dramatic change of the entire mode of production and the whole working life of the countryside even where tillage does not directly involve an electric plough. And secondly, it occurred through the spreading use of tractors in cultivating the soil. State tractor detachments of 8–10 machines functioned as mobile, large-scale farming units, which, through their work on peasant fields, linked the peasantry with the large-scale production that provided these tractors, repaired them, and supplied them with fuel and skilled workers. But the linkage also occurred in other ways. The peasant economy became dependent on the large-scale state economy when it acquired fertiliser from state chemical plants, when it received improved seed varieties from a neighbouring Soviet farm, when it used state stock-breeding facilities, and so on. Finally, it depended on large-scale production to undertake enormous and costly land improvements that were impossible without state assistance. If we add to this the influence of state and cooperative trade, along with long-term credit, which involved part of the peasants' harvest being sold to the state several years in advance, i.e., if we add to production influences the influences through exchange that we described earlier, then taking all of this together permits us to speak of a peasant economy within 'a socialist encirclement'.

But these were only tendencies. During the period that we are discussing, development in this direction was only beginning to occur. Mechanised cultivation was not very widespread in agriculture; the district power stations, projected in the plan of electrification, were not yet all built; and even those that were completed still did not provide service to the rural areas. Hence, in this period 'socialist rationality' only reached the peasant economy indirectly: through the banking system, through state and cooperative trade, through credits, and through the productive and agricultural work of Narkomzem. Still, even in this period, one could perceive at several points a *smychka* in production, operating alongside the *smychka* with the peasant economy through exchange. This *smychka* in production provided the content of a second and more protracted period, during which Gosplan used not merely the capitalist reins of Gosbank but also the transmission cables from regional power stations in order to include the village within the orbit of the planned economy.

Lecture No. 10

6   New Forms of Labour Payments: The NEP Insurrection against the
       Proletarian Dictatorship

To people such as us, living more than fifty years after the period we are describing, the psychology of that time is not fully comprehensible. We are all drawn to the 1920s as years of the greatest heroism, both in war and then in the economic sphere. We are inclined to see our grandparents' generation only in a dazzling, bright red light and heroic tones. In brief, we see the poetry but not the prose. It is difficult even for the historian to avoid this kind of psychological error when he turns to study the documents of that epoch and tries to catch the tone of life and day-to-day events, the great diversity of a real historical picture.

For instance, it is difficult for you to believe that the great deeds of that epoch were accomplished by people with such weaknesses, shortcomings, occasional criminal tendencies and a level of culture that for the most part was abysmally low. Yet this was the reality in so far as we are talking about the great masses of the people rather than individuals or small groups. In the newspaper chronicles of that time – *Pravda, Izvestiya, Rabochaya Gazeta, Bednota* and others – you will read, alongside some historical decree or news of undertakings whose benefits we still enjoy today, reports of the execution by firing squad of a group of citizens for stealing a couple of boxes of matches from a vehicle; of a trial of bribe-takers in some economic organ; of speculation by Soviet officials who were previously merchants and industrialists; of outcries concerning the theft of state property, etc.

The most remarkable poet of the time, Demyan Bednyi, writes with bitter sarcasm and indignation of the *sovdury* (Soviet idiots who allowed themselves to be led about by the nose by all sorts of crooks from the Soviet institutions). In the newspapers of the time, you will read articles by the talented journalist Sosnovsky concerning some affair involving bourgeois specialists. You will be dumbfounded when you run across comrade Trotsky's article, where he speaks of the need to clean one's boots and not to throw cigarette ends on the floor. Moreover, you can even read of crimes sometimes committed by communists themselves, usually provoked by the most dreadful needs.

On the one hand, you will find the great task of building socialism and heroic struggle for it with arms in hand – on the other, the misappropriation of a couple of poods of flour belonging to the treasury. Is this crime too great, and the shame of the person who committed it eternal by comparison with the great cause for which he was fighting? Or does the greatness of the cause, on the contrary, make the crime seem trivial? In the general opinion of later generations, the second interpretation is the one that prevails.

But even if we reconstruct the real circumstances of the time, if we put everything in its place and preserve light and dark in their proper proportions, we have no reason to be disappointed when appraising this epoch. On the contrary, I personally believe that if a thousand people build a great bridge, this thousand are all the more astonishing if they are not healthy and well-fed but rather people who are hungry and sick, who have blisters on their hands and feet, and who quarrel over a crumb of bread. The same applies to the construction of socialism. When this system is being built by those who were most corrupted by capitalism, whose psychology was a battlefield between 'yesterday' and 'tomorrow', who together carried on their own shoulders all the barbarism of capitalism while enduring the ignorance to which capitalism condemns the majority, all of this merely amplifies our amazement concerning this epoch.

That is how matters stood in terms of the human material available for the reconstruction of state industry. Communists had never previously studied how to manage enterprises, to trade, or to conduct banking affairs. They learned all of this in the process of work, just as they had earlier learned how to build an army, lead it, and emerge victorious. Here though, because the task was more complex, the process took much longer. At first a swarm of former merchants, entrepreneurs and simple hustlers of every sort robbed the state and conducted matters for their own profit, etc. But these cadres were gradually eliminated from the state apparatus. From the ranks of specialists, on the one hand, emerged a number of reliable and honest people; and a large section of the Communist Party, on the other hand, went through training in high schools, specialised schools and courses, and a practical training course within the existing institutions of state trade and industry. Later, as it became evident that private trade and industry faced limited prospects of development, and most importantly no future, the best representatives of the defeated class consciously and in good faith undertook to serve the state. In this connection, an especially favourable reaction came after the failure of a bourgeois-kulak uprising that occurred at the end of the period we are considering and about which we shall have more to say later. Within industry, engineers from among the workers played the decisive role, building state industry as their own project and with support from some of the engineer-specialists who understood the spirit of the time and realised that socialist state production is a higher type than capitalist production and gives broader scope for development of the productive forces and for the progress of science and technology.

Of great importance also was the change in the psychology of the Communist Party itself, especially amongst communist youth. During the civil war, it was absolutely imperative for a communist to know everything, even if only in a superficial way. The revolution threw party members from tens of causes of one kind into hundreds of another kind, while sabotage by the old intelligentsia compelled them to fulfil the role of that class or else, in the role of Commissars, to supervise them. Conversely, the task of organising state industry, trade, banking matters and socialist enlightenment in the broadest sense of the word demanded that the party reject amateurism and the superficiality of know-it-alls, that its cadres specialise in specific areas of practical work and science, and that each study thoroughly the task he chose for himself or to which he was assigned by the party. This promoted emergence within the ranks of the Communist Party of cadres of genuine specialists in various fields.

You and I, as workers of a socialist society that is gradually being transformed into a communist one, are in yet another respect separated by an entire epoch from the period we are considering. I have in mind the incentives to work under capitalism and socialism. You have already seen from our previous account that War Communism provided no psychological stimulus to increase production in an individual enterprise or for the individual worker to raise his own labour productivity. The question is: How did matters stand with regard to these incentives during the period we are examining?

In this respect, we have already seen that with the New Economic Policy there was a turn to capitalist incentives that had already begun to play a role in the period of War Communism. Piece-work ultimately became the prevailing form of payment for labour wherever production conditions allowed. In general, the worker received more, the greater was his output, and all of the enterprises acquired more resources from the market or from the state if they produced more.

This system began to change gradually as the state raised wages from year to year both to eliminate the artificial sales crisis and, most importantly, as its own resources grew. Experience demonstrated that there was no reason why wage increases should be paid out as part of the piece-work system. On the contrary, a wage increase could become a more powerful lever for raising labour productivity if distributed in the form of a collective bonus. An experiment in collective supply, introduced during the first year of NEP, already showed that when an increase in the individual worker's earnings is made dependent not only on what he produces himself but also upon production by the whole enterprise, workers develop a keen interest in the work of shop-mates, of the neighbouring shop, and ultimately of the enterprise as a whole. The worker then monitors not just himself but others as well, while they in turn monitor him. The result is a kind of obligatory production morality. To individual incentives is added a collective incentive, and this is already a higher level of production discipline compared to the individual responsibility of each and dealing with each individually.

Thus, when the state raised wages it left the old capitalist incentive to apply to one part of the worker's income, but it simultaneously introduced a system of collective bonuses for the workers of enterprises that completed their production programme or exceeded their assignments. Moreover, the enterprise was required to produce not just a certain quantity of goods but also goods of a corresponding quality. At the same time the enterprise itself, out of considerations of economic accounting, was interested in the least wastage of materials and fuel, the maximal use of production capacity of the entire enterprise, and so forth. Recourse to collective bonuses had actually been mentioned in a War

Communist decree, but it remained a dead letter because, in circumstances where a bonus was due but there was nothing to distribute, the workers were being cheated. During that period the state was not up to providing bonuses because it could not secure a minimum of food not just for the workers but even for the army. It is true that during the period of War Communism there were individual enterprises that showed enormous heroism on the economic front even with nutrition so paltry that workers were fainting at their benches. It was heroism at the time just to work at all. The same sort of upsurge occurred as in the struggle at the front, but it could not continue for long and the production results were modest. Conversely, an industrial upswing and an increase of the state's material resources made collective bonuses materially possible and expedient in terms of production. Consider an example. On a railway there is a congress of representatives of various railway services. It turns out from the production report that if the railway carries a certain amount of freight or more, if the depot workshops complete repair work on a certain number of carriages and locomotives, if the railway does not consume more fuel than expected and even saves some compared to the norm, then all the railway workers will receive a corresponding bonus. In the name of all the services, the congress resolves to achieve the maximum bonus, and this is made known to every watchman, every switch operator and every fireman along the line. Everyone is interested in seeing that the locomotives and carriages are repaired more quickly, that less fuel is consumed and none stolen, that loads are delivered intact, etc. The entire economy of the railway is already operating under the surveillance of thousands of eyes. And at the same time, payment by piece-work is preserved as an incentive where it is technically feasible and useful.

This use of collective bonuses was the forerunner of a new form of payment that is characteristic of socialism. The new form grows on the basis of workers' collective responsibility for production results, on the basis of mutual control, and finally on the basis of a higher cultural level and awareness of the whole working class in general. If piece-work encourages competition between individual shop workers, collective bonuses encourage competition between entire enterprises and, in future, between entire branches of production. In this form the state essentially distributes the surplus values that are produced by workers throughout the entire economy. Later on, depending upon the increase of labour productivity throughout industry, the *greater part* of wages in general comes to be paid through the bonus system. Every year there is a relative decline in the role of piece-work in the total sum of wages. But piece-work dies out not only materially but also psychologically, insofar as performance of a certain average minimum of work becomes a kind of labour instinct, a habit for which no special remuneration is given.

True, progress in this area was generally very slow, because the triumph of a new form of labour remuneration is closely linked, as we have already mentioned, to the growth of working-class culture and consciousness, which is not achieved in just a few years. From the fact that we ourselves have not yet achieved communist distribution, you can see how difficult progress is in this direction. It requires remaking human character in the expectation that what once required coercion or the promise of a sweet reward, or else was an act of collective enthusiasm and self-sacrifice, will become instinctive. A change of generations is needed and a new kind of upbringing before the new collective man replaces the individualist of the period of commodity production. The moment when collective incentives prevail over individual incentives amongst the working class is a solemn one in the construction of socialism – a moment no less important for the future than socialisation of the instruments of production. And although we have not yet achieved communist distribution, we have made a substantial advance compared to the period we have been discussing, when the worker had to be led like a child towards awareness of the need for a certain amount of work – not by familiarisation with the country's production or consumption statics but by promising to give out an extra pound of bread or a greater sum of money.

As for the work of foreign capital in Russia during this period, the extent of this capital's influence on the country's domestic economic life, compared to the role of foreign capital in external trade, was not particularly significant. The reasons for this were the following. Generally speaking, foreign capital was allowed to enter Russia either as loans or as industrial or commercial capital. As far as loan capital is concerned, in the decade that we are considering the Soviet government did conclude a few loans with different countries, but these were small loans and primarily in commodity form. Capital did not subscribe to large loans that it considered to be risky. In industry the situation was somewhat better. But we must remember that capital, at the time in question, was entering a period of senility and decrepitude in all countries. It feared large undertakings or big risks, and because of its senile cowardice it could not be tempted even by significant profits. German capital was the sole exception.

Obviously, foreign capital was not very interested in going into branches of industry that worked for the domestic market, since this market was almost completely satisfied by the output of Russian industry. This was especially true during the period when commodities produced within the country were selling for depreciating paper currency. Foreign capital was naturally attracted to industries that produced products of export significance, for example, the oil industry, gold and platinum, forest products, copper, etc. At the same time, it did not favour investments that could produce results only after a long period. It made no sense for the Soviet government, however meagre its own circulating capital, to hand over to foreign capital those enterprises that yielded benefits without particularly large expenditures.

The attraction of German capital was in general a great success for the economy of Soviet Russia, especially for the large-scale development of vacant spaces of the South, South-East and Western Siberia, and the creation there of large tractor and livestock farms. German capital was more enterprising and flexible than English capital. It was also forced to take greater risks than English capital, which still had unexploited opportunities in the colonies. German capital wedged itself into Russia's economy and, without realising it, contributed to the creation of a single powerful economic combination of Russian agriculture and German industry, the benefits of which socialism was destined to reap in the future. From German capital our agriculture acquired significant sums of commodity credits in the form of agricultural machinery and equipment, which allowed the agricultural bank to organise an extensive programme of long-term agricultural loans. As for American capital, its involvement in the economic life of Russia was the most significant following German capital. But it was interested almost exclusively in our oil, manganese and platinum industries, i.e., those branches whose products were needed by America's own economy.

As for external trade with foreign countries, it grew from year to year, and by the end of the decade exports of material and grain had already surpassed those of pre-war times. The Soviet government sought to limit foreign commercial capital to wholesale trade, regulating it through participation in mixed trading companies. It worked to prevent any penetration by private foreign capital into domestic retail trade. Thus, foreign commercial capital was confined to the borders of the state and to the environs of the external ports and was not allowed, unless there was some special need, to extend its tentacles into the interior of the country. This was a source of serious misunderstandings with foreign merchants, especially at the outset, when foreign commercial firms, especially speculative ones, burst into the country looking for maximum profits. Later on they accepted the situation and confined themselves to participation in wholesale trade and their admission to the largest fairs, where they made the majority of their transactions with cooperatives, state trading bodies and the trusts. As for the monopoly of foreign trade, it was formally abolished after the state became the actual monopolist in foreign trade. The formal monopoly remained only for trade in a definite and strictly enumerated number of commodities.

In any event, notwithstanding the expectations of the White Guards, foreign capital failed to have any seriously disintegrating influence on the Soviet economy. Its role in the Soviet economic system was limited to approximately 10 % of the total production of state enterprises. Even during the uprising of the NEP bourgeoisie against the dictatorship of the proletariat, it was unable to form a united front in support of the insurgents, having split into two groups, one of which remained neutral.

We now turn to this final attempt at capitalist restoration.

From the moment of the New Economic Policy's introduction, acute manifestations of class struggle by all the bourgeois and part of the petty-bourgeois forces against the proletarian dictatorship, which peaked with the Kronstadt uprising, ended completely. NEP provided sufficient scope for capitalist accumulation and generally for the development of capitalist relations within the limits of what capitalism itself was capable of. The country's productive forces had declined so far that their development could proceed by various means, and the path of reconstruction by capitalist methods, in areas where the state deliberately curtailed its commitments, could proceed in parallel with the restoration of large-scale industry using socialist methods. With regard to the restoration and intensification of individual small-scale production, given the lack of objective conditions for reconstructing it in the form of a large-scale cooperative economy, its recovery was an absolute necessity and the fundamental precondition for rebuilding large-scale state industry. From this point of view, NEP represented a combined method of restoring the economy by socialist methods (a planned state economy, large-scale industry and transport, etc.), by purely capitalist methods (the market, capitalist accounting even in state industry, private capitalist enterprises in trade and industry, concessions capital), and finally, by the method of intensifying petty commodity production, mainly small-scale peasant farming.

During the early years, all of these methods coexisted with one another; the territory for their operation allowed sufficient space. But the basic directions of the capitalist and socialist paths to reconstruction were entirely different. The spontaneous aspiration of all capitalist forces and tendencies involved relying upon the country's pretty-bourgeois base, gathering strength, connecting with foreign capital and thereby linking it with the petty-bourgeois base of the Soviet countryside, freeing itself of the restrictions that the socialist state imposed on capitalist accumulation to transform it into socialist accumulation, overthrowing the Soviet state, denationalising industry, and subordinating the country's petty commodity production to the capitalist elite that existed in pre-revolutionary Russia. Conversely, the task of socialism was to use capitalist forms up to a certain point in order to develop the country's productive forces, limiting these forms to playing the role of timber in erecting the socialist building. It had to rely on them where they represented a more progressive principle compared to petty production (the average capitalist enterprise is more advanced than handicrafts; orderly private trade, given the prevalence of petty commodity production in the country, is better than speculation and the bag trade; and large-scale concession capital is more advanced than all these forms). Socialism's task was to adapt these inferior capitalist forms to higher socialist forms whenever, wherever, and so long as that was possible and useful for socialism, and to eliminate them where adaptation was impossible or not required and they could be replaced by higher socialist forms. In the countryside, socialism's task further included making it possible for small-scale, commodity-producing agriculture to develop at the expense of petty subsistence farming. The aim was to lean one foot temporarily on capitalist relations, and then to lift that foot and closely adjust small-scale rural production to large-scale socialist industry through cooperatives.

Today, it seems ridiculous to us that our grandfathers, having captured such positions as large-scale industry, transport, wholesale trade, banking and control of the currency, and having in their hands a powerful state apparatus and the army, still feared that they would be superseded and defeated by the Kolupaevs and Razuvayevs,[9] i.e., the representatives of an historically more primitive mode of production that was already on the decline in all the capitalist countries. But we should not fall into one mistake that is psychologically quite possible. For instance, the feudal-serf mode of production and its corresponding property form could not defeat the bourgeois form once the large factory appeared and the bourgeois revolution brought the Third Estate to power; however, this in no way rendered hopeless, *without any exception*, all attempts by the nobility at counter-revolution. In France itself, several revolutions were necessary before the bourgeoisie was firmly in power. It was the same in Soviet Russia during the so-called NEP. The capitalist form, represented by wretched speculative capital and resurgent kulaks in the village, was a lower form compared to socialism, and the basic line of development involved these forms adapting to socialist ones, just as feudalism, defeated but not yet finished, adapted to bourgeois forms. Nevertheless, this did not exclude the possibility of capitalist restoration in individual cases. In general and on the whole, the victory of socialism in the twentieth century was assured, but this by no means implied the inevitable and unconditional failure of all counter-revolutionary bourgeois uprisings. The same was true in Soviet Russia during the period under review.

---

9   [That is, kulaks and merchants.]

Let us consider what the balance of forces was between the two types of economy and between the two class groupings, each of which represented its own mode of production. To ascertain the balance of forces means first of all to measure the balance of economic forces and take into account the cultural levels of the struggling groups. The capitalist forces were: small and medium private trade; mid-sized private industry, mainly leased; the farms of the kulaks and well-to-do strata in the countryside, representing most of commercial agriculture; and foreign concessions capital. In addition, we must also take into account kulak cooperatives, the clergy, the bourgeois intelligentsia, and finally the remnants of former ruling classes who, although they were of no economic significance, still possessed 'living human weight'. All of these elements were oriented first and foremost toward the middle peasantry, hoping to win support from this multi-million infantry, which, owing to its intermediate class position, alternated historically between serving as the infantry of revolution at then as the cannon fodder of counter-revolution.

The socialist forces included: the urban proletariat, which at the end of the decade was no longer declassed as it was at the beginning and was no less numerous than before the war; the poorest strata of the village and the enormous masses of powerless peasants, who benefited from privileged long-term credit and whose farms depended upon the Soviet state; and that part of the petty-bourgeois intelligentsia who had made their peace with socialism and now constituted the main element in the state apparatus. Finally, there were the purely political forces represented by the Communist Party, the Young Communist League, the Red Army and the state apparatus. As for the share of national income that each of the class groupings represented, the state represented the larger portion if the production of the middle-peasant sector is not included in either grouping.

With respect to cultural levels, the state socialist sphere was, if not higher then not much lower than its adversaries. In the course of this decade, the proletariat and its state recognised the enormous danger threatening them due to the cultural superiority of the defeated classes and undertook enormous work to raise the cultural level of the entire proletariat.

The immediate social-economic causes of the movement were the following. Urban private trade, which had become firmly established, began to be squeezed out of its positions by state and cooperative trade, while taxes consumed an important share of commercial profit. On the other hand, the State Bank took a certain part of the profit in the form of interest on loans. The well-to-do section of the peasantry – subjected to progressive income taxation, restricted in their attempts to exploit the peasant poor, and not permitted to indulge quietly in capitalist accumulation – each year became more and more resentful and tried to break free of the chains of the socialist state. Medium-sized industries were similarly hostile to the state, complaining of the burden of state taxes and lease payments.

But there was no unity in the bourgeois camp. Numerous capitalist enterprises, both commercial and industrial, were so closely interwoven into the whole economic organism that they were deprived of any freedom of movement and feared, at the same time, that an unsuccessful attempt at bourgeois restoration would cause them to lose all the gains they had made under NEP. Nor was there any unity among foreign capitalists. In principle, and from the standpoint of bourgeois class interests in general, they were all in favour of restoration. But their interests diverged insofar as any specific attempt at restoration was concerned. With the existing international power groupings, a victory for counter-revolution would have resulted in German capital being squeezed out of Russia by French capital. Since the bourgeoisie usually makes decisions on the basis of short-run gains, in this case German capital, due to antagonism with French capital, turned out to oppose restoration. French capital, which supported restoration, had no significant economic influence in the country.

The ideologists of the counter-revolutionary movement were representatives of the bourgeois intelligentsia. Within the intelligentsia, however, many of the foremost specialists were against restoration. Since the time of the October Revolution, certain changes had occurred in these circles. As we know, the majority of the Russian intelligentsia had fought against the autocracy under the socialist flag, but their socialism was merely a pseudonym for bourgeois democracy, as October demonstrated when it drove the entire intelligentsia into the camp of bourgeois counter-revolution. However, ten years of building a large-scale state economy under Soviet authority, in which bourgeois specialists also participated, forced some of them to reassess their values. In the experience of economic construction, especially the experience of electrification, they were convinced not only of the social but above all the technical superiority of socialist economic forms over those of private capitalism. And when the air smelled of bourgeois-kulak counter-revolution, which could and would have delayed development of large-scale production and thrown the country back to pre-war conditions, this group of specialists stood together with the proletariat for the state form of economy.

On the contrary another group, mainly from the old emigration who had mostly returned to Russia by this time, headed up the counter-revolutionary movement. But these people by no means represented the Kadet[10] elements of

---

10   [The reference is to the Constitutional Democratic Party, which comprised bourgeois-liberal opponents of the autocracy prior to the Bolshevik Revolution.]

the previous emigration. The orthodox old Kadets had become inveterate liars, lost all credibility and been superseded by the *Smenovekhovtsy*.[11] The latter created an organised ferment on Russian territory, affecting both the returning emigrants and the intelligentsia who had remained in Russia. They gave the intelligentsia an ideology and reconciled it temporarily with the Soviet authority. Later they split, and their right wing captured the movement. The slogans of the movement were: defence of economic liberalism; struggle against restrictions on the private economy; struggle against tax increases on private production; struggle against the continuous increase in wages, which in their opinion delayed economic development; and struggle for universal suffrage and a parliamentary system. They also propagated ardent anti-Semitism.

Of course, the new bourgeoisie had its own literature and press, partly legal and partly foreign. In the first years of NEP, the new bourgeoisie, especially the commercial bourgeoisie and the kulaks, were quite indifferent to the ideological work of the bourgeois intelligentsia. They were busy accumulating and had no time for politics. In addition, the old-fashioned intellectual ideology was psychologically incomprehensible to the new bourgeoisie. But soon the bourgeois intelligentsia found ways to the soul of Nepman, both urban and rural, adapted to his needs and began to fabricate the ideology he needed.

The movement began in the cities with large demonstrations in which merchants played the most active role. Pointing to high taxes, they mutually agreed to raise the selling prices of all commodities and in this way attempted to involve the broad masses of consumers. This urban movement was joined by wealthy elements of the village, who refused to pay state taxes and supported the opposition of city merchants. However, with the exception of certain outlying regions, where kulak banditry erupted, the whole movement was not able to take the open form of armed and organised struggle against Soviet power and was smashed before it could create an all-Russian organising centre. Bourgeois representatives who had been involved in the movement saw their property confiscated. The groups of city merchants were particularly affected. Their

---

11   [The *Smenovekhovstvo* movement originated with Russian émigrés whose journal, *Smena Vekh* (Changing Signposts) began publication in Prague in 1921. Adherents of *Smena Vekh* advocated reconciliation with the new Soviet state on the grounds that it was fulfilling the national interest and would eventually give way to traditional, Russian nationalism. Lenin commented in March of 1922 that the *Smenovekhovtsy* 'express the sentiments of thousands and tens of thousands of bourgeois, or of Soviet employees whose function it is to operate our New Economic Policy'. See 'Political Report of the C.C., RCP(B), March 27', in Lenin 1966b, p. 287.]

shops were nationalised and incorporated into the network of state cooperative shops, and their goods were requisitioned by the state. The cooperative
societies of rural kulaks were also suppressed, and their assets were used to
strengthen the cooperative organisations of poor and middle peasants. Heavy
fines were imposed on the kulak strata who participated in the movement,
without, however, destroying their farms. Suppression of the movement was
then followed by the 'Communist reaction', which, although it did not create a new situation, did accelerate socialisation of those branches of trade
and industry for which suitable conditions for socialisation already existed.
In particular, the setback suffered by private trade both strengthened state
and cooperative trade and facilitated a change of relations between the state
and the private merchants who continued to operate. The latter were transformed by degrees into something resembling commissioned agents of large-
scale state industry and thus were absorbed into the system of planned, state
distribution.

Lecture No. 11

7   **The Beginning of the Economy's Transition to a Higher Level: The
     Economic Impasse**

In my previous lectures, I have sketched a brief outline for you of the economic
development of Soviet Russia during approximately the first decade of the New
Economic Policy. During this period, as I have already said, the pre-war proportions of the economy were achieved and partly surpassed. The mixed form of
commodity-socialist economy opened up sufficient scope for development of
the productive forces, and the capitalist context did not create any constraints
on growth. On the contrary, it was only by making capitalist calculations that
the working class in general could learn to manage production at the given level
of development of large-scale production. Soon, however, the socialist content
of the economy's nationalised sector began to be restricted by its capitalist
context and began to burst out of it, demanding new forms. Moreover, relations with small-scale peasant production entered a new phase as well, when
trade and credit links with it were already insufficient for development of the
country's economy as a whole. This new period can be characterised, therefore, as a painless and gradual one in which the socialist economy shed the
husks of its capitalist forms. This process was merely speeded up by NEP's failed
uprising against the proletarian dictatorship, although it had begun long before
that uprising.

At this time the Soviet Republic's international position also changed fundamentally as a new wave of proletarian revolution began in Europe, for which suppression of the NEP uprising was a kind of introduction.

But let us return to Russia.

In my survey of this period I shall not dwell upon production statistics for large-scale industry, much less those of its individual branches. My concern will only be the change of economic forms. Let us begin with the peak of the economic pyramid, with state industry. We left industry in a position where it was financed in the great majority of cases by Gosbank and the Trade-Industrial Bank, managed operationally by the Supreme Council of the National Economy together with the Bureau of Industrial Congresses, kept capitalist-style accounts, and bought and sold for money not only in its trade relations with the non-socialised sector of the economy but also in trade relations between state enterprises. This market chaos within the state sphere proper had to be abolished first of all, since this chaos made it impossible to establish strict proportionality in the development of individual branches of large-scale industry even when the state sector itself was the market. Some state enterprise – let us say a textile plant – needed a certain amount of machinery, fuel and so on. The suppliers of both were also state enterprises, but they did not know for each production year what the demand for their output would be from other enterprises. Each enterprise made purchases where it could do so most cheaply. As a result, purchases were spread over a much greater territory than necessary, funds were spent on commission charges, and this meant considerable cross-haulage for transport. The organs of economic planning began by eliminating this market chaos within the state economy.

The first step, taken already during the early years of NEP, was that all state enterprises were obliged to make not only financial but also economic estimates. These estimates were summed up by VSNKh, so that all quantities of the same kind were combined and it was clear how much oil, coal, steel, etc. were needed for the state sector itself. The demands placed upon industry by industry itself, and by government institutions, could thereby be ascertained. To begin with, this made it possible to foresee what products and what quantities must be produced for the state sector. Secondly, it became possible to distinguish by degree of importance those enterprises that required different products of state industry but could not pay for them in full. This established which enterprises should receive support from public funds in order to expand production. Moreover, it became possible to clarify for all state enterprises the amount of their production that they could definitely dispose of within the state sector itself as well as the volume they would have to sell in the market of the non-socialised sector. Finally, it was possible both to anticipate the threat of under-production of any products and also to foresee the possible extent of any over-production. It was already possible with such a system to take measures in advance to purchase the missing products abroad and to introduce a compulsory planned distribution of such products, which by deliberate decision would be in short supply for all state consumers. Obviously, the state also had to know the volume of production to be expected from all private enterprises that were of more than local significance, and to oblige all private enterprises to provide the state with data on their production plan and the scale of expected output.

I have already mentioned that this work of socialist accounting began in the most crucial branches before the period we are considering, but now it was carried out for the whole of industry, including the most important branches of cottage and handicraft industry. The next step was to distribute orders and purchases in accordance with a definite plan. The state planning organs had no desire to strangle the initiatives of individual enterprises by introducing the old system of distribution by orders or trade by command. But they did try to link a certain group of state consumers with certain groups of state producers, basing these decisions on economic calculation and economy of transport. At the same time, a number of measures were worked out allowing a buyer to disassociate himself in cases when one or another producer provided an unsatisfactory product.

All of these steps helped state industry to function as a united front in dealing with the non-socialised part of the economy, so that individual state enterprises did not weaken the position of state industry as a whole on the free market. The new form of accounting and placing orders was at the same time both flexible and elastic: it left scope for the initiative of individual trusts while protecting the interests of the whole, and at the same time it preserved the interests of the whole in the most rapid advance of the entire economy with the least expenditure of resources.

It was very difficult, however, to regulate production in those industries that were oriented towards the non-socialised, mainly peasant economy. Both the scale of effective demand and the volume of materials that the peasant sector could supply were difficult to estimate with any precision. To get even an approximate production figure for the non-socialised economy and to anticipate the possible conjuncture, the state used every type of statistics, dispatches from correspondents in the localities, and statements from all the trade and credit organisations that came into contact with the free market and could assess its supply and inventories.

Before the peasant economy began to adjust its production to large-scale industry, which radically altered the entire situation, the system of long-term credit played an enormous role in estimating the resources of the countryside and in subordinating small-scale production to the tasks of large-scale industry. Long-term credits to the countryside were used on a much greater scale in Russia than in any country previously. Thanks to the extensive use of short-term credits, through all types of cooperatives and state trading organs, it was already customary for the countryside's autumn harvest to be sold to the state in the spring, six months in advance. The peasantry received not only commodity credits but also cash deposits for the future harvest. This system was used in the procurement of technical crops (such as flax and hemp) and also for different types of livestock raw material products such as wool, leather, bristles, etc. Such a system of trade on credit inevitably required an estimate of the solvency of millions of credited farms, and to avoid enormous losses for the lenders all the state organs involved were compelled to take into consideration the total resources of the peasant economy. Socialist accounting ultimately grew out of this commercial capitalist accounting.

Long-term loans were even more influential in this respect. Through the special agricultural bank for long-term credits, the peasantry each year received such things as agricultural machinery, fertiliser, improved seeds, etc., and even cash loans of tens of millions of gold roubles, loans for new buildings, for the purchase of cattle, for land improvement works and so on. The annual sum of loan values increased in pace with the development of industry, foreign trade, and the production of the peasant economy itself. But the sum of peasant repayments also grew, involving not so much money as payments in kind: grain and other foodstuffs, raw materials, and partly labour. Cartage work, logging for the factories and railways, road repairs etc. could all serve as repayments for loans received from the state. But long-term credit requires more accounting of the client's credit-worthiness than short-term commercial credit. Hence, from this direction too there was an accounting of the volume of production from the peasant economy and its quality.

Now, it was not enough simply to reconnoitre the market; it was necessary to have a permanent agency, a permanent, systematic and scientific-statistical stocktaking of the peasant economy in general and the solvency of individual peasants. With long-term credit, the peasantry pre-sells not only the current year's harvest but also the harvest for several years ahead. If we now add up the three sums – 1) the amount the state currently receives in repayment for short-term commercial and long-term credits; 2) the amount coming from the tax in kind;[12] and 3) what is consumed by the peasant economy itself – and

---

12   Although the tax in kind was formally abolished once the currency was stabilised, allowing the peasantry to pay in cash, in the majority of cases payments were in kind because

then deduct these three[13] sums from the total of all production, the remaining balance will the peasantry's resources for the free market. This sum, which escaped state control, was now not so great, and it declined each year because it was more profitable for the peasantry to deal with the state than with intermediaries. That is to say nothing of the fact that the peasantry sold much of its production to the cooperatives. On the actual free market, the peasantry only sold that portion of agricultural products that exchanged for products from the cottage industry and craftsmen along with what peasants exchanged with each other. Naturally, the accounting process that we have been describing also had to consider and ascertain this share of peasant production that did not fall into state hands.

In any case, when drawing up the general production programme for the next year, the state planning bodies not only knew everything that was accountable in the state sector itself, but they could also quite accurately take into account the volume of that part of small-scale production that was to enter the channels of the state economy in the form of raw materials and food. At the same time, they were able to derive an approximate estimate of how much production the peasant economy could absorb from large-scale industry in the coming year, given an average harvest. At this stage it was no longer quite proper to speak of a peasant market in the traditional sense, because the state itself determined what amount of production from large-scale industry would be provided to the peasantry on credit. The state itself knew, first and foremost, how much it could provide on credit, and secondly, through the tentacles of commercial credit and statistical bodies and agents, how much the peasantry could absorb on credit.

It is also necessary to mention the enormous role played by state insurance against fires, hailstorms, cattle losses and the like, since this insurance also required registration of the insured's property and meant mobilisation of significant peasant funds in the form of insurance premiums.

It will be apparent therefore, that by using mainly capitalist calculations and supplementing these with the methods of scientific-statistical accounting, the state was able to compile overall social accounts covering not only the state sector but also the entire sphere of its contact with the non-socialised economy. The question now is whether the state could not only take into account the resources of small-scale production, not only divert most of its products into the state's own channels of circulation, but also affect the volume and the

---

the peasantry sought to avoid the middle-men, while the state benefited from receiving the tax in kind in order to increase its stock of grain for export.

13   [There is an error in the text, which refers to 'these two sums'.]

quality of output. It was important for the state not just to know what it could acquire from the peasantry and in what volume; it was also vitally interested in seeing that the peasant produced the kinds of raw materials and foodstuffs required and in specific quantities, in accordance with the state's plan for the development of industry and the demand coming from the foreign market. Furthermore, the state was interested in seeing that some crops expanded at the expense of others and that the development of all crops not lag behind the tempo of industrial expansion, in other words, that the backwardness of agriculture not hold back the process of developing industry.

The first task already turned out to be achievable on the basis of credit and trade connections between the peasant economy and state industry. Indeed, when the state planning organs concluded, on the basis of their calculations, that it was necessary to increase flax cultivation at the expense of grain in the North, to expand hemp and reduce potato production in the Central provinces, etc., etc., they then addressed not only the Commissariat of Agriculture but also gave a directive to all the organs of capitalist regulation to settle their accounts with the peasantry in such manner that all of these areas would achieve the desired effect. That was accomplished when Gosbank, the Agricultural Bank, and the state and cooperative bodies announced to the peasantry that in repayment for loans and goods provided on credit they would accept flax and hemp but not grain, that prices would be raised on leather and wool, etc. At the same time, the lending agencies could expand loans to peasants who increased production of the required crops. From the standpoint of the economy as a whole, such premium prices and increased advances were something like a loan to support expansion of the production branches that were indispensable to the state; they were an increase of the fixed and circulating capital of these branches of the economy and had to be continued until, thanks to expanded production, equilibrium was achieved with large-scale industry and its requirements. Conversely, the contraction of one crop or another was achieved in the opposite manner, i.e., by refusing to accept these crops in payment for loans and by reducing their prices.

If a similar decree were issued in the same situation during War Communism, agitators would go to the village, vigorous appeals would be written to the peasantry, and none of this would lead to the desired result if the necessary economic incentives were lacking. Now, with the economic power that the state had acquired, it could be accomplished by a skilful *manipulation of the price lever. Market prices, having once been the spontaneous regulator of the economy, were now converted, in the hands of a powerful state, into a subordinate instrument of planned economy.* Those capitalist forms that were most resilient and suitable for the economy of the transition period were in this way transformed, adjusted, and made to serve socialism. The movement of prices in the market, which at the beginning of NEP forced state industry to dance to its tune and mocked the planned economy, now became the means of socialist regulation of the non-socialist part of the economy. We shall see below how such a transformation also occurred with money and its function in the commodity-socialist economic system.

The methods that we have been describing for regulating the peasant economy were for the time being sufficient for the socialist state. But then it became apparent that the pace of agricultural development was beginning to lag behind that of industry and the requirements for foreign trade. True, large-scale Soviet farms in the outlying regions mitigated the onset of the crisis, and their rapid development played the role of a safety valve, but it was not enough. What was needed was such a change in the whole technology of peasant farming as would signal a rapid and decisive expansion of the agricultural base for industry both in Russia and in Germany, which was economically linked with it. Credit and commercial relations with the peasantry could serve the purposes of regulation only up to a certain point. When that limit was passed, it was necessary to change the mode of production itself in the peasant economy and begin cultivating new areas of idle land in the South-East of Russia and in Western Siberia.

In accordance with calculations by economists and statisticians of the time, the task was formulated approximately as follows: with the existing supply of agricultural labour, grain output, technical crops, fats, meat and animal products would have to increase immensely in all regions; where terrain allowed, cultivation of the soil must be done with tractors and electrical ploughs; all the improvements made in agricultural technology and the science of agronomy must be introduced; crops must be distributed between districts according to plan; and outlying regions must be settled together with the organisation of large-scale farming for the migrants. All of this must first and foremost enormously increase the productivity of the land, and secondly free up from peasant farming the vast amount of labour power required for developing industry.

In the period that we are considering, over a hundred million people were involved in Russian agriculture, about one-half of whom were able-bodied. The projected revolution in agricultural technology was to free up approximately one-third of the able-bodied. Through rationalising agriculture, the economists proposed to move this redundant labour force into colonisation of empty areas on the periphery. Thus, through a revolution in technology and the redistribution of forces within agriculture itself, a much larger area of land could be brought under cultivation and better crops could be grown in the older areas of peasant agriculture. This would provide a vast increase in the grain and raw materials needed for industry and export and thus ensure, for an indefinitely long period, the unhindered and rapid advance of Soviet industry.

But despite the obvious persuasiveness of these arguments, it was almost impossible to implement this plan more or less rapidly. There were obstacles in every direction. To begin with, the regional electrical stations were not yet all completed, and the state did not have sufficient disposable resources to accelerate the pace of construction. These stations could not serve the whole vast area of peasant agriculture; they could only form islands of electrified agriculture in the boundless peasant sea. As for tractor cultivation, it would require about a million tractors and consequently an enormous supply of drivers, repair workers, petrol, and most importantly, colossal free funds from the state in order to service the entire area where electrical ploughing was impracticable.

The third obstacle was the peasantry themselves. The great rural over-population of that time, and the passion for small-scale intensive cultivation, led to agricultural stagnation. An extensive stratum of homestead farms had formed, and they stubbornly clung to their 'Danish methods' of cultivation, which, although they produced high yields per desyatin, demanded an enormous expenditure of labour per unit of output on the part of the farmer and his family. The rest of the peasant masses, though less attached to their [strip] holdings than farmers with consolidated homesteads, feared a massive breakdown in the economic system and even more a mass migration to far-flung regions, which was absolutely inevitable. Earlier, during the tsarist period, land was so scarce in the peasant's place of birth that life was extremely difficult and resettlement was very attractive. But once the peasantry managed to get the farm working in their home area, improved their cultivation and raised yields, the majority, especially the older peasants, had no desire to leave familiar surroundings. Only the young people, who had spent some time in the city or barracked with the Red Army, had higher ambitions and no objection to mass resettlement in the borderlands.

Despite the fact that this colossal task could not be resolved in a short time by the forces of Soviet Russia itself, and that achieving an economic revolution in Russian agriculture required a political revolution in Europe, something was nevertheless accomplished with Russia's own resources. Mechanised cultivation was introduced on a small percentage of peasant holdings, and in a number of places electrification did reach into the countryside. But the process had to be accelerated in every way possible. Resettlement, likewise, occurred every year, although again on a limited scale. The state needed agricultural workers in order to expand the acreage of its large Soviet farms in the outlying areas and its livestock farms on the steppes. On the other hand, some settlers were recruited, mainly from the central provinces where land was in short supply, and moved voluntarily to outlying areas on their own initiative. The young people were mainly attracted after land repartitions among their elders. Due to lack of the necessary funds, at the outset the state was limited to staking out holdings in the resettlement areas for individual peasant farms and providing the most essential assistance for travel and initial construction.

In the new locations, peasants continued to farm in the old way. But when the state became wealthier, it organised the settlers differently. Buildings were erected in the settlement areas for large collective farms, equipped with machinery and everything else required for large-scale agricultural production. In these cases, the settlers changed not merely their abode but their way of farming as well. From being individualists and petty bourgeois they became collective farm workers and sometimes, if everyone agreed, they became communards. True, these large farms were not always state enterprises like the Soviet farms, and the resettled farmers did not always feel that they were workers in a state enterprise. That depended upon the agreement they concluded with the state during the relocation. In cases where the settlers acquired the equipment for a large farm in the form of a long-term loan, they looked upon the farm as their own. They freely disposed of the product of their labour with the exception of the portion that went to pay down the loan. Thus, the state already began during that time to implement a socialist policy alongside of the old resettlement policy. Besides the extension of petty production to the periphery, i.e., in addition to petty bourgeois colonisation, *socialist colonisation of the borderlands also began to develop.*

The next step was to give much greater scope for this progress in agriculture, in particular by turning to construction of new power stations especially for agricultural electrification. As I previously mentioned, such an enormous task was beyond the power of the Soviet Republic. Here the productive forces of Russia encountered the need for a proletarian revolution in the West and a new regrouping of productive forces on a European scale. As regards the monetary system, it proved to be very hardy not only during the first period we have looked at, i.e., when socialist and capitalist economic relations existed side by side, but also during the second period, when socialism began to triumph all along the line. The monetary system turned out to be very adaptable to the new type of economy, although the functions of money, of course, changed dramatically in a planned economy. Generally speaking, the abolition of money is inevitable in a communist society, where neither individual nor social accounts will be kept of who takes how much. On the contrary, socialism (because socialism, by the way, is not communism) does have such accounting, although accounting in the future applies only to a portion of the products entering into distribution. Moreover, socialism does not entirely exclude the market for those branches of the economy, small-scale production for instance, that are not yet socialised. It is true that these branches, and at the same time the market, gradually die out under socialism. But they die out *gradually*, just as socialism – being only incomplete, unfinished and under-developed communism – gradually turns into actual communism.

Finally, with socialism so-called amateur industry and amateur art also grow up; workers of the socialist state busy themselves after they have put in their obligatory working time, and these products also exchange for money as they do today. But the role of money in such circumstances is, of course, completely different from its role in either a capitalist or a commodity-socialist type of economy. There it was the measure of the value of commodities, the medium of circulation, and the means of payment. It was one of the means for spontaneous regulation of the process of production and exchange. To the contrary, when all the decisive areas of the economy become planned, when accumulation is planned on the one hand and the distribution of means of consumption on the other – then money is transformed into merely a *subsidiary instrument of planned distribution*. It retains its former status only for the non-socialised part of the economy, but even then not for the whole but only for the market in the narrow sense of the word, i.e., for the market in which material exchange occurs within the non-socialised sector.

We have already seen, however, that petty non-socialist production disposes of only a small portion of its output in the free market. Moreover, this output is already accounted for in the country's general economic plan, and that includes production in the petty economy as well as in all the processes of this surviving market, which in many respects is already regulated by the state. Thus, money is here 'in a socialist encirclement' and its economic role becomes extremely limited.

During the period that we are examining, the state fully mastered the task of regulating the circulation of money. In this area it encountered no insurmountable problems. It also solved the problem of replacing gold with a paper circulation, while retaining for paper money all of the basic functions fulfilled by gold. It was in no rush to drive money from circulation and artificially curtail the sphere of monetary settlements because, as we shall see below, non-monetary payments successfully disposed of money in a natural way. With the existence of a mixed system of economy, money had major advantages and could not be displaced by any 'labour unit' or other artificially invented accounting methods.

Still, something in the nature of a monetary crisis was pending. The root of this crisis was the following. During the first decade of NEP the volume of commodities that circulated with the use of money grew from year to year, although the possibilities for non-monetary payments grew simultaneously in connection with credit and the banking system. As the currency was stabilised, people no longer tossed money from hand to hand. The commodity turnover absorbed it in enormous quantities, and as foreign trade developed there was a great demand abroad for the Russian state's stable currency. There was also a significant growth of accumulation in the form of money. I have already pointed out that the government and Gosbank took advantage of this situation in order to increase their own working assets. Each year they added to the money supply to the extent required by a growing commodity turnover and the needs of accumulation. But then a fundamental change began to occur.

Although industrial and agricultural production continued to increase each year, the circulation of commodities with the use of money began to contract due to the narrowing sphere of monetary payments. The planned distribution of orders within the state sector reduced monetary circulation between state enterprises to a minimum. Only outstanding balances were settled in cash, and the sums involved were merely a small percentage of the total transactions occurring within the state sector.

As for the method of wage payments, here essential changes were also under way. Workers left most of their wages, and in some areas almost the whole sum, with the cooperatives and state trading organs, where they acquired everything they needed. The cooperatives purchased their supplies either from state enterprises (the major share) or on the free market (a much smaller share). As regards agricultural products in particular, for example bread, meat, fats and so forth, whereas previously the cooperatives purchased most of these products in the village as part of normal trade, now they were acquired mainly from the state, which had enormous quantities resulting from the tax in kind, payment of bank loans, payment for commodity loans from state trading organs, etc.

Thus, instead of monetary settlements between state enterprises and their workers, between workers and the cooperatives, and finally between cooperatives and the state and its organs, it was much simpler and more convenient for cooperatives to settle accounts with state organs by way of the bank so that only the difference was paid in monetary form. As for purchases by workers, the cooperatives were obliged by agreement with the state to pay the entire wage in the form of commodities according to the workbook if the worker so requested. For this purpose, the cooperatives were provided with sufficient credit from state organs. At the end of the month, the worker received in cash only what he had not spent, according to his workbook, on commodities in the cooperative shop. In most cases the worker spent more than his monthly wages by using credits from his cooperative. In concrete terms, if a worker took goods over the course of a month valued at 60 gold roubles, whereas he was supposed to receive 70 roubles as wages, the factory office made the deduction and he received only the difference of 10 roubles in cash. In many places, especially where the workers normally left all or nearly all of their wages with the cooperatives, a system even began to be used whereby the factory management and the cooperative would agree that the final cash balance would be paid by the cooperative itself.

All of this meant the displacement of money from a vast area of commodity turnover and payments, and this was accomplished without the slightest loss to state organs and cooperatives or to workers. The peasantry's payment of the tax in kind to the state was also predominantly non-monetary; in most instances, loan repayments to Gosbank were likewise non-monetary; and the peasants frequently dealt with cooperatives without the use of cash by purchasing commodities on credit. Moreover, thanks to development of the credit system, monetary payments[14] were curtailed even within the non-socialised part of the economy. The need for money declined, therefore, year by year. Whereas it previously served the entire commodity turnover of the country, both inside the state sphere and beyond, now it was entirely displaced from the sphere of intra-state payments and also largely from the sphere of exchange between the state and non-socialised production. The only field that remained to it was the free market in the proper sense of the word, and the limits of the free market continually narrowed due to the growing role of socialised production in the country's economy.

The sphere of monetary settlements contracted still further when it was made obligatory not only for state and cooperative enterprises but also for private ones (except for the smallest) to keep current accounts with Gosbank, the Trade-industrial Bank and other credit institutions associated with them. Thus, Gosbank and the other credit organs gradually became not only the repositories of free resources and the treasury for the country's surplus capital, but also the accounting office of the entire socialist economy, including even some enterprises belonging to the private sector.

What now was the role of money?

For the workers who received cash for the difference between their monthly pay and what they had already acquired, money was a means with which to buy one thing or another outside of the cooperatives, that is, for a freer choice on

---

14   [There is an error in the text, which speaks of 'non-monetary' payments when the intended meaning is clearly 'monetary payments'.]

the free market. For state enterprises, money was a means of settlement among themselves, with the cooperatives, and with the peasantry; in other words, money was a means of payment. If these payments did not balance, the residual constituted a fund for purchases on the free market, which in turn made purchases from state enterprises. Here, money served as means of circulation between the two economic systems. Was money also a means of accumulation? It was, but given the credit system, whereby the country's whole accumulation normally flowed into the banks, it was the banks that put this money into circulation and, upon deposit in the bank, money merely served as evidence of a certain share of the national income.

Finally, how did matters stand with money's most important function in the commodity economy, namely, its role as the measure of value? Once most of the country's production originated in the economy's socialised sector, led by the planning organs; once the market did not control the state economy but rather the state began to control the market, which now acted only as a corrective for the planned economy; and in particular, once the market did not determine prices as the spontaneous resultant of supply and demand but prices were instead specified *for the market* – from that point on the role of money, as the measure of value, gradually began to wither away. Society no longer needed to take such a circuitous route in determining what underlies value, that is, the average socially necessary labour time expended for one or another mass product. This magnitude could be determined directly through calculations in the central accounting department, with data for the predominant part of the economy, and *then* be expressed in terms of money. In these conditions money remains a technically necessary means for the public expression of value. But *what it had to express in its language of figures* is dictated to it by the bookkeeping and statistics of the socialist economy. In other words, money retained only those functions required for a planned economy. Basically, it was gradually transformed into symbols for a certain portion of the national income, or in this case coupons, or else into evidence of receiving a certain quantity of raw materials and means of production, i.e., a permit or an order issued by the planned economy. Money retains its former role only on the free market of the economy's non-socialised sector, which itself no longer plays any independent role in the country's economy. This process occurs quite naturally and imperceptibly, without any shocks, just as the commodity-socialist economic system, with the dictatorship of the proletariat, imperceptibly turns into a socialist-commodity system and the latter becomes purely socialist.

What happened then with all the 'unemployed money'? After all, according to the laws of monetary circulation, should not the processes we have been discussing lead to its depreciation from one year to the next?

In fact, that did occur. The value of the stable rouble did begin to decline domestically, yet it did so not due to the economy's disintegration but because of its progressive development. There were two ways to avoid this depreciation, which is most inconvenient for economic development. One was to reduce the quantity of money in the country each year by withdrawing it from circulation and either destroying it or preserving it in bank vaults for posterity. The other was to regulate the process through annually replacing all cash in the country with new money of reduced nominal value (10 old roubles, say, would be equal to 9 full-valued new roubles). The government was quite strong enough, both politically and economically, to take the second course, which was more advantageous from a narrow financial viewpoint. But this measure was too cumbersome to take just about every year. The state opted, therefore, for the first route, i.e., deflation, and carried out several domestic loans for this purpose. Thus, the quantity of money in the country was adjusted to the needs of commodity circulation; in other words, it was reduced each year. Money not only lost its former economic functions by being gradually converted into coupons but also physically withered away.

Now we must say a few words regarding the fate of small-scale industry in this period. During the collapse of large-scale industry, the role of cottage and handicraft industries greatly expanded throughout the economy. If the net pre-war product of artisans and handicraftsmen was equal in value to one-third or one-quarter of that originating in capitalist industry, during the revolution its value was almost the same as the product from state industry. When large-scale industry began to recover, when its output returned to the pre-war level, the role of artisan and handicraft industry began to decline markedly. This decline became all the more apparent when the state undertook, as one of its immediate production tasks, to extinguish those branches of artisan and handicraft industry in which small-scale production could have been replaced long ago by machines. It still survived in Russia because pre-war capitalism barbarously exploited labour power and had no interest in introducing machinery in a number of branches where wages were low. At the same time, in areas where electrical power stations were operating, preservation of certain types of handicrafts clearly became pointless from an economic point of view. Thus, the restoration of industry led to displacement of small-scale production not only from the areas it had penetrated during the temporary collapse of large-scale industry but also from those in which it operated before the war.

However, the handicrafts did display considerable vitality, first of all because the very improvement of technology in agriculture reduced the peasant's working time and prompted him to take up handicraft work as an auxiliary and secondary occupation. Even during the period of War Communism, collective labour in agricultural communes and artels – especially the emancipation of women from the kitchen – led to the communards having more time free from agricultural work than the peasants had in neighbouring villages. The communards generally made use of this time for work in various side-line activities. Finally, as a result of the seasonality of agricultural work, the peasantry had a great deal of free time in the winter, which they usually devoted to hand weaving and various handicrafts. All of these factors delayed the elimination of mediaeval hangovers in small-scale industry.

One more circumstance was also significant, namely, the fact that large-scale industry, while replacing crafts, could not always absorb the resulting surplus labour. If, for instance, machine production enables 1,000 workers to do the work of 5,000 artisans, the remaining 4,000 have to find places somewhere in large-scale industry. With a very rapid industrial expansion, this transfer of the labour power displaced from craftwork occurs more or less normally. But if there is a delay in the development of large-scale industry, some of these ruined craftsmen remain unemployed, which usually drives the crafts to attempt to compete with large industry by notoriously exploiting the labour power of the craftsman and his family and by reducing personal consumption to a minimum.

But we have already noted that the rapid advance of Soviet industry began to stall after a certain time due to agricultural backwardness. This Achilles heel, the stagnation of agriculture, affected every aspect of the struggle against handicrafts. At this point, all roads led to Rome, meaning the proletarian revolution in the West.

•••

My brief account of Russia's economic development may give you the false impression that the entire struggle of socialism against capitalist forms, and against all the other forces of the past that surrounded the island of proletarian socialist economy in a peasant country, was straightforward and painless until the moment when the NEP counter-revolution broke out. That view would be incorrect. You need only take a close look at the Soviet press of the time, at the reports, debates and resolutions of party and Soviet congresses, to become convinced of the numerous threats that the regime of proletarian dictatorship encountered at every step of the way. It is true that our grandparents exaggerated some of those threats and were too late in seeing others that were more urgent, but the dangers did exist and they resulted in a fierce struggle.

The proletarian power lived through several critical moments: the period of the Brest peace; July and August of 1918, when White Guard forces were on the brink of victory and the Red Army had only begun to organise; the period when Yudenich and Denikin enjoyed their greatest successes; the time of the Kronstadt uprising. Transition to the New Economic Policy averted the danger of a petty-bourgeois counter-revolution at a time when it was all the more serious because some of the urban workers, in conditions of hunger and deprivation, were strongly influenced by the peasants' mood. The first years of NEP brought the Soviet state a period of relative peace. State industry was in ruins, and the proletariat had largely ceased to exist as a class, but then capitalism had not yet gathered strength because it was just entering a period of 'secondary accumulation'.

The danger began from the moment when development of capitalist relations gained momentum and capitalism in Russia threatened, in economic terms, to outstrip socialist construction. This danger was especially acute during the first half-decade of the New Economic Policy, when the working class and the Communist Party, in their struggle against capitalism, were forced to depend not so much on their own economic base as on non-economic means of pressure. In order to exert such pressure, it was imperative that all proletarian and communist forces be drawn together into a solid phalanx that would both ideologically and organisationally oppose the corrosive influences emanating from the bourgeoisie and the petty bourgeoisie. This was an extremely difficult and internally contradictory task, because large-scale industry could economically subordinate petty production and capitalist relations not through economic isolation from them but only through becoming bound together with them. At that moment, the cultural superiority of the defeated class over the victors posed an enormous threat.

Socialism could not manage its economic construction without assistance from bourgeois elements, for construction itself required a level of culture higher than what was accessible to the proletariat of this epoch. The bourgeois specialists represented an even greater threat during this period than during War communism; all their bourgeois habits and their psychological hostility to the new order were fed from the inexhaustible resources of those same capitalist relations that socialism was forced to use in order to develop the country's productive forces. The most dangerous and critical years for the proletarian power were those when large-scale industry had not yet fully recovered and the working class had yet to produce sufficient numbers of leading cadres to replace the old bourgeois specialists in all spheres of economic construction. This was a time when bribery, theft of state property, and the scoffing of bourgeois elements at the misfortunes of the state economy reached their peak; it was a time when even a section of the Communist Party was in danger of being demoralised.

The Communist Party launched an aggressive struggle to raise the cultural level of the working class and to conquer science and higher education for the proletariat. Thanks to these efforts, the schools of higher education gradually did become truly proletarian. At the same time, the Communist Party underwent a new purge to rid itself of those elements who had been corrupted by NEP influences, who had 'moderated' their attitudes towards the bourgeoisie, and who in effect became enemy agents at the command posts of the proletarian dictatorship.

This was the period when the struggle also began for the new Soviet man, for transformation of the national type of the Russian worker. Soviet industry could not rapidly advance until the working class itself overcame not merely ignorance and lack of culture, but also laziness, dishonesty in work, and sloppiness. Soviet industry could not triumph without the introduction of a new, scientific organisation of labour and creation of the type of worker who would correspond to a higher type of industry.

My history is not one of culture during the Soviet period: I cannot dwell upon all the problems that our grandparents struggled to overcome except to say that they solved them with honour. But in the cultural as well as the economic field, there was a moment during the New Economic Policy when survival of the proletarian regime in Russia was in question. The victory of socialism only became clear when the reconstruction of large-scale industry began to outpace the development of capitalist relations, when the working class began to overtake the defeated class in terms of culture, and when the economic bankruptcy of capitalism became clear in Western Europe and a new wave of world proletarian revolution began to swell.

The proletarian revolution in Europe will be the subject of my next lecture.

Lecture No. 12

8   The Capitalist Crash and Civil War in Europe

From previous lectures you have seen that at a certain point in its economic development the Soviet authority, much more acutely than before, began to feel the limitations of its economic resources for a powerful advance. Only a new redistribution of Europe's productive forces, aimed at applying new resources and instruments of production to Russian agriculture, to the rich and uncultivated lands of the South-East and Siberia, only the mechanisation of agricultural labour on a mass scale, could provide a strong impetus for advance. Psychologically, this was expressed in a certain 'westward thrust', in an increasingly nervous anticipation of proletarian revolution in the West and an impatience that resembled that of 1917–20.

With capitalism, this task could not be resolved, since capitalism excluded any possibility of a planned economy in Europe without regard to national borders, or the regionalisation of Europe along production lines; it excluded such an enormous rupture in the distribution of productive forces, whereby only those areas of land that yield the maximum income would be cultivated. Because of the self-centred interests of individual groups of entrepreneurs, capitalism could not concentrate production or eliminate the 'rotten boroughs' of industry, whose existence was economically senseless if production were regionalised and concentrated. They could only be preserved with the protection of customs duties imposed by nation-states. Finally, capitalism did not risk placing large funds in Russia, with the partial exception of German capital.

Meanwhile, only a revolution in railway transport with electrified super trunk lines, and the cutting of a number of canals for water transport, could bring the sources of raw materials and Russian grain to Europe's industry. Thus, development of Russia's productive forces now drove Russia to the West in order to accelerate the West's movement towards Russia. If the revolution in the West had been delayed too long, this situation could have led to an aggressive socialist war between Russia, supported by the European proletariat, and the West. That did not occur because by that time the proletarian revolution, by the laws of its own internal development, was already knocking at the door. It is quite true, as you know, that the development of further events did lead to war, but war was not the chief agent in solving this imminent historical problem; it was not the obstetrician but merely his technical assistant in helping to facilitate the childbirth.

What were the reasons for the second wave of proletarian revolution in Europe?

The post-war crisis of European industry began gradually to dissipate by the mid-twenties. The improvement in the conjuncture occurred, first and foremost, at the cost of deterioration in the position of the working class. Capital's economic onslaught against the working class, especially in the victorious countries, where the currency was stable, led to the general victory of capital and a corresponding general reduction of wage levels, which enabled the capitalists of those countries to cheapen the costs of commodities and thereby compete more successfully against Germany. On the other hand European capital, and above all English capital, began to search strenuously for new markets and sources of raw materials in the colonies and in several agrarian countries of Europe and Asia. This was crowned with some success. The raw material and market bases of European industry were expanded. The establishment of economic relations between Europe and Russia had a similar influence, and Russia increased its exports and imports every year.

However, this temporary improvement could not be stable and long-lasting. The steady progress of industry very quickly came to a halt at a general level of production that did not even reach pre-war levels. And this meant that capitalism since 1914, that is, the first year of the war, was already stagnant or degenerating. These fifteen years of stagnation or decline demonstrated beyond any doubt that capitalism had already exhausted itself as a specific economic system, that history had squeezed from it all it could give, and like the Moor who had done his duty, capitalism now had to go. We shall discuss later how the Moor 'made his exit' and how he was also pushed so that he would depart quickly. But here we face one very important theoretical question. Capitalism died or was killed (depending upon which aspect of the process we emphasise), and socialism made possible a much more rapid and unhindered development of the productive forces. These are established historical facts. But the question is: Why, in purely economic terms, was capitalism unable to develop after the world war? Why did a development of the productive forces in *capitalist forms* become objectively impossible? In other words, what was the economic cause of the stagnation of the European economy during the 1920s, when the first proletarian attack on the bourgeois order had been repulsed in 1917–20 and the capitalist regime had regained its balance?

The explanation is to be found in the following. The very fact of the world war was a manifestation of profound crisis in capitalism. If previously capitalism had been conquering a world in which areas still existed that had not yet been touched by its tentacles, now the issue was merely one of how to divide a world that had already been conquered. One part of the capitalist whole could develop further only by crushing another part; capitalism began to tear its own body to pieces. As a matter of fact, the answer to our question is partly contained in the answer to another: What were the economic causes of the world war? Before the war, European capitalist production had generally reached an all-time high. After the war, the capitalist countries were able to do no more than rearrange the basic requisites for any industrial production, but they could not create a broader basis for it. Indeed, several colonies passed from Germany to France, but there was no increase in the number of markets and their absorptive capacity. One or another source of raw materials passed from England to America, yet there was no increase in either the sources of materials or the materials themselves. Capitalism had fallen into a vicious circle.

That was not the case in the pre-war decades, because then there were still undistributed markets and new sources of raw materials, providing a basis for the capitalist economy to take its next leap ahead. These new material sources and markets for sales enabled capitalism to climb to the next, higher stage of expanded production, and that expansion of production itself, to a certain extent, created additional new markets and the preconditions for further growth. As for the surplus population, who either accumulated in the European countryside or were drawn from the ranks of the petty bourgeoisie – who were being ruined by capitalism and could not find work within the capitalist system – all of these masses flowed to America through the canals of emigration. Before the war, Europe dispatched beyond its borders from 800,000 to 1,000,000 emigrants every year. Since this emigration was aimed at the new lands of America, what occurred here was a spontaneous redistribution of productive forces in the world economy, which meant expanding the basis of world capitalism: new areas of land being cultivated, new masses of grain and materials, new strata of solvent buyers for industrial products. During and after the war, emigration halted; instead, several countries, such as Poland and Czechoslovakia, had a return movement of emigrants, for whom, alas, Europe had no work, no bread, and no land – even less land than before.

In the pursuit of profit, capitalism became entangled in its own contradictions. Private property in the instruments of production, freedom for management and initiative, competition – these were the strongest incentives for economic growth in the phase of capitalism when the world was not yet dismantled down to the last colony, when there were reserve outlets for redundant population, when even a slight expansion of raw materials and markets for sales enabled a significant expansion of production. All of these opportunities had narrowed. On the other hand, agriculture in the world economy generally did not keep pace with the development of industry. Dragging its remnants of mediaeval modes of production along behind, and constrained by the institution of private property not just in the instruments of production but even in the very object of agricultural labour, the land, agriculture could not catch up with industry, which had raced ahead and was incapable of proportionally increasing the output of raw material with a minimum expenditure of labour. Had capitalist agriculture solved this problem, the result would have been to guarantee uninterrupted industrial development with nothing more than a change in the distribution of productive forces between industry and agriculture. But that was impossible as long as the capitalist mode of production survived; the valve of rapidly progressing agriculture could not be opened, and different parts of the capitalist organism were driven to seek an outlet in mutual extermination. With this thrombosis in the agricultural sector, capitalism began increasingly to develop its negative features until they soon outweighed its positive tendencies. What it achieved at one pole on the basis of competition, freedom of economic activity and initiative, it destroyed at the other in world war, crises and massive unemployment. During the war and immediately afterwards, both bourgeois circles and even the majority of socialists believed that the world war, although unprecedented in scope, was still only a setback for capitalism and not the beginning of its collapse. It seemed that the world war of 1914–18 did not really differ in principle from earlier imperialist wars, only in degree. Most observers claimed that on the basis of a new relation of forces and a new world division, capitalism would resume its gradual advance after a brief setback and decline. But the years following the world war demonstrated that the period of capitalism's flowering, its high point, had already passed. It became increasingly clear to everyone that the very fact of the war was evidence of the inescapable cul-de-sac into which capitalism had fallen. It could throw existing and strictly limited raw materials and markets for sales from the hands of one nation into those of another, but it could no longer expand them on the basis of capitalist production. On the contrary, this very redistribution had itself already become the most powerful factor in the collapse of the world economy's capitalist ties, and it threw the economy of the entire world back to a lower level compared to the pre-war period.

Capitalism was in no position quickly and decisively to open the valve in agriculture and remove the cause of the stagnation that had begun, i.e., to avoid the very impasse from which the capitalist states looked for an exit through war. The struggle for markets, materials and investment spheres took the form of armed hostilities only because the necessary economic effect could not be achieved on the basis of a new redistribution of productive forces on a world scale. Capitalism could not take decisive measures to abolish private property in land, to allocate productive forces in the world economy irrespective of national borders, or to introduce improvements to the whole agricultural system, so that on the basis of this new distribution of productive forces, and beginning with technical advances in agriculture, the world economy could set new records of coal mining, steel smelting, machinery production, grain harvests, etc. If capitalism could have achieved all of this, it would already have ceased to be capitalism. In the best of cases, it would be state capitalism organised on an international scale.

The first decade after the conclusion of the world war was a time when capitalism, having bled itself white, tried once again to climb the rungs of the ladder whence it had been hurled by the war; and it did so, moreover, having retained all of the old capitalist economic methods. It failed. The few successes that it did achieve in this direction were too small and lagged too far behind the growing crisis. This crisis took the form of chronic mass unemployment, which for years excluded five to ten million people from production in both hemispheres.

It took the form of an unprecedented accumulation of surplus population in agrarian countries and in the agricultural regions of industrial countries. Once the overflow canal of emigration was closed, surplus population began to accumulate within Europe along with unemployment in the cities, rising discontent and indignation, and the thunderous growing energy of the lower classes before the revolutionary storm. In the form of surplus population, capitalism accumulated all of the forces that in every revolution have played the role of assault troops in overthrowing an existing social-political order that has become obsolete.

What exactly was the task that capitalism could not resolve by its own methods and bequeathed to the epoch of proletarian dictatorship? The problem, as we see it, was the following. At the moment when division of the world was by and large completed, when emigration had to be curtailed, when the impetuous development of capitalist industry could not continue through expanding the base of capitalism in new regions of the world, the centre of gravity had to be transferred to reform of agriculture in the decisive areas of world agricultural production. First and foremost, it was imperative to implement a revolution in the technique of Russian peasant agriculture. But this reform was too profound and radical for capitalism; not only could it not cope with this task, it could not even really contemplate it. The category of profit and free enterprise was too weak a weapon to break through the barriers to progress posed by the institution of private property in the land, the division of the world into nation-states, and the senseless anarchism of the entire capitalist system. Capitalism might have been saved only by some unexpected discoveries in the area of agricultural machinery and technology in general, such as the mass manufacture of protein from the air, etc. The obstacle was partly the surplus population itself, which was both a consequence of the crisis and also a complicating cause. The cheapness of labour did nothing to promote technical progress in agriculture. True, a rise in the prices of grain and materials stimulated agricultural development to a certain extent, but on a scale that lagged far behind the rapid pace of capitalism's industrial chariot.

Once the war ended, European industry found itself facing not only a decline in agricultural production on its own territory, but also the fact that a great many of its non-European markets and sources of material were lost, having been captured by American or by native industry. Like an enormous ocean-going steamship, intended to navigate the deep water of the oceans, European industry was now stuck fast in the sands of a shallow sea.

Capitalism not only failed to cope with an appropriate distribution of productive forces on a world scale; it was also incapable of rational economic organisation within individual countries. In the decade after the world war,

Europe was increasingly dominated by the psychology of a blind-alley and hopelessness. True, immediately after the war ended, the prevailing mood was one of protest against economic controls, all types of regulations, rationing and the regimentation of economic life in general. It seemed that economic coercion was not the result of want but rather the reverse. The capitalist press very successfully used this attitude to discredit the very idea of a state planned economy. The reaction against hunger, want, queues and rationing was thus converted into a reaction against socialism and a demonstration in favour of free competition and capitalist initiative. Very soon, however, this reaction inspired its own reaction. The longer triumphant Manchesterism prevailed, the more clearly it revealed its bankruptcy. You can have as much free enterprise as you want, but the economy's production did not expand, wages declined, taxes increased, and the numbers of unemployed could not be reduced. Financial bankruptcy spread from one country to another. The workers of England, Germany and America – even those who were not affected by communist propaganda – each year more insistently demanded nationalisation of railways, mines and other key branches of the economy, especially during the massive strikes in these branches, which were usually liquidated with the direct participation and at the initiative of the state. This entire period can be regarded as one of spontaneous struggle by the working class for a system of state capitalism. At the time, important groups of bourgeois economists likewise began to lean towards recognising the need for a planned economy on a global scale, and they obviously fed the illusion that capitalism was capable of carrying out such a plan.

The attention of the masses was focused upon the most striking external manifestations of capitalism's bankruptcy, which had already begun. A succession of state financial bankruptcies swept through Germany, France, Austria and several small countries. The complete bankruptcy of the Versailles Treaty was revealed and even French nationalists repudiated it, replacing it in fact by a number of temporary agreements. Bourgeois politicians scratched their heads in vain over the problem of squaring the capitalist circle. But the circle held firm, and no tricks of any agreements or conferences, either political or economic, could find a way out. A deep conviction gradually seized the masses that it was impossible to get things moving again so long as the bourgeois system lasted. This conviction of the helplessness of the capitalist class appeared everywhere: in the press of the day – not only the labour but also the bourgeois press – in cartoons, jokes, and sayings, and in the concluding words of resolutions adopted by every workers' meeting without exception. It is said that even before the war, during Italian parliamentary elections, the incumbent government was criticised by its opponents on the grounds that during its administration the cows and goats gave less milk. Something similar was repeated now. Capitalism began to be held responsible even for events over which it had no control.

'Under capitalism nothing gets better and there is no progress' – that was the general slogan. Even the capitalist class became conscious of the hopelessness of the situation. That was reflected in the literature of the time. The philosophy of Spengler[15] and his followers found more and more adherents. The conviction took hold that the whole of European culture was following in the footsteps of the Roman Empire; mysticism intensified; people were drawn to Indian philosophy; the bourgeoisie and the bourgeois intelligentsia returned to the crudest of faith in a personal God; bourgeois morality began to collapse. The speculator, with his slogan of 'capture the moment', more than ever before became the hero of the day. The nervousness and anxiety in social psychology coincided with a similar loss of confidence, unsteadiness and feverishness in the economy as a whole. At the same time, a certain group of the bourgeoisie emerged who were prepared to defend their positions to the last drop of blood. They took the view that a transition to state capitalism would be a backward step in all economic development and an organised degradation of all human culture; capitalism, on the contrary, could heal its own wounds and surmount its predicament through free economic initiative and competition.

It was typical of the time that while important groups of the actual bourgeoisie vacillated, and while one group in particular supported state capitalism and a workers' government, the most principled and implacable force for state capitalism was another class; namely, part of the pretty bourgeoisie, a section of the intelligentsia, former officers and some of the clergy. This historical paradox recurs in every bourgeois revolution. In the English, French and Russian revolutions, the petty bourgeoisie sought to carry the bourgeois-democratic revolution through to its culmination despite the wishes of the supposed initiator of the festivities – the big bourgeoisie. All of this occurred regardless of the fact that the development of capitalism not only fails to improve but in fact worsens the position of the petty bourgeoisie, especially the economically independent petty-bourgeois strata. Similarly, in a counter-revolution certain groups of the petty bourgeoisie, along with some intermediate class groups, have proven to be more consistent than the bourgeoisie itself and have courageously perished for its interests as the cannon-fodder of counter-revolution, even though socialism could not have worsened their situation. These strata, whose objective role has simply been that of shock battalions in capitalism's

---

15   [The reference is to Oswald Spengler's *The Decline of the West*.]

self-defence, often elude the bourgeoisie and its state organisations and independently undertake to save the bourgeois regime, refusing any manoeuvres,
retreats or temporary concessions to the working class. Italian fascism was
merely the first harbinger of this peculiar division of roles in the class struggle
of this period.

By the late 1920s, the common slogan of the working masses gradually
became state capitalism in the economy and a workers' government in politics.
In different countries the transition to a so-called workers' government followed different paths. In England, for example, the Labour party came to power
with left-wing liberals as a result of their victory in parliamentary elections.
In Austria and Germany, workers' governments were formed despite bourgeois
majorities in parliament. In Germany the transfer occurred through the proletariat's struggle against rising reaction. The result was emergence of so-called
dual power; that is, the real power of the workers' organisations on the one
hand, and the purely formal power of the Reichstag on the other. At a time
of soaring inflation, crisis, and the greatest unrest among the working class –
manifested in demonstrations, clashes with the police and reactionaries, and
general strikes, when it seemed that the entire structure of German capitalism
was shaking to its very foundations – the Reichstag thought it fitting to cast a
majority of bourgeois votes for creation of a workers' government and gave it a
vote of confidence.

This government, in which people like Scheidemann[16] naturally played the
leading role, was soon responsible not to the Reichstag but actually to the
Social-Democratic party and the trade-union centres. There were many simpletons at the time who proclaimed that power had been painlessly transferred
from the bourgeoisie to the proletariat without any of the bloody horrors that
attend a civil war. These simpletons did not even suspect that no real transfer
of power had occurred at all. Events very quickly demonstrated that a workers' government was not in fact the class power of the proletariat in the proper
sense of the word, but only the final trench of bourgeois society in the struggle
against the real workers' power that was yet to come.

The bourgeoisie consciously and voluntarily 'surrendered' power to the
workers' government and only feigned some resistance to cover up their manoeuvre. In reality, they were simply temporising and preparing for the decis-

---

16   [Philipp Heinrich Scheidemann (1865–1939) was a Social Democrat and head of the Wei-
      mar government from February to June 1919. He resigned in protest against the terms of
      the Versailles Treaty but remained a member of the Reichstag until the Nazis seized power.
      Scheidemann's name was popularly associated with all of the problems and failures of the
      Weimar system.]

ive battle. Particular energy was thrown into these preparations by the intermediate groups of society, who, as we have already mentioned, turned out to be more consistent, principled, steadfast and self-sacrificing defenders of the bourgeois system than the bourgeoisie themselves. The bourgeoisie calculated that the workers' parties, once in power, would accomplish nothing in the way of real improvements for the working masses: they would compromise themselves and the very idea of a workers' government, and then a purely bourgeois government would return to power and be much stronger, for example, than the coalition government of Wirth[17] and others. In one respect the calculations of the bourgeoisie were justified. Once in power, the reformists actually lost no time in compromising themselves in the eyes of the working masses. The masses, however, did not draw quite the same conclusion from all the previous events as the bourgeoisie had expected. Very soon the same masses who had supported the Scheidemanns began to denounce their leaders for doing nothing and for not wanting to do anything to pressure the bourgeoisie and turn to real socialist construction. These masses quickly began to abandon the reformist camp and move on to the Communists.

Where workers' governments, under pressure from the proletarian masses, made a real attempt to begin regulating production and distribution and to impose serious limitations on the incomes of the propertied classes, they met with desperate resistance and open defiance and drove the bourgeoisie and landlords to defend their interests with arms in hand. As a result, the workers' government enabled the proletariat to make better preparations for the real conquest of power, to draw its more backward sections into the struggle, to unify them and unmask the reformists completely and irreversibly in practice. Thus, the workers' government not only failed to resolve the central problem of the entire class struggle in the twentieth century, that is, to bring labour's struggle against capital to an end, but only postponed any denouement of the conflict for several years.

It turned out that to realise the most important and urgent measures in the spirit of state capitalism is impossible not just for capitalism itself, in the form of bourgeois power, but also for a workers' government that has achieved power not as the conclusion of a victorious proletarian civil war but rather as the result of a conciliatory manoeuvre by the bourgeoisie. Even for serious measures in the spirit of state capitalism, the ground had to be cleared by class war; it

---

17   [Joseph Wirth (1879–1956) represented the Catholic Centre Party. He was briefly Chancellor in 1921–22 and held several important posts until the Nazis seized power.]

was imperative to bring down the bourgeoisie and all the so-called privileged classes from their key positions and compel them to submit to the proletariat. Insubordination and a spiteful, ironic attitude towards the workers' government were typical for the European bourgeoisie of the time. It was perfectly natural that the bourgeoisie should not take seriously a government whose historical mission was not to pressure the bourgeoisie but to defend it against a proletarian revolution.

If we recall that there was a similar attitude to proletarian power in Russia even immediately after the October Revolution, i.e., after the actual triumph of the proletarian dictatorship, how could we expect anything else from the still *undefeated* bourgeoisie of the West? Due to this attitude of the bourgeoisie towards the workers' government, which it regarded as the result of its own manoeuvre, not only was there no expropriation of large landed property, not only were the most important branches of industry not nationalised, not only could there be no tolerable regulation of economic life and price movements, but even ordinary taxes were not punctually paid by the propertied classes. On the one hand, this bourgeois resistance made it impossible even to begin surmounting the crisis that had produced the workers' government in its first phase. And on the other hand, this resistance terribly embittered the masses of the proletariat, who wanted real workers' power and not one made of margarine, who wanted seriously to implement their programme of state capitalism, and for whom the position of the workers' government must be one of waging a further offensive. In the midst of an increasingly heated atmosphere of class struggle, the masses moved rapidly to the left and more and more insistently demanded decisive measures from their leaders. But the reformists were incapable of such action and never intended seriously to wage a struggle against the bourgeoisie, at least as far as their leading elements were concerned. Among the reformists in general, including their lower ranks, three trends appeared. The first favoured sabotaging the struggle against capitalism and discouraging the workers from decisive actions. The second group was for implementation of all the urgent measures against the propertied classes and opposed to anarchy in production and distribution. Yet this group hoped to 'persuade' the propertied classes to yield without a fight. Finally there was the third group, who were openly disenchanted with reformism and took rapid steps to merge with the Communists. To the first two groups belonged almost all the trade-union and party bureaucracy of the reformists along with practically the entire reformist intelligentsia, while the overwhelming majority of the rank-and-file masses of the reformist parties and the trade unions gravitated towards the third group. This shift of the working masses to the left was especially evident at every successive re-election in the trade unions and the Soviet of workers' deputies.

I must note that simultaneously with the transfer of power to the workers' parties in all the countries of the West, Soviets of workers' deputies were created with great enthusiasm. At first the reformists had a stable majority in both the Soviets and the trade unions. At this stage it seemed that the Soviets were merely an extraordinary form used to keep the masses under reformist control and thus obedient to capital, since the growth of excitement and discontent made the usual measures inadequate. But the Soviet form contained within itself the cure for the proletariat's reformist disease. The reformist Soviets already carried the seed of future revolutionary Soviets. The dominance of reformists in the Soviets was neither eternal nor even particularly long-lived, even though they reigned here much longer than in Russia during the interval from February to October.

During this period there were two characteristic and significant dates. The first occurred in Berlin, the central city of the central country of Europe, when the compromisers with the bourgeoisie were defeated by Communists in elections to the Soviet. The second date is the victory of Communists at the next all-German congress of Soviets, in which delegates from Austria also always participated. Even earlier, the Communists had won a majority in the Soviets of workers and peasants deputies in Bulgaria. The reformists desperately resisted at each stage of their expulsion from the workers' movement. Yet when they had a majority in the Soviets, their workers' government was in fact accountable to the Soviets of workers' deputies. Although parliaments were not dissolved and the institution of parliamentarism itself was not abolished, they nevertheless eked out a miserable existence as some kind of rudimentary organs.

Once the reformists lost their majority in the Soviets, they suddenly remembered that the actual 'lawful' power in each country was not the Central Executive Committee of Soviets, and not congresses of the Soviets of workers' deputies, but parliaments elected by 'the whole people'. This enlightenment in the field of constitutional law came to the reformists with astronomical precision wherever they lost the majority in the Soviets. But their loss of the majority led to other consequences that prompted the counter-revolution to act more openly and to group itself around the parliaments.

Soviets with a communist majority resorted everywhere to more vigorous action. First of all, they deprived local authorities of the most important functions of local self-government except where the municipalities were also communist. In their rent policy, in local taxation, labour conscription etc., they began to put pressure on the bourgeoisie. All of this made the bourgeoisie turn to open struggle against the Soviets. The national centres of this struggle now naturally became the parliaments, protracting their miserable existence like flags sagging when the wind of class struggle did not carry them aloft. Now, the storm of revolution and counter-revolution lifted them again and made them serve as a unifying banner for all bourgeois, monarchist and reformist elements. I shall not dwell here on the specific reasons that led to open civil war in Central Europe. That war now began.

The events unfolded in the following sequence. The declaration of proletarian dictatorship in Prussia, Saxony and Central Germany led to armed victory of the workers in urban and factory centres. Here the vast majority of the proletariat, and hence the majority of the population in general, was on the side of the revolution. As might be expected, the majority of reformists fought on the side of the bourgeoisie and landlords against the working class. As for the rural areas of Germany, there the struggle took on a more protracted, fierce and bloody character. The Red Army of urban workers, together with guerrilla squads of farm labourers, had to take practically every landlord's estate and every castle by storm. In their homes, the Junkers maintained considerable quantities not only of rifles, machine guns and grenades, but on a number of estates even artillery pieces that had been hidden since 1918. The Junkers were mostly former officers, and they quickly organised military detachments from the counter-revolutionary peasantry, who played the role of infantry in their hands. Overall this was an enormous force, but its power, fortunately, was geographically scattered. Without any base of support in the cities, with no railway transport, and meeting with stubborn resistance from the railway workers at every turn, the Junkers were unable to organise a united front and were defeated piecemeal.

In the south of Germany events took a completely different path. The Bavarian counter-revolution managed to crush the workers' movement before help could arrive from the north. In addition, France supported Bavaria and helped to organise a proper front against the Northern German Republic. The struggle here became protracted. Defeated bourgeois elements fled to Bavaria from the north. As for Bavaria's frontier with Austria, there was another front here, because in Austria Soviet power was likewise proclaimed and Soviet Austria provided armed support to northern Germany. The positions taken by France, Poland, England and North America proved to be decisively important for the further course of events.

By mutual agreement, France and Poland simultaneously invaded northern Germany. But their attacks met with armed, domestic proletarian resistance in both countries. The mobilisation of reserves, the intervention against Germany, and the entry of French troops into the Ruhr basin led to an armed uprising in Paris and the northern departments. That uprising saved the revolution in Germany. It focused the forces of French imperialism on the domestic struggle at the very moment when the Red Army of North Germany was just being formed, when the Junker *Vendée* was still undefeated, and when help had not yet arrived from Soviet Russia. It is true that the domestic uprising was suppressed in France and failed to establish a proletarian dictatorship, but its world-historical significance lay in the fact that it prevented the French bourgeoisie from using regular military operations to occupy insurgent Northern Germany and thus to roll back the wheel of history. The French managed to occupy only part of the Ruhr basin with forces that were not involved in suppressing the unrest. But the occupation of the Ruhr met with desperate resistance from local partisan detachments of the workers' Red Guard. By the time the French government put down the insurrection, thus freeing its forces for a frontal assault on Germany, North Germany was in a position to send regular detachments of the Red Army to the Ruhr, forestalling any further French advance.

As for Poland, after some hesitation its ruling circles decided to attack North Germany in alliance with France and launched an offensive against Prussia. Romania simultaneously attacked Bulgaria, where Soviet power had been proclaimed somewhat earlier than in Germany and Austria. Immediately afterwards, Soviet Russia formally declared war on Poland and Romania, while the Red Army launched an offensive to the west with two separate columns moving at completely different speeds. In Poland, as in France, there was an insurrection of proletarians and farm labourers. The insurrection was suppressed in the cities – Warsaw, Lodz and the Dombrowa basin – but in a number of rural areas the insurgents held out until arrival of the Red Army. The uprising was particularly successful in Belarussia, Volhynia and Eastern Galicia, where the Red Army met with enthusiastic support from the broad masses of peasants. However, the Red Army's advance beyond the ethnographic frontier of Poland encountered pronounced resistance. To lend a hand to the German proletariat from this direction, in the shortest possible time, proved to be very difficult and impracticable.

On the Romanian front, things were quite different. The Romanian army was completely defeated on the Dniester and steadily retreated. Soviet power was proclaimed in Bessarabia. Budyonny's cavalry swept like an avalanche across the Romanian steppes, smashing the occupying Romanian army in the north of Bulgaria, and established contact between Soviet Bulgaria and Soviet Russia at the same time as the right wing of the south-eastern army broke through Eastern Galicia into Hungary, helping the insurrectionary Hungarian proletariat to victory and establishing the second Hungarian Soviet Republic.[18] This was a sol-

---

18   [The first Hungarian Soviet Republic lasted from March to August of 1919 under the lead-

emn moment in the proletarian struggle. The circle of proletarian dictatorship was now closed, describing an arc from Petrograd through Budapest to Vienna and on to Berlin and Königsberg.

Soviet power was also proclaimed by the Czech proletariat, who immediately began sending reinforcements to German workers on the Bavarian, French and Polish fronts. Yugoslavia was forced to withdraw behind its own frontiers following initial successes against Austria and Bulgaria, but at the same time a number of violent national uprisings began in Montenegro, Bosnia and Herzegovina, Croatia, and Macedonia. The civil war that had broken out in Italy ended with the victory of the Italian proletariat in the industrial north, while in central Italy and the south the Fascists prevailed. North of Rome, the Apennine Peninsula was cut in two by civil war. The Soviet of northern Italy was given extensive support by the country's fleet, including both the merchant marine and most of the navy. From the very outset the fleet sided with the proletariat, helping Italian workers to launch a peasant uprising in Sicily and southern Italy, i.e., to the rear of the Fascists. Breaking through the Romanian ring, the combined forces of Austria, Bulgaria and Yugoslavia advanced and eliminated the threat to the Italian Soviet Republic from the north-east. A direct link was established between Soviet Italy and the Soviet Balkans, thereby connecting Italy and Russia. This was enormously important for Soviet Italy, which was now being blockaded by the American and French fleets and was encountering serious difficulties with food supplies. With assistance from the north, that problem was now solved.

When Soviet Russia's Red Army approached the national frontiers of Poland, there was an outbreak of Polish chauvinism, which, given the weakness of the Polish proletariat, threatened the Red Army with an extremely difficult struggle on Polish territory. On the other hand, the struggle on the Franco-Bavarian front was also protracted, making it impossible to count on a rapid and successful conclusion. Believing that the results already achieved were sufficient for establishing a proletarian dictatorship in most of Europe, Soviet Russia, Soviet Germany and the other Soviet states offered peace to bourgeois France and Poland on the following terms: bourgeois Poland would remain within its purely ethnographic frontiers; the French would evacuate the Ruhr and Saar basins and withdraw their troops from the Bavarian front; Poland would allow free transit, with no customs duties, in economic relations between Germany and Russia. These proposals caused considerable dithering among the ruling

ership of Béla Kun, who was in constant contact with Lenin until Hungary surrendered to Romanian forces.]

circles of Poland, which was forced to reject the peace under pressure from France. The French bourgeoisie opposed peace, although support for it was also quite strong in France. Finally, having financed the Franco-Polish-Romanian alliance, America was categorically opposed to peace and intent on completely destroying the proletarian revolution in Europe.

Once the peace proposals of the Soviet states were rejected, the war resumed with a vengeance. After concentrating sufficient forces, Soviet Russia launched an offensive on Polish territory and soon the Red Army entered Warsaw.

From the other direction, Soviet Germany passed from defence to the offensive on its Polish frontier and occupied a section of Poznan. At the same time, a successful assault began on the Bavarian front. Seeing that its eastern ally's defeat was completely inevitable, and taking into account its refusal to continue the war, the bourgeois government of France agreed to peace on the original terms. But these terms were no longer acceptable to the alliance of Soviet states. The war continued; bourgeois Poland ceased to exist; the Polish proletariat assumed power on the territory of ethnographic Poland; and a direct connection was established between Soviet Russia and Soviet Germany. This allowed Russia's Red Army to assist Soviet Germany on the French front, and the French armies were driven from the Ruhr and Saar basin. By this time the United States of America began to send its forces to the French front, but this help was already too late. The French bourgeoisie thought they might still defend their own frontiers, but they had no chance to wage an offensive struggle against all of Soviet Europe. Accordingly, they withstood the growing pressure of American capital and agreed to new peace proposals based on the *status quo* resulting from the war.

Thus ended the great period of civil war in Europe. The Labour government of England took no direct part in the war, despite the fact that its fingers itched to join with bourgeois France against the revolutionary European proletariat. The sympathy of English workers for the European proletarian revolution was too strong, and the leaders of England's so-called Labour Party could not risk an adventure against the will of a majority of their own proletariat.

The military alliance of the Soviet states of Europe naturally grew into an economic alliance. The Federation of Soviet Republics of Europe undertook to organise a planned economy throughout its territory. Not being in a position to introduce socialist organisation of the economy immediately, the victorious proletariat implemented full nationalisation only in the most important branches of industry and in large and medium-sized farms; for a time it also had to preserve certain capitalist methods in its own state economy, especially where questions of economic calculation were concerned. It did not consider it necessary even to abolish private commerce until all the preconditions were in place for socialist distribution of products. It did, however, bring both its own state economy and the non-socialised sector – above all the small-scale peasant economy – under conscious regulation, using both socialist methods and the methods of large-scale capital. Practice very quickly established two basic types of state economy of the proletariat: a higher type in the industrial countries such as Germany, Czechoslovakia and Austria, and the agrarian type in more backward countries like Russia, Poland, Bulgaria, etc. Neither type of transitional economic system was socialist in the full sense of the word, but they had already passed beyond state capitalism, which turned out to be an unattainable ideal for capitalism and was already a bygone stage for the epoch of proletarian revolution.

The new Soviet Europe turned a fresh page in the area of economic development. Germany's industrial technique was united with Russian agriculture, and on the territory of Europe a new organism rapidly began to develop and flourish, revealing enormous opportunities and a mighty breakthrough for development of the productive forces. Soviet Russia, having previously outstripped Europe in political terms, now modestly took its place as an economically backward country, following behind the advanced industrial countries of the proletarian dictatorship.

E.A. Preobrazhensky,
От непа к социализму (Взгляд в будущее России и Европы),
Moscow, 'Moskovskii Rabochii', 1922, pp. 3–138.

Letter from E.A. Preobrazhensky to L.D. Trotsky and Nataliya Ivanovna [Sedova] (Early March 1928)

Dear Lev Davidovich and Nataliya Ivanovna,

I received the postcard from you L.D. that you sent while in transit, but I did not respond to it because I was waiting for an 'address'. Now I know the address and can actually write to you.

First of all, you must admit that while all of the characters that I used to write looked the same, I have now made some progress with my *handwriting*.[1] And how could I write in my customary way to Radek – he cannot even read clear handwriting – and deliberately add the problem of reading my letters to his inevitable troubles on Freedom Street (his address is: 49 Freedom Street, Tobolsk)? I also want to spare your eyes so that in future letters you will not be making the same jokes. It must also be miserable for the reader from the GPU.[2] Finally, if you use the word 'revolution' in a letter, in a report to the Executive Committee of the Comintern they will quote the letter as saying 'counter-revolution', and 10 years later they will justify themselves by saying that all the characters in the letter looked the same.

That is why I have resolved to do better.

Ad vocem international conditions.

An Anglo-American conflict is maturing very rapidly. In the foreign press nowadays (here I get to read mainly 'Berliner Tageblatt') they treat the things they write on this theme as if they were routine and obvious, whereas a year and half ago they would have caused a sensation. I see the future course of events this way. American capital will get through its current industrial depression without resorting to war. Its rivals, England first and foremost, *still have something to lose*. South America and Canada can still be pressured, increasing the absorptive capacity of the market by extending the term of loans and increasing the export of capital (which, on the part of such a highly industrialised country, is more than half the export of commodities). This depression has shown that American capitalism now responds even to a mild over-

---

1 [Preobrazhensky's handwriting was minuscule in size and notoriously difficult to read.]

2 [State Political Directorate. The official name of this secret police organisation after 1923 was 'Joint State Political Directorate under the Council of People's Commissars of the USSR', known by the acronym OGPU.]

production toothache by raising its fists, cursing and threatening others. That is as far as it has gone. But we can imagine what this expansionist gentleman might do when facing a real crisis! And that is what is beginning. America has become deeply involved in the world economy, and each day it gets in more deeply. And now the time is coming when the rate of industrial accumulation in America will markedly surpass accumulation elsewhere [...][3] and their personal consumption, which are the co-proportional factors of American *productive accumulation*. A rupture of tempos is inevitable here; it comes from the gap between overall American development and the development (and sometimes the standing still) of other countries. While America, in its rush ahead, relied mainly on growth of the domestic market – and the [American] farmer, in turn, profited from Europe's difficulties with raw material – or on the wartime and post-war economic feebleness of Europe, this difference of tempos could not lead to a general worldwide crisis. But now this 'uneven development of capitalism' is creating an upheaval in America that is directly proportional to its previous breath-taking successes and technical achievements. And that is what will put war on the agenda, because it will have to resolve the disproportion by physically removing competitors and, most importantly, by inevitably creating an enormous military market for heavy industry. Construction of new warships, and an insanely wasteful policy of building up a merchant marine larger than England's, is significantly allaying the crisis.

But when will all this happen?

I think it will be in three-four years. And if they should tear themselves apart before marching against us, then we, i.e., the USSR, are saved because then the cunning of history, or more accurately the constructive folly of capitalism, will override all of our stupidities.[4]

Some very important facts are occurring in our domestic economic policy. Did you read the editorial in 'Pravda' on 15 February? If you have not read it, then stop reading this letter and find the editorial because I don't want to chat and spend time with people who are hopelessly behind the times.

The editorial of 15 February, which, judging by the style, was written by Stalin, is a proclamation of *our* course in the countryside, and it was based on the quotation from Lenin that we use as the basis for the agrarian part of our platform.

---

3 [Part of the text is illegible.]
4 At least the publicly funded stupidity, because it is outweighed by the 'funding' of capitalism's constructive folly.

In 'Ekonomicheskaya zhizn'' Krumin, who always grows wiser upon command from the Politburo, writes in italics that 'the most important cause of the difficulties with grain procurements is that we did not draw conclusions in good time from the obvious fact of the growth in recent years of rural economic life as a whole'. Concerning the village, he writes that 'it is growing fat with the accumulation of commodities and money'. 'We did not sufficiently take into account that grain procurements, in our soviet conditions, are not just a commercial-technical but also a crucially important social-economic task' ... and so on.[5]

To be sure, you [Krumin] did not consider the matter in 'good time', but we studied it and shouted about it, and in return you, who have objectively protected this village 'fat', imprisoned and exiled us!

But I am interested in facts here, not in the distribution of awards for foresight.

The about-turn by the CC is a *new* political fact of enormous importance. It would be a mistake to evaluate the situation by thinking that Kobe[6] could not remove Syrtsov[7] and do further reshuffles, and that for that reason he is getting at Syrtsov and A. Smirnov[8] through barns full of peasant grain, i.e., that he has *paid* dearly in political terms for an organisational measure and the opportunity to complete his organisational plan. Even if something of the sort did occur on the surface, it would not be correct to make this the basis for a political analysis. Here is how it looks to me.

1) We predicted the inevitability of an onslaught from the right. That was an algebraic foresight (although we often spoke concretely about the kulak). History has now provided the arithmetic. The pressure originated economically, coming from the most important and strongest detachment of our bourgeoisie, the kulaks, who have undertaken a boycott of the state economy and dug in to

---

5   The taxman Lifshits demonstrates the inadequacy of the single tax (how they crucified me for 'plundering the countryside') and is preparing the ground for significantly increasing it. Finally!

6   [A pseudonym used by Stalin, adopted from the novel *The Patricide* by Alexander Kazbegi.]

7   [Sergei Ivanovich Syrtsov (1893–1937) was a close associate of Stalin from 1922 onwards. He headed the Urals party organisation at the time of the grain crisis of 1927–28 and supported Stalin's use of the 'Siberian method' of grain collection and later the policy of forced collectivisation. By 1930 he plotted to remove Stalin due to the violence of the collectivisation campaign and was expelled from the party. He was executed in September 1937.]

8   [Aleksandr Petrovich Smirnov (1877–1938) was Deputy People's Commissar for Agriculture in the Russian Republic from 1923–28, and from 1928–30 Deputy Chairman of the RSFSR Council of People's Commissars. He was expelled from the party at the end of 1934, arrested in 1937 and executed in 1938.]

defend the free circulation of commodities. The result is a shortfall of 120 million in grain, problems in supplying the cities, disruption of the export plan, etc.

2) Foreseeing this, we proposed to begin the fight earlier, and had it begun two years earlier it would have been far less costly for us, because with heavier taxation of the countryside for the sake of industrial accumulation, implemented *at that time*, there would have been fewer problems with the commodity turnover and less need to turn to non-economic pressure to achieve *exactly the same results*. [...][9] less violation of free trade and the established practice of NEP.

3) A great deal of time has been lost, but we still have to solve the fundamental problem of putting out a fire on our roof. There are two possible ways out, *both of them realistic* but with different social outcomes. Sokol'nikov's[10] way: a) sticking with market methods, b) the Dreyfus concessions and, in general terms, partial disarmament of the foreign trade monopoly, c) reduced spending on heavy industry, and d) a general line not of struggle against the kulak but instead working together on the basis of concessions to him in economic policy. (This would inevitably bring a sharp rise in grain procurement prices.)

The opposition's way: 1) struggle against the kulak; 2) non-economic measures if necessary (a compulsory grain loan of 100 million poods); 3) the integrity of the [foreign trade] monopoly; 4) increased capital investment in industry, especially heavy industry; 5) increased taxation of the part of the village that is 'growing fat'; 6) a focus on tillage by poor and small farms rather than by the kulak.

4) The Central Committee is choosing the second way, the way of the opposition, although it is committing *a number of secondary stupidities*. For instance, a compulsory loan would be better and create less panic in the soul of *every* petty bourgeois than the current charges against kulaks under Article 107 for speculation. Implementing a loan, the government would declare: the state is short of 100 million poods of grain, and you wealthy peasants have that grain. *This year* we are taking it from you. That would involve no violation of NEP, because *every* bourgeois government has the right to requisition in the social interest.

---

9   [Part of the text is illegible. Trotsky and Preobrazhensky both believed that NEP was being abandoned prematurely by Stalin.]

10   [Grigory Yakovlevich Sokol'nikov frequently advocated capital imports into the USSR by leasing resource assets as concessions for foreign exploitation. He was Commissar of Finance from 1922–26 and principally responsibility to stabilising the currency. For Sokol'nikov's role in the Soviet economic debates of the 1920s, see Day 1973.]

But now *any* grain accumulation is called into question, along with freedom to trade and any economic planning by the petty bourgeois. This will affect the acreage sown in the village, if not in the form of a reduction of spring ploughing then in limiting its possible expansion. But, despite these follies (for instance, inspecting peasants' barns under the pretext of eliminating weevils and vermin), *the general course adopted is correct*, it is our course.

5) Such a course in the countryside must be complemented by reinforced industrialisation and serious attention to improving the daily life of workers. The kulaks will fight back in the Ural provinces; for example, they are already selling off cattle and *have no interest in spring ploughing* or else they are curtailing it. This struggle demands a mobilisation of forces on the other side. The kulak, with his pressure, is trying to impose a change in the line of policy, he has already lost Narkomzem. The workers must gain something. *This is inevitable.* Consequently, I think that we (ideally you personally) should send a brief letter to the editors of *Pravda* and declare that we consider the course adopted in agrarian policy to be fundamentally *correct*.

An objection might be that if we declare the course to be basically correct, then we must also say what is *incorrect*. We cannot just send compliments to the CC, all the more so since we *still have no idea of how this music will end*.

Nevertheless, we must make such a statement. It seems to me that the authors of the about-turn have not thought through for themselves just *what* they have done.

I have several other thoughts and suggestions concerning political questions, but I will write about them next time. When I can see that our 'superintendents' are not mocking our correspondence and that letters reach their addressees.

I am generally less interested in politics nowadays and am willing to send it to hell for a year or so. I have now begun to write a major work of *Essays on the Theory of Capitalist Society*. I have to re-read a lot of material, particularly *on the history of capitalism*, including even a lot of fiction, i.e., artistic portrayals of certain capitalist social processes and relations. For now, *this* interests me more than Coolidge, grain procurements and Van'ka Kubik (that is how Bezhetsk workers in the Bryansk organisation referred to Kubyak, who was then a modest, hard-working fellow).[11] Speaking generally, politics has always interfered with my theoretical work. That was the case before the revolution, under Lenin following the revolution, and after Lenin's death. Now, I have resolved to make

---

11   [Nikolai Afanasyevich Kubyak was a secretary of the Central Committee during 1927–28 and Commissar of Agriculture for the RSFSR in 1928–29, the period of 'preparation for all-round collectivisation'. He was executed in 1937. 'Van'ka Kubik' means 'Van'ka the brick'.]

full use of my forced 'removal from political affairs' and seek revenge on the scientific front. Nowadays I have had enough of writing brochures! Now I am only writing scientific and substantial work, and only after lengthy tractor-ploughing through scientific material and *primary sources*. (I am now reading what Tacitus had to say about the Germans.) By the way, I have a hypothesis concerning the origin of logic, which, if proven, would produce a revolution in the theory of knowledge. I say that in all modesty, but it requires major exper-imental work with dogs and mainly on monkeys, as well as observations of children. Prior to my exile from Moscow, I already agreed in principle to organ-ise experiments at the Brain Institute of the Communist Academy, but I did not manage to finalise the programme. Professors have been interested in this theme, but the observations must not be made using their methods. I am now busy with the theoretical (not the experimental) aspect of *this topic*. There is also some work to be done (two printer's sheets)[12] on the first part of the second volume of *The New Economics*, although I have already grown somewhat tired of economics and am now interested in sociology.

This is how I am living here. I am renting a small but bright and neat room. I eat at the Tserabkop[13] canteen for 60 kopeks a day. In material terms, everything is quite fine. I am working as an economist for the provincial planning agency (150 roubles per month) alongside of and on equal terms with Timofeev, a former member of the central committee of the right SRs who was convicted along with Gots.[14] My planning work takes little time. Then I translate the second volume of *The Renegade Kautsky* (from the latest two-volume work). That takes two hours a day, and in terms of content (not style) the translation is more interesting than 'your' Marx.[15] (I will write more to you about Kaut-sky.) The rest of the time I spend on my former assignment, i.e., my theoretical work. I am reading all the newspapers and have subscribed to *The Economist*. I should stop reading newspapers because that nonsense takes up an hour of my day, but the habit has become second nature. They say that the hunting here is *great*. In a month or so the spring [hunt] will begin. I will send you a complete account of my results. Concerning the son of Cambyses. You are a bit confused. My Eva-Diana had four pups. Two went to the owner of Cambyses, I gave you

12 [One printer's sheet (*печатный лист*) was the equivalent of 16 published pages or approximately 24 typewritten sheets.]
13 [Tserabkop refers to the Central Workers' Cooperative.]
14 [Avram Rafailovich Gots (1882–1940), a leader of the SR faction in the Petrograd Soviet in 1917, spent 1925–27 in prison, followed by exile.]
15 [While in Alma Ata, Trotsky earned a modest income by translating work by Marx for Ryazanov and the Marx-Engels Institute, and by proofreading and editing some of the volumes of works by Marx and Engels that were being prepared for publication.]

the black female, and I kept the *male* myself. You have confused the male with the female, and even after the rough and tumble that we have been through such a *'petite différence'* should be obvious. I saw the keeper of your Alka or Alma before leaving. Her senses are sharp, but she is *very sick* with some kind of worm infection. That is why there was no point in sending her to you. I will take my black male with me to Ural'sk if he lives. There are vast numbers of snipes[16] here. (The district, incidentally, is quite malarial).

Your temperature very much distresses me. There is no one there to turn to if you have complications. I am eagerly anticipating spring. They say it is wonderful here. I embrace you warmly and shake your hand.

E.P. [Trotsky Archive Document 1182]

_____

16   [Preobrazhensky was an avid hunter. A Snipe is a wading bird found in marshes and wet meadows.]

Theses by E.A. Preobrazhensky on 'The Left Course in the Countryside and Its Prospects' (April 1928)

I) The current economic crisis in the USSR is neither a conjunctural nor merely an economic crisis: this is a prolonged social crisis. It is rooted in two facts: first of all, the lag of industry behind agriculture, i.e., the delay in the country's industrialisation; and secondly, the intensifying contradiction, which is inherent in our system, between the state economy and capitalist development, which until now has been expressed primarily in the growing concentration of raw materials and grain stocks in the hands of the kulaks. Up to a certain point, the growth of raw material and grain procurements, with the existing prices for industrial commodities (i.e., with restoration and reconstruction prices) could depend upon the kulaks' increasing supply, the growth of commodity production by middle-peasant farms, and the strengthening of weak farms. This has, in fact, been the basis of the Central Committee's centrist agrarian policy of recent years. But once the kulaks completed their own 'reconstruction' process, they entered into implacable contradiction with the entire system of the state economy to the extent that the latter is forced to develop with the existing prices. *The kulak economy, at a certain level of its development, is beginning to boycott the state economy, to boycott state procurements, to accumulate stocks in kind and to lead an isolated economic existence, so that the portion of state land that has been seized by prosperous and kulak elements, along with its output, is becoming a weapon for disrupting state pricing policy.* This kulak offensive against the state economy, first seen in 1925, became perfectly obvious in 1926. The opposition issued a timely warning to the party about the approaching threat, and especially about the insufficient taxation of upper strata in the village. Its warnings were not heeded.

II) In 1927 and early 1928 the kulaks continued their offensive. This pressure on the Soviet authority, coming from the principal counter-revolutionary force in the country, is taking the state by surprise: with a shortage of grain reserves, an inadequate fund of industrial commodities destined for the village, the currency in a state of latent inflation, limited credit resources and without grain reserves. A boycott of grain procurements by the wealthy kulak strata is not only disrupting the plan for grain exports and impeding procurement of certain kinds of materials (flax), but also directly threatening a collapse of the whole system of state supply for the cities, seeds for poor peasants, and grain for parts of the country that produce raw materials. There was no other way out of the situation other than the one the CC had to adopt, i.e., to coerce those who are on strike in the grain market and to use force to constrain free commodity circulation between the city and the part of the village that is economically attacking Soviet power. I am not aware of what the right-wing groups in the party have suggested in connection with the supply crisis, but one thing is clear from the general situation: they have not been able to suggest anything articulate, anything that would provide a speedy way out of the situation. This adoption by the party of a state-organised struggle against capitalist elements in the village is a new fact of enormous importance, and it is fraught with great consequences. This is a new fact in terms of the whole economic and general policy of recent years, and thus a new fact in terms of relations over the past several years between the opposition and the party majority.

III) The pressure on the kulak in recent months has made it possible for the state forcefully to include kulak grain in total state resources, but the next question is: Who, what strata in the village, what sources will cover the annually increasing state demand for raw materials and grain in the future?

Only two kinds of policy are now possible for the party and the state: a) a policy of gradually surmounting the crisis, calculated over a number of years and based upon a struggle against the kulaks and an increase of commodity production on the farms of middle and poor peasants, i.e., development of the course adopted in January–February; and b) a policy of loudly and decisively repudiating any future recourse to all that has been done from January to March, along with any left course in general, and an attempt to rely, in terms of developing the raw material base and export resources, on the growing kulak strata in the village, thus increasing commodity production without spending state resources for that purpose. Each of these two courses of action has its own logic of development, its own prospects, and its own Achilles heel.

IV) The prospect of a left course in the countryside is based upon replacing growth in the supply of grain and materials from kulaks with supply from middle and poor peasants, while simultaneously increasing production by small farms through cooperative production among the poor, and finally by taking state farms seriously. The change in the general policy of Narkomzem, already outlined in precisely this direction, is no left-wing declamation but rather the most immediate and imperative necessity for moving along the first path. This about-turn will objectively turn out to be a leftist gesture only in the event that there is a general halt to the whole new course, which is entirely possible, of course, with an unfavourable balance of forces and crude mistakes and inconsistency on the part of the leadership. The Achilles heel of this first path is the unfortunate fact that growth of production by small farms, by the poor and in part by the middle peasants, will go mainly to increasing the level of natural consumption by these strata and 'primitive' natural-economic accumulation, and only in much smaller measure to increasing the market supply of grain and materials. A rough example: the kulaks fail to sow a million desyatins, and this is compensated by a million desyatins sown by poor and middle peasants, which will not mean restoration of the former volume of commodity surpluses but instead a significant curtailment. In that case – not just in the event of a poor harvest but even with an average one – to restore equilibrium in supplying the cities with materials and food may require returning time and again to the January–March measures, which will become economically 'tiresome' to the strong middle peasant and may cause a more dangerous reduction of sowing among this stratum, with whom it is especially dangerous to quarrel precisely during the first year of implementing the new course in the countryside. This is the second Achilles heel.

v) The prospects of the right course in agrarian policy are the following: immediate artificial abortion of the left course; reconciliation with those who are striking in the grain market on the basis of making concessions to them; a rise in grain prices; removal of all restrictions on their leasing of land from poor peasants; adjustment of the commodity supply in the village to the demand from those strata who are capable of fighting for their interests with a grain and raw material strike; and, given the limitations of our own domestic commodity fund, *import of commodities for the countryside from abroad with the probability of a breach in the monopoly of foreign trade.* This policy would inevitably demand increased pressure on the working class in the cities (a rise of bread prices, higher output norms, etc.) while in the village it would be connected with an increase of agrarian over-population and a slowing of the country's rate of industrialisation. The natural culmination of this course would be rehabilitation of the kulak and acknowledgement that he is a helpful worker in the Soviet economic system. The fifth Achilles heel of this right-wing policy is the fact that the January–March measures are already an accomplished fact; they have already terrorised the kulaks, and it will be no easy matter to reassure them and restore their confidence. To do so would require paying an unheard-of price – the price of such a sharp turn to the right that even the furthest right of our rightists, who are accustomed to slowly creeping into the position of a rightist NEP, will not dare to undertake. Half-measures here will accomplish nothing. Moreover, there are times when abortion is altogether impossible without endangering life.

vi) Which of these courses will ultimately be adopted?

For the moment, there is no categorical answer to that question, although one thing is clear: there are no other courses, and a choice cannot long be postponed. During the current year, and even within the next few months (with the spring and autumn sowing), the question will be decided. In the event of a victory for the rightist course, which in the wake of the January–March measures can only be a decisively right-wing course, we shall have the following general scheme for the party's entire policy over the ten-year period:

1) From 1917 to 1923, a proletarian-Leninist agrarian policy;

2) From 1923 to 1928 (i.e. following defeat of the opposition in 1923), a centrist policy based upon resurgence of all the commodity-producing strata in the countryside (apart from the poor peasants);

3) From 1928 onwards, the rightist policy relying increasingly upon an upsurge of the kulak and well-to-do strata in the village first and foremost.

In the event of a victory for the left course, we shall have a different scheme in which the first two stages are the same as before, but in 1928 a return to the Leninist agrarian policy begins, relying upon the rise of poor and middle peasants in the countryside and struggle against capitalist tendencies. The social-economic basis for the about-turn will then be the growth of domestic class contradictions and the economic offensive by the kulak, which hones the currently rusting tool of proletarian dictatorship and forcibly interrupts the process of drift. The external cause is growth of class contradictions in the capitalist countries and of the pre-war contradictions between them.

VII) A lasting victory for the left course requires the following:

1) Replacement of materials and grain coming from the kulaks with those coming from middle and poor peasants makes it particularly urgent to accelerate the pace of industrialisation, because grain can be taken from these strata *only by using economic methods*, only through commodity exchange aiming also, in economic ways, for a reduction in the rural consumption of agricultural products through an increase in demand for industrially produced consumer items. And that requires a certain rate of growth in all industrial production under penalty of a rupture of all the mandatory proportions of exchange between city and village. The time for a lukewarm, centrist attitude to the problems of industrialisation has come to an end.

2) An anti-kulak policy on the part of Soviet authorities, coupled with pressure on the Nepmen, cannot but aggravate our relations with the whole of world capitalism, reducing our already paltry chances of receiving foreign loans for industrialisation. (The sole exception might be America if, as the result of a growing crisis of sales and the search for a way out, it might prefer an agreement with the USSR involving capital investment here rather than financing a European war against us.) The relationship between us and world capitalism is also becoming more strained due to the intensifying struggle of imperialist countries in the world market and reinforcement of the workers' class struggle

against combined capital. In such conditions, a left policy within the USSR must inevitably be organically combined with a left policy in the Comintern, among other things guaranteeing a greater defensive capacity of the USSR in the event of war.

3) It is impossible to quarrel with one part of the countryside without simultaneously reinforcing our positions in the cities. Currently the attitude of the average worker – under the influence of a near total halt in wage increases, rising living costs, queues, higher output norms and universal bureaucratic pressure – is not important. Thus far the left course in the village means no improvements for the worker, because up to now it has simply saved workers from an inevitable deterioration of their food situation under the old course. The extraordinary measures against the kulak have merely managed somehow to maintain the old level of supply in the cities, which was previously achieved by commodity exchange without applying Article 107. But it is a known fact that the masses do not say thank you for such things. So long as the average worker does not really feel any benefit from the left course in the village, it can always be thwarted by a regrouping of forces on the part of its opponents and their supporters among the leading cadres of the party. In addition to any economic improvements in the position of the working class that the state can manage, we need something that is far more achievable, namely, speedy improvement in the legal status of workers, especially at the bottom, in the factory, which means implementation of a regime of workers' democracy and exposing the worst elements of the apparatus and the worst practices of management and trade-union leadership to real rank-and-file worker's criticism.

4) It goes without saying that logical implementation of the left course makes nonsense of all acts of repression against the opposition, which can only be associated with the first movement described above, i.e., with the right-wing option. We must not forget, however, that the people who are currently directing the new course are not implementing THEIR OWN POLICY,[1] and for that reason they cannot be expected to be consistent, particularly with regard to this question.

VIII) Following the party's transition to a left course in the village and in Comintern policy, what must the opposition do? *If, in the event of an unfavourable outcome for the spring sowing campaign, the majority of the CC does not repudiate the line they have taken, I consider a collective declaration by the opposition, in support of the party majority, to be absolutely imperative and overdue, regardless of any follies and abominations that are being committed and will*

---

1   [Preobrazhensky means the 'new course' is in fact the opposition's policy.]

be committed against us. The declaration must include an analysis of the new situation that has been created due to the aggravation of class contradictions within the country and abroad, an appraisal of the about-turn in the policy of the CC, and *an announcement that we take responsibility for the left course in the countryside and for its logical conclusion in the Comintern and will help to reinforce it.* It seems to me that the document should make no request for our re-admission to the party nor any reference to eliminating repression. Zinoviev and Kamenev declined to defend their views, pretending that some sort of new situation has emerged, when all that has happened was condemnation of us at the Congress, that is, change FOR THE WORSE. We would now be making the opposite mistake if we start from the view that there has been no change FOR THE BETTER, when *a very important (and possibly decisive) change has actually occurred due to the intensified class struggle within the country, a possibility that we ourselves frequently predicted.* This intensification impedes a latent 'Thermidorian' type of change in the balance of forces within the country to the benefit of capitalist elements. *The leaders of the opposition have waged a struggle for return of the party majority to a Leninist policy. They must now do everything within their power to facilitate return to the party by the opposition's supporters at a time when the possibility is emerging for a gradual correction of the party's line in a different direction. Should it be disrupted, let there be no guilt whatever on our part.*

In practical terms, I suggest that our comrades who signed the latest statement to the XV Congress,[2] which Comrade Smilga announced, appeal to the CC with a request that they be permitted to come together to work out a statement such as I have proposed (provided, of course, that we are in agreement on this matter) and publish it. Politically, it would be most appropriate for Lev Davidovich to contact the CC, geographically – for comrade Rakovsky or me.

I am circulating my proposal for discussion by the comrades who signed our last address to the Congress, and I request that they advise me of their opinion either in writing or by telegram.

E.A. Preobrazhensky
[Trotsky Archive Document T 1262]

---

2 See 'Déclaration au XV Congress du P.C de l'URSS concernant la demande d'exclusion de l'opposition (1)', in *Cahiers Leon Trotsky: Numero Special, Les Trotskystes en Union Soviétique*, No. 6 (Paris: Institute Leon Trotsky, 1980), pp. 71–3. The document was signed by I.T. Smilga, Kh.G. Rakovsky, N.I. Muralov and K.B. Radek.

Excerpts from Correspondence by
E.A. Preobrazhensky (Probably Late May 1928)

1   [Preobrazhensky] to [Ishchenko]

'Excerpts from Preobrazhensky's letter to comrade A.G. Ishchenko'[1]
The harmful attitudes that you note among some members of the opposition really do exist .... We often do not realise that we have young oppositionists who, in the numbing party circumstances ... of recent years, have only begun to experience real party life in the opposition. It must seem to them that any end of the opposition means the end of all political life for them .... Politics always involves risk. We devised our tactics in 1927 while struggling against the worst variant of events .... The risk we faced then was *pessimism* .... We so compromised the rightist policy that we cut off any retreat for the CC in a rightist direction .... At that time we had one working hypothesis for policy, and now we need a different one – we need to take a risk in the direction of *optimism* .... If Thermidor 'has not occurred', we must rejoice in that fact and move towards rapprochement with the party, otherwise we face conversion into a small sect of 'true Leninists' resembling the true sects of the past.

[Trotsky Archive Document T1497]

25 May 1928
[K. Radek] to [Preobrazhensky?]
The central question is: Can we take the about-turn to be decisive, you do not think so yourself, and I do not think it is decisive. As to why – I wrote about that in my first letter. We must, therefore, support this about-turn in order to make it decisive, but we *cannot, as you are proposing, take responsibility for it.* How can we take responsibility for something upon which we do not have the

---

1   [A.G. Ishchenko (1895–1937) was formerly leader of the Transport Workers' Union. In April 1928 he wrote to Trotsky concerning the 'appearance of a turn to the left': 'Such a situation makes it possible for us to take a more concrete course to rejoin the party and not to defer this return for an indefinite time. Keeping the opposition outside the party for a prolonged period would be very dangerous for the dictatorship of the proletariat', See Broué 2007, pp. 137–60.]

slightest influence? Such a declaration would be ridiculous: we are sitting in exile and we take responsibility!

... The declaration must end by pointing out that, given a development and continuation of the left course in the party, our exile and expulsion would be some kind of monstrous nonsense, weakening even the current leadership of the party, or that *they can count on our total support for implementing the goals that they are proclaiming* ....

[Trotsky Archive Document T1521]

Letter from E.A. Preobrazhensky to L.D. Trotsky (Spring 1928)

Dear Lev Davidovich!

I have received from you a total of three sealed letters (and two opened ones) and have responded to all of the sealed ones. My first two responses were quite detailed, probably about a quarter of a printer's sheet each,[1] and I included quite a bit about political themes. Since you still have not received them, and I neither enjoy nor have any time to write for the entertainment of GPU agents, this letter, in response to your last one (i.e., the one based on your letter to Iv. Nikit.,)[2] is being written without any real appetite and will be brief.

Your information that I am unhappy in Ural'sk and in a 'melancholy' mood is not true. I merely wrote to Polina[3] a couple of times about the local boredom. Generally speaking, if I may say so, I take no notice of Ural'sk and am just ignoring it. I have no time to be bored. I allocate my time strictly and am working like a machine. My room is my workshop, and I even find it quite lovely (even though it is in Ural'sk) as I do any room for literary work. This one suits me just fine. I shall complete my work on the sociology of capitalist society within a year or so, and it will take no more than a year to exhaust all of the literature that can be sent here, at which point I'll need to get sources that cannot be sent (things Ryazanov[4] has and unique works) by travelling to the Institute for a couple of months. Since I'll be sitting here for at least a year, I have brought my gramophone, ordered the dog, and so on.

I already wrote to you that with permission from the CC I spent 10 days in Moscow when Polina was due. She gave birth an hour before the caesarean section that the professor had scheduled. In Moscow I collected all sorts of information and impressions. One of my impressions is that there has been a dramatic increase of the number of women in our capital, women whose

---

1 [One printer's sheet (*печатный лист*) was the equivalent of 16 published pages or approximately 24 typewritten sheets.]

2 [Apparently a reference to Ivan Nikitich Smirnov, an oppositionist since 1923 who was condemned to exile in December 1927 and denounced 'Trotskyism' in October 1929.]

3 [Preobrazhensky's wife: Polina Semenovna Vinogradskaya.]

4 [David Borisovich Ryazanov (Gol'dendakh) (1870–1938) was founder and Director of the Marx-Engels Institute, the world's major repository for documents on the history of socialism and communism.]

husbands have been exiled, scores of whom visited Polina, me and the baby because they were interested in seeing the three of us together. I got the impression that Moscow has become 'She town'.

As for your suggestion that I move to Verny,[5] it is true that we are both living in the same Kazakh Republic, but that suggestion is just too utopian to consider. I would certainly welcome the prospect in every way, especially because the newspapers are 10 days late getting to Verny. I would read fewer newspapers and more of the books that I need for my main work. But the disadvantage is that it would be more difficult for me to get books, which would be a serious drawback for my factory since it cannot function without timely delivery of such raw material.

By the way, I already wrote to you that my interest in politics has seriously waned and my interest in 'pure' science has correspondingly grown. Science is what endures. Politics drains away with all the debris, like water in the spring. And when you reach a mature age, you want to give something lasting to society. So now I want to do a decent job for the reader, especially since no Marxist has ventured into the subject and I am the first to take the initiative.

I shall soon send you a long letter with my assessment of the situation. You can tell me by telegram when you receive it.

In Moscow I was always besieged by visitors on the one hand and by the crying baby on the other. The crying went on day and night (we've had only a single room since my departure from house number 1)[6] and it so scrambled my mind that I have found some relief in my Ural'sk room. You can imagine what this does to poor Polina, who was never involved in this business. And here I am selfishly enjoying the tranquillity!

As far as the hunting is concerned, it is also being delayed by the late spring. In the office of the provincial Executive Committee an announcement has been prepared saying hunting will be allowed two weeks after the first [...][7] flight, but there has been no flight yet and we are waiting day by day. The weather is good, we had sun last week, and the snow is melting quickly. I have everything ready, even my boots are greased. We have to stand in the water all the time here because the best flights arrive in the so-called 'straits'. Hunting is permitted only for drakes and geese, but there is almost nothing else here in any case.

---

5   [That is, Alma-Ata, where Trotsky was in exile.]
6   [The reference apparently is to the First House of Soviets, the former National Hotel, where Preobrazhensky resided before he was politically 'disgraced'.]
7   [A word here is illegible. The sentence appears to refer to the first major inflight of migratory birds.]

I am very glad to hear of your health. But it is very sad to hear that things are so bad for Natalya Ivanovna! Maybe it would be better for her to leave Alma-Ata, since the deterioration is probably somehow connected with the change of location?

It is good that you have finally sat down to write the memoirs. I suggested to Rakovsky that he do the same, but you also supported the idea, with the result, as his letter shows, that he is doing so.

Well, that is all for now. Warm regards to Nataliya Ivanovna and Lev.

I shake your hand firmly.

E. Preobrazhensky
P.S. Try to send this letter by fast post.
[Trotsky Archive Document T1294]

Letter from E.A. Preobrazhensky to L.D. Trotsky (2 June 1928)

Dear Lev Davidovich,

I have delayed answering you (I sent a telegram immediately) because I wanted first to outline some theses concerning the content of the proposed declaration to the Comintern. It took a long time, and it is difficult to do 'hand-written' correspondence on a typewriter. I am now writing just a few observations and sending them to you only after typing my handwritten correspondence for comrades. That is what explains the delay.

I take what you sent to be an outline of some of the main ideas for the appeal to the Congress, not a complete draft and still less the actual text. I will therefore discuss not so much what you sent as the text and appropriate content for the appeal.

In our appeal, which should be absolutely objective in assessing the past, we must very carefully separate the consequences of the general world situation of the workers' movement over the past 5–7 years from the results that are directly connected with the Comintern's mistakes.

If we talk about missed opportunities, we must not forget that the main opportunity missed by the proletariat and its parties was the possibility of overthrowing the bourgeoisie immediately after the war; that possibility did exist, at least in the defeated countries and in Italy. The leading role in the (revolutionary) European workers' movement after 1917 belonged to our party, and within our party, to Lenin. But can anyone say that our party is answerable for all the opportunities missed by the European proletariat up to and including 1920, even though we undertook to assist the European proletariat with such an heroic effort as the attack on Warsaw, which was beyond our capacity? No one has made, is making, or can make such an accusation.

And what follows from this indisputable fact?

It follows that the opportunities not seized after 1920 were lost on the basis of a situation that was already created by the hiatus in 1917–20. These opportunities occurred when the general trend of the worker's movement was already declining. The objective preconditions for these defeats were already much more serious than in the previous period. These created the historical context, with its reduced possibilities for success, that the Comintern faced in Europe from 1920 to 1928. It is within these limits that the mistakes of the Comintern must be assessed. I understand perfectly how difficult it is, in an historical process, to separate the subjective errors of organisations and leadership from the objective causes of ensuing events. Nevertheless, some sort of distinction can be made in broad outline (in this case the abbreviated revolutionary epoch). It is better to accuse the Comintern leadership of less, but of things that can be fully proven, things that everyone knows something about but does not mention aloud. By accusing them of things that are difficult to prove in a comparatively brief document, and even more of things that are difficult to prove at all, we would risk counter-criticism and clearly appropriate denunciations. Better fewer, but better.

Take Germany for example. We certainly must not try to prove, say, that the Comintern squandered *all chances* for a victorious proletarian revolution in 1923. That cannot be proven. But we can certainly prove that having failed to begin preparations for an armed uprising immediately following the occupation of the Ruhr, it did miss the opportunity to fight for the dictatorship of the proletariat. The opportunity to fight really was missed. But how that might have ended is something no one knows, and we must not discuss that issue. We cannot say that we wasted the chance in China for a victorious establishment of Soviet power. That cannot be proven. But what can be proven? It can be proven that in China, thanks to the Menshevik errors of the Comintern during an epoch of general realignment of class forces, the opportunity to create strong proletarian class organisations was lost along with all of the ensuing consequences for the further course of events.

When speaking of Estonia, Bulgaria or Canton, bear in mind the need to keep things secret from the world bourgeoisie, or else stipulate that this section is only for internal use and not for publication. In connection with Canton, don't forget to make the elementary point that we can distinguish the fatal tactical error of the leadership from the historical importance for future struggle of every attempted workers' uprising.

It is imperative to say something about the organisational side of things, i.e., the bureaucratic methods of the Comintern leadership, and how dangerous all of this is, especially in a period of approaching battles, when the leadership of each party must accept responsibility for extremely important and urgent decisions.

It is no great honour for revolutionaries to beat someone when he is down, nevertheless, we must quite clearly disassociate ourselves from the *Leninbund* for general political reasons. We should drop the idea that just as pre-war opportunism engendered the opposite distortion in the form of revolutionary syndicalism, so the mistakes of the Comintern not only provoked Bolshevik opposition but also drove some revolutionary workers to create a second party and unacceptable methods of criticising the USSR, which is something we always condemned even at the height of our struggle with the CC.

But the centre of gravity of our appeal to the Congress must still be the 'Russian question'. The primary goal of the appeal: we want to reconcile with the official party majority on the basis of further development of the course being taken both in agrarian policy and in the Comintern, and for our part we think this is possible and will do everything we can for such reconciliation, ruling out in advance only falsehoods, politicking and tarring ourselves in advance. It has to be emphasised that our struggle was against the worst of two possible variants for the course of events, and that we warned against an about-turn in policy to the right under pressure from hostile class forces. Pressures from the kulak and intensification of class contradictions on the world scale have shifted the policy of the CC away from the former centrist rails, but to the left rather than to the right. The past can be evaluated in different ways – if there can be no agreement regarding the past, all that means is that members of the opposition cannot teach party history for the years 1923 to 1928 – but what is fundamental and of immediate practical significance is the narrowing of our differences with the party majority concerning the concrete and topical issues of the day and the opportunity for us, in the event that we are accepted back into the party, really to fulfil our obligation concerning the elimination of factional activity.

I do not agree that in our document we should be afraid of over-estimating the significance of the about-turn in the policy of the CC or of optimism *in that area*. It must be one or the other. Either there has been no serious change in the policy of the CC, in which case there is no point in writing any document at all – everything has already been said in that case, and our silence would be the most emphatic affirmation of our final word on the matter – or else an about-turn in the policy of the CC has really begun. But in that event our risk is exactly the opposite: rather than exaggerating, the risk is that what we say to the Congress (which does not meet every day) will very quickly turn out to be timid, inadequate, half-hearted and behind the times. It will be up to the Congress to decide, on the basis of this half-hearted declaration, whether we made a mistake in submitting it. A Marxist and a Leninist policy is not simply a reaction to statistical facts already recorded, it always includes a prognosis, a probable hypothesis, *and therefore a risk*. We must now take a risk on the side of optimism, just as we had to take risks on the side of pessimism.

We must also say that the party majority has demonstrated, in its struggle against the kulak, the ability to find a way out along the lines of a return to the Leninist policy. This was an extremely important test of the party's general preparedness for battle, and it occurred despite all of the negative consequences of the CC's previous agrarian policy for the party, the working class and the poor peasants. *In this connection we also can and must mention our own exag-*

gerations and harshness in the course of polemics (even though they cannot be compared to the CC's 'polemical' methods).

Speaking of the internal party regime, we must point out that on this question the CC faces exactly the same situation as during the kulak offensive against Soviet power. The most extreme bureaucratic methods have brought them to the point where, under cover of bureaucratism, spontaneous philistine corruption is swamping entire organisations. The struggle against it has begun only after a delay of several years. Spurious policies provoked heightened opposition activities that are fatal not just to the opposition but also to party life in general.

At one point in your text you have included exaggerations that I am firmly opposed to repeating in the appeal to the Comintern. I'm talking about the third paragraph on the second page. You say there that the cause of the aboutturn in the CC was – the opposition. That is very flattering for all of us, but the way you formulate it is not correct. The opposition was around in 1926 and 1927 – in the Central Committee and in the Politburo – but there was no change of direction. The change began due to the kulak assault on Soviet power. That is true both chronologically and in terms of the essence of the matter. And from the other direction, the *increasingly acute class struggle in Europe*, which has nothing to do with relations between the CC and the opposition, has made a change in Comintern policy more urgent. Of course, we were always a factor in this change, but we were too weak. Specifically, our role lay in the fact that we so thoroughly drummed home the idea of the danger of degeneration and so compromised the right-wing policy that we made a diversion in that direction extremely difficult in political terms. That much can be demonstrated but no more, and it would be damaging to try to prove anything more.

As I mentioned before, I withdraw my proposal[1] and subscribe to your idea of an appeal to the Congress.

I do not consider it at all utopian to think that we might receive permission to get together in order to work out the document. Even If we use your text as the basis, such a statement is politically beneficial to the CC, not to mention the party, although it is totally unacceptable to them as a basis for returning to the party.

I take it for granted that as far Chinese affairs are concerned, the statement will not include anything not yet discussed.

---

1 [This comment possibly refers to Preobrazhensky's proposal in Appendix 3, suggesting that Trotsky send a letter to the editorial board of Pravda declaring that the agrarian policy of the Central Committee was 'fundamentally correct'.]

Apart from political issues, I also have theoretical corrections to make to the draft programme of the Comintern. I shall formulate them and send them to you. What do you think must be done by 'citizens' who have been expelled from the party and the Comintern but wish to improve the programme of the latter? The fact that they have been expelled seems to suggest that it is not their concern. But they cannot avoid being concerned, first of all because they do not consider 'all that exists' to be actually 'rational' – that is, enduring in Hegel's terms – and on the other hand they do not want the irrationality in the Comintern's draft programme to become actual in the long term. Should we not in future send something on this theme for a discussion article in *Bol'shevik*?

I'll not include anything more in this letter. One of these days I'll write you another letter about numerous things, including books. I expect that you are more involved with the details of correspondence than with work, and that the memoirs, in particular, are not getting the attention they deserve.

Warm greetings to Nataliya Ivanovna and to Lev.

I shake your hand.

    E. Preobrazhensky
    Ural'sk, 2 June 1928.
    [Trotsky Archive Document T1593]

Letter from E.A. Preobrazhensky to L.D. Trotsky (June 1928?)

Dear Lev Davidovich,[1]

Four days ago, I sent to you my comments on your counter-theses. Now I am sending my outline of what I think should be said to the Congress. I have only written the outline so far and shall not write the text itself: it would be late and of no use. The point is that Rakovsky wrote a draft of theses and sent them to you, and Radek must have sent his (I have still not received them). If you add my comments and synopsis, plus my original theses concerning the course in the countryside, then I think that is enough of a contribution from me for formulating the text. If you have not written the draft, it must be done quickly and dispatched to friends.

I am confident that the public, reluctantly and gradually, will in coming weeks move closer to my point of view. That is why I insist that *the question of our reconciliation with the party be at the centre of the appeal to the Congress*. Of course there must be an assessment, without any concealment, of what divides us from the cc, but the *statement* must serve this practical objective even if we have no illusions as to when it might be realised.

In your brochure on Lenin there is one excellent comparison about extracting nails when Lenin changed his position.[2] I very much fear that this operation

---

1 [To the right there is an insertion saying 'to Polina' (Vinogradskaya), E.A. Preobrazhensky's wife, which is crossed out. There is no further explanation.]

2 [In his essay on Lenin, Trotsky wrote:

Lenin's speeches are characterized by what is so essential in all his activity: the intentness on the goal, his purposefulness. The speaker is not out to deliver an oration, but to guide towards a conclusion which is to be followed by action. He has different ways of approaching his audience: he explains; he convinces; he shames it; he jokes with it; and then again tries to convince it and again expounds his idea. What makes for the unity of his speech is not a preconceived formal plan, but a practical aim, clearly defined and valid for that particular moment, which the audience must take in and absorb into its consciousness. Even the humor has to serve that purpose. The jests themselves are utilitarian. A racy word has its practical significance: it has to stir some and curb others. This is why so many of the expressions coined by Lenin have entered into our political vocabulary. Before he coins such a word, the speaker seems to go round and round as if searching for some central point. Then he finds it and as if placing a nail in position, glances round once more, lifts his hammer with great vigor and hits it on the head once, twice, three times, ten times, until the nail holds firmly, so firmly that it is hard to pull out even when no longer needed. When it is needed no longer, Lenin knocks it from the left, from the right, loosens it, draws it out, jokingly throws it on the pile of scrap-

is taking us too long, which is a great pity: the nails are so well and thoroughly hammered in, and the problem is amplified by the beating to which we have been subjected ....

You did very well at getting the counter-theses out quickly. I really wanted you to have the opportunity to weigh everything more thoroughly. *I have received a long letter from Radek. Essentially, we have no disagreements.* He just thinks that my analysis is too one-sided, creating the possibility of ignoring the past errors of the CC (I didn't mention them because I didn't discuss *every* issue), but his main objection is that when we are sitting in exile we cannot 'accept responsibility'. To that I reply: *the left policy in the countryside is our policy, and the inconsistency in implementing it – that is the responsibility of the CC. We answer for our policy as such, and not for the methods by which it is or is not implemented.* There are many who oppose it, and all philistines are against any struggle with the kulak. We must say that we have nothing in common with that sort of opposition. Aside from that, I agree completely with Radek. But here is the main thing: Smilga was in transit and saw Radek in Tomsk (he is there now), and Radek writes that after half an hour of conversation they agreed, with only shades of difference in assessing the situation .... Hence Radek concludes that the misunderstandings between us in assessing the situation are merely the product of our being scattered geographically. Muralov[3] sent me a brief answer: I reject your proposal (nothing new). I.N. Smirnov sent theses in which he takes an entirely different route but ends up essentially sharing my political views. Sosnovsky[4] sent a letter in which I see no major disagreements (he is for considerable caution on the issue of optimism). Beloborodov[5] supports working out a statement, but he is sceptical of how I assess the situation. Mrachkovsky[6] has not replied. (Something must be done about him or he will die before he says anything).

That is all for now. I shake your hand firmly. Greetings to all of yours.

E. Preobrazh[ensky]
[Trotsky Archive Document T1593]

---

iron in the archives to the great regret of all those who have grown so much accustomed to it (Trotsky 2018, p. 309).

3   [N.I. Muralov (1877–1937), party member from 1903, one of the main leaders of the Red Army, member of the Left Opposition, executed in 1937.]

4   [L.S. Sosnovsky (1886–1937), party member from 1904, journalist for 'Pravda', expelled from the party in 1927, capitulated in 1934, executed in 1937.]

5   [A.G. Beloborodov (1891–1938), party member from 1907, expelled in 1927, capitulated in 1928, executed in 1938.]

6   [S.V. Mrachkovsky (1988–1936), party member from 1905, member of the Left Opposition, executed in 1936.]

Letter from E.A. Preobrazhensky to L.D. Trotsky (Early June 1928)

What must be said to the Comintern Congress

THE POLICY OF THE COMINTERN

The general situation following the First World War. The Comintern is acting in circumstances created by the proletariat missing the opportunity to overthrow the bourgeoisie immediately after the world war. The opportunity to fight for the dictatorship [of the proletariat] was lost in Germany in 1923. Mistakes were made in Estonia and Bulgaria. The greatest mistakes in China. Over-estimation of the length of the breathing-space that capitalism allows to the USSR. Slow preparation of fighting cadres, despite parliamentary successes, slow growth in party membership, terrible weakness of leadership in the Communist parties, weakness in the trade-union movement, terribly harmful consequences of carrying over bureaucratic methods of leadership from the RCP to the Comintern, damaging consequences of the opportunistic policy (the Anglo-Russian Committee etc.) implemented up to the recent about-turn to the left. Prospects of an approaching moment when contradictions between the USSR and capitalism will explode. The duty of Comintern sections is to be ready not just to defend the USSR, but also for armed uprising and seizure of power in their own countries. The duty of communist workers in other countries is to provide support in the struggle against opportunistic tendencies in our party.

We have waged a long and stubborn struggle with the CC and the party majority, which reached an extreme degree of bitterness. We were driven to this struggle by the seriousness of our disagreements with the majority and the impossibility of defending them by the normal statutory route. Our disagreements come down to five basic points. I) The Policy of the Comintern. The content of disagreements is mentioned above. *At the present moment many of these disagreements have been eliminated due to the about-turn in Comintern policy following the most recent plenum of the IKKI.*[1] II) Policy in the countryside. The essence of the disagreements: the CC's under-estimation of the growth of kulaks, growing dependence of the state economy on kulak materials and grain,

---

1 [The Executive Committee of the Communist International.]

opportunistic and non-Leninist views regarding peaceful co-existence with the kulak economy, theoretical attempts to justify these utopian hopes, ignoring the process of increasing kulak-isation of certain groups of communists and the danger of losing ties with the poor, *insufficient taxation of the kulaks*, concessions to them in land law, failure to create a union of the village poor, inattentiveness to the development of soviet farms, etc. *The assault by the kulaks, the crisis in grain procurements and other facts forced the CC to change policy abruptly in the countryside in the sense of returning to the Leninist path. We welcome such an about-turn and are prepared to support it in every way (which is difficult, however, when we are not in the party and hundreds of our supporters are in exile).*

III) The internal party regime.

Our criticism of the internal party regime and our persistent demands for real internal party democracy are fully justified by all the officially established facts concerning the disintegration of a number of organisations. We attach great importance to the proclamation from the CC, published in *Pravda* on 30 June. Since it has been several years late in coming, we very much fear that attempts by the CC to return to the internal party regime that existed under Lenin – given their fear of allowing criticism of their past and present errors in the area of general policy and the continuation of repression against the opposition – will not produce any serious results. Their willingness to struggle against the evil is not proportional to the sickness.

IV) Our disagreements with the CC on the question of the workers and industrialisation were set out in our platform and counter-theses. *We acknowledge that our fears concerning a retreat from the monopoly of foreign trade, associated with a general retreat to the right in terms of economic policy as a whole, were not justified. But there has been no serious improvement in the area of policy concerning the workers, and we cannot detect any increase in the rate of industrialisation*; in particular, the changes in trade-union policy enunciated in the CC proclamation have yet to be implemented.

Results and prospects.

During the period when our struggle with the majority was most acute, i.e., with the intensification of disagreements concerning Chinese issues in April of last year, we feared the worst variant in the development of events, i.e., we expected a further turn of policy to the right and the growth of Thermidorian forces and threats. The transition on the part of the party majority towards active struggle with the kulak, so long as it lasts, removes this danger. This is the most important of the changes that have occurred in the general political situation. We note a decline in our disagreements with the CC on a number of urgent questions of international and domestic policy. The sharpening of class contradictions at home and abroad excludes any possibility of continuing the old policy of the CC: neither the economic nor the social preconditions for it any longer exist. The only possibility now is for either a consistent left policy or a decisive right policy. It goes without saying that on the basis of a rightist domestic policy the party cannot be victorious either in the struggle against domestic capitalist forces or in the inevitable and rapidly approaching foreign war. We are prepared to apply all of our efforts in support of every step by the CC along the line of Leninist policy, we wish to reconcile with the party majority on the basis of carrying out the new course. We ask the Congress to return us to the party, in whose ranks we will loyally and sincerely accept our obligation not to engage in factional activity.

To quote our last appeal to the Congress.

E. Preobrazhensky
[Trotsky Archive Document 1594]

PART 5

Conclusions

CHAPTER 1

E.A. Preobrazhensky: Instead of an Afterword

M.M. Gorinov and S.V. Tsakunov

In the history of political economy in the 1920s, Evgeny Alexseevich Preo-brazhensky stands out strikingly as a prominent figure in the Bolshevik Party, member of the Presidium of the Communist Academy, economic theorist, journalist and writer. Born in 1886 to the family of a priest and religious teacher at the Bolkhovsky parish school in Orel province, E.A. Preobrazhensky took up revolutionary activity at an early age.[1] Already in 1905, while enrolled at Moscow University, he was a leading propagandist in Moscow's Presnensky district and took part in the battles of the armed uprising in that city. Preo-brazhensky rightfully belongs to the second, younger generation of the Bol-shevik 'Old Guard', who took up revolutionary activity during the first Russian revolution.

Preobrazhensky's pre-revolutionary path was perfectly typical of a Bol-shevik: active revolutionary involvement, work in a social-democratic cell un-der a party committee, followed by arrest, exile, escape and return to revolu-tionary activity. In documents kept by the Police Department, he is referred to as 'a prominent member of the Russian Social-Democratic party'.[2] Dur-ing his years in the underground and in exile – also typical of Bolsheviks – Preobrazhensky managed independently to read and study the basic works of Marxism, particularly those dealing with financial problems and the agrarian

---

1 For political reasons, the multifaceted activity of E.A. Preobrazhensky for a long time re-mained in the shadows and was practically never studied in the Soviet period. References to him in the literature on party history and economic history have a one-sided and extremely fragmentary character. In Anglo-American literature concerning problems in the history of Soviet society during the 1920s, Preobrazhensky's views are presented much more fully and objectively. Edward H. Carr, Robert V. Daniels, Alexander Erlich, Stephen F. Cohen, Alec Nove and others describe in their works various aspects of Preobrazhensky's political and scientific activity. Nevertheless, there are no specific studies devoted to his life and creative work. Bio-graphical information is given in Blaug (ed.) 1983 and also in Schultz et al. (eds) 1972. In the Russian language, biographical information was published in: *Deyateli sssr i revolyut-sionnovo dvizheniya Rossii*; *Entsiklopedicheskii slovar' 'Granat'* (reprinted in Moscow, 1989); *Politicheskie partii Rossii: Konets XIX – pervaya tret' XX veka* (Moscow: Entsiklopediya, 1996), pp. 482–3. See also Preobrazhensky 2014, pp. 3–12.
2 GARF. F. 102. DP OO. 1908. D. 12. Ch. 67. L. 4–4 ob.

question, and contributed a number of publications on these subjects to the Novonikolaevsk newspaper, 'Obskaya Zhizn' (1912).[3] It was understandable, therefore, that while in Ekaterinburg in the Urals during 1918, Preobrazhensky delivered a course of lectures at the People's University – the regional party school of the Urals – on political economy, Russian economic history, and financial and agricultural issues. As a member of the editorial board of the newspaper 'Ural'skii rabochii', he managed the political and economic sections of the paper along with G.I. Safarov.[4] This was the time when Preobrazhensky had the opportunity not only to express openly his own economic views, but also to exercise a direct influence on formation of the Bolshevik Party's position regarding economic questions.

1   As a Left Communist

In January–February of 1918, Preobrazhensky actively contributed to 'Pravda', where his articles were published just about every day on topical political themes. As a member of the Bolshevik faction, Preobrazhensky attended and spoke twice at the sessions of the historic Third Congress of Soviets: in debates concerning the report on the work of the SNK[5] (by Lenin), and on the national question and foundations for the future constitution (by Stalin). The end of the winter of 1917 and the beginning of the spring of 1918 were a special period in the history of the Bolshevik Party and the Soviet state: this was the time of the establishment of Soviet power and the 'Red-Guard' attack on capital.

The Bolsheviks aimed for development of the political and economic creativity of the popular masses. However, during the first months of Soviet power the practical realisation of 'mass creativity' led to even greater intensification of the social and economic problems inherited from the Provisional Government. At the same time, the continuing state of war with Germany made it impossible to concentrate on solving domestic problems and diverted significant resources and funds to preserving the front line. All of this prompted Lenin to support the idea of a 'breathing space' from the war by immediately concluding a separate and annexationist peace with Germany. Beyond the purely military rationale of such a step, in the spring of 1918 Lenin moved to the wider conception of a temporary pause in revolutionary reforms as a necessary tac-

---

3   See Preobrazhensky 2014, pp. 71–6, 94–104, 182–3.
4   See Ural'skii rabochii, 25 April, 5 May and 10 May 1918.
5   Council of People's Commissars.

tical step on the road to socialism. Such a sharp about-turn by Lenin provoked a heated discussion within the party.

Representatives of an emergent faction of 'Left Communists', with the journal *'Kommunist'* as their organ, claimed that Lenin's programme threatened society with a slide into state capitalism, leading to collapse of the revolution. They formulated a programme for 'building proletarian socialism',[6] which subsequently, in the years of Civil War and War Communism, would become widespread in the RCP(B).

Preobrazhensky actively participated in the theoretical and practical work of the 'Left Communists'. On 21 January 1918, at an expanded meeting of the Central Committee with representatives of different views on the question of concluding the Brest peace, Preobrazhensky took a position that was very close to the views of N.I. Bukharin.[7] When the question of the Brest peace became particularly urgent in March, Preobrazhensky fully identified with the views of the 'Lefts' and promulgated them widely in the party organisation of the Urals district. At the same time, his writing activity shifted from the pages of *'Pravda'* (simultaneously with Bukharin's departure from his post as editor) to the pages of *'Ural'skii rabochii'*. Here, Preobrazhensky published a series of articles under the heading 'War or Peace', devoted to the problem of the Brest peace. He concluded that 'Comrade Lenin's entire plan is essentially an attempt to save the life of the Soviet authority by committing suicide'.[8] Almost the entire party organisation of the Urals endorsed the position of the 'Left Communists'.[9]

In April–May 1918, Preobrazhensky participated just as actively in the second phase of the discussion, involving questions of the economic organisation of society, the focus of which proved to be a dispute over the question of state capitalism.[10]

In order to understand the original views that Preobrazhensky took with him into the revolution and that subsequently determined his approaches to questions of economic construction, it is necessary to analyse in detail the resolution of the Urals regional party conference that was prepared and adopted with his direct involvement. Preobrazhensky thought very highly of this resolution; he considered its positions to be not merely a product of theorising but

---

6   Osinsky 1918, p. 5.
7   For more detail see *Izvestiya TsK KPSS*, No. 2, 1989, p. 183.
8   *Ural'skii rabochii*, 3, 6, 7, 9 March, 1918. See also Preobrazhensky 2014, pp. 318–31. The comment about suicide is on p. 325.
9   *Ural'skii rabochii*, 6 March 1918.
10   Preobrazhensky 2014, pp. 346–54.

also the result of the first practical experience 'in the matter of socialist reconstruction of the Urals'.[11] First of all, what we find in this important document
is a statement of two objectively possible ways of developing the country's
productive forces: either admission of foreign capital into the country, restoration of the capitalist regime and gradual elimination of all the socialist reforms
already begun, or else restoration of industry with its own resources, recourse
to foreign capital only to purchase means of production, the final liquidation
of bourgeois property, and completion of the entire reconstruction of the economy according to socialist principles. The resolution stated: 'There cannot be
any compromise, any middle-way between these two methods of economic
reconstruction of the country: they are the only ones possible, and at the same
time they are mutually exclusive'.[12] In general, the Urals Communists believed
that 'the only path possible for a proletarian Communist Party is to pursue
economic reconstruction of the country based on steadfast, resolute and consistent construction of a socialist economy'.[13] Regarding practical proposals for
organisation of such an economy, many of the economic measures suggested
at the time did not go beyond the well-known positions of the Sixth Congress
of the RCP(B): putting the organisation of all social production and consumption under the direct control and leadership of workers' production unions
and the relevant economic associations of poor peasants; state trustification
of all branches of large-scale industry, with small and backward enterprises
being brought within their sphere of influence; establishment of the social
organisation of production in agriculture; establishment of proper exchange of
products between the city and the countryside by way of state supply organs;
organisation of consumer communes with mandatory enrolment of all consumers, and so forth.

This was also the period when E.A. Preobrazhensky's first relatively long economic work, *Anarchism and Communism*, was published. Its appearance was
due to the fact that the revolution fostered a growing popularity of anarcho-
syndicalist ideas among the working class. For that reason, an important part
of the book was devoted to a comparative analysis of the communist and
anarchist programmes. The communist ideal of organising production was
seen by Preobrazhensky as a strictly centralised planned economy, in which
'every branch of industry must be assigned its task, which is calculated according to the whole country's need for its product',[14] and 'the distribution of

---

11   Preobrazhensky 1918a, p. 13. See also Preobrazhensky 2014, p. 349.
12   *Ural'skii rabochii*, 9 May 1918. See also Preobrazhensky 2014, p. 351.
13   Ibid.
14   Preobrazhensky 1921, p. 44. See also Preobrazhensky 2014, p. 620.

labour between industry and agriculture must also satisfy a plan consciously developed on the basis of statistics'.[15] 'Under communism', wrote Preobrazhensky, there will be no 'squandering of social labour because the role of the market ... will be replaced by the work of statistics'.[16]

Against the 'economic ideal of anarchism', Preobrazhensky made the interesting argument that it was, in his words, 'a reactionary utopia', 'a petty-bourgeois variant of capitalist commodity economy', and 'a step backwards even by comparison with developed capitalism'.[17] The anarchists called for 'transferring the instruments of production not to all the toilers as a whole, but to separate groups of comrades or *artels* of toilers'; they opposed 'any regulation of production from a special economic centre elected by the toilers'; and they supported direct product exchange between communes of producers on the basis of voluntary agreements.[18] Preobrazhensky points to an insoluble contradiction of anarchist doctrine: 'They can have free trade between separate communes ... (buying and selling also means voluntary agreement), in which case the distribution of labour-power will take place just as in capitalism but at the cost of equality – long live free competition .... Or else there must be accounting and control over production on the scale first of the country and later of the entire world – away with the independence of each commune from the others ...'.[19] The practical social result of implementing the anarchist economic model, according to Preobrazhensky, would be emergence of the most pronounced income inequality between different communes, which would create the soil for a civil war within the working class. 'Every independent commune-factory can become a stronghold for protecting the narrow group-interests of that factory alone, instead of all the workers of society, and this will lead to such inequality in distribution that must horrify every honest anarchist',[20] wrote Preobrazhensky. He also gave an example (in the second edition of the book) of how in 1918, during the bitter Civil War, the workers at the Cheremkovo mines, taking advantage of increased demand from the railways for coal, raised prices and began to receive five times more than workers at other enterprises in Siberia.[21]

---

15   Preobrazhensky 1921, p. 50. See also Preobrazhensky 2014, p. 623.
16   Preobrazhensky 1921, p. 50. See also Preobrazhensky 2014, p. 620.
17   Preobrazhensky 1921, p. 44. See also Preobrazhensky 2014, p. 619.
18   Preobrazhensky 1921, pp. 43, 55. See also Preobrazhensky 2014, pp. 620, 624.
19   Preobrazhensky 1921, p. 58. See also Preobrazhensky 2014, p. 627.
20   Preobrazhensky 1921, p. 65. See also Preobrazhensky 2014, p. 633.
21   Preobrazhensky 1921, p. 65. See also Preobrazhensky 2014, pp. 634–5.

2   Co-author of the 'ABC'

In 1919, Preobrazhensky was called to Moscow, where he began to work in the editorial office of 'Pravda'. He was delegated to the VIII Party Congress by the Penza provincial party organisation of the RCP(B). E.A. Preobrazhensky was elected to the Presidium of the Congress along with V.I. Lenin, L.B. Kamenev, G.E. Zinoviev, G.L. Pyatakov, G.E. Evdokimov, and P.G. Smidovich. He also joined the commission that edited and prepared the final draft of the programme that the Congress adopted. Following the Congress, and using material from the text of the programme, in just three weeks Preobrazhensky and Bukharin wrote *The ABC of Communism*, a popular textbook of communist literacy for party schools, based on materials in the new programme of the RCP(B). Bukharin took it upon himself to cover mainly the general theoretical aspects of the programme;[22] Preobrazhensky wrote the chapters on agricultural organisation, distribution, banks, money circulation, and finances in the proletarian state. This division also corresponded to the scientific interests of each author. The result, according to Lenin, was a 'highly valuable book' in which the party programme was 'perfectly explained'.[23]

A lengthy chapter of the *ABC* was devoted to the organisation of agriculture and the tasks of the RCP(B) in relation to the peasantry. Like all Marxists of that time, E.A. Preobrazhensky associated the future of agriculture with large-scale collective production. He was distinguished in that regard by a sober and realistic view of the prospects for transformation in the Russian countryside: '... whatever successes we enjoy in the area of organising Soviet farms and communes, the small peasant farm will long exist and for a significant part of that time will be *the prevailing form of agriculture in Russia* ...'.[24] For that very reason, the party programme scheduled transitional measures that would help the small peasant farmer to see the advantages of collective agriculture. 'Instead of taking a direct route to socialist reconstruction in agriculture', Preobrazhensky had written in his much earlier work *Peasant Russia and Socialism*, 'we must follow a long, difficult and roundabout path'.[25]

---

22   For a more detailed analysis of *The ABC of Communism* and the chapters written by Bukharin, see Tsakunov 1989.

23   Lenin 1970, p. 157. See also Lenin, 'Report on the Work of the Council of People's Commissars, December 22', in Lenin 1966a, p. 514. See also Preobrazhensky 2014, pp. 569–798.

24   Bukharin and Preobrazhensky 1920, p. 265. See also Preobrazhensky 2014, pp. 706–7.

25   Preobrazhensky 1918b, p. 6. See also Preobrazhensky 2014, p. 573.

However, Preobrazhensky would not have been a Marxist had he failed to note the social differentiation of the peasantry. His attitude towards the kulak (which, incidentally, was the same as Lenin's in this period) was emphatically hostile:

> Until the kulak class is fully liquidated, it must inevitably emerge as an implacable enemy of the proletarian state and its land policy, and, in turn, it can expect from the Soviet authority only the most merciless struggle against all attempts at counter-revolution. The possibility also cannot be excluded that the Soviet authority will have to conduct a planned expropriation of the kulaks, mobilising them for public work and, above all, for work on improving the lands of the peasants and the state.[26]

Let us note that the possibility of employing such measures in relation to the kulak class does not imply any necessity; Preobrazhensky associated the latter only with kulak 'attempts at counter-revolution'. Moreover, it must be remembered that this was written in the midst of the Civil War, when the kulaks were fighting against Bolshevik power with arms in hand. Later on, Preobrazhensky changed his position and was less extreme. Thus, when he predicted early in 1918 an intensification of the struggle within the peasantry, he called upon the party to 'see to it that this struggle does not take the form of a spontaneous rebellion, with a lumpen-proletarian tendency towards "equalisation" and the plundering of household-treasures, but that it leads to an economic union of the poor so that ... they will be able to begin working their share of the former landlords' land through *artels*'.[27]

A characteristic feature of Preobrazhensky's thinking was his constant concern for the criteria of economic efficiency and rationality. Developing his ideas concerning poor-peasant artels and communes, in *The ABC of Communism* he wrote:

> But this will already cease to be a dictatorship of the poor, in the proper sense of the word; it will not be the rule of 'beggars and freeloaders', as the kulaks complained (and sometimes with good reason) during the period of poor people's committees. It will be rule by the leading stratum of working people in the countryside, and they will be two centuries ahead of the majority.[28]

---

26   Bukharin and Preobrazhensky 1920, p. 270. See also Preobrazhensky 2014, pp. 710–11.
27   Preobrazhensky 1918b, p. 6. See also Preobrazhensky 2014, p. 573.
28   Bukharin and Preobrazhensky 1920, p. 272. See also Preobrazhensky 2014, p. 712.

He added that '... in struggling for a socialist reconstruction of agriculture, we must avoid irritating the middle-peasant with the carelessness and hastiness of our own measures, and this means completely avoiding any attempt to force him into communes and *artels*'.[29]

Preobrazhensky devoted considerable space in the ABC to problems of organising distribution, the banks, the circulation of money and finances. All of this was subordinated to showing the steps involved in elimination of commodity-money relations and the transition to a system of natural economy. In Preobrazhensky's thinking, the process of liquidating money would pass through several stages. Initially, money would vanish from the nationalised economy – in the factories, railways, state farms etc., as well as from settlements between the state and the workers and employees of Soviet enterprises. At the second stage, money would be replaced by commodity exchange in the turnover between the state and petty production. In the final stage, money would vanish from the sphere of the small-scale economy, being eliminated as a social phenomenon only 'along with the disappearance of the small-scale economy as such'.[30] The latter demonstrated that Preobrazhensky took a rather cautious approach to devising such social projects and understood the concrete conditions of Russia within which the Bolsheviks must realise their socialist ideal.

Shortly after the ABC of Communism, Preobrazhensky continued his research in the field of the Marxist theory of money and the prospects for monetary circulation within the country. The result was the book *Paper Money in the Era of Proletarian Dictatorship*, which was published in 1920 and was highly regarded by Lenin. Despite the obvious influence of the experience of 'War Communism' in terms of the elimination of money, this work typified the scientific integrity of the author. In a review of Preobrazhensky's book, M. Ol'minsky noted that 'the author takes rapid strides towards freeing himself of the prevailing nonsense concerning the imminent elimination of money as an indicator of the rapid establishment of "socialism"'.[31] Preobrazhensky demonstrated in the book that he was well aware of the objective roots of commodity-money relations and the conditions in which they must inevitably continue. He wrote that 'Money, as a means of circulation and accumulation, will die out together with the commodity economy';[32] the source of commodity-money relations –

---

29   Bukharin and Preobrazhensky 1920, p. 271. See also Preobrazhensky 2014, p. 711.

30   Bukharin and Preobrazhensky 1920, p. 286. See also Preobrazhensky 2014, p. 723.

31   M. Ol'minsky, *Rets. na kn*: E.A. Preobrazhensky, *Bumazhnie den'gi v epokhu diktatury proletariata*, in *Proletarskaya revolyutsiya*, No. 1, 1921, pp. 184–5.

32   Preobrazhensky 1920, p. 84. See also Preobrazhensky 2014, p. 798.

the peasant economy – would co-exist for a long time with socialist production. '... [T]he slow withering away of our paper rouble', emphasised Preobrazhensky, 'is connected with the economic peculiarities of Russia'.[33] On these grounds, he subsequently conceived the idea of introducing a 'silver currency', which he defended in an address to the Tenth Congress of the RCP(B). The idea was to create a stable currency as the basis for the monetary portion of wage payments to workers[34] for their 'free-market' purchases of commodities from the peasantry. In addition, the 'silver currency' would provide a basis for issuing new paper money, which, in the absence of other revenues, would allow the state to collect a special 'issuance' tax.

3   At the Head of the Financial Commission

The transition to NEP further increased the need for restoring order in the country's monetary system. 'We are now faced with the need to review the question of financial and wage-rate policy in its entirety', Preobrazhensky told the Tenth Congress of the RCP(B).[35] Following a decision of the Congress to adopt fundamental financial reforms, the party's Central Committee appointed a commission headed by Preobrazhensky. It also included N.N. Krestinsky, A.O. Alsky, O.Yu. Shmidt, F.F. Syromolotov, I.T. Smilga, A.M. Lezhava, Yu. Larin, A.S. Kiselev, A.M. Krasnoshchekov and G.Ya. Sokol'nikov. The commission took up the basic questions of credit, monetary circulation, the budget, and tax legislation in conditions of the transition to NEP. Thus, during the first years of NEP almost all the basic concerns of Preobrazhensky came to focus on the elaboration of financial problems and the rationale for ways in which to stabilise monetary circulation. He outlined his position in numerous articles in *Pravda* and *Ekonomicheskaya Zhizn'*, in contributions to discussions, and in several pamphlets devoted to financial problems. It was during this period, as Chairman of the financial commission set up by the Central Committee and the Council of People's Commissars, and as a member of the collegium of the People's Commissariat of Finance, that he thoroughly investigated the mech-

---

33   Preobrazhensky 1920, p. 40. See also Preobrazhensky 2014, p. 761.
34   Preobrazhensky believed that with development of a non-commodity economy, wages would increasingly be naturalised and would reach the worker not through the market but with the help of the apparatus for state distribution of products. Such views corresponded to the practice of 'War Communism' and the prevailing opinion of the time. See also Preobrazhensky 2014, p. 794.
35   *X S'ezd RKP(B). Stenograficheskii otchet* (Moscow, 1963), p. 246.

anism of monetary circulation, the formation of items in the state budget, and taxation policy. Preobrazhensky dealt with questions of implementing a general financial and monetary reform within the context of significant improvement of conditions in the national economy as a whole and the state sector in particular. But the reality of 1921 was such that the only source of state revenues was the tax in kind, levied on the peasantry, and significant issuance of new currency. Consequently, the first step towards monetary reform had to be curtailment of currency issues and expansion of the state budget through taxation and other economic sources in order gradually to eliminate the deficit. These were the challenges that members of the financial commission tried to cope with during the first years of NEP.

Due to the novelty of the impending tasks and the Bolsheviks' lack of any experience with carrying out financial reforms, not all of the practical measures taken to improve the economy's financial health were initially successful. A typical example was the sad history of the Republic's first budget for nine months of 1922. G.Ya. Sokol'nikov, the deputy Commissar of Finance, commented at the time that 'the budget – which, of course, is a great step forward and the basis for our further work – this budget had numerous inadequacies, mainly because it was drawn up with extraordinary haste, and because of this haste and the lack of statistical materials, it included fundamental errors'.[36]

Compiled for January–September of 1922 – with the participation of G.Ya. Sokol'nikov, N.N. Krestinsky, E.A. Preobrazhensky, Yu. Larin and others, and affirmed by the Ninth Congress of Soviets – the 'stable budget calculated in terms of gold' failed to ensure currency stabilisation or curtailment of emissions. On the contrary, in late 1921 and early 1922 there was a sharp increase in the rate of issuance and further depreciation of the currency, which was primarily due to the harvest failure and famine of 1921.

In the conditions of an aggravated financial crisis, in March 1922 the Eleventh Congress of the RCP(B) gathered in Moscow, where for the first time in the party's history one of the central issues was discussion of a programme for financial stabilisation. Preobrazhensky followed Sokol'nikov with a co-report to the congress on the financial question. In view of the acute budget deficit, the rapporteurs ruled out any 'possibility of rapid monetary reform aimed at creation of a stable currency'.[37] The immediate task of the moment was to devise a set of special economic measures aiming for overall financial recovery of the

---

36   *XI S'ezd RKP(B). Stenograficheskii otchet* (Moscow, 1961), p. 302.
37   *XI S'ezd RKP(B). Stenograficheskii otchet* (Moscow, 1961), p. 676.

national economy. Drafted by Sokol'nikov and Preobrazhensky, the resolution that the congress adopted on the financial question included extensive development of all forms of trade, de-naturalisation of the national economy, radical curtailment by the Soviet state of the ballast of small and medium enterprises nationalised during the Civil War, and a severe contraction of the administrative apparatus.

Along with the need for rapid financial recovery of the country, the national economy increasingly required a stable measure for the value of commodities. In the economic literature, the periodical press and numerous financial-economic reports, a widespread discussion developed in 1922 over whether gold might serve as the measure of value and a gauge of prices in the new economic conditions. Preobrazhensky was also part of these discussions,[38] in the course of which three principal viewpoints were expressed. Sokol'nikov and his associates at Narkomfin thought gold was already becoming the measure of value, and calculations must be guided by that fact (i.e. a real gold rouble). S.G. Strumilin and some others suggested not only that gold is not the measure of value, but also that it could generally be supplanted in its functions by paper money, with the state and its planning organs replacing gold in its role as spontaneous regulator of the economy. Finally, Preobrazhensky and a rather large group of supporters at VSNKh[39] and Gosplan thought the measure of value in such conditions might be the pre-war gold rouble, which could be used pending establishment of a stable paper currency that would be quoted abroad and based upon gold as world money. This position had good theoretical and practical justification. During 1921 and part of 1922, most of the main financial transactions in the country were carried out with the help of the so-called 'commodity rouble', i.e., a rouble with the purchasing power of 1913, adjusted for the commodity price index of 1913–21. It is important to note that Preobrazhensky recognised the transitional character of these ideas and by no means denied the need for ultimately introducing a stable, gold-based currency once the price of gold stabilised.[40] Despite all its limitations, the use of monetary settlements in the national economy, based upon the 'commodity rouble', laid the groundwork for the ensuing stage of financial reform: that is, for introduction of the *chervonets*[41] and real restoration of the gold content of Soviet currency, which

---

38   For more detail see Preobrazhensky 1923, pp. 58–64, 73.

39   Supreme Council of the National Economy.

40   Preobrazhensky 1923, p. 73. (That is, when the exchange rate between paper money and gold stabilised.)

41   In the monetary reform of 1922–23, Soviet token money, the *sovznak*, was replaced by the *chervonets* rouble, which corresponded in terms of gold value to the 10-rouble pre-revolutionary coin.

came about without the active involvement of E.A. Preobrazhensky, who by 1924 had become one of the theorists of the 'Left Opposition'.

4 The Agrarian Question and the Prospects for NEP

At the Eleventh Congress of the RCP(B), Preobrazhensky spoke on other questions besides financial policy. At the very beginning of work by the congress, he proposed that the agenda include the question of the party's policy in the countryside as a special item.[42] This question did not, in fact, appear in the congress agenda, which was published in *Pravda* on 27 January and 12 February. Preobrazhensky had prepared theses in which he attempted, taking into account the processes of commodity-money relations in the village, to show the tasks of the party with regard to different strata of the peasantry. After reviewing them, the Bolshevik leader [Lenin] sent a letter to members of the Politburo in which he considered the theses to be 'inappropriate' and suggested instead that a meeting of rural delegates be organised at the congress to examine local practical experience. 'All comrade Preobrazhensky's theses are ultra- and super-academic; they smack of the intelligentsia, the study circle and the littérateur, and not of practical state and economic activity' – such was Lenin's harsh appraisal.[43] Precisely because Lenin, as leader of the party and government at the time, was interested in the first practical experience of NEP, he scarcely touched upon the content of the theses.

Meanwhile, they did merit attention. The theses, which Preobrazhensky entitled 'Basic Principles of the Policy of the RCP in the Countryside', discussed the fact that since the end of requisitioning, and in connection with the increased absorptive capacity of the urban commodity market, peasant farming was beginning to be reoriented away from consumption and towards production of marketable commodities. The process of rural stratification was also resuming. Although the social-class contours of the village were only beginning to emerge, in Preobrazhensky's opinion the party had to define its policy and its attitude towards these processes. Without predetermining the question of practical rural reforms, in the theses he proposed the general principles upon which the party must construct its policy for the near future in relation to the

---

42 See *XI S'ezd RKP(B). Stenograficheskii otchet* (Moscow, 1961), p. 6. The Eleventh Congress met from 27 March to 2 April 1922.
43 V.I. Lenin, *Pol. sobr. soch.*, t. 45, p. 44. See Lenin 1966b, p. 238. Lenin's letter was written on 16 March 1922.

kulaks and well-to-do peasantry, the middle and small-holding peasantry, as well as the agricultural proletariat.

It is important to note that Preobrazhensky's views had changed somewhat compared to 1918–20. Much of what he wrote about in the form of theses in 1922 would later be developed in his articles and books. In this connection, it is appropriate to emphasise that in 1922 he had no thought of using non-economic coercion against the peasantry. Of course, the final sentence of his theses confirms that their author, like the entire Bolshevik party, stood for development of large-scale production, including collective farming in the countryside, as the primary condition for a transition to socialism. However, in terms of the means for such a transition, Preobrazhensky referred only to economic levers for all strata of the peasantry.

The most controversial and difficult point of the party's agrarian policy during the years of NEP proved, of course, to be the 'kulak question'. Preobrazhensky attempted in his theses to work out approaches to a solution. In his view, the rapid growth of kulaks and the well-to-do peasantry objectively resulted from commodity economy in the conditions of NEP. This stratum of the peasantry represented a necessary link in the formation of new economic relations in the village because it promoted the intensification of agriculture with its own petty-bourgeois methods. Thus, Preobrazhensky wrote that 'a policy of hostility to this stratum and its brutal suppression by the methods of poor-peasant committees, as in 1918, would be a grave error'.[44] Taken in abstraction, with no concrete links to politics and economics, this remark was totally justified. But Lenin, who read the theses during a most complicated period of our history, was not thinking only in terms of scientific categories. Consequently, he objected that 'a war, for example, may compel us to resort to the methods of the Poor Peasants' Committees'.[45]

What Preobrazhensky had to say about the kulaks does not mean that he came out in his theses as a defender of their interests. On the contrary, when referring to the inadmissibility of non-economic coercion, he spoke of the need for state measures to limit the exploitative aspirations of the kulaks with the help of higher taxes. It would be a gross error, according to Preobrazhensky, to support this stratum at the cost of others and under the pretext of a more rapid expansion of agriculture. Lenin supported that position but suggested that it be formulated differently, pointing once again to the unsoundness of general phrases and the impossibility of accepting such an approach once and for all.

---

44   GRASPI. F. 170. Op. 2. D. 77. L. 5.
45   V.I. Lenin, *Pol. sobr. soch.*, t. 45, p. 44. See Lenin 1966b, p. 238.

Finally, great importance attaches to Lenin's remark concerning the final sentence in the paragraph that dealt with relations with the kulaks. Preobrazhensky spoke there of the need 'to use, within available limits, the process of capitalist accumulation that has already begun in the countryside for socialist accumulation'. Lenin noted: 'The last words in § 11 are correct, but they are abstruse and insufficiently enlarged upon. This must be explained in greater detail'.[46] It follows from this that Lenin was also reflecting upon the possibilities of using capitalist accumulation in the countryside in the interests of socialist construction. In our view, therefore, the theories of socialist accumulation and industrialisation that were developed in the mid-1920s by Preobrazhensky and his opponent, Bukharin, were attempts to implement by different economic methods one and the same idea, which was supported by Lenin, in relation to the wealthiest group in the Soviet countryside. However, Bukharin torched himself with the slogan 'Enrich Yourselves!', and Preobrazhensky became a 'theorist of Trotskyism'.

With his reflections on prospects of rural development in the conditions of NEP, Preobrazhensky to some degree anticipated events: what he wrote about in his theses became, as we know, topical for the Bolshevik Party only in 1925. It is no wonder that Lenin repeated several times in his comments that the author's views were 'ultra-unpopular' and belonged in 'another opera'. Moreover, Lenin did not think it necessary for the congress to revise the party's policy towards the peasantry; the basic principles had already been established by the party programme and the decisions taken at the Tenth Congress of Soviets. Accordingly, Lenin suggested that the author entitle his theses 'On the Organisation of work by the RCP in the Countryside at the Current Moment', putting the main emphasis on analysis of practical experience. 'It must be formulated quite differently, without repeating the bare slogan: "Cooperate!" but *showing concretely* what *practical experience* has already been acquired in the field of cooperation, and *how* it can be promoted'.[47]

Despite the fact that Lenin told the Eleventh Congress of the RCP(B) to 'Stop philosophising and arguing about NEP',[48] there was a growing need in the party for a more substantive development of the theoretical problems of the New Economic Policy, especially concerning socialist prospects. One of the first people who clearly recognised this need and attempted to elaborate it concretely was Preobrazhensky.

---

46   V.I. Lenin, *Pol. sobr. soch.*, t. 45, p. 44. See Lenin 1966b, p. 239.
47   V.I. Lenin, *Pol. sobr. soch.*, t. 45, pp. 43–4. See Lenin 1966b, pp. 237–8.
48   V.I. Lenin, *Pol. sobr. soch.*, t. 45, p. 92. See Lenin 1966b, p. 285.

At the Eleventh Congress of the RCP(B) he spoke of the need for a theoretical interpretation of questions posed by the unique character of the economic system that was taking shape on the basis of NEP principles, since, in his opinion, 'on this issue the party completely lacks any clear picture'.[49] At the same time, Preobrazhensky raised the question at the congress of the need to reconcile the party programme of War Communism with the new political and economic circumstances of NEP.

Perhaps it was premature in 1922 to formulate the question that way, since NEP was not yet fully established and developed, and the initial experience was not sufficiently typical. Nevertheless, as one of the authors of the *ABC of Communism* and a participant in developing the programme of the RCP(B), Preobrazhensky was acutely aware of the growing contradiction between the practice of NEP and the old programme formulated by the party. Motivated by these reflections, in the same year Preobrazhensky wrote one of the first generalising works on NEP, *From NEP to Socialism* (*A Glance into the Future of Russia and Europe*), where he attempted in a popular-scientific manner to outline the country's prospective development towards socialism during 'decades' of NEP. The work was written in the form of lectures, supposedly given in 1970 in the Moscow Polytechnic Museum by a professor of Russian history, Minayev, who was also a mechanic in the railway workshops. In terms of form, the book was a futurological sketch by a Marxist theorist; in content, it was the result of a deep understanding of the essence of the emerging NEP and its main tendencies of development.

In the book Preobrazhensky quite comprehensively and distinctively formulated his view of the course of economic and political development in the country during the years of NEP. His approach combined the traditional Marxist landmarks of the time (a large-scale socialised economy, the elimination of money, proletarian revolution in the West), with new theoretical constructions regarding the transition period (widespread use of commodity-money relations and cooperatives) and a realistic appraisal of Russia's economic potential for a speedy transition to socialism (the weakness of small-scale commodity production and the time required for the productive forces to recover).

The model of future development that Preobrazhensky provided in the book was based on an understanding of NEP as a mixed type of economy:

> This mixed type of economy can best be portrayed in the shape of a pyramid, divided into several bands, with the main band (4/5 of the

---

value of annual production) consisting of roughly two dozen million petty-bourgeois undertakings with a stratum of patriarchal-tribal economy ....the whole upper part of the pyramid represented a solid unit of socialist relations that were not yet the dominant ones but were struggling for dominance. This system as a whole, with its two main bands – an upper socialist band and a lower band of small commodity production – could be called a commodity-socialist system of economy.[50]

Exactly how, in 1922, did Preobrazhensky imagine the further development of NEP? The first stage of NEP, in his scheme, involved the restoration of industry and agriculture. The connection between them occurred through trade. With the development of commodity-money relations in agriculture, the process of social differentiation began quickly, with the middle peasantry constituting the principal element. The state would economically and administratively limit the growth of capitalist elements in the rural areas. Parallel with this, state farms would strengthen and grow. Preobrazhensky expected that during this first decade of NEP, Russian agriculture would not merely reach the pre-war level but also surpass it. In addition, with the help of trade and long-term credits for the peasantry, it would be possible to establish quite a strong tie with large-scale state industry. However, 'more substantial changes' within the agricultural economy would only begin 'with the second decade'.[51]

As far as industry was concerned, Preobrazhensky thought that during the first decade of NEP it would be able to strengthen its technical base; with the help of a system of professional-technical education, it would dramatically improve the training of skilled workers, and a mixed administrative-market system would be introduced for management and regulation of production. But all of this, for Preobrazhensky, meant only creation of the preconditions for transition to socialism: '... the task of socialism was to use capitalist forms in order to develop the country's productive forces up to a certain point, limiting these forms to playing the role of timber in erecting the socialist building'.[52]

According to Preobrazhensky, any attempts in future to dispose of this capitalist 'timber' of NEP, for the sake of a direct turn to socialist construction, must lead to a 'bourgeois-kulak' counter-revolution. 'The slogans of the movement were: defence of economic liberalism; struggle against restrictions on the private economy, struggle against tax increases on private production ... and

50   Preobrazhensky 1922, pp. 19–20. In this volume, p. 356.
51   Preobrazhensky 1922, p. 34. In this volume, p. 368.
52   Preobrazhensky 1922, p. 90. In this volume, p. 402.

struggle for universal suffrage and a parliamentary system'.[53] Precisely this kind of 'NEP uprising' would bring the first period, the first decade of NEP, to a close. But during that period the mixed commodity-socialist system of economy would give sufficient scope for development of the productive forces. However, Preobrazhensky believed that development along the path of NEP would decelerate due to its unresolved internal contradictions. This process would begin long before 'NEP's failed uprising against the proletarian dictatorship'.[54] By the late 1920s, the country would run into an economic impasse (the term used in the title of one of the book's sections); according to Preobrazhensky's prognosis, the way out would involve assistance from the European proletariat, who would be victorious in a European revolution by the late 1920s or early 1930s.

Modern readers may be amazed by the way results corresponded to the social-economic forecast for the development of NEP that Preobrazhensky made in 1922. 'The danger', he wrote, 'began from the moment when development of capitalist relations ... threatened, in economic terms, to outstrip socialist construction'.[55] Does this mean as some writers claim, that Preobrazhensky justified the 'Stalinist' variant of shutting down and discarding NEP? There is no disputing the fact that in Stalin's actions of the late 1920s one can find direct repetition of many of the ideas of L.D. Trotsky, E.A. Preobrazhensky, N.I. Bukharin and other theorists of the Bolshevik Party, not to mention V.I. Lenin (though they were expressed at a different time and applied to different historical circumstances). However, such an explanation would be too simple: it would reduce the whole of historical development to the 'fault' of one or another historical personality, leading us away from any consideration of those *objective* factors of which the ideas of Bolshevik theorists were the fruit and which propelled Stalin to make decisions at the end of the 1920s.

In the most general terms, it should be acknowledged that after Lenin's death the thinking about NEP and socialism among members of the party leadership – the 'Old Guard' – followed a direction that ultimately facilitated the creation, both in theory and in practice, of an insoluble contradiction between NEP and the need to move further in the direction of socialism, understood as a social-economic system beyond commodity production. Unfortunately, Lenin was unable in the closing years of his life to direct theoretical reflection towards a search for ways of combining NEP with socialism, and in his final writings he merely noted certain general approaches to such an about-turn. Thus, both in

---

53   Preobrazhensky 1922, p. 93. In this volume, p. 406.
54   Preobrazhensky 1922, p. 97. In this volume, p. 407.
55   Preobrazhensky 1922, p. 115. In this volume, p. 422.

1922 and subsequently, NEP was regarded as a path leading to the traditional model of socialism. It was precisely this path (without any modification of the characteristics of the final objective – socialism in Russia), that Preobrazhensky described in detail and according to scientific logic in his book *From NEP to Socialism*. Had his portrayal of the 'blind alleys' of NEP been properly understood and accepted in a timely manner, perhaps the outcome of the first decade of NEP would have been different.

5   Theorist of Trotskyism

During the summer and autumn of 1923, economic difficulties began to increase in the country: prices for agricultural and industrial products diverged, creating an acute 'sales crisis' that seized up the peasant market. This was the trigger mechanism for a number of prominent members of the Bolshevik Party, including Preobrazhensky, to demand a review of the party's political and economic line in the conditions of NEP, and the development and implementation of greater planning, competence and democracy.[56] Trotsky became leader of the emergent opposition. Preobrazhensky also played a prominent role in working out the opposition's economic and political program, as well as in propagating and defending it as an alternative to the majority views: his signature was the first on the famous 'Letter of the 46' – the opposition's manifesto – and he frequently appeared in the press and at the most important party forums, including two speeches as the Thirteenth Party Conference and one at the Thirteenth Congress of the RCP(B).

The 'Left Opposition' explained the emergence of the economic crisis of 1923 primarily in terms of subjective causes: the chaotic character of industrial construction and credit policy.[57] It was noted that during the spring and summer of 1923 an expansion of credit occurred for industry and trade, but there was no sum of credit kept as a reserve. In the autumn, the credits going to industrial and trade organisations were cut off unexpectedly and without any advance warning. The result was an increase in the number of strikes. The personnel in trade also had to be paid. In consequence, the trade organisations were forced to throw an array of commodities into the market at a time when the peasants were paying their agricultural tax and had no money. The situation was aggravated by the state's insufficient purchase of grain for export, which sharply drove

---

56   For the Discussion of 1923 see Polov (ed.) 1927.
57   For more detail on the events of 1923 and the problems of the national economy, see Gorinov 1990. See also Day 1973.

down grain prices. The result was the sales crisis. According to the authors of the 'Letter of the 46', 'The haphazardness, rashness and unsystematic character of the decisions of the Central Committee, which has failed to make ends meet in the economic sphere, has led us to ... a grave general-economic crisis'.[58]

The anti-crisis programme of the opposition included several elements. The 'motor' of further economic development was expansion of industry, without which there could not possibly be any genuine reduction of industrial prices that would benefit the consumer. Since industrial development lagged behind the growth of demand from agriculture, a reduction of industrial wholesale prices on the part of industry would never reach the village. After buying industrial commodities at cheap prices in the city, the private trader, who was predominant in the village, would make use of the shortage by selling them for three times the price in rural districts, pocketing the difference between the wholesale and retail prices for himself. The proposed solution to current economic difficulties was to reduce the prices of state industry and simultaneously alleviate the shortage by importing certain commodities from abroad for certain localities ('commodity intervention'), which must have the effect of reducing prices on industrial products. In terms of regulating the economy, priority was assigned to strengthening the planning principle in the activity of the state sector.[59]

In the political sphere, the opposition called for implementation of far-reaching party reforms that would be capable of stimulating collective initiative in the party, developing broad democracy, and liquidating apparatus tendencies.

At the height of the internal party discussion, Preobrazhensky tried to give a theoretical summary of the critical situation in the national economy while continuing his general study of the laws of the Soviet economy during the NEP period. He wrote that 'We cannot understand anything about the current crisis – neither its causes, nor how it is presently developing, nor future prospects – unless we address this problem of sales and clarify both the basic elements of proportionality in the present economic system and when material exchange between city and village can proceed normally'.[60] By undertaking a study of the conditions for achieving a balanced commodity market and general proportionality of all components of the national economy of the day, he was the first to pursue an important direction of analysis of the emerging eco-

---

58   Polov (ed.) 1927, p. 61. See *Documents of the 1923 Opposition* 1975.
59   For more detail see Erlich 1960.
60   Preobrazhensky 1923b, p. 305. [In this volume, p. 154.]

nomic system.[61] In the following years, he would continue his analysis from that same point of view. Meanwhile, in 1923 Preobrazhensky pointed out, first of all, that proportionality of the market, as the basis for overcoming crises, requires state regulation that takes into account the dynamics of the main elements of the economy through a forecast of conjunctural changes and, most importantly, of those associated with the seasonal character of agriculture. Secondly, the Soviet economy of the time needed a unified economic centre for regulating and controlling the conjuncture and for commodity-money regulation in place of the existing 'five centres' (Gosplan, Narkomfin, Gosbank, Komvnutorg and VSNKh). At the same time, Preobrazhensky criticised the position of those economists who relied fully, in terms of economic practice, upon the 'organising will of the state', assuming *a priori* that the state would prove to be stronger than all the 'lower', 'spontaneous' forms of economy and could therefore guarantee the elimination of economic crises. The reality of the economy of that period, as Preobrazhensky had already emphasised, was the coexistence and interaction of various economic forms; it was impossible not to take into account the fact that the main part of the NEP economy was regulated by and functioned on the basis of the spontaneous laws of commodity production. 'In general and on the whole, all of these forms are in direct contact with one another, and there are already grounds for speaking of a single economic organism ...'.[62]After his defeat in the political debate of 1923, Preobrazhensky became deputy chairman of the Communist Academy and was able to continue his theoretical studies of the Soviet economy. Relying upon many ideas that he had previously expressed, during 1924–26 he worked on his principal undertaking, the two-volume work entitled *The New Economics*, devoted to analysis of the theoretical laws of the Soviet economy's development and the concrete paths of a transition to socialism in the conditions of NEP Russia.

Following Bukharin's *Economics of the Transition Period*, this was perhaps the second most serious and penetrating investigation of such a theme undertaken during the Soviet period by a Bolshevik theorist. His conception, as we have already seen, was already beginning to mature at the end of 1922. A conviction of the need to write such a work grew stronger in 1923 during the internal party discussion. Unable any longer to argue and defend his political views, Preobrazhensky tried to give a detailed interpretation of a number of the

---

61   Preobrazhensky, together with V.G. Groman and S.G. Strumilin, worked on a special commission to calculate the commodity-money balance of the national economy in 1923.

62   Preobrazhensky 1923b, p. 305. In this volume, p. 154.

assumptions he had made in 1922–23. In particular, he discussed ideas concerning the commodity-socialist character of the Soviet economy, the forms and
methods of achieving national economic balance and dynamic equilibrium in
the processes of socialist accumulation, and the need for a pace-setting development of industry and a strengthening of planning in the state sector. The
whole book was Preobrazhensky's unique response to his own challenge that
he often repeated during this period – to investigate the prospective tendencies
of NEP and theoretically to justify further steps in socialist construction.

Moreover, there were also objective reasons for Preobrazhensky's preoccupation in 1924–25 with problems concerning the laws of development of the
Soviet economy and ways to stimulate more rapid economic growth of the
state sector. As early as 1923, it became clear that a dangerous disproportion
was emerging in development of the national economy: the restoration of state
industry began to lag far behind the analogous process in agriculture. Technical
backwardness, low labour productivity, and the high cost of industrial production created a palpable limit to the reconstruction of large-scale state industry
on the basis simply of increasing production and bringing idle equipment back
into operation. The nearer this limit, the clearer became the problem of finding sources for the modernisation and reconstruction of industry. In circumstances where the fixed capital of industry had long been neglected – from
1914–24 there was virtually no replacement, and capital was merely depleted
more intensively – a solution to this problem demanded significant financial
resources. In turn, the country's agriculture had significantly greater mobil-
ity not only in terms of rapidly restoring production (in the first harvest year
of 1922, agricultural production reached 75% of the pre-war level), but also
from the standpoint of accumulating the necessary monetary resources for
its expansion and improvement. In such circumstances, state economic policy
ran into a new round of interconnected problems whose solution would mark
a new stage of NEP. The issue involved working out a strategy for a pace-
setting development of state industry on the basis of accelerated accumulation, accompanied by expansion and growth in other branches and areas of
the national economy, beginning with the peasant sector. Projects were put
forward at the time by almost all the leaders of the Bolshevik Party, including prominent economists and economic leaders such as N.I. Bukharin, G. Ya.
Sokol'nikov, L.B. Krasin, V.A. Bazarov, A.V. Chayanov, N.D. Kondrat'ev and others. Preobrazhensky provided his own detailed and scientifically grounded project.

The initial version of a programme of socialist industrialisation, put forth by
Preobrazhensky in 1924,[63] immediately provoked a sharp protest from

---

63   See Preobrazhensky 1924.

Bukharin.[64] As soon as the first part of *The New Economics* appeared in the form of a book, Bukharin responded with a series of articles in 'Pravda' entitled 'On the Question of the Laws of the Transition Period'. During 1925–26 these replies from Bukharin often appeared in various publications devoted to criticism of the economic theories of so-called 'Trotskyism'.[65] In turn, Preobrazhensky answered Bukharin and other opponents in the second edition of *The New Economics*.

Unfortunately, the polemic between Bukharin and Preobrazhensky immediately went beyond the limits of scientific debate and acquired a pronounced political overtone.

The 'Trotskyist past' of 1923 re-emerged, now in the form of accusations of creating a special scientific theory to justify Trotskyist policy. Preobrazhensky emphatically rejected such parallels and was extremely upset that the results of his scientific research were persistently represented as a particular political platform. He had no intention of renewing political debates on that issue. 'Comrades, I have listened here to several remarks that are political in character', he commented at a discussion in the Communist Academy of one of the chapters from *The New Economics*. 'My report is not a political report but a scientific-theoretical one. For that reason, I have no intention to do battle in this auditorium with those comrades who have made political sorties'.[66] In Preobrazhensky's opinion, his 'chief' opponent, Bukharin, 'has sacrificed the theoretical integrity of research to the polemical tasks of today'.[67]

What was the essence of the debate that emerged over the idea of the 'new economics', and what was Preobrazhensky's actual position, as distinct from the distorted interpretation by his critics?[68] When studying the laws of development in the soviet economy in the concrete conditions of early 1920, Preobrazhensky, as we have already seen, first of all distinguished the dual character of the economic system that arose following the transition to NEP. Despite the

---

64   See Bukharin 1924. See also Bukharin 1982, pp. 151–82.

65   See Bukharin 1925a, 1925b, 1926. English translation of the latter in Bukharin 1982, pp. 109–50.

66   Preobrazhensky, 'Zakon tsennosti v sovetskom khozyaistve, Preniya po dokladu', in *Vestnik Kommunisticheskoi akademii*, No. 15, 1926, p. 232. [In this edition, see Volume II p. 395.]

67   Preobrazhensky 1926, p. 250. [In this edition, see Volume II p. 308.]

68   In Soviet literature on the history of economic thought, not a single attempt was made to provide an objective appraisal, without political labels, of Preobrazhensky's debate with Bukharin; nor were Preobrazhensky's replies to his critics published, although they would have clarified a great deal. This was the case even after Bukharin's critical articles against Preobrazhensky became accessible to the scientific community.

existence of various social-economic structures, in Preobrazhensky's view of prospective future development two economic forms would play a determining role: the planned state economy and small-scale peasant commodity production. Accordingly, two systems of regulation co-existed in the national economy: one of them, as Preobrazhensky saw it, was based upon specific planning regulators; and the other, on commodity-money and market regulators that corresponded with the law of value. The overall economic movement in such conditions was formed as a result of interaction between these two systems of regulation and the struggle between them. The latter description was completely consistent with orthodox Marxist thinking of the time, when socialism was viewed as a non-commodity and plan-organised system – the antithesis of capitalism and commodity production. State industry was considered to be mainly socialist or 'consistently socialist', and the petty commodity economy underpinned market relations. It was perfectly legitimate and logical, therefore, for Preobrazhensky to view the soviet economy as a mixed 'commodity-socialist economy' in which socialism and planning stood opposed to modes that function on the basis of private property and the market.

At the same time, recognising the unity of the country's economic organism and the interconnection of all its structures, Preobrazhensky was adamant on the question of the confrontation and struggle between socialist and commodity-capitalist forms and regarded any retreat from such positions as Menshevism.

The socialist perspective, for him, was inseparable from growth of large-scale industry and the strengthening and expansion of the state economy. In proposing his own version of a solution for the associated problems, Preobrazhensky understood that in Russian conditions an industrial breakthrough required assistance from all social classes, not merely the working class, which at the time was a minority in society. 'The worker', wrote Preobrazhensky, 'is not an exploiter of the peasant but a partner in making deductions for expanded reproduction, which is necessary not only to him but to Soviet society as a whole, to all the toiling classes'.[69] The condition of industry during the first half of the 1920s, when Preobrazhensky was working out the initial variant of industrialisation policy that we are examining here, was such that industry could not survive on its own without state support (subsidies from the state budget plus state loans) and the gratuitous transfer of part of the surplus product of peasant farming (the food tax).

---

69   Preobrazhensky 1926, p. 255. [In this edition, see Volume II, p. 311.]

What ways did Preobrazhensky suggest for accumulating this initial social capital, which was necessary in order for industry to 'get to its feet' and begin to accumulate the sums required independently of assistance from the state or the peasantry? We know that as early as 1919–20 he used the term 'primitive socialist accumulation'. The issue, of course, was not the term, which Preobrazhensky himself used in a 'conditional sense', but rather the content of the processes it helped to express insofar as 'the material substance of what it stands for remains'.[70] During the years of 'War Communism', this content was expressed through the system of food requisitioning; in the years of NEP, through the food tax and later the money tax on the peasantry. Both represented state alienation (partially or in total) of the surplus product of peasant farms in favour of the state budget, whose resources were directed mainly to the needs of industry. By then it was already obvious that, with development of the market and the restoration of industry and agriculture, the tax in kind or money coming from the peasantry would have to diminish and gradually disappear as a source for the state budget, being replaced by production sources of accumulation and economic ties between town and country based upon equivalent exchange. Preobrazhensky characterised this period as the transition from 'primitive' accumulation to accumulation on a 'production basis'. However, that sort of transition would not come any time soon. The reality in 1924 was non-equivalent exchange between industry and agriculture.

On the basis of these arguments, Preobrazhensky sought to identify the general tendency of development of the state sector's economic relations with all the other sectors, and particularly with the small-peasant economy. He formulated the 'law of primitive socialist accumulation', which he thought would describe development of the interaction between town and country until the restoration of normal equivalent exchange between them based upon creation of a highly developed socialist industry. The full formulation of the law was as follows:

> *The more economically backward, petty-bourgeois and peasant is one or another country that is going over to the socialist organisation of production, and the smaller is the inheritance that the proletariat of a given country receives at the moment of social revolution for its fund of socialist accumulation, the more will socialist accumulation be compelled to depend upon alienation of part of the surplus product of pre-socialist forms of economy, and the less will be the relative weight of accumulation on its own produc-*

---

70   Preobrazhensky 1926, p. 93. [In this edition, see Volume II, p. 154.]

tion base, i.e., the less will it be nourished by the surplus product of workers in socialist industry. Conversely, the more economically and industrially developed is one or another country in which the social revolution wins, and the greater is the material inheritance in the form of highly developed industry and capitalistically organised agriculture that the proletariat of this country receives from the bourgeoisie after nationalisation, the less will be the relative weight in the given country of pre-capitalist forms of production, the more imperative will it be for the proletariat of the given country to reduce non-equivalence in the exchange of its products for products of the former colonies, and the more will the centre of gravity of socialist accumulation shift to the production base of socialist forms, i.e., depend upon the surplus product of its own industry and its own agriculture.[71]

The objections that Bukharin formulated in a polemical article in 'Pravda' amounted basically to the following idea. Acknowledging the existence of non-equivalent exchange between town and country, Bukharin did not consider it acceptable to use the term 'exploitation'. 'Can this process be described as one involving the *exploitation* of small producers? No, it must not be described that way. To do so would involve setting aside the whole uniqueness of the process, misunderstanding its objective significance ...', wrote Bukharin.[72] In his opinion, this uniqueness consisted of the fact that 'we are heading not toward a *reinforcement* of relations among classes, but toward their elimination. And the faster accumulation takes place within the socialist economic sphere and its periphery, which is becoming socialist, the faster does the elimination of the antithesis proceed as well'.[73] This argument missed the target, since Preobrazhensky never interpreted non-equivalent exchange to be a permanent phenomenon, forever enshrining the supremacy of the proletariat. Moreover, as Preobrazhensky wrote, 'Having acknowledged both the fact and the necessity for non-equivalent exchange with the private economy ... he accepted my basic way of posing the question and thereby deprived himself of any possibility of waging a principled dispute concerning all the essential conclusions that follow from this position'.[74]

The second point of Bukharin's criticism was that Preobrazhensky's conception involved an incorrect, 'non-Leninist' understanding of the process of interaction between state industry and the peasant economy, in which the first

---

71   Preobrazhensky 1926, p. 138. [In this edition, see Volume II, p. 190.]
72   Bukharin 1925a, p. 69. Also Bukharin 1982, p. 157.
73   Ibid. Also Bukharin 1982, pp. 156–7.
74   Preobrazhensky 1926, p. 253. [In this edition, see Volume II, p. 310.]

'devours' the second, as Bukharin thought, rather than 'transforms' it. Further-more, in Preobrazhensky's scheme 'there is *no* place for *Leninist* cooperation, which leads the peasantry to socialism'.[75] In response to this, Preobrazhensky provided some very interesting and pointed arguments. He claimed that 'Com-rade Bukharin fastens upon the word "devouring" not for a debate over the essence of the matter ... but rather to attribute to me a concrete plan for this devouring ... After composing such a scheme for me, which has no rela-tion to what I in fact said, comrade Bukharin decisively announces that "all of this is fundamentally incorrect"'.[76] With regard to the role of cooperatives in development of the peasant economy, Preobrazhensky points out, in the first place, that in his book *From NEP to Socialism*, two years earlier, he already 'analysed this question in detail';[77] secondly, if he had disagreed with Lenin concerning the role of cooperatives he would have written about it directly. Preobrazhensky explains his caution concerning a projection of the peasant economy's future paths of development on the way to socialist agriculture by the fact that 'for the present, *no one knows or can know* how agriculture will be concretely transformed into a type of agricultural cooperation in production that will be the transitional stage to the socialisation of agriculture'.[78] In Lenin's article 'On Cooperation', he continued, 'what Bukharin demands of me ... is not to be found ... there is nothing concerning the forms and paths of producers' cooperation in the countryside, only a statement in principle concerning the role of cooperation in a peasant country. Lenin could say nothing on this point because he had no love for utopias and never involved himself in composing them'.[79]

A recitation of the dispute between Bukharin and Preobrazhensky could be extended further, but its meaning will not be changed by adding arguments and counter-arguments from one side or the other. If we abstract from political motives, in our view the essential aim of the debate between these two talented theorists of the Bolshevik party was to develop further the Leninist heritage. It is not surprising that Preobrazhensky claimed that his 'conception of accumu-lation not only does not contradict Lenin's last article "On Cooperation" but, on the contrary, has a direct internal connection with it'.[80] Similarly, Bukharin traced a direct connection between his views and works by Lenin.

---

75   Bukharin 1925a, p. 74. See Bukharin 1982, p. 161.
76   Preobrazhensky 1926, pp. 258–9. [In this edition, see Volume II, p. 314.]
77   Preobrazhensky 1926, p. 260. [In this edition, see Volume II, p. 315.]
78   Ibid.
79   Preobrazhensky 1926, p. 261. [In this edition, see Volume II, p. 316.]
80   Ibid.

The two party theorists each read Lenin's works from the NEP period in his own way. Since the theory of the path to socialism, in conditions of NEP, remained incomplete and involved a number of theoretical problems not resolved by Lenin, his works could provide validation for the views of both Bukharin and Preobrazhensky. Only Bukharin, in our opinion, placed more emphasis in 1924–25 on Lenin's views concerning development of peasant market principles during NEP, whereas Preobrazhensky emphasised the industrial proletarian principle. It is noteworthy that following the bitter fight of 1924–25, their positions will begin to converge: Bukharin will be forced to acknowledge the seriousness of the problem of industrialisation and its sources, and Preobrazhensky will pay increased attention to the problem of commodity-money equilibrium in the course of social reproduction.[81] However, the tendency towards mitigation of their disagreements on questions of principle was blocked by escalation of the political confrontation, which for Preobrazhensky ended in expulsion from the party and deportation from Moscow to Ural'sk.

6   No Matter What

Exile did not break Preobrazhensky. He continued to correspond with colleagues and analysed the processes that were occurring in both the country and the party. One of the interesting documents from this period is 'The Left Course in the Countryside and its Prospects', a set of theses by Preobrazhensky dated 23 April 1928.[82] Analysing the grain procurement crisis that shook the Soviet economy at the beginning of 1928, Preobrazhensky saw it as confirmation of the validity of the left opposition's economic programme. He wrote:

> The current economic crisis in the USSR is neither a conjunctural nor merely an economic crisis: this is a prolonged social crisis. It is rooted in two facts: first of all, the lag of industry behind agriculture, i.e., the delay in the country's industrialisation; and secondly, the intensifying contradiction, which is inherent in our system, between the state economy and

---

81   See, for example, Preobrazhensky 1927; Preobrazhensky, 'Ekonomicheskie zametky', *Pravda*, 15 December 1925; *Bol'shevik*, No. 6, 1926, pp. 15–16; No. 6, 1927. [In this volume, see Part 1, Chapter 2; Part 2, Chapter 4; Part 2, Chapter 5.]

82   This document is in the Trotsky Archives at Harvard University (No. T-1262). Professor V.P. Danilov provided the authors with a copy. [In this volume, see Part 4, Appendix 3.]

capitalist development, which until now has been expressed primarily in the growing concentration of materials and grain stocks in the hands of the kulaks.[83]

Preobrazhensky modelled two possible alternative ways out of the crisis. He saw the 'right course' as 'an attempt to rely, in terms of developing the raw material base and export resources, on the growing kulak strata in the village, thus increasing commodity production without spending state resources for that purpose'.[84] He added that 'This policy would inevitably demand increased pressure on the urban working class (a rise of bread prices, higher output norms, etc.), while in the village it would be connected with an increase of agrarian over-population and a slowing of the country's rate of industrialisation'.[85] Moreover, since the kulaks were terrorised by the recent use of 'extraordinary measures', to inspire their confidence would require paying 'some kind of unheard of price – the price of such a sharp turn to the right that even the furthest right of our rightists ... will not dare ...'.[86] This road also entailed the danger of losing political power.

The 'left course' was 'the policy of a gradual way out of the crisis, calculated over a number of years, based upon ... an increase of commodity production on the farms of middle and poor peasants' through cooperatives in production and the creation of state farms. In order to block any counter tendencies, which would objectively result from the 'left course' (a possible curtailment of production on major commodity-producing farms belonging to well-off peasants and kulaks), Preobrazhensky suggested a system of inter-related measures: 1) 'to accelerate the rate of industrialisation, because grain can be taken from these strata *only by using economic methods*, only through commodity exchange aiming also, in economic ways, for a reduction in the rural consumption of agricultural products through an increase in demand for industrially produced consumer items';[87] 2) conduct a left policy in the Comintern, 'guaranteeing a greater defensive capacity of the USSR in the event of war';[88] 3) expand the party's social support in the city, in which case, to the extent that significant improvement in the material position of the workers was objectively

---

83   In this volume, see p. 447.
84   Ibid., p. 448.
85   Ibid., p. 449.
86   Ibid.
87   Ibid., p. 450. Italics added.
88   Ibid., p. 451.

impossible, there would be need for 'a speedy improvement in the legal status of workers, especially at the bottom, in the factory, which means implementation of a regime of workers' democracy'.[89]

Preobrazhensky's 'left course', therefore, was radically different from the Stalinist 'revolution from above' and the latter's typical expansion of non-economic methods of coercion.

However, the package of measures suggested by Preobrazhensky was quite vulnerable. To increase commodity production by poor and middle peasant farms, using economic methods, in fact presupposed an acceleration in the rate of industrialisation, but the latter, in turn, required growth in agricultural commodity production (in order to secure materials for industry and food for workers). To force industrialisation at the cost of 'belt tightening' by workers would fit poorly with the suggestion to increase social support in the city. As in his earlier works, Preobrazhensky probably was hoping for the second form of the 'left course' – a revolutionary policy in the Comintern, whose success could lead to the victory of socialist revolutions in developed European countries, which would solve the problem of industrial commodities for the village.

In connection with Trotsky's deportation from the USSR in 1929 and the sharp 'shift to the left' by Stalin, vacillation increased in the ranks of the opposition. On 13 July 1929 'Pravda' published a 'Declaration to the Central Control Commission by former leaders of the Trotskyist opposition, comrades E. Preobrazhensky, K. Radek and I. Smilga, concerning a break with the opposition'. Preobrazhensky and other 'leftist' leaders sincerely believed that the majority of the Central Committee, headed by Stalin, had gone over to their position after striking a blow at the 'rightists'.[90] And once the political basis of the disagreements had vanished, they must put aside past grievances and return to the party. Preobrazhensky did not yet know the methods Stalin would employ in struggling to implement the 'general line'. Once he saw those methods, he could not fully support them: '... I could shoot the way I wanted to, but not as the party was shooting ... And so I was expelled from the party a second time ... (during the fierce battles for collectivisation in the village)'.[91]

In the interval between the two expulsions from the party, Preobrazhensky managed to publish a number of works. Their scientific orientation was no mere coincidence. The situation in the country's national economy in the late 1920s convinced Preobrazhensky once again to study the problems of paper-money circulation. The fact is that the state returned to issuing money as a

---

89   Ibid.
90   See Preobrazhensky 1960 and 1929.
91   *XVII S'ezd VKP(B). Stenograficheskii otchet* (Moscow, 1934), p. 238.

means for implementing forced industrialisation independently of the peasant market. That, along with a goods famine, curtailment of the private capitalist sector, nationalisation of cooperative trade, and obstacles to any reduction in the cost of production through growth of labour productivity in state enterprises, led to rising prices and destabilisation of the currency. The about-turn in 1929 restored command-administrative methods of managing the national economy and, at the same time, meant an abrupt curtailment of NEP and commodity-money relations.

Since his view of the content and basic features of the socialist economic system remained unchanged in those years, Preobrazhensky assessed the prospects for further economic development, including monetary circulation, within the context of a planned economy and gradual elimination of commodity production. It is interesting to note his remark about the fate of the planned economy, which, in his opinion, began to take form in the years of 'War Communism' (thus Preobrazhensky, like many others, identified planned economy with an administrative-command system, a natural economy). He wrote: '... The planned economy of the period of War Communism was not eliminated [in the years of NEP] but was only transformed in the context of the market system of connecting the state economy with the private economy. All of the subsequent changes in the nature of our money, which have already occurred *during the NEP period*, were thereby predetermined.'[92] With this remark, Preobrazhensky accurately and astutely grasped the meaning of the processes that had taken place with the transition from War Communism to NEP. Indeed, one of the internal obstacles to development of NEP was the weak development of commodity-money relations in the state sector and the considerable and long-term preservation, within the economic mechanism of NEP, of administrative-command methods of management.

> After a certain period of confusion and weakening of the planning principle in managing industry, we entered a period during which, on the one hand, we had more rapid restoration of the state economy and growth of its accumulation and production, while on the other hand we began a period of strengthening the planning principle within the state sector and increasing the elements of regulation and the regulating influence of this state economy on the entire private economy in general.[93]

---

92   Preobrazhensky 1930a, p. 62.
93   Preobrazhensky 1930a, p. 63.

Given these tendencies, Preobrazhensky interpreted many new phenomena of the late 1920s as a gradual approach to the moment of the final collapse of paper-money circulation and the elimination of most of money's functions. When analysing these processes, he thought the laws of capitalism's monetary circulation must not be uncritically transferred to the Soviet economy, especially to the sphere of the state economy. This reflects, on the one hand, Preobrazhensky's well-known position concerning the extremely limited effect of the law of value in the state sector, and on the other hand, in our view, the scientific intuition that told him that large-scale state intervention in economic life, and especially in the mechanism of functioning commodity-money relations, required a different approach and a special investigation that Marx could not carry out. What was involved, essentially, was further development of the Marxist theory of the circulation of money.

'The rising cost of living and the depreciation of gold, which began in the 1890s. have posed for Marxist theoretical thought the question of the causes of this phenomenon', wrote Preobrazhensky.[94] In his book *The Theory of a Falling Currency*, he undertook a thorough investigation of general processes in the development of currency systems in terms of currency issues and inflation. As we have already noted, Soviet practice in the late 1920s provided plenty of material for studying these phenomena.

Unlike an analysis of the laws of stable money circulation, which was carried out in *Capital*, Preobrazhensky concentrated on studying the factors that lead to instability of a currency system. In this case, he was interested not in ways to restore a stable currency system (the country had already gone through that experience), but rather in the mechanisms of monetary circulation in conditions of an unstable currency system and its destabilisation. Decline of the currency, in his opinion, was a feature of crisis in the system of money circulation. As a result, he considered changes in money circulation by analogy with a cyclical crisis: the currency first declines, followed by a sharp acceleration and collapse of the monetary system, then comes restoration and stabilisation of the currency, followed by another destruction of equilibrium.[95]

In this respect, Preobrazhensky was able to formulate one of the promising lines of analysis that many non-Marxist, western economists soon followed.

The ability to think broadly, to capture underlying trends and predict their subsequent development, was confirmed in another book written by Preobrazhensky during these years, *The Decline of Capitalism: Reproduction and*

---

94   Preobrazhensky 1930b, p. 112.
95   See Preobrazhensky 1930c, p. 27.

Crises in Imperialism and the World Crisis of 1930–1931.[96] The theme had a broad scope: in the preface the author mentioned that the book was part of an extensive work on contemporary imperialism and its demise. The world economic crisis, which had begun in 1929, added relevance to the problem of studying the prospects of capitalism as a system. This question was debated frequently in Soviet economic literature, in numerous discussions and in the press. Preobrazhensky undertook to solve it from the standpoint of analysing a change in the capitalist cycle of reproduction during the period of monopoly capitalism as compared to the cycle during the time of free competition, which was analysed by Marx. 'What has happened', asked Preobrazhensky, 'to the very mechanism of capitalist society to deprive it of the ability to move from one cycle of expanded reproduction to another, as it used to do in the epoch of free competition?'[97] He showed in the book that the phenomena of monopolism – resulting from concentration of production – deformed the cycle of capitalist reproduction, with the result of creating extraordinary difficulty in the transition on a world scale to a new cycle of expanded reproduction.

Preobrazhensky's conclusions typified the 'optimism' of the time. After showing that in the new epoch the mechanism of capitalist reproduction itself demanded intervention by the state, he believed, as did most of his Marxist contemporaries, that the 'decline of capitalism' was under way, for 'Capitalism and a planned economy are ... incompatible. Capitalism might well find itself in a blind alley and begin to have need of a planned economy, but a planned economy has no need of capitalism'.[98] In real life, however, things turned out not to be so simple. Indeed, the old capitalism of free competition as well as the monopoly capitalism of the early twentieth century actually had run into a blind alley. But 'bourgeois' science (particularly J.M. Keynes) worked out methods for state regulation of the capitalist economy. As a result, world capitalism was able to overcome the structural crisis of the 1930s through transition to a system of state-monopoly capitalism.

In fairness, it should be pointed out that scientific intuition still suggested to Preobrazhensky that capitalism might find a way out. He wrote, among other things, that *'if it does not lead to a world war, or is not interrupted by a technological revolution*, a general economic crisis under monopolism must outgrow its economic framework and become a general social crisis of the entire historical system of capitalism'.[99] It is not so much the unjustified forecast of

---

96   See Preobrazhensky 1985, republished by Random House in 2018.
97   See Preobrazhensky 1985, p. 7.
98   See Preobrazhensky 1985, p. 13.
99   See Preobrazhensky 1985, p. 111 (italics added).

the imminent 'decline of capitalism' that is important here, but rather Preobrazhensky's mention of possible reserves for a future 'second wind' for capitalism: 1) state involvement in the process of capitalist reproduction; 2) expansion of the military-industrial complex; 3) use of the achievements of a scientific-technical revolution.[100]

The works of Preobrazhensky that we have analysed testify to the fact that he had entered a period of creative maturity. In 1931 he was 45 years old – the age when a scholar flourishes. Freely working with a colossal volume of material from English, American, French,[101] German and Russian sources, Evgeny Alekseevich drew broad generalisations concerning the development of world economic processes and continued to work on fundamental problems of political economy. But persecution was mounting in the press. The accusation of 'Trotskyist contraband'[102] – a murderous charge for those years – was levelled against Preobrazhensky. At the end of 1931 Preobrazhensky sent to the editors of the journal 'Problemy ekonomiki' an article 'On the Methodology for Compiling a General Plan and the Second Five-Year Plan'. The article was not published, but it was excoriated. A few paragraphs were quoted from it, accompanied by detailed commentary, or else there were simply 'commentaries'.[103]

This renewed hounding in the press culminated in expulsion from the party. Although Preobrazhensky made a penitent speech at the Seventeenth Congress of the RCP(B) on 31 January 1934, it was already too late to have any significant effect on his fate. On 13 July 1937, Preobrazhensky was murdered in Stalin's torture chambers.

M.M. Gorinov, S.V. Tsakunov

---

100 [Debates between Soviet economists concerning the counter-cyclical potential of the capitalist state are discussed in Day 1981. See 'The Preobrazhensky Affair', pp. 229–47.]

101 In particular, Preobrazhensky published a book on France in 1926: *Ekonomika i politika sovremennoi Frantsii* (Moscow, 1926).

102 See Borilin 1931.

103 See Butayev 1932. It is important to note that in his unpublished article, as revealed by critics, Preobrazhensky also criticised the excessive pace of industrialisation projected in the second five-year plan, warning that 'the hypertrophy of tempos in the development of heavy industry' must give way to a period of adjustment and widening of existing bottlenecks. (See Day 1980, p. 230).

Preobrazhensky and Trotsky: The Transition to Socialism and the Afterlife of NEP

Richard B. Day

Evgeny Preobrazhensky is best known to historians as the author of *The New Economics*. Preobrazhensky's economic research was characterised by a rigorous commitment to scientific integrity that sustained him through years of heated debates with N.I. Bukharin and abusive denunciations from lesser-known party functionaries. His scholarship inevitably involved him in the political struggles of the 1920s, but he was never primarily a political actor. Writing to Leon Trotsky in 1928, he declared that 'my interest in politics has seriously waned and my interest in "pure" science has correspondingly grown. Science is what endures. Politics drains away with all the debris, like water in the spring. And when you reach a mature age, you want to give something lasting to society'.[1]

Leon Trotsky was an altogether different sort of revolutionary. Trotsky lived and breathed politics, regarding himself first and foremost as an agent of world history. Trotsky's understanding of economics moved on the scale of the world economy and world history. The result was that Trotsky and Preobrazhensky responded quite differently to Stalin's adoption of the 'left course' in the countryside in 1928. Preobrazhensky welcomed Stalin's attack on the kulak as a triumph for '*our course* in the countryside'[2] and a final vindication in his decade-long struggle over primitive socialist accumulation. Trotsky, in contrast, regarded Stalin's change of policy as a mere manoeuvre and another desperate chapter of a much larger struggle over 'Socialism in One Country'.

In this essay, I intend to look at NEP from three perspectives. First, I shall consider the debate within the Soviet Union and the differences between Trotsky and Preobrazhensky that ultimately fractured the Left Opposition. Next, I shall assess NEP as a general model for industrialising an agrarian economy. Finally, taking the 'afterlife of NEP' in China as my point of reference, I want to emphasise the critical importance of political life in socialist society. Preobrazhensky

---

1   In this volume, p. 456.
2   In this volume, p. 441.

never considered a *political* theory of socialist transition; the political state would wither away with the growth of scientific economic planning. In exile, however, Trotsky's articles in the *Bulletin of the Opposition* and his work on *The Revolution Betrayed* fundamentally reassessed the relation between political life and socialist forms of economic organisation.

1   Preobrazhensky, Trotsky and NEP

Many readers of this volume will be surprised by the Appendices in Part 3. By the spring of 1928, only months after being sent into exile, Preobrazhensky was considering how he and other exiles might endorse Stalin's measures against the kulaks and thereby reconcile with the party. He objected to the brutality of Stalin's methods, yet in principle he regarded the 'left course' as fulfilment of the programme expounded by the Left Opposition since at least 1923. Preobrazhensky urged that the opposition must 'accept responsibility' for the policy of primitive accumulation even if the Central Committee was inconsistent in implementing it: '*the left policy in the countryside is our policy, and the inconsistency in implementing it – that is the responsibility of the CC. We answer for our policy as such, and not for the methods by which it is or is not implemented*'.[3] Karl Radek's initial reaction indicated the bewilderment of many exiles upon hearing of Preobrazhensky's proposal: 'How can we take responsibility', exclaimed Radek, 'for something upon which we do not have the slightest influence? Such a declaration would be ridiculous: we are sitting in exile and we take responsibility!'[4]

In *The Prophet Unarmed*, the second volume of his widely acclaimed biography of Trotsky, Isaac Deutscher described Trotsky's response: 'Trotsky was dead set against Preobrazhensky's proposal ... The jailer and the jailed were not allies'.[5] Deutscher explained Trotsky's intransigence by pointing to fundamental differences of conviction and temperament between the two men:

> Trotsky had never committed himself to the view that the workers' state must as a rule 'exploit' the peasantry – at any rate, he had never expounded the view as bluntly as Preobrazhensky had done. Nor had he advocated a pace of industrialization as forcible as that which Preobrazhensky anticipated. Preobrazhensky's theorem of *The New Economics*

---

3   In this volume, p. 464.
4   In this volume, p. 454.
5   Deutscher 1965, p. 418.

had ... implied that primitive accumulation, the most difficult part of the transition from capitalism to socialism, might be accomplished within a single industrially underdeveloped nation-state. Finally, unlike Trotsky, Preobrazhensky had dwelt on the 'objective force of the laws' of the transition to socialism, a force which would assert itself and compel the party leaders to act *malgré eux-mêmes* as the agents of socialism. Nationalization of all large-scale industry, [Preobrazhensky] held, led ineluctably to planned economy and rapid industrialization.[6]

Deutscher spoke of these differences as being 'implicit' up to 1928. They contained 'only the seed of political disagreement'.[7] Yet by the summer of 1929 Preobrazhensky repudiated 'Trotskyism', and in January 1930 he was readmitted to the party. Three years later he was again exiled. On 13 July 1937 he was sentenced to death and shot. Trotsky was deported from the Soviet Union in January 1929. He continued to denounce Stalin's economic policies and the bureaucratic corruption of Soviet society until he was assassinated by Stalin's agent in Mexico on 20 August 1940.

Deutscher's biographical insights were accurate, but they require elaboration with reference to the documentary sources. Trotsky and Preobrazhensky certainly agreed on the urgent need for industrialisation. Nevertheless, by the late 1920s their core ideas led them to react differently to the issue of 'Socialism in One Country'. For Stalin, this slogan stood for a programme of industrialisation aiming for 'independence' from the capitalist world economy, which in turn implied a manic focus upon domestic heavy industry along with forced collectivisation to extract necessary resources from the peasantry. When Stalin spoke of 'Socialism in One Country', he declared that 'our country ... possesses all that is necessary for the construction of a full socialist society':

> [We must] conduct our economic construction in such a way as to convert the USSR from a country which imports machines and equipment into a country which produces machines and equipment ... In this manner the USSR ... will become *a self-sufficient economic unit building socialism*.[8]

The documents in this volume show how easy it must have been for Preobrazhensky to conclude that Stalin's rhetoric reflected the objective requirements of the law of primitive socialist accumulation. Trotsky, on the other

---

6   Deutscher 1965, p. 416.
7   Deutscher 1965, p. 238.
8   Stalin 1926, p. 28 (italics added).

hand, had always insisted that Soviet industrialisation could not be conceived in abstraction from the world economy. This was a crucial difference between the two men, and it needs to be specified at the outset.

For Preobrazhensky, a socialist economy must co-exist with *but no longer be part of* the world capitalist economy. Trotsky, in contrast, claimed that to ignore the Soviet Union's dependence upon the world economy would be equivalent to walking naked in the streets of Moscow during mid-winter – trying to ignore the cold.[9] In July 1925 Trotsky wrote:

> The international division of labour flows from both economic and his-torical causes. The fact that our country has gone over to a socialist organ-isation of its economy, while the rest of mankind lives in capitalist con-ditions, in no way eliminates the international division of labour or the bonds and dependencies which result from it. One of the causes of our economic collapse during the first years of the revolution was the block-ade. Escape from the blockade means a restoration of economic links, which grow out of the world division of labour; that is ... out of the differ-ent economic levels of the various countries.[10]

Trotsky regarded the world economy as an irreversible historical fact, a contra-dictory unity that after 1917 also embraced the struggle between capitalism and socialism. Until proletarian revolution came in Europe, the Soviet Union must use its export revenues to draw upon the 'reserves' of the capitalist countries both to facilitate industrialisation and also to regulate the domestic market and class contradictions between the proletariat and peasantry. The alternative was to rely upon 'the curbed and domesticated productive forces, that is ... [on] the technology of economic backwardness'.[11]

> We must renew our basic capital, which is presently passing through a crisis. Whoever imagines that we will be able to build all of our equipment in the coming years, or even the greater part of it, is a dreamer. The indus-trialisation of our country ... means ... not a decrease, but on the contrary a growth of our connections with the outside world, which means ... our growing dependence ... on the world market, on capitalism, on its tech-nical equipment and its economy.[12]

---

9   Trotsky 1927, p. 530.
10   *Trotsky Archives*, No. T-2977.
11   Trotsky 1957, p. 53.
12   *Pravda*, 14 December 1926.

It is impossible to opt out of the world economy. What is export? ... And what are imports? ... There you have it. On the question of imports and exports the whole theory of [Socialism in One Country] ... at once falls to pieces. The success of socialist construction depends on the tempo, and the tempo of our economic development is presently most directly ... determined by the import of materials and equipment.[13]

This is the context in which Trotsky began to worry by the mid-1920s that Preobrazhensky's emphasis upon domestic accumulation, financed by turning the domestic terms of trade against the peasantry, might lend support to Stalinism. Preobrazhensky's primary concern was always to protect Soviet industry from the competition of cheaper foreign commodities that he feared would thwart primitive socialist accumulation. To minimise the threat of contraband, the foreign trade monopoly must 'fence off Soviet territory from the disintegrating operation of the world law of value'.[14] In practical terms, this meant severing Soviet domestic prices from world prices – or the domestic law of value from the world law of value – in order that industry might acquire the resources it needed from agriculture.

If economic relations in our country were currently formed on the basis of free operation of the world economy's law of value [i.e., if domestic prices were determined by world prices], this would lead to a situation in which, with today's prices on the world market and the present over-industrialisation of Europe, two-thirds of our large-scale industry would be eliminated due to its unprofitability and redundancy *from the viewpoint of the world division of labour on the capitalist basis*.[15]

Industrial prices that exceeded those on the world market, combined with relatively low state procurement prices for agricultural commodities, would be the formula of primitive socialist accumulation: 'the basic line of struggle of the socialist sector of our economy with the bourgeois system corresponds precisely with the line of struggle against the world capitalist economy ...'.[16] Furthermore, '[T]he import fund that the state acquires through ... exports ... cannot to any significant extent be committed to imports of peasant means

13   Trotsky 1927, pp. 530–1.
14   In this edition, see Volume II, p. 376.
15   In this edition, see Volume II, p. 428.
16   In this edition, see Volume II, p. 359.

of consumption'.[17] 'More rapid accumulation in heavy industry' must always occur 'prior to expanded reproduction' in other branches of the economy.[18]

In May 1926 Trotsky commented that Preobrazhensky's concept of a domestic struggle between the law of primitive socialist accumulation and the domestic law of value – or the control of domestic prices in support of industrial accumulation – was 'in the highest degree productive, more accurately, the only correct way' of studying the Soviet economy. But Preobrazhensky's methodology, which began by modelling domestic relations and then added a supplementary role for foreign trade, could also be seen as implying a prospect of socialist self-sufficiency. 'It was necessary', Trotsky cautioned, 'to begin this investigation within the limits of a closed Soviet economy. But now the danger is growing that this methodological approach will be converted into a finished economic perspective for the development of "Socialism in One Country".'[19]

Preobrazhensky was clearly aware of important potential benefits from international trade. In his essay on the conditions of equilibrium he even specified the need for 'maximal contact with the world economy' in order to import capital equipment.[20] The problem was that Trotsky did not agree with Preobrazhensky's notion of 'the completely unique character of our exports and imports',[21] which for Preobrazhensky meant a continuous priority of producer needs over those of consumers. Stalinist propaganda portrayed both Trotsky and Preobrazhensky as 'super-industrialisers', but Trotsky's commitment to industrialisation was tempered by a conviction that peasant interests must also be incorporated into industrialisation and foreign-trade strategy if NEP was not to collapse.

These two crucial issues – 1) the contradictory universality of the world division of labour, and 2) the implications of foreign trade for Soviet domestic policy, including both industrialisation and agrarian policy – provide the framework for explaining the differences between Trotsky and Preobrazhensky that ultimately fractured the Trotskyist Opposition.

---

17   In this volume, pp. 125–6.
18   In this volume, p. 110.
19   *Trotsky Archives*, No. T-2984.
20   In this volume, p. 105.
21   In this volume, p. 106.

2   'Socialism in One Country' and Soviet Russia's Place in the World
        Economy

In many respects Preobrazhensky's *New Economics* followed ideas first set out
in *From NEP to Socialism*. This early work, written in 1921 and published in
1922, showed remarkable prescience in anticipating a general capitalist crisis by
the early 1930s. Convinced that this crisis would finally precipitate a European
revolution, Preobrazhensky projected what Soviet Russia might accomplish in
the meantime:

> In contrast with the industrial countries of Europe, and especially with
> England or Germany, Russia was a country that possessed everything
> needed in order to develop into *a self-sufficient economic organism*. The
> economic and geographical requirements, together with the required
> social character, were all present. In the first place, Russia possessed all
> the natural resources needed to create a powerful industrial-agricultural
> complex. Coal, oil, peat, timber, iron and other ores, cotton, all kinds of
> raw materials except rubber, unlimited possibilities for agricultural devel-
> opment and for increasing the output of materials from livestock produc-
> tion: all these were at hand. Thus all the requirements were there for a
> rapid expansion after the American pattern.[22]

Preobrazhensky also anticipated, however, that the USSR would eventually face
its own acute crisis – an attempted bourgeois counter-revolution, led by kulaks,
private traders and small commodity producers – that would coincide with
the coming cyclical crisis in the capitalist countries. The threat of counter-
revolution would result from failure to complete the one major task that Soviet
Russia could not accomplish on its own; that is, a revolutionary transformation of agriculture, through electrification and mechanisation, in preparation
for gradual, voluntary collectivisation.

   Just one year after publication of *From NEP to Socialism*, however, the revolutionary timetable in Europe appeared for a short interval to change dramatically. France occupied the Ruhr, and the ensuing German inflation seemed
briefly to portend a German revolution. Preobrazhensky's response revealed
a view of the world economy that was fundamentally different from Trotsky's.
In a 'Pravda' article entitled 'Two Lines of World Economic Development', Preobrazhensky now spoke of two emerging 'systems of world economy', one cap-

---

22   In this volume, p. 351 (italics added).

italist and the other socialist. Revolutionary Germany would exit the capitalist world economy to join with Soviet Russia in a newly emerging world socialist system.

> Russia's withdrawal from the world war and from the world economy, the creation of its own *shut-in [zamknutovo] economic whole*, the transition to socialist rails of large-scale industry and transport, with the aspiration of the whole complex to establish contact with the [capitalist] world economy as a single organised entity (the monopoly of foreign trade), marks the beginning of a new era ... The world economy has *broken up* into two unequal halves with economic systems that are different in principle and with two socially opposed classes at the helm of state power ... [A] new successful proletarian revolution will not just repaint a part of the geographical map of the earth in red, but will also divert the corresponding part of the productive forces from the channel of one system to the other.[23]

Trotsky, on the other hand, attributed the world division of labour to the fact that modern industrial production had irreversibly outgrown the limits of political frontiers, an argument that he developed long before the Russian Revolution and continued to uphold throughout the debate over 'Socialism in One Country'.[24] As early as 1915 he had argued that a socialist United States of Europe was 'the only political form in which the proletariat can resolve the implacable contradiction between the contemporary productive forces and the limitations of nation-state organisation'.[25] Imperialism and the world war were capitalism's testimony to the irreconcilable contradiction between the requirements of modern industry and the archaic limitations imposed by tariff barriers and narrow national markets.

> To the extent that capitalist development became constricted within the limits of the state, the latter was supplemented by annexations and colonial appendages ... The competition for colonies led to the struggle of the capitalist states among themselves. The productive forces have finally become cramped within the limits of the state ... The place of the *shut-in*

---

23   Preobrazhensky 1923c, italics added.

24   Technological change entailed a continuously rising 'organic composition of capital', meaning that per-unit costs of production could only be minimised by continuously expanding the volume of output, which in turn accounted for the division of labour and growth of international trade.

25   *Nashe Slovo*, 23 February 1915.

[*zamknutovo*] *national state* must inevitably be taken by a broad democratic federation of the leading states, with the abolition of all tariff divisions.[26]

Trotsky applied the same thinking to Stalin's slogan of 'Socialism in One Country'. The 'scheme for a self-contained socialist development' was the result of 'a national limitation supplemented by provincial conceit'.[27] Repudiating the formula of a 'shut-in', 'closed' and 'self-sufficient' economy, in 1926 Trotsky wrote:

> Actually the most essential line of our economic growth is precisely the fact that we are at last leaving behind our *shut-in (zamknutoe) state-economic existence* and are entering into increasingly profound ties with the European and world markets. To reduce the whole question of our development to the internal relation between the proletariat and peasantry in the USSR, and to think that correct political manoeuvring ... frees us from world economic dependencies, means falling into a dreadful national limitation. Not only theoretical considerations, but also the difficulties with exports and imports provide the evidence of this fact.[28]

On countless occasions throughout the 1920s Trotsky repeated such comments. The continuity of his thinking on these issues is remarkable. In 1928, at exactly the time when Preobrazhensky was expressing support for Stalin's 'left course', Trotsky was writing his own blistering denunciation of Stalinism that was later

---

26   Trotsky 1915, italics added. It should be noted that the one occasion when Preobrazhensky expressed many of the same views as Trotsky concerning the world economy and the limitations of nation-states came in his essay on *The Results of the Genoa Conference and Economic Prospects for Europe*, published in 1922. In that essay he wrote with genuine enthusiasm of the possibility of a comprehensive restoration of Soviet Russia's economic ties with Europe even prior to a European revolution. He hoped that the Treaty of Rapallo, signed by Russia and Germany in April 1922, might lead to closer economic ties based upon export of Russian grain and raw materials in exchange for access to German technology, principally for the development of agriculture and the extractive industries. In an Appendix to his essay, he also included a visionary proposal for an international loan to finance an electrified railway linking London with Vladivostok. See Preobrazhensky 1922b, pp. 45–51. (A translation of this essay will appear in *The Preobrazhensky Papers*, Volume IV.). But following the failure of the Genoa Conference and the collapse of hopes for a German revolution in 1923, for the rest of the 1920s he consistently emphasised that Soviet Russia must finance its own industrialisation through primitive socialist accumulation.

27   *Trotsky Archives*, No. T-3004.

28   *Trotsky Archives*, No. T-3017. Italics added.

published as *The Third International after Lenin*. Trotsky devoted whole sections of the book to topics such as 'The United States of America and Europe', 'The Slogan of the Soviet United States of Europe', 'The Criterion of Internationalism', 'The Dependence of the USSR on the World Economy', and 'The Contradiction Between the Productive Forces and the National Boundaries as the Cause of the Reactionary Utopian Theory of "Socialism in One Country"'.[29]

In 1926 Trotsky told the Executive Committee of the Communist International that a newly industrialising country, including a country building socialism, must inevitably be drawn more deeply into the world market. 'This is the basic fact, and for this reason even the attempt to look at the economic and political fate of a separate country [*otdel'naya strana*], tearing this country away from its links and interdependencies with the world economy as a whole, is basically false'. 'The road back to the isolated state no longer exists'. Russia's previous historical development, benefitting from imports of capital during the tsarist period, was a perfect illustration. Russia's past would also leave its imprint upon the Soviet future:

> The precondition of socialism is heavy industry and machine-building – these are the most important levers of socialism. On this … we are all agreed. But let us ask ourselves how things really stand with the technical equipment in our factories and works. According to statistical calculations … before the war 63 per cent of our industry's equipment consisted of imported machines. Only a third was of domestic manufacture, and even this third consisted of the simplest machines; the most important and complicated items came from abroad. Consequently when you look around at the technical equipment of our factories you see with your own eyes the materialised dependence of Russia – and also of the Soviet Union on the world economy.[30]

Trotsky believed that 'This dependence has hardly decreased in our own time, which means that it will scarcely be economically profitable for us in the next few years to produce at home the machinery we require, at any rate, more than two-fifths of the quantity, or at best more than half of it'.[31] He emphasised that committing excessive resources to heavy industry would necessarily deprive light industry of the machinery and materials required to satisfy peasant needs and alleviate the chronic 'goods famine'. Instead, the Soviet Union must import

---

29   Trotsky 1957, pp. 3–74.
30   *Pravda*, 14 December 1926.
31   Trotsky 1926, p. 89.

equipment that was technically more advanced and could be purchased more cheaply abroad. A refusal to fill the 'gaps' in Soviet equipment with imports would be the equivalent of a socialist Munroe Doctrine. Certainly, in 10 or 20 years Soviet metallurgy and engineering might make self-sufficiency feasible. But 'this would inevitably mean an extraordinary lowering in the tempo of our economic growth ... Moreover, the tempo of development is the most decisive factor: ... thus far an isolated socialist state exists only in the dreams of journalists and resolution-makers'. 'Whoever discusses the theory of Socialism in One Country', was 'ignoring the fact of "co-operation" and struggle between our economy and the world capitalist economy [and] occupying himself with empty metaphysics'.[32]

A single socialist state, despite its monopoly of foreign trade, could never fully escape the effects of the world law of value. The pressure of foreign commodities and the threat of contraband demanded caution in primitive socialist accumulation. Too wide a divergence between foreign and domestic prices could evoke a flood of imports that would destroy the monopoly of foreign trade. While the monopoly must accord the highest priority to imports of machinery and equipment, when necessary it must also accommodate domestic demand originating with the peasantry. Domestic price relations could not be arbitrarily imposed without reference to world prices determined by the world law of value.

> The interaction of the [domestic] law of value and the law of socialist accumulation must be put in contact with the world economy. Then it will become clear that the law of value, within the confines of NEP, is supplemented by a growing pressure from the external law of value, which emerges on the world market.[33]

> We are part of the world economy and find ourselves in the capitalist encirclement. This means that the duel of 'our' law of socialist accumulation with 'our' law of value is embraced by the world law of value, which ... seriously alters the relationship of forces between the two laws.[34]

---

32 *Pravda*, 14 December 1926.
33 *Trotsky Archives*, No. T-2984.
34 *Trotsky Archives*, No. T-1015. In Volume II, p. 381, Preobrazhensky does mention that expansion of foreign trade 'opens up a wider area for the world economy's law of value to affect our economy', but his focus remains 'a maximal increase in the import of foreign equipment'. In other words, without the rapid restoration of Soviet industry, contraband would threaten the prospect of industrialisation.

3   The Question of 'Exploiting' the Peasantry

Isaac Deutscher was correct when he spoke of the differences between Trotsky and Preobrazhensky. Trotsky never contemplated Soviet Russia's independence of the world economy, nor did he advocate 'a pace of industrialization as forcible as that which Preobrazhensky anticipated'.[35] Preobrazhensky had only one answer when it came to alleviating the goods famine and reducing domestic prices on consumer goods, namely, to *accelerate* primitive socialist accumulation in order first to expand heavy industry and then to provide domestically manufactured equipment for light industry. 'Proportionate development' of the Soviet economy involved constant struggle against

> both the capitalist world and the capitalist and petty-bourgeois elements within our own economy. This sort of equilibrium is an unstable balance in the struggle between two systems, which is achieved on the basis not of the world law of value but through constant violation of this law, constant violation of the world market, and complete or partial withdrawal of an enormous economic area from the world market's sphere of regulation.[36]

The priority that Preobrazhensky attached to heavy industry and 'strict protectionism'[37] led him to discount the importance of importing consumer goods to alleviate chronic rural shortages. In December 1925 he spoke of such imports as the 'line of the least socialist resistance' and 'a system for undermining socialist industry'.[38] Trotsky, on the other hand, hoped to establish a virtuous circle of foreign trade that would enable both industry and agriculture to benefit from drawing upon the 'reserves' of the world market. The essential problem was to set an appropriate trade pattern in motion, thereafter allowing it to gain its own momentum. Trotsky summarised this way:

> Our economic system has become part of the world system. This has made new links in the chain of exchange. Peasant grain is exchanged for foreign gold. Gold is exchanged for machinery, implements, and other requisite articles of consumption for town and village. Textile machinery acquired for gold and paid for by the export of grain provides new equipment for the textile industry and thus lowers the prices of fabrics sent

---

35   Deutscher 1965, p. 416.
36   Volume II, Part 1, Chapter 2.
37   Ibid.
38   In this volume, p. 188

to the rural districts. The circle becomes very complicated, but the basis remains the same – a certain economic relation between town and village.[39]

By the autumn of 1925 retail prices for industrial consumer goods were more than 50 percent above agricultural procurement prices (calculating the two indices in terms of 1913 prices). Throughout 1925 and 1926 Trotsky warned that unless the needs of the countryside were satisfied, the peasant would spontaneously create his own *smychka*, or alliance, with foreign capital through illegal imports. To determine the pressure of foreign goods on the trade monopoly, he proposed a system of comparative coefficients that would measure the efficiency of Soviet production in terms of price and quality against that of other countries. These coefficients would then serve as a guide to both the import plan and new investments. Domestic production would be rationalised and standardised in order to lengthen runs and reduce per-unit costs.[40] In cases where the coefficient was least satisfactory, lower-cost foreign goods were to be imported and sold in the Soviet market, the profits being used to subsidise retail prices for the corresponding commodities manufactured domestically.[41] The idea of discouraging contraband by using foreign trade as a reserve for light industry clearly indicates the absurdity of the allegation that Trotsky ignored, or was bent upon exploiting, the peasantry. His desire to husband scarce capital, to maximise the political and economic return from investments in the shortest possible time, actually led directly to the conclusion that an important share of investments should be devoted to the less capital-intensive consumer goods industries.

In order to expand grain exports and set the virtuous circle in motion, Trotsky was even prepared, for a time at least, to contemplate the expansion of *kulak* agriculture. In June 1925 he said it would be a 'reactionary policy' to interfere prematurely with the development of rural productive forces that were

---

39 Trotsky 1926, pp. 44–5.
40 Trotsky 1926, pp. 69–71. In Volume II, pp. 433–4, Preobrazhensky also briefly mentioned comparative coefficients as a most productive way of 'comparing our economy with the world capitalist economy', but he did not draw the same conclusions for industrialisation strategy as Trotsky did. Preobrazhensky's concern was to use such coefficients to determine the weakest branches of Soviet industry and to target investment resources there. He did not, however, countenance the need to support light industry with imports of machinery or finished commodities (e.g. textiles) in cases where the coefficients were dangerously low. For Preobrazhensky, the way to support light industry was always first to expand domestic investments in heavy industry.
41 For a more detailed analysis of Trotsky's view of the *smychka*, see Day 1982, pp. 55–68.

currently growing in capitalist or semi-capitalist forms.[42] On another occasion he claimed that concessions to the *kulak*, assuming the growth of state industry continued without interruption, would not pose any threat of 'economic surprises' or of a 'sharp turn to capitalism'.[43] 'There may be periods when the state, sure of its economic power and desirous of increasing the rate of development, purposely allows a temporary increase in the weight of private enterprise in agriculture in the shape of capitalist farms ...'.[44] In November 1925 he contrasted the initiative of the *kulak* with the complacency of poor-peasant communes and approved of the Central Committee's decision to ease anti-kulak restrictions on land leasing and the hiring of agricultural labour. Trotsky thought such concessions – which directly contradicted the principles of Preobrazhensky's model of primitive socialist accumulation – must be treated as 'purely a matter of expediency'.[45]

In a speech on 19 January 1926, Trotsky described the *smychka*, or the worker-peasant alliance – as an 'endless ribbon of cloth that is stretched out between town and country. A cloth conveyor – that is what the *smychka* is'.[46] But at precisely the time when the cloth *smychka* needed to be supplemented gradually by a tractor *smychka*,[47] the link between town and country was breaking down. As early as 1923 Trotsky had become convinced that contraband imports of consumer goods could only be forestalled by a more or less continuous programme of 'commodity intervention', meaning the planned import of foreign consumer commodities to alleviate the domestic 'goods famine'. In one manner or another, the laws of the world economy would make themselves felt. 'Contraband is inevitable', he warned the twelfth party congress, 'if the difference between internal and external prices goes beyond a certain limit ... [and] contraband, comrades, ... undermines and washes away the [foreign trade] monopoly'. The peasant would say 'Open up the frontier, "Down with the monopoly of foreign trade"; he wants to have cheap commodities ... Well, if the peasant says: "Down with the monopoly of foreign trade" – that will be a lot worse than our wavering and hesitations in Moscow on this question'.[48] As for the party's

42   *Pravda*, 29 July 1925.
43   Trotsky 1926, pp. 26–7.
44   Trotsky 1926, p. 41. Cf. *Pravda*, 7 November 1925.
45   *Izvestiya*, 28 November 1925.
46   *Pravda*, 29 January 1926.
47   Ibid. In 1927 there were an estimated 7,000 tractors in the whole of USSR. It was expected at the time that 250,000 would be required for collective farming. [http://spartacus-educational.com/RUSfive.htm] accessed 10 June 2019.
48   Trotsky 1923, p. 372.

mistrust of commodity intervention, he attributed it to 'a passive fear of the foreign market ... [which] led to the theory of a closed (*zamknutoe*) national economy'.[49]

In January 1925 Felix Dzerzhinsky, in his capacity as VSNKh chairman, received a major commitment from the Central Committee to expand metal-lurgical output in anticipation of new capital construction. This was the first programme for heavy industrial expansion to receive the explicit sanction of the party leaders. Although G.L. Pyatakov, deputy chairman of VSNKh and a frequent ally of Trotsky, enthusiastically endorsed Dzerzhinsky's plan, Trotsky was quick to communicate his misgivings. He recounted the incident as follows:

> Returning from the Caucasus in May (1925), I found a typical picture of speculation. All the trusts were following a course of capital invest-ments. The operations of the Prombank [the Industrial Bank] were cease-lessly expanding. In June I wrote to Dzerzhinsky and Pyatakov with a warning that this fever was fatally leading to a financial and industrial crisis. Neither Dzerzhinsky nor Pyatakov understood this, and accused me instead (especially Pyatakov) of an intervention 'against' industrial-isation. I showed them that the overall material base, with a proper policy, could be considerably expanded, but that with the given material base it was impossible to push industrialisation forward with the aid of unreal credits. Probably everyone recalls that in September 1925 a serious crisis occurred, accompanied by the dismissal of workers etc.[50]

When the Central Committee met in plenary session in April 1926, Trotsky suggested a five-year plan to overcome the goods famine by 1931, including a reduction of retail prices through 'commodity intervention' for 1926–27.[51] There are reasons to think that if Trotsky's proposals for 'commodity intervention' had been implemented from the mid-1920s, collapse of the *smychka* and forced collectivisation might not have occurred. The principal error of the party lead-ership was to commit excessive resources to heavy industry at the height of the goods famine. A preoccupation with industrial self-sufficiency, involving the production of equipment never before manufactured in the country, and

---

49   *Trotsky Archives*, No. T-2972.

50   Trotsky 1955, p. 186. For Preobrazhensky's appraisal of Gosplan's intentions at this time for the year 1925/27, see Volume II, Part 2, Appendix 1. On p. 306 Preobrazhensky mentions 'a 380 million deficit of commodities and an expected deficit of 500 million in 1926–1927'.

51   *Trotsky Archives*, No. T-2983.

at costs that were up to twice as high as foreign imports on average, was Stalin's contribution to industrialisation strategy. The historians E.H. Carr and R.W. Davies described the consequences:

> The individual peasant, having little inducement to spend, developed the traditional peasant propensity to hoard. Grain, whether as a reserve for future contingencies or as a speculation on higher prices, was the most stable and convenient form of wealth. The existence of large holdings in individual hands meant that the holders would surrender the grain only on terms – involving an adequate supply of consumer goods at acceptable prices – which were incompatible with the ever increasing investment in heavy industry.[52]

Trotsky's proposals would have seen a portion of the resources expended on capital-intensive projects used instead to purchase consumer goods and foreign equipment for *both departments* of Soviet industry.[53] The USSR, he argued, should specialise in the simpler types of products that were in greatest demand, maximising scale economies within the country and importing more complex items from abroad. In this way acute shortages could be avoided, the danger of inflation would be reduced, and the 'reserves' of the historically formed world division of labour would be deployed in the service of socialism. In his chapter in *Capital* on primitive accumulation, Marx had shown how capitalism grew out of feudalism. Trotsky thought the dialectics of historical development would now see capitalist reserves utilised in support of socialism in the same way as merchant-capitalists drew from the 'reserves' of feudalism. 'Well', he remarked, 'has not capitalism been nourished at the breasts of feudalism? History has honoured the debt'.[54]

In March 1926, however, Preobrazhensky published an article in the journal *Bol'shevik* and warned against 'petty-bourgeois pressure' in support of exactly the ideas that Trotsky was promoting:

---

52 Carr and Davies 1969, p. 245.
53 Construction costs in the Soviet Union were even higher in the 1920s, relative to pre-war prices, than manufacturing costs. Nevertheless, the Soviet government pressed ahead with prestigious projects such as the Dnieper power station, the Stalingrad tractor factory, the metallurgical works of Krivoi Rog and Kuznetsk, and the Sverdlovsk engineering works – in every case holding the import of capital goods to a minimum. Up to one-third of all industrial investments by 1928–29 were allocated to construction of new factories rather than the re-equipping of existing ones, even though new investments in Department I generally result in new production only after a period of from 3 to 5 years.
54 Trotsky 1926, p. 92.

With the growth of our harvests and export potential, we shall inevitably face such pressure from the private economy on our tariff system and our monopoly of foreign trade (i.e., on the barriers that we erect to paralyse the operation of the world economy's law of value) that our artificial obstacles will be completely shattered and our import plan will be constructed not in accordance with a plan for industrialising the country but instead like Trishkin's caftan,[55] so that patches in the form of imports of consumer goods will grow from year to year.[56] We concede that such a line in economic policy has its own rationale, but it ... is dictated by petty-bourgeois pressure on the economic policy of the proletarian state. This line is leading us in exactly the direction that the capitalist countries want from us: it means liquidation of the foreign trade monopoly, liquidation of socialist protectionism, inclusion of the USSR in the system of the world division of labour on the basis of the operation of the world law of value, and *preservation of Europe's existing level of industrialisation through increasing the relative agrarianisation of our country.*[57]

In his chapter on 'Economic Equilibrium in the USSR', Preobrazhensky acknowledged that 'participation in the world division of labour is beneficial and necessary for us *in general, regardless of the structure of the economy and the level of its development*'. He added, however, that 'What I have in mind is the import of means of production ...'. In a footnote on the same page he elaborated:

Of course, from the viewpoint of private production and its interests, the disproportion ... can also be solved by the direct import of means of consumption from abroad, but it is perfectly obvious that such a solution to the problem entails *a serious delay, if not the elimination, of expanded socialist reproduction.* Many problems of the private economy, generally speaking, can be solved by the *elimination of socialist industry or even just by elimination of the monopoly of foreign trade.* The whole struggle between the state and private sectors of the Soviet economy leads directly

---

55 In a popular fable by I.A. Krylov, Trishkin repairs a hole in his caftan by cutting off material from another part of the caftan, creating another hole to be repaired. The comparable English expression would be 'robbing Peter to pay Paul'.

56 [There is an obvious misprint here in the text, which says 'patches in the form of *exports* of consumer goods will play a growing role from year to year'. What Preobrazhensky clearly had in mind is that *imports* of consumer goods would be increasing from year to year.]

57 In this volume, pp. 194–5.

to the issue of the basis upon which equilibrium in the Soviet economy can be established: on the basis of inclusion in the world economy under 'normal conditions', i.e., on the basis of the law of value [world prices], or by way of something new and unprecedented in economic history – planned imports that are subordinated to the task of primitive socialist accumulation.[58]

By 1928 Preobrazhensky actually described '*import of commodities for the countryside*' as part of a right-wing programme of concessions to the kulak, which was the antithesis of primitive socialist accumulation.[59] In *The New Economics* he illustrated his concern with a numerical example. Suppose, he suggested, there was an unsatisfied rural demand of 200 million roubles in the form of agricultural products that peasants resist bringing to market due to the shortage of manufactured consumer goods. If the state could somehow acquire those products and exchange them for imports of consumer items, the formal requirements of domestic proportionality would be met. But Preobrazhensky objected that 'in practical terms' this solution was impossible:

> ... given the shortage of export resources even for importing the most important means of production, *this turns out to be impossible* for the Soviet state during the early years of the reconstruction process. In order to draw these 200 million of additional export resources into circulation, it would first be necessary to purchase the products of light industry abroad at a cost to this year's import fund, i.e., at the expense of curtailing the import of means of production that are already in short supply.[60]

If the import of consumer goods was 'impossible', and if the rate of industrialisation was not accelerated, the obvious threat was that the Soviet countryside would begin 'the familiar process of increasing its own consumption of eggs, butter and so on, increasing its stocks of grain beyond the levels required for insurance against a bad harvest along with a number of related phenomena'. That, of course, was precisely the formula for the 'grain strike' that brought the end of NEP in 1927–28.

Later in the same chapter, Preobrazhensky considered in further detail the potential benefits that Trotsky thought would result from drawing upon the

---

58   In this volume, p. 106 (italics added).
59   In this volume, p. 449.
60   In this volume, p. 113 (italics added).

'reserves' of the world economy for commodity intervention. If the 200 million of peasant exports could be used to purchase 200 million of foreign consumer goods, the latter might be sold with a considerable mark-up at prevailing domestic prices, making a substantial profit for the purpose of socialist accumulation. Alternatively, just 100 million might be used for imported consumer goods and the other 100 million to purchase means of production. In this case, too, the state would acquire a significant profit from the sale of imported goods that might then be used to purchase additional means of production for socialist industry.

No sooner had Preobrazhensky considered these possibilities, however, than he again rejected them:

> Although such a solution to the problem is fully possible in theory, it is perfectly obvious that in practice, given our existing conditions, it would only alleviate the difficulty we have described but not eliminate it. The point is that even in this case we would have *to advance* 100 million roubles from the import fund for the purchase of means of consumption.[61]

The logical reply would be that *this year's* import fund might be considerably larger had commodity intervention occurred *last year*. In other words, to begin by *alleviating* the difficulty might be the first, necessary step towards *eliminating* it, which was precisely the rationale of Trotsky's proposed strategy of industrialisation. This difference also explains why, by 1928, Trotsky could not possibly join Preobrazhensky in endorsing Stalin's attack on the peasantry as 'our policy'. Trotsky hoped to preserve the *smychka*; Stalin's policy was a return to coercive seizures of grain.

---

61   In this volume, p. 114. At the height of the 'sales crisis' in 1923–24, Preobrazhensky did briefly endorse 'commodity intervention', but only as an emergency measure. By March of 1927 he also belatedly mentioned supporting the domestic textile industry with increased imports of materials and even of equipment, although by that time NEP was about to collapse. In an article in *Bol'shevik* (in this volume, pp. 236–7) he wrote in a footnote:

> In particular, it would be terrible bungling on our part if we did not take full advantage of the exceptionally favourable conditions in the world cotton market and failed this year to produce sufficient textiles. Since development of the textile industry encounters obstacles from the equipment side as well, we must ensure that it quickly receives imports of new equipment. The expansion of production in the textile industry that is already planned is clearly inadequate.

4   The Role of Objective Forces and Political Will in History

This brings us to the third point mentioned by Isaac Deutscher, namely, that Trotsky also could not agree with Preobrazhensky concerning

> the 'objective force' or logic of primitive accumulation which would impose itself on the party leaders and make them its agents, regardless of what they thought and intended. This was a view which must have appeared to Trotsky to be too rigidly deterministic, even fatalistic, and to rely too much on the automatic development of socialism and too little on the consciousness, the will, and the action of fighting men.[62]

There is no doubt that Preobrazhensky vested enormous confidence in the objective inevitability of primitive socialist accumulation. In his chapter of *The New Economics*, dealing with 'The Method of Theoretical Analysis of the Soviet Economy', he wrote:

> If we poorly understood the need to act – and to do so with increasing speed and energy in the spirit of accumulation – the objective facts would whip us onwards, such as growth of the goods famine, the growth of private accumulation, the threat to the whole system's existence due to the weakness of our industry and its military-industrial base, etc. In such circumstances, any objection to the term 'law', simply on the grounds that its form of appearance changes, or its character changes in terms of the way it determines people's will, would amount to nothing more than philological doctrinairism ... *Failure to understand the fact that* [the law of primitive socialist accumulation] *exists, that it has compulsory force for the state economy and also influences the private one, is not only a theoretical mistake, not only mental stubbornness and conservatism, but also dangerous in practice, dangerous from the point of view of the struggle for existence of our entire system of collective economy.*[63]

As Deutscher notes, Trotsky had a totally different view of the relation between historical determinism and human agency. He believed that the laws of *political* economy are not just economic; they are also *political*, and they change with successive modes of production through the conscious intervention of

---

62   Deutscher 1965, p. 238.
63   In this edition, see Volume II, p. 131 and p. 140.

the revolutionary class. Preobrazhensky's conviction of objective inevitability contrasted strikingly with Trotsky's emphasis upon class consciousness and political struggle:

> ... politics grows out of *economics* in order for it in turn to influence the [economic] base by levers of a superstructural [political] character .... in both instances the actions of living people are involved; in one instance they are grouped together for production, in the other – under the pressure of demands of the very same production – they are grouped politically and act with *the levers of politics* upon their own production grouping [i.e. they change the mode of production].[64]

In his *Notebooks* on philosophy, Trotsky said human consciousness must always play 'an autonomous, that is, within certain limits, an independent role in the life of the individual and the species'.[65] If consciousness did not play such a role, then 'it is unnecessary, useless; it is harmful because it is a superfluous complication – and what a complication'.[66] Consciousness was an inseparable part of history and dialectics. Human history did not just *objectively happen* – at critical junctures it was *consciously made*.

This is certainly not to say that Preobrazhensky was indifferent to the role of politics and class consciousness. But such comments do pinpoint an important difference of temperament; they help to explain why Trotsky was a flamboyant political actor and Preobrazhensky a disciplined theorist of objective economic laws. Trotsky was a man of brilliant insight, whose flashes of vision were never expressed with the same systematic rigour as Preobrazhensky exhibited in *The New Economics*. But Preobrazhensky was a man of systematic rigour who also became *trapped* within his own insight. Together, they were for a time powerful allies who understood, more than any of their peers, both the necessity and the frailty of the New Economic Policy. Yet their paths parted by 1928 when Preobrazhensky accepted 'responsibility' for Stalin's 'left course', a decision that profoundly conflicted with Trotsky's convictions concerning Soviet Russia's 'dependence' upon the world economy and the perilous futility of 'Socialism in One Country'.

---

64   Trotsky 1986, pp. 106–7.
65   Trotsky 1986, p. 106.
66   Trotsky 1986, p. 104.

5   China and the 'Afterlife' of the New Economic Policy

There is certainly no disputing the fact that Stalin's first five-year plan and forced collectivisation of a hundred million peasants was perilous. But was it totally futile? However repulsive Stalin's regime, however numerous its victims of famine and purges, such questions are ultimately judged not just by the participants themselves and their victims but also by history. And with the benefit of hindsight we must acknowledge that the Great Depression and the Second World War cast a different light upon the issues debated in the 1920s. During the debate over Soviet industrialisation, no one could have anticipated the consequences of Hitler's ascendancy in Germany.

On the other hand, many have argued, most notably Trotsky, that Stalin brought Hitler to power by denouncing German Social Democrats as 'social-fascists' and by dictating to the German Communist Party a political strategy that divided the left and opened the door to the Nazis. Moreover, Trotsky's reasoning suggested that the debacle of NEP's collapse, including the famine of 1932–33, which cost millions of lives and vast losses in output and productivity, could have been avoided had relations with the peasantry been better managed during the previous decade. Putting aside speculation, however, the major contribution of the five-year plans was to shift the USSR's industrial centre of gravity eastward, including the major iron and steel centres at Magnitogorsk in the Urals, Kuznetsk in Siberia, and even Komsomolsk in the Far East on the Amur River. Major chemical and machine-building plants were also constructed in the southern part of Western Siberia. Had it not been for this strategic re-positioning of heavy industry, in all probability the outcome of the Second World War would have been a Nazi triumph.

For more general purposes of economic theory, however, Stalin's autarkic industrialisation must also be assessed with reference to countries such as Japan and the other Asian 'tigers', especially mainland China, all of which have followed a strategy of industrialisation through integration into the world economy. In other words, the countries that have been most successful in rapid industrialisation followed a strategy that was quite reminiscent of Trotsky's thinking in the 1920s. Today, it is China that is setting records of economic development, whereas the Soviet Union fell apart three decades ago. The case of China is particularly important since it began post-war modernisation with a five-year plan directly patterned on the Stalinist model, giving priority to steel, coal, electric power and cement.[67] Following Mao's death in 1976, however, his

---

67   During the 'Great Leap Forward' of 1957–60, Soviet-style planning was replaced by the

successors initiated a new model of economic development that drew upon the Soviet experience of NEP. In that sense, we can consider China as a kind of historical test of the economic potential inherent in the NEP model as well as the long-run implications.

When Lenin implemented NEP in 1921, he astutely described the new policy as one of 'state capitalism'. After the experience of War Communism, his object-ives were to stabilise the currency and reintroduce a mixed economy; to restore trade with the capitalist countries and possibly secure capital imports; and to replace grain requisitioning and failed attempts at communal agriculture with traditional forms of land cultivation and the tax in kind. The principle of the tax in kind was to re-create economic incentives: once the tax was paid, any remaining produce could be sold by the peasant household at market prices.

The reforms implemented by Deng Xiaoping in China after 1978 followed the same NEP pattern. The first change came in agriculture with the 'house-hold responsibility system'. Communal farming, imposed under Mao, began to be dismantled. Households were permitted to contract for land and equip-ment; state delivery quotas were significantly reduced; purchase prices were raised, and once the state delivery target was met, any remaining output could be sold at market prices. Deng dismantled Mao's communes just as Lenin, following War Communism, abandoned grain requisitioning and premature experiments in collective farming. By 1983 the land contract system in China was nearly universal; from 1978–83 per capita rural incomes doubled, and China became self-sufficient in food production.

Whereas the grain strike in the Soviet Union resulted from scarcity of man-ufactured consumer goods, Deng's second major reform was to promote a return of traditional local industry, or 'township and village enterprises', as part of the strategy of 'growing out of the plan'. Beginning in 1921, Lenin had also leased numerous small enterprises to private investors and lifted restric-tions on private handicraft production. Although the small enterprises encour-aged by Deng have often been described as local-government enterprises, most were privately owned and protected by local authorities as sources of rev-enue. Deng, in other words, co-opted small capitalists just as Lenin intended to do with the introduction of NEP.[68] By the mid-1990s town and village enter-

---

creation of giant communes that were intended to join collective farming with 'backyard' industry. The result was the greatest famine of the twentieth century. From 1961–65 there was a period relative stabilisation, but in 1966 Mao unleashed the 'Great Proletarian Cul-tural Revolution', causing the paralysis of most government institutions from 1969–71 and their replacement by military control.

68   One element of Lenin's strategy was to lease small undertakings, which could no longer be

prises produced more than 16 percent of GDP and employed up to 135 million people.[69]

In further accordance with Lenin's idea of NEP, the Chinese state retained total control of all the 'commanding heights' – aviation, coal, shipping, petroleum, heavy metallurgy, electricity, telecommunications and military supply, as well as 'relative control' over other key industries, including automotive and chemicals production, the construction industry, exploration and design, electronic information, equipment manufacturing, nonferrous metals, and science and technology. The ultimate outcome of Deng's reforms was a mixed economy resembling Lenin's initial concept of NEP as 'state capitalism'.

Most important in terms of the issues of foreign trade that divided Trotsky and Preobrazhensky, Deng Xiaoping also 'opened' China to the world economy. For almost three decades, China's economic growth has been driven by manufactured exports and imports of foreign capital and technological know-how. Under Mao, foreign trade was controlled by a state monopoly. Like Stalin, Mao intended China to be independent of the world economy and the capitalist encirclement. But Deng adopted the export-oriented strategy pioneered by Japan, using labour-intensive exports to finance the import of foreign capital equipment.[70] Deng treated foreign trade as a learning experience in economic development.

China 'entered' the world economy, and foreign capital also entered China – on strictly Chinese terms. In 1992 Deng made his 'Southern tour' and endorsed 'special economic zones' reminiscent of the treaty ports of the nineteenth and early twentieth centuries. Deng called them 'bird cages' for foreign investors, who were given reduced taxes, duty-free import of materials to manufacture for export, and a diligent work force disciplined by party control. This policy, too, was reminiscent of Lenin's effort to attract foreign investment during the early days of NEP in Soviet Russia.

In this context, it is also worth remembering that in 1925 Trotsky pursued the same policy after being posted to the Soviet government's Main Concessions Committee. Trotsky frequently spoke of the potential importance of concessions and his hope of attracting foreign capital into Soviet electrification and other projects involving 'the transfer to our country of foreign plant, foreign productive formulae, and the financing of our economy by the resources of

---

supported by the state, to private entrepreneurs, including foreign investors. Some were also converted into 'mixed' private-public enterprises.

69   [https://en.wikipedia.org/wiki/Township_and_Village_Enterprises] accessed 15 July 2018.

70   Export-led growth did not, of course, exclude a parallel strategy of import substitution.

world capitalist savings'.[71] In 2001 China joined the World Trade Organization, and today direct foreign investment supports tens of millions of jobs. After the US and the UK, China is the world's third largest recipient of foreign capital.

6   Market Socialism and Political Life

Our brief comparison of the Soviet NEP of the 1920s and the Chinese 'after-life' of NEP since 1978 is sufficient to highlight the importance of integration into the world economy during a period of socialist transition. Obviously, the Chinese case differs from the Russian one because the USSR faced increasingly grave international threats during the 1930s, whereas China has enjoyed four decades of relative stability in its international relations.

The second key question posed by China's NEP is the relation between plan and market in a transitional economy. When Trotsky surveyed the results of Stalinist planning from exile during the 1930s, he became increasingly interested in the possibility that some form of market socialism should accompany planned industrialisation, beginning with the dismantling of under-equipped collective farms and a return of up to 80 percent of peasant households to commercial farming.[72] Blaming the 1933 famine on the attempt to plan everything from the number of hectares of wheat to the number of 'buttons on a waistcoat', he stressed the need to correct a socialist plan through the expression of supply and demand in a market:

> The innumerable living participants in the economy, state and private, collective and individual, must announce their needs and their respective intensities not only through the statistical calculations of the planning commissions, but also by the direct pressure of supply and demand. The plan ... [must be] verified, and in an important measure must be achieved through the market.[73]

Readers of this volume will be well aware of Preobrazhensky's view that the plan and the market were dialectical opposites. A Marxist might well conclude,

---

71   See Day 1973, pp. 132–4. Preobrazhensky thought resource concessions, in forestry or agriculture for example, were acceptable, but he opposed any concessions involving foreign industrial investment (Volume II, pp. 202–3.): 'a cautious attitude towards concessions is integrally connected with my whole conception in general' (Volume II, p. 340.).

72   *Trotsky Archives*, No. T-3485.

73   *Trotsky Archives*, No. T-3542.

however – as Trotsky evidently did – that the higher synthesis to emerge from such a contradiction would be a transitional *planned market*. The important point that Trotsky emphasised is that the corollary of a mixed form of economy must also be more participatory forms of socialist political life:

> The struggle of vital interests, in the form of a new factor of planning, brings us to the role of politics, which is concentrated economics. The equipment of the social groups of Soviet society is (and must be); the Soviets, the trade unions, the co-operatives, and above all the ruling party. Only the interaction of the three elements; of state planning, of the market, and of soviet democracy, can provide the economy with proper leadership in the transitional epoch.[74]

In particular, Trotsky emphasised the autonomy of trade unions and their direct participation in the political-economic process of drafting a plan.

> The relative independence of the trade unions is a necessary and important corrective in the Soviet *state system* [my emphasis], which finds itself under pressure from the peasantry and the bureaucracy. Until such time as classes are liquidated, the workers – even in a workers' state – must defend themselves with the help of their professional organizations. In other words, *the trade unions must remain trade unions just as long as the state remains a state, that is, an apparatus of compulsion. The statification of the trade unions can only take place parallel with the destatification of the state itself.*[75]

The 'statification' (*ogosudarstvlenie*) of trade unions was the dialectical counterpart of the 'workerisation' (*orabochenie*) of the state. The two processes would combine control from above with control from below, i.e., workers' self-control in the factory would be the counterpart of macroeconomic self-determination through a democratic plan. Trotsky envisaged a 'coalescence' of workers' organisations with the state planning commission, involving direct trade-union representation on the highest planning bodies and a corresponding representation of planners in the leadership of the trade unions. 'Consequently, in the same measure as the elimination of classes deprives the state of its functions of compulsion, causing it to dissolve itself into society, the trade

---

74   *Byulleten' Oppozitsii*, XXXI (1932), pp. 8–9.
75   *Trotsky Archives*, No. T-3542.

unions lose their special class functions and dissolve into the state, which is withering away'.[76]

Until the state withered, however, the diverse interests of socialist society would also require representation through competing political parties. Trotsky was perfectly clear in arguing that 'classes are heterogeneous; they are torn by inner antagonisms, and arrive at the solution of their common problems in no other way than through an inner struggle of tendencies, groups and parties'.[77] Social opinion in a socialist society required 'several parties';[78] new values could only emerge from 'a free conflict of ideas'[79] and 'spiritual creativeness'.[80] 'Humiliating control'[81] by Stalinist bureaucrats must be replaced by workers' self-control and 'cultural discipline'[82] growing out of 'education, habit and social opinion'.[83] Self-control by the associated producers was the final reconciliation of freedom with necessity and of autonomy with responsibility. Subjective emancipation of the workers was as essential to socialism as social ownership of the means of production.

7   Is China Socialist?

If we now measure China's NEP against the expectations of Trotsky and Preobrazhensky, we can see clearly both the limitations of Preobrazhensky's concentration upon economics at the expense of a theory of socialist political life and also the dramatic failure of China to avoid some of the worst consequences of both market forms of economic relations and the political forms of Stalinism. The Chinese NEP has produced a dramatic skewing of income distribution and class differentiation. In 2014 China's coefficient of income inequality was higher than in South Korea, Indonesia, India and even the United States. In 2015 the top 20 percent of recipients acquired nearly 50 percent of total income while the bottom 20 percent received less than 5 percent.[84] To preserve control of the mixed economy, the Communist Party has sacrificed any prospect of

---

76   *Trotsky Archives*, No. T-3542.
77   Trotsky 1972, p. 267.
78   Ibid.
79   Trotsky 1972, p. 276.
80   Trotsky 1972, p. 180.
81   Trotsky 1972, p. 258.
82   Trotsky 1972, p. 262.
83   Trotsky 1972, p. 46.
84   [https://blogs.wsj.com/economics/2015/03/26/china-is-one-of-most-unequal-countries-in-the-world-imf-paper-says/] accessed 15 July 2018.

socialist democracy and preserved a structure of imperial hierarchy and ritual-ised political life.

Since 2001 the Party has fortified its 'leading role' by co-opting the newly rich into its own ranks. By 2017 there were more than 150 billionaires in the National People's Congress and the People's Political Consultative Conference. By January 2021 China had 1,058 dollar-billionaires compared to 696 in the United States.[85] At the same time, the only trade unions with a legal right to exist are those authorised by the state and jointly controlled at the factory level by a party committee and the enterprise management. The Trade Union Law of the People's Republic of China excludes any reference to the right to strike. In the common formulation, China has built 'Socialism with Chinese Character-istics'. It would probably be more accurate to say that China remains 'Chinese with Chinese Characteristics'. Xi Jinping, the current president and potential ruler for life, nowadays cites Confucian virtues in order to legitimate political hierarchy and ceremonial rule.[86]

8 Conclusions

The Chinese experience clearly demonstrates that the mixed economy of NEP, viewed as a model of development, involved significantly more potential than was realised in the Soviet Union. Preobrazhensky's theory of primitive social-ist accumulation brilliantly grasped the contradictions inherent in the Soviet NEP of the 1920s – given the geopolitical circumstances of the time – but the Chinese case shows that he was mistaken in his conviction that any under-developed and mainly peasant country must necessarily replicate the Soviet pattern of moving from a period of NEP to completely centralised planning.[87]

In the architecture of Preobrazhensky's theory there was little room for political choice if the market was to be replaced by the logic of statistics. When Stalin leaped backwards to the methods of War Communism, including renewed class war in the countryside, Preobrazhensky could see in such actions both objective necessity and his own self-vindication. His repudiation of 'Trot-skyism' in 1928 represented acceptance of political defeat but also affirmed his own triumph as an economic theorist: Stalin's course was 'our course'. Preo-brazhensky accepted the ends proclaimed by Stalin but despised the means.

---

85 [https://www.hurun.net/en-US/Info/Detail?num=LWAS8B997XUP] accessed 11 July 2021.
86 Jinping 2015.
87 In this volume, see pp. 142–151.

The problem was that by accepting the ends he found himself compelled, however reluctantly, to abide the means.

Trotsky, by emphasising greater scope for conscious historical choice, ultimately contemplated a completely different outcome for NEP – a transitional form of market socialism that would be integrated into the world economy, would minimise domestic contradictions by drawing upon the 'reserves' of the world economy, and most importantly would include workers' democracy and trade-union participation in planning. In *The Revolution Betrayed* he commented that a transitional society might choose socialism as its goal, but other questions must still be answered: 'How to go toward socialism, with what tempo, etc. The choice of the road is no less important than the choice of the goal. Who is going to choose the road?'[88]

If Trotsky were asked to assess the experience of China, he might well say that the principal obstacle to socialism in China has turned out to be the hierarchical political monopoly of the Communist Party itself. A Stalinist form of political organisation, superimposed upon an impressively successful NEP-like economy, represents a contradictory social formation that has yet to reach any determinate outcome. Although Trotsky and Preobrazhensky would quite probably continue to differ over specific issues, this seems to be the general conclusion upon which they would be in full agreement.

In March 1928 Preobrazhensky wrote to Trotsky that he was 'generally less interested in politics nowadays and ... willing to send it to hell for a year or so'. Nevertheless, in his theses on the 'Left Course in the Countryside', he also emphasised the need for 'speedy improvement in the legal status of workers, especially at the bottom, in the factory, which means implementation of a regime of workers' democracy and exposing the worst elements of the apparatus and the worst practices of management and trade-union leadership to real rank-and-file worker's criticism'.[89] Despite their differences over the priorities of primitive socialist accumulation, Preobrazhensky and Trotsky both understood that industrialisation on its own – without workers' democracy and real trade unions – was a formula for betraying the socialist revolution.

---

88   Trotsky 1972, p. 268.
89   In this volume, p. 451.

Biographical Index

Adoratsky, Vladimir Viktorovich (1878–1945), historian, member of the Academy of Sciences of the USSR (1932). Participated in the revolution of 1905–07. From 1220 one of the leaders of the Central Archival Administration. In 1931–39 Director of the Communist Party's Institute of Marx-Engels-Lenin.

Andreev, Leonid Nikolaevich (1871–1919), Russian writer.

Astrov, Valentin Nikolaevich (1898-?), party journalist during the 1920s and a supporter of N.I. Bukharin. Purged and subsequently rehabilitated.

Babeuf, Gracchus (Francois-Noël) (1760–1797), French utopian communist. One of the leaders of the 'Conspiracy of Equals' to replace the bourgeois Directory; in 1796 led preparations for the uprising to enforce the constitution of 1793. Guillotined.

Ballivet, French worker-mechanic and syndicalist, delegate of the mechanics union at the Second Working-Class Congress at Lyons in 1878. Called for collectivisation of the land and the instruments of labour.

Bebel, August (1840–1923), one of the founders and leaders of the Social-Democratic Party of Germany and the Second International. Elected several times to the Reichstag.

Bedny, Demyan (Efim Alekseevich Privdorov) (1883–1945). Russian writer. Published in the Bolshevik papers 'Sevzda' and 'Pravda'.

Bentham, Jeremy (1748–1832), English philosopher, founder of modern utilitarianism.

Bergson, Henri (1859–1941), French philosopher, exponent of 'intuitionism' and 'creative evolution'.

Berin, a participant in discussing a report by E.A. Preobrazhensky.

Bernstein, Eduard (1850–1932), one of the leaders of German Social Democracy and the Second International, a leading advocate of reformism and the 'revision' of Marxism. Rejected scientific socialism and regarded socialist society as an ethical ideal.

Berth, Édouard (1875–1939), French syndicalist and a disciple of Georges Sorel.

Birmann, German legal theorist associated with the neo-Kantian school of Rudolf Stammler.

Bismarck, Otto von (1815–1898), first Chancellor of the German Empire from 1871–90.

Blanqui, Louis Auguste (1805–1881), French utopian communist. While in prison, elected *in absentia* as a member of the Paris Commune. Believed the

Diehl, Karl (1864–1943), German economist.

Dietzgen, Joseph (1828–1888), German Social Democrat and philosopher.

Dostoyevsky, Fyodor Mikhailovich (1821–1881), Russian writer and philosopher

Dvolaitsky, Shalom Moiseevich (1893–1937), political figure and economist. Purged and posthumously rehabilitated.

Dühring, Eugen (1833–1921), German political economist and philosopher of economics and law. Considered violence to be the most important factor in history. Opposed Marxism.

Dzerzhinsky, Felix Edmundovich (1877–1926), political figure, one of the leaders of the revolution of 1905–07. In October 1917 member of the party's Military-Revolutionary Centre and the Petrograd Military-Revolutionary Committee. From 1917 chairman of the All-Russian Extraordinary Committee for Struggle Against Counter-Revolution (Cheka: GPU from 1922–23, OGPU from 1923–34). People's Commissar of Internal Affairs for the RSFSR in 1919 and 1923, Commissar of Communications from 1921. From 1924 Chairman of VSNKh of the USSR. Member of the Bolshevik Central Committee 1907–12 and from 1917. Candidate member of the Politburo of the Central Committee from 1924.

Engels, Friedrich (1820–1895), principal associate and co-author of Karl Marx.

Epicurus (341–270 BC), ancient Greek philosopher.

Fourier, Charles (1772–1837), French utopian socialist.

Frumkin, Moses Il'ich (1878–1938), until 1929 Deputy People's Commissar of Finance of the USSR, in 1932–35 Deputy People's Commissar of Foreign Trade. Purged and rehabilitated posthumously.

Gallifet, Gaston Alexandre August, Marquis de (1830–1909), French general involved in crushing the Paris Commune.

Gol'denberg, E., party journalist.

Griffuelhes, Victor (1874–1922), French syndicalist, leader of the *Confédération Générale du Travail.*

Groman, Vladimir Gustavovich (1874–?), Social Democrat and Menshevik economist. Purged.

Grünberg, Karl (1861–1940), Austrian Social Democrat, lawyer, economist and historian.

Guesde (Bazile), **Jules** (1845–1922), one of the founders of the French Workers' Party, active in the Second International, Marxist propagandist.

Guloyan, Abram Abramovich, party journalist, economist and Vice-Rector of the Transcaucasian Communist University.

Hegel, Georg Wilhelm Friedrich (1770–1831), German philosopher and objective-idealist dialectician.

Heinzen, Karl (1809–1880), German revolutionary author.

Hesse, Albert, German lawyer associated with the Stammler school.

Jaurès, Jean (1859–1914), one of the first social-democratic reformists, became leader of the French Socialist Party in 1902 (after 1905 the French Section of the International). Founder of 'Humanité' in 1904. Opposed colonialism, militarism and war. Assassinated in 1914 on the eve of the First World War.

Kan, a participant in the dispute over E.A. Preobrazhensky's report to Proletkult.

Kant, Immanuel (1724–1804), German philosopher, a founder of German classical philosophy. Professor at the University in Königsberg. Foreign honorary member of the Petersburg Academy of Sciences (1794).

Kapitonov, Ivan Petrovich (1900-?), Soviet economist.

Kareev, Nikolai Ivanovich (1850–1931), historian, corresponding member of the USSR Academy of Science. Corresponding member of the Petersburg Academy of Science from 1910. Corresponding member of the Russian Academy of Science from 1917. Honorary member of the USSR Academy of Science (1929).

Karev, Nikolai Afanasyevich (1901–1936), party journalist. Purged, posthumously rehabilitated.

Karyshev, N.A. (1855–1905), economist and statistician.

Kats, a participant in the discussion of a report by E.A. Preobrazhensky.

Kautsky, Karl (1854–1938), a leader and theorist of German Social Democracy and the Second International. Took a pacifist position from the beginning of World War I. Hostile to the Russian Revolution.

Kerensky, Aleksandr Fedorovich (1881–1970), politician and lawyer. In the Provisional Government held the posts of Minister of Justice, Minister of the Army and Navy, Prime Minister, and Supreme Commander. Lived in France after 1918 and from 1940 in the US.

Kestner, Fritz, German economist and specialist in cartel law.

Kogan, a participant in discussing a report by E.A. Preobrazhensky.

Kon, Aleksandr Feliksovich (1897–1941), economist. From 1935 worked at Institute of Marx-Engels-Lenin in preparing a new edition of the economic writings of Karl Marx.

Kondratiev, Nikolai Dmitrievich (1892–1938). Author of the theory of long cycles of the conjuncture and their relation to qualitative changes in the economic life of society. Purged, posthumously rehabilitated.

Kritsman, Lev Natanovich (1890–1941), public official and economist specialising in agricultural questions during the 1920s.

Ksenofontov, F.K., a party journalist.

Kugelmann, Ludwig (1828–1902), physician and participant in the revolution of 1848–49 in Germany. Friend of Karl Marx and Friedrich Engels.

Kviring, Emmanuel Ionovich (1888–1937), 1925–27 Deputy Chairman of the USSR VSNKh. 1927–30 Deputy Chairman of the USSR Gosplan. 1931 Deputy People's Commissar of Railways of the USSR. 1932–34 Deputy Chairman of the Committee of Commodity Funds of the Council of Labour and Defence. From 1934, First Deputy Chairman of the USSR Gosplan. From 1930 headed the Economic Institute of Red Professors (in 1932–36, the Economic Institute of the Communist Academy). Purged.

Labriola, Arturo (1873–1959), economist and a leader and theorist of syndicalism in Italy.

Lafargue, Paul (1842–1911), one of the founders of the French Workers' Party, a member of the First International. K. Marx's son-in-law, the husband of his daughter Laura.

Lagardelle, Hubert (1874–1958), French anarcho-syndicalist, follower of Georges Sorel and Minister of Labour in the Vichy government from 1942–43. Convicted in 1946 of collaboration.

Lange, Friedrich Albert (1828–1875), German neo-Kantian philosopher and economist.

Larin, Yu. (Lur'e, Mikhail Zal'manovich (Aleksandrovich)) (1882–1932), economist active in the Social-Democratic movement from 1900. Member of the RSDRP(B) from August 1917. After October advocated a coalition government with Menshevik and SR representatives. From late 1917 to early 1918 member of the Presidium of VSNKh. Worked in several Soviet economic organs.

Lenin (Ulyanov), **Vladimir Il'ich** (1870–1924), Russian politician. In 1887 entered the law faculty of Kazan University. In December expelled from the university for participation in the student movement. In 1891 passed the exams for the Faculty of Law at St. Petersburg University. Assistant attorney in Samara. In 1893 moved to St. Petersburg. In 1895 participated in creation of the St. Petersburg 'Union of Struggle for the Emancipation of the Working Class', then arrested. In 1897 exiled for three years to a village in Shushenskoe Yenisei guberniya. In 1900, together with G.V. Plekhanov and others, began publishing the newspaper 'Iskra'. At the second congress of the RSDLP (1903) led the Bolshevik Party. From 1905 in St. Petersburg. Emigrated in December 1907. In April 1917 arrived in Petrograd. Principal leader of the October uprising in Petrograd. At the Second All-Russian Congress of Soviets, elected chairman of the Council of People's Commissars, at the same time (from

1918) chairman of the Council of Workers' and Peasants' Defence (from 1919 the Council of Workers' Defence). Member of the All-Russia Central Executive Committee and the Central Executive Committee of the USSR. From March 1919 in Moscow. Fell seriously ill in 1922 and after December did not participate in political activity.

An early adherent of the ideas of Karl Marx and Friedrich Engels. Concluded that Russia had entered the path of capitalist development and saw the need for a bourgeois-democratic revolution that would develop into a socialist revolution.

Leone, Enrico, Italian syndicalist.

Liebknecht, Karl (1871–1919), one of the founders of the Communist Party of Germany. Murdered (together with Rosa Luxemburg) by counter-revolutionaries.

Lloyd George, David (1863–1945), British Prime Minister from 1916–22.

Lukács, Georg (1885–1971), Hungarian writer and philosopher. First a Social Democrat and later a Communist.

Luxemburg, Rosa (1871–1919), Marxist theorist and a leader of Polish Social Democracy and the left-radical wing of German Social Democracy and the Second International. One of the organisers of the 'Spartacus League' and a founder of the Communist Party of Germany. Murdered (together with Karl Liebknecht) by counter-revolutionaries.

MacDonald, James Ramsay (1866–1937), one of the founders and leaders of the Labour Party of Great Britain, Prime Minister in 1924 and in 1929–31.

Marx, Karl (1818–1883), philosopher, economist and revolutionary. Founder of Marxism. In 1835–41 studied at the Law Faculty of Bonn, then the University of Berlin. From 1842 editor of the democratic 'Rheinische Zeitung'. Met with representatives of the socialist and democratic movement in Paris in 1843. During the revolutionary events in Europe in 1848–49, participated in the international 'Union of Communists' and, together with Engels, wrote its 'Manifesto of the Communist Party' (1848). Marx was the organiser and leader of the First International (1846–76). In 1867, his main work was published, Volume 1 of *Capital*. He did not complete the work on the following volumes. Engels prepared them for publication (Vol. 2, 1885; Vol. 3, 1894). In the last years of his life, Marx actively participated in the formation of proletarian parties.

Marx worked out the principles of the materialist interpretation of history (historical materialism), the theory of surplus value, studied the development of capitalism and anticipated its inevitable collapse and the transition to communism by way of proletarian revolution.

Mendel'son, Lev Abramovich (1899–1962), economist.

Merezhin, A.N. (1880-?), party worker and journalist.

Mikhailovsky, Nikolai Konstantinovich (1842–1904), journalist, literary critic, sociologist.

Mikoyan, Anastas Ivanovich (1895–1978), political figure. In 1926–46 People's Commissar for Foreign and Domestic Trade, People's Commissar of Supply, People's Commissar for the Food Industry, People's Commissar for Foreign Trade of the USSR and simultaneously, from 1937, deputy chairman of the USSR Council of People's Commissars. In 1942–45 member of the State Committee for Defence. From 1946 Deputy Chairman then First Deputy Chairman of the Council of Ministers of the USSR. In 1964–65 Chairman of the Presidium of the USSR Armed Forces. Member of the Central Committee of the party from 1923–76. Member of the Politburo (Presidium) of the Central Committee from 1935–66 (candidate from 1926).

Millerand, Alexandre Étienne (1895–1978), political figure, lawyer and journalist. In 1920 Prime Minister and Minister of Foreign Affairs. President of France 1920–24.

Milyukov, Pavel Nikolaevich (1859–1943), politician, historian, journalist, theorist and leader of the Cadet Party. Emigrated after the October Revolution.

Milyutin, Vladimir Pavlovich (1884–1937), from 1917 People's Commissar of Agriculture. In 1918–21 Deputy Chairman of VSNKh. From 1928 headed the Central Statistical Department and was deputy chairman of Gosplan. From 1934 Chairman of the Academic Council attached to the Central Executive Committee of the USSR. Member of the Central Committee of the party in 1917–18 (candidate in 1920–22). Purged, rehabilitated posthumously.

Morgans – a reference to the J.P. Morgan Company.

Morris, William M. (1834–1896), British artist, writer, art theorist. From the 1880s participated in the British labour movement.

Motylev, Wolf Evnovich (1899–1967), economist.

Nagiev, J., journalist.

Napoleon I (Napoleon Bonaparte) (1769–1821), French emperor in 1804–14 and March–June 1815.

Oerter, Freidrich (*Fritz*) (1869–1935), German syndicalist.

Ol', P.V., statistician.

Olivetti, Angelo (1874–1931), Italian syndicalist. Joined the Italian Socialist Party in 1892, began editing a syndicalist journal by 1906, and in 1914 authored a fascist manifesto.

Owen, Robert (1771–1858), British utopian socialist.

Rosenberg, David Iokhelevich (1879–1950), economist, corresponding member of the USSR Academy of Sciences.

Rosengol'ts, Arkady Pavlovich (1889–1938), 1930–37 USSR Commissar of Foreign Trade. Purged, rehabilitated posthumously.

Rousseau, Jean-Jacques (1712–1778), French writer and philosopher.

Ruskin, John (1819–1900), British writer and art critic.

Ryazanov (Gol'dendakh) David Borisovich (1870–1938), political figure, member of the Academy of Sciences of the USSR (1929). In 1921–31 Director of the Institute of Karl Marx and Friedrich Engels. Purged, rehabilitated posthumously.

Rykov, Aleksei Ivanovich (1881–1938), participant in the revolution of 1905–07 and the October 1917 revolution. Commissar of Internal Affairs (November 1917) in the first Soviet government. In 1917–21 and 1923–24 chairman of VSNKh and from 1921 deputy chairman of the Council of People's Commissars and the Council of Labour and Defence. In 1924–30 Chairman of the Council of People's Commissars of the USSR, and in 1924–29 Chairman of the Council of People's Commissars of the RSFSR. In 1926–30 chairman of the Council of Labour and Defence. 1931–36 Commissar of Posts and Telegraphs, Commissar of Communications of the USSR. Member of the Party Central Committee in 1905–07, 1917–18, and 1920–34 (candidate in 1907–12 and 1934–37). Member of the Politburo of the Central Committee 1922–30. Member of the Organising Bureau of the Central Committee in 1920–24. Purged, rehabilitated posthumously.

Saint-Simon, Claude Henri de Rouvroy (Henri de Saint-Simon) (1760–1825), French utopian socialist.

Scheidemann, Philipp (1865–1939), one of the leaders of the Social-Democratic Party of Germany, first Chancellor of the Weimar Republic.

Schmidt, Conrad (1863–1932), German economist and philosopher, initially a supporter of Marx and Engels, from the 1890s supported revisionists.

Shanin, Lev M. (Shapiro L.G.), economist, Social Democrat, Menshevik and then Bolshevik from 1918.

Skvortsov-Stepanov, Ivan Ivanovich (1870–1928). From 1925 editor of 'Izvestia', deputy editor of 'Pravda', editor of 'Leningradskaya Pravda'. Translator of *Capital* by Karl Marx.

Smilga, Ivar Tenisovich (1892–1938), political figure and economist. From 1921 deputy chairman of VSNKh, deputy chairman of the USSR Gosplan, rector of the Plekhanov Institute of National Economy. Purged, rehabilitated posthumously.

Smirnov, Vladimir Mikhailovich (1887–1937), member of the RSDLP from 1907. After October, member of the Presidium of VSNKh. A 'Left Communist' in

1918 and one of the leaders of the 'military opposition' in 1919. In 1920–21 active in the 'democratic centralism' group. Joined the Trotskyist opposition in 1923. Purged.

Sokol'nikov (Brilliant), Grigory Yakovlevich (1888–1938). In 1921 Deputy Commissar, in 1922–26 Commissar of Finance. From 1926 Deputy Chairman of Gosplan. From 1928 chairman of the Oil Syndicate. Engaged in diplomatic work from 1929. In 1935–36 first Deputy People's Commissar of the USSR forest industry. Candidate Member of the Politburo of the Central Committee of the RCP(B) in 1924–25. Purged, rehabilitated posthumously.

Solntsev, Elizar Borisovich (1900–1937), Bolshevik economist and historian. Member of the Trotskyist Opposition, exiled in 1928.

Sorel, Georges (1847–1922), French philosopher of anarcho-syndicalism.

Stalin (Dzhugashvili) Joseph Vissarionovich (1878–1953). Joined the Georgian Social-Democratic organisation 'Mesame-dasi' in 1898. In 1902–13 arrested six times and exiled, escaped from places of exile four times. Joined the Bolsheviks in 1903. Supporter of V.I. Lenin, on whose initiative he was co-opted in 1912 into the Central Committee and the Russian Bureau of the Central Committee of the RSDLP. In 1917 member of the editorial board of the newspaper 'Pravda', the Politburo of the Central Committee, and the Military-Revolutionary Center. In 1917–22 People's Commissar for Nationalities and in 1919–22 People's Commissar of State Control, head of the Workers' and Peasants' Inspection, and from 1918 member of the Revolutionary War Council of the Republic. In 1922–53 General Secretary of the Central Committee of the party. From 1941 chairman of the Council of People's Commissars (Council of Ministers) of the USSR. Served during the war as chairman of the State Defence Committee, People's Commissar of Defence, and Supreme Commander. In 1946–47 Minister of the Armed Forces of the USSR.

Stammler, Rudolf (1856–1938), German neo-Kantian legal philosopher.

Stepanov – see Skvortsov-Stepanov.

Stetsky, Aleksei Ivanovich (1896–1938), party activist and economist. In the 1920s a supporter of N.I. Bukharin.

Stolzmann, Rudolf (1852–1930), German neo-Kantian philosopher of law and economics, adherent of the Stammler school.

Strumilin (Strumillo-Petrashevich), Stanislav Gustavovich (1877–1974), economist and Statistician, Academician of the USSR (1931).

Struve, Peter Berngardovich (1870–1944), political figure, philosopher, economist, historian, journalist, member of the Russian Academy of Sciences in 1917, excluded in 1928. In the 1890s theorist of 'legal Marxism' and author of the Manifesto of the RSDLP (1898). From the early 1900s a leader of Russian liberalism and of the 'Union of Liberation'. From 1905 a member of the

Cadet Party and its Central Committee. Deputy of the second State Duma. After October 1917 opposed the Bolsheviks. In exile from 1920 onwards.

Thalheimer, August (1884–1948), German Social Democrat. In 1918 one of the founders of the German Communist Party. In 1929 expelled from the Communist Party of Germany and the Comintern.

Thiers, Adolphe (1797–1877), French statesman and historian. President of France 1871–73.

Timofeev, party activist.

Trotsky (Bronstein), **Lev Davidovich** (1879–1940), politician and statesman. In the social- democratic movement from 1896. After 1904, advocated unification of the Bolsheviks and Mensheviks. In 1905 the principal leader of the Petrograd Soviet. In 1908–12 editor of the newspaper 'Pravda'. In 1917 chairman of the Petrograd Soviet of Workers' and Soldiers' Deputies. One of the leaders of the October armed uprising. In 1917–18 Commissar for Foreign Affairs. In 1918–25 Commissar for Military Affairs, Chairman of the Revolutionary Military Council of the Republic, one of the creators of the Red Army. Member of the Central Committee in 1917–27, member of the Politburo of the Central Committee in October 1917 and in 1919–26. The struggle with Stalin for leadership in the party ended in the defeat of Trotsky. In 1924 his views (so-called Trotskyism) were declared a 'petty-bourgeois deviation' in the RKP(B). In 1927 expelled from the party, sent to Alma-Ata, exiled from the USSR in 1929. Murdered in Mexico by an NKVD agent.

Viviani, René (1863–1925), French political figure and social reformist. In 1914 Prime Minister of France and Minister of Foreign Affairs.

Vladimir Il'ich – see Lenin, V.I.

Vollmar, Georg von (1850–1922), social-democratic reformist politician.

Vol'skii, Stanislav (Sokolov, A.V.) (1880-?), author, philosopher, Social Democrat and Bolshevik. No party affiliation after 1917.

Weitling, Wilhelm (1808–1871). German worker and member of the 'League of the Just'. Regarded revolution as a spontaneous process in which the major role belongs to declassed elements. Advocated egalitarian communism.

Yudenich, Nikolai Nikolaevich (1862–1933), General of the Infantry (1915), one of the leaders of the White forces in North-West Russia. After the failure of the 'advance' on Petrograd (October–November 1919), retreated to Estonia with the remnants of his army. Emigrated in 1920.

Zander, a participant in the dispute over E.A. Preobrazhensky's report to Proletkult.

References

Berth, Édouard 1908, *Ideologiya proizvoditelei: Sotsial'noe dvizhenie v sovremennoi Frantsii*, Moscow: Izd. Dorovatovskovo i Charushnikova.

Berth, Édouard 1925, *Les Derniers aspects du Socialisme*, Paris: Marcel Rivière.

Blanqui, [Louis] Auguste 1871, *La Patrie en Danger*, Paris: A. Chevalier.

Blanqui, [Louis] Auguste 1885a, *Critique Sociale*, edited by Felix Alcan, Tome premier: *Capital et Travail*, Paris: Ancienne Librairie Germer Baillière et Cie.

Blanqui, [Louis] Auguste 1885b, *Critique Sociale*, edited by Félix Alcan, Tome second: *Fragments et Notes*, Paris: Ancienne Librairie Germer Baillière et Cie.

Blaug, Mark (ed.) 1983, *Who's Who in Economics: A Biographical Dictionary of Major Economists 1700–1980*, Brighton: Wheatsheaf Books.

Borilin, B. 1931, 'Protiv izvrashchenii marksistsko-leninskoi teorii na ekonomicheskom fronte', *Problemy ekonomiki*, no. 10–12.

Broué, Pierre 2007, 'The Bolshevik-Leninist Faction', *Revolutionary History*, 9, no. 4: 137–60.

Bukharin, N.I. 1924, 'Novoe otkrovenie o sovetskoi ekonomike, ili kak mozhno pogubit' raboche-krest'yanskii blok', *Pravda*, 12 December.

Bukharin, N.I. 1925a, *K voprosu o trotskizme*, Moscow-Leningrad.

Bukharin, N.I. 1925b, *Nekotorye voprosy ekonomicheskoi politike*, Moscow.

Bukharin, N.I. 1926, *Kritika ekonomichsoi platformy oppozitsii*, Leningrad.

Bukharin, N.I. 1969, *Historical Materialism*, Ann Arbor: University of Michigan Press.

Bukharin, N.I. 1982, *Selected Writings on the State and the Transition to Socialism*, edited and translated by Richard B. Day, New York: M.E. Sharpe.

Bukharin, N.I., and E.A. Preobrazhensky 1920, *Azbuka kommunizma*, Moscow.

Butayev, K. 1932, 'K Voprosu o material'noi base sotsializma', *Problemy ekonomiki*, no. 1.

Cabet, Étienne 1842, *Voyage en Icarie: Roman Philosophique et Social*, Paris: J. Mallett et Cie.

Carr, E.H., and R.W. Davies 1969, *Foundations of a Planned Economy*, Vol. I, Part 1, London: Macmillan.

Day, Richard B. 1973, *Leon Trotsky and the Politics of Economic Isolation*, Cambridge: Cambridge University Press.

Day, Richard B. 1980, *The 'Crisis' and the 'Crash': Soviet Studies of the West (1917–1939)*, London: NLB.

Day, Richard B. 1982, 'Leon Trotsky on the Problems of the Smychka and Forced Collectivization', *Critique*, 13, no. 1: 55–68.

Day, Richard B. 1987, 'Democratic Control and the Dignity of Politics – An Analysis of *The Revolution Betrayed*', *Comparative Economic Studies*, 29, no. 3: 4–29.

Day, Richard B. 1988, 'Leon Trotsky on the Dialectics of Democratic Control', in *The Soviet Economy on the Brink of Reform*, edited by Peter Wiles, Boston: Unwin Hyman.

Day, Richard B. 1992, 'Between Hegel and Habermas: The Political Theory of Leon Trotsky', in *The Trotsky Reappraisal*, edited by Terry Brotherstone and Paul Dukes, Edinburgh: Edinburgh University Press.

Day, Richard B., and Mikhail M. Gorinov (eds) 2014, *The Preobrazhensky Papers*, Vol. 1, Leiden: Brill.

Deutscher, Isaac 1965, *The Prophet Unarmed*, New York: Vintage.

Documents of the 1923 Opposition 1975, London: New Park.

Engels, Frederick 1926, *The Peasant War in Germany*, New York: International Publishers.

Engels, Frederick 1954, *Anti-Dühring: Herr Eugen Dühring's Revolution in Science*, Moscow: Foreign Languages Publishing House.

Engels, Frederick 1959, *Anti-Dühring: Herr Eugen Dühring's Revolution in Science*, Moscow: Foreign Languages Publishing House.

Erlich, A. 1960, *The Soviet Industrialisation Debate, 1924–1928*, Cambridge, MA: Harvard University Press.

Fourier, Charles 1841, *Oeuvres Complètes*, Tome 5, Deuxième edition, Paris: Société pour la Propagation et pour la Réalisation de la Théorie de Fourier.

Fourier, Charles 1846, *Oeuvres Complètes*, Tome 1, Troisième édition, *Théorie des Quatres Mouvements et des Destinées Générales*, Paris: Librairie de l'École Sociétaire.

Fourier, Charles 1876, *The Theory of Social Organization*, in *Sociological Series*, no. 11, Introduction by Charles Brisbane, New York: C.P. Somerby.

Fourier, Charles 2001, *Théorie de l'Unité universelle*, Vol. 11, Paris: Les Presses du reel.

Gianinazzi, Willy 1989, *L'itinerario di Enrico Leone: Liberismo e sindacalismo nel movimento operaio italiano*, Milan: Franco Angeli.

Gol'denberg, E. 1926, 'Delayed Reflex', *Bol'shevik*, no. 7–8.

Gorinov, M.M. 1990, *Nep: poiski putei razvitiya*, Moscow.

Griffuelhes, Victor 1908, *L'Action Syndicaliste*, Paris: Marcel Rivière.

Hegel, Georg Wilhelm Friedrich 2010, *The Science of Logic*, edited and translated by George Di Giovanni, Cambridge: Cambridge University Press.

Jinping, Xi 2015, *How to Read Confucius*, New York: CN Times Books Inc.

Kautsky, Karl 1910, *The Social Revolution*, Chicago: Kerr.

Kautsky, Karl 1918, *Ethics and the Materialist Conception of History*, Chicago: Charles H. Kerr & Company.

Kestner, Fritz 1912, *Der Organisationszwang. Eine Untersuchung über die Kämpfe zwischen Kartellen und Aussenseitern*, Berlin: C. Heymann.

Kon, Aleksandr Feliksovich 1923, *Opyt programmy po politicheskoi ekonomii*, Moscow: Krasnaya Nov'.

Koshkarev, N.N. 1918, *O proletarskoi etike*, Moscow.

Krementsov, Nikolai 2011, 'From "Beastly Philosophy" to Medical Genetics: Eugenics in Russia and the Soviet Union', *Annals of Science*, 68, no. 1: 61–92.

Kritsman, L.N. 1926, *Klassovoe rassloenie v sovetskoi derevne. Po dannym volostnikh obsledovanii*, Moscow: Izd. Kommunisticheskoi akademii.

Labriola, Arturo 1907, *Reformizm i sindicalizm*, translated by G. Kirdetsov, edited by A. Lunacharsky, St. Petersburg: Shipovnik.

Lagardelle, Hubert 1906, 'Mannheim, Rome, Amiens', *Mouvement Socialiste*, 179 and 180 (October and November), 5–25 and 250–65.

Lenin, V.I. 1929, *Leninskii Sbornik*, XI, edited by N.I. Bukharin, V.M. Molotov, and M.A. Savelyev, Moscow and Leningrad: Institut Lenina pri TsKVKP(в).

Lenin, V.I. 1960, *Imperialism, The Highest Stage of Capitalism*, in *Selected Works*, Vol. 1, Moscow: Foreign Languages Publishing House.

Lenin, V.I. 1961, *Selected Works*, Vol. 1, Moscow: Foreign Languages Publishing House.

Lenin, V.I. 1962, *Collected Works*, Vol. 13, Moscow: Progress Publishers.

Lenin, V.I. 1963, *Collected Works*, Vol. 17, Moscow: Foreign Languages Publishing House.

Lenin, V.I. 1964a, *Collected Works*, Vol. 23, Moscow: Progress Publishers.

Lenin, V.I. 1964b, *Collected Works*, Vol. 25, Moscow: Progress Publishers.

Lenin, V.I. 1965a, *Collected Works*, Vol. 29, Moscow: Progress Publishers.

Lenin, V.I. 1965b, *Collected Works*, Vol. 32, Moscow: Progress Publishers.

Lenin, V.I. 1966a, *Collected Works*, Vol. 31, Moscow: Progress Publishers.

Lenin, V.I. 1966b, *Collected Works*, Vol. 33, Moscow: Progress Publishers.

Lenin, V.I. 1970, *Polnoe sobranie sochinenii*, Tom 42, Izdanie Pyatoe, Moscow: Izdatel'stvo Politicheskoi Literatury.

Leone, Enrico 1907a, *Il sindacalismo*, Milano, Palermo and Napoli: Remo Sandron.

Leone, Enrico 1907b, *Sindikalizm*, translated by G. Kidretsov, St. Petersburg.

Marx, Karl 1970, *A Contribution to the Critique of Political Economy*, Moscow: Progress Publishers.

Marx, Karl 1976, *Capital*, Vol. 1, introduced by Ernest Mandel, translated by Ben Fowkes, London: Penguin.

Marx, Karl 1978, *Capital*, Vol. 2, introduced by Ernest Mandel, translated by David Fernbach, London: Penguin.

Marx, Karl 1981, *Capital*, Vol. III, introduced by Ernest Mandel, translated by David Fernbach, London: Penguin.

Marx, Karl, and Frederick Engels 1962, *Selected Works in Two Volumes*, Moscow: Foreign Languages Publishing House.

Marx, Karl, and Frederick Engels 1964, *The German Ideology*, Moscow: Progress Publishers.

Marx, Karl, and Frederick Engels 1965, *Selected Correspondence*, Moscow: Progress Publishers.

Marx, Karl, and Frederick Engels 1976, *Collected Works*, Vol. 6, New York: International Publishers.

Marx, Karl, and Frederick Engels 1977, *Collected Works*, Vol. 7, New York: International Publishers.

Marx, Karl, and Frederick Engels 1987, *Collected Works*, Vol. 42, New York: International Publishers.

Marx, Karl, and Frederick Engels 1988, *Collected Works*, Vol. 43, New York: International Publishers.

Marx, Karl, and Frederick Engels 1989, *Collected Works*, Vol. 24, New York: International Publishers.

Marx, Karl, and Frederick Engels 1991, *Collected Works*, Vol. 45, New York: International Publishers.

Marx, Karl, and Frederick Engels 2001, *Collected Works*, Vol. 49, New York: International Publishers.

Marx, Karl, and Frederick Engels 2010, *Collected Works*, Vol. 46, New York: International Publishers.

Motylev, V.E. 1924, *Tsena i stoimost' v kapitalisticheskom khozyaistve i v khozyaistvo SSSR*, Krasnodat: Burevestnik.

Motylev, V.E. 1925a, *Kurs politicheskoi ekonomii*, Vol. 1, Moscow: Gosizdat.

Motylev, V.E. 1925b, *Pribavochnaya stoimost' i sotsialisticheskoe nakoplenie na SSSR*, Rostov n/D: Burevestnik.

Oerter, Fritz [Friedrich] 1920, *Was wollen die Syndikalisten?* Berlin: Kater.

Owen, Robert 1817, *A New View of Society; or, Essays on the Formation of the Human Character*, 3rd edn, London: Longman (and others).

Owen, Robert 1849, *The Book of the New Moral World*, London: J. Watson.

Olivetti, Angelo Oliviero 1906, *Problemi del socialismo contemporaneo*, Lugano: Società editrice Avanguardia.

Olivetti, Angelo Oliviero 1908, *Problemy sovremennovo sotsializma*, Moscow: Izd. S. Dorovatovskovo i A. Charushnikova.

Osinsky, N. 1918, 'Stroitel'stvo sotsializma', *Kommunist*, no. 2.

Paul, Diane 1984, 'Eugenics and the Left', *Journal of the History of Ideas*, 45: 567–90.

Pelloutier, Fernand 1921, *Histoire des Bourses du Travail*, Paris: Ancienne Librairie Schleicher.

Polov, K.A. (ed.) 1927, *Diskussiya 1923 g. Materialy i dokumenty*, Moscow and Leningrad.

Pouget, Émile 1910, *La Confédération Générale du Travail*, Paris: Librarie des Sciences Politiques & Sociales Marcel Rivière.

Preobrazhensky, E.A. 1918a, 'S'ezd neobkhodim', *Kommunist*, no. 4: 13.

Preobrazhensky, E.A. 1918b, *Krest'yanskaya Rossiya i sotsializm (K peresmotru nashei agrarnoi programmy)*, Petrograd.

Preobrazhensky, E.A. 1920, *Bumazhnie den'gi v epokhu diktatury proletariata*, Moscow.

Preobrazhensky, E.A. 1921, *Anarkhizm i kommunizm*, Moscow.

Preobrazhensky, E.A. 1922a, *Ot Nepa k sotsializmu (Vzglyad v budushchee Rossii i Evropy)*, Moscow.

Preobrazhensky, E.A. 1922b, *Itogi Genyezskoi Konferentsii i khozyaistvennye perspektivy Evropy*, Moscow: Gosudarstvennoe izdatel'stvo.

Preobrazhensky, E.A. 1923a, '*Teoreticheskie osnovy spora o zolotom i tovarnom ruble*', *Vestnik Kommunisticheskoi akademii*, no. 2, 58–74.

Preobrazhensky, E.A. 1923b, 'Ekonomicheskie krizisy pri nepe', *Vestnik Kommunisticheskoi akademii*, no. 6.

Preobrazhensky, E.A. 1923c, 'Dve linii ekonomicheskovo razvitiya mira', *Pravda*, 11 July.

Preobrazhensky, E.A. 1924, '*Osnovnoi zakon sotsialisticheskoi nakopleniya*', *Vestnik Kommunisticheskoi akademii*, no. 8, 47–116.

Preobrazhensky, E.A. 1925, 'Socialist and Communist Conceptions of Socialism', *Vestnik Kommunisticheskoi akademii*, no. 12: 19–75; no. 13: 3–33.

Preobrazhensky, E.A. 1926, *The New Economics*, 2nd edition, Moscow: Izdatel'stvo Kommunisticheskoi akademii.

Preobrazhensky, E.A. 1927, 'Khozyaistvennoe ravnovesie v sisteme SSSR', *Vestnik Kommunisticheskoi akademii*, no. 22.

Preobrazhensky, E.A. 1929, 'Zayavlenie v TsKK byvshikh rukovoditelei trotskistskoi oppozitsii', *Pravda*, 13 July.

Preobrazhensky, E.A. 1930a, 'Ekonomicheskaya priroda sovetskikh deneg i perspektivy chervontsa', *Pod znamenem marksizma*, no. 4.

Preobrazhensky, E.A. 1930b, 'Izmeneniye v stoimosti zolota i tovarnye tseny', *Problemy ekonomiki*, no. 1.

Preobrazhensky, E.A. 1930c, *Teoriya padayushchei valyuty*, Moscow, Leningrad.

Preobrazhensky, E.A. 1960, 'Za chto nas isklyuchili iz partii (pis'mo k partiinomu s'ezdu)', in *Kommunisticheskaya oppositziya v SSSR*, T.4, Moscow.

Preobrazhensky, E.A. 1985, *The Decline of Capitalism*, translated and edited by Richard B. Day, Armonk, NY: M.E. Sharpe.

Preobrazhensky, E.A. 2014, *The Preobrazhensky Papers, Archival Documents and Materials, Volume I: 1886–1920*, Leiden: Brill.

Prokpovich, S.N. 1918, *Opyt ischisleniya narodnovo dokhoda 50 gub. Evropeiskoi Rossii v 1900–1913 gg*, Moscow.

Saint-Simon, Claude Henri de 1859, *Oeuvres Choisies*, Tome III, Brussels: Fr. Van Meenen et Cie.

Schecter, Darrow 1994, *Radical Theories: Paths Beyond Marxism and Social Democracy*, Manchester: Manchester University Press.

Schultz, Heinrich E., et al. (eds) 1972, *Who was Who in the USSR*, Metuchen, NJ: The Scarecrow Press.

Sorel, Georges 1901a, *L'Avenir socialiste des syndicats*, Paris: Librairie G. Jaques et Cie.

Sorel, Georges 1901b, *La ruine du monde antique: Conception matérialiste de l'histoire*, Paris: Librairie G. Jacques et Cie.

Sorel, Georges 1908, *La Décomposition du Marxisme*, Paris: Librairie des Sciences Politiques et Sociales, Marcel Riviére.

Sorel, Georges 1919, *Materiaux d'une théorie du proletariat*, Paris: Marcel Rivière et Cie.

Sorel, Georges 1921, *Les illusions du progress: Suivi de L'avenir des syndicates*, 3rd edn, Paris: Librairie des Sciences Politiques et Sociales Marcel Rivière et Cie.

Sorel, Georges 1950, *Reflections on Violence*, translated by J. Roth and T.E. Hulme, introduced by Edward A. Shils, New York: Collier.

Sorel, Georges 2009, 'The Decomposition of Marxism', in *Radicalism and the Revolt Against Reason: The Social Theories of Georges Sorel with a Translation of his Essay on 'The Decomposition of Marxism'*, by Irving Louis Horowitz, New York: Routledge.

Stalin, J.V. 1926, *Chetyrnadtsatyi S'ezd Vsesoyuznoi Kommunisticheskoi Partii (B): Stenograficheskii Otchet*, Moscow: Gosudarstvennoe Izdatel'stvo.

Stammler, Rudolf 1906, *Wirtschaft und recht nach der materialistischen gesichtsauffassung*, Leipzig: Veit.

Trotsky, Leon 1915, 'Natsiya i khozyaistvo', *Nashe Slovo*, nos. 130 and 135, 3 and 9 July.

Trotsky, Leon 1923, *Dvenadtsatyi S'ezd Rossiskoi Kommunisticheskoi Partii (Bol'shevikov): Stenograficheskii Otchet*, Moscow: Izdatel'stvo Krasnaya Nov'.

Trotsky, Leon 1926, *Towards Socialism or Capitalism?* London: Methuen & Co.

Trotsky, Leon 1927, *Pyatnadtsataya Konferentsiya Vsesoyuznoi Kommunisticheskoi Partii (B): Stenograficheskii Otchet*, Moscow.

Trotsky, Leon 1955, *Écrits 1928–1940*, T. I, Paris: Librairie Marcel Rivière et Cie.

Trotsky, Leon 1957, *The Third International After Lenin*, New York: Pioneer Publishers.

Trotsky, Leon 1972, *The Revolution Betrayed*, New York: Pioneer Publishers.

Trotsky, Leon 1986, *Trotsky's Notebooks 1933–1935*, edited and translated by Philip Pomper, New York: Columbia University Press.

Trotsky, Leon 2007, *Terrorism and Communism*, London: Verso.

Trotsky, Leon 2018, *Trotsky on Lenin*, Chicago: Haymarket Books.

Tsakunov, S.V. 1989, 'Formirovanie vzglyadov Bukharina na ekonomiku perekhodnovo perioda', *Istoki*, 1.

Name Index

Printed in the USA
CPSIA information can be obtained
at www.ICGtesting.com
JSHW011024151123
52135JS00004B/17

9 781642 599947